THE BOOK OF THE
SHETLAND SHEEPDOG

Distributed in the UNITED STATES by T.F.H. Publications, Inc., 211 West Sylvania Avenue, Neptune City, NJ 07753; in CANADA by H & L Pet Supplies Inc., 27 Kingston Crescent, Kitchener, Ontario N2B 2T6; Rolf C. Hagen Ltd., 3225 Sartelon Street, Montreal 382 Quebec; in ENGLAND by T.F.H. Publications Limited, 4 Kier Park, Ascot, Berkshire SL5 7DS; in AUSTRALIA AND THE SOUTH PACIFIC by T.F.H. (Australia) Pty. Ltd., Box 149, Brookvale 2100 N.S.W., Australia; in NEW ZEALAND by Ross Haines & Son, Ltd., 18 Monmouth Street, Grey Lynn, Auckland 2 New Zealand; in SINGAPORE AND MALAYSIA by MPH Distributors (S) Pte., Ltd., 601 Sims Drive, # 03/07/21, Singapore 1438; in the PHILIPPINES by Bio-Research, 5 Lippay Street, San Lorenzo Village, Makati Rizal; in SOUTH AFRICA by Multipet Pty. Ltd., 30 Turners Avenue, Durban 4001. Published by T.F.H. Publications Inc., Ltd. the British Crown Colony of Hong Kong.

THE BOOK OF THE SHETLAND SHEEPDOG

Chris

by **Anna Katherine Nicholas**
*With special features by Dona Hausman,
Linda More, Leslie B. Rogers, Jean Daniels
Simmons, and Joseph P. Sayres, D.V.M.*

Dedication

To Betty Whelen and to Lee Reasin,

who have been such good friends to me and to this book,

and to the memory of Eugene Cohen, a friend whom we miss.

Contents

In Appreciation.............................7
About the Author 9

Chapter One
Early History of the Shetland Sheepdog 11

Chapter Two
Shetland Sheepdogs in England............15
Kyleburn—Mountaincrest

Chapter Three
Shetland Sheepdogs in the United States.....27
Early Shetland Sheepdog Champions—The
American Shetland Sheepdog Association

Chapter Four
Kennels in the Continental United States 65
Ardencaple—Astolat—Belle Mount—Birch
Hollow—Bran Gay—Caper Hill—Carmylie—
Catamount—Cedarhope—Chisterling—Chosen
—Conendale—Edlen—Enchanted—Fran-Dor—
Gay Acres—Happy Glen—Hoch Haven—Jade
Mist—Karral—Ken-Rob—Kensington—Kismet
—Legacy—Lochanora—Lynnlea—Macdega—
Mainstay—Malashel—Marwal—Meadow Ridge
—Montage—Pixie Dell—Pocono—Rickgarbob—
Rockwood—Rorralore—Rosewood—Rosmoor—
Rustic—Sea Isle—Severn—Starhaven—Sumer-
Song—Summit Lane—Velveteen—Villager—
Water's Edge

Chapter Five
Shetland Sheepdogs in Canada 241
Some Canadian Firsts—Best in Show Shelties
and Top Sires and Dams—Cavatina—Chicwin—
Crinan—Forever—Gallantry—Genson—Loch-
lana—Marchwind—Meridian—Sheldon—Shiel
—Sovereign

Chapter Six
Shetland Sheepdogs in Australia...........281

Chapter Seven
Standards of the Breed 285
British and Australian Standard—Early Ameri-
can Standard—Current American Standard—
What To Look For in a Sheltie, *drawn by Jean
Daniels Simmonds*

Chapter Eight
Some Comments on Sheltie Type
by Leslie B. Rogers 321

Chapter Nine
Random Thoughts on Judging Shelties
by Dona Hausman.....................327

Chapter Ten
Selection of a Shetland Sheepdog 331

Chapter Eleven
Caring for a Sheltie Puppy 345
Advance Preparation—Joining the Family—
Socialization and Training—Feeding

Chapter Twelve
Grooming the Shetland Sheepdog
by Linda More 361
General Good Care—Trimming the Sheltie—
Grooming at the Show

Chapter Thirteen
Showing Your Shetland Sheepdog.........385
General Considerations—A Note on Sheltie
Puppy Ears—Match Shows—Point Shows—
Junior Showmanship—Pre-Show Preparation—
Day of the Show

Chapter Fourteen
Obedience and Shetland Sheepdogs 417
Obedience—Some Outstanding Obedience
Shelties—A Very Special Sheltie-Am., Can.,
Mex. Ch. and O.T.Ch. Merriley's Steely Dan,
Am., Can., and Mex. U.D.

Chapter Fifteen
Breeding Shetland Sheepdogs 449
The Stud Dog—The Brood Bitch—Pedigrees—
Gestation, Whelping, and the Litter

Chapter Sixteen
You and Your Sheltie 507
The Shetland Sheepdog Personality—Responsibilities of Shetland Sheepdog Owners—Travelling With Your Shetland Sheepdog.

Chapter Seventeen
Veterinarian's Corner
by Joseph P. Sayres, D.V.M...............519
Congenital Defects—Vaccines—Infectious and
Contagious Diseases—External Parasites—Inter-
nal Parasites—Home Remedies and First Aid—
Care of the Older Dog—Canine Nutrition

Index

Gae Goldilocks, C.D., a sable and white female by Taddy of Laurel ex Bil-Bo-Dot Doll's Delight, born September 1961. Owned by Mr. and Mrs. Charles A. Kuhn. From Lee Reasin's collection.

In Appreciation

There are many people to whom we owe gratitude for their assistance in making this book informative and interesting. The cooperation I have received from the Sheltie people has been tremendous; without it, the book could not possibly be nearly so complete.

The first two who came through most helpfully were Lee Reasin and Betty Whelen, both with photographs, time, and a wealth of historic information. Lee has shared his albums and scrapbooks with me, giving permission to use whatever I might need. I have done so quite lavishly, and it is to this gentleman that we owe thanks for a great many of our photos from the 1960's and earlier, together with facts about important dogs all along the way.

As for Betty Whelen, on a warm afternoon during July 1983, when she was visiting her friends the Frothinghams at Rye, New York, Marcia Foy and I spent a fabulous afternoon with her. We came away loaded with photographs, memorabilia, and a copy of her own wonderful book on Shelties, now out of print, with permission to use anything and everything I might wish to incorporate into this new book. Consequently the Pocono Kennel story here is filled with facts not only about Betty's own famous dogs but also with her comments on many others which she personally knew, making for an invaluable presentation of the breed from the early 1930's.

Then Jean Simmonds gave me permission to select and use some of her drawings from her outstanding *Illustrated Standard of the Shetland Sheepdog,* which is one of the best presentations of this type I have seen on any breed. We have taken advantage of her permission in this regard, and at the same time I urge every student of this breed to acquire one of Mrs. Simmonds's books immediately, as they are complete and helpful beyond words for those wishing to truly know what is, and is not, correct in a Sheltie.

Dona Hausman did a very interesting feature about judging for us, which we appreciate. Charlotte Clem McGowan, with the owner's consent, shared her "Sea Isle" story with us; again, our appreciation. Leslie Rogers, noted Canadian authority, has submitted, with permission for us to use, his thoughts on type and coat which we feel honored to include, along with other information about Shelties in Canada, supplied by him. And of course our wonderful veterinarian, Dr. Joseph P. Sayres, has done his usual outstanding job with his veterinarian's section geared especially toward Shetland Sheepdogs.

Along with these folks are the dozens of others who have played an important part by submitting kennel stories, photographs, and pedigrees of their dogs to be included. The kennel story features are always especially well received by readers of these books, and I feel proud to say that in this book we present an outstanding assortment for the information and pleasure of our readers.

Marcia Foy has sent out many letters which helped to gather needed information. The Sheltie handlers have been great about providing material we've needed pertaining to their own and their clients' dogs. To each and every fancier who has helped, we extend our heartfelt thanks. We hope that you will all thoroughly enjoy the book, and we feel it to be an outstanding addition to the literature of the Sheltie world!

Anna Katherine Nicholas

CARTER

Ch. Kismet's Conquistador, a 14½″ mahogany sable by Ch. Banchory High Born ex Cee Dee's Annandale, born December 1973. Bred and owned by Guy and Thelma Mauldin, Kismet Shetland Sheepdogs.

About the Author

Since early childhood, Anna Katherine Nicholas has been involved with dogs. Her first pets were a Boston Terrier, an Airedale, and a German Shepherd Dog. Then, in 1925, came the first Pekingese, a gift from a family friend who raised them. Now her home is shared with a Miniature Poodle and a dozen or so Beagles, including her noted Best in Show and National Specialty winner, Champion Rockaplenty's Wild Oats, an internationally famous Beagle sire, who as a show dog was top Beagle in the nation in 1973. She also owns Champion Foyscroft True Blue Lou and, in co-ownership with Marcia Foy who lives with her, Champion Foyscroft Triple Mitey Migit.

Miss Nicholas is best known in the dog fancy as a writer and as a judge. Her first magazine articles were about Pekingese, published in *Dog News* magazine about 1930. This was followed by a widely acclaimed breed column, "Peeking at the Pekingese," which appeared continuously for at least two decades, originally in *Dogdom* and, when that magazine ceased to exist, in *Popular Dogs*.

During the 1940's she was Boxer columnist for the American Kennel Club *Gazette* and a featured East Coast representative for *Boxer Briefs*. More recently, many of her articles of general interest to the dog fancy have appeared in *Popular Dogs, Pure-Bred Dogs/American Kennel Gazette*, and *Show Dogs*. She is presently a featured columnist for *Dog World, Canine Chronicle*, and *Kennel Review* in the United States and *Dog Fancier* in Canada. Her *Dog World* column, "Here, There and Everywhere," was the Dog Writers Association of America selection for Best Series in a dog magazine which was awarded her for 1979. And for 1981 her feature article, "Faster Is Not Better," published in the *Canine Chronicle*, was one of four nominated for the Best Feature Article Award from the Dog Writers Association. She also has been a columnist for *World of the Working Dog*.

It was during the 1930's that Miss Nicholas' first book, *The Pekingese*, was published by the Judy Publishing Company. This book completely sold out two editions and is now an eagerly sought-after collector's item, as is her *The Skye Terrier Book*, published through the Skye Terrier Club of America during the early 1960's.

Miss Nicholas won the Dog Writers Association of America award in 1970 for the Best Technical Book of the Year with her *Nicholas Guide to Dog Judging*. Then in 1979 the revision of this book again won the Dog Writers Association of America Best Technical Book Award, the first time ever that a revision has been so honored by this association.

In the early 1970's Miss Nicholas co-authored with Joan Brearley five breed books for T.F.H. Publications. These were *This is the Bichon Frise, The Wonderful World of Beagles and Beagling, The Book of the Pekingese, This is the Skye Terrier*, and *The Book of the Boxer*. *The Wonderful World of Beagles and Beagling* won a Dog Writers Association of America Honorable Mention Award the year that it was published.

All of Miss Nicholas' recent releases from T.F.H. have been received with enthusiasm and acclaim; these include *Successful Dog Show Exhibiting, The Book of the Rottweiler, The Book of the Poodle, The Book of the Labrador Retriever, The Book of the English Springer Spaniel, The Book of the Golden Retriever* and *The Book of the German Shepherd Dog*.

In addition to her four Dog Writers Association of America awards, Miss Nicholas has received the Gaines "Fido" as Dog Writer of the Year on two occasions, in the late 1970's and again in 1982; and she has received, on separate occasions, two "Winkies" from *Kennel Review* as Dog Journalist of the Year.

The very important English dog Ch. Peabody Pan, imported into the United States and owned by Elizabeth D. Whelen, Pocono Kennels.

CHAPTER ONE

Early History of the Shetland Sheepdog

A Collie, Int. Ch. Blue Minstrel of Ronas Hill, and a Sheltie, Ch. Blue Flag of Ronas Hill, circa 1955. Both bred and owned by Mrs. G.F. Lovett, Ontario. This photo, loaned to us by Mr. L.B. Rogers, Forever Kennels, shows the differences in size and type between the two breeds.

The original Shetland Sheepdogs were exactly what the name describes—sheep-dogs indigenous to the Shetland Isles, developed there as herding dogs. Since all of the animals from the Shetland Isles were diminutive in size, so too were these dogs, closely resembling one of the best loved breeds of all, the Collie.

To the average person, a Shetland Sheepdog even to this day is frequently referred to as a "Miniature Collie"—an inaccurate reference in these modern times, when purebred Shetland Sheepdogs have been raised of undiluted Sheltie bloodlines over a great many generations. In the earliest days, however, the relationship quite obviously did exist.

In both the early Collies and the early Shetland Sheepdogs there were two definite and distinct types of dog: show type and working type. Unfortunately both types in both breeds were registered under the same name and judged together, despite the fact that the one type was more like the Collie of the eighteenth and nineteenth centuries while the other represented a dog far more similar to the show-type Collie of the present day—and the show-type Shetland Sheepdog.

Obviously, opinion must have been sharply divided as to the rights and wrongs of each type during this period. The "Shetland Island Dogs" were handsome little animals of definitely utilitarian type; the "show Collie-type Shetland Sheepdog" was far more advanced in beauty and elegance—toward the type we admire today. Leader of the island breeders was a gentleman from Bixter in the Shetland Isles, Dr. Bowie, who was the principal advocate for retaining the Shetland Sheepdog in its original form, not a dog of "show Collie type." He and his followers "stuck to their guns" about this, showing their working Collie-type Sheepdogs in competition side by side with the other faction's show Collie-type Sheepdogs. The decisions of the judges, thus (even as now in judging dogs), was based largely on which type the judge happened to prefer; and since the standard's description was along those lines, the majority obviously were in favor of the show-type dogs.

There were very wide variations in the type of sheepdogs raised on the Shetland Isles, for while some were working Collie type others bore little resemblance to Collies (or Shelties), especially in head qualities which we have read of as being sometimes fox-like in appearance, with short muzzles.

As the controversy raged, Dr. Bowie is quoted as having objected to efforts to alter or standard-

Ch. Eltham Park Eureka, by Ch. Specks of Mountford ex Princess of Mountford, won at least seven Challenge Certificates at English shows for owner E.C. Pierce. Miss E.P. Humphries was the breeder.

ize the breed's appearance on the grounds that by doing so a show Collie-type Sheepdog was being created which actually had nothing to do with the islands. Those in favor of producing Shetland Sheepdogs, which were miniature show Collies in appearance, defended their stand with the contention that their actions were not an attempt to change the breed. Rather they regarded it as a step to improve it and achieve

uniformity which they felt at that point to be essential unless the dogs which, in many cases, they felt were mongrels be permitted to cause deterioration in the breed by uncontrolled continuation along those lines.

Still further controversy was caused by the fact that the advocates of the working type dogs felt that the title "Shetland Sheepdog" should be applicable only to the island breed and its use not permitted for dogs of the miniature show Collie-type.

Then, to really compound the problems, some of the show Collie-type breeders started to create a Toy Collie, a toy-sized dog which might well have been a success as a Toy had it been given its own classification, but it never had that chance.

There is little known of the history of Shetland Sheepdogs other than that they attracted much attention of early visitors to the Shetlands by their small size and business-like efficiency. No one could recall a time when they had not been present or when they had been other than their diminutive size. Some felt that since the famous Shetland ponies, tiny sheep, and small cattle as well as the dogs were miniature editions of their kind, perhaps something about the climate of the Shetlands had dwarfed them all. Others wondered if, in the case of the dogs, there might not have been interbreeding between working

Ch. Eltham Park Ena, a daughter of Ch. Eltham Park Eureka ex Eltham Park Emmie. She won her first Challenge Certificate in 1927 and was bred by Mr. Pierce of the famous Eltham Park Kennels.

Kilvarock Specks, by Ch. Max of Clerwood ex Nan of Mountfort, born in 1929. Bred by Mrs. E.E. Sparrow, this dog became widely known under the ownership of Miss B. Thynne.

Collies and smaller dogs, perhaps spaniels or terriers, to create the smallness of size. One thing about the latter theory (if it had been practiced at all): the Collie had been dominant, for despite tremendous diversity of color, markings, head type, and expression, the appearance of the Collie had, in various degrees, remained.

Even as Shetland Sheepdogs were being taken off the islands by visitors, island breeders were moving toward the establishment of their dogs officially as a breed and for recognition as such in the Kennel Club Stud Book. So it was that the first of the Shetland Sheepdog Clubs was formed, at Lerwick, capital of the Shetlands, in 1908. Even the official naming of the breed and club had not been without its problems, as the title "Shetland Collie" had been considered for the breed and club; this was objected to strongly by the Collie Club of Great Britain who felt that the dogs, being of island type, did not conform to their show type standards.

In 1908, the Scottish Shetland Sheepdog Club was organized, with the British Shetland Sheepdog Breeders Association following shortly and then the English Shetland Sheepdog Club. Two of the three survived. Also in 1909 the Kennel Club agreed to recognize Shetland Sheepdogs as a "distinct variety of show Collie type," with the standard drawn up accordingly. Twelve inches was established as the height limit.

Mountaincrest's Wee Laird of Hillyacres, from Mrs. Frances Ruth Williams's noted kennel at South Wales.

CHAPTER TWO

Shetland Sheepdogs in England

Ch. Eltham Park Petite was widely acclaimed in England during 1923 when he gained his championship in three shows within five weeks. Mr. E.C. Pierce, one of the period's most famous breeders, was his owner.

The year 1909 was an important year in the history of the Shetland Sheepdog, for not only did the breed receive its recognition from the Kennel Club; but it also received, for the first time, classification at Crufts Dog Show, albeit no Challenge Certificates were offered to the winners until 1915.

The first championship awarded was to Clifford Pat, owned by the Misses E. Dawson and J. Wilkinson. Pat was born in 1914 and was a descendant of Lerwick Jarl and Lerwick Sigurd. This bitch gained her three Certificates at Crufts, Richmond, and Kensington.

Early Shetland Sheepdog exhibitors included Mrs. C. Ashton Cross, owner of the world-famous Alderbourne Pekingese, and I believe another Pekingese breeder as there is a Mrs. Hunloke listed on an early Sheltie entry which I have read. There also were four gentlemen active as exhibitors: Mr. Clark, Mr. Hoggan, Mr. Loggie, and Mr. Thompson.

Woodvoid, another descendant of Lerwick Jarl, bred by Mr. Keith and Mr. Ramsey, was shown prior to World War I by Miss B. Thynne and finished in 1914. Miss Thynne was very active as a Shetland Sheepdog exhibitor, and as the war began she was the only one with several win-

ners in competition, which included Caliph of Kilvarock, Iona Modee, and Kilvarock Spriggie.

Yet another Lerwick Jarl progeny, Frea, a homebred belonging to Mrs. B. Huband, was a pre-World War I winner, while Phoebe of Pix Hall, owned by Misses Dawson and Wilkinson, and Erica, shown by Miss M. Grey, are to be found in show records of that period, too.

Nettie of Mountford gained the title, while Freshfield Fad brought home numerous awards for Mrs. T. Harrison.

By about 1923 things were sufficiently returned to normal following the war; Shetland Sheepdog activities again were on the upswing. Both show entries and number of registrations were recording a rising trend, the latter numbering 258 that year. It is interesting that of the nineteen champions recorded, a considerable portion of them showed one parent or another to be unregistered.

As the 1920's progressed, so did Shetland Sheepdogs, with some truly excellent specimens appearing at the leading shows. Early postwar favorites included Champion Hurly Burly, Champion Walesby Select, and the lovely sable and white dog who was widely acclaimed for his quality and for his beneficial influential as a sire who produced the true show Collie-type Shetland Sheepdog—Champion Specks of Mountford, born in 1922 and bred by Mr. MacGregor.

One of the most famous, successful, and admired of the early kennels was Eltham Park, where Mr. E. C. Pierce made a worthy contribution to the breed, both in England and in the United States, with a whole succession of winners. Eltham Park Petite was said to be one of his best and is said to have truly excelled as an outstanding example of desirable type. Coming out in 1923, he quickly gained his championship at three consecutive shows. Champion Eltham Park Esme came to Miss Fredericka Fry in the United States. Eltham Park Evan and Eltham Park Evette were littermates. Champion Eltham Park Eureka, by Champion Specks of Mountford, won seven or more Challenge Certificates and became the sire of Champion Eltham Park Ena, from Eltham Park Emmie, a big winner of the late 1920's. Another Specks son with the Eltham Park prefix was Eltham Park Perfection, who was shown by Miss Thynne. Mr. Pierce also owned Wistonian Pixie, who was shown by A.R. Cox. Eltham Park Erling was another seen frequently in the winners' circle.

Miss Thynne's prewar activity continued into the postwar period with notable winning done by her Champion Kilvarock Nettie and her Goldfinger. Mr. Saunders was winning with

Margawse of Cameliard, a daughter of Ch. Gawaine of Cameliard ex Eltham Park Elise, was born in 1927. Bred by Mrs. J.A. Allen.

Farburn Advance, and Mrs. M. C. Tod was also winning with good dogs.

Tilford has been mentioned in the pedigrees of early dogs important in the United States. Champion Tilford Tinette was one doing well for the home kennel, owned by Mrs. and Miss Allen while Champion Tilford Tay came out during the early 1930's period, accounting for Challenge Certificate winning.

Probably the two English kennels most influential on Shelties in the United States were Clerwood and Peabody. The great American Champion Wee Laird of Downfield was a son of Braeberry of Clerwood, and the kennel's owner, Mrs. I. Warren, also gained fame with her Champion Euan of Clerwood and Champion Lochinva of Clerwood, the latter a leading winner of 1932.

It was from Miss Montgomery's Peabody Kennels that Betty Whelen bought the Shelties behind the blue line at Pocono; they were Peabody Silver Phantasy and, later that same year, Peabody Pan who became, as any Sheltie historian has found to be the case and can write about or tell you, the sire of the great and so very influential American sire, Champion Merrymaker of Pocono. At home in England, Peabody Panache became a champion for Miss Montgomery, in 1931.

Eng. and Am. Ch. Eltham Park Esme came from Mr. Pierce's kennel in Great Britain to that of Miss Fredericka Fry in Connecticut.

Ch. Ashbank Actress, winner of four Challenge Certificates, became a noted campaigner for Miss B. Thynne. She was bred by Mrs. A. Copland in 1928, starting her winning career the following year as a youngster.

This early English champion, Downfield Olaf, was a dog of tremendous importance to the breed, both in England and in the United States. Bred and owned by Mrs. J.C. Ramsay, he was a well-known Challenge Certificate winner for her abroad; then he came to the United States to Mr. and Mrs. Nichols' Walnut Hall Kennels, where he proved a valuable asset and quickly became an American champion. Olaf is a brother to the famed Eng. and Am. Ch. Wee Laird O'Downfield, who was so influential in the American Sheltie world when imported by Mrs. Dreer. Both dogs were by Blaeberry of Clerwood ex Downfield Ethne and were born in the late 1920's.

Other British Shetland Sheepdogs whose photos have taken my attention include a lovely bitch owned by Miss Thynne—Champion Ashbank Actress, who had won four Challenge Certificates, thus becoming an English Champion prior to reaching one year of age. She was bred by Mrs. Copland and born during 1928.

The features considered important to Shetland Sheepdogs in the British show ring of the 1930's placed emphasis on pretty dogs with *particular* emphasis on head and expression.

Flat skull, moderately wide between the ears, tapering towards the eyes with only a slight depression at the stop; cheeks neither full nor prominent; muzzle of fair length tapering towards the nose with no sign of weakness, snippiness, or a "lippy" condition. Nose black regardless of color of the dog. Sound teeth as nearly level as possible, although a very slight unevenness was permissible (and noticed in some of the dogs coming from England to the States and in their progeny). Clean-cut powerful jaws. Eyes medium size, set obliquely, almond shaped and close together, color brown. Ears small, moderately wide at the base, placed fairly close

Eng. and Am. Ch. Rob Roy O'Page's Hill, 1934-1949, from Mr. Gallagher's kennels. Photo courtesy of Lee Reasin.

together at top of skull. In repose thrown back, but at attention brought forward and carried firmly erect, tips drooping forward. The neck somewhat arched and fairly long and in proportion to the body which was moderately long and level with ribs well sprung and good length of loin, plus deep chest. Straight muscular forelegs. Hindlegs muscular at the thighs with hocks well bent. Oval feet with soles well padded, close, nicely arched toes. Tail moderately long with abundant hair, carried low with a slight upward swirl when the dog is quiet, gaily carried (but never over the back) when excited. The outer coat was described as being of hard hair, the undercoat resembling fur—short, soft and close, with abundant mane and frill; mask on face and tip of ears smooth. Forelegs well feathered. Hindlegs above the hocks profusely covered with hair, fairly smooth below the hocks. Any color acceptable except brindle. The general appearance of a Shetland Sheepdog that of a rough-coated Collie in miniature (Collie character and type adhered to), the height not exceeding 15 inches at maturity, which is at ten months old.

Faults: Short nose; domed skull; large, drooping ears; weak jaws; snipy muzzles; full or light eyes; crooked forelegs; cow hocks; tail carried over back; and overshot or undershot mouth.

Points were allotted as follows:
Head and expression.....15
Ears.................15
Neck and shoulders.......5
Legs and feet..........10
Hindquarters..........10
Back and loins..........5
Tail.................10
Coat and frill..........15
Size 15

Total.........100

It will be noticed that the standard of England and Scotland as adopted in 1930 gave a total of thirty points for head properties, almost a third of the total dog.

Both the Scottish Club and the English Club, revising their standards jointly in 1930, also stated that "the Shetland Sheepdog should resemble a Collie (Rough) in miniature."

Throughout the 1930's and on until World War II, Shelties continued a steady progress among English breeders. One kennel we have

Ch. Hallinwood Robin Hood of Marl, an English import owned by Mr. and Mrs. Willard K. Denton, Ardencaple Kennels.

heard mentioned for longevity and excellence is Riverhill, belonging to the Misses Felicity and Patience Rogers, which was founded back in 1931.

In post-World War II England, the Shelert Kennels had the first Sheltie puppy to win a Junior Warrant, and then this same Sheltie became famous in both England and the United States. This was English and American Champion Sigurd of Shelert, about whom you will read in the story of Hoch Haven Kennels further along in this book.

We wrote to numerous English breeders whose names we found as having been active since World War II, and we received very interesting and informative replies from Mrs. Eaves of the Kyleburns and from a South Wales breeder, Mrs. Williams of Mountaincrest. We are delighted to include them on the following pages, as they give some idea of what is taking place in the British Sheltie kennels of the present.

Golden Eagle puppies, one now a Danish champion, at about five months of age. Owned by Kyleburn Shelties, Mrs. Eaves, Kyleburn Kennels, Bucks, England.

A typical Sheltie puppy from Mountaincrest Kennels owned by Mrs. Frances Ruth Williams in South Wales.

Kyleburn

Kyleburn Shetland Sheepdogs are among the most famous and successful to be found in present-day Great Britain. Owned by Margaret D. Eaves at Askett, Aylesbury, Bucks, the kennel has earned a long and illustrious history, about which we shall let Mrs. Eaves tell you in her own words.

I first became interested in Shelties when, as a child at home, my sister was given permission to have a dog, something which I had longed for all my life. I remember adopting a neighbouring mongrel which practically lived at our house, on which I lavished my attentions and tried to train to a high standard, being then very interested in the obedience world. That poor dog had to put up with the somewhat crude methods of a complete novice, in between spells of living a life of unrestricted bliss chasing bitches in the streets.

When we moved to the country, I was leaving home, so it was my sister, who now shows horses, not dogs, who was able to keep a dog. This, on my father's advice, turned out to be a Sheltie. Every weekend I went home and again adopted a dog which was not my own. I was even then keen on showing and entered this bitch by Ellington Encore, a top postwar sire. She went Best of Breed at a local show and was even placed at a championship show, this at 16½ inches high, very dubious ear carriage, and a tail at times over her back. I was caught on dog shows, well and truly! I remember travelling by rail to one show and seeing Mrs. Thatcher get a top award with a lovely tri bitch. She even spoke to me—and made my day!

Dogs and dog shows became my dream after that. I desperately wanted my own, and I would invent illness to get to a show to see the Shelties if I couldn't get time off. My foundation bitch was eventually bought (in 1958, when I was twenty-six years old) from Mrs. Charlton of the Melwaig prefix, by Champion Heatherisle Rufus ex Champion Honeybunch of Melwaig. She was a tri-colour and ten weeks old. I have always loved the tri-colours above all else, possibly partly the reason for now adding Bernese

Eng. Ch. Kyleburn Athena, owned by Mrs. Eaves, Kyleburn Shelties, England. Diane Pearce, photographer.

Mountain Dogs to my kennel. I've also been an advocate for stronger bone in Shelties, though a Bernese is possibly going too far! The thing which worried me the most about Shelties when I started, apart from the prevalent fine bone, was the very nervous temperament. I was determined from the outset to breed Shelties which were of the right type but very hardy, moving as a working dog should, with the look of a worker in bone and substance, and a good temperament. Now I also add to this list freedom from eye defects, a fault I had not realized was so widespread until more recently. I do not mind if my dogs are not the fashionable type of the day. While I love to win in the ring, my first consideration is to breed what will justify in my eyes the worth of breeding at all, and hopefully to better the breed.

Even now, my dogs must be capable of being "rough." They are not pampered show dogs. I go hiking and regularly take some, who must be prepared to walk twelve miles times two, for they usually double my distance, through brambles and fences regardless of coat left hanging on every bit of barbed wire, and then go home to mate a bitch or go in the show ring a few days later, mud up to their bellies washed off and the remaining coat hopefully brushed into some semblance of a "show dog."

My initial efforts at breeding produced a superb bitch, by Champion Dilhome Blackcap. Beginner's luck, I'm sure. Unfortunately she hated shows, and with a young baby myself I could not really campaign her. She was called simply Black Belle. This was a mating within the CHE bloodlines though subsequently most of my stock has been BB due to an outcross to Oastwood Unique which produced Kyleburn Coppelia, one of the four pups Black Belle ever managed to rear out of three litters. Coppelia was a wonderful brood, producing six pups every time, with quality in most litters. Her first litter really started off the Kyleburn line and also the Midnitesun Kennels, for as I was having a baby and moving shortly afterwards I could not cope with a litter and Mrs. Wilbraham took over Coppelia for me, and we shared the resultant litter by one of the top dogs of the day, Champion Antoc Sealodge Spotlight, whom I loved for his bone, type and personality. He was also a grandson of Carousel of Melvaig, another offspring of Champion Honeybunch, the dam of my first bitch. I mated my Spotlight offspring mainly to Loughrigg dogs, for again I fell for the bone, movement and temperament they produced, and it was a Spotlight granddaughter mated to Loughrigg Concert Master (by Champion Trumpeter of Tooneytown) who produced Kyleburn Chiff Chaff, the dam of Champion Kyleburn Golden Eagle. Chiff Chaff was then mated to another Spotlight grandson who also had in his pedigree Tooneytown and Shelect bloodlines, the outcome being one of the "great" stud dogs who has made a lasting mark on the breed.

Strangely, Mrs. Wilbraham also went to similar bloodlines to produce her winning line and used Champion Trumpeter with great success. I personally had my success mainly from Concert Master, and we each tried the other dog, but it did not work out, yet one was the son of the other, and we each started with puppies from the same litter.

Golden Eagle happened at the right time for me. Until then I'd been struggling to breed and show a little whilst bringing up a young family and on a very limited budget indeed. I was willing to do almost anything to bring in the money to keep my dogs and hopefully breed the type of Sheltie I thought would both do the breed justice and please me personally. Born in 1970, he is still fit and well and has been outstanding as a stud being now behind many, many winning dogs in this country. He never did himself justice in the ring being "bored stiff" by the whole thing. I have had him swaying on his feet in the middle of the ring when called to "show your dogs" with his

Kyleburn Bundle of Joy (left), championship and open show winning puppy 1982, and Kyleburn Sweet William (right), by Adonis of Kyleburn, S/W puppy of 1982. Owned by Mrs. M.H. Eaves, Kyleburn Shelties, England.

Eng. Ch. Kyleburn Golden Eagle, by Loughrigg Harbour Pilot ex Kyleburn Chiff Chaff, born in 1970 and still alive and well in 1983. He has been an outstanding stud dog for the noted Kyleburn Kennels owned by Mrs. M.H. Eaves, England. Diane Pearce, photographer.

eyes closing as I dangled every tidbit I could think of before his complete unconcerned disinterest. He finally achieved four Challenge Certificates. But as a stud dog he was much more successful, passing on his own friendly temperament, beautiful coat, strong bone and lovely movement, qualities his sons and grandsons are still passing on. I finally got a good photo of him by banging car doors pretending to go away whilst the photographer patiently tried to get a picture of the true dog really using himself as he could at home. He was the leading stud dog in the country for several years running, and this was then taken over by one then another of his sons. He in total produced three champions, an overseas champion, and a Challenge Certificate winning dog in addition to many other first prize winners and Best of Breed winning children. His sons have produced more champions, and the line remains very strong.

Apart from Golden Eagle, I have since bred Champion Kyleburn Athena, to my mind still the best I have ever bred, and a joy to show as she loved the ring. She was by Champion Laughing King Minstrel who was 75% the same breeding as Golden Eagle. She gained five Challenge Certificates and seven Reserve Challenge Certificates before retirement, and her daughter by Champion Kyleburn Golden Eagle produced Adonis of Kyleburn who at the moment is siring so many winners. Other champions from here are Champion Kyleburn Penny Royal, Champion Kyleburn Star Laird, Champion Kyleburn Wild Thyme, Champion Laiderette of Kyleburn, and Champion Kyleburn Razzle Dazzle. There are also several overseas Kyleburn champions and I have lost count of the number of Reserve Challenge Certificate winners.

Over the past year or two (early 1980's) I have deliberately introduced some new blood, both from the Shelect bloodline and some more Riverhill and the CHE line. This has brought rewards and corrected some faults which can develop with too much inbreeding. My policy is still to mainly line-breed with an occasional introduction of new blood. Since I have now limited myself to keeping only CEA free males here, it has been a struggle to breed the ones who will really "keep the flag flying" in the ring as the best pups seem to be the ones with CEA, but I feel the ends will justify the struggle.

I hope that breeders always will consider the good of the breed before their achievements in the show ring, and remember that we must also think of the public who buy 75% of our stock as pets and do not mind show faults but do want a dog with a good temperament and free of defects.

We have brought you Mrs. Eaves' story of Kyleburn Shelties in her own words because many of her comments and remarks are of value to those who will read this book. We appreciate her time and interest in having replied so fully to my inquiry about her Shelties, and we wish her many years of continued success.

Above: Mountaincrest's Sparkler, by Hazelhead Drummer Boy, the winner of 149 first prizes plus numerous other awards. This is a grandson of the late Ch. Trumpeter of Tooneytown. Mrs. Frances Ruth Williams, owner, Mountaincrest Shetland Sheepdogs, Caerphilly, Mid Glam, South Wales. **Below:** An adorable litter sired by Mountaincrest's Wonder Boy and owned by Frances Ruth Williams, Mountaincrest Shetland Sheepdogs.

Mountaincrest

Mountaincrest Shetland Sheepdogs, owned by Mrs. Frances Ruth Williams, are located at South Wales. This lady is a Sheltie breeder of long duration, and although she feels pleased with the results of all her bloodlines, she is especially pleased with the one descended from the late Champion Trumpeter of Tooneytown.

Mrs. Williams purchased Trumpeter's winning son, the well-known Hazelhead Drummer Boy, who was widely used at stud. She had two sired by Drummer Boy: Mountaincrest's Sparkler (winner of 149 first prizes along with numerous other awards) and Mountaincrest's Wonder Boy. Both of these beautiful dogs are now deceased, but both left a quality heritage behind.

Dervan Pompadour is Wonder Boy's son, by whom Mrs. Williams has a litter of six which look to be extremely promising as we write this in 1983. The other stud dog presently at Mountaincrest is Glenmist Copper Cassanover, purchased at eight weeks of age.

Above: Mountaincrest Welsh Star, sold to Ireland, won two Green Stars and a Reserve Green Star before being tragically killed in the road. Bred by Mountaincrest Shetland Sheepdogs, Mrs. Frances Ruth Williams. **Below:** Sovereign of Mountaincrest is one of the fine Shelties bred by Frances Ruth Williams in South Wales.

Christmas at Mountaincrest in South Wales. Dervan Pompadour of Mountaincrest and Sovereign of Mountaincrest **belong** to Mrs. Frances Ruth **Williams. The baby belongs to a friend.**

Above: Dervan Pompadour of Mountaincrest is a present-day stud dog at Mountaincrest Shetland Sheepdogs owned by Mrs. F.R. Williams at South Wales. This popular dog is by Mountaincrest's Wonder Boy, who is by Hazelhead Drummer Boy, the latter a son of the late Ch. Trumpeter of Tooneytown. There is a most promising young litter by him at Mountaincrest as we write. **Below:** Glenmist Copper Cassanover at Mountaincrest is one of the present-day stud dogs owned by Mrs. F.R. Williams, Mountaincrest Shetland Sheepdogs. This lovely dog, a son of Lysebourne Quick March, was purchased at eight weeks of age as a breeding outcross.

Both of these two young Shelties have gone to show homes: Mountaincrest Welsh Queen (right) to a fancier in Sweden; Mountaincrest's Welsh Model (left) to another exhibitor. Bred by Mountaincrest Shetland Sheepdogs, Mrs. Frances Ruth Williams, South Wales.

The lovely Mountaincrest's Wee Laird of Hillyacres won his way to Crufts and will never be forgotten. Unfortunately he was not a good stud dog, although he has a winning son in Germany, namely Mountaincrest's Easter Lad. Mountaincrest Irish Maid, a daughter of Mountaincrest's Wonder Boy, was also exported to Germany, where she produced International and National Champion Etzel vom Stormarner Land and several other winners.

Another very excellent Sheltie, Mountaincrest's Welsh Star, was sold to Ireland where she did a lot of winning including two Green Stars and one Reserve Green Star. Then tragedy struck when someone left a gate open and she was killed instantly after wandering out into the road. She was a daughter of Dervan Pompadour of Mountaincrest.

Mrs. Williams has cut back sharply on her exhibiting since 1980, as she is judging instead and cannot manage to do both. A widow since the early 1970's, she is devoted to her dogs and only regrets that circumstances since that time have made it impossible for her to campaign them as she would have enjoyed doing so. They are surely a credit to her and, we know, a source of enormous pleasure.

Ch. Badgerton Alert Alec, the first Shetland Sheepdog in the United States ever to achieve three Bests in Show. Between the mid-1950's and his retirement in 1965, this handsome dog, in addition to his Best in Show victories, was Best of Breed 116 times and won sixty-six Group placements of which ten were firsts. Mrs. Joan J. Rejholic, owner. Photo courtesy of Lee Reasin.

CHAPTER THREE

Shetland Sheepdogs in the United States

Truly a priceless picture from the early 1930's! Mrs. Dreer's so very renowned early importation Ch. Wee Laird O'Downfield with his, at that time, young son, the future Ch. Mowgli. Anahassitt Kennels. Photo courtesy of Lee Reasin.

At the time of the breed's recognition by the American Kennel Club, and inclusion in the A.K.C. Stud Book, three members of the breed were listed. They were Lord Scott, 148,760; Lerwick Bess, 148,761; and the daughter of these two, Shetland Rose, 148,762, who thus became the first American-bred Shetland Sheepdog to be registered, her parents both having been imported from Scotland. Mr. J.G. Sherman of New Rochelle, New York, was the owner of Bess and the breeder of Rose. E.H. McChesney of New York City owned Lord Scott, and Shetland Rose's owner was Mrs. K.D. McMurrich of Minotto, New York. All three of these dogs were sables.

Another Scottish import, also carrying the Lerwick prefix, was the first Sheltie to become an American champion, an honor he attained in 1916. He remained the only one of the breed to hold the title in the United States for more than ten years. This was Champion Lerwick Rex, descended from Lerwick Jarl owned by the Scottish breeder Mr. Loggie, Rex being by Berry ex Bee.

During the few years immediately following the breed's acceptance by the American Kennel Club, Shetland Sheepdogs appeared in competition at all-breed dog shows and at shows held by the Toy Spaniel Club. But there was really very little stir of interest within the breed until the summer of 1923 when Mrs. Byron Rogers, then living on Long Island, imported four of them. A dog and a bitch of this group went to Mr. E.R. Stettinius, who kept the dog, English Champion Walesby Select, and sold the bitch, while the other two would seem to have been retained by Mrs. Rogers. The bitch Mr. Stettinius sold, Kilvarock Lassie, was purchased by a young fancier named Catherine Coleman, thus becoming the foundation bitch of the future very influential and important Sheltieland Kennels. Between 1923 and 1929 ten other Shelties arrived from overseas: three for Miss Coleman, two for Mrs. Dreer of Anahassitt, and five for Miss Frederica Fry of Far Sea Kennels at Cos Cob, Connecticut. Thus were the roots planted for the future! There was also another dog whom I have noticed Sheltie folk seem loath to mention, one named Nettle of Mountford, an English champion, whose papers were accepted for registration by the American Kennel Club and then later cancelled, along with those on a litter he had sired. It seems that Nettle of Mountford was accepted without question in England as an English champion; but War Baby of Mountford, his sire, was the son of a Collie, Teena, which did not in any way satisfy the requirements of the A.K.C.

When the "ice was finally broken" and a second Sheltie gained the honor of a championship title in the United States, some twelve years after Lerwick Rex had done so, it was the imported Farburn Captain who did so, owned by Catherine Coleman. To this lady goes tremendous credit for her contributions to and accomplishments within this breed! This lady's dogs and knowledge were extremely impressive and one notes with considerable awe that almost without exception the Shelties of note whelped in the United States during the 1920's were of her breeding. The already mentioned bitch, Kilvarock Lassie, had five litters during this time, while two of her daughters each produced one. Misty of Gray Hill and Champion Farburn Captain, both imported dogs belonging to Miss Coleman, were the sires used.

The Anahassitt Kennels is another to have become Sheltie-oriented in the late 1920's. Mrs. William F. Dreer, the owner, was a Collie breeder whose interest included Shelties, too. This became apparent when in 1927 she imported one of the famed Eltham Park Shelties, named Eltham Park Anahassitt; and Merlyn of

Mrs. William F. Dreer of the Anahassitt Shetland Sheepdogs with two of the very first puppies sired by Ch. Wee Laird O'Downfield. The photo, courtesy of Lee Reasin, is marked on the back: "Gift of J. Nate Levine, 30 Dec. 63."

Ch. Dancing Master of Anahassitt, the sire of Ch. Syncopating Sue, was a very famous Sheltie around 1930. Owned by Mrs. Dreer.

Cameliard, dog, the latter never heard from further so far as history is concerned. Eltham Park Anahassitt did leave her mark on the breed; she was sold to Mr. Harkness Edwards whose daughter, Katherine, became Mrs. H. W. Nichols, Jr., owner of the prestigious Walnut Hall Shelties; and this bitch became the dam of American and Canadian Champion Tiny Betty of Walnut Hall who was sired by Champion Downfield Olaf of Walnut Hall. Olaf was an English Challenge Certificate winner of 1929.

In researching for this book I have heard and read words of glowing praise for that most wonderful little dog Champion Wee Laird O' Downfield who came to America to Anahassitt Kennels. He had been selected by professional handler J. Nate Levine for his client when Mrs. Dreer sent him to England and Scotland during 1928 to choose some Shelties and some Collies for her. Mr. Levine was an inspired "dog man" with an eye for a good one second to none. Time and time again he proved this over the years, to the advantage of those for whom he showed dogs. Wee Laird was selected by him, along with an older full sister, Downfield Grethe, and a tricolor half-sister, Natalie of Clerwood; all of them were sired by English Champion Blae-

Ch. Syncopating Sue of Anahassitt was Pocono's second champion and was the first Sheltie owned by Miss Elizabeth D. Whelen, who purchased her at Morris and Essex in 1933. Sue was by Ch. Dancing Master of Anahassitt ex Anahassitt Atalanta; and in her first litter, by Ch. Bodachan of Clerwood, she produced the first of Betty Whelen's many homebred champions, this one Ch. Autumn Leaf of Pocono.

berry of Clerwood. Wee Laird, a young puppy at the time, and Grethe were from Downfield Ethne, while Natalie's dam was a bitch named No No Nanette. All three of these importations were listed in the Stud Book of July 1929. Wee Laird did not come to America until he was nine months old, we are told, having been left behind, we assume, to mature a bit more. These three new Shelties brought the number of Shelties in the United States to thirty: sixteen imported and fourteen American-bred. Of the total number, fortunately sixteen were bitches.

Despite his immaturity and the fact that he was not as yet a proven sire, less than a year after his arrival Wee Laird's stud career was underway. Natalie of Clerwood, his half-sister, became the dam of two noteworthy Shelties. One, Champion Adorable of Anahassitt in her turn added Shelties to the breed population who figured importantly in its progress in the United States. She had at least one litter for Mrs. Dreer and then was sold to Betty Whelen where she became the dam of other litters. One of them included a daughter, Astolat Lady Harlequin, who became the female ancestor behind Connie Hub-

bard's dogs. Adorable later became the property of Allan B. McLaughlin. The second, a son of Natalie and Wee Laird, became Jock of Walnut Hall, who sired six champions in his role as foundation stud at the Nichols' kennel.

Black Eyes Susan also produced well by Wee Laird, providing some good stock for the Longleigh Kennels belonging to Mrs. Wander.

Downfield Grethe, Wee Laird's full sister, produced little of importance by him in her first litter. But Mrs. Dreer tried it again, this time with far more exciting results in the form of a son, Wee MacGregor of Anahassitt, and a daughter, Jean of Anahassitt. Wee MacGregor daughters played an important role in the breeding programs at Bagaduce, Beach Cliff, and Captivator Kennels. Jean of Anahassitt became the foundation bitch of Mr. William W. Gallagher's Page's Hill Kennels, thus starting sixteen years of fantastic success of Sheltie breeding for this gentleman who remained ac-

Ch. Peabody Pan, by Peabody Paulet ex Peabody Plume, was imported from England in 1934 by Elizabeth D. Whelen from Miss Montgomery. Ch. Syncopating Sue of Anahassitt and this dog produced one of the most important early sires in the breed, Ch. Merrymaker of Pocono, born in October 1935, who became the sire of twenty-five champions and is credited by many as having a major share in changing the very appearance of the breed.

Two famous Shelties of the 1935 period: on the left, Ch. Autumn Leaf of Pocono, Betty Whelen's first homebred champion, and on the right, Ch. Merry Memory of Pocono. Pocono Kennels, Elizabeth D. Whelen.

tively involved throughout the balance of his lifetime. As foundation bitch at Page's Hill, Jean was bred back twice to her sire and became the dam of Champion Mowgli and Champion Piccolo O'Page's Hill.

Returning to Wee Laird himself, he was a super show-dog who aroused admiration upon sight. His career began at Westminster in 1929 where he won Best of Breed, following this up with an almost unbroken chain of twenty-six Bests of Breed over the next forty months. Considering how very few and far between dog shows were in those days by our modern standards, this was truly a very notable accomplishment. In 1929, 1930, and 1932 he won the breed at Westminster, and on the third of these occasions added excitement for the Sheltie world with a Working Group placement there, the breed's first. Wee Laird had a Working Group first to his credit as well, gained at Rochester in 1932. His brother, Champion Downfield Olaf of Walnut Hall, was the dog who interrupted his Westminster Best of Breed victories, being the one who took the honor in 1931.

As a sire, Wee Laird produced seventeen litters from breedings to thirteen bitches. Sadly, he

only lived to become seven and a half years of age—his loss sincerely mourned by all who knew or had ever seen him!

You will read more about the Anahassitt dogs as you enjoy our kennel stories, since these dogs have been instrumental in the founding or background of many noted members of the breed.

Wee Laird's son, Champion Mowgli, was the first American-bred Shetland Sheepdog to attain championship honors. He himself sired nineteen champions, and he was grandsire of fifty-four champions, certainly a very impressive total. Added to this is the fact that many of these champions were dogs of tremendous influence on the breed. While he himself was the foundation dog at Mr. Gallagher's Page's Hill Kennels, his sons were equally important to the success of Beach Cliff, Noralee, and Pixie Dell. His grandsons numbered among them Champion Mountaineer O'Page's Hill (sire of twenty-two champions), Champion Prince George O'Page's Hill (thirteen champions including Champion Nashcrest Golden Note who sired twenty-six champions), and Champion Timberidge Temptation (sire of thirty-two champions).

Mr. Gallagher was a wonderful gentleman from all we have read about him, and I only regret never having known him personally. Although we speak of Jean of Anahassitt as having started him off with Shelties, actually he was already a Sheltie owner when he purchased her,

Ch. Timberidge Temptress, the dam of Dot Foster's well-known Ch. Timberidge Temptation, a popular winner of the early 1940's. Dorothy Allen Foster had many fine Shelties under the "Timberidge" identification and was an important breeder of that period.

bred her back to her sire, and produced Mowgli. This earlier dog was acquired by Mr. Gallagher through his long-time friend Mr. James Saunders, noted Terrier expert from Scotland, who sent to Mr. Gallagher in 1930, a tricolor English Champion named Helensdale Laddie, known to his friends as "Peter," who was five years old at that time (he lived to be nearly eighteen). He has to his credit the distinction of being the first English champion Shetland Sheepdog male to gain an American championship as well, plus having been the sire of the first American-bred Sheltie bitch, Miss Blackie (also owned by Mr. Gallagher), who finished just two weeks later than Mowgli. Bred by Catherine Coleman, Miss Blackie was by English and American Champion Helensdale Laddie ex Sheltieland Thistle, who was from Helensdale Lassie, litter-sister to Laddie. Incidentally, Thistle made history, too, by becoming America's first blue-merle champion.

Ch. Mountaineer O'Page's Hill, born in 1941, was a tremendously important influence on the breed as the sire of twenty-two American champions. Photo courtesy of Lee Reasin.

Best of Breed at the American Shetland Sheepdog Association Specialty, June 1946 at Framingham, Massachusetts, was Ch. Timberidge Temptation, owner-handled by Dorothy (Dot) Allen Foster. The gentlemen in the picture are William Gallagher (left) whose Page's Hill Kennel was one of the breed's most successful in the early days, and Willis H. Nichols who, with Mrs. Nichols, owned the noted Walnut Hall Shelties.

Mowgli's show career is of interest as it was very brief and completed while he was still a puppy. He made his debut at Westminster in 1932, taking Reserve. The following week at Hartford he gained five points by taking Winners Dog, and then he went on to Best of Breed. He went Reserve again the following day at Elm City, and then on to the Eastern in Boston for Best of Winners and another five points. The following month, at Providence, Mowgli took Best of Winners for his third five-point major, then again on to his second Best of Breed. Eight months and ten days old, Mowgli now was a champion and did not again compete in the show ring. Nate Levine, his handler, in writing of Mowgli some years later said of him,

> He was the greatest balanced Sheltie of his day. His legs, feet, body and gait were absolutely perfection. He had a full, bang up muzzle, flat skull, very good eye, perfectly even teeth, strong underjaw, very clean cheeks, ears correctly placed but pricked, nice reach of neck, a full white collar and was a dark mahogany sable in color. With a little less stop at the eyes, and naturally tipped ears, he might well have been considered perfect.

Mowgli's son, Champion Pegasus O'Page's Hill, became the foundation male at Beach Cliff

Kennels. Another son, Champion Sheltieland Laird, was exported to England prior to World War II. A third son, Champion Ronalee Norseman, became the foundation male for Noralee Kennels. Still another of his sons, Champion Cock O'The North O'Page's Hill, became foundation male for the Pixie Dell Kennels.

The Pacific Coast has long been a busy place for activity within the Sheltie world, and many fine breeders are now located there, as well as some highly important and active Specialty clubs in California among other areas. Generally credited with being the trailblazer for all this was Mrs. Vance Callan O'Bryan who had moved to the West Coast from Michigan around 1930, prior to her marriage. As Miss Callan, she met and became associated with a Collie breeder of note on the Pacific Coast, Mrs. Florence B. Cleveland, owner of Geronimo Kennels. In 1931, Vance Callan purchased a blue-merle Sheltie bitch puppy from Catherine Coleman, which was named Bluebell and which was a litter-sister to Mr. Gallagher's tricolor Champion Miss Blackie already referred to here. The Sheltie so completely won over Mrs. Cleveland that it was decided by the two ladies to merge their interests, adding Shelties to the Collies

Ch. Sheltieland Laird O'Page's Hill was exported to England just prior to World War II. Photo courtesy of Lee Reasin.

The great Ch. Cock O'The North O'Page's Hill, one of the breed's all time greats. Photo courtesy of Lee Reasin.

already owned by Mrs. Cleveland. At first the Shelties were registered under "Cleveland and Callan," which we are sure must have proven burdensome in naming dogs due to the limit on the number of letters permissible in registered names. For awhile Miss Callan used "Sunset" but could not register it due to a St. Bernard breeder's previous use of that name. "O' the Picts" came from references Vance Callan had read of a small warlike ancient people in the Shetland Islands. She liked the sound of it, so she applied for registration of this kennel name, which was approved in 1936.

O' the Picts Kennels appeared for the first time in a show catalog at Marin North Bay Kennel Club on September 27th of that year, an occasion memorable not only for the inclusion of this new kennel but also for having been the very first time on the West Coast when the Sheltie entry totalled a sufficient number of Shelties in competition for a major, three points in this case. Shadow o' the Picts and Petticoat o' the Picts took Winners Dog and Winners Bitch respectively, gaining both the majors. There were three dogs and four bitches comprising the Sheltie entry, the dog going Best of Winners.

Vance Callan was married to W.L. O'Bryan in 1937, following which she terminated the association with Geronimo, taking her Shelties to her new home at Petaluma, California. Soon

The great and important Ch. Will O'The Mill O'Page's Hill, one of Mr. Gallagher's early winners. Photo courtesy of Lee Reasin.

Mountaineer arrived at his new home in California in 1942 at less than two years old. He sired, the records tell us, ninety-four litters from sixty-three bitches. The progeny of those dogs and bitches which had accompanied Mrs. O'Bryan to her new home at the time of her marriage provided ideal daughters for breeding to Mountaineer, since they were from backgrounds so similar to his own.

It is interesting that Mrs. O'Bryan kept Corriedale lambs and ewes at her home on its seventeen acres, which she had acquired specifically to prove that the Sheltie is not too small to train for herding and obedience. Scottish Mist o'the Picts was the first Sheltie on the West Coast to earn an obedience degree.

When Mrs. O'Bryan started with Shelties in California, the West Coast entries were extremely small, interest there having in no way kept

after that she lost Bluebell, purchasing as a replacement Sheltieland Shades O'Night and the dog Dazzler O'Page's Hill (Dazzler by Mowgli from Miss Blackie, Bluebell's litter-sister), who was intended to become a stud dog but died prior to ever being used. Upon losing Dazzler, Mrs. O'Bryan purchased Pickaninny O' Page's Hill, and this was the real beginning of the o'the Picts line. Bred to Mowgli, Pickaninny produced Champion Petticoat o'the Picts. Bred to Jack O'Page's Hill she produced Geronimo Red Knight. When Miss Callan became Mrs. O'Bryan she took along with her Pickaninny Petticoat, Pinafore, two blue females from Pastel o'the Picts, and three new purchases. The latter were Pocono Penelope of Bagaduce, Champion Royal Scot O'Page's Hill, and Harbinger O'Page's Hill. In 1942, halfway through his second year, Champion Mountaineer O'Page's Hill was added to the kennel after a whirlwind Eastern show career. Mountaineer took Winners Dog from the American-bred Class at Westminster judged by Mrs. Nichols. From there he went to First and Best American-bred in the Working Group at Elm City and Best of Breed at Eastern Dog Club. He finished in March with Best of Breed and first in the Working Group at Saw Mill (one of the very rare occasions when Saw Mill has permitted Group competition at its shows), and six days later in Chicago for the International he took Best of Breed from Alva Rosenberg and third in the Working Group from R.L. Patterson.

Ch. Stronghold O'Page's Hill, still another fine example of the quality for which Mr. Gallagher's noted kennel was so widely respected. Photo courtesy of Lee Reasin.

Ch. Pinafore o'the Picts, left; Ch. Royal Scot O'Page's Hill, center; and Popinjay o'the Picts with the sheep at Vance Callan O'Bryan's in California in the early 1940's. Photo courtesy of Lee Reasin.

pace with the rise on the East Coast. By 1942, however, a sharp increase had developed. Champion Magic Master of Pocono was the first of the breed to become a champion there, and Petticoat o'the Picts was the first California-bred. Then came Shepherd, Pinafore, and Pastel o'the Picts; Geronimo's Little Jemima; and Mrs. Cooley's Toonie Bridget of Crawleyridge. In 1942, the Pacific Northwest Shetland Sheepdog Club was formed, with a membership of about twenty people located from El Cajon to British Columbia!

Mr. O'Bryan passed away suddenly in 1949, leading to changes for his widow, which led to the temporary dispersal of the o'the Picts Kennels. Mountaineer went to Mrs. Cleveland's Geronimo Kennels, where he was cared for and used at stud until his death.

It was not until 1935 that Sheltie registrations in the United States passed the 100 mark, which they did that year when the total reached 120. Things picked up after that, however, and by 1942 there were 456 registrations, making Shetland Sheepdogs twenty-eighth on the registration lists that year.

One cannot write about Sheltie history in the United States without paying special tribute to Champion Elf Dale Viking, who had the longest and most exciting list of consecutive victories of his day. Bred and owned by Frank and Velma Sanders, and handled by Wayne Baxter, Viking during the mid-1960's gained, among other

The great Ch. Elf Dale Viking taking one of his Bests in Show, this time at Silver Bay Kennel Club under judge Rex B. Foster in February 1964. Handler, W. Baxter; owner, Elf Dale Kennels. This dog held a phenomenal show record, with the longest and most exciting string of consecutive wins in Sheltie history of the 1960's. Photo courtesy of Lee A. Reasin.

honors, thirteen Bests in Show, forty-two Working Group firsts, fifty-one additional Group placements, and Best of Breed at two Specialty shows. He was Number Five all-breeds in 1963, Number Three all-breeds in 1964, and Number Nine all-breeds in 1965.

The sire of Viking was Champion Noralee's Forecaster, owned by Dr. and Mrs. Earle E. Hansch, for whom they had named their kennel when they brought this magnificent dog from the East in about 1954. Forecaster Kennels were appropriately named for him, and the role he played in Sheltie history during the 1950's was one of tremendous importance. Forecaster died on October 22nd 1962, and the kennels disbanded in that same year. Prominent among Forecaster's progeny were, as already mentioned, Champion Elf Dale Viking and his littermate Champion Forecaster Son of Heidi, C.D., and Champion Timberidge Scarlet Phantasy.

Following Mrs. Cleveland's death (she was the "Geronimo" lady already mentioned), some of her Shelties joined Forecaster at the Hansch's kennel. One of these was Champion Geronimo Crown Prince.

Lee Reasin of the Tambrae Shelties has been actively associated with this breed over a great many years. Living in Santa Barbara at that time, it was he who arranged for and brought the lovely Champion Kawartha Mr. Alpha to the Coast during the 1950's, shown by him in co-ownership with Gerald J. Carey. Mr. Alpha was by Champion Sheltielore Diablo ex Champion Kawarthas Sabrina Fair.

Special "stars" of the 1960's include those who belonged to the coveted Century Club for which any Sheltie who has gained more than one hundred Bests in Show is eligible. Among the distinguished membership of those days was Champion Dark Lagoon O'Page's Hill, retired

Ch. Noralee Forecaster, by Ch. Noralee Bronze Nugget ex Noralee Indian Summer, June 1951-October 1962. Owner Dr. Earle J. Hansch, Forecaster Kennels, looks on as Noralee takes Best of Breed at Santa Barbara in 1957. Wayne Baxter, handler; Virgil Johnson, judge. Bred by Noralee and Timberidge Kennels. Photo courtesy of Lee Reasin.

Ch. Dark Lagoon O'Page's Hill, one of the many important winners handled by Frank Ashbey, a very talented professional. Here winning at Rock Creek Kennel Club in 1962 under judge Ed Pickhardt. Photo courtesy of John L. Ashbey.

on September 3rd 1967; he was bred by Florence Levine and was sold to Karol A. O'Connell of Suffern, New York, in 1961 at about a year old. In joining the Century Club, which was established in 1955 by Champion Frigate's Emblem of Astolat (with 101 Bests of Breed), he found himself a fellow member to Champion Nashcrest Golden Note (105 times Best of Breed), Champion Mori-Brook's Country Squire (104), Champion Badgerton Alert Alec (117), Champion Elf Dale Viking (170), Champion Mori-Brook Icecapade, C.D. (151), and now Lagoon—these between 1955 and 1961.

A son of Champion Brandell's Break-a-Way II ex Champion Dark Mist O'Page's Hill, both of whom were Best in Show winners, Dark Lagoon was handled, as were so many famous Shelties of that day, by Frank Ashbey of Ballston Spa, New York. He was the father of our tremendously gifted professional photographer of the present, John Ashbey, who possesses the talent with a camera that his father had with a lead and brush—that of making a dog look its best. Frank Ashbey was extremely popular with Sheltie exhibitors and always had a choice of outstanding dogs with which to work as he was known for his ability, especially with the "coated" breeds which for so many less capable people can present a real problem.

Ch. Pixie Dell Theme Song (left) and Ch. Nashcrest Golden Note (right) at the Tri State Shetland Sheepdog Association Specialty on October 11th 1953.

Early Shetland Sheepdog Champions

The following is a list of the earliest Shetland Sheepdog champions in the United States, from the first in 1916 through December 1938, originally compiled by *Dog World* magazine. Since there were only eighty-one of them, we feel that our readers will find the list of interest and that it should be included here.

Ace of Anahassitt, by Wee Laird O'Downfield ex Ariadne of Anahassitt

Adorable of Anahassitt, by Wee Laird O'Downfield ex Natalie of Clerwood

Adoration, by Merrymaker of Pocono ex Sheltieland Tillie

Alice of Anahassitt, by Wee Laird O'Downfield ex Adriadne of Anahassitt

Anahassitt Adoration, by Wee MacGregor of Anahassitt ex Adorable of Anahassitt

Anahassitt Aphrodite, by Sprig of Houghton Hill ex Anahassitt Atalanta

Ardland Actress, by Ardland Actor ex Ardland Ann

Ardland Admiral, by Melchior of Anahassitt ex Keep Goin'

Ch. Carrico's Port of Entry, a famous winner owned by Mr. and Mrs. Willard K. Denton of Southbury, Connecticut, during the 1950's. Photo of a portrait done by Betty McConnell.

A lovely and historic photo of highly successful professional handler Frank Ashbey, who piloted many a splendid Sheltie to top honors, with Ch. Bonnie Lass of Hatfield. Photo courtesy of John L. Ashbey.

Ardland Adorable, by Rob Roy O'Page's Hill ex Keep Goin'

Ardland Ann, by Melchior of Anahassitt ex Keep Goin'

Ardland Artist, by Melchior of Anahassitt ex Keep Goin'

Ardland Atom, by Rob Roy O'Page's Hill ex Keep Goin'

Ariadne of Anahassitt, by Bodachan of Clerwood ex Ashbank Fairy

Ashbank Fairy, by Blaeberry of Clerwood ex Ashbank Sheila

Autumn Leaf of Pocono, by Bodachan of Clerwood ex Syncopating Sue of Anahassitt

Avocation, by Melchior of Anahassitt ex Adventuress of Lea

Beach Cliff's Mischief, by Merrymaker of Pocono ex Dark Elegance of Pocono

Black Sachem O'Page's Hill, by Rob Roy O'Page's Hill ex Feldgate Biddy

Bodachan of Clerwood, by Euan of Clerwood ex Bradken of Clerwood

Captivator Candy O'Beech Tree, by Melchior of Anahassitt ex Ada of Anahassitt

Coltness Commander, by Mowgli ex Nattie Gallagher O'Page's Hill

Dancing Master of Anahassitt, by Uam Var of Houghton Hill ex Ballet Girl of Houghton Hill

Ch. Merry Memory of Pocono, at six months of age. Elizabeth D. Whelen, breeder-owner, Pocono Shetland Sheepdogs.

Downfield Grethe, by Blaeberry of Clerwood ex Downfield Ethne

Downfield Jarl, by Blaeberry of Clerwood ex Downfield Ethne

Downfield Olaf of Walnut Hall, by Blaeberry of Clerwood ex Downfield Ethne

Eltham Park Elyned of Far Sea, by Tilford Tartan ex Judy of Clerwood

Eltham Park Esme, by Eltham Park Erling ex Eltham Park Emmie

Evening Chimes, by Jack O'Page's Hill ex Dixie Belle

Farburn Captain, by Forward ex Farburn Bo Bo

Gigolo of Anahassitt, by Dancing Master of Anahassitt ex Anahassitt Atalanta

Golden Girl of Walnut Hall, by Sport ex Kate of Kateville

Golden Harriet of Brunstane, by Golden Boss ex Golden Girl

Gregor MacGregor of Bagaduce, by Peabody Paladin ex Eroica O'Page's Hill

Helensdale Forget Me Not, by Rob Roy O'Page's Hill ex Helensdale Jewel

Helensdale Laddie, by Chestnut Bud ex Aberland Wendy

Helensdale Marigold of Walnut Hall, by Helensdale Emerald ex Helensdale Nugget

Helensdale Sapphire, by Farburn Marshall ex Helensdale Ruby

Kalandar Prince O'Page's Hill, by Mowgli ex Pandora O'Page's Hill

Kelpie, by Coltness Commander ex Brenda

Kim O'Page's Hill, by Mowgli ex Natalie O' Page's Hill

Lady Precious O'Page's Hill, by Mowgli ex Pandora O'Page's Hill

Lady Tamworth O'Page's Hill, by Mowgli ex Natalie O'Page's Hill

Lerwick Rex, by Berry ex Bee

Light Brigade O'Page's Hill, by Rob Roy O' Page's Hill ex Anahassitt April Lady

Magic Master of Pocono, by Masterpiece of Pocono ex Peabody Silver Phantasy

Mazeppa O'Page's Hill, by Kalandar Prince O'Page's Hill ex Anahassitt April Lady

Meadow Sweet O'Page's Hill, by Rob Roy O'Page's Hill ex Anahassitt April Lady

Merry Maid of Anahassitt, by Merrymaker of Pocono ex Sunny Girl of Anahassitt

Merrymaker of Pocono, by Peabody Pan ex Syncopating Sue of Anahassitt

Merry Memory of Pocono, by Melchior of Anahassitt ex Syncopating Sue of Anahassitt

Miss Blackie, by Helensdale Laddie ex Sheltieland Thistle

Mowgli, by Wee Laird of Downfield ex Jean of Anahassitt

Neilsland Nuffsaid, by Bodachan of Clerwood ex Glenisla Elegance

Nicholas of Exford, by Puck of Exford ex Wonder of Exford

Peabody Pan, by Peabody Paulet ex Peabody Plume

Pegasus O'Page's Hill, by Mowgli ex Miss Blackie

Peter Pan O'Page's Hill, by Mowgli ex Miss Blackie

Petticoat o'the Picts, by Mowgli ex Pickaninny O'Page's Hill

Piccolo O'Page's Hill, by Wee Laird of Downfield ex Jean of Anahassitt

Pied Piper O'Page's Hill, by Mowgli ex Helensdale Sapphire

Promise O'Page's Hill, by Mowgli ex Helensdale Sapphire

Qui Vive O'Page's Hill, by Rob Roy O'Page's Hill ex Anahassitt April Lady

Rob Roy O'Page's Hill, by Helensdale Emerald ex Helensdale Nuggett

Rockwood Lady Astolat, by Wee Cubby of Far Sea ex Anahassitt Aphrodite

Ronalee Norseman, by Mowgli ex Lady Diana of Rowcliffe

Sable David of Runnymede, by Jock of Walnut Hall ex Golden Lady of Walnut Hall

Sheltieland Butterscotch, by Sheltieland Little Tay ex Sheltieland Bittersweet

Sheltieland Laird, by Mowgli ex Sheltieland Little Ideal

Sheltieland Little Boy, by Mowgli ex Sheltieland Bittersweet

Shepherd o'the Picts, by Geronimo Red Knight ex Sheltieland Shades o'Night

Sprig of Houghton Hill, by Uam Var of Houghton Hill ex Chestnut Garland

Syncopating Sue of Anahassitt, by Dancing Master of Anahassitt ex Anahassitt Atalanta

Tilford Tulla, by Euan of Clerwood ex Tilford Tontine

Tiny Betty of Walnut Hall, by Downfield Olaf of Walnut Hall ex Lassie of Walnut Hall

Tiny Chloe of Walnut Hall, by Mowgli ex Tiny Betty of Walnut Hall

Tiny Lelani of Walnut Hall, by Nicholas of Exford ex Tiny Hildeburh of Walnut Hall

Tiny Margaret of Walnut Hall, by Kim O'Page's Hill ex Helmsdale Marigold of Walnut Hall

Tiny Rex of Walnut Hall, by Nicholas of Exford ex Golden Lady of Walnut Hall

Wee Cubby of Far Sea, by Wee Tommy II of Far Sea ex Eltham Park Eclat of Far Sea

Wee Laird O'Downfield, by Blaeberry of Clerwood ex Downfield Ethne

Winsome Brownie, by Melchior of Anahassitt ex Adventuress of Lea

Ch. Tiny Toby of Walnut Hall, by Ch. Blue Heritage of Pocono ex Leatha of Walnut Hall, went Best of Breed at the American Shetland Sheepdog Association Specialty Show in 1960. Mrs. Gray, judge; Mr. and Mrs. H.W. Nichols, Jr., owners; Elizabeth D. Whelen, handler. Photo courtesy of Miss Whelen.

Ch. Colvidale Soliloquy taking Best of Opposite Sex at the American Shetland Sheepdog Association National in 1959. Louis Murr, judge; Mary Van Wagenen, handler. Photo courtesy of Charlotte McGowan.

The American Shetland Sheepdog Association

It was in 1929, during the Westminster Kennel Club event in Madison Square Garden, New York, that a group of Shetland Sheepdog enthusiasts gathered together to organize a Specialty club for their breed, which subsequently became known as the American Shetland Sheepdog Association. This first meeting was called to order at 9:00 P.M. on February 12th, 1929, to be exact, and the first panel of officers elected consisted of Miss Fredericka Fry (who later became Mrs. del Guercio) who was elected President; Mrs. William F. Dreer, First Vice-President; A.A. Parker, Second Vice-President; Miss Catherine E. Coleman, Secretary; and George W. Carr, Treasurer.

It was an unlimited membership, open to all who owned, had owned, or intended to own Shelties. Annual awards were lined up to be competed for by members only, and all members were under agreement to work for the good of the breed and for the club's accomplishments.

Since Sheltie fanciers were scattered throughout the country, it was decided to hold just one formal meeting annually, during Westminster in New York. To keep the membership abreast of any new developments or subjects under discussion, a newsletter was created to be circulated among all members.

The first membership list of the ASSA included, in addition to those already named as officers, Mrs. Gladys A. Funke, New York City; Mr. and Mrs. C.J. Spill, Garden City, New York; Mrs. Florence L. Hough, New York City; Oscar Day, Fulton, New York; Mrs. J. Edward Shanaberger, Ravenna, Ohio; J. Nate Levine, Philadelphia, Pa.; Walter J. Graham, Red Bank, New Jersey; Misses Florence and Mabel and Master Anthony Garvin, Roslyn, New York; S.W. Wright, Reading, Pennsylvania; Miss Agnes Mills (companion and secretary to Mrs. Dreer); Mrs. Gerry A. Morgan, Garden City, New York; Mrs. Natalie Stonington, West Brighton, New York; Miss Constance Brainard, Hartford, Connecticut; Miss Jean Carter, Locust Valley, New York; and Benjamin Richardson of Cos Cob, Connecticut.

A supplementary meeting took place ten days later, in conjunction with the Eastern Dog Club Show in Boston, when discussion of by-laws and work on setting up a system was begun. Two months later, in April 1929, Miss Fry presented the club with an especially appreciated gift—the membership fee enabling it to become a member of the American Kennel Club.

The American Shetland Sheepdog Association has grown steadily over the years, always watchful for the breed's best interests. The Sheltie's swift rise to popularity, as is always the case under these circumstances, has brought about problems. ASSA has handled these well, sticking to its steady course as a stabilizing force in the breed.

There are many regional clubs, ASSA members, throughout the country. These clubs give successful Specialty shows and offer local Sheltie fanciers the opportunity of adding to their breed knowledge through educational programs and match shows as well. ASSA prefers, we understand, that new fanciers start out by joining a regional club, several years' active participation in which is considered to be excellent background and preparation for eventual membership in ASSA, the parent club of the breed.

Specialty shows have been held by ASSA since the beginning of the 1930's and are now on a rotating basis in various sections of the country, usually combined with a local Specialty as well as other events for a very impressive Sheltie "happening." Now hundreds of dogs turn out for these events, a win at which is considered to be the breed's most prestigious of any year.

Ch. Pixie Dell Royal Jester (left) and Ch. Pixie Dell Bright Promise (right), handled by J. Nate Levine, at Wilmington Kennel Club. April 1956. Photo courtesy of Lee A. Reasin.

"V for Victory" in 1945. From left to right: Pandora of Pocono, C.D.; Ch. Larkspur of Pocono, C.D.X.; Ch. Merry Meddler of Pocono, C.D.X.; Ch. Sea Isle Merle Legacy, C.D.; and Ch. Victory of Pocono, C.D.X.—all from the Pocono Kennels, Elizabeth D. Whelen, now at Albuquerque, New Mexico.

Ch. Malpsh Great Scott, famous Best in Show winner handled by Frank Ashbey. Photo courtesy of John L. Ashbey.

Ch. Alandie Blue Lily, C.D.X., by Ch. Little John of Alandie ex Bil-Bo-Dot Thimble, an important Sheltie of the 1950's. Photo courtesy of Lee A. Reasin.

Above: Ch. Carrico's Port of Entry in May 1955. This famous winner of the period was owned by Mr. and Mrs. Willard K. Denton. Below: Ch. Kiloren Silvertone winning Best of Breed at the S.S.C.S.C. Judge, Betty Whelen.

Above: Ch. Tiny Honey of Walnut Hall, by Ch. Browne Acres Statesman ex Tiny Bly of Walnut Hall. Shown exclusively by Betty Whelen for owners, Mr. and Mrs. H.W. Nichols, Walnut Hall Kennels. Below: Tiny Talisman of Walnut Hall, C.D.X., a 15½-inch sable and white weighing twenty-five pounds, by Golden Web of Houghford ex Tiny Hannah of Walnut Hall. Born in 1955, bred by Mr. and Mrs. H.W. Nichols, Jr., Walnut Hall Kennels, and owned by Josephine Sagebeer. Photo courtesy of Lee Reasin.

Ch. Sea Isle Serenade in June 1958 with handler Frank Ashbey. Photo courtesy of John L. Ashbey.

Ch. Wansor's Dusky Lassie in June 1957 with noted professional handler Frank Ashbey.

Ch. Nashcrest Ensign in August 1960 making a good win under judge Bob Wills with handler Frank Ashbey, father of photographer John L. Ashbey who so kindly got together many photos from his dad's collection for us.

Ch. Tentagel David Copperfield, from the 1960's. Photo from Lee Reasin's collection.

Above: Ch. Browne Acres Diplomat. Below: Browne Acres Barrister. Photos courtesy of Lee Reasin.

Above: Ch. Forecaster Francesca, by Ch. Forecaster Son of Heidi ex Geronimo Golden Gossimer, in December 1960. Bred, owned, and handled by Sallie Hansch, Francesca completed title in September 1962 under six judges with one Best of Breed and five Best Opposites. Below: Alandie Am I Blue, owned by Alandie Kennels, Miss Joan Morley and Mrs. Helen Reinertsen, El Monte, California. Photos courtesy of Lee Reasin.

Above: Ch. Little John of Alandie, well-known Sheltie of the 1960's. **Below:** Ch. Wendemere's Bold Venture, by Ch. Jim Jon Ard Geronimo ex Browne Acres Bouffant, C.D.X., in January 1962. Bred by T.D. Parkhurst and J.W. Brown; owners, Don and Margaret Parkhurst. Photos courtesy of Lee Reasin.

Above: Forecaster Sweet William, by Ch. Forecaster Son of Heidi ex Forecaster Lady Ellen, in July 1962. Handled by Bill Holbrook for owner, Irene C. Rowlands. **Below:** Am., Mex., and Can. Ch. Playwater Beau of Thadane, Am. U.D., Mex. P.C.E., Can. C.D., by Ch. Little Shepherd of Thadane ex Ch. Pixie Lass of Thadane, whelped April 1959. Breeder, Teresa M. Brooks; owner, Betty W. Ross. Photos courtesy of Lee A. Reasin.

Forecaster Prince of Sharlin at Santa Ana Valley in 1964; judge, Mrs. E.C. Edmiston. Co-owners, Barbara Haegele and breeder-handler Sallie Hansch. Photo courtesy of Lee Reasin.

Ch. Forecaster Morning Mist, by Ch. Forecaster Song of Heidi ex Forecaster Song of Norgay, born September 1964. Barbara Riepe, owner, Calabasas, California. Photo from Lee Reasin's collection.

Ch. Sharlin's Tempting Teressa, by Ch. Forecaster Son of Heidi ex Forecaster Willow Wren, born April 23rd 1961. Bred by Richard Haegele; owned by Carl and Barbara Jackson. Photo courtesy of Lee Reasin.

Ch. Forecaster Song of Norgay, by Forecaster Scarlet Duke ex Forecaster Francesca, on February 6th 1962. Photo courtesy of Lee Reasin.

Above: Ch. Forecaster Wee Bairn of Heidi, by Ch. Pixie Dell Bright Vision ex Ch. Forecaster Francesca, in 1967. Whelped in September 1964. Breeder, Kambrae Kennels; owners, Jack P. and Flora C. Hall; handler, Jack Hall. Photo from the collection of Lee Reasin. **Below:** Ch. Pixie Dell Revelry, handled here by Howard Tyler, winning at Bucks County in May 1962.

Above: Rorralore Renata, August 1964. **Below:** Ch. Rorralore Robert The Bruce, an important dog you may find in your pedigrees, in May 1962. Photo courtesy of Lee Reasin.

Above: Ch. Elf Dale Captain's Choice, by Ch. Elf Dale Viking ex Playmate's Prima Dona, C.D., at Reno Kennel Club, October 1967. Breeder, Frances L. Travis; owners, Frances L. Travis and Richard D. Travis. **Right:** On the back of this lovely painting of Ch. Hatfield's Stardust is the following note written by the owner: "Star refuses to pose and makes such a fuss when she sees a camera that I have never gotten a really good photo of her." The artist was Louise Lopina, and the portrait is dated 1964. Photos courtesy of Lee Reasin.

Elf Dale My Fair Lady at Golden Gate in 1968; judge, Langdon Skarda; Bob Hastings handling for owners, Mr. and Mrs. Harry O. Merrill. Photo courtesy of Lee Reasin.

Mrs. Frances Ruth Williams, owner of the Mountaincrest Shetland Sheepdogs at South Wales, pictured here in an informal moment with Sovereign of Mountaincrest.

Ch. Macdega The Family Man. Bred by Mr. and Mrs. Willard K. Denton and Dorothy Atkins; owned by Macdega, Thomas Coen. Photo courtesy of Mrs. Denton.

BEST OF BREED

Ch. Madselin's Grand Slam, a son of Ch. Banchory Backstop ex Can. Ch. Banchory Misty Blue, at five years of age winning Best of Breed at Palm Beach in 1983; judge, Joe Gregory. Bred by Susan Jensen; owned by George and Melanie Williams.

Birchcrest Once In A Lifetime, by Ch. Bran Gay Golden Quest ex Ch. Bran Gay Sweet Vision. Bred by Brandol and Gayle Eads, Bran Gay Kennels.

BEST IN SHOW
WYOMING VALLEY
KENNEL CLUB, INC.
MAY 21 1978

Ch. Romayne's Special Edition, sable dog by Ch. Severn Spellbinder ex Ch. Beltane Romayne, winning Best in Show at Wyoming Valley in 1978, the same year he finished. Handled by Linda More; judged by Denise Kodner; bred by G. and T. Danforth, now owned in Japan.

Ch. RobCary Jubil'nt Expectation, by Ch. Chosen Jubilation, C.D., taking Best of Winners at Corpus Christi Kennel Club. Bred by Caryl Fennel; owned by Ron McGee and Pat Inguaggiato.

Above: Ch. Severn Comedy Tonight, sable bitch winning under judge Robert White. Bred by Linda More, Tom Coen, and Steve Barger; owned by Joanne G. Timpany. **Below:** Ch. Macdega Mainstay. Tetsuo Miyama and Stephen W. Barger, owners.

Ch. Meadow Ridge Hello Bunny taking Best of Opposite Sex at Devon in 1978. Owned by Dona Hausman.

Happy Glen's Royal Dream, the very exciting son of Ch. Windhover Sweet Music Man ex Happy Glen's Flaming Fantasy, who gained a four-point major by winning a Best in Show from the classes. Barbara and Marvin Ross, who own this lovely little dog, hope to have him finished by the time you are reading this, when he will become their first *homebred Sheltie* (they have some Schipperkes, too) *champion.* Living in Wyoming as they do, majors are not easily come by or we are certain that Royal Dream would have been sporting "champion" before his name far sooner!

Ch. Karelane Royal Flush O'Kismet. This exquisite Sheltie has broken all records for the breed with his thirty-three Bests in Show. Owned by Thelma and Guy Mauldin, Kismet Kennels.

Ch. Jade Mist Suntide, by Ch. Barwood Weather Report ex Ch. Jade Mist Woodwind Chimes. Owned by Jade Mist Kennels, Dr. and Mrs. Keith B. Howell.

Ch. Carmylie Rosmoor Silvertip, by Ch. Nathan Hale of Carmylie ex Rosmoor Winter Wind o'Tuwin, C.D. Jean D. Simmonds, Carmylie Kennels.

Sterling's Enchanted Spirit, by Ch. Rockwood the Hustler ex Valdawn's Heather of Rockwood, now being shown as we go to press. Owned by Debra Elkin, Enchanted Shelties.

BEST OF
OPPOSITE SEX
WINNERS BITCH
KENNESAW
KENNEL CLUB SHOW
MAY 3 1981
PHOTOS BY ALVERSON

Ch. Chisterling Smoke Signals, by Ch. Banchory High Born ex Chisterling Silver Song, winning Best of Breed at the Combined Specialties of Atlanta, April 1978. Bred and owned by Don Combee.

Facing page: Ch. Chisterling Anniversary Blu, by Ch. Chisterling Smoke Screen ex Chisterling Blu Sequin, taking Winners Bitch and Best of Opposite Sex at Kennesaw Kennel Club Dog Show, May 1981. Owned by Don Combee.

Ch. Macdega Proof Positive winning the breed at Sir Francis Drake Kennel Club in 1981; judge, Thelma Von Thaden. Handler, Jerry Machado; owners, Chris and Jerry Machado, Montage Shelties.

Ch. Marwal Struttin' The Blues, by Am. and Can. Ch. Macdega Mainstay ex Marwal Bluesette, in 1983. Bred by Marwal Kennels, Margaret and Walt Huening.

Canden Count The Ways, by Ch. Banchory Reflection ex Ch. Canden Kinni Carisma, taking Winners Bitch and Best of Winners at the 1981 Northern California Specialty. Handler, Chris Machado. Owners, Jerry and Chris Machado and Glennis and Buddy Carroll.

Ch. Delamantha's Debonair taking Winners at Del-Otse-Nango in 1975. Handled here, and finished, by Steve Barger; owned by Mr. and Mrs. Willard K. Denton.

CHAPTER FOUR

Kennels in the Continental United States

Ch. Carrico's Port of Entry in May 1955. Owned by Mr. and Mrs. Willard K. Denton, Ardencaple Kennels, Southbury, Connecticut.

There is no better way to describe the progress of a breed than by telling you of the individual breeders and kennels that have contributed along the way. On the following pages we are proud to present summary descriptions of these breeders and their kennels and of many important Shetland Sheepdogs and the background from which their success was attained. We tell you not only about the long-time breeders, many of whom are still active; but we also pay tribute to the comparative newcomers as well. Each has contributed to the well-being and development of these splendid dogs; and on the shoulders of the newcomers in particular squarely rests the task of carrying on and preserving what has already been accomplished and the responsibility for the future well-being of the breed. Study these pages well and you will come away with an increased knowledge of where the best Shetland Sheepdogs have been bred, the care and forethought expended toward their progress and improvement, generation after generation, and the exciting results these breeders have accomplished.

Ardencaple

Ardencaple was registered as her kennel name in 1949 with the American Kennel Club by Mrs. Willard K. (Mimi) Denton, now of Southbury, Connecticut. The name came from her grandmother's home, better known as Ardencaple Castle, in Edinburgh, Scotland. Since Shelties were descended in part from the Scotch Collie, Mimi explains, and she herself has some Scotch blood, she felt that the name was fitting.

Mimi Denton has always been a dog lover, in fact an animal lover in general. As a child her family travelled extensively, which curtailed her desire to have dogs, although somehow she always managed to latch on to one, and sometimes two, much to her mother's chagrin.

Her first Sheltie was a blue-merle which was just a pet. In 1947 she bought a sable and white bitch from Elsie Hydon, which also ended up being just a pet, as she never grew large enough. She did have considerable quality, however, and the temperament and disposition to melt anyone's heart. She loved the Dentons' son, who was then at the playpen age, and she would get

Ch. Ardencaple's Cute Trick. Owned and bred by Mr. and Mrs. Willard K. Denton.

through the wooden bars of the pen and play with him. A Sheltie of the correct size could never have accomplished this feat.

In 1949 it was decided to breed this bitch, and the stud Mimi Denton chose was Champion Pixie Dell Roy's Boy. From this litter she kept one bitch, Ardencaple's Summer Eve, who later became the dam of Champion Ardencaple's Cute Trick.

Cute Trick's career started with a Best in Match at the Tri-State Shetland Sheepdog Association Match Show under Betty Whelen. In 1952 he was Best of Breed at Westminster and fourth in the Working Group—owner-handled. With limited showing that year he garnered twenty-one Bests of Breed, a Group first, and numerous placements, along with being chosen the outstanding Sheltie in the East.

In 1954, at Westminster, the Dentons saw what Mimi considered came as close to the ideal

Ch. Ardencaple's Cute Trick (left) with a friend. Both owned by Ardencaple Kennels, Mr. and Mrs. Willard K. Denton, Southbury, Connecticut.

Sheltie as is possible, a nine-month-old tri bitch who moved and showed like a million. She lived up to Mimi's expectations, not only for her five-point win at Westminster but also for her later wins. Acquiring her was not easy but took a great deal of persuasion and negotiating, not only with her owner but also with her handler. Carrico's Port of Entry, fondly called "Candy," finished while still a puppy and then went on to over forty Bests of Breed, six firsts in the Working Group, and numerous Group placements. Here Mrs. Denton quotes Betty Whelen from her article in the Shetland Sheepdog periodical:

It was not quite as easy to find tricolor and blue-merle Shelties in the old days that I felt were tops and close to the standard, as there were not as many of them, but will go with the ones I remember as being the best. The sables far outnumbered the two other colors and it was easier to find quite a few very excellent ones. . . . I would put Champion Carrico's Port of Entry, a very sound, lovely bitch, a little ahead of her time, as she was on the extreme side, but her quality was not to be denied. She was an outstanding mover, and the year I showed her for Ardencaple Kennels she was Best of Breed at over fifteen shows and won four Working Groups and many other placings. She might have gone further but she took dislikes to certain judges at times and would not make the best of herself. She carried a very heavy coat, had great length of neck, a beautiful topline, dark almond shaped eyes, perfect natural ears, flat skull, and good round muzzle. She never came in season, so never produced anything to carry on her outstanding qualities.

The bloodlines on which the Ardencaple breeding program was started were predominantly Pocono and Astolat. However, there were other breeds that intrigued Mimi Denton; and wanting to broaden her knowledge,

Ch. Carrico's Port of Entry winning the Working Group at Heart of America in 1954; judge, Lloyd Brackett. Owned by Mr. and Mrs. Willard K. Denton.

Ch. Carrico's Port of Entry with Betty Whelen handling at Ladies Kennel Association in May 1955; judge, Percy Roberts. Mr. and Mrs. Willard K. Denton, owners, Ardencaple Kennels, Southbury, Connecticut.

From a painting by Jeanne Mellin in 1953—Ardencaple's Winning Ways, by Ch. Ardencaple's Cute Trick ex Ch. Fortune's Fancy of Pocono had 11 points including both majors. Bred and owned by Ardencaple Kennels, Mr. and Mrs. Willard K. Denton.

she decided to try her hand elsewhere for awhile, namely with Dachshunds and Whippets. As the years went by, her love for Shelties again took over, however, and so she acquired another bitch, Berridale The Critic's Choice, who should have finished but lacked the desire and spark that is so necessary in the show ring; she never did gain her title. Instead she became a good producer, and Mimi feels she would have been a top producer had she not had various complications and problems leading ultimately to premature spaying. "Sally," as she is called, was bred to Champion Gerthstone's Jon Christopher, from which litter came Champion Ardencaple Berridale Belove, who finished as a puppy in nine shows within one month. She has also been a good producer for her owners, Jesse and Glennis Carroll.

As the Dentons were in a state of upheaval, making a second move in barely two years, it was necessary to cut back on the number of dogs, so Sally went to Dorothy Atkins on a co-ownership. It was there that she was bred to Champion Banchory Reflection and produced Champion Macdega The Family Man now owned by Mr. and Mrs. Buddy Character.

In the number of years she has bred and shown Shelties, there were numerous other

Ch. Ardencaple Berridale Belove, sable and white by Ch. Gerthstone's Jon Christopher ex Berridale The Critic's Choice, born June 1976, completed title in July 1977. Bred by Mr. and Mrs. Willard K. Denton; owned by Jesse R. and Glennis Carroll, Tolland, Connecticut.

Above: Ch. Fortune's Favorite of Pocono owned by Mr. and Mrs. Willard K. Denton, Ardencaple Kennels. Below: Reno, a pointed young Sheltie by Ch. Nashcrest Golden Note ex Nashcrest Debutante, from a painting in 1954 by Jeanne Mellin. Mr. and Mrs. Willard K. Denton, owners.

Ch. Hallinwood Robin Hood of Marl (standing) and Hallinwood Token (sitting), from a painting by Betty M. Cornell. These two fine Shelties from the Ardencaple Kennels, Mr. and Mrs. Willard K. Denton.

Ardencaple dogs with the title "champion" in front of their names, but the ones mentioned stand out in Mimi Denton's mind. She comments:

I will probably always have a Sheltie or two, along with the Dobes and the Toy Poodles who share our household. My husband, who does not share the same enthusiasm about dogs that I do, is however unusually tolerant—to the point of having reached far away shores to surprise me, usually for Christmas or my birthday, in acquiring dogs for me. Two Shelties came this way from England, a dog and a bitch, Hallinwood Robin Hood and Hallinwood Token who did not quite make it in the show ring. More recently he bought a male from Canada, Delamantha's Debonair, who was by the illustrious Champion Halstor's Peter Pumpkin. Stephen Barger finished him for me, and at home he is a joy to live with, the kind of dog there are too few of. Very sadly, he had to be put down due to cancer.

Ch. Frigate's Emblem of Astolat, by Ch. Frigate of Faunbrook, C.D., ex Astolat Snow Flurry (bred, as was her dam, by Constance B. Hubbard), born in 1947. Emblem was one of the most famous and important Astolat Shelties from Constance B. Hubbard's illustrious kennel.

Astolat

Astolat was chosen for the kennel name, from Tennyson's *Idylls of the King*, by the lady who was to become Mrs. Constance Hubbard and one of the world's foremost Shetland Sheepdog breeders. She chose the name in 1929, when she owned white Collies and was still in high school; the following year the name was registered by her on a lifetime basis with the American Kennel Club. The kennel, at Effort, Pennsylvania, remains active to this day.

It was not until 1934 that Shelties took Mrs. Hubbard's attention. Then she purchased Anahassitt Aphrodite, who went on to become a champion. The white Collies, however, continued to share her interest. Those were busy days for her with the operation of a successful restaurant business as well. Thus it was not until following World War II that her concentration on the Shelties began.

Ch. Astolat Headliner, C.D., by Amer., Can., Bda., Mex., and Col. Ch. Astolat Gold Award, Int. C.D., ex Astolat Mayrime, in 1974. Bred, owned, and handled by Mrs. Constance B. Hubbard, Astolat Kennels, Effort, Pennsylvania.

Am., Can., and Bda. Ch. Astolat Jupiter, C.D., a fifth generation descendant of Ch. Frigate of Faunbrook, C.D. Bred and owned by Constance B. Hubbard, Astolat Kennels.

A handsome homebred bitch of the Pocono line was bred to Champion Frigate of Faunbrook, C.D., and in 1947 a puppy, to become Frigate's Emblem of Astolat, was born. Emblem finished his championship in seven shows with two five-point majors along the way (Golden Gate and Morris and Essex, the former from the Puppy Class) in addition to two three-point majors. Emblem was the first Sheltie in the United States to win Best of Breed more than one hundred times. He also won four Working Groups and twenty-two additional Group placements, always owner-handled. When he died, he left fifteen champion offspring.

Emblem's influence is seen at Astolat right down to the present day. His great-grandson, Champion Astolat Headliner, C.D.; his great-great-grandson, Champion Astolat Galaxy, C.D.; and his fifth generation descendant,

Champion Astolat Jupiter, are eloquent examples of his contributions to the breed. He stands behind almost every Sheltie bred at Astolat over the years.

The dam of Emblem was a third generation homebred, Astolat Snow Flurry, and had been bred by Constance Hubbard, as had his grandam. The latter was from a bitch Mrs. Hubbard had purchased from Betty Whelen of Pocono Kennels.

Emblem was Best of Breed at Westminster in 1953. Thirteen years later his grandson, Canadian and American Champion Astolat Gold Award repeated this win at the Garden, handled, as Emblem had been, by his breeder-owner, Constance (called Connie by her friends) Hubbard.

Gold Award's sire was Champion Astolat Golden Symbol; his dam was Scotswold Gretta, by Champion Bykenhall St. Andrew ex Champion Timberidge Scarlet Phantasy. Golden Symbol sired among others, two noteworthy sons in addition to Golden Emblem: Champion Astolat Gold Twist and Champion Astolat Gold Award. Then Champion Astolat Golden Touch, an Award son, from a granddaughter of Golden Symbol and Gold Twist, produced a lovely star of the early 1970's, Champion Heather's Bruce of Remlap, American and Bermudian C.D. Bruce was a 15½-inch golden-sable who goes back in his pedigree four times to Golden

Am. and Can. Ch. Astolat Galaxy, C.D., by Ch. Halstor's Peter Pumpkin ex Ch. Astolat Stardust. Bred and owned by Constance B. Hubbard.

Symbol and also proved to be an excellent sire. His progeny included Champion Astolat Spice Drop and Champion Astolat Gilded Lily.

Early in the 1960's Astolat campaigned Champion Piper's Pride of Astolat, the aforementioned Gold Twist, Champion Astolat Peggy of Faunbrook, Award, Astolat Rock and Roll, Astolat Radiance, and Astolat Springtime to their titles.

Champion Astolat Galaxy, by Champion Halstor's Peter Pumpkin, is an Award grandson. Champion Astolat Headliner, another Westminster winner, is a son of Award. American, Bermudian, and Canadian Champion Astolat Enchantor, a homebred son of Champion Lingard Sealect Bruce, and five champion bitches and a daughter of Award, Heather's Bruce and Enchantor, were doing well for themselves in the 1970's from Astolat.

By 1980, Connie Hubbard had finished thirty-three champions in the conformation ring and seven C.D. dogs in obedience, plus dozens of customers' dogs who have taken top awards in obedience, the most outstanding of which are the Obedience Trial championships won by two Galaxy sons.

Champion Astolat Jupiter, C.D., the aforementioned fifth generation descendant of Cham-

Ch. Heather's Bruce of Remlap, C.D., at Delaware County in 1968. Judge, James Walker Trullinger. Owner, Mrs. Constance B. Hubbard, Astolat Shelties.

Am. and Can. Ch. Astolat Enchantor, by Ch. Lingard Sealect Bruce ex Ch. Astolat Peggy of Faunbrook, C.D., in 1970. Owned by Astolat Shelties, Constance B. Hubbard.

Ch. Astolat Astronaut snapped informally. One of the memorable Shelties from Astolat Kennels, Mrs. Constance B. Hubbard.

Above: Am. and Can. Ch. Astolat Gold Touch, by Am., Can., and Bda. Ch. Astolat Gold Award ex Astolat Symbol's Radiance. Handled by Frank Ashbey for Mrs. Constance B. Hubbard, Astolat Kennels. **Below:** Ch. Astolat Gilded Lily, by Ch. Heather's Bruce of Remlap, at the Interstate Specialty in 1972. Mrs. Constance B. Hubbard, owner.

Ch. Conendale Challenger O'Akirene winning Best of Breed at Bucks County in May 1982. This was Gene Cohen's dog, left to Connie Hubbard upon Gene's untimely death.

pion Frigate's Emblem of Astolat, is by the Peter Pumpkin son and Award grandson, Champion Astolat Galaxy, C.D., from Park Crest Cinnamon Twist, a Peter granddaughter. He is a 15½-inch golden-sable who in addition to his American championship also has earned titles in Bermuda and Canada. As of 1982, Jupiter, Champion Astolat Headliner, C.D., and Champion Astolat Galaxy, C.D., are the stud force at Astolat, joined recently by Champion Conendale Challenger O'Akirene, a heavily coated 15½-inch tricolor who was inherited, along with another of his Shelties, by Mrs. Hubbard upon the tragic death of Eugene Cohen (who died from a heart attack at far too young an age). Challenger finished with three majors, two Bests of Breed, and a Working Group third.

It is interesting to read Mrs. Hubbard's statement, made during 1982, that she has three predominantly white Shelties which she hopes one day will *again* be allowed to be considered in the show ring.

Am. and Can. Ch. Astolat Enchanting Lady, by Ch. Astolat Enchantor ex Astolat Cherry Bounce, winning at Trenton Kennel Club in 1969. Bred, owned, and exclusively handled by Mrs. Constance B. Hubbard, Astolat Shelties.

Belle Mount

Belle Mount was registered in 1942 with the American Kennel Club as the kennel name for Alice Burhans and her family, of Troy, New York. One could not possibly find a more completely dog-oriented family than this one, as Alice at age nine was in the ring exhibiting her parents' Collies; and Alice's daughter, Rebecca, in her turn showed at matches from five years onward, handling a puppy to win its first points when she was eight years old. Belle Mount bred and showed Collies and Golden Retrievers to championship right from the beginning, but a completed championship on a Shetland Sheepdog eluded them for years.

Finally they reached the elite circle in Shelties with their Champion Belle Mount Wee Tobias. Although he was shown by several handlers along the way, Toby's major wins were gained with Rebecca and Alice Burhans personally showing him. And Alice remarks, "My greatest thrill was piloting him to his first major, going on to Best of Breed and then to second in the Working Group." Nowadays Alice is having a great deal of fun showing Toby (Champion Belle Mount Wee Tobias) and Cookiebush (Belle

Ch. Belle Mount Wee Tobias, homebred son of Am. and Can. Ch. Astolat Galaxy, C.D., ex Belle Mount Wee Lena, C.D., taking the breed from the classes at Westchester in 1982 under judge Seaver Smith. "Toby" then had thirteen points, one major, six Bests of Breed and a Working Group second. Handled by Rebecca Burhans for Alice A. Burhans, Belle Mount Kennels, Troy, New York.

Mount Wee Duke of Orange) as a brace, who in three shows have won Best Working Brace three times and Best Brace in Show twice.

Alice Burhans has been extremely active in obedience with her Shelties. She has served on the Board of the Petroon Dog Training Club for more than fifteen years and served as that club's secretary for five years. The determination to get a finished conformation Sheltie to the kennel's credit moved their emphasis away from obedience, but they still continue to score well in obedience competition when given the chance. The newest obedience star from there is Belle Mount Wee Silver Shore, American and Canadian C.D., owned by R.J. and Linda J. McAuley, trained and shown by Linda. Other obedience headliners in Belle Mount history include Belle Mount Wee Gypsy, C.D., Belle Mount Wee Sugar, C.D., Belle Mount Wee Lena, C.D., Belle Mount Wee Melody, C.D. (Urda), Belle Mount Wee Gemini, C.D.X. (Crain), Belle Mount Wee Peggy, C.D. (Hamlin), Belle Mount Wee Sarah, C.D. (Rowe), Belle Mount Wee Pieman, C.D. (Kitchie), Belle Mount Wee Isabelle, C.D. (Webber), Lakehill Wee Rachel, C.D., Pixie Dell Lovin Heart, C.D., and Belle Mount Wee Nebucadnezar, U.D.—certainly a very impressive lineup.

Kylo Clowning MacGregor, Belle Mount's foundation Sheltie, combined the best of the East coast with the best of the West Coast of his day, which was during the mid- to late-1950's. His dam, Geronimo Diamond Lass of Kylo (sired by Champion Geronimo Son Rey ex

Belle Mount Wee Lena, C.D., major pointed toward her conformation title, too, was by Fair Play of Sea Isle ex Belle Mount Wee Gypsy, C.D. (this daughter of the foundation dog at this kennel, Kylo Clowning Wee MacGregor, was important in the background of the Belle Mount sable line). Alice A. Burhans, owner.

Belle Mount Wee Sesame. Owned by Alice A. Burhans, Belle Mount Shelties.

Belle Mount Wee Nebucadnezar, C.D. Owned by Belle Mount Kennels, Alice A. Burhans, Troy, New York.

Belle Mount's foundation dog, Wee MacGregor. Alice Burhans, owner.

Above: Alice A. Burhans with some of the Belle Mount gang in 1977. **Below:** Belle Mount Wee Snow White. Owned by Alice A. Burhans.

Belle Mount Wee Gypsy, C.D. Alice A. Burhans, owner.

Champion Geronimo Diamond Lil) was shipped East to be bred at Sea Isle to the most suitable stud. Champion Sea Isle Cadenza (litter-brother to Champion Sea Isle Serenade) was the choice. Wee MacGregor was the happy result. He came to live with the Burhans at six weeks of age and immediately established himself as top dog and guardian of the household which he continued to rule for sixteen years.

Wee MacGregor's daughter, Belle Mount Wee Gypsy, C.D., bred to Fair Play of Sea Isle produced the major-pointed bitch Belle Mount Wee Lena, C.D. She then was bred to Champion Beltane the Buccaneer and to Champion Astolat Galaxy, C.D. The progeny from these two litters, by sons of Champion Halstor's Peter Pumpkin, gave to Belle Mount their main line of basically Sea Isle sables. Lena was also bred to Best in Show-winning Champion Pixie Dell Epicure, establishing a second line of sables which Mrs. Burhans has line-bred back to Epicure.

Belle Mount's tricolor, Lakehill Wee Rachel, C.D., (Champion Calcurt Luke ex Lakehill Special Request, she by International Champion Blue Quest of Pocono from Kiloren Moonbeam) came to the Burhans when she was seven weeks old. She promptly got underfoot and broke a bone in her paw, as the result of which it was necessary for her to spend a week thumping about in a cast. At five months of age she won Best Puppy at the Mohawk Shetland Sheepdog Club match show. She became Rebecca

Belle Mount Wee Eloise, by Ch. Pixie Dell Bairn of Cluaron ex Belle Mount Wee Hyacinth, third generation homebred blue winning at Southern Maryland Kennel Club in 1983. Handled by Mildred B. Nicoll for Belle Mount Shelties, Alice A. Burhans.

Lakehill Wee Rachel, C.D. Owned by Alice Burhans, Belle Mount Shelties.

Above: Belle Mount Wee Elisabeth. Owned by Alice A. Burhans. **Below:** Belle Mount Wee Betsy, by Pixie Dell Epicure ex Belle Mount Wee Lena, has thirteen points, including one major. Bred and owned by Alice A. Burhans.

Burhans' Junior Showmanship dog, the two of them doing well together.

Wee Rachel was bred to Champion Philidove Benevolent Anthony (Champion Banchory High Born ex Champion Philidove Carmylie In A Mist), producing the tricolor Belle Mount Wee Nebucadnezar, C.D., and the blue-merle Belle Mount Wee Elizabeth (five points), establishing the Belle Mount blue-tri line. Crosses to Champion Chenterra Thunderation and to Champion Pixie Dell Bairn of Cluaron resulted in the Burhans' current winning blue, Belle Mount Wee Eloise, with ten points including both majors at the time of this writing.

By judiciously crossing their three foundation lines, Belle Mount is developing its own strain of Shelties, elegant in outline with pleasing Sheltie character and sound working minds and bodies. The Burhans prefer, and strive for, rich color in their sables, tricolors and blue-merles. It is their hope that the Belle Mount Shelties will supply a different but compatible gene pool from which to work.

Above: This magnificent bitch, Ch. Birch Hollow's Once Upon A Time, Best in Show at Farmington Valley in July 1983, has to her credit a total record of one all-breed Best in Show, two Specialty Bests in Show, fifty-two Bests of Breed, nine Group firsts, and twenty-five Group placements. She is temporarily retired for motherhood, having been bred to the Best in Show winner Ch. Rorrelore Sportin' Chance. "Crissie" belongs to, and is handled by, Millie Nichols, Birch Hollow Shelties, Easton, Connecticut. Below: A particularly good example of correct Sheltie expression, Ch. Birch Hollow The Choirboy, born in 1975, is one of the handsome Shetland Sheepdogs owned by Mildred B. Nicoll.

Birch Hollow

The Birch Hollow Kennel, of Mildred Nicoll at Easton, Connecticut, acquired its first Sheltie in 1949 and exhibited for the first time during 1950. Bonnie Heather, as the dog was named, eventually attained thirteen championship points and a Utility Dog degree, thereby introducing her owner to dog shows, handling, training, and breeding.

Two more bitches earned Utility degrees and championship points before Bagaduce Lark of Birch Hollow, C.D.X., became the foundation bitch for the current Birch Hollow dogs. Lark was a combination of Bagaduce and Page's Hill bloodlines and was bred to Meadow Ridge Hundred Proof, a son of Champion Pixie Dell Bright Vision. These are still the bloodlines which are concentrated in the Birch Hollow Shelties.

Because of professional handling commitments, only one Birch Hollow champion has been campaigned after finishing her title. This is the current (1983) winning bitch Champion Birch Hollow Once Upon A Time, who represents seven generations of Birch Hollow breeding and is a Specialty show, Group, Westminster, and all-breed Best in Show winner.

Once Upon A Time's sire, Champion Birch Hollow The Choirboy, was a Specialty show and multiple Group-winner from the classes. Other titleholders include Champion Meadow Ridge Baby Jane and her litter-sister Champion Meadow Ridge Bright Holiday (co-owned with Meadow Ridge Kennels); Champion Pixie Dell Miller's High Life, C.D., co-owned with Pixie Dell; and Specialty winners Champion Meadow Ridge Mint Julep, C.D., Champion Meadow Ridge of Birch Hollow, C.D., and Champion Birch Hollow Sprig O'Bagaduce, C.D. Sprig, co-owned with Bagaduce Kennels, was both a Westminster Best of Breed and a Highest Scoring Dog in Trial winner.

Another significant Sheltie at Mildred Nicoll's kennel is the talented and beautiful Birch Hollow The Matinee Idol, C.D., sire of Champion Birch Hollow The Choirboy. Trained and shown by ten-year-old Pam Nicoll, he is also a Highest Scoring Dog in Trial winner. As his name implies, he is as well a show business star, having had a successful career as a cast member of the television soap opera, *Love Is A Many Splendored Thing*. In addition he has appeared as a model in *Vogue* and other prestigious magazines. He is certainly an ambassador of good will for the entire Sheltie breed!

Ch. Birch Hollow Once Upon A Time, Best in Show winning bitch by Ch. Birch Hollow The Choirboy ex Graham's Loradel Kandi Kane, moving out with the excellent "reach and drive" so important in this breed. Mildred B. Nicoll, owner-handler, Birch Hollow Kennels.

Ch. Pixie Dell Miller's High Life, C.D., born in 1972, co-owned by Marie K. Miller of Pixie Dell Kennels and Mildred B. Nicoll of Birch Hollow Kennels.

Shawn Campbell ("Ricky") with Pamela J. Nicoll's Birch Hollow The Matinee Idol ("Irving") pictured at six months of age, on the set of *Love Is A Many Splendored Thing*.

Esthof Misty Morn, the Eads very first dog and very first Sheltie, going Winners Bitch under John Stanek. Brandol and Gayle Eads, Bran Gay Shelties, Rialto, California.

Bran Gay

Ever since childhood, Gayle Eads had wanted to own a Sheltie. But it was not until she had reached twenty-seven years of age that her husband, Brandol, bought her an eight-week-old female, Esthof Misty Morn, as a birthday gift, thus making the first move toward the establishment of the now highly successful Bran Gay Shetland Sheepdog Kennels at Rialto, California.

The Eads did not become interested in showing their new puppy until her breeder saw her at six months of age and urged them to do so, feeling that Misty had potential for success in the ring. She went third in a large 6-9 Month Class at her first match show.

Gayle Eads then started attending a training class which met a couple of nights each week, and both she and her husband joined the Santiago Shetland Sheepdog Club of Southern California after they joined the American Shetland Sheepdog Association. By then both had become keenly interested in show dogs—

Gayle in handling, Brandol through his books and charts.

When it came time for the first Sheltie breeding at Bran Gay, the Eads had already been looking around a lot at many stud dogs. Champion Cherden Light My Fire seemed a logical choice for Misty, and in due time a litter of four bitches and a dog arrived.

One from this litter was Champion Bran Gay Cricket, who finished very quickly, owner-handled. She was bred to Champion Scotspride Legionaire, and in her turn produced Champion Bran Gay Jessica and Champion Bran Gay Sweet Vision.

Jessica has a young son, Bran Gay Time Traveler, by Noradel Cimarron, who is one year old and has been very impressive at Specialties. Champion Sweet Vision has a son from her half-brother, Champion Bran Gay Golden Quest, who has ten points including a major. Also in Misty's first litter was Bran Gay Georgie Girl who was bred to Lingard Golden Idol, an inbred

The Eads' youngsters with the very first Sheltie litter at Bran Gay. Brandol and Gayle Eads.

Above: Ch. Bran Gay Golden Quest, the sire of Best in Show winner Ch. Bran Gay Unchained Melody. Quest finished January 1980, Gayle Eads's third champion. Gayle Eads, owner, Bran Gay Shelties. **Below:** Ch. Bran Gay Dream Maker, finished in November 1980, the Eads' fourth champion, the second from Memory. Bred by Brandol and Gayle Eads.

Sealect Bruce son, and produced Memory Maker who was also bred to Legionaire, the first time producing three males, Champion Bran Gay Golden Quest, and Champion Bran Gay Dream Maker; and in a repeat breeding Champion Bran Gay Golden Fawn who became the dam of the Best in Show-winner, Champion Balinbrea Buck Rogers.

Georgie Girl had only one litter due to her death of an illness at two and a half years of age, one week before her sister Cricket finished with less than six months of showing.

The Eads boarded and cared for Champion Cherden Light My Fire during the period when his owners, Guy and Judy Okayama, were getting a divorce, and the Eads had permission to use him at stud during this time. He was bred twice—a repeat to Misty that did not take and then to a nice-bodied tri bitch named Feiffie that produced Champion Bran Gay Sweet Charity.

Bran Gay Georgie Girl, by Ch. Cherden Light My Fire ex Esthof Misty Morn, dam of Bran Gay Memory Maker. Brandol and Gayle Eads, Rialto, California.

Ch. Bran Gay Unchained Melody, a bright red-orange sable measuring 14 ¾", up in the snow with Wendy Eads (holding her) and Cindy Eads, daughters of her owners, Brandol and Gayle Eads. This lovely Best in Show winner (under breeder-judge Hayden Martin) took the Best in Show award on November 7th 1982 at K.C. of Riverside.

Ch. Bran Gay Sweet Charity, by Ch. Cherden Light My Fire ex Feiffer, has been in the Top Ten and the Top Twenty Shelties several times in a two-year period. Gayle Eads, owner, Bran Gay Shelties.

Ch. Bran Gay Unchained Melody winning Best of Breed under Lynette Saltzman one week after completing her title, defeating eight champions, at Superstition Kennel Club. She then went on to third in Group. Owned by Bran Gay Shelties.

Ch. Bran Gay Golden Fawn, by Ch. Scotspride Legionaire (finished in 1981, the Eads' fifth champion) ex Bran Gay Memory Maker, dam of Best in Show winner Ch. Balenbrae Buck Rogers. Bred by Brandol and Gayle Eads; owned by Anne De Witt.

Above: Ch. Bran Gay Sweet Vision, the seventh champion for the Eads, finished November 1982. **Below:** Ch. Bran Gay Jessica, the eighth champion for the Eads, finished March 1983. Judge, Jane Kay. Both Sweet Vision and Jessica are by Ch. Scotspride Legionaire ex Ch. Bran Gay Cricket, and both are owned by Brandol and Gayle Eads.

This lovely bitch took her first five points at the Southern California Specialty, handled by Guy Okayama, who put three more points on her. Then Gayle Eads took over, putting on an additional six points, and the final point was gained for her handled by the Eads' sixteen-year-old daughter, Cosette, who also had put the first point on Champion Cricket.

All of the Eads' dogs are very dearly loved and mean a great deal to their owners. A particular favorite is Melody, of whom Gayle Eads writes,

> Melody is the neatest Sheltie. She finished at eighteen months at the last show in the National week in San Diego. Within the next ten months she had Specialty Best of Breeds and an All Breed Best in Show! She was bred to Noradel Cimarron and produced two very nice young males that look very promising. Melody is "Miss Personality." She loves people and knows everyone loves her. But most of all she loves dog shows, and she loves the sport almost as much as I do!

The Eads can well take pride in their record of eight champions in a very short length of time and with only a limited breeding program. There are, however, more on the way, among them Birchcrest Once In A Lifetime and Bran Gay Centerfold, both picking up points at a very satisfactory rate of speed. Gayle Eads does the handling of Bran Gay Shelties almost exclusively.

Caper Hill

Caper Hill Shetland Sheepdogs are a small kennel, owned by Dr. James L. Smith and Lynette Smith at Califon, New Jersey. Currently there are in residence seven adult dogs and a couple of promising puppies.

The foundation of this kennel came about through the acquisition of a darling tri puppy from Banchory Kennels in about 1978. She is Canadian Champion Banchory Picture Perfect. From her first litter came the beautiful and widely admired blue bitch, American and Canadian Champion Caper Hills Song Sung Blue, the dam of three Canadian champions, one American champion, and three awaiting maturity to start out in the United States. Song's sisters have likewise been splendid producers, as seen in their offspring—Caper Hills I Mean To Shine, Caper Hills In The Sky, Caper Hills I Like Dreamin', and Caper Hills I Have Dreamed. Some of these sisters are awaiting a return to full coat to start out on ring careers.

The Smiths have elected to keep Caper Hill a small kennel, where the emphasis is on top quality, not quantity. Lynette Smith has written several articles for both of the Sheltie breed magazines and lacks one hour of having her Masters in reproductive physiology. Dr. Smith

Can. Ch. Banchory Picture Perfect, by Am. and Can. Ch. Banchory Backstop ex Banchory Love Is Black, at two years of age in September 1979. Bred by Donna Olson; owned by Lynette Smith.

Am. and Can. Ch. Caper Hills Song Sung Blue, by Am. and Can. Ch. Banchory Deep Purple ex Can. Ch. Banchory Picture Perfect, at three years of age. Breeder-owner, Lynette Smith, Califon, New Jersey.

Caper Hills I Write The Songs, by Banchory Reflection ex Am. and Can. Ch. Caper Hills Song Sung Blue, at eighteen months of age. Bred by Lynette Smith, Califon, New Jersey; owned by Yasko Jitosho, Japan.

Caper Hill For Your Eyes Only, bi-blue male by Ch. Macdega The Piano Man ex Caper Hill Angels In The Sky, three months old here. Bred by Lynette Smith; owned by Cindy Beadley. Photo by Diana Ricucci.

Above: Caper Hills Cool Change, one year old, by Am. and Can. Ch. Banchory Deep Purple ex Banchory Picture Perfect. **Below:** Caper Hills Captain Sunshine, one year old, by Ch. Naripa Sunlight Etude ex Am. and Can. Ch. Caper Hills Song Sung Blue. Bred and owned by Lynette Smith.

is a practitioner of equine veterinary medicine. The Smiths originally owned Collies.

The Caper Hill dogs have a "look"; head detail is of utmost importance to their owners, followed by an overall body balance and pretty lines. Because they live closely with their dogs, temperament is crucial to the Smiths. They do not like "spooks," but neither will they tolerate "terrier" temperament; these types of temperament are *not* a pleasure to live with and are definitely not the sweet temperament called for by the Sheltie standard. Linda More has handled the Caper Hill Shetland Sheepdogs for the past four years.

A group of famous "Carmylies" from the noted kennel of Jean D. Simmonds at Chatham, New York. Left to right, Badgerton Red Riot of Carmylie, C.D.X.; Ch. Jomar Carmylie Bundle of Love; Ch. Vanity Fair of Carmylie, C.D.; Carmylie Duchess of Karalane; Banchory Bi Jingo of Carmylie; and Leewayne Lark of Carmylie.

Jomar Carmylie By Request, by Ch. Jomar Carmylie Rob of Perkasie ex Carmylie Black Lace, the first black and white in U.S. breed history to gain a Specialty win; Reserve Winners Bitch, in a five-point entry from the Puppy Class, at the Cleveland Shetland Sheepdog Club, June 1971. Jean D. Simmonds, owner.

Carmylie

Carmylie Shetland Sheepdogs are located at Chatham, New York, where they are owned by Jean D. Simmonds. This kennel has produced, as of August 1983, nineteen American champions, numerous Canadian champions, and one Japanese champion.

It all began back in 1949 when Jean, barely a teenager at that time, acquired her first Sheltie. This turned out to be a high-scoring obedience dog who in no time at all had given this young fancier a taste for showing dogs. Although she never suspected it at the time, her second Sheltie, purchased a year later, was destined to become the foundation dog of the future Carmylie Kennels (named after a Scottish rock formation) which is now one of the most respected in the Shetland Sheepdog world.

Walnobr's Golden Promise, C.D.X., with two points on a conformation title, too, was line-bred several times from the great Champion Timberidge Temptation. Through her daughter by Champion Nightfall of Perkasie (also line-bred on Temptation), the Sea Isle lines were introduced, this by crossing her with a later acquisition, Badgerton Red Riot O'Carmylie, C.D.X. (who was by Champion Sea Isle Serenade ex Champion Badgerton Impersonator, C.D.). Mrs. Simmonds describes him as "one of the greatest Shelties I have ever had the pleasure of owning—one of those rare 'nearly human' companions, who almost knew everything that was said to him." A delight to train, Red Riot scored

Milord Marmalade, sable male by Badgerton Red Riot o'Carmylie, C.D.X. from a daughter of Ch. Katie-J's Ronny ex Bi Jingo, on New Year's Day, 1970. Photo courtesy of Jean D. Simmonds.

Am. and Can. Ch. Carmylie Elusive Dream. Handsome representative of Jean Simmond's Carmylie Shelties.

numerous High in Trials, several times with 199 points, and once with 199½. He crept slightly over the height limit as he matured, so he had to be content with eight conformation points which consisted of both majors; but he made up for that by producing two champions and figuring prominently in the background of one of the breed's leading sires, Champion Calcurt Luke. An inbred Red Riot daughter, from the original Golden Promise, when bred to Champion Halstor's Peter Pumpkin produced American and Canadian Champion Carmylie Call To Promise, who in turn produced Champion Carmylie Some Pumpkin and is influential in several of the Mainstay dogs as well through her daughter by Luke, Carmylie Candle Dancer.

Serious breeding actually began at Carmylie in 1961 with the acquisition of Champion Kawartha's Fair Game, who was Peter Pumpkin's grandam, later to make the Top Producing lists as the dam of five champions. She was by Champion Sheltieland Kiltie O'Sea Isle ex Champion Kawartha's Sabrina Fair, and she came to Mrs. Simmonds bred to Champion Lindhurst Comanchero, the breeding her late owner had planned for her. There were four puppies in the litter, all of which became backgrounds for later champions. Carmylie Comanche had six points

including a major when a virus rendered him sterile, after which it seemed unimportant to try to finish him since he would no longer be a stud dog. His first litter, conceived before this had occurred, contained the lovely Champion Jomar Carmylie Bundle of Love, who played a significant role in the Carmylie program. A daughter of hers by Champion Katie-J's The Gay Prince when bred to Champion Halstor's Peter Pumpkin gave Mrs. Simmonds one of her most influential dogs, American and Canadian Champion Carmylie Elusive Dream. This dog gained his title with ease, starting out by going Best of Winners at the American Shetland Sheepdog Association National Specialty when only nine months old; he finished at thirteen months of age. He was also a dominant sire, with nine champions to his credit, several of which have become foundations of other successful kennels.

Mrs. Simmonds pauses here to comment, "I cannot write a kennel log without paying tribute to a great lady, the late Mae Freeman, and her now defunct Katie-J dogs, as they played an important part in my success." Wanting to take advantage of the Note-Kiltie cross, Mrs. Simmonds decided to breed Fair Game to the inbred Note son, Champion Sea Isle Serenade. Two of the three pups born became Champion Carmylie

Ch. Kawartha's Fair Game, by Ch. Sheltieland Kiltie O'Sea Isle ex Ch. Kawartha's Sabrina Fair, dam of five champions. Jean Simmonds, owner.

Bravo O'Banchory and Champion Vanity Fair of Carmylie, C.D. When bred to Champion Katie-J's The Gay Prince, Vanity Fair also presented Carmylie with a two-champion litter, in this case Champion Carmylie Heatherland So Fair and Champion Carmylie Lady Fair. The former never produced, and Lady Fair was leased by Heatherland, where she figures strongly in present pedigrees. Katie-J's Early Bird was bred to Banchory Heatherland On High, a son of Lady Fair by Champion Banchory High Born, producing American and Canadian Champion Carmylie Shine On High, American and Canadian C.D., the foundation for Judy Brown's Dury Voe Kennels. While at home, Lady Fair was bred to Champion Halstor's Peter Pumpkin, from which came Carmylie Walter Watermelon,

Ch. Vanity Fair of Carmylie, C.D., by Ch. Sea Isle Serenade ex Ch. Kawartha's Fair Game. Bred and owned by Jean Simmonds.

Above: Ch. Katie-J's The Gay Prince. Owned by Ralph and Mae Freeman, Katie-J Kennels. **Below:** Ch. Carmylie Lady Fair, by Champion Katie-J's The Gay Prince ex Champion Vanity Fair of Carmylie, C.D. Jean Simmonds, owner.

the dog with the unforgettable name and a great deal of quality, who had to be content with eight points due to low-breaking ears.

Bred to another pointed son of Champion Lindhurst Comanchero from Champion Jomar Carmylie Bundle of Love, Lady Fair produced a darling little daughter who, when bred to Peter Pumpkin, presented Mrs. Simmonds with another of her better bitches, Champion Carmylie Carioca of Kaher. This one now has several gorgeous and pointed daughters, including the very excellent bitch Carmylie Dance To The Music who was sired by Champion Windhover Sweet Music Man, whose grandam is a later sister to Elusive Dream.

Vanity Fair's life was tragically snuffed out by a fatal airplane ride, and her loss is a sad one as she had so much to offer with her exquisite type, body structure, and effortless movement.

Due to extraneous circumstances, Fair Game was sold in whelp to Joan Wilk in Canada, and that combination gave the Terian Kennels an outstanding start with a Best in Show winner, Champion Terian's Amber Fair, who in turn produced one of Canada's top winners, Champion Terian's Aire Fair. Amber Fair later came to Carmylie and was finished in the United States by Mrs. Simmonds. Amber Fair produced a son who was close to the title when he was lost, plus a lone daughter who, when bred to Elusive Dream's son, Champion Heatherlands Simon Says, became the dam of a current Carmylie winner, Champion Carmylie Jillian Lauradon.

Above: Ch. Carmylie Carioca of Kaher, by Ch. Halstor's Peter Pumpkin ex Carmylie Scottish Charm. Jean D. Simmonds, owner, Carmylie Shetland Sheepdogs. **Below:** Carmylie Dance To The Music, by Ch. Windhover Sweet Music Man ex Ch. Carmylie Carioca of Kaher. Jean D. Simmonds.

Above: The black and whites Carmylie Kaher Bi Now (right) and Checkerchance "Jenny." Both owned by Jean D. Simmonds. **Below:** Ch. Carmylie Jillian Lauradon, 14″, by Ch. Heatherland's Simon Says ex Carmylie Cinnamon Flare. Breeder-owners, Jean D. Simmonds and Judith C. Brown.

Ch. Diamond's Robert Bruce as painted by Jean D. Simmonds.

Am. and Can. Ch. Carmylie Shine On High, Am. and Can. C.D., as a water dog! Owned by Judy Brown.

Carmylie Taplrac Nelli Bi, the bi-blue-merle by Taplrac Sound of Silence ex Ch. Carmylie Polly Paintbrush, with eight points including one major. Jean D. Simmonds, owner.

Banchory Bi Jingo of Carmylie, by Ch. Thistlerose Arcwood Alladin ex Lodgewood Queen of Banchory, at thirteen years of age. Owned by Jean D. Simmonds, Carmylie Shetland Sheepdogs.

Ch. Philidove Carmylie In A Mist (above), sired by Ch. Philidove Heir Presumptive, and Ch. Carmylie Polly Paintbrush (below). Both owned by Jean D. Simmonds, Carmylie Kennels.

Concurrent with the love for sables was a love for the black and white and blue and white bicolors at Carmylie. Mrs. Simmonds notes:

> The bicolor Sheltie was a much misunderstood phenomenon in those days—often considered a misfit by breeders and judges alike. In 1965, Banchory Bi Jingo of Carmylie came into my life and changed my course. "Inky" was born 10 years too soon. An exquisite black and white of superior type, she could never get out of the ribbons, while sables or tan-pointed tris of obviously lesser quality defeated her for the high awards.

These injustices inspired Mrs. Simmonds to write a series of detailed articles on the bicolor Sheltie for the national breed magazine. Not only did they receive a Dog Writers Association of America Award, but they helped pave the way for the bicolors in the breed ring. Acceptance was emerging!

Bi Jingo contributed well to the breed by way of the whelping box, producing two champions and two others with major points. Her daughter, Champion Philidove Carmylie In A Mist, produced a smashing litter of four males, affectionately known as the "Misty Banger Wrecking

A family portrait of Shelties with their people. Courtesy of Jean D. Simmonds, Carmylie Kennels, Chatham, New York.

Crew" when young, two of whom finished, one with major wins and one who, in spite of his quality, absolutely refused to show. Because of these sons of In A Mist, and her own son Champion Carmylie The Real McCoy, Bi Jingo figures in many pedigrees throughout the country. A later sister to In A Mist, Carmylie Black Lace, was bred to the non-showing Misty son, Philidove Neva Can Say Goodby, and from this litter came another of Mrs. Simmonds's more influential champions, Carmylie If Bi Chance. A classic black and white, Chance truly opened doors for this color. Judges were unable to deny her quality, and she became the first modern black and white to attain Specialty wins. Mrs. Simmonds reminds us that the very first Sheltie champion in the United States was Champion Lerwick Rex—yes, a black and white! He, however, was imported from Scotland.

Because she took time out for litters, another black and white beat Chance to the title for the modern times. But shortly thereafter, Mrs. Simmonds tells us, Chance became the first *bitch* champion of her color in breed history in the U.S.A., finishing smartly with three-, four-, and five-point major wins. Pyometra claimed her in mid-life, but not before she had given Mrs. Simmonds a blue version of herself, the renowned Champion Carmylie Polly Paintbrush, sired by Champion Banchory Deep Purple. Going back into the Deep Purple line, through his double grandson Taplrac Sound of Silence, Polly has produced a pair of major-pointed littermates, the bi-blue Carmylie Taplrac Nellie Bi and the blue-

tan Taplrac Carmylie Blueprint, co-bred by Pat and Carl Strauser of Taplrac Shelties.

Bi Jingo was bred to another of the Misty sons, Champion Philidove Kismet Heir Borne, and a lovely son was lost but a daughter, bred to Deltem's In Sunshine or Shadow (thus doubling up on High Born and adding one-third Katie-J through Shine On High) resulted in the handsome tricolor Champion Nathan Hale of Carmylie. A stud-fee puppy of his ex Rosmoor Winter Wind O'Tuwin, C.D., became Champion Carmylie Rosmoor Silvertip, who in his turn is a champion producer.

Being an artist by trade, dog portraits naturally have been Jean Simmonds's favorites, and she has painted many of the leading Shelties over the years. Always feeling the need for some sort of visual aid for the newcomer, she has authored and illustrated the book, *The Illustrated Shetland Sheepdog Standard*, depicting "rights and wrongs" of the Sheltie, both in words and pictures. We are honored that she has permitted us to use a few of these drawings in our own book, which you will find in the chapter on Sheltie standards. Study these drawings well, and do by all means add the very useful little volume to your library, as it is an invaluable and beautifully done study of the subject.

Mrs. Simmonds has judged Collies and Shelties since 1971, having officiated throughout the United States and Canada. She describes her pleasure in having recently officiated in Melbourne, Australia, where she found the "people, places and dogs all truly engrossing."

Ch. Catamount Black Phantom, by Ch. Sutter's Golden Masquerade ex Catamount Flower Power. Bred and owned by the Stanley Saltzmans.

Above: Catamount Come September and Catamount Commuter owner-handled by Lynette and Stanley Saltzman at Trenton Kennel Club, May 1962. First and second at both the National Specialty Futurity and the Interstate Futurity, these two Shelties were also Winners Dog and Winners Bitch at Long Island Kennel Club in addition to their wins at Trenton pictured here. Mr. and Mrs. Stanley S. Saltzman, Catamount Kennels, Westport, Connecticut. **Below:** Ch. Lingard Catamount Cameo finishing at twelve months of age, Best of Breed over Specials under judge Vincent Perry; handled by Lynette Saltzman. Owned by Stanley and Lynette Saltzman.

Catamount

Catamount Kennels, owned by Mr. and Mrs. Stanley S. Saltzman at Westport, Connecticut, came into being when, in 1959, the couple purchased a six-month-old puppy, Golden Glory O' Page's Hill, from J. Nate Levine. She made her debut at the National the following month, where she went Best in Futurity and Reserve Winners Bitch, repeating her wins the following day at the Interstate Specialty. She completed her championship in very short order but unfortunately died before producing a litter.

Next, Saphire O'Page's Hill was purchased from Nate. She was by Champion Musket O'Page's Hill ex Champion Kacing Summer Sprite, a large bitch but very typey and very sound. She had one litter before a baby sitter let her out of a run and she disappeared. Bred to Champion Pixie Dell Penrod, she produced Catamount Come September and Catamount Commuter, first and second in both National and Interstate Futurities.

Come September, bred to Champion Dark Lagoon O'Page's Hill, produced the Interstate Futurity winner, Catamount Excalibur; and bred to Champion Pixie Dell Bright Vision she produced the American Shetland Sheepdog Association Futurity winner, Catamount Count Down. Both of these were sold as puppies. Bred to Champion Pixie Dell Royal Jester, Come September produced Catamount Chiffon, who had both majors by seven months but died of heartworm before finishing.

The Saltzmans purchased Blossom Girl O'Page's Hill and bred her to Dark Pilot O'Page's Hill. She produced Catamount Calla Lilly, a very plain tri of excellent personality with a number of Specialty Reserves and about five points. The Saltzmans, in those days, were showing almost exclusively at Specialties. Calla Lilly bred to Champion Pixie Dell Bright Vision produced the beautiful Catamount Flower Power; this was unfortunate so far as timing was concerned because it was just before Lynette Saltzman was about to have her second child and her interest in showing the dogs was taken away for a bit. Flower Power was bred to her half brother, Champion Sutter's Golden Masquerade, producing Champion Catamount Black Phantom and Champion Catamount Charade along with the Specialty winner, Catamount Charisma. Phantom finished with five majors at nine months; Charade finished with three majors, including five points at Trenton; and Charisma was Winners Bitch at Tri-State her only time as an adult, before being shipped to Venezuela. Phantom sired champions on both coasts of the U.S.

Flower Power, bred to Champion Crawford's Matchless, produced Champion Catamount Classy Chassis, who won both Interstate and Tri-State Futurities at six months, accumulated ten points as a puppy, and as an adult won three

Above: Ch. Catamount Magic Dragon, by Ch. Catamount Black Phantom ex Champion Pixie Dell Blue Thistle, a 1973 champion for the Saltzmans. **Below:** Ch. Catamount Charade, one of the many lovely winners bred and owned by the Stanley Saltzmans.

Catamount Charisma, by Ch. Sutter's Golden Masquerade ex Catamount Flower Power, taking Winners Bitch at the Tri-State Specialty. Bred and owned by the Stanley S. Saltzmans.

of the first four shows in which she was entered to finish. She was Best of Breed her first time in Specials at the Harrisburg Show and was shown only a handful of times as a Special, primarily on Specialty weekends. Her record includes Best of Opposite Sex at the National Specialty weekend in 1977 in an entry of 217, thirty-five of which were Specials, and Best of Breed at an Interstate Specialty from the Veterans Class.

Bred to Champion Kismet's Conquistador, Classy Chassis produced Champion Catamount Caress, who accumulated fourteen points including both majors by ten months of age with wins which included Best of Opposite Sex at the Interstate Specialty over Specials. She returned to the ring as an adult to finish with her third major and a Group third from the classes.

Bred to Champion SumerSong Hurry Sundown, Classy Chassis produced Catamount Moonglow, Best in Sweepstakes at the Interstate Specialty with a major from the Puppy Class, and several major Reserve wins.

The Saltzmans have never kept more than six or eight adult dogs, always with old-timers among them. They have never kept dogs that they have felt "could finish," preferring to keep only dogs that they consider to be superior specimens in every way.

Above: Catamount Charade, Ch. Sutter's Golden Masquerade ex Catamount Flower Power, finishing title with a five-point win at Trenton Kennel Club. Lynette Saltzman handling. **Below:** Ch. Catamount Classy Chassis, Best of Breed from the Veterans Class at the Interstate Specialty in 1979, then on to a breed win and a Working Group fourth the following day at Penn Treaty. Stanley and Lynette Saltzman, breeder-owners.

Above: Ch. Catamount Caress, winner of her third major under J.D. Jones at Baton Rouge Kennel Club. Mr. and Mrs. Stanley Saltzman, owners, Catamount Kennels. **Below:** Catamount Moonglow, Winners Bitch for three points from the Puppy Class at Northern New Jersey. Stanley and Lynette Saltzman, owners.

Cedarhope

Cedarhope Shetland Sheepdogs are owned by Dr. and Mrs. Dale Gouger and are located at Mohnton, Pennsylvania. This is the home of one of the most influential and respected dogs in our present-day Sheltie world, American and Canadian Champion Banchory Deep Purple, who, as we are going to press (late 1983), has just broken the record of top producing blue-merle sire in Sheltie history, with eighteen champion of record offspring—a record which will undoubtedly have been added to even before you are reading this, as several others by him are very close to the finishing line.

Deep Purple was bred by Donna Tidswell Harden and was sired by Champion Sundowner Mr. Bojangles, C.D., ex Horizon White Ice. Bojangles is by Champion Tentagel David Copperfield (Champion Diamond's Robert Bruce ex Tentagel Mrs. Robinson) ex Champion Tentagel the Genie (Champion Vikingsholm Vilhelm ex Champion Sharlin's Oh Suzanna). White Ice is a daughter of Champion Banchory Thunder Blue (Champion Cherden Sock It To 'Em ex Clan Duncan Banchory Bluette) ex Banchory Flash of Blue (Champion Banchory High Born ex Banchory Pamper of Maywood).

"Jake," as Deep Purple is known to his friends, was the youngest stud dog to appear on the list of Top Sheltie Sires, and his influence as a sire has certainly contributed enormously to the breed, making him internationally famous for producing clean heads with full muzzle and underjaw, sweet expression, well-boned substance, and an excellent strong rear.

Most recent of his winning offspring as we write are his fifteenth champion, Waldenwood Moon Frost, belonging to H. Smith in Georgia; his sixteenth champion, Piper's Tamarac O'Revelree, C.D., owned by P. Graham in Arizona; his seventeenth champion, Harvest Hill's Soft Spoken Blue, owned by Cathy Loesch of Harvest Hill Kennels in Washington, who bred and finished an entire all-champion litter by him; his eighteenth champion, Banchory Future Shock, owned by M. Illg in Minnesota; and Canadian Champion Harvest Hill's Tom Jones, owned by K. Dickenson in California.

The Gougers are dedicated Sheltie fanciers who are very proud of "Jake's" strong and favorable influence on his breed.

Ch. Cherden's Sock It To 'Em, a very important Sheltie of the late 1960's-early 1970's. Owned by Cheryl Anderson. Photo courtesy of Lee A. Reasin.

Ch. Astolat Future Emblem, by Ch. Frigate's Emblem of Astolat ex Astolat Emblem of Hope, the first Sheltie at Chisterling and the sire of thirteen champions. Breeder, Constance Hubbard; owner, Don K. Combee.

Chisterling

The Chisterling Kennels were established in 1948 as a Collie kennel when their owner, Don K. Combee, was fourteen years old. In 1952, this young Georgia fancier changed breeds, having become interested in the Shetland Sheepdog. Since he had already gone through the various learning processes, and had made his share of mistakes with the Collies (such as beginning with the typical pet and so on), Don came into Shelties with a better understanding of breeding and showing dogs than might otherwise have been the case.

Champion Astolat Future Emblem, his first Sheltie, was purchased by Don Combee from Constance Hubbard of Astolat Kennels, at seven months of age. He proved to be a very good start for his new owner, as he eventually became the sire of thirteen champions, the most famous of which was Champion Chisterling Florian, who in his turn sired seventeen champions including the all-breed Best in Show bitch, Champion Chisterling Scarlett O'Hara. Scarlett was the

Ch. Chisterling Brandy, the sire of three champions. Owned by Don K. Combee, Chisterling Kennels.

third bitch in the history of the breed to go Best in Show from the classes.

Another dog who added to the fame of this kennel was Champion Chisterling's Falkirk's Flame, who produced five champions including Scarlett O'Hara. The Combees have had a great many bitches at Chisterling, champions and non-champions, each of whom have produced three or even four champions. A good number of their males have sired three or four champions each, among these being Champion Chisterling Brandy (three champions), Champion Chisterling Tradewinds (three champions), Champion Chisterling Black Fortune (three champions), and Champion Chisterling Smoke Screen (four champions). Some of the most outstanding features the Combees have strived for over the years have been the beautiful and correct eye which gives a Sheltie the sweetest of expressions and the lovely high-set natural ears for which Chisterling dogs are known.

Don Combee comments that "since the Sheltie was a rather shy breed when I first started, I have put a great deal of emphasis into improving temperament. Fortunately, there are very few shy Shelties today."

To date, Don Combee has finished more than sixty champions—certainly a very impressive total. Among them are Champions Chisterling Devl Made Me Do It, Chisterling Woodwink Peach, Chisterling Bourbon Delux, Chisterling Gold Windjammer, Chisterling Sweet and Love-

Ch. Chisterling Smoke Screen (above), by Ch. Chisterling Smoke Signal ex Ch. Sherrillon Lark O'Wadegate, and Ch. Chisterling Hot Toddy (below), by Ch. Chisterling Brandy ex Chisterling Gold O'Perimist. Both owned by Don K. Combee.

Ch. Chisterling Florian, by Ch. Astolat Future Emblem ex Ch. Lillegard Golden Charm, the sire of seventeen champions. Breeder-owner, Don Combee, Chisterling Shelties.

Ch. Chisterling Exquisite Dream, by Ch. Chisterling The Phantom ex Ch. Chisterling Dreamboat. Breeder-owner, Don K. Combee, Chisterling Kennels.

Ch. Chisterling Highland Fling completing title at the 1955 Georgia Specialty, judged by Betty Whelen. Don Combee, owner-handler.

ly, Chisterling Hot Toddy, Chisterling Falkirk's Flame, Chisterling Pipe Dreams, Chisterling Bold Venture, Chisterling Bronze Prince, Chisterling Scarlett O'Hara, Chisterling Trade Winds, Chisterling Highland Fling, Chisterling Dawn O'Maryknoll, Chisterling The Phantom, Chisterling Dreamboat, Chisterling Exquisite Dream, Chisterling Cadet O'Taralane, Chisterling Golden Boy, Chisterling Black Fortune, Chisterling Mainstay O'Fide, Chisterling All A Glow, Chisterling Florian, Chisterling The Heiress, Chisterling Timtone's Sunrise, Chisterling Extra Special, Chisterling Florian's Image, Chisterling Brandy, Chisterling Copper Glow II, Chisterling King of Diamonds,

Above: Ch. Chisterling Woodwink Peach, by Ch. Alynphyll Whispering Wind ex Chisterling Bloody Mary, taking Best in the Working Group at Kennesaw Kennel Club Dog Show, October 1979. **Below:** Ch. Chisterling Extra Special, by Ch. Chisterling Florian ex Timtone's Bright Star. Both dogs bred and owned by Don K. Combee.

Ch. Feracres Daisy Mae, one of the first champion Shelties owned by Don K. Combee at the start of the Chisterling Shelties in 1954.

Ch. Chisterling Saucy of Tamaron. Owned by Don K. Combee, Chisterling Kennels, Marietta, Georgia.

An informal head-study of Ch. Chisterling Extra Special. Breeder-owner, Don K. Combee.

Chisterling Smoke Signal, Chisterling Smoke Screen, Chisterling Vintage Wine, Chisterling Candy of Jamar, Chisterling Saucy of Tamaron, Chisterling Anniversary Blu, Chisterling High Tide, Chisterling Center Stage, and Chisterling Piper O'Beckward.

Champion Astolat Future Emblem was, as mentioned herein, Don Combee's first Sheltie. Champion Ardencaple's The Highlander, Champion Bykenhall's Honey Love, and Champion Lanbur Tarheel Lassie each produced three champions for him when introduced into the breeding program. Six champions were sired at Chisterling by Champion Edanjo After Glow of Marjan. Two were sired by Champion Ken-Rob's Crown Royal. Champion Timtone's Amber Lady and Champion Sherrilon Lark O'Wadegate each produced two. And champions at Chisterling have also come from Champion Bee-Jay's Cayenne of Aron-Kar, Champion Fawley's Highland Piper, Champion Gra-Jon's High Ho, Champion Habilu the Herald, and Champion Lillegard Golden Charm, among others.

In 1958, Don Combee started judging Collies and Shetland Sheepdogs; then about fifteen years later he decided to add on some other breeds. He is now approved for eighteen breeds in the Working and Herding Groups.

Chisterling Shelties are located at Marietta in Georgia.

Chosen

Chosen Shetland Sheepdogs belong to Barbara B. Thompson and are located at Boerne, Texas.

The fifteen-inch dog, Champion Chosen Jubilation, C.D., would seem to be "top man" here, and he is indeed a dog in whom to take pride. Bred by Patsy Edmonson, he is a son of International, Mexican, and American Champion Macdega The Chosen, C.D. (Champion Halstor's Peter Pumpkin ex Shu-La-Le's Sincerity O'Macdega) from September's Highly Likely (Champion September's Hi Time at Catomco ex Champion September's Sasha in Satin). His date of birth is May 8th 1976.

As we write, this splendid dog is the sire of nine American champions, two Canadian champions, plus a daughter with fourteen points in-

Above: Ch. RobCary's Return Engagement, owned by Caryl Fennell and Jan Johnson, San Antonio, Texas. **Below:** Ch. Notoriety O'Barwood, by Ch. Banchory Formal Notice ex Ch. Barwood's Chosen Sensation. Bred and owned by Barbara Thompson, Chosen Kennels, Boerne, Texas.

Above and below: Two views of Ch. Chosen Jubilation, C.D. Owned by Barbara B. Thompson, Chosen Kennels.

Ch. RobCary Jubilant Image, by Ch. Chosen Jubilation, C.D., taking Best of Breed at Trinity Valley Kennel Club under judge James Noe. Bred and owned by Caryl Fennell, San Antonio, Texas.

The eight-month-old male, Chosen Richly Sunblest. Chosen Kennels, Barbara B. Thompson.

cluding both majors and a Specialty win plus a Group first.

Chosen Notoriety of Barwood, by Champion Banchory Formal Notice ex Champion Barwoods Chosen Sensation, a young bitch now being campaigned, is off to a good start and was Best Puppy and Reserve Winners Bitch at the recent West Texas Shetland Sheepdog Club Specialty.

Then there is a smashing youngster, Chosen Richly Sunblest, by Champion Jubilation ex September Poppin' Fresh, for whom hopes are high.

Three lovely champions, all by Jubilation from Benayr Robcary Moonshine, are Champion Robcary Jubilant Image (male), American and Canadian Champion Robcary Jubilant Expectations (male), and the lovely bitch, Champion Robcary Return Engagement.

101

A very historic photo from the late 1960's. On the right, Frank Ashbey handling Ch. Astolat Enchantor owned by Mrs. Constance Hubbard, sire; on the right, Gene Cohen with future champion Conendale Lord of Astolat, son. "Lordy" was Gene's very first Sheltie companion who was still alive and well and placed in a good home following Gene's death in 1981.

Conendale

Conendale Shetland Sheepdogs were owned by the late Eugene (Gene) Cohen and located at Wilton, Connecticut. One could not possibly find a more dedicated Sheltie enthusiast than Gene—or one with a better eye for the breed.

Gene's very first Sheltie champion was purchased in the late 1960's as a puppy from Mrs. Constance Hubbard of Astolat fame, Gene's close friend whom he held in tremendous esteem through the remainder of his lifetime. "Lordy" was a son of the great Champion Astolat Enchantor and a credit to him in every way. He gained his title in short order, had an exciting show career, and was Gene's adored companion and pet right up until the time Gene passed away. A good home was found for "Lordy," and the last we heard he was well and going strong although in his "teens."

Other well-known Shelties at Conendale included the lovely Champion Willow Wand Blueberry Sundae, Champion Babinette Tagetta, Champion Benayr Lil Tartan O'Conendale, Champion Waldenwood British Sterling, Champion Wade Gate's Honor Bound, Champion Tull-E-Ho Enterprise, and a number more with points toward their titles.

The bitch, Tull-E-Ho Curtain Call, was one over which Gene was especially excited. He saw and fell in love with her, and at the time of his death she was well on the way to her title. It was she whom he was campaigning at the time of his

The very handsome mahogany sable dog, Ch. Benayr Lil Tartan O'Conendale, one of the excellent Shelties owned and handled by the late Eugene Cohen, Conendale Kennels.

sudden tragic death of a heart attack in his motel room on a dog show weekend. That day she had won well for him, a three-point major under Stanley Saltzman, over which Gene had been much elated.

Champion Tull-E-Ho Enterprise was Curtain Call's sire, Champion Tull-E-Ho Desiree O'Barwood her dam. She had been Winners Bitch at the Chicagoland Specialty the previous February for a five-point major, and she had won a long list of admirers on each of her show ring appearances.

Conendale Challenger O'Akirene was left by Gene, close to his title, to Connie Hubbard. She

Above: Ch. Willow Wand Bluberry Sundae taking Winners Bitch for a five-point major under noted specialist judge Ms. Elizabeth Babin at the SCIOTO Shetland Sheepdog Club Specialty Show in April 1977. Owned and handled by Eugene (Gene) Cohen. **Below:** Gene Cohen showing his very pretty blue bitch, Ch. Babinette Tagetta, to judge A. Peter Knoop at a dog show during 1970.

Above: Tull E-Ho Curtain Call went Winners Bitch for a three-point major under Stanley Saltzman on the eve of Gene Cohen's death and thus was the last Sheltie he showed. Here she is taking a five-point major, three months earlier, at the Chicagoland Specialty, handled by Gene's friend and partner Eddie Abramowicz. **Below:** Ch. Conendale Challenger O'Akirene winning Best of Breed at Riverhead Kennel Club in 1981. This lovely dog was Gene Cohen's greatest pride and joy. Shortly after Gene's death, Joe Malloy took Challenger to two Working Group firsts.

Ch. Waldenwood British Sterling, taking the points here, in 1979, under judge Howard Tyler. Sterling was finished owner-handled, by Eugene (Gene) Cohen in about ten shows.

Ch. Wade Gate Honor Bound in 1975, winning some of his first points, owner-handled by Eugene Cohen.

Ch. Wade Gate Honor Bound in 1977 with his owner-handler Gene Cohen adding still another to his string of Best of Breed successes.

Eugene Cohen's first Sheltie judging assignment, at Harrisburg Kennel Club in 1980, where he drew a four-point major entry. Linda More is handling the winner.

Babinette Ballad of the Blues at nine months of age taking Winners Dog and Best of Winners for a three-point major at Columbiana Kennel Club in 1980. The judge is Eugene Cohen, owner of the Conendale Shetland Sheepdogs.

sent him out with professional handler Joe Malloy to be finished, and he made quite a triumphant tour of it, returning with two Working Group firsts to his credit. Gene had brought "Chally" out originally while still a puppy, his first two points having been gained from the Puppy Class. Now he is proving a popular and successful stud dog at Connie Hubbard's Astolat Kennel.

Champion Wade Gate's Honor Bound was one of Gene Cohen's most widely admired Shelties. His thirty-five Bests of Breed gained in keenest Eastern competition certainly speak for themselves, as do the lovely photos of him appearing in the pages of this book.

Gene Cohen had received his judging approval in the beginning of 1980 and showed promise of becoming one of the best and most popular, immediately receiving assignments from the East Coast to Texas. He was a member of the Interstate Shetland Sheepdog Club, the American Shetland Sheepdog Association, the Nutmeg Afghan Hound Club (another breed with which he was actively involved), and the Trap Falls Kennel Club.

We are grateful to Gene's good friend Eddie Abramowitz for having collected the pictures reproduced here for this book.

Ch. Addup Mount Mist of Jer-Nic. Bred and owned by Edmund and Helen Scherer, Edlen Kennels, Ravenna, Ohio.

Ch. Extraspecial of Edlen, by Am. and Can. Ch. Markris Red Baron of Edlen ex the Peter Pumpkin daughter, Marscott's Scotch Mist. Edmund and Helen Scherer, owners.

Am. and Can. Ch. Markris Red Baron of Edlen, between fifteen and nineteen months of age. Edlen Kennels, Edmund and Helen Scherer.

Edlen

Edlen Kennels, owned by Edmund and Helen Scherer, at Ravenna, Ohio, started out when the Scherers had the good fortune, in the spring of 1969, to purchase a seven-week-old son of Champion Kerrylance Bossman, C.D.X., ex Kerrylance Witacism who was to become American and Canadian Champion Markris Red Baron of Edlen and was to complete his championship in the United States with two four-point majors, back to back, on one weekend.

In the summer of 1973, when Baron was four years old, he was shown over a three and a half month period, during which he became Number Ten Sheltie in the United States for that year.

Since the Scherers were new in the fancy and unknown at that time, it remained for them to prove what Baron could produce. They were able to buy what Helen Scherer describes as "a plain little Peter daughter, Marscott's Scotch Mist," to be bred to Baron. From their first litter, she produced Champion Addup Mount Mist of Jer-Nic, Champion Extraspecial of Edlen, and Extraordinary of Edlen, who gained twelve points. All three of these have produced champions or pointed get.

Champion Addup Mount Mist of Jer-Nic, bred to Merri-Jon's Outlaw O'Connemara, produced Champion The Rifleman of Jer-Nic and Champion Addup N Over of Jer-Nic. Then bred to Champion Banchory Formal Notice she produced Easdale's Notice Me of Jer-Nic.

Champion Extraspecial of Edlen, bred to Theresa Ann of Edlen, produced Woodlyn

Special of Jer-Nic, owned by Easdale Kennels in North Carolina.

Extraordinary of Edlen, bred to Sea Wind's Song, C.D., produced Champion The Mark of Edlen.

A bitch by Champion Rorralore Mickey Dazzler ex Champion Rorralore's Sma' Primsie was leased and bred to Baron, producing Champion Galahad of Edlen and Gina of Edlen who won a large Specialty Match judged by Betty Whelen, but she was sold to someone who I assume did not continue showing her.

Sugar N Spice of Edlen, an inbred Champion Barwood's Bold Venture daughter, bred to Baron, produced Hector of Edlen, who had nine points when he, too, was sold to what turned out to be not a show home.

The Scherers purchased Tiny Dian of Walnut Hall, by Champion Tiny Tuck of Walnut Hall ex Tiny Amanda of Walnut Hall. Bred to Baron, she produced for the Scherers the handsome Champion Knock On Wood of Edlen, whose progeny include Maryne Backburner of Edlen (with thirteen points including two five-point majors), from Theresa Ann of Edlen; and two sons, My Lucky Bit of Edlen (eleven points including three three-point majors) and Little Bit of Luck of Edlen (seven points including a five-point major Specialty win), from Lazy K. Honey Bit of Edlen. This same bitch was bred to Baron

Theresa Ann of Edlen, a lovely example of the Shelties raised at this kennel.

Ch. The Mark of Edlen owned by Edlen's Shetland Sheepdogs, Edmund and Helen Scherer.

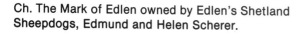

Ch. Galahad of Edlen, three years of age. Owned by Edmund and Helen Scherer, Edlen Kennels.

Above: Little Bit of Luck of Edlen, by Ch. Knock On Wood of Edlen (Am. and Can. Ch. Markris Red Baron of Edlen ex Tiny Dian of Walnut Hall) ex Lazy K Honey Bit of Edlen, has seven points including a five-point Specialty win as of August 1983. Bred and owned by Edmund and Helen Scherer, Edlen Shetland Sheepdogs. **Below:** Ch. Merri-Lon Count On Me of Edlen, at Erie Kennel Club Dog Show in 1974, taking Best of Opposite Sex for Edmund and Helen Scherer.

for his last litter, from which the Scherers have Baron's last show-daughter, Natalie of Edlen.

As of August 1983, Baron, despite being fourteen years of age, is still a happy, healthy, loving Sheltie and sharing a run with two lively young bitches. The Scherers feel, understandably, that they were lucky in getting him. He has always loved shows and has reproduced his splendid temperament in many of his progeny. A true mahogany sable, he measured 15¾ inches at one year of age, but he had settled to 15¼ inches by the time he had reached age two.

Kerrylance Minority Wit was the Scherers' first show bitch, acquiring all but one three-point major. In her last litter she had six pups, most of whose birth weight was more than twelve ounces each. Her hindquarters never recovered. Mrs. Scherer says that "apparently we never found just the right male to breed her to," and her only claim to fame may come through her daughter, by Champion Badgerton Proud Prince, Prim Princess of Edlen, who when bred to Champion Merri-Lon Count On Me of Edlen produced Windrush Summer Sunshine, a lovely bitch who should have been shown. She was bred to Baron, by whom she produced Sea Sprite of Jer-Nic, on the way to championship. Also, bred back to Count On Me, she gave the Scherers Summer Melody of Edlen

Ch. Knock On Wood of Edlen while en route to the title taking Best of Winners at Dan Emmett in 1981. Edmund and Helen Scherer, owners.

who now has three small and lovely daughters by Knock On Wood.

Count On Me came to the Scherers from the Pattersons at Merri-Lon Kennels when they wanted another show male for breeding, to "cross fault" Red Baron. He came with all the credentials, a Peter Pumpkin son, heavy boned and heavy coated with a lovely neck. His dam was Champion Merri-Lon Sunburst Serena, a daughter of Champion Barwood's Bold Venture (whom Count closely resembled). Count produced two types of bitches: one little, 13½ to 14½ inches tall, and the other always 15¼ to 15¾ inches tall, never anything in between.

Sherlynn Fancy Nancy, one of the Edlen Shelties, relaxing. Owned by the Scherers.

Above: Gypsy Lore of Edlen, one of the many fine Shelties at Edlen Kennels, is an example of the larger type of bitch produced by her sire, Ch. Merri-Lon Count On Me of Edlen. **Below:** Sea Wind's Countess of Edlen, with twelve points, is an example of the small type Sheltie bitch sired by Ch. Merri-Lon Count On Me of Edlen. Owned by Edmund and Helen Scherer, Edlen Kennels.

Winning his first points from the Puppy Class at nine and a half months of age, Count became Champion Merri-Lon Count On Me when just past two years of age.

The Scherers had bought two Champion Bossman daughters, Kerrylance Gypsy Mol of Edlen and her dam, Sherlynn Fancy Nancy. Mol, bred to Champion Rorralore Mickey Dazzler, gave them Gypsy Dazzle of Edlen who, when bred to Champion Galahad of Edlen, produced Champion Weslan Chairman of the Board and Champion Weslen Hedera. The breeding was repeated, the second time producing Weslan Lucky of Jer-Nic and My Fancy of Edlen, both pointed. Champion Hedera, bred to Champion Lingard Centurian O'Cahaba, produced Champion Weslan's Southern Comfort. Then Mol was bred to Count On Me, producing Gypsy Lore of Edlen. Although Lore was shown twice, she came in season every five and a half months and never seemed to grow sufficient coat to really compete. She was bred back to her grandsire, Champion Halstor's Peter Pumpkin, to produce Champion Captain Cully of Edlen. Punkinette of Edlen, Captain's full sister, bred to Champion Knock On Wood, produced Morgan of Edlen whose career is just now starting as we write. Countess of Edlen also came from this breeding and has given the Edlens probably their best bitch to date, sired by Champion Lingard Cen-

Ch. Captain Cully of Edlen, right, with his son, Hicliff Impression of Edlen. Edmund and Helen Scherer, owners, Ravenna, Ohio.

Ch. Knock On Wood of Edlen, by Am. and Can. Ch. 'Markris Red Baron of Edlen (Ch. Kerrylance Bossman, C.D.X., ex Kerrylance Witacism) ex Tiny Dian of Walnut Hall (Ch. Tiny Tim of Walnut Hall ex Tiny Amanda of Walnut Hall), whose progeny include at least several close to championship honors. Edmund and Helen Scherer, owners, Edlen Kennels.

turian O'Cahaba, the lovely Everything Nice of Edlen.

Sherlynn Fancy Nancy was also bred to Count On Me, producing Sea Wind's Countess of Edlen, who, with twelve points, lost a tooth on a fence, preventing her finishing. Also in this litter came Theresa Ann of Edlen (dam of two aforementioned pointed sons). Another sister, Precious Nancy, was bred to Champion Knock On Wood, from which a daughter, Timeless Tash of Edlen, bred to Captain Cully has produced the colorful showman Hicliff Impression of Edlen, already pointed, although she just started her show career in August 1983.

Future attractions coming up are two litters by Champion Knock On Wood out of Eva of Edlen, the first so good that the breeding was repeated. Holiday Spirit of Edlen is from the first of these litters and Wood Nymph of Edlen from the second. Wood Nymph is now bred to Count.

It is this back and forth breeding between the two lines, Baron-Bossman and Count On Me-Peter Pumpkin that is giving the Edlens the youngsters with many of the improvements needed when they started out. Recently they have been adding a touch of the Banchory line through their Backstop daughter, Banchory Back Fence Gossip, and through Banchory the Candidate in the pedigree of Champion Merridon's Riding Shotgun. Also, Pollyanna has recently had puppies by Banchory Reflection, with the hope of incorporating something from that breeding into the younger ones now at Edlen.

Sterling's Enchanted Spirit at six months of age with his mom, Valdawn's Heather of Rockwood, aged two years. Both owned by Debra Elkin, Enchanted Shelties, Meriden, Connecticut.

Enchanted

Enchanted Shetland Sheepdogs started out in 1980 when their owner, Debra Elkin of Meriden, Connecticut, purchased her first of the breed from Barbara Kenealey. This was Valdawn's Heather of Rockwood, a daughter of Champion Rockwoods Nite Enchantment, C.D., ex Valdawn's Taste of Honey.

In 1981, Miss Elkin bred Heather to Champion Rockwoods The Hustler, owned by Shirley Bond, whose married name is now Kulneski. Valdawn's Heather of Rockwood had a litter of four, two males and two females, from which her owner kept one male who became Sterling's Enchanted Spirit. This young dog is now being shown as we write. Debra Elkin also co-owns a female with Kathleen and Herbert Searle, named Valdawn's Sterling Nugget, who has done very well at matches.

A very pretty picture of Valdawn's Heather of Rockwood, Sterling's Enchanted Spirit, and Valdawn's Sterling Nugget, courtesy of Debra Elkin.

Seven-week-old Enchanted Shelties. Debra Elkin, owner.

Sterling's Enchanted Spirit with owner Debra Elkin winning at the Farmington Valley Kennel Club Match Show, May 1st 1983. Spirit also took Group first at the Newton Kennel Club Match Show the preceding week. This handsome young Sheltie will probably be a champion when you are reading this.

Nugget has been bred to Barbara Kenealey's Champion Rockwoods Night Enchantment, C.D. During 1983, Heather was again bred, this time to Rockwoods Gold Strike, owned also by Barbara Kenealey, a son of Champion Rorralore Sportin' Chance from Champion Rockwood's Sweet Charity. Valdawn's Simply Enchanted is also bred to Champion Rockwoods Gold Strike, Enchanted being a daughter of Champion Benayrs Peter Principle ex Valdawn's Taste of Honey.

Thus the Enchanted Shelties are off to a good start, and their owner is looking forward to a highly successful future with her favorite breed.

Enchanted Shelties relaxing at home. Left to right: Valdawn's Sterling Nugget, Champion Rockwoods The Hustler, Sterling's Enchanted Spirit, Valdawn's Heather of Rockwood, and Valdawn's Simply Enchanted. All are owned by Debra Elkin excepting The Hustler who is just visiting.

Fran-Dor

Doris A. Homsher, owner of Fran-Dor Shelties at Perkasie, Pennsylvania, has been "in dogs" since the beginning of the 1970's, first with Collies and Bichons Frises, then later with Shetland Sheepdogs. Remarking that she owes most of her early success to luck, she goes on to tell us that in her very first litter she bred a Collie who went on to become a Best in Show winner. In retrospect, she adds, "At that time the smartest thing I did was to sell her to someone who not only knew her potential, but how to promote it."

After Collies and a number of Bichon champions, as a favor she took a young Sheltie puppy home to socialize it, and she became drawn to the endearing qualities of the breed. That was in 1974, and now the Shetland Sheepdog is the only breed she owns at present and the only one she will ever own in the future.

Fran-Dor's breeding program from the start has been a conservative one and one as carefully researched as possible. Having been involved with dogs all of her life, Doris Homsher has spent much time studying and learning about them, in hopes of constantly improving not only on her own stock but also on the breed in general. She has a very small operation, and once a line shows improvement the older stock is replaced with the younger generation.

The Fran-Dor sables are basically line-bred on "Peter"; the blues and tris are from the Banchory line.

The most successful of the Fran-Dor Shelties to date, who have come from the Fran-Dor breeding program, is Champion Fran-Dor's Kelty. In the first two months following completion of her championship, Kelty gained seven Bests of Breed and three Group placements, which put her in the Top Twenty Sheltie listing.

Next perhaps is the blue bitch, Champion Glenwood Ice Dancer O'Fran-Dor, C.D. This one, purchased as a puppy, has become the foundation bitch at Fran-Dor for the blue-tri line. Her sire is Champion Banchory Deep Purple, her dam a Thunderation daughter. "Crystal," as she is known, went Best of Breed over eight different Specials on the way to her title. She now has three pointed daughters from her first litter.

Fran-Dor puppies, owned by Doris A. Homsher, Fran-Dor Farm, Perkasie, Pennsylvania.

Ch. Glenwood Ice Dancer O'Fran-Dor, C.D., from the Fran-Dor Kennels owned by Doris A. Homsher.

Gay Acres

Gay Acres Kennels has been in existence since 1946, started then by Melvin and Florence Roberts breeding Collies—good ones, too, including their homebred Champion Gay Acres Ensign and Champion Gay Acres Harbor Master along with other point-winning dogs and bitches.

Ten years later, in 1956, the Roberts introduced Shetland Sheepdogs into their kennel. It was not until quite recently, however, that they began exhibiting them, although in earlier days they did own the well-known and beautiful Champion Ardencaple's Sugar 'N Spice. Since the beginning of the 1980's, the Roberts have started taking a really active part as Sheltie exhibitors. Champion Gay Acres Hullabaloo, a handsome sable dog bred by Betty Hall, was owned by them, but he met with a tragic death in 1981 on the Florida Circuit when fumes from a motor home found their way into his crate—a hard loss, indeed, to bear!

Now the Roberts have and own, in co-ownership with Steve Barger, an excellent sable bitch with points already garnered from the Puppy Classes, Gay Acres Glory of Mainstay. They also have Whitegates Wish Upon A Star, blue-merle bitch who was second in her Puppy Class at the Futurity and winner of her regular class at the American Shetland Sheepdog Association National Specialty; as we write this she has

A lovely head-study of Ch. Gay Acres Hullabaloo, sired by Ch. Chenterra Thunderation. Bred by Betty Hall, handled by Steve Barger, and owned by Florence Roberts, Gay Acres Shelties, Winsted, Connecticut.

Whitegates Wish Upon A Star, blue-merle bitch by Ridgeside Star Wars ex Whitegates Salute to Mainstay. Bred by Joan and Terry Pavey and owned by Florence W. Roberts, Gay Acres Shelties.

earned seven points including a major. Along with these two at Gay Acres there is Whitegates Anything U Can Do, whom they have recently acquired; he is a blue-merle dog, winner of the 1983 A.S.S.A. Futurity, with points toward his title. All three of these current Shelties were bred by the Paveys and are handled by Steve Barger.

Additionally there are a number of young show-prospects coming along for whom the Roberts's hopes are high. Another noted winner here is Canadian Champion Whitegates Most Happy Fellow, also bred by the Paveys; he was sired by Reflection.

Gay Acres Kennels are located at Winsted, Connecticut. The dogs come from a background mostly of Champion Chenterra Thunderation and the Macdega and Mainstay lines.

Happy Glen

Happy Glen Shetland Sheepdogs are located at Evansville, Wyoming, and are owned by Marvin and Barbara Ross. A small kennel right from the beginning, the intention is to keep it that way in order for the dogs to enjoy all of the love and individual attention possible. First Shelties here were two bitches which came to the Rosses as a gift: Ross's Happy Girl and Lady Reamali, both of whom were shown in obedience. Lady Reamali was never bred, but Ross's Happy Girl (for whom the kennel was named) became the dam of Sir Toby's Happy Man, who won his C.D. degree and also started the Rosses' interest in conformation when he won a Best of Breed over several Specials.

Marv and Barb Ross purchased a brood bitch who was sold to them "because she disliked being shown." This was Shannasy Flicker O'Flame. Bred several times, she produced show-quality offspring, including Happy Glen's Starting Stone, who is close to the title as we write, sired by Champion Banchory The Cornerstone, C.D., a Champion Halstor's Peter Pumpkin son from a daughter of Champion Banchory High Born.

Next a puppy dog destined to become Champion Banchory Stand Back, C.D., was purchased from Banchory Kennels. This good son of American and Canadian Champion Banchory Back Stop from Banchory Angelique (Champion

Above: Lady Reamali was one of the two Shelties with whom Marvin and Barbara Ross started their Happy Glen Kennels in Evansville, Wyoming, during the late 1960's. Sired by Gra-John's Whiz Kid (Ch. Gra-John's Country Gentleman ex Ch. Gra-John's Diamond Lil) ex Gra-John's Red Angel (Ch. Gra-John's Little G Man ex Gra-John's Dark Angel).
Below: Sir Toby's Happy Man, C.D., two points, by Sir Sebastian's Little Toby, C.D., ex Ross's Happy Girl, is the dog who started Marv and Barb Ross out in Shelties in breed competition. Although seldom shown, Happy Man has won a Best of Breed over Specials plus, of course, his successes in obedience.

Happy Glen's Starting Stone, by Ch. Banchory The Cornerstone ex Shannasy Flicker O'Flame, has thirteen points including a major. Barbara and Marvin Ross, owners.

Banchory Bit O'Stone, by Ch. Banchory The Cornerstone (Ch. Halstor's Peter Pumpkin ex Banchory High Glow) ex Banchory I'll Live On (Am. and Can. Ch. Banchory Back Stop ex Forever Alana). Bred by Donna Harden; owned by Marvin and Barbara Ross.

Shannasy Flicker O'Flame, C.D., with Rita Ross taking Best of Winners at Rapid City for two points. Flicker was purchased as a brood bitch by Happy Glen Kennels and has produced several splendid litters for Barbara and Marvin Ross. Among her outstanding progeny is Happy Glen's Starting Stone. **Below:** Ch. Banchory Stand Back, C.D. One of the lovely Shelties from Barbara and Marvin Ross' Happy Glen Kennels.

Halstor's Peter Pumpkin ex Banchory High Glow, the latter an American and Canadian Champion Banchory High Born daughter) was owner-handled by Marv Ross all the way to his title—as his owner comments, "no easy chore from the state of Wyoming."

Then came Banchory Bit O'Stone, by Champion Banchory The Cornerstone ex the Back Stop daughter, Banchory I'll Live On, whose dam is a daughter of Champion Thistlerose Arcwood Aladdin from Banchory Sweet Dream, a daughter of Champion Philidove Heir Presumptive. This bitch has become the backbone of the Happy Glen Kennels and has produced some truly handsome youngsters for the Rosses.

A breeding by Champion Banchory Stand Back, C.D., to Shannasy Flicker O'Flame produced Happy Glen's Flaming Fantasy. Due to an accident, her fang tooth was kicked out by a horse, so she was not shown until she was four years old and then, to help make a major, she was entered at two shows. She took Reserve Bitch the first day and Best of Opposite Sex for a four-point major the second day. At these same two shows, Happy Glen Kennels had ten Happy Glen Shelties entered and placing both days, which included Reserve Dog both days, Reserve Bitch and Winners Bitch, Winners Dog, and Best of Winners. All of these wins indeed in-

Happy Glen's Autumn Amber at eight months of age taking Best of Opposite Sex under judge Fernandez Cartright at Ft. Collins in 1981, handled by Marvin Ross. Owned by Marvin and Barbara Ross.

dicate that the breeding program at Happy Glen is progressing well!

Flaming Fantasy has been bred only once, and that was to Champion Windover Sweet Music Man. A very outstanding male puppy was included in this litter, Happy Glen's Royal Dream, who already has twelve points including a four-point major as we write; this major was acquired by the impressive win of Best in Show from the classes! It certainly is an accomplishment to bring pride! Now the Rosses are looking for majors at which to finish him—somewhat of a problem in so distant an area. When he finishes, Royal Dream will be Happy Glen's first homebred Sheltie champion, a day to which they look forward with keen anticipation. There are already several homebred Schipperke champions at this kennel, we understand, as the owners share their interests between these two breeds. The owners refer to the Schips as their "Sheltie Syndrome Relief."

Marvin and Barbara Ross have also become interested in handling Shelties for other breeders, doing so very successfully. One of these dogs is Windover Sweet Music Man, on whom Marv has put at least one Best in Show, and he has finished several other dogs as well.

Happy Glen's Flaming Fantasy, by Ch. Banchory Stand Back, C.D., ex Shannasy Flicker of Flame, C.D. (eight points). Bred and owned by Happy Glen Shelties, Barbara and Marvin Ross.

Eng. and Am. Ch. Sigurd of Shelert, top winning Sheltie in England for 1962, who finished in five shows following his importation to the United States by Mr. and Mrs. Haworth F. Hoch for their Hoch Haven Kennels.

Ch. Pixie Dell Charm O'The North, by Ch. Cock O'The North O'Page's Hill ex Pixie Dell Dutchess, born May 4th 1950, shown here at eleven years of age. Mr. and Mrs. Haworth F. Hoch, owners, Hoch Haven Kennels, Sweetbriar Farms, Villa Ridge, Missouri.

Hoch Haven

Hoch Haven Kennels are located at beautiful Sweetbriar Farms, owned by Mr. and Mrs. Haworth F. Hoch at Villa Ridge, Missouri. Although he is now thought of most frequently as an excellent multiple-breed judge and as an American Kennel Club Director, Haworth Hoch is, as well, a dedicated fancier of Shetland Sheepdogs; and there have been some very outstanding members of this breed living at this kennel, all of them owned, loved, and enjoyed by both Haworth and Peg Hoch over the years.

The Hochs have the top basic American bloodlines represented in their dogs: Pixie Dell, Page's Hill, Pocono, and others. They also have brought over some excellent importations from England, the best known of these being English and American Champion Sigurd of Shelert, with an interesting story behind him.

In 1961, when he was in England, Mr. Hoch saw and enormously admired Sigurd as a six-month-old puppy. He had the privilege of showing this puppy at Chester (England), and needless to say he must have been more than a little delighted when he won the Challenge Cer-

Ch. Hoch Haven Very Merry, by Ch. White Wings Dusky Davey ex Ch. Pixie Dell Charm O'The North. Bred and owned by Mr. and Mrs. Haworth F. Hoch, Hoch Haven Shelties.

Left to right, Ch. Pixie Dell Little Hobo, Sea Haze of Shelert, C.D., Ch. Hoch Haven Tiny Memory, and Eng. and Am. Ch. Sigurd of Shelert—a very handsome quartet of Shelties owned by Mr. and Mrs. Haworth F. Hoch, Hoch Haven Kennels, during the 1950's-1960's.

Ch. Hoch Haven Todhunter (left), by Eng. and Am. Ch. Sigurd of Shelert ex Thorpehill Hoch Haven Harriet, C.D.; and Ch. Hoch Haven Blue Chip, by Ch. Larkspur Finalist of Pocono ex Shelt-E-Ain Lady o'the Knight. Mr. and Mrs. Haworth F. Hoch, owners, Hoch Haven Kennels, Sweetbriar Farms.

Ch. Pixie Dell Little Hobo, by Ch. Magnet O'Page's Hill ex Ch. Va-Gore's Bright Promise, born in July 1956, shown here at six years of age. This beautiful Sheltie owned by Mr. and Mrs. Haworth F. Hoch, Hoch Haven Kennels.

Ch. Hoch Haven Tiny Memory, by Ch. Blue Flame of Pocono, C.D., ex Ch. Hoch Haven Tiny Pocono Patty. Mr. and Mrs. Haworth F. Hoch, owners.

Ch. Hoch Haven Blue Chip of Pocono, by Ch. Larkspur Finalist of Pocono ex Shelt-E-Ain Lady o'the Knight. Owned by Mr. and Mrs. Haworth F. Hoch.

tificate, considering the puppy's youth! A year later this was the Top Winning Sheltie in England. The Hochs brought him to the United States, where he finished in five shows—nice going, indeed! Sigurd was the first Sheltie to be awarded a Junior Warrant following the close of World War II. He has made his presence felt as a sire, too, with champion progeny to his credit.

Other well-known winners belonging to the Hochs include Champion Pixie Dell Charm O'The North, by Champion Cock O'The North O'Pages's Hill ex Champion Pixie Dell Dutchess, who is the dam of their Champion Hoch Haven Very Merry (by Champion White Wings Dusky Davey) and Champion Hoch Haven's Maida's Memory (by Champion Pixie Dell Little Hobo), whom they also own. Little Hobo is by Champion Magnet O'Page's Hill ex Champion Va-Gore's Bright Promise.

Then there is Champion Hoch Haven Todhunter, by English and American Champion Sigurd of Shelert ex Thorpehill Hoch Haven Harriet, C.D.; Champion Hoch Haven Blue Chip, by Champion Larkspur Finalist of Pocono ex Shelt-e-ain Lady o'the Knight; and Champion Hoch Haven Tiny Memory, by Champion Blue Flame of Pocono, C.D., ex Champion Hoch Haven Tiny Pocono Patty.

Sea Haze of Shelert, C.D., is also a member of the Hoch Sheltie family, having come from the same kennel as Sigurd in England.

120

Jade Mist

Jade Mist Shetland Sheepdogs belong to Keith B. Howell, D.V.M., and Carol G. Howell of Davidsonville, Maryland. Like so many Sheltie breeders, the Howells started in obedience. Their first Sheltie was purchased in 1967. After a long search for a quality conformation Sheltie, they were fortunate in buying their foundation bitches from the leading West Coast breeder of that time, Valerie Daniels of Dan-Dee Shelties. From her the Howells purchased Dan-Dee Study in Scarlet, whom they showed to twelve points including a major, and her dam, the pointed Dan-Dee Petite Regards, whose championship the Howells completed in 1967. Petite was by Champion Pixie Dell Bright Vision. Her dam was Champion Dan-Dee Prima Donna, a blend of the old Browne Acres and Elf Dale bloodlines. All of the Howells' present Shelties descend from Petite's daughter, Study in Scarlet, who was sired by Champion Elf Dale Golden Legacy. Study in Scarlet had one litter (consisting of one dog and two bitches) sired by Champion Apache of Karelane. The bitch pup

Dan-Dee Study in Scarlet, twelve points, one major, owned by Dr. and Mrs. Keith B. Howell. All of the present-day Jade Mist Shelties are descended from her.

Ch. Jade Mist Twilight Song the day she finished at nine and a half years of age. Dr. and Mrs. Keith B. Howell, Davidsonville, Maryland.

became Champion Jade Mist Twilight Song at nine and a half years of age, and she set a record by becoming the oldest Sheltie to have finished at that time.

In 1972, the Howells leased Champion Sutter's Golden Cassandra for a litter (she was by Champion Lingard Western Heir ex Champion Dan-Dee's Samantha) by Champion Ilemist Impossible Dream, C.D.X. From this breeding, the Howells finished Champion Jade Mist Inherit A Dream. Although they seldom Special their dogs, much preferring to compete for the points, the Howells did show Inherit A Dream to ten Bests of Breed and three Working Group placements. He was also Best of Breed at the 1978 Interstate Shetland Sheepdog Club Spring Specialty.

A male puppy, Dorlane's Scalawag, was purchased by the Howells in 1974. He is by Champion Beltane The Mutineer ex Champion Lobo Dell Tangerine O'Dorlane. He finished his championship in 1977, and he became, at just under 14″, the smallest male in recent breed history to finish. Champion Jade Mist Twilight Song was bred to Scalawag, and they produced Champion Jade Mist Woodwind Chimes. Thus far (August 1983) Woodwind Chimes has produced four champions for the Howells (she tied

Ch. Jade Mist Inherit A Dream, by Ch. Ilemist Impossible Dream, C.D.X., ex Ch. Sutter's Golden Cassandra. Owned by Dr. and Mrs. Keith Howell, Jade Mist Shelties.

for Top Producing Sheltie Bitch in 1982, *Canine Chronicle* System), two of them by Champion Barwood's Weather Report and two by Champion Wayanet's Dallas Cowboy. The Dallas Cowboy champions were sold as youngsters, Champion Jade Mist Down Memory Lane going to William and Suzanne McCullough and Champion Jade Mist Westernway Marshall co-owned by Linda and Charles Davis but finished by the Howells. The Weather Report youngsters remained at Jade Mist, becoming Champion Jade Mist Suntide and Champion Jade Mist Windspell. In addition to these two litters, Woodwind Chimes was bred to the Howells' Champion Inherit A Dream, from which breeding a bitch was kept, Jade Mist Sunbrite Cedar. Mrs. Howell notes, "From all indications, Windspell, Suntide, and Sunbrite Cedar will be top-producers like their dam. Windspell has two young sons, both with Reserve Winners Dog at their first show, Suntide has already sired eight pointed progeny, and Sunbrite Cedar has a son with eight points from her only litter, sired by Suntide."

The Howells are proud of what they have accomplished in their years in the Sheltie Fancy, as they are very small breeders averaging only

about one litter yearly, and they do all of their own handling. Starting out with the top West Coast bloodlines (Elf Dale and Browne Acres), they blended these in their breeding program with the East Coast's Pixie Dell and Sea Isle lines, especially through Champion Halstor's Peter Pumpkin and Champion Lingard Sealect Bruce. Their present-day pedigrees have a very strong Sea Isle influence.

Ch. Dorlane's Scalawag, by Ch. Beltane The Mutineer ex Ch. Lobo Dell Tangerine O'Dorlane, the smallest present-day Sheltie dog to finish title. Jade Mist Shelties, Dr. and Mrs. Keith B. Howell.

Ch. Jade Mist Westernway Marshal, a son of Ch. Wayanet's Dallas Cowboy ex Ch. Jade Mist Woodwind Chimes, at eleven months of age. Dr. and Mrs. Keith B. Howell, Davidsonville, Maryland, breeders; Linda and Charles Davis and the Howells, co-owners.

Ch. Jade Mist Down Memory Lane, a lovely daughter of Ch. Wayanet's Dallas Cowboy ex Ch. Jade Mist Woodwind Chimes, at eight months of age. Owned by William and Suzanne McCullough.

Dr. and Mrs. Keith B. Howell's favorite photograph of their well-known Ch. Jade Mist Woodwind Chimes.

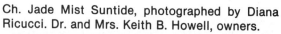

Ch. Jade Mist Suntide, photographed by Diana Ricucci. Dr. and Mrs. Keith B. Howell, owners.

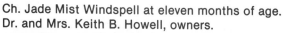

Ch. Jade Mist Windspell at eleven months of age. Dr. and Mrs. Keith B. Howell, owners.

Karral

Karral (pronounced "Corral") Shetland Sheepdogs, owned by Karen and Ralph Elledge of Baytown, Texas, began in January 1974 with the arrival of Champion Barwoods Bonanza O'Merri-Lon, the sire of three champions, who was purchased as an eight-year-old from Merri-Lon Kennels. Merri-Lon I Hear Bells, a daughter of Champion Barwoods Bold Venture (full brother to Bonanza) was purchased at seven months of age, and eventually, bred to Champion Lingard Centurian O'Cahaba, produced Champion Karral Liberty Bell.

For her second litter, I Hear Bells was bred to the Centurian son, Champion Cahaba's Magic O'Marion, which produced Karral Southern Bell.

The Elledges then purchased another Centurian daughter, Char-Nan's Carrie O'Cahaba

Karral Southern Bell, by Ch. Cahaba's Magic O'Marion ex Merri Lon I Hear Bells, photographed at ten months of age. Dam of Karral Happy Times. Karen and Ralph Elledge of Baytown, Texas, owners.

Ch. Karral Liberty Bell, by Ch. Lingard Centurian O'Cahaba ex Merrilon I Hear Bells, shown here handled by Ralph Elledge to a five-point major at the Alamo Area Shetland Sheepdog Club Specialty Show. Bred and owned by Karen and Ralph Elledge, Karral Shetland Sheepdogs.

Barwood's Dominator, by Ch. Halstor's Peter Pumpkin ex Ch. Barwood's Treasure (a Peter daughter), is close to his title as we go to press. Owned by Karen and Ralph Elledge, Karral Shetland Sheepdogs.

Ch. Karral Good Times, by Barwood's Dominator ex Karral Ramblin' Rose, winning first in the Herding Group at Danville Kennel Club, March 1983. Breeder-owners, Karen and Ralph Elledge.

Karral Happy Times at twenty months of age taking a five-point major at Carroll Kennel Club in 1983 from judge Ernest Loeb, handled by Jon Woodring. Bred and owned by Karen and Ralph Elledge, Karral Shetland Sheepdogs.

whom they bred to Champion Dorlane's Kings Ransome to produce Karral Ramblin' Rose. The next purchase was Barwoods Dominator (with twelve points including one major), an inbred Peter Pumpkin son. Ramblin' Rose bred to this dog produced Champion Karral Good Times, known as "Tuffy," who finished his championship at barely two years of age with three majors including a Specialty win, all owner-handled. As of June 1983, "Tuffy" has had fifty-one Bests of Breed and twenty-four Group placements including five Group firsts, which makes him the Number Two Sheltie in the United States according to the Sheltie International tabulations—all this at the age of three years. His first litter produced Karral Happy Times (ex Southern Bell), who won the Open, Sable and White, Class at the 1983 American Shetland Sheepdog Association National and who currently has five points including one major. Good Times produced in his second litter Canadian Champion September Chiffon Ruffles, and in his third litter he produced Cahaba Lanbur This Is Dream'n who currently has eleven points with one major.

Karral is a very small kennel, having only one or two litters annually and maintaining no more than eight adult dogs at a time, which includes the Elledges' only foray into another breed, a Bearded Collie bitch whom they finished as a youngster in about a dozen shows.

Above: Ch. Stylish Miss of Hatfield, a daughter of the famous Ch. Nashcrest Golden Note (Ch. Prince George O'Page's Hill ex Nashcrest Rhythm) ex Ch. Bonnie Lass of Hatfield (Ch. Sheltieland Kiltie O'Sea Isle ex Golden True of Achmore), at six months of age. This gorgeous bitch was an outstanding producer and the dam of seven champions. Ken-Rob Kennels, owners, Kenneth E. Poole and Robert W. White. **Below:** Am. and Can. Ch. Ken-Robs Kenny, by Ch. Malpsh Great Scott (Ch. Lingard Sealand Bruce ex Malpsh Her Royal Majesty) ex Ch. Stylish Miss of Hatfield (Ch. Nashcrest Golden Note ex Ch. Bonnie Lass of Hatfield), born August 15th 1966. One of many fine Shelties owned by Ken-Rob Shelties, Kenneth H. Poole and Robert W. White.

Above: Ch. Ken-Robs Gay Blade, by Ch. Sea Isle Serenade (Ch. Nashcrest Golden Note ex Ch. Sea Isle Serenata) ex Ch. Bonnie Lass of Hatfield (Ch. Sheltieland Kiltie O'Sea Isle ex Golden True of Achmore). Owned by Ken-Rob Shelties, Kenneth E. Poole and Robert W. White, Easthampton, Massachusetts. **Below:** Ch. Ken-Robs Partners Choice, by Ch. Sea Isle Serenade (Ch. Nashcrest Golden Note ex Ch. Sea Isle Serenata) ex Ch. Stylish Miss of Hatfield (Ch. Nashcrest Golden Note ex Ch. Bonnie Lass of Hatfield), born September 1965. Owned by Ken-Rob Shelties, Kenneth E. Poole and Robert W. White.

Ken-Rob

Ken-Rob Shelties at Easthampton, Massachussetts, were started in 1962 by Robert W. White and Kenneth E. Poole, based principally on foundation stock from Sea Isle Kennels. Mr. Poole had owned and shown dogs since 1954, beginning with Collies, and is a judge (since 1969) of these two breeds.

Among the noted Shelties from this kennel have been Champion Highland Laird of Hatfield, Champion Bonnie Lass of Hatfield, C.D., Champion Stylish Miss of Hatfield (who became the dam of seven champions), Champion Hatfield Star Dust (a Best in Show winner), Champion Ken-Robs Gay Blade, Champion Ken-Robs Partners Choice, Champion Ken-Robs Kenny, Champion Ken-Robs Bobbie, Champion Ken-Robs That's Life, and Champion Astolat Song of Bambi.

Mr. White belongs to numerous Collie Clubs (he founded the Collie Club of Western Massachusetts in 1963-64) and to the American Shetland Sheepdog Association, Mohawk Shetland Sheepdog Club, and the Springfield Kennel Club.

Ch. Highland Laird of Hatfield, a son of Ch. Sheltieland Kiltie O'Sea Isle (Ch. Bagota Blaze ex Ch. Sheltieland Peg o'the Picts) ex Ch. Stylish Miss of Hatfield (Ch. Nashcrest Golden Note ex Ch. Bonnie Lass of Hatfield). From the Ken-Rob Shelties of Kenneth E. Poole and Robert W. White.

Ch. Bonnie Lass of Hatfield, a daughter of Ch. Sheltieland Kiltie O'Sea Isle ex Golden True of Achmore, from the 1960's. The dam of Ch. Stylish Miss of Hatfield, she was a foundation bitch at Ken-Rob Kennels. Frank Ashbey handling.

Ch. Ken-Robs Benchmark, by Ch. Ken-Robs Kenny ex Country Glenn Miss (daughter of Ch. Sea Isle Merchant Prince). Owned by Ken-Rob Shelties, Kenneth E. Poole and Robert W. White.

Ch. Arthea Blue Sparkler, by Ch. Merry Meddler of Pocono ex Peabody Silver Phantasy (imported), a well-known winner of forty Bests of Breed in the 1940's. Bred and owned by Dr. and Mrs. Arthur W. Combs, Fostoria, Ohio. Photo courtesy of Rhea Butler.

Kensington

Kensington Shelties, now located at Albuquerque, New Mexico, had their beginnings back in the 1940's. Owner Rhea Butler recalls that it was in the late summer of 1946 when Mr. and Mrs. Lee Bailey drove with their daughters, Mary Ellen Wallace and her husband Bill and Rhea Jane Bailey and her fiance Bob Butler, to Fostoria, Ohio, where Dr. and Mrs. Arthur Combs had their Arthea Kennels. The Baileys had heard about this "new" breed of lovely little dogs and so drove from their summer home in Michigan with the intention of "just looking."

First to catch their eyes was Champion Arthea Blue Sparkler, the Combs's blue sire who had won forty Bests of Breed. The Baileys were completely captivated by this happy little dog. Then they saw Portia, Champion Pocono Portia of Arthea, an endearing tri-bitch. And as Rhea Butler says, "Indeed it worked out that we were able to take home our first Shetland Sheepdog, Arthea Blue Sparklette, sired by Sparkler and out of the lovely Portia." Rhea remembers "Sparkie" sleeping in her father's hat all the way home to Michigan.

In 1948, the first Kensington litter was born, "Sparkie" having been shipped by train to West Chester, Pennsylvania, where she was bred to

Arthea Blue Sparklette, by Arthea Blue Sparkler ex Ch. Pocono Portia of Arthea, snapped in the ring at the Jackson, Mississippi, Dog Show in the summer of 1949; Rhea Butler handling under judge Robert Wills. Owned by Mrs. Lee F. Bailey.

The first Kensington litter, sired by Ch. Night Rider of Pocono (Ch. Merry Meddler of Pocono ex Larkspur of Pocono) from Arthea Blue Sparklette (Ch. Arthea Blue Sparkler ex Ch. Pocono Portia of Arthea), on October 19th 1946. The puppy in the middle became Bluet of Kensington, C.D.X.

Champion Night Rider of Pocono, Mrs. Alan Robson's tricolor, a litter-brother to Betty Whelen's Champion Tailor Made of Pocono. Mrs. Lee F. Bailey was officially the breeder of this litter, and the puppies were born at Kensington Road (from where the kennel name was taken), East Lansing, Michigan. Mrs. Bailey's two daughters, Mary Wallace and Rhea Butler, both became very interested in the breed. Mary Wallace took a puppy from Sparklette's first litter, finishing a C.D.X. on this blue-merle bitch, Bluet of Kensington, in a blaze of glory when she won top honors over all the obedience trial entries at an early 1950's dog show of the Gary, Indiana, Kennel Club, making a score of 198. Her two earlier scores had been in the 190 bracket. Mrs. Wallace went on to teach obedience in the Kalamazoo area for many years. Her initial training was under famous German Shepherd breeder Virginia McCoy of the Longworth Kennels. Eventually Bluet of Kensington was bred back to her sire, Champion Night Rider of Pocono, shipped back to Pennsylvania by rail as her dam had been. Out of this litter came a blue female, Kensington's Blue Frost, who went to Mary Jane Morey of Allegan, Michigan, her first Sheltie; this puppy became the foundation bitch for Mori brook Kennels and eventually the grandam of Best in Show and National Specialty winner, Champion Moribrook's Country Squire.

Mrs. Lee Bailey died in 1975 and Mrs. Wallace has not had Shelties since the 1950's.

A lovely head-study of Kismet Bi Surprise of Pocono, by Ch. Karelane Royal Flush O'Kismet ex Ch. Harvest Hill's Ribbon 'N Lace. Bred by Elizabeth D. Whelen; owned by Rhea J. Butler, Albuquerque, New Mexico.

Above: Kensington's C-Note, U.D., in December 1978 at eleven years of age. Owners, Carole and Gordon Walter, Bakersfield, California. **Right:** Kismet Bi Surprise of Pocono taking Winners Bitch, Best of Winners, and Best of Opposite Sex for a three-point major at Texas Kennel Club in 1983; judge, Dorothy Welsh. Handler, Guy Mauldin; owner, Rhea J. Butler. **Below:** Kensington Ribbon O'Pocono, 14″, by Kismet Classic of Pocono ex Ch. Harvest Hill's Ribbon 'N Lace, winning the Puppy Class from judge Laura Wills at San Antonio in 1983. Breeders, Elizabeth D. Whelen and Rhea J. Butler; handler, Elizabeth D. Whelen; owner, Rhea J. Butler.

Mrs. Butler has been with Shelties since 1948, and her active interest in them continues into plans for the future. The Butlers were married in 1947, and throughout the years they have always had Shelties. In the late 1960's, they bred their Champion Mori brook's Knight On The Town daughter to Champion Richmore Gamblin Man. This litter gave them the tricolor male Kensington's C-Note, U.D., who at this time is still ruling his domain, owned by Carole and Gordon Walter of Bakersfield, California, who breed Borzois and Arabian horses. C-Note was handled by Mr. Walter through to his U.D.

In 1980, the Butlers purchased from Betty Whelen a Champion Banchory Thunder Blue daughter bred to Banchory Passport of Pocono. In 1981, they acquired Kismet Bi Surprise from Betty, shortly after Surprise had gone Reserve Bitch at the Cleveland Specialty at the age of six months. She is a daughter of Best in Show winning Champion Karelane Royal Flush O'Kismet out of Champion Harvest Hill's Ribbon 'N Lace and now has eleven points including both majors.

Rhea Butler comments: "In October of 1981 Betty Whelen came to live with us in New Mexico. Having the Pocono Sheltie lady here is a rare privilege. Kensington and Pocono continue a limited breeding program. Shelties have always been part of our lives, and will continue to be in the future."

Kismet

Guy and Thelma Mauldin, owners of Kismet Kennels in Richmond, Texas, have been the breeders and/or owners of over eighty champions, and their kennel is the home of many of the most prestigious top producers and outstanding winners.

Bloodlines here are based on the tricolor Champion Banchory High Born, who holds the distinction of being the second top-producing Sheltie sire of all time, with seventy-four champions to his credit. Although shown at only a few all-breed shows, High Born was a Group winner and won nineteen Specialty Bests in Show, in addition to having sired many top winners and top producers.

The Mauldins' first really big winner was Champion Philidove Kismet Heir Borne, sired by Champion Banchory High Born ex Champion Philidove Carmylie In A Mist, bred and co-owned by Irene Brody. Guy Mauldin piloted him to seven all-breed Bests in Show and

Ch. Philidove Kismet Heir Borne, blue-merle, tan, and white by Ch. Banchory High Born ex Philidove Carmylie In A Mist, sire of ten champions. Bred by Irene Brody; owned by Guy and Thelma Mauldin, Kismet Kennels, Richmond, Texas.

Ch. Banchory High Born in 1975 at the age of seven years. The Kismet breeding program is based on this Sheltie. Owned by Thelma and Guy Mauldin, Kismet Shetland Sheepdogs.

The great Ch. Karelane Royal Flush O'Kismet with a Playboy bunny in an informal photo. Guy and Thelma Mauldin own "Acey," but we have no particulars on the bunny.

Above: Ch. Kismet's Status Assured, by Ch. Kismet's Conquistador ex Ch. Fiesta's Fazzle Dazzle. Bred by Guy A. and Thelma Mauldin; owned by Guy A. Mauldin and Lloyd H. Graser. **Below:** Ch. Kismet's Centurian en route to the title was Best in Show at Clearwater, Florida, judged by Maxwell Riddle, and (pictured) completed championship by taking Best Working Dog at Texas Kennel Club, Dallas, Texas, judged by Arthur K. Zane. Breeder-owners, Guy and Thelma Mauldin.

eighteen Specialty Bests in Show. He, too, has made his mark as a stud dog, being the sire of ten champions, including the blue bitch, Champion Kismet's Cee Dee Pollyanna, the dam of the Mauldins' current big winner, Champion Karelane Royal Flush O'Kismet (by High Born). Royal Flush has broken all Sheltie records with his thirty-three all-breed Bests in Show.

Also bred by the Mauldins, later co-owned by them, is Kismet's Rubaiyyat, second top-pro-

Ch. Kismet's Status Symbol, by Ch. Kismet's Conquistador ex Ch. Fiesta's Fazzle Dazzle. Bred and owned by Guy and Thelma Mauldin, Kismet Kennels.

Ch. Kismet's Seasons In the Sun, by Ch. Kismet's Conquistador ex Ch. Fiesta's Fazzle Dazzle. Bred and owned by Guy and Thelma Mauldin, Kismet Kennels.

ducing dam in the breed with thirteen champions, all of them sired by Champion Banchory High Born. One of the offspring from this combination, Champion Fiesta's Fazzle Dazzle, bred to the High Born son, Champion Kismet's Conquistador, produced Champion Kismet's Status Quo, who is a Group winner and who won the National Specialty twice. Champion Kismet's Status Symbol, Champion Kismet's Seasons in the Sun, and Champion Kismet's Status Assured were also bred by the Mauldins.

Champion Kismet's Conquistador, in addition to being a great sire, is a multiple Group-winner and winner of thirteen Specialty Bests in Show. His champions produced number thirty-four.

The Mauldins also bred another Best in Show winner in Champion Kismet's Centurian, by Champion Banchory High Born ex Champion Kismet's Coquette. Other Group winners bred and owned at Kismet include Champion Kismet's El Cid and Champion Kismet's Saint or Sinner.

Above: Ch. Kismet's Conquistador, famous homebred owned by Guy and Thelma Mauldin. **Below:** Ch. Kismet's Saint or Sinner, by Can. Ch. Sovereign Winning Spirit ex Kismet's Lovesong. Owned by Guy A. Mauldin.

Ch. Kismet's El Cid, C.D., by Ch. Banchory High Born ex Kismet's Caprice, winning a Working Group.

Ch. Kismet's Crown Jewel, by Ch. Century Farm's High Roller ex Ch. Alibi's Blue Is Blue at Sun-up. Handled by Guy A. Mauldin for himself and Thelma Mauldin, Kismet Kennels.

Am. and Can. Ch. Banchory The Midnight Hour, bi-black dog by Ch. Harvest Hills Shoeshine Boy ex Banchory Orchid Blue. Owned by Nancy Howard, Legacy Shelties, Woodbury, Minnesota.

Legacy Song of Love winning Best of Breed at Duluth in July 1982; judge, Mrs. Michele Billings. Nancy Howard, owner, Legacy Kennels.

Legacy

Legacy Shetland Sheepdogs, located at Woodbury, Minnesota, belong to Nancy Howard who is a breeder of considerable talent judging by the quality of her beautiful dogs.

Champion Legacy Steela Breeze, a stunning blue-merle, white, and tan homebred whelped April 19th, 1980, is the "head man" representing this kennel as we write in mid-1983. A grandson of Champion Banchory Deep Purple, Steela Breeze is by Banchory Private Enterprise ex Banchory Flow Blue. He has been going great guns in Specials and Group competition, and he was the Best of Opposite Sex dog at the American Shetland Sheepdog Association National Specialty in 1983. He is also fast becoming an important sire, with winners in the ring starting their careers as we write.

American and Canadian Champion Banchory The Midnight Hour is another important dog at Legacy. He is a bi-black son of Champion Harvest Hills Shoeshine Boy from Banchory Orchid Blue, and he, too, is a sire of some excellent progeny. Among them are several who have been in the winners circle recently, these including Legacy Seventh Heaven, a young homebred bitch from Banchory Flow Blue, C.D., owned by Nancy Howard, and her litter-sister, Legacy String of Pearls, owned by Brian Cleveland and Helen A. Hurlburt.

Legacy Dot To Dot exhibiting beautiful Sheltie expression. Owned by Nancy Howard, Legacy Shetland Sheepdogs.

Ch. Legacy Steela Breeze, by Banchory Private Enterprise ex Banchory Flow Blue, a lovely blue-merle, white, and tan homebred from Legacy Kennels, Nancy Howard.

Legacy Autumn Breeze, by Ch. Legacy Steela Breeze ex Legacy Sweet Success, winning Best in Sweepstakes under judge Sandra Alters at Midlands Shetland Sheepdog Club in 1983. Nancy Howard, owner, Legacy Shelties.

Lochanora

Lochanora Shetland Sheepdogs, at Lakeland, Florida, are owned by George and Melanie Williams and were originally established during the late 1960's. The time-consuming responsibilities of raising four children have in many ways curtailed the Williams's active show and breeding participation, although both take tremendous pleasure in the dogs. George Williams enjoys the breeding end of the sport and Melanie the showing, making for a very happy partnership.

The Williams have had three separate and distinct lines of Shelties over the years before settling on a type and consistency upon which they could agree. Several years ago they found a dog whom they considered suitable to build upon, Champion Banchory Backstop. Since then they have utilized his pedigree, making breedings planned on his sire, Banchory Reflection.

It was the Williams's good fortune that Champion Madselin's Grand Slam, a son of Champion Banchory Backstop, was made available to them through the generosity of Irene Oishi of Akirene Kennels in Canada. Thus they were able to start building a genetic pool with which to work. Irene Oishi is the owner of Backstop, a multiple Specialty and all-breed Best in Show winner. The Williams began their foundation line through their bitch, Champion Diamond's Gingerbread Girl and her breeder, Barbara Byrd of Diamond Kennels. Researching her pedigree, they noted an especially dominant bitch there who appears in many other pedigrees through her sons, Champion Diamond's Robert Bruce (by Champion Lingard Sealect Bruce) and Champion Diamond's Redbud (by Champion Sea Isle Serenade). Her name was Champion Diamond's Black Velvet.

Champion Diamond's Gingerbread Girl (tri-factored sable) was bred to Champion Banchory Thunder Blue, producing Lochanora Forbidden Fruit, so named, to quote Mrs. Williams "because at the time it was not fashionable or acceptable to breed sables to blues." Forbidden Fruit was a typey, small bitch who was shown only a handful of times but managed a respectable Reserve Winners Bitch at a major show in the Midwest. She in turn was bred to tri-factored Champion Banchory Backstop, the Williams hoping that they might produce a bicolor. They did, and she turned out to be Lochanora Back-

Ch. Madselin's Grand Slam, five years of age. Bred by Susan Jensen; owned by George and Melanie Williams, Lakeland, Florida.

gammon, an elegant bi-black bitch who was a point winner from the Puppy Classes.

During this period the Williams's children were quite small and they, naturally, came first in their parents' time and consideration. Also the family was living in Korea when Forbidden Fruit was whelped, and it was quite difficult to get involved in any way with dogs over there. But when they moved back to the United States, the Williams made the breeding to Backstop and moved twice before settling in Florida. While George was travelling in the Pacific Northwest, he frequently dropped in to visit the Oishis, who kept trying to get him to take home "this large, hairy puppy." Finally, when the puppy was eight months of age, he told the Oishis that this was just too much dog to please him.

Then the Williams and the Oishis all attended the National in Texas, and Irene showed the Williams pictures of the dog. They still said "no." Finally about a year later, when George Williams was at the airport in Vancouver, having a bit of spare time he phoned Irene. She said, "Wait for me, I'm coming right over with the dog," and she did! Melanie comments, "How she made it, I'll never know as the flight was due to leave in less than an hour and she lived over an hour away." She did, though, and next morning, before the sun came up, a very surprised Melanie was being awakened by her husband telling her to "go get the dog out of the car."

That is how Champion Madselin's Grand Slam came to Lochanora! The Williams decided to keep him on a co-ownership agreement with the Oishis for awhile, to see how he was going to work out. His first A.K.C. show was to be at Central Florida Kennel Club, at Orlando, where Melanie had "just entered him to see how he would show." He went Winners Dog, Best of Winners for a three-point major, and then on to Best of Breed over several Specials, by which time Melanie was flying high. This was under Helen Miller Fisher, who was also doing the Group. When that was over, "Matt" as he is called, had added a Working Group third to his day's victories, and Melanie was quickly getting him entered for the rest of the shows in Florida that spring. By the end of the year he had finished. Shown out of coat most of the time, he was entered in a total of seventeen shows when he gained his title. By that time the Williams had purchased him outright and thought perhaps he might do well in Specials competition when he came into coat, which had certainly not been helped by the move from Canada's cool climate to Florida's much warmer climate. It took him almost two and a half years to become acclimated.

Champion Madselin's Grand Slam was the second bi-blue male Sheltie champion in the United States.

At present the Williams are building on Grand Slam's lines, he being by Champion Banchory

Lochanora Grand Larceny, at ten weeks of age. Bred by George and Melanie Williams and Marcella Jewett; owned by the Williams, Lochanora Kennels.

Backstop out of Canadian Champion Banchory Misty Blue who is an inbred Champion Banchory Thunder Blue daughter. Forbidden Fruit was bred to him, producing the major-pointed Lochanora Wendy Iceberg, a lovely small bi-blue who resembles her sire in many ways but is very feminine. She is just two years of age now (in 1983) and the Williams have high hopes for her to finish this year.

The Williams also bred Grand Slam to a Backstop daughter, Banchory Badgerton Babe, a major-pointed tri-factored sable belonging to friends of theirs, and she produced the Best in Sweepstakes and point-winning puppy, Lochanora Southern Accent, a tri-factored sable. Before her first birthday she has accumulated three points, with more to come shortly, it seems certain. And the Williams are "growing out" a bi-black male whom they feel has tremendous potential, Lochanora Grand Larceny, who is by Grand Slam out of the Williams's Backstop daughter, Lochanora Backgammon.

During 1983 as we write, Champion Madselin's Grand Slam is being shown and to date has won thirty-four Bests of Breed under twenty-nine different judges; he has also won the Herding Group twice, and placed second, third, and fourth. To the Williams's knowledge, Grand Slam is the only Group-winning bi-blue Sheltie. He topped out 1982 in Number Eighteen position according to the *Sheltie Pacesetter* system—an owner-handled dog who has surely made his presence felt. The Williams are justly proud!

Lochanora Wendy Iceberg, at one and a half years of age. Breeders, George and Melanie Williams; owner, Kathy Randolph, Miramar, Florida.

Ch. Lynnlea Forever Amber, C.D., by Ch. Barwood's Gentle Persuasion ex Westwood Leo Piper of Ashford, C.D. Amber was Best of Breed at the American Shetland Sheepdog Association National Specialty in 1983 from the Veterans Class, winning over seventy-five champions entered in Specials and a total entry of close to six hundred Shelties. Bred and owned by Ray and Dorothy Christiansen, Lynnlea Shelties, Lockport, Illinois.

Lynnlea's Josh of Water's Edge, by Barwood's Formal Attire ex Ch. Barwood Ashford Vanity Fair, C.D. Owned by Pat Stewart, Chicago, Illinois.

Lynnlea

Lynnlea Shetland Sheepdogs, owned by Ray and Dorothy Christiansen, have been active in the Sheltie world for about fifteen years, participating in both conformation and obedience competition. They are located at Lockport, Illinois.

We are certain that one of the very most exciting days of their years in Shelties is the one which took place at the American Shetland Sheepdog Association National Specialty in May 1983, when their homebred bitch, Champion Lynnlea Forever Amber, C.D., swept all before her to win first the Veterans Class and then Best of Breed in an entry of 600 which included about seventy-five competing in Specials. Making this all the more a noteworthy achievement is the fact that this lovely bitch was eight years old at the time of this triumph and that she was the dam of four litters over the years.

Ch. Halstor's Peter Pumpkin with his dam, Ch. Sea Isle Rhapsody of Halstor, photographed at the 1976 Colonial weekend. Peter was almost eleven years of age then, Rhapsody almost twelve. Photo courtesy of Thomas W. Coen, Macdega Shelties, Samsonville, New York.

Macdega

Thomas W. Coen is the owner of the Macdega Shetland Sheepdogs at Samsonville, New York. It was in 1959 when he started out to study Shelties; in 1961, he attended his first National Specialty Show; and in 1963, he made up his kennel name. Since that time he has been steadily and heavily involved with the breed—very successfully, we might add!

During most of the 1960's, Tom was in school, and his first few Shelties were cared for by Irene Brody, a dear friend to whom, we quote, he feels "much indebted." Again quoting, "What we lacked in experience and finances was definitely made up in intention and enthusiasm. At one point we had two young males housed in the attached garage, and we were certain they were destined for greatness and posterity in Sheltie history. Every novice's dream!" This time the dream was not in vain, however, as those two Shelties became Champion Halstor's Peter Pumpkin and Champion Philidove Heir

Ch. Halstor's Peter Pumpkin with his sire, Fair Play of Sea Isle, in the summer of 1975. Photo courtesy of Thomas Coen.

Ch. Banchory Arabesque, by Ch. Halstor's Peter Pumpkin, dam of Ch. Banchory Formal Attire by Banchory Reflection. Photo courtesy of Thomas Coen.

Presumptive. Now, almost twenty years later, Peter is the top sire in breed history with more than 156 champions; and Heir Presumptive is the sire of the breed's second top sire, Champion Banchory High Born. What more can one possibly say?

In 1966, Tom Coen saw and purchased Halstor's Peter Pumpkin, a young male of the Kiltie-Note cross, the combination that was responsible for many of the successes of the Sea Isle Kennels. Though he advises newcomers to start with the best bitch possible, again quoting Tom, "I blithely set to the task of building a family of dogs based on Peter." At that time inbreeding was not widely practiced, at least not in Shelties. However, Tom chose a Peter daughter from a distantly related complementary family (Lindhurst) to use as a foundation for the sable program. The original bitch, Habilu Macdega Marni, was bred to her sire several times and returned the complementary progeny to him again. There are currently about thirty-five champions descending from Marni, which is quite remarkable as mostly bitches were retained and they, rather than a top sire, are responsible for the figure.

Only recently did Macdega have a suitable male to retain from this tail bitch family, and she

Ch. Philidove Heir Presumptive, by Ch. Karelane Heir Apparent ex Wansor's Flashy Flame. Handled by Steve Barger; owned by Irene Brody.

is Best in Show-winning Champion Macdega Canden Coming Home. The individual dams most well known through modern pedigrees are Macdega Apple Annie, Macdega Sara of Long Hill, Champion Macdega All In The Family, and Champion Macdega The Farmer's Daughter.

After several generations of tight breeding, it was felt that the faults and virtues had become set, and it was time to introduce some new blood. In 1972, Tom purchased a six-month-old Peter son out of a bitch of Pocono-Sea Isle lines. Not only did he excel in the areas where the inbred bitches needed improvement, but also his dam was an excellent complement to Marni. This dog became Champion Calcurt Luke, Peter's top-producing son with twenty-one champions and the sire of numerous bitches who have contributed to the success of many kennels. Tom Coen notes, "Each year at the National his influence is evident in many of the winners, and the Luke daughters are possibly the most sought-after commodity in the breed today." Luke's contribution through the Marni descendants include such well-known bitches as Champion Macdega Fantasy World, Berridale The Critic's Choice, Champion Berridale Alnphyll Brigette, and Macdega Leave It To Beaver.

Calcurt Black Angie, dam of Ch. Calcurt Luke. Photo courtesy of Thomas W. Coen, Macdega.

Ch. Northcountry Westering Son, exported before his fourth birthday, sire of eleven champions. Owned by Macdega, Thomas W. Coen.

In 1977, Tom Coen acquired another inbred Peter son, and he became Champion Northcountry Westering Son. His dam, Champion Malpsh Count Your Blessings, was one of Peter's best daughters and of strong Sea Isle lineage. "Blazer" was bred to daughters of Luke, Thunderation, and Jon Christopher before he was exported when he was three years old. His siring record is quite remarkable as he did produce eleven champions in this short time.

For several years previous to 1977, the Luke and Peter daughters were bred to two triple Peter descendants: Champion Chenterra Thunderation, two times American Shetland Sheepdog Association Best of Breed and twenty-two times all-breed Best in Show winner, and Champion Gerthstone's Jon Christopher, who was at Macdega on lease for several years. The best known results of these combinations are Champion Canden Fantasia, Champion Ardencaple Berridale Belove, Champion Sharmont Ruby Slippers, and Champion Benayr Chimera Colloguy.

In late 1978, Banchory Reflection, an Heir Presumptive grandson, was purchased as a complement to the line-bred Peter individuals and as an addition to the AOC program. The success of this breeding is evident in numerous National Specialty winners, Group winners, and those going on to Best in Show.

Both Luke and Reflection were tri-factored and along with Thunderation have been of great importance to the AOC program which began in the early 1970's and has been steadily on the increase. Again quoting Tom, "Almost all our AOC individuals trace to Champion Lake Hill Portrait In Blue, Champion Philidove Carmylie In A Mist, both great blue bitches; or to the well-known bi-black, Champion Nadia. Results of this program include the well-known sires Champion Macdega Proof Positive, Champion Macdega The Piano Man, and Champion Macdega Times Square, and bitches such as Macdega Under The Rainbow, Macdega Marrakech, and Champion Macdega One Day At A Time."

Ch. Nadia, a Specialty winning bitch and the dam of Ch. Macdega The Piano Man. Owned by Macdega Kennels, Thomas W. Coen.

Ch. Macdega Proof Positive, sire of numerous champions and multiple Specialty winners. Macdega Kennels, Thomas W. Coen.

Banchory Reflection, the sire of twenty champions including three Best in Show sons. Owned by Macdega Shetland Sheepdogs, Thomas W. Coen.

Mainstay

Mainstay Shetland Sheepdogs are owned by Stephen W. Barger, situated at Old Chatham, New York. Steve, who is now a highly successful professional handler, has been showing dogs since the age of nine years, doing so professionally since the late 1960's. The first dog Steve finished was an Afghan Hound. However, his greatest successes, and the breeds he most completely enjoys, are Collies and Shelties.

Steve, as a child, was another Albert Payson Terhune reader and enthusiast. No animals were permitted while he was a child, but his interest was already well under way as he dreamed of a pony beneath his Christmas tree and pored over the Terhune stories and his uncle's copies of *Dog World* magazine. From its pages he learned a good deal about various breeds prior to his decision that his first dog, when it finally came, would be a Collie. When family friends started taking him to dog shows, Steve admired and

Head-study of Ch. Chenterra Thunderation, the great Best in Show dog.

Ch. Chenterra Thunderation, one of the most important winning Shelties in the history of the breed and a superlative stud dog as well. Owned by Tetsuo Miyama and Stephen W. Barger, Old Chatham, New York.

Ch. Macdega Mainstay, by Ch. Chenterra Thunderation ex Macdega Leave It To Beaver. Owned by Tetsuo Miyama and Stephen W. Barger.

Ch. Banchory Strike Me Silver, by Ch. Banchory Formal Notice ex Banchory Ice Follie. Owned by Tetsuo Miyama and Stephen W. Barger.

learned technique by watching such handlers of that day as Jane Kamp Forsyth and Anne Rogers Clark.

When one even hears Steve Barger's name, immediately the fantastic dog with whom he is so closely associated, Champion Chenterra Thunderation, comes to mind—for this magnificent dog and Steve made history together, a combination never to be forgotten in Sheltie circles!

Winning his seventeenth Best in Show (which he shortly thereafter surpassed with his eighteenth), Thunderation is the dog who broke the record (held since the mid-1960's by Champion Elf Dale Viking), this under Langdon Skarda, on February 25, 1979 at Elm City Kennel Club at but five years of age. This was a never-to-be-forgotten occasion, we are sure, in Steve's life! Thunderation had first come to Steve Barger's attention at one of the Nationals just after he had completed his championship. It was a busy day, but even so Steve observed the dog with admiration, noting especially his balance, coat, and pleasing overall outline. Later he availed himself of the opportunity of going over the dog, who was then handled by Dianne Wolcott, really liking everything he saw. The breeding, as listed in the catalog, meant little to Steve at the time; but he did recall that he had especially liked the little dog's double grandam when she had been sent to him and Tom Coen for breeding to Peter Pumpkin.

In selecting a stud for the lovely Portrait In Blue, Steve felt that the ideal dog for her would be this handsome newcomer; the problem was that Steve did not want to ship this bitch, yet there was no other dog but "Thunder" to whom he *really* wanted her bred. Numerous telephone calls later, "Thunder's" owner, Jody Chenoweth, had been persuaded, reluctantly as

Above, left: The beautiful youngster Whitegates Anything U Can Do, by Ch. Macdega Mainstay ex Whitegates On A Clear Day, Best in Futurity in 1983. Handled by Steve Barger; owned by Joan and Terry Pavey. **Right:** Ch. Banchory Arabesque, by Ch. Halstor's Peter Pumpkin ex Banchory High Glow, one of the many outstanding Shelties owned by Tetsuo Miyama and handled by Stephen Barger. This lovely bitch is the dam of Ch. Banchory Formal Notice.

Ch. Lakehill Portrait In Blue, by Ch. Kiloren Night Apache ex Kiloren Moonbeam. Owned by Stephen W. Barger.

she was loathe to part with him even temporarily, to send "Thunder" on to Steve, "to stay six months, but no longer."

Picking up the dog at the airport, Steve admits to having had mixed emotions. Had he been overly enthusiastic at the Specialty, which had been such a rushed and busy day? Was the dog *really* so super, or had it been his imagination? He could hardly wait to get the dog safely home and look him over again. And the moment Thunderation stepped from the crate and entered the house for Tom Coen to see, Steve knew he had been right. "Thunder," according to Steve, checked things out, put his head in the lap of the man sitting in the chair by the fireplace, and promptly made himself at home. Steve knew right then that there was no way he would let this dog leave him, and so there were more phone calls, plus considerable worry and anticipation until finally Jody Chenoweth agreed to let him remain and the sale wás closed.

Champion Chenterra Thunderation was shown 228 times. On these occasions he won 220 Bests of Breed (120 of them consecutively), twenty-one all-breed Bests in Show, and seventy-eight Working Group firsts. "Thunder" was shown almost exclusively by Steve Barger (excepting a few times by his then partner Tom Coen, and Jane Hammett), and watching the two of them work together was a joy, as the rapport between handler and dog was so very evident.

Mainstay Kennels came about when Steve Barger and Tom Coen dissolved their partnership and Steve needed a new kennel name that was strictly his own. The name of one of his important dogs is "Mainstay" and although Steve had not intended naming the kennel after any individual Sheltie, somehow as he thought over possible names, that one kept coming to mind. Checking out the meaning he found "main supporting structure, backbone," which certainly was appropriate and so the name was chosen. It has already identified a goodly number of important Shelties as we write this, and we feel sure will continue to do so over the years.

Steve has owned, bred, or finished for others an impressive list of champions and important winners. Two of his favorites have included Champion Lakehill Portrait In Blue, one of the "best Shelties I have ever known," to quote him, bred by Ginny Cavallaro; and Champion Mainstay Rumor Has It, from a bitch leased by him to Gulie Krook, another very beautiful one.

Of the young stock at Mainstay, watch for Mainstay Pieces of Dreams, whom you will have seen, I am sure, before this book comes out. Steve describes this young blue bitch as coming "close to what I want."

Ch. Mainstay Rumor Has It, by Ch. Macdega Mainstay ex Montage Pardon My Past. Owned by Jo Ann McNeal and Stephen W. Barger.

Malashel

Malashel's Fortune Cookie, U.D., Can. C.D., by Ch. Rockwoods Bac Talk ex Creekview's Heather Wish-Now, C.D., pointed toward conformation championship in the United States and Canada. Bred and owned by Elaine Wishnow.

Malashel Kennels, located in Brooklyn, New York, are owned by Elaine Wishnow, who has been "in" Shelties since the late 1960's when she purchased her first bitch, Trumark's Little Miss Tommy, U.D., Canadian C.D.X. Miss Wishnow had not been too experienced with the breed when she made this purchase and Little Miss Tommy did not turn out to be a show dog. She was, however, a wonderful obedience dog.

Since that time most of the Shelties at Malashel have been line-bred on Peter Pumpkin, and their owner has been very happy with the results. Malashel's Fortune Cookie, U.D., Canadian C.D., is pointed in the United States and in Canada while Malashel's Autumn Amberglo, U.D., Canadian C.D.X., has points toward an Obedience Trial championship and is a *Dog World* Award winner. Both are excellent obedience dogs and good brood bitches.

Since her kennel is in the heart of a big city, Miss Wishnow tries to have her dogs contribute to the community as much as possible. All of them do breed and obedience demonstrations in public schools and have also done work in nursing homes, entertaining the patients.

"The gang" from Malashel Kennels. Left to right: Schipperke, Am. and Can. Ch. Malashel's Hug-A-Love Bug, C.D.X.; Malashel's Fortune Cookie, U.D., Can. C.D.; Malshel's Autumn Amberglo, U.D., Can. C.D.X.; Lingard My Precious Peach, C.D.X.; and Malashel's Patches of Blue, C.D. All owned by Elaine Wishnow, Brooklyn, New York.

Above and below: Malashel's Autumn Amberglo, U.D., Can. C.D.X. Owned by Miss Elaine Wishnow, shown below with Amberglo.

Above: Malashel's Lost in a Fun House at five weeks of age. Miss Elaine Wishnow, owner.
Below: Malashel's Patches of Blue, C.D., by Ch. Rockwood Nite Enchantment, C.D., ex Creekview's Bi Betsy Blue. Elaine Wishnow, owner.

149

Marwal Kennels, home of the Shelties owned by Margaret and Walt Huening at Ballston Spa, New York.

Highland Huey of Shelcort, the first pet Sheltie owned by Margaret and Walt Huening back in 1960. He was a grandson of Ch. Nashcrest Golden Note and a son of Ch. Timberidge Target, and he lived to be twelve years old.

Marwal

Margaret and Walt Huening of Ballston Spa, New York, had their first encounter with a Shetland Sheepdog in 1954 through knowing Margaret's sister's dog, Spud, who came from E-Danha Kennels in Idaho, hence the name "Spud." That was the beginning of a long-lasting love between the Huenings and the Sheltie breed.

In March of 1956, Margaret and Walt purchased their first pet Sheltie, Highland Huey of Shelcort, the name "Huey" derived from their own last name. He was a grandson of Champion Nashcrest Golden Note and a son of Champion Timberidge Target. He lived to be twelve years old. In addition to Huey, the Huenings had numerous other pet Shelties, three of which came from the Kiloren Kennels in Ohio.

In 1967, two more Shelties joined the family, Jason Laird Woodhaven for the Huenings' son and Shel-T-Lane Cutey from Montana, both pets; but in 1969 their mating (and the Huenings' first attempt at dog breeding) produced Marwal Princess Tara and the first use of the Marwal kennel name, derived from the first names of the owners, MARgaret and WALter. Tara passed away at age twelve. Jason and Cutey are still alive as we write this, both age sixteen.

In 1970, the Huenings started their first serious attempts to breed quality Shelties with the purchase of Kiloren Friendly Persuasion II.

He was shown a few times, but he was never comfortable in the ring and he was eventually sold to a pet home, where he lived to the good age of fourteen. From one of his breedings, however, he did produce Marwal Princess Lana, who in 1972 was bred to Champion Carmylie Elusive Dream, producing Marwal Pennies From Heaven, with whom began the long tradition of the Huenings naming their Shelties with song titles. Pennies was shown a few times, acquiring three points. In 1975, she was bred to Champion Calcurt Luke, from which came the Huenings' first champion, the widely admired Champion Marwal Joshua of Jericho, who finished in 1981, and Marwal Belle of the Ball, who is the dam of one champion. "Penny" is now retired at Marwal.

Also in 1972, Princess Tara was bred to Banchory Heatherland High Noon producing Miss Priscilla of Marwal, the Huenings' first tricolor Sheltie. Priscilla was bred twice to Champion Philidove Benevolent Anthony, first in 1974 producing Marwal Satin Doll and again in 1977 producing Marwal Blue Denim. Blue Denim's breeding to Champion Centerra Thunderation in 1976 produced Marwall Sister Kate, the Huenings' bi-factored tricolor brood bitch.

Marwal's Pennies From Heaven, by Ch. Carmylie Elusive Dream ex Princess Lana of Marwal, at eight years old in 1981. Pennies was the dam of Marwal's first champion, Marwal Joshua of Jericho, who finished in 1981. Margaret and Walt Huening, owners.

Ch. Marwal Joshua of Jericho, a homebred son of Ch. Calcurt Luke ex Marwal's Pennies From Heaven. This is the first champion owned by the Walt Huenings of Marwal Kennels, Ballston Spa, New York.

Am. and Can. Ch. Carmylie Elusive Dream, by Ch. Halstor's Peter Pumpkin ex Jomar Carmylie Love's Magic, the sire of nine champions as of summer 1983.

Rallyround Lady Ice (Banchory High Power ex Banchory A Blue Delight) was acquired in 1973, the first blue-merle at Marwal and a "very special dog." Although Ice was timid in the show ring and thus gained only a few points herself, her breeding to Champion Chenterra Thunderation in 1976 produced Champion Marwal Bluesette, who finished in 1983, and her breeding to Champion Reflection of Sealect produced Barwood Marwal Mirage. Her last breeding, out of five, to Champion Marwal Joshua of Jericho produced Marwal Fire and Ice who is being readied for her show career as we write this in October 1983. The Huenings will never stop feeling grief over the sad loss, of cancer at only eight and a half years, of Lady Ice, whom they dearly loved for her personality and devotion—truly one of those "once in a lifetime" favorites.

Champion Lanbur's Look of Love was purchased from Waldenwood Kennels in Georgia during 1974. She has a great pedigree, and three of her littermates also became champions; but she was bred three times, produced only pet puppies, and was retired. At age thirteen (in 1983) she is the Huenings' dearly loved "gentle old house lady," a job she fills most happily.

Marwal Bluesette was bred to Champion Chenterra Thunderation in 1977, producing Mainstay Night Fever (eleven points as we write) owned by the Troups in Maryland. In 1980, she was bred to American and Canadian Champion Macdega Mainstay which produced Champion Marwal Struttin' the Blues,

Above: Rallyround Lady Ice, the first blue-merle and a very special Sheltie to her owners, Margaret and Walt Huening, who lost this beautiful bitch to cancer at eight and a half years of age in 1981. Margaret Huening comments: "We doubt we'll ever see her likes again. Her love of life and her devotion to her friends were unsurpassed and we will forever miss her." Lady Ice was a granddaughter of Am. and Can. Ch. Banchory High Born and Am. and Can. Ch. Cherden Sock It To 'Em. **Below:** A fabulous head-study of the lovely bitch Ch. Marwal Bluesette. "Becky" belongs to Margaret and Walt Huening, Marwal Shelties.

Ch. Marwal Struttin' the Blues, who finished title in 1983. This dog is a homebred from Marwal Kennels, Margaret and Walt Huening.

Ch. Macdega Mainstay, by Ch. Chenterra Thunderation ex Macdega Leave It To Beaver, sire of Ch. Marwal Struttin' The Blues. Owned by Tetsuo Miyama and Stephen W. Barger, Mainstay Kennels.

A head-study of Marwal Bobbin' Along in 1982. Margaret and Walt Huening, owners, Marwal Kennels.

"Bobby," who finished in 1983. Two bitches from this litter are Marwal Liza Jayne, who has eight points including both majors, owned by Diane Bostwick, and Marwal Annie Laurie with two points. Bluesette, who is now seven years old, spent a long time on the show circuit and is now enjoying a well-earned vacation at home, during which she will take some time to have a few more offspring.

In 1980, the Huenings acquired Marwal Bobbin' Along. Her breeding to American and Canadian Champion Sir Joshua of Winslow produced Champion Marwal Steppin' Out, who is also owned by Diane Bostwick. This handsome dog finished with all his wins from the Puppy Classes.

In May 1983, Champion Marwal Joshua of Jericho won Best Veteran at the American Shetland Sheepdog Association National Specialty Show in Boston—a very exciting occasion. Margaret Huening notes that they have been members of the ASSA for nine years and have attended five National shows.

It has taken a few years to get where Marwal consistently produces potential show-quality Shelties, mainly because the Huenings also accumulated a few pets along the way. They are especially proud of Marwal's line of silver-blue-merles. As of this writing there are four homebred champions at Marwal and high hopes for more in the future. This writer especially admires Mrs. Huening's comment that "though the kennel consists of 'stars' and pets, we love them all like family."

Dona Hausman showing one of her lovely Shelties.

Meadow Ridge

Meadow Ridge Shetland Sheepdogs, at Stamford, Connecticut, belong to Dona (Mrs. James E.) Hausman, who is a third-generation dog breeder, her grandfather having imported some of the first St. Bernards to have come to the United States from Switzerland and her father having bred Airedales. Dona was brought up on stories of her father's Airedale, Champion Red Raven, and of his having gone Best of Breed at Westminster for three successive years in the days when Airedales were at a popularity peak; thus it must have given her very special pleasure later on when one of her Shelties duplicated this triple series of Bests of Breed at our most prestigious dog show, which Westminster is generally considered to be.

Dona Hausman started breeding and showing dogs back in 1937, Cocker Spaniels at that time, and her first to gain the title was Champion My Own of Meadow Ridge. She then imported a Springer Spaniel who became Champion Trevillas Peggy of Meadow Ridge, and this one is behind some of the winning Springers today. Then in 1950, her husband became interested in shooting game, and the Hausmans acquired a Brittany who became Champion Meadow Ridge Trashman; he did some Group placing while the breed was almost unknown in the show ring. In 1957, James Hausman needed a larger dog to hunt over the rough Maryland terrain; thus a Gordon Setter was purchased who became Champion Meadow Ridge Gillie Adair.

It was Dona's decision to "go into" Shetland Sheepdogs because she had always wanted a Collie, but they "were just too big." So in 1941, she bought her first Sheltie from Betty Whelen, and this good little bitch became Champion Meadow Ridge Golden Dawn. This was the foundation bitch of Dona Hausman's Sheltie line and produced four champions: Champion Meadow Ridge of Bagaduce, Champion Meadow Another Ridge, Champion Meadow Ridge Rascal, and Champion Meadow Ridge Cold Saturday, all sired by different stud dogs.

Dona's next decision was to work with a combination of Pixie Dell and Pocono in establishing her breeding program. Thus she bought from Mr. and Mrs. A. Raymond Miller a young puppy who was to become Champion Pixie Dell Bright Vision. Born June 17th 1957, this exquisite dog was a mahogany sable and white son of Champion Brandell's Break-A-Way II ex Champion Va-Gore's Bright Promise (a very outstanding bitch who had done considerable winning for Mr. and Mrs. George Howard). Vision was both a great stud dog and an outstanding campaigner in the show ring. He sired nineteen champions when breeders were not yet in the habit of shipping their bitches all over the country to be bred, which was an imposing total. As a show dog, he was Best of Breed on eighty-six occasions which included three successive

Ch. Pixie Dell Bright Vision, one of the big winners of the breed. Owned by Dona Hausman, Meadow Ridge Kennels, Stamford, Connecticut.

Ch. Sutter's Golden Masquerade. Owned by Dona Hausman, Meadow Ridge Kennels.

Ch. Meadow Ridge It's Me, handled here by R. Stephen Shaw for Mrs. Dona Hausman, Meadow Ridge Kennels.

Ch. Elf Dale Golden Legacy winning at Chicago International in 1964. Owned by Mrs. Dona Hausman.

years (1960, 1961, and 1962) at Westminster, plus winning Best of Breed at three Inter-State Specialties, one Tri-State Specialty, and one American Shetland Sheepdog Association National Specialty. Additionally he had twenty Working Group placements.

Vision's top winning son was Champion Sutter's Golden Masquerade, who was co-owned by Dona with Valerie Daniels until such time as she persuaded that lady to let her have him outright. His top producing daughter was Champion Sherlin's Penny Bright. Vision's winning grandchildren are far too numerous to list, but they include Champion Lencrest Rabel Rouser and Champion Meadow's Fire of Bryce Star Lit.

Masquerade won two all-breed Bests in Show, 116 Bests of Breed, and thirty-eight Group placements. He was first in the East in 1968, and then in 1969 Dona herself handled him to first among *all* Shelties in the United States that year. He also was twice Best of Breed at Westminster.

As an exhibitor, Dona's two greatest thrills have been when Vision won Best of Breed for the third time at Westminster; and Masquerade's first Best in Show which, as she comments, had taken place after something like thirty-five years of showing and breeding dogs and when the accomplishment was especially noteworthy as Shelties were not taking many top awards back in 1969.

Other Meadow Ridge champions include Champion Meadow Ridge Hot Sunday and her litter-brother Champion Meadow Ridge Stitch In Time, Champion Meadow Ridge Busy

Dona Hausman at Queensboro in October 1965 winning under James W. Trullinger with her Ch. Meadow Ridge Bright Holiday.

Ch. Meadow Ridge Baby Face finished in 1964 to become the fifth champion by her noted sire, Champion Pixie Dell Bright Vision. Both owned by Mrs. Dona Hausman, Meadow Ridge Kennels.

Night, Champion Meadow Ridge Bright Monday, Champion Meadow Ridge Hello Edith, Champion Meadow Ridge On Time, Champion Meadow Ridge Good Night Steve, Champion Meadow Ridge Baby Jane and her litter-sister Champion Meadow Ridge Bright Holiday, Champion Meadow Ridge of Birch Hollow, Champion Meadow Ridge Mint Julep, Champion Meadow Ridge So What's New, Champion Meadow Ridge It's Me, and Champion Meadow Ridge Hello Bunny. The latter, by the way, Dona's last Sheltie champion, is out of Vision's last daughter.

Dona Hausman always has kept her kennel small, usually with about ten dogs including pensioners among the grown-ups, and she annually breeds at the most one litter—sometimes not even that. "It's Me" is the Hausmans' house dog, and he is going on sixteen years old as we write this in October 1983.

Dona is an extremely popular dog show judge, kept busy by a full schedule of assignments, which includes around thirty-four shows each year. For this reason she has practically stopped showing and has cut back sharply on her breeding activities.

Above: Ch. Berridale Alnphyl Brigette, by Ch. Calcurt Luke ex Ch. Macdega's The Farmer's Daughter. Owned by Montage Kennels, Jerry and Chris Machado. **Below:** Banchory A Blue Nun, by Ch. Banchory Deep Purple ex Banchory Night Glow, at six months of age in 1976. Jerry and Chris Machado, owners, Montage Kennels.

Chris Machado holding two puppies sired by Ch. Banchory Formal Notice. Montage Kennels, the Machados, Scotts Valley, California.

Montage

Montage Shetland Sheepdogs, at Scott's Valley, California, are owned by Jerry and Chris Machado, who "met in the 6-9 Puppy Bitch Class at the 1978 National Specialty in Omaha, Nebraska, where Champion Berridale Alnphyll Brigette went Reserve Winners."

The Machados have a family of dogs based on their two foundation bitches, Champion Berridale Alnphyl Brigette (sable) and Banchory A Blue Nun (bi-blue).

Brigette is by Champion Calcurt Luke ex Champion Macdega's The Farmer's Daughter. Blue Nun is a daughter of Champion Banchory Deep Purple from Banchory Night Glow.

All of the current winners at Montage relate closely to these two original girls. The Montage breeding program is a blend of certain Banchory dogs and certain Macdega dogs, which are obviously combining well together.

The Machados own five acres in a northern coastal California town, on which they keep their twelve dogs, a miniature Arabian (27 inches), a French Lop rabbit, and two children.

Above: Head-study of Banchory By Invitation Only, at one and a half years of age. Jerry and Chris Machado, Montage Kennels. **Below:** Ch. Macdega Proof Positive taking Best of Breed at the 1981 Fall Specialty; judge, Lois Hillman. Handler, Jerry Machado; owners, Jerry and Chris Machado, Montage Kennels.

Above: Ch. Banchory Classic Image, by Ch. Banchory Formal Notice ex Banchory A Blue Nun. Bred by Jerry and Chris Machado; owner-handled by Donna Harden of Banchory Kennels. **Below:** Montage A Painted Pony, by Ch. Banchory Formal Notice ex Montage Last Tango, at one year old. Painted Pony was Winners Dog at the Dallas Specialty for four points. Owned by Jerry and Chris Machado, Montage Shelties.

Above: The great Ch. Pixie Dell Little Gamin, born in 1944. This fabulous dog was a Best in Show winner, a multiple Working Group winner, and Westminster's 1945 Best of Breed. Owned by Mr. and Mrs. A. R. Miller, Pixie Dell Kennels, Scarsdale, New York. Below: Ch. Pixie Dell Epicure winning his first Best in Show, at Elm City Kennel Club in 1970. Anna K. Nicholas, judge; Mildred B. Nicoll, handler; Mr. and Mrs. A. R. Miller, owners.

Pixie Dell

The Pixie Dell Shetland Sheepdogs began back in 1939 when Mr. and Mrs. A. Raymond Miller (Ray and Marie) of Scarsdale, New York, purchased their first of the breed as a gift for their daughter. Supposedly show quality, it soon became apparent to the Millers that actually she was not. But by this time they had become sufficiently enthusiastic about dog shows as to have learned what they considered to be excellent type and that the place from which to purchase it was Page's Hill Kennels.

Thus it was that Champion Cock O'The North O'Page's Hill and Champion Dunrobin Bijou O'Page's Hill were selected and brought home by the Millers, becoming the first of the long line of champions made famous under their banner.

Pixie Dell was chosen as their future kennel identification and registered as such by the Millers in 1941. The following year, 1942, found them with their first champion homebred, Champion Pixie Dell Blue Splendor. Their motto, "A kennel founded on champion stock with a record that speaks for itself" has been fully

Ch. Va-Gore's Bright Promise, dam of five champions (including Ch. Pixie Dell Bright Vision), American Shetland Sheepdog Association Best of Breed in 1955 and 1956, and Westminster Best of Breed in 1954. Owned by the Millers; handled by Nate Levine.

justified, as the Millers have owned and/or bred more than fifty champions over the years.

Among the most famous of the Pixie Dell standard-bearers were Champion Pixie Dell Little Gamin and Champion Pixie Dell Epicure (who lived to the grand old age of eighteen years), both noted and widely admired winners with Best in Show to their credit. Others included American Shetland Sheepdog Association Specialty Best of Breed winners (Gamin took this honor in 1945), Champion Pixie Dell Theme Song (the 1952 Best of Breed), Champion Va-Gore's Bright Promise (1955 and 1956), Champion Pixie Dell Royal Blue (1961), and Champion Pixie Dell Bright Vision (1962) who was owned by Meadow Ridge Kennels.

Pixie Dell Shelties also were dominant at Westminster over a long period of time, winning

Pixie Dell Thistledown at Interstate Shetland Sheepdog Club, 1969. Mr. and Mrs. Miller, owners. Photo courtesy of Lee Reasin.

Above: Ch. Pixie Dell Epigram, June 1966. Handled by Mildred B. Nicoll for Mr. and Mrs. Miller's Pixie Dell Kennels. **Below:** Ch. Pixie Dell Blue Thistle at Penn Treaty Kennel Club in April 1972. Mildred B. Nicoll, handler; Mr. and Mrs. A. W. Miller, owners.

Pixie Dell Morning Glory and Pixie Dell Thistledown, a beautifully matched brace winning second in the large Working Dog Brace Class at Westminster some years back. Millie Nicoll handling for owners Mr. and Mrs. A.R. Miller. Photo courtesy of Lee Reasin.

The Millers' Ch. Pixie Dell Epicure, winner of Best Shetland Sheepdog at Westminster for three consecutive years.

Best of Breed there with Champion Pixie Dell Roy's Boy in 1944, Champion Pixie Dell Little Gamin in 1945, Champion Songstress O'Page's Hill in 1948, Champion Bandmaster O'Page's Hill in 1950, Champion Va-Gore's Bright Promise in 1954, Champion Pixie Dell Bright Beacon in 1958, and the Meadow Ridge-owned Champion Pixie Dell Bright Vision in 1960, 1961, and 1962. Champion Pixie Dell Epicure then became the second Sheltie to win Westminster's Best Shetland Sheepdog award for three consecutive years, in this case in 1969, 1970, and 1971.

The Pixie Dell dogs spent their lives in luxurious heated and air-conditioned kennels with acre-sized fenced runs. They were a source of tremendous pleasure to the Millers, both of whom were dedicated fanciers in every sense of the word. Following Mr. Miller's death some years back the kennel was disbanded; since then a number of the dogs remained with Mildred Nicoll, living out their lives in happy comfort.

The kennel sign at Pocono in 1940. Elizabeth D. Whelen, owner.

Pocono

Pocono Shetland Sheepdogs is a kennel which very richly deserves the designation "a legend in their own time." The name was selected when Elizabeth D. (Betty) Whelen's first Collie bitch whelped her first litter, all the way back in May 1928, at which time Betty and her family were living at Mt. Pocono, Pennsylvania. Betty had selected Collies for her first purebred dogs for the same reason so many others have done so over the years—because she was an enthusiastic reader of the Albert Payson Terhune stories of his Sunnybank Farm Collies. There were six puppies in this first litter, of which Betty sold all but two (her mother decidedly did not share her enthusiasm for dogs) and then eventually placed one of these in a good home leaving her just with a male, Pocono Prince. Prince really "triggered" Betty's interest in the dog show world. She subscribed to all the dog publications of the day and joined the Interstate Collie Club in Philadelphia, and in 1929 she attended her first dog show, that of the Westminster Kennel Club in New York City. There she saw, and loved, her first blue-merle, this one a Collie, but undoubtedly that was the occasion on which the seed was sown which led to all those fantastic blue-merle Pocono Shelties!

Betty remained "in Collies" for awhile. As she has said in her book, *Off To The Shows*, she "never did any spectacular winning with the Collies, but learned much that I was able to apply later to the Shelties. The Collies taught me how to correctly feed, condition, train and groom for the ring."

Around 1935, Betty and her mother moved from Mt. Pocono to Atlantic City, where Betty took over the management of Glenara Kennels, belonging to Mr. Leeds, who was a breeder of Collies and Scottish Terriers.

Betty Whelen saw the first Shetland Sheepdog that truly impressed her back in 1929, attending the "old" Kennel Club of Atlantic City Dog Show. He was the famous Champion Wee Laird O'Downfield, and he had been imported, selected to come to the United States by the noted professional handler J. Nate Levine for his client, Mrs. Dreer, owner of the Anahassitt Sheltie Kennels. Again quoting Betty, "Wee Laird was the epitome of elegance and beauty and I was so impressed by him standing there in the Working Group that I decided then and there to have a Shetland at the first opportunity."

William Gallagher, whose kennel was in Massachusetts, imported a tricolor Sheltie, English Champion Helensdale Laddie, for whom he needed a handler. Someone who had seen Betty handle her Collies suggested her name to this gentleman, and Betty was duly contacted. Yes, indeed, it could be arranged for her to show this dog for Mr. Gallagher at the 1931 Westminster. Betty thoroughly enjoyed doing

Mr. and Mrs. Robert Frothingham of Rye, New York, holding their new puppies, which mark their fiftieth year of owning Pocono Shelties bred by Betty Whelen.

so, and she feels that he was a nice little dog who did very well. When Mr. Gallagher came to Betty for advice regarding the purchase of a bitch for breeding, she suggested Anahassitt Kennels with the result that he purchased Jean of Anahassitt from them. On Nate Levine's recommendation, Jean was bred to Wee Laird, which produced a very outstanding little dog, Champion Mowgli, thus starting Mr. Gallagher's kennel on its way. This was Page's Hill Kennels—one to command respect wherever Shetland Sheepdogs are known and whenever Sheltie pedigrees, right up until the present day, are studied!

It was in 1933 that Betty Whelen purchased her first Sheltie, at the Morris and Essex Kennel Club Dog Show, a tricolor bitch named Syncopating Sue of Anahassitt. She was sired by Champion Dancing Master of Anahassitt ("a very correct tricolor of outstanding head qualities") from Anahassitt Atalanta. Syncopating Sue, again quoting Betty, "possessed a very nice head, full round muzzle, good skull and stop, and lovely small natural ears. She was very sound with a good body; her eyes were dark and moderate in size; her tan markings red and rich; her coat very black and shiny, although it was rather soft and wavy. She had a lovely expression in spite of her wide blaze."

These are the *first three blue-merle American-bred champions in the United States:* Ch. Larkspur of Pocono, C.D.X., the second to finish; Ch. Sea Isle Merle Legacy, C.D., the first; and Ch. Bil-Bo-Dot Blue Flag of Pocono, the third. Elizabeth D. Whelen, owner, Pocono Kennels, then in Pennsylvania.

Ch. Autumn Leaf of Pocono, by Ch. Bodachan of Clerwood ex Ch. Syncopating Sue of Anahassitt, Betty Whelen's first homebred champion. Pocono Kennels.

Syncopating Sue's first litter was whelped in November 1933 when she was one year old. The sire was Champion Bodachan of Clerwood. There were two sable bitches and three tricolor dogs, the pick of which, a sable bitch, went to Mrs. Dreer. Betty kept the other bitch, naming her Autumn Leaf of Pocono, while Mrs. Dreer called hers Autumn Leaf of Anahassitt. The best tricolor male from the litter was sold to Mrs. Neva Wray of Kiloh Kennels, becoming her noted Pocono Pirate. The other two were sold as pets.

Autumn Leaf of Pocono became Betty Whelen's first homebred champion.

Syncopating Sue had another litter in January 1935, these puppies sired by Melchior of Anahassitt. The 14½-inch sable and white bitch, Champion Merry Memory of Pocono, came from this litter. Syncopating Sue also became a champion, completing her title when she was six years old, by which time she had produced three of her champion offspring.

During this period Nate Levine left Anahassitt and opened his own kennel in Philadelphia, where Mr. Gallagher housed the majority of his Page's Hill dogs. Another change in the Sheltie world was that of Betty's close friends from her earliest Collie days (Betty continued breeding Collies until 1955, then switched to Shelties exclusively) taking over the management at Anahassitt. Mrs. Dreer had imported a number of new Shelties. Wanting another female, Betty visited Anahassitt, where Mrs. Huhn led her to a run with some twenty puppies playing. Finally Betty's selection was made—a nicely marked tricolor with good ears and a fair head with correct size for her age. She was named Pocono Promise; unfortunately she turned out to be a disappointment and so was finally resold by Betty as a pet. That day visiting Anahassitt was not wasted, as Betty did see a little fellow who won her heart immediately with his style, personality, and good looks. At the time they would not sell him, but eventually, as Mrs. Dreer's health failed and necessitated cutting down of the kennel, he did come to Pocono. He was Artful Dodger of Anahassitt, by Champion Sprig of Houghton Hill from the same dam as Champion Syncopating Sue, thus ideal for Betty's breeding program. When bred to Betty's imported bitch, Peabody Silver Phantasy, he sired Gray Mist of Pocono; thus he is behind all of the Pocono blues, so he did contribute some qualities to that line, mostly beauty of coat and body, good ears, dark eyes, and stable temperament.

Along with Artful Dodger, Betty also purchased the Wee Laird daughter, Champion Adorable of Anahassitt, a tricolor with an exceptionally good head. She became the tail female ancestor behind the Astolat dogs (Connie Hubbard) through her daughter Astolat Lady Harlequin, a mostly white Sheltie with tricolor markings who was sired by Artful Dodger and was sold by Betty to Mrs. Hubbard. Betty noted,

As Pandora of Pocono was a daughter of Astolat Lady Harlequin, Artful Dodger played a part in the older breedings of sables. Pandora was the dam of Champion Timberidge Temptress, placing Artful Dodger behind the good sable lines of today; not only through the Astolat dogs but also through both Temptation and his brother, Champion Prince George O'Page's Hill, the sire of Champion Nashcrest Golden Note.

It was in the early 1930's (1933 or 1934, I would say) when Betty imported the blue bitch, Peabody Silver Phantasy, from Miss Montgomery in England. Her excitement was great as she had been so anxious to get started with this color. Mrs. Dreer had not imported any blue dogs. Catherine Coleman did have a few, one of which Betty had acquired while she was still living at Mt. Pocono. That dog was Blue Jacket of

Ch. Peabody Pan as a ten-month-old puppy. Imported by Elizabeth D. (Betty) Whelen, Pocono Shetland Sheepdogs.

Pocono, by Champion Pegasus of Page's Hill ex Kinnersley Blue Morn of Sheltieland, but he was never used for breeding and Betty eventually gave him to Eleanor Mann, Noralee Kennels, who showed him occasionally.

Silver Phantasy turned out to be exactly what Betty had wanted. Of her she says,

She was small, around 14 inches, her color very beautiful, and she was very well marked. She had good legs, front and rear, and a lovely type head with correct stop, flat skull with dark eyes, and excellent small, natural ears. Most of all she had the prettiest expression, which followed on down through the years in all of my Pocono line of blues, as did the dark eyes.

For her first litter, "Fancy," as Silver Phantasy was called, was bred to Artful Dodger by whom she produced two lovely puppies, born July 2nd 1935. They were far and away the best Betty had had to that date, and she was quite elated over them. They progressed nicely until five months old when the dread distemper struck, and the bitch, the better of the two, died with pneumonia on top of the distemper. The male survived, becoming Gray Mist of Pocono, C.D. He went Reserve at several shows and Winners once, but aside from being part of Betty Whelen's fantastic team which won Best Team in Show at Westminster four years in a row, he did little that was exciting in the ring.

Two all-time great producers who contributed inestimably to the progress of the Sheltie breed: Ch. Larkspur of Pocono, C.D.X., the dam of sixteen champions; and Ch. Merry Meddler of Pocono, C.D.X., sire of twenty-one champions. Both owned by Elizabeth D. Whelen, Pocono Kennels.

Later that same year, Betty imported Peabody Pan from Miss Montgomery. Again she was delighted with her purchase! Shortly after Pan's arrival, Syncopating Sue was bred to him. Sue had a problem with her milk supply and Betty managed to save just one puppy, a sable male, by giving him to one of the Scotties who had a new litter to raise. Betty speculates: "I wonder what the outcome would be today, and what difference to the breed it would have made, if that puppy had died. He was a small and runty puppy that never grew over 13 inches. Whelped October 10th 1935, his name was Merrymaker of Pocono." This dog developed into a gorgeous coated, very heavy shaded sable with exquisite head quality, eyes, and ears. Betty says, "I know he was a little cow hocked and had a poor bite, being a bit overshot, but he was a very attractive looking little dog and from the beginning sired outstanding Shelties." Shown as a young dog at Westminster, a price was put on him in the catalogue of $200.00, but there were no takers—very fortunately, as Merrymaker went on to become one of the pillar sires of the breed with a total of twenty-five champions to his credit.

Dorothy Allen Foster, of the Timberidge Shelties, wrote a most beautiful tribute to Merrymaker (who was known as "Cricket") upon his death. In part she said,

How could the fanciers know that Destiny had marked this pretty but relatively inconspicuous young dog as her own and that he was to have a major share in changing the very appearance of the breed? He was never a sensational show dog, though he completed his championship in 1938 and received his C.D. title the following year. He proved to be one of the few very great sires.

Merrymaker linked to bloodlines of proven quality. He was the carrier of a fortunate combination of genes, and stamped his progeny, particularly his daughters, with a winsome beauty, with head quality and a certain style easily identified, and with a tendency toward smaller and correct size. He also transmitted much sweetness of disposition and quick intelligence as proven by the numbers of his children attaining their C.D. and C.D.X. titles.

I shall never forget little "Cricket," whose name, Champion Merrymaker of Pocono, C.D., is indelibly graven in the Sheltie Hall of Fame.

Merrymaker's first litter was with Merry Memory of Pocono, and she had three puppies on January 2nd 1937. The tricolor male looked promising right from the start and was named

Ch. Sea Isle Merle Legacy, C.D., by Ch. Gray Mist of Pocono, C.D., ex Parkswood Little Symphony, the first American-bred blue-merle Sheltie champion. Bred by Mary Van Wagenen, Sea Isle; owned by Elizabeth D. Whelen, Pocono Kennels. Photo courtesy of Betty Whelen.

A lovely head-study of Ch. Larkspur of Pocono at six months of age. This bitch became the dam of sixteen champions and was one of the most dominant producing Sheltie bitches in history. Elizabeth D. Whelen, owner, Pocono Kennels.

Ch. Pollyanna of Pocono was the first of the Meddler-Larkspur champion progeny bred and owned by Elizabeth D. Whelen, Pocono Kennels.

Merry Meddler of Pocono. Merry Memory had several other litters, completed her title in 1937, and was sold to Add-A-Bit Kennels in New York.

Champion Larkspur of Pocono was born at the close of the 1930's, by Sea Isle Merle Legacy ex Merry Medley of Pocono. Merle Legacy was a son of Mary Van Wagenen's tricolor Parkswood Little Symphony from Gray Mist. Larkspur was "an exceptionally beautiful puppy at two months, with sweet expression, very dark eyes, and a medium sized blaze with very little black mottling on her face. She had a proper neck and topline, flawless front and shoulders, rich tan markings and gorgeous natural ears." She made her debut at the 1940 Westminster, taking Winners Bitch. The Richard C. Kettles, Jr., owners of some very famous Boxers, wanted to buy her but felt the asked price of $500.00 was "too much." Again luck was with Betty

Above: Ch. Blue Petal of Pocono and Ch. Forget-me-not of Pocono, by Ch. Merry Meddler of Pocono, C.D.X., from Ch. Larkspur of Pocono, C.D.X., at four months of age. Elizabeth D. Whelen, Pocono Kennels. **Below:** Ch. Pocono Trinket O'Windy Oaks, by Ch. Merry Meddler of Pocono, C.D.X., from Ch. Larkspur of Pocono, C.D.X. Bred, owned, and finished at Pocono by Betty Whelen.

Whelen, who says, "I would estimate that, with the sale of her offspring, she earned close to $10,000." This was the only time Larkspur ever was offered for sale.

For the benefit of new Sheltie judges who may be reading this book, we shall quote Betty Whelen's story on what ended a very promising show career for Champion Larkspur of Pocono, C.D.X.

Larkspur continued winning the spring after her five-point win at Westminster, and had fourteen points when I took her to the Bryn Mawr Show which was just before the American Shetland Sheepdog Association National Specialty at Katonah. I wanted to show her in the classes at the Specialty under Nate Levine. She won Best of Breed at Bryn Mawr, and I was utterly unprepared for what happened in that Working Group. I suspect the judge felt that he had to be especially careful with Shelties, so he put out both hands and stealthily crept up to Larkspur. She took one look at him, went into a panic, and would not let him near her. I was heartsick as it only takes one incident like that to ruin a good show dog (Larkspur always in the past had been a perfect show dog), and ruined she

Above: Ch. Blue Elegance of Pocono, by Ch. Merry Meddler of Pocono, C.D.X., from Ch. Larkspur of Pocono, C.D.X., one of the famous early Pocono champions. Bred and owned by Elizabeth D. Whelen. Below: Ch. Blue Petal of Pocono, by Ch. Merry Meddler of Pocono, C.D.X., from Ch. Larkspur of Pocono, C.D.X. Bred by Elizabeth D. Whelen; owned and finished by Mrs. Beckwith of Iowa.

Ch. Pocono Penny Royal o'Sea Isle, by Ch. Merry Meddler of Pocono, C.D.X., ex Ch. Larkspur of Pocono, C.D.X. Bred by Betty Whelen; owned and finished by Sea Isle Kennels. Photo courtesy of Betty Whelen.

was. At the Specialty she would not let Nate Levine near her either and was consequently out of the ribbons—a bitter disappointment. In fact she would not let a judge near her for the remainder of the year, and it was not until the following year that she completed her championship.

So, judges, please approach Shelties in the same friendly, confident manner you would *any* dog, and do not try any fancy tactics such as those just described as they are not only unnecessary but also may backfire on you as happened in this case!

Larkspur was bred to Merry Meddler, producing four puppies, two tri females and two blue males. As Betty had no suspicion that Larkspur

Ch. Pollyanna of Pocono and Phantasy of Pocono at seven months of age. Pollyanna was one of the sixteen champions produced by Ch. Larkspur of Pocono and really "did her mother proud" as she gained her title in three five-point majors in one month, winning the largest show of the year, Westminster (Winners Bitch from the Novice Class), the National Specialty, and the Cincinnati Specialty. Bred and owned at Pocono by Elizabeth D. Whelen.

The handsome Ch. Tailor Made of Pocono, by Ch. Merry Meddler of Pocono, C.D.X., from Ch. Larkspur of Pocono. This was one of Larkspur's many fine children who sired a number of excellent dogs that were sold to various parts of the country. Tailor Made himself was eventually sold to new owners in British Columbia. Bred and originally owned by Elizabeth D. (Betty) Whelen, Pocono Kennels.

would one day become the top champion-producing bitch in Sheltie history, she sold both blue males while they were going through the "teen-age stage" we are accustomed to think of as "the uglies." The bitches she kept, later selling them to other breeders. One became Phantasy of Pocono, who is behind Champion E-Danha Just My Bill. Larkspur went on to have one good litter after another until her total number of champions reached the astounding number of sixteen. Once more quoting Betty,

> The interesting thing about Larkspur's children was that every year, from the time Pollyanna went Winners from the Novice Class there, one of her offspring won one, and sometimes two, of the top awards in Shelties at Westminster. Larkspur's Finalist did it in 1950 while still a puppy, making it ten years in a row. I always entered them in the Novice Class, and most times they were under a year old.

Champion Tailor Made of Pocono was one of Larkspur's sons who sired many nice children who went to different places all over the country. He was later sold to fanciers in British Columbia.

In 1938, Betty Whelen acquired Penstemon of Beech Tree, who had been sold as a puppy, back from Ruth Taynton. She was by Gray Mist ex Jonquil of Pocono, and Betty bred her to Merry Meddler and then shipped her to the Bil-Bo-Dot Kennels in California. From the nice litter which resulted, Mr. McLaughlin (owner of Bil-Bo-Dot Shelties) kept three blue males and a blue female, which he showed to eleven points before she suddenly died. Two of the males were purchased by Betty at four months of age, one of which became Blue Banner of Pocono, C.D.

Mr. McLaughlin wanted to concentrate on his sable line at Bil-Bo-Dot, so Betty bought back Penstemon from him, along with the other male puppy from her litter which she named Bil-Bo-Dot Blue Flag of Pocono. This dog completed his title with ease and became one of the breed's top blue sires.

As time went on, Betty Whelen acquired some other dogs to use in her breeding program. Sunny Girl of Anahassitt and Lady Diana of Rowcliffe were two of these, both producing outstanding progeny. Lady Diana bred to Gray Mist became the dam of Champion Pocono Blue Thistle of Noralee before going to Peggy Thomforde's kennel. After that she was bred to Blue

Above: Ch. Penstemon of Beech Tree, the fourth blue-merle American-bred Shetland Sheepdog to become a champion. Elizabeth D. Whelen, owner; Pocono Kennels. **Below:** The top blue sire up until 1982, with fourteen champions to his credit, Ch. Bil-Bo-Dot Blue Flag of Pocono, by Ch. Merry Meddler of Pocono, C.D.X., from Ch. Penstemon of Beech Tree, C.D. Elizabeth D. (Betty) Whelen, owner.

Flag which gave her three of her six champion offspring. Sunny Girl was bred to Merrymaker by whom she produced well, including Champion Victory of Pocono who finished before she was eight months old and then grew to be 16½ inches. Bred to Temptation, Sunny Girl produced Champion Wayfarer of Pocono, sire of eight champions including the foundation bitch of Elaine Samuels' Karelane Kennels, the sable bitch Champion Wayfarer's Girl of Pocono.

Dempsey's Blue Bill was also acquired; he was by the Blue Flag son Champion Laurelridge Fuzzy Wuzzy out of Blue Flag's daughter, Blue Feather of Pocono. Bill swept through to his championship in 1945 and also sired Champion Blue Silhouette of Pocono from Champion Blue Treasure of Pocono; Silhouette in her turn became the dam of three champions, one of them the three-time Best in Show winner Champion Blue Quest of Pocono. Later Bill was sold to Shelmar Kennels, leaving several good litters at Pocono.

Pocono Carefree eventually came back to Betty's, completing her title in 1946. A Merry Meddler-Larkspur daughter you recall, she became the dam of three champions, among them Champion Happy Go Lucky of Pocono and Champion Albelarm Echo of Pocono. Then there was Timberidge Truth of Pocono, who was bred to Meddler to produce the National Futurity winner, Champion Blue Iris of Pocono.

Two sable bitches were purchased by Betty from Connie Hubbard, these from the Champion Peabody Pan-Astolat Lady Harlequin litter. They were Pandora of Pocono and Merry Mischief of Pocono. The latter went oversize and was sold as a pet to a Philadelphia family who wanted to breed her; so Merrymaker was used and Betty took the pick of the litter. This became Champion Mischief Maker of Pocono and she eventually was owned by Dot Foster.

The other of the sable bitches purchased by Betty from Connie Hubbard, Pandora of Pocono, was "not a small bitch, but was very

Ch. Victory of Pocono, C.D.X., by Ch. Merrymaker of Pocono, C.D.X., from Sunny Girl of Anahassitt. Victory was the dam of four champions. Owned by Pocono Kennels, Elizabeth D. Whelen.

good in body and legs. She had good natural ears, but a rather large round eye which was, however, dark." Pandora was not just a *good* producer—she was a *great* one. Betty loaned her to Dot Foster (these two did considerable swapping back and forth with their Shelties over the years) for a litter by Champion Merrymaker of Pocono, C.D. In this litter she produced Champion Timberidge Temptress, dam of Champion Timberidge Temptation and Champion Prince George of Page's Hill, both by the beautiful Champion Kalandar Prince O'Page's Hill. Again in Betty's words,

> This Page's Hill-Pocono cross was a very successful one and is behind most of the winners today. Kalandar Prince was an extremely elegant dog of approximately 15 inches with a lovely head, ears and conformation. He and his lovely sister, Champion Lady Precious O'Page's Hill, were two of the top Shelties produced to that date, and of all the Page's Hill Shelties, Kalandar Prince was my favorite.

Betty Whelen's kennel was a busy place in those days, with demand for Pocono dogs coming from all parts of the United States. Dr. Arthur Combs, from Ohio, purchased Peabody

Ch. Blue Quest of Pocono, by Ch. Larkspur's Finalist of Pocono ex Blue Silhouette of Pocono, a three-time Best in Show winner for Elizabeth D. Whelen, Pocono Kennels.

Silver Phantasy bred to Merry Meddler, from which litter came the very famous Champion Arthea Blue Sparkler, the exquisite blue with whom he won Best of Breed more than forty times and who placed well in Working Groups. He also purchased the tricolor Champion Pocono Portia of Arthea, sired by Meddler. The Page's Hill blue line came from these dogs, and Champion Dark Mist O'Page's Hill, a granddaughter of Blue Sparkler, was a Best in Show winner.

Ch. Pocono Carefree o'Sea Isle, by Ch. Merry Meddler of Pocono C.D.X., from Ch. Larkspur of Pocono, C.D.X. She was finished by Betty Whelen in 1946 and produced Ch. Happy Go Lucky of Pocono and Ch. Albelarm Echo of Pocono among her winning progeny. Photo courtesy of Betty Whelen.

Ch. Timberidge Temptress, by Ch. Merrymaker of Pocono, C.D., with her mother, Pandora of Pocono, C.D., by Ch. Peabody Pan ex Astolat Lady Harlequin. Temptress was the dam of Ch. Timberidge Temptation and Ch. Prince George O'Page's Hill, both by the handsome Ch. Kalandar Prince O'Page's Hill. The Pocono-Page's Hill cross was highly successful and is to be found behind numerous present-day winners.

Mr. and Mrs. Haworth Hoch, of Missouri, purchased a sable puppy by Peabody Pan which they finished, she becoming Champion Hoch Haven's Tiny Pocono Patty. The Hochs also purchased Champion Blue Flame of Pocono from Betty and Champion Tiny Ebony of Walnut Hall from the Nichols.

Since there were very few shows in Georgia at that period, in 1944 Dot Foster sent Timberidge Temptation to Betty to campaign, following which Betty applied for a professional handler's license. Of this dog, Betty says,

> Temptation was without doubt the best Sheltie I had seen. He was a beautifully colored shaded golden sable with a lovely coat, sound movement, excellent neck, lovely head, eye and ears, and a great temperament. It was during that period that I bred Sunny Girl of Anahassitt to him with the resulting Champions Wayfarer of Pocono whom I kept and Gingerbread Lady of Pocono who was shown to her title by her owner, Harry Heinen of Loveland, Ohio.

Betty had a "fling" with Afghan Hounds during the early 1940's, having purchased several extremely worthy ones from Lil and Charles Wernsman of Arken fame. However, they were a great deal of work.

Betty lost her mother in 1947, a crushing blow as they had been so close and shared many good and bad times together. At this time she put her

Betty Whelen with her famous Sheltie team going Best in Show Team at Westminster on one of the four occasions they did so early in the 1940's (1940, 1941, 1942, and 1943). Dr. Samuel Milbank is the judge here. The team consisted of Timberidge Truth of Pocono, C.D.; Ch. Sea Isle Merle Legacy, C.D.; Ch. Bil-Bo-Dot Blue Flag of Pocono; and Ch. Penstemon of Beech Tree, C.D.

Ch. Night Rider of Pocono, by Ch. Merry Meddler of Pocono, C.D.X., ex Ch. Larkspur of Pocono, C.D.X. Bred by Elizabeth D. Whelen and owned and finished by Mrs. Alan Robson of Westchester, Pennsylvania.

farm up for sale and moved to a small house with about two wooded acres near Kimberton, a section of Chester County she had grown to love and where she had many friends. The smaller quarters necessitated cutting down on the number of dogs, so Betty sold or placed about half of them in good homes. Mrs. Alan Robson, of Albelarm fame, now a noted Dalmatian breeder, bought several including Champion Happy Go Lucky of Pocono (by Champion Blue Flag ex Champion Pocono Carefree of Sea Isle), Gallant of Pocono (sable male by Champion Valiant of Pocono), and Night Rider of Pocono, a tricolor son of Meddler and Larkspur. She finished the latter two, later purchasing Champion Blue Treasure of Pocono.

Many of Betty's original dogs were gone by this time. The younger ones, Champion Tailor Made of Pocono and Champion Wayfarer of Pocono, were producing very nice stock, however. Champion Valiant of Pocono and several females went to Peg Ferry of Feracres Kennels. Champion Dempsey's Blue Bill went to Claire Barnet Keyburn for her Shelmar Kennels.

171

Ch. Valiant of Pocono, by Ch. Merry Meddler of Pocono, C.D.X., ex Ch. Larkspur of Pocono, C.D.X. Bred and owned by Elizabeth D. Whelen, Pocono Kennels.

Betty had, and kept, a very nice blue bitch by Blue Bill from Champion Blue Legacy of Pocono who, due to the war and for various other reasons, was not seriously campaigned. She was bred to Champion Finalist and thus became the dam of the noted Best in Show Champion Blue Quest of Pocono and Surprise Package of Pocono, both familiar to students of tricolor and blue-merle pedigrees.

The lovely bitch Blue Mist of Pocono II, by Champion Blue Storm of Pocono, had been winning well when an occurrence similar to what had happened to Larkspur (being unintentionally frightened by a judge) completely ruined her for future shows, making it impossible for her to finish. Betty bred her to Champion Wayfarer of Pocono ("I really don't know why, except that he would correct certain faults. He never sired anything but sables; but I suppose I thought that I might get a tri-factored sable that would have the head quality I was looking for in the blues"), with the resulting litter of five all sable merles. All were sold as pets excepting one which was very pretty with very dark eyes which Betty gave to her aunt and cousin and then did not see again until she was around eight to ten months old. What a pleasant surprise, as Betty found her then to be "the most beautifully colored sable. None of the merling showed, and she was a brilliant orange color with black tipped hairs around her ruff, head, tail, and down her back. She could have finished easily but her ears were incurably pricked, and they had not made an effort to correct them as she grew up." This bitch

was bred to Champion Tailor Made of Pocono, producing two sable males (one normal colored and one sable-merle), a tricolor, and a very lovely blue male. Betty kept the blue male, named Blue Legacy of Pocono. "He developed into a very beautiful Sheltie that carried a simply gorgeous profuse silver blue coat with correct texture. He was such a picture in full bloom!" Blue Legacy was a winner from the moment he entered the show ring and almost a champion when sold to Louis Carrico of Texas, by whom he was finished. He became an important dog in future generations of Carrico Shelties.

Ch. Blue Legacy of Pocono, by Ch. Tailor Made of Pocono. Bred and originally owned by Elizabeth D. Whelen; later owned and finished by Louis Carrico.

Several Shelties were sold to Mrs. Natalie Reeves at Huntington Valley, Pennsylvania, who bred a number of good ones from these dogs.

Fortune's Favorite of Pocono was purchased by Mrs. Willard Denton, for whom Betty finished him. He became the sire of Champion Fortune's Flower of Pocono and Champion Fortune's Fancy of Pocono, plus other winners. Flower was the dam of Mrs. Denton's highly successful winner, Champion Carrico's Port of Entry, sired by Champion Blue Storm of Pocono.

Larkspur produced her last litter in 1949, just before Betty decided that keeping her own place was too much for her alone and moved in with her recently widowed long-time friend and neighbor Esther Graham. In this litter Larkspur produced a blue male puppy that after many misfortunes, and Betty several times giving up all hope of raising him, started to come into his own. He was named Larkspur's Finalist of

Ch. Carrico's Port of Entry, by Ch. Blue Storm of Pocono ex Fortunes Flower of Pocono, winning the Working Group at Chester Valley Kennel Club in 1955. Elizabeth D. Whelen handled for Ardencaple Kennels, Mr. and Mrs. Willard K. Denton.

Pocono and, entered at Westminster that year, pleased his owner enormously in what had become the Pocono tradition at this show by going from the Novice Class to a five-point major. He quickly completed his championship, thus becoming Larkspur's sixteenth offspring to gain the title! Finalist sired nine champions, having the ability to produce excellent offspring in each of his litters. Unfortunately, he died at only age seven. Who knows how great his stud record might have become?

In 1950, Betty Whelen saw and loved a three-month-old puppy belonging to Toby Ain which she bought. This one became Champion Shelt-E-Ain Reflection O'Knight, and eventually Mrs. Alan Robson bought him, leaving him with Betty to be shown. He was by Champion Shelt-E-Ain Black Knight ex Shelt-E-Ain Lucky Penny, and he proved very dominant behind the blue line of Shelties. Betty also acquired a really nice blue female puppy from Mae Freeman, sired by Champion Larkspur's Finalist of Pocono out of Katie-J's Blue Dawn of Pocono, who was Winners Bitch at Westminster the same year that Blue Legacy took Winners Dog. The Millers, of Pixie Dell, were looking for a blue, so they bought her when she had finished. She became the dam of Champion Pixie Dell Royal Blue who in turn sired several splendid blue champions for Marie and Ray Miller. Royal Blue's sire was Champion Dark Stream O'Page's Hill,

"a beautiful headed dog out of Champion Dark Miss O'Page's Hill. As Blue Dawn's dam was sired by the Millers' Champion Cock 'O The North O'Page's Hill, her breeding fit in well with their line."

Betty found herself missing having her own home, where she could have dogs with her as house pets as well as in the kennel, and so she looked for and again found a house to buy, near Kimberton in the middle of the hunt country. This was in 1954.

A very good tricolor bitch, Carolynann's Pixie, by Champion Tailor Made of Pocono, was bred to Finalist producing three puppies, blue-merles, one of which Betty took as the "stud-fee puppy," at the same time purchasing the other two. The stud-fee puppy was sold to Mr. and Mrs. Reed in New Jersey and handled by Betty to become, quite easily, Champion Little Blue Pearl of Pocono. Another of the puppies she kept for herself, naming her Larkspur's Replica of Pocono; she finished with three five-point majors and then was sold to the Art Alexanders of Ohio. Kiloren Kennels later acquired her. Although she did not finish she did gain eleven points, and both she and Replica are behind the Kiloren blue and tricolor lines. Later, Betty bought their dam and bred her to her grandson, Champion Blue Heritage of Pocono. She had three tricolor bitches and one blue bitch. One of the tricolors was Black Sprite of Pocono, the dam of Champion Black Knight of Pocono and Champion Golden Sprite of Pocono II, both to be found in many pedigrees of the best Shelties in the Texas, Colorado, and Midwest areas.

Ch. Katie-J's Blue Dawn of Pocono, by Ch. Larkspur's Finalist of Pocono, an important factor behind the blue line at Pixie Dell Kennels, to whom she was sold by Betty Whelen.

Larkspur's Replica was born in March 1955, was sold to fanciers in Texas, but was handled by Betty at Westminster in 1956. As they did not seem too happy with her, Betty bought her back, sending the people in Texas a male who became Champion Blue Heirloom of Pocono. Again things had worked out to Betty's advantage, as Replica won three five-point majors in March and April to finish her title and then made a record as a producer second only to that of her grandmother, Larkspur.

In June 1955, Betty bred Blue Silhouette of Pocono to Finalist. In the resulting litter was a fabulous male puppy, obviously destined for greatness. The Reeds, owners of Little Blue Pearl of Pocono, saw him and then gave Betty no peace until she had agreed to sell him to them. This was the great Best in Show dog, Champion Blue Quest of Pocono, a fantastic winner and a superb stud dog.

Betty lost Finalist following her return from the 1956 Westminster show where there had been so much sickness among the dogs. "His passing was a great loss, as he was Larkspur's last son and my constant companion, and a top sire with nine champions. I have always felt that he was the last of the true line of beautiful Pocono blues and tricolors. I was now left without a top blue male."

Having been showing Ken Sta Quixote Lad for the Staples in Indiana, Betty bred Replica to this very handsome tricolor before his returning home. This produced The Lone Ranger of Pocono, a good tricolor male whom Betty had intended to keep. But when Fran Phillips, who became Fran May, called to see Betty's dogs, that was the one she wanted, so Betty was persuaded to let him go. He adjusted well to his new home, finished his title, and in one year was the leading sire for his new owner.

Shelt-E-Ain Reflection O'Knight was still with Betty and owned again by her as Mrs. Robson had given up her Shelties and he was a gift, then, from her to Betty. Replica produced an outstanding litter by him. One of the puppies, sold at an early age, became Champion Blue Blend of Pocono. Betty kept the remaining blue male and named him Blue Heritage of Pocono. He went Winners Dog at Westminster for five points as a puppy, following with another major at Northern New Jersey. Then he took a back seat while Betty finished Tiny Tag of Walnut Hall for the Nichols, after which he returned to competition, again at Westminster, where he

Ch. Blue Heritage of Pocono, by Ch. Sheltie-E-Ain Reflection O'Knight ex Ch. Larkspur's Replica of Pocono, the sire of ten champions. Elizabeth D. Whelen, Pocono Kennels.

completed his title with his third five-point major. His younger brother, Blue Echo of Pocono from a repeat breeding of their parents, went from Puppy Class to Reserve Winners that same day.

Karelane Fair Lady of Pocono, sold by Betty to Elaine Samuels, produced three very noteworthy winners and producers by Heritage: Champion Heir Apparant of Karelane, Champion Northwood Regent of Karelane, and Champion Northwood Heiress of Karelane. Heritage also sired Champion Tiny Toby of Walnut Hall, a very successful sire in his own right. Heritage sired ten champions, definitely leaving his mark on the breed!

In 1956, Mr. John Lafore needed to relocate his Collies and approached Betty regarding placing them in her care. An agreement was reached, additional property next to Betty's purchased by the Lafores, and the Chantwood Collies had a new kennel built and moved in. Betty handled the Collies for the Lafores (who at the same time, through her Kees which she had acquired from Mrs. Petersen, developed an interest in that breed, too) and also continued her own activity with the Shelties—quite an enormous undertaking!

After a particularly stormy winter, with all the hardships that are inherent where there are dogs and kennels involved, Betty began suffering with a severe case of fallen arches which necessitated that she discontinue caring for the Lafores' dogs and cut back on her own. She sold most of her good young dogs to people wanting to start with the Pocono line. A number of them went to Stephanie Kennedy in Texas, including Champion Black Night of Pocono whom she purchased as a young puppy. She also bought Champion Golden Sprite of Pocono II, a half-sister to Black Night and sired by Champion Browne Acres Statesman. Faharaby Blue Babe of Pocono, by Heritage from Tiny Leatha of Walnut Hall, was sold to the Chappels in North Carolina, where she became the foundation of their blues and tricolors, producing many champions and winners.

It was in 1962 that Betty purchased a young sable dog, Browne Acres Statesman, from Browne Acres Kennels in Texas, having been looking for a sable male. Of the many good Shelties he sired, the most notable was Champion Tiny Honey of Walnut Hall, an outstanding winner who finished with ease and then had a splendid career in Specials. Betty had bred Tiny Bly of Walnut Hall to Statesman while she was showing her, and Betty kept and raised

Ch. Browne Acres Statesman, bought as a puppy and finished by Betty Whelen of Pocono. He sired several champions and went back in his pedigree to Ch. Syncopating Sue of Anahassitt and to Gray Mist of Pocono. His daughter, Ch. Tiny Honey of Walnut Hall, owned by the W.H. Nichols, was a popular winner in the 1950's and 1960's.

Ch. Tiny Honey of Walnut Hall, by Ch. Browne Acres Statesman ex Tiny Bly of Walnut Hall, winning Best of Opposite Sex at Westminster, 1965. Handled by Betty Whelen for Mr. and Mrs. Willis H. Nichols of the famed Walnut Hall Shelties.

Honey, from this litter, for the Nichols. Bred to Champion Tiny Tuck of Walnut Hall, she produced Champion Tiny Vicky and Champion Tiny Rip of Walnut Hall.

When Nate Levine stopped handling, Betty showed Pixie Dell dogs for the Millers for awhile. In 1968, she flew to California to judge the Shetland Sheepdog Club of Southern California Specialty (she had judged the Northern California Specialty three years earlier), during the period when handlers were permitted and extremely popular as judges of important Specialties. While there she saw O'Melron Blue Sabre, "one of the most beautiful blues I had seen in a long time," who reminded her of Larkspur. Of course she had to bring him East with her, which she finally persuaded owner Lila McGuire was the thing to do. He was admired here for his quality but not for his lack of showmanship, until one fine day, at the Interstate Specialty in May 1970 to be exact, he suddenly decided that the shows were not all *that* bad, and, doing a fairly creditable job, he took Best of Winners. Another major and two points followed, bringing his total to seven and both his majors when he started dropping coat and never did finish—a disappointment, I am sure, to all concerned. He sired two nice champions for Betty, though: Black Sabre and Piercrest Blue Hope of Pocono.

Until 1975, when Betty gave up her handling license, she continued to show a number of the

Walnut Hall dogs for Mrs. Nichols. These included Champions Tiny Toby and Tiny Honey, plus Honey's daughters Tiny Vicky and Tiny Wendy of Walnut Hall, and her son Tiny Rip of Walnut Hall. Vicky and Rip eventually completed their titles. All of these were sired by Champion Tiny Tuck of Walnut Hall who was by Champion Lingard Sealect Bruce out of a Tiny Toby daughter.

Betty Whelen left her beloved Pennsylvania in 1969, to go to live with her niece and nephew who had purchased a beautiful home near Medina, Ohio, where there was a nice cottage for her behind the main house; one end of the garage was prepared to house the dogs. The old Pocono line of Shelties was now virtually nonexistent, and Betty was regretting having neglected it while her interest in horses had increased. She

bought back Black Sabre of Pocono, but since she was still showing dogs for Mrs. Nichols, Black Sabre had to remain at home while Tiny Thomas of Walnut Hall took preference. Sabre was siring very nice puppies, and Betty had purchased Starhaven Snow Leopard which she bred to him and which produced a litter of six. In 1974, she decided it was useless to try to show dogs of her own while handling for others, so she sold Black Sabre to Jeanne Roland in Iowa, who managed to get a few more points on him.

While attending a party following the 1974 Cleveland Specialty, Betty struck up a "mutual admiration fest" with a tiny blue-merle whom she describes as "the image of Finalist as a puppy." When she asked Patty Kazar if she could buy the puppy, Patty made her a gift of him. He is Rallyround Reward of Pocono, a source of

Rallyround Reward of Pocono, 14″, by Ch. Banchory Color Me Blue ex Banchory Blue Delight. This was the first Sheltie Betty Whelen acquired in 1974 when she started serious breeding again, trying to get the good qualities of the old Pocono line. Now nine years old (in 1983), he is Betty's beloved companion and has sired many winners for her. Pocono Kennels, Albuquerque, New Mexico.

Betty Whelen in 1975 with a group of the old Pocono-line Shelties and her beloved "Cricket," Sho-om Bay Bruk, an Arabian gelding.

Ch. Banchory Blue Mist of Pocono, by Ch. Sundowner Mr. Bojangles ex Horizon White Ice, Betty Whelen's first champion after trying to get back the old Pocono line. Larry Downey is the judge.

tremendous pleasure due to his resemblance in both looks and temperament to the old Poconos! He is a son of Champion Banchory Color Me Blue, C.D., ex Banchory A Blue Delight.

Upon giving up her handler's license in 1975, Betty's next move was to apply for judging approval; and in June 1976, she began her career as a judge. She also started to entertain thoughts of again starting up the Pocono line. At the American Shetland Sheepdog Association National in 1975, Rivendell Ransom caught Betty's eye and she purchased him from Carol Leach. That same spring Betty also leased a bitch, of E-Danha and Babinette breeding, from Marybeth Gollon of Illinois. A tricolor, she went back to Champion The Lone Ranger of Pocono, and the E-Danha line has Victory and Larkspur behind it. This bitch was bred to Rallyround Reward of Pocono, producing four blues and two tricolors. Betty kept the blue female, who placed second in an enormous class of puppy bitches at the Northern California Specialty the day after the National in 1976. This bitch was later bred to Ransom.

At this point, Betty comments:

> Because I was impressed with Reward and Ransom and their resemblance to my old Pocono blues in temperament and in type, I decid-

Ch. Harvest Hills Ribbon 'n Lace, by Ch. Banchory Deep Purple ex Harvest Hills Twilight Tear, from a litter of four, all of which became champions. Elizabeth D. Whelen, now of Albuquerque, New Mexico, owner.

Northwest and the National Specialties. It was a marvelous experience, for I still become excited at seeing all the famous dogs one reads about, plus the young ones just starting out. I fell in love with a red gold sable male, Catomco's Rain or Shine, and gave Carol Cronin, his breeder, no peace until she let me have him. He has been a great joy to me, fits in with my little band of Shelties very nicely. He and "Speedy" (Reward) are my regular house dogs, going everywhere with me.

In June 1976, Betty's three provisional judging assignments came along—very appropriately, considering this lady's background in the breed, consisting of three Specialty Shows: the Colonial Shetland Sheepdog Club, the Denver Specialty, and the Cleveland Specialty, all within a matter of days. Betty delights in judging, "especially when I can find what I am looking for," and at those three shows she found it "wonderful to have so many good ones in each color." She adds:

> One cannot help but feel sad when now and then an older type Sheltie comes along. I will love them as long as I live, but they are gone forever so

ed to obtain additional stock of Banchory breeding. They seemed to possess the qualities I was looking for in the blues and the tricolors. I purchased Ransom's dam, Rivendell Silver Scandal, from Carol Leach in 1975 and bred her to Reward. She greatly resembles Champion Penstemon of Beech Tree, dam of Blue Flag, but with better head qualities. The result of her litter was six blue-merle puppies, all males but one.

These puppies were sold to people whom Betty hoped would give them an opportunity to fulfill their promise as future winners.

Betty next says,

> 1970 was the advent of my seventieth birthday and some rather exciting experiences for an old lady. In March, June Koranko and I left the Cleveland area during a severe snowstorm to fly out to California to attend the

Ch. Calico Lace of Pocono, by Ch. Karelane Royal Flush o'Kismet ex Ch. Harvest Hills Ribbon 'n Lace, taking Best of Breed at Plainview, Texas, over two of the top winning blue-merle Shelties in the country. Elizabeth D. (Betty) Whelen, Pocono Shetland Sheepdogs.

Banchory Passport of Pocono, by Ch. Banchory Backstop ex Banchory High Glow. Bred by Banchory; owned by Elizabeth D. (Betty) Whelen, Pocono.

far as any consistent winning is concerned. They are fast disappearing from the show ring, with their larger, expressive eyes, shorter heads, and wider backskulls, finer bone and sound little bodies. However, the standard was written with the goal of improvement, and the improvement in head qualities certainly has come about. If we could keep that and retain the soundness and keep the size down to a happy medium I think the breed will survive and progress in the right way.

In the fall of 1980, Rhea Butler telephoned Betty from New Mexico to inquire about the purchase of a Pocono blue bitch. Betty sold her one, bred to Banchory Passport of Pocono. As the puppies arrived, Betty and Rhea kept in touch by letter. Then Rhea purchased Kismet Bi Surprise of Pocono, an exciting young show bitch, and the friendship grew. Since Betty was suffering quite badly with arthritis, which had been plaguing her for several years, Rhea suggested that Betty escape the severe Ohio winter by coming to spend some time with her and her husband Bob at their home in Albuquerque, New Mexico. Betty finally decided that she would try it and, planning to return to Ohio that spring, she took off for Albuquerque in October with her dogs and many of her belongings. Betty absolutely adores New Mexico and has done so

almost from the moment she set foot there. The warm welcome she received from the Butlers—both Rhea and Bob—the pleasant life they all are enjoying, shared with her own and the Butlers' Shelties and this exciting mutual interest, has made for a delightful association, thoroughly enjoyed by all involved.

In June 1982, while I was working on this book, I received a telephone call from New Mexico from Betty Whelen. She asked if we would be able to get together sometime the following week, when she would be visiting long-time friends, Mr. and Mrs. Frothingham in Rye, New York, which is less than an hour away from me, and she would bring me photos and other material for the book. Needless to say I was thrilled! We all spent a truly memorable afternoon, talking about Shelties, reminiscing about the dog show world, and selecting Pocono photos to be included here. What a wealth of wisdom this charming lady possesses! And what a lovely person she is, with her obvious enthusiasm for all animals, her zest for life, and her devotion to the fancy! This was one of the red-letter afternoons I can recall, and the time flew so quickly it seemed only to have been a few moments. I hope that our paths will cross again one day soon, for she is definitely a person to command both liking and respect.

Kismet Bi Surprise of Pocono, by the Best in Show winning Ch. Karelane Royal Flush of Kismet (thirty-three Bests in Show) ex Ch. Harvest Hill's Ribbon 'n Lace, with eleven points including both majors in July 1983. Bi Surprise is from a litter of four, all of which have become champions. Bred by Elizabeth D. Whelen; owned by Rhea J. Butler, Albuquerque, New Mexico.

Rickgarbob

Rickgarbob Shetland Sheepdogs are owned by Bob Carlough and Mrs. Marie Carlough at Blue Point, New York. The story here starts not with a Sheltie but with a German Shepherd Dog back in 1968 when Bob Carlough's dad brought home a German Shepherd Dog for an anniversary gift for Bob's mom, Marie Carlough. Little did they anticipate at the time that this bitch puppy was going to launch them right into the middle of the Dog Fancy!

The first step was to select a kennel name, which they did by combining the names of Bob and his two younger brothers, Rick and Gary, coming up with Rickgarbob. The German Shepherd was named Rickgarbob's Heidi Girl, and she had the Carloughs involved in obedience in no time flat. Once Heidi had received her C.D.X., she had to be retired as her hips became very weak, to the point that her owners feared further jumping involved in obedience work would become harmful to her.

It was along about this time, in 1970 , that the Carloughs purchased their first Sheltie. Rickgarbob Robert Bruce, whom Bob Carlough took through to a C.D.X. degree as they had done with the Shepherd. "Ro," as he was called, was not very correct as far as the breed standard went, which the Carloughs discovered by entering him in conformation classes, losing, and trying to analyze the reasons. By reading the stan-

Left and above: Ch. Rickgarbob Jonathan, by Ch. Gerthstone's Jon Christopher ex Rickgarbob Lotsa Luck. Jonathan won all of his points from the Bred-by-Exhibitor Class; and in the photo above, he is receiving one of his back to back majors at about fourteen months old. Owned by Bob Carlough and Mrs. Marie Carlough, Blue Point, New York.

dard and discussing it with breeders and successful handlers, they were able to gain a clearer picture and more knowledge of the breed.

The next purchase turned out to be the Carloughs' foundation bitch, Rickgarbob's Pumpkin Promise, C.D.X. "Cory," as she is affectionately called, will be twelve years old in September 1983, and she is the one on whom Bob Carlough really learned the art of showing dogs. The two of them were in obedience, the conformation ring, and also Junior Showmanship. Cory still lacks one major for her championship, like many others, having tons of major Reserves. She is an inbred Champion Halstor's

Rickgarbob Pumpkin Promise, C.D.X., by Ch. Halstor's Peter Pumpkin ex Cherryglen Shady Lady, C.D., the foundation bitch belonging to Rickgarbob Shelties, Bob Carlough and Mrs. Marie Carlough.

Above: Ch. Halstor's Peter Pumpkin, the sire of Rickgarbob's Pumpkin Promise, C.D.X. Photo courtesy of Charlotte McGowan. **Below:** Rickgarbob Katie, by Ch. Gerthstone's Jon Christopher ex Rickgarbob Lotsa Luck, pointed. She is the dam of Ch. Rickgarbob Dianamation and is another homebred from Rickgarbob Shelties, Bob Carlough and Mrs. Marie Carlough.

Peter Pumpkin daughter. The Sea Isle line is basically the line which runs through the Carloughs' entire breeding program. Cory produced just one litter of seven puppies for the Carloughs—this is it!

One of the bitches from Cory's litter was bred to Champion Gerthstone's Jon Christopher, from which a dog and a bitch were kept. The dog is Champion Rickgarbob Jonathan, who is his owners' very first homebred champion. Jonathan finished at sixteen months of age entirely from the Bred-by-Exhibitor Class, and one of his most exciting weekends was when he gained both of his majors back to back. The bitch, Rickgarbob Katie, has a few points, many Reserves, and in general is the Carloughs' "resident mother." She was bred to Champion Chenterra Thunderation and produced the Carloughs' second homebred champion, Rickgarbob Dianamation. "Diana" has the great asset of being truly "a show dog," loving every moment in the ring. She finished in just three short months with five Best of Breed wins over Specials, three majors (Best of Winners each time), and two Working Group placements from the classes. Shown through the 1979 season, she became the Top Winning Sheltie Bitch in the United States, she was Number Two on the East

Macdega Blue Note, by Ch. Chenterra Thunderation ex Banchory Blue Petal, with thirteen points. Owned by Rickgarbob Shelties, Bob Carlough and Mrs. Marie Carlough.

Coast behind her sire, Thunderation, and ended up the year overall as Number Seven.

Currently the Carloughs have in competition Macdega Blue Note, lacking just one major; Rickgarbob Genuine Risk with four points, by Blue Note ex Rickgarbob Katie; Rickgarbob Ebony and Ivory, bi-black bitch who is just starting; Stevie, by Champion Macdega The Piano Man ex Rickgarbob Katie; and Rickgarbob Jade Mist Brian, the newest six-month-old puppy dog, about to hit the point shows, by Champion Rickgarbob Jonathan ex Champion Jade Mist Windspell.

The Carloughs have now been involved in breeding and in showing for approximately fourteen years. Their kennel is small, but despite limited space and a limited breeding program they are consistently producing Shetland Sheepdogs who are a credit to the breed and to themselves.

Rickgarbob Genuine Risk, by Macdega Blue Note ex Rickgarbob Katie, pointed. The judge here is Gene Cohen. Bred and owned by Rickgarbob Shelties, Bob Carlough (handling) and Mrs. Marie Carlough, Blue Point, New York.

Ch. Rock N' Seawood The Townsman, by Ch. Valdawn's Talk Of The Town ex Meadow Ridge Rockwood It's Me. Bred by Barbara Kenealy; owned by Marjorie Tuff.

Rockwood

Rockwood Kennels (also known as Our Own Rockwood Kennels), at Ridgefield, Connecticut, came about when Barbara M. Kenealy bought her first Sheltie from Dona Hausman's Meadow Ridge Kennels in 1970. Her name was Meadow Ridge Rockwood It's Me, and she became the dam of three champions, all sired by Champion Valdawn's Talk of the Town, who were Champion Rock N' Seawood The Townsman, Champion Rockwoods Tattle Tales, and Champion Rockwoods Talk To Me.

Champion Rockwoods Talk To Me was bred to Champion Halstor's Peter Pumpkin, producing four champions: Champion Our Own Rockwoods Bewitched, Champion Rockwoods Sweet Charity, Champion Rockwoods Bac Talk, and Champion Rockwoods Bohemian Rhapsody. "Mi Mi" was also bred to Champion Whipperwil Grand Master, this producing only one puppy, Rockwood Arista's Master Plan, who gained twelve points including one major.

A very plain but beautiful eight-week-old female puppy was bought from Shirley Bond of Shylove Kennels. She was eventually bred to Champion Rockwoods Bac Talk with very exciting results. This little bitch, Shylove Rockwood Show Off, C.D., won four points, but

Above: Ch. Rockwoods Tattle Tales, by Ch. Valdawn's Talk Of The Town ex Meadow Ridge Rockwood It's Me, in July 1976 winning under judge Bill Warhurst. Handler, Barbara Kenealy; owner, Jo Anne Pilzer. Below: Meadow Ridge Rockwood It's Me, by Ch. Sutter's Golden Masquerade (Ch. Pixie Dell Bright Vision ex Ch. Dan-Cee's Samantha) ex Meadow Ridge Starlight (Ch. Pixie Dell Bright Vision ex Meadow Ridge Venus). It's Me, Barbara Kenealy's foundation bitch, was the dam of three champions.

Above: Ch. Rockwoods Talk To Me, by Ch. Valdawn's Talk of the Town ex Meadow Ridge Rockwood It's Me, the dam of four champions. Bred and owned by Barbara M. Kenealy. **Below:** Ch. Rockwoods Sweet Charity. Bred, owned, and handled by Barbara M. Kenealy, Rockwood Kennels.

Ch. Rockwood Prin Du Misty Blue, by Ch. Rockwoods Nite Enchantment ex Carmylie Gentian Blue Fringe. Bred by Howard G. and Rosalie Wirkus; owned by Barbara Kenealy.

Ch. Our Own Rockwoods Bewitched, by Ch. Halstor's Peter Pumpkin ex Ch. Rockwood Talk To Me, a full sister to Ch. Rockwoods Bac Talk and Ch. Rockwoods Sweet Charity. Bewitched is shown here winning Best of Breed at St. Hubert's, July 1976, under judge Mrs. Peggy Adamson. Bred and owned by Barbara and Robert Kenealy, Ridgefield, Connecticut.

most of all she became the dam of five champions: Champion Rockwoods Nite Enchantment, C.D., Champion Rockwood Repeat Performance, Champion Rockwood Sylvan Seafarin' Man, Champion Alician Rockwood Talk Bac, and Champion Mirluc Full of the Devil.

Champion Rockwoods Bac Talk sired six champions to date, while his son, Champion Rockwood Nite Enchantment, C.D., belonging to Barbara Kenealy, has six who are finished with several more only a few points short of their titles. The former include Champion Rockwood Prin Du Misty Blue (Kenealy), Champion Mirluc Starry Nite, C.D. (Ieronimo and Edelheit), Champion Sylvans Snowfrost (Gunzel), Champion Sherwyn's Chasing The Blues (Picherd), Champion Sylvan Rockwood Silversmith (Lexington), and, pending A.K.C. confirmation, Champion Milbrook Macalester Lad (Olson).

Currently (summer of 1983), Barbara Kenealy has some half dozen other Shelties busily making names, and titles, for themselves. These include the brothers, Rockwood Keepsake and Rockwood Kintyre Rymin' Simon. Keepsake was first in the 12-18 Month Futurity Class at the American Shetland Sheepdog Association and took a major Reserve at Harrisburg Kennel Club; Simon has ten points including both majors.

Then there is Rockwoods Prin Du Midnite Hour with four points, and Rockwoods Gold Strike with twelve points in three majors.

Two of the Rockwood Shelties are Best of Breed winners in Specialty Shows: Rockwoods Prin Du Misty Blue at the Northern New Jersey Shetland Sheepdog Club and Champion Rockwood Repeat Performance at the Tri-State Shetland Sheepdog Specialty.

Above: Rockwoods Gold Strike, by Ch. Rorralore Sportin' Chance, C.D., ex Ch. Rockwoods Sweet Charity, with twelve points in three majors in August 1983. Bred and owned by Barbara M. Kenealy, Our Own Rockwood Kennels. **Below:** Ch. Sylvan Rockwood Silversmith, by Ch. Rockwoods Nite Enchantment ex Sylvan Blue Mist. Bred by Lynn Gunzel; handled by Barbara M. Kenealy; owned by Susan and Harlan Leckington.

Above: Ch. Rockwoods Bohemian Rhapsody, by Ch. Halstor's Peter Pumpkin ex Ch. Rockwoods Talk To Me. Breeder, Barbara M. Kenealy; owner, Jo Anne Pilzer. **Below:** Ch. Alician Rockwood Talk Bac, by Ch. Rockwoods Bac Talk ex Shylove Rockwood Show Off, C.D. Bred by Barbara M. Kenealy and owned by Alice Kurlburg.

Rorralore

Rorralore Shetland Sheepdogs, at Newton, Massachusetts, belong to Charlotte Clem McGowan who, in her own words, "grew up as a tomboy favoring all kinds of animals from frogs, turtles, snakes, rabbits and even a pet skunk to the more accepted toys associated with little girls." When she won tickets to the Eastern Dog Club Show, in a contest in 1956 at age eleven, it was the beginning of a long and continuing love affair with dog shows and dog breeding.

The first Rorralore Sheltie, Rip Rorry, mainly contributed his name to make the kennel name. After a series of less than successful dogs, Charlotte purchased American and Canadian Champion Rorralore Robert the Bruce from Blanche and Kenneth Poole of Hatfield as a puppy. Bruce was not only a champion but was also Charlotte's Junior Showmanship dog, and they went to Westminster together having qualified for the Junior Showmanship competition there.

The real foundation for Rorralore Shelties came from two bitches purchased from the Pooles. Rorralore Renata, a daughter of the Champion Nashcrest Golden Note son, Champion Sea Isle Serenade, from the Note daughter Champion Stylish Miss of Hatfield, heads one main branch of Rorralore Shelties. Renata was inbred to Serenade, producing the very sound

Can. Ch. Rorralore Maurya, by Ch. Sea Isle Serenade ex Rorralore Renata. Bred and owned by Charlotte Clem McGowan, Rorralore Kennels, Newton, Massachusetts. Maurya's daughter, Rorralore Pegeen O'Pine Knoll, is one of the two foundation bitches of the Beltane Kennel.

Ch. Hatfield's Stardust, by Ch. Nashcrest Golden Note ex Ch. Bonnie Lass of Hatfield (dam of four champions), the foundation bitch at Rorralore. She was Best in Show at Riverhead Kennel Club in 1966, judged by Mrs. Leonard W. Bonney, making her only the sixth bitch in Sheltie history to attain this honor. Bred by Blanche Poole and owned by Charlotte Clem McGowan.

Ch. Rorralore Curst Kate in July 1965. Photo courtesy of Lee Reasin.

and elegant Canadian Champion Rorralore Maurya. This handsome bitch appears in many important pedigrees today through her daughters Champion Rorralore Sma' Primsie, Rorralore Royale of Swizaine (back of many Ilemist and Someday Shelties), and Rorralore Pegeen of Pine Knoll (one of the foundation bitches at Beltane). Renata was also the dam of Champion Beltane Solitaire who produced a number of champions for the Currys.

Champion Hatfield's Stardust, purchased from Blanche Poole as a four-year-old champion, set Rorralore on the real path to glory. In Charlotte's hands, Stardust blossomed and became one of the top winning bitches in the breed. She was just the sixth Sheltie bitch to win an all-breed Best in Show when she did so at Riverhead Kennel Club in 1966. From about twenty-five times in the ring with Charlotte handling, "Star" compiled a record of nineteen Bests of Breed and eight Group placements including three firsts. Stardust was a structurally outstanding Sheltie with beautiful balance, a very feminine appearance, lovely eye and expression, and outstanding character and intelligence. She also loved shows, totally tuned into Charlotte in the ring. From her have come many

Ch. Rorralore Mickey Dazzler, by Ch. Willow Acres Golden Note ex Ch. Rorralore Curst Kate, the sire of nine champions who through his daughters is grandsire of many outstanding champions including the current star Ch. Rorralore Sportin' Chance, C.D. Charlotte Clem McGowan, Rorralore Kennels.

outstanding Shelties, which was really no surprise since she was by the great Champion Nashcrest Golden Note from the Kiltie daughter, Champion Bonnie Lass of Hatfield. Stardust's daughter, Champion Rorralore Curst Kate, was the first homebred Rorralore champion, and she heads a line of outstanding sons and daughters. Kate was by Champion Rorralore Robert the Bruce and thus tightly line-bred on the Note-Bonnie Lass combination. Bred to the double Note grandson, Canadian Champion Willow Acres Golden Encore, Kate produced the justly famous "brood bitch sire," Champion Rorralore Mickey Dazzler. Mickey was never enamored of dog shows, but he was a beautifully balanced, typey, highly intelligent dog. He was noted for his standard-correct head with beautiful muzzle, eye and expression; a lean, clean skull; and moderate proportions. Mickey sired nine champions, but his greatest contribution was as the sire of outstanding brood bitches, who reproduced so many of his excellent qualities.

Kate was also the dam of Champion Rorralore Zodiac, C.D.X. "Gordon" is alive and well at this writing and is approaching his seventeenth birthday; like many of the Rorralore Shelties, he has enjoyed a very long life and lasting quality. "Gordon" was a double Specialty winner during his show career and sired five champions. He

Ch. Mistimoor Stonehenge, bred by Jill and Tap Holt, at sixteen months of age. Charlotte McGowan discovered this handsome son of Ch. Beltane Druid's Disciple ex Ch. Kiloren Sugarplum when judging at a Florida Specialty, where she awarded him Reserve Winners Dog and then purchased him. Later she sold him to Ken and Ann Flessas who won a Best in Show with him.

Ch. Thistlerose Glittering Gem, by Ch. Halstor's Peter Pumpkin ex Thistlerose Torchsong, dam of Ch. Rorralore Diamond Dust.

Ch. Rorralore Diamond Dust, by Ch. Brigadoon Merri Lou I'm Ready. Bred by Charlotte Clem McGowan; owned by Elizabeth Hall, Checkerchance Kennels.

carries forward in a number of the Lobo Dell dogs and via his daughter, Champion Rorralore Rosmarin O'Swizaine, who went to Julie Maust's Ilemist Kennels. "Gordon" is a double Note grandson, by the beautiful Champion Katie-J's Ronnie. Curst Kate was also bred to Champion Shu La Le Royal Orleanian, grandson of the two inbred Note brothers Champion Sea Isle Serenade and Champion Sea Isle Cadenza. From this litter came Champion Rorralore Anne Boleyn, Best of Winners at the Colonial Specialty under English authority Mary Davis. Anne Boleyn, bred to Champion Brigadoon Merri Lou I'm Ready, produced the noted Group-winner Champion Rorralore Star Echo, an amazing accomplishment in Shelties as this was the fifth consecutive generation of female champions. In a breed which does not breed true, Charlotte points out, this is most unusual. Star Echo already has a champion son and will, it is hoped, have more before her career is over.

Rorralore also has acquired a number of outstanding Shelties in addition to the two foundation bitches. Among those who have resided with Charlotte are American, Canadian, and Bermudian Champion Sea Isle Rhapsody of Halstor, co-owned with Edith Overly, the dam of Champion Halstor's Peter Pumpkin and grandam of Champion Rorralore Play Fair; Champion Thistlerose Glittering Gem (dam of Champion Rorralore Diamond Dust); Champion Ilakai's Mi Lady Ambassador (grandam of the 1981 American Shetland Sheepdog Association National Winners Bitch, Champion Rorralore Rejoice); and Jeanie of Mary Dell, who is a Mickey Dazzler daughter from Beech Tree Cindy of Mary Dell, dam of the gorgeous Champion Colleen of Mary Dell, also acquired by Charlotte.

Jeanie was placed for awhile in co-ownership with Nancy Boomhower for two litters. Because Jeanie was a "substantial, extraordinarily sound bitch with a long neck and beautiful skull," again quoting Charlotte, "she was paired with the outstanding small, tightly bred Champion Romayne's Sportin' Life." From this litter came one American champion and two Canadian champions. Charlotte sold Champion Rorralore Sportin' Chance, C.D., initially to Bill and Helen Wadsworth but co-owned him to pilot him to his championship. He made a record as the first Sheltie in breed history to complete his title in three consecutive shows, all five-point major Best of Winners awards at Specialties!

These were Northern New Jersey under Marilyn Schultz, Colonial under Barbara Curry, and the 1979 National of the American Shetland Sheepdog Association under Mary Van Wagenen.

Chance was re-purchased by Charlotte in the fall of 1981, and he has amassed a spectacular show record with fourteen Specialty Show Bests of Breed, Best in Show all-breeds, seventy-five Bests of Breed, and thirty Group placements including eight firsts. He has also proven to be an outstanding stud dog with five champions to his credit through 1983 and many more to come. Chance is a very moderate dog with a truly

Above: Ch. Rorralore Rosmarin O'Swizain, from Rorralore Royale of Swizaine, a Specialty winner. Bred by Bob and Nancy Paine; owned by Charlotte Clem McGowan and later by Julie Desy Moust. **Below:** Ch. Rorralore Anne Boleyn. Breeder-owner, Charlotte Clem McGowan.

Ch. Colleen of Mary Dell, by Ch. Halstor's Peter Pumpkin ex Beech Tree's Cindy of Mary Dell. Bred by Peter Devaney; owned by Charlotte Clem McGowan, Rorralore Kennels.

melting expression in a perfectly balanced head. He is a strong, sound mover and exemplifies correct breed type.

Charlotte, like Mary Van Wagenen, became fascinated with records on the breed. She has an extensive card file with the producing records of Shelties from the first champions in this country and has thousands of photos of Shelties. She has lectured to many clubs and judges groups with her slide program on Sheltie type. Charlotte served on the American Shetland Sheepdog Association Board for thirteen years and was the founder and first President of the Colonial Shetland Sheepdog Club in Massachusetts. She is also a highly successful breeder of Dandie Dinmont Terriers.

After studying the Sheltie's history and standard over many years, Charlotte believes that the key to understanding the breed is a full appreciation of the importance of overall balance and harmony, moderation, refinement, and correctness of detail. This must come in an individual who has real quality or the ability to attract one's eye because of virtue. Balance cannot come about without correct structure and correct type detail. Temperament has always been an important consideration, with intelligence highly valued. Charlotte has admitted to having "personality conflicts" with dogs who do not seem to be very intelligent and responsive, and so most of the Rorralore dogs have been strong characters, with more than one "alpha" in residence.

Charlotte has always been a student of breeding theories and strong emphasis has been placed on the female portion of any pedigree. A course of strict line-breeding with occasional in-breeding has been the rule at Rorralore. The original plan was to combine the best descendants of Champion Nashcrest Golden Note and Champion Sheltieland Kiltie of Sea Isle, including Champion Bonnie Lass of Hatfield. As the years have passed, that basic plan has been augmented with the idea of remaining primarily within the basic Sea Isle line framework, adding new threads only where it was not a complete outcross. The tightness of Rorralore pedigrees may account for the basic look the kennel has achieved.

Rorralore has always been a very small kennel with an average of four to eight dogs kept at any one time. The demands of Charlotte's many other interests have always made this necessary.

Charlotte has been a judge of Shelties since 1971 and has done the National twice, along with a great many regional Specialties. Currently she judges twenty-eight breeds, including most of the Herding breeds, all Working breeds and the Working Group, and Best in Show.

Ch. Rorralore Sportin' Chance, C.D., winning the Herding Group at Pioneer Valley; owner-handled by Charlotte Clem McGowan. Chance is a noted Best in Show and Specialty winner, and he went Best of Breed at Westminster in 1984.

Rosewood

Rosewood Shetland Sheepdogs were established in 1973 by Rosemary Petter of Kent, Washington, who breeds on a small scale with outstanding quality the goal.

The kennel is best known as the home of the spectacular blue-merle who holds the record of being the Top Winning Sheltie Bitch in the history of the breed. She is American and Canadian Champion Rosewood's Christy The Clown, a daughter of American and Canadian Champion Sundowner Mr. Bojangles, C.D. (Best of Breed at the American Shetland Sheepdog Association National Specialty in 1975) ex American and Canadian Champion Forever Pawthorne Blue Eclipse (Group first and Specialty winner). Handled throughout her career either by Mrs. Petter herself or her daughter Linda, Christy has won a total of seven all-breed Bests in Show, two Bests in Specialty shows, nine firsts in the Working Group, and twelve additional Group placements.

Christy was campaigned for three years as a Special (1980, 1981, and 1982), holding her position as Number One Sheltie bitch throughout this period. She retired in May 1983 with five Bests of Breed for that period, plus two firsts in the Group.

Christy's potential as a show bitch became obvious almost the moment her career began. She finished her United States title with three majors, acquiring in so doing two Best of Breed awards over two Best in Show males. In Canada it was more of the same, as she finished with four Group firsts and two Group fourths.

Retired in May 1983, Christy was bred back to her sire, Bojangles. Five puppies were the result,

Am. and Can. Ch. Rosewood's Christy The Clown, by Am. and Can. Ch. Sundowner Mr. Bojangles, C.D., ex Am. and Can. Ch. Forever Pawthorne Blue Eclipse. Christy holds the record as Number One Sheltie Bitch in the history of the breed. Seven times Best in Show (all-breeds), she has held the Number One position through 1980, 1981, and 1982, always handled by Rosemary Petter, her breeder-owner, or Rosemary's daughter, Linda Petter. Here Christy is shown taking first in Group under judge Janet Wilcox at a California show in 1983.

Four Wind's Duchess O'The Glenn, by Ch. Halstor's Peter Pumpkin ex Four Wind's Frolic, pictured at ten years of age with Brenda Petter, daughter of owner Rosemary Petter of Kent, Washington. Duchess is the foundation bitch for Rosewood Shetland Sheepdogs and is the dam of three American-Canadian champions.

but unfortunately only one was born alive. This one is full of promise, however, and is being raised at Rosewood where hopes are high for his future.

Christy has a famous littermate who has also contributed well to the breed, American and Canadian Champion Rosewood Texas Blue Horizons, who is the sire of the young Best of Breed winner, Rosewood's Mr. Hobo, whose dam is inbred American and Canadian Champion Cherden Sock It To 'Em, C.D.

Rosewood's foundation bitch in sables is Four Wind's Duchess O'The Glenn, a littermate to the American Shetland Sheepdog Association National's Winners Dog, Champion Four Wind's Baron O'The Glenn, C.D.X. She is by Champion Halstor's Peter Pumpkin ex Four Wind's Frolic (dam of three champions). Duchess bred to Champion Cherden Sock It To 'Em, C.D., produced American and Canadian Champion Rosewood Lady, American and Canadian Champion Vandell's Little Powder Keg, C.D., American and Canadian Champion Rosewood Power Pumpkin, and Rosewood Dutchess Jolene (dam of two champions).

Mrs. Petter is breeding all colors at Rosewood, working with the male lines of Champion Sundowner Mr. Bojangles, C.D., Champion Cherden Sock It To 'Em, C.D., and Champion Dorlane's King's Ransome. At present Rosewood is working on the formation of their own line, and the anticipation is that the next few years will be most exciting for them in all colors.

Ch. Faharaby Blue Larkspur, C.D., a daughter of Ch. Faharaby Replica of Don Juan ex Faharaby Blue Babe of Pocono, and Reid Tomlin in 1965. This was Rosmoor's first Sheltie, bred by Mr. and Mrs. Frank Chappell and owned by Rose and Don Tomlin.

Rosmoor

Rosmoor Shetland Sheepdogs are located in Pelham, in Westchester County, New York, and belong to Rose Tomlin and her daughter Jennie. Rosmoor's uniqueness lies in the fact that its self-imposed limit is four adult dogs, yet it has averaged over one champion each year since 1966, finishing Shelties in all three colors, almost always owner-handled. Suburban location and outside interests have resulted in this kennel remaining small, yet its owners feel that this fact has worked to their advantage since everything they keep on the premises is show quality.

Rosmoor's first Sheltie was purchased in 1964 following a search of several years. Acquired at four months of age from the Frank Chappells of Asheville, North Carolina, Champion Faharaby Blue Larkspur, C.D., won the Working Group the day she became a champion. She was out of a full sister to Champion Tiny Toby of Walnut Hall and was sired by the Chappells' prominent stud, Champion Faharaby Replica of Don Juan, who had considerable Timberidge stock behind him.

The second foundation bitch at Rosmoor was Champion Rosmoor Brae-Carel Bonnie, purchased at six weeks of age from Becky Elliott of

Brae-Carel fame. She was a sable, sired by Champion Diamond's Robert Bruce out of a Lingard bitch.

Rose Tomlin attributes Rosmoor's early success to their having been so fortunate as to acquire these two very sound, showy, outgoing bitches with which to begin and the tremendous amount of help received from other breeders, especially Beth Chappell of Faharaby. Every dog now owned by Rosmoor goes back to one, or in many cases to both, of these two original bitches. Each bitch produced a champion, and Rose feels they would have produced more had she been a more experienced breeder.

Rosmoor moved from South Carolina to New York in 1969 and won Winners Bitch that year

Above: Ch. Rosmoor Robert of Migadala, by Ch. Banchory Deep Purple ex Rosmoor Symphony of Migadala. Bred by Betty Savitch; owned by Rose and Jennie Tomlin. **Below:** Ch. Rosmoor Lark's Legacy, by Ch. Waldenwood Bonny's Blue Clyde ex Rosmoor Night Lark. Bred by Rose Tomlin and Tony Tumlin; owned by Rose and Jennie Tomlin and Elizabeth Cathcart.

Ch. Rosmoor Night Sprite, by Ch. Rosmoor Robert of Migadala ex Rosmoor Katy-Did. Bred and owned by Rose and Jennie Tomlin, Rosmoor Kennels.

at Westminster with Champion Rosmoor Raven, C.D., its first homebred champion from Larkspur's first litter. Raven and her sire, Champion Faharaby Gold King, C.D., were both finished by Rosmoor and sold to Carol Noelle of Elfenfolk Kennels.

Larkspur's last litter was sired by Champion Banchory High Born, from which a 16¼-inch bitch, Rosmoor Night Lark, was retained for breeding and co-owned with Toni Tumlin of Tuwin Shelties. Bred to Champion Waldenwood Bonny's Blue Clyde, she produced two champions in her first litter: Champion Beau Blackguard of Tuwin and Champion Rosmoor Lark's Legacy, who figures prominently in the Tomlin's breeding program.

Bred to Champion Sundowner Mr. Bojangles, Lark produced Champion Cambro Independence and Rosmoor Symphony of Migadala. Symphony, 13¼ inches, is the dam of Champion Rosmoor Robert of Migadala and Champion Migadala Deep Blue Song.

From Robert's first litter, out of Champion Rosmoor Katy-Did, a great-granddaughter of Champion Rosmoor Brae-Carel Bonnie, came two champions: Champion Rosmoor Night Sprite and Champion Rosmoor Sally Forth. When being campaigned, Robert was at one time rated in sixth place according to the *Sheltie Special* system.

Rosmoor Winter Wind O'Tuwin, C.D., dam of Ch. Carmylie Rosmoor Silvertip. Mr. and Mrs. Willard K. Denton, owners, Ardencaple Kennels.

A sister to Champion Rosmoor Lark's Legacy, Rosmoor Winter Wind O'Tuwin, C.D., produced Champion Carmylie Rosmoor Silvertip when bred to Champion Nathan Hale of Carmylie.

Champion Rosmoor Lark's Legacy whelped a litter in 1981 by Banchory Reflection which produced Rosmoor Lark's Reflection. The latter, in turn, when bred to Champion Macdega The Piano Man in 1982 produced two puppies which at this writing are pointed, one with a major. They are B'field Cryst'l Blue Persuasion and B'field Chelsea Star Born, co-bred with Nancy Butterfield.

Lark's Legacy has been bred twice to her grandson, Champion Rosmoor Robert. From the first litter, co-bred with Elizabeth Cathcart, a son, Edgelea a Summer Legacy has major points; and from the second litter, Rosmoor Living Legend, a blue puppy bitch, is Rosmoor's latest hopeful as we write.

A granddaughter of Lark's Legacy, Rosmoor Burravoe Ebb Tide, was bred to Champion Sundowner Mr. Bojangles, resulting in a blue bitch, Rosmoor Star Spangled, who should be finished

Ch. Rosmoor Honey Do with Rose Tomlin just after winning a four-point major—how sweet it is! A daughter of Ch. Carmylie Elusive Dream ex Rosmoor Inkling of Hope, Honey is he dam of the three-champion litter sired by Ch. Romayne Sportin' Life. Breeder, Joseph Marks; owners, Rose and Jennie Tomlin.

Ch. Rosmoor Sally Forth, a daughter of Ch. Rosmoor Robert of Migadala ex Ch. Rosmoor Katy-Did. Bred and owned by Rose and Jennie Tomlin, Rosmoor Shetland Sheepdogs.

Rosmoor Lark's Reflection, by Banchory Reflection ex Ch. Rosmoor Lark's Legacy, a homebred from Rosmoor Kennels owned by Rose and Jennie Tomlin.

Rosmoor Silver Sprite (left) and Ch. Carmylie Rosmoor Silvertip (right). Sprite is by Silvertip from Ch. Rosmoor Night Spirit. Silvertip is by Ch. Nathan Hale of Carmylie ex Rosmoor Winter Wind of Tuwin, C.D. Jean Simmonds owns Silvertip. Rose and Jennie Tomlin are the breeders of Silvertip and the breeder-owners of Silver Sprite.

Ch. Rosmoor Fancy That, one of three champions in a litter by Ch. Romayne Sportin' Life ex Ch. Rosmoor Honey Do. Fancy That was Winners Bitch at Westminster in 1978. Bred by Rose and Don Tomlin; owned by Rose and Jennie Tomlin.

before you are reading this and who will be the twentieth champion for Rosmoor.

Champion Rosmoor Brae-Carel Bonnie produced Champion Rosmoor Repete when bred to Champion Halstor's Peter Pumpkin, but the offspring who carries on her line for Rosmoor most successfully is Rosmoor Inkling of Hope, by Champion Diamond's Clemson Tiger. Bred to Champion Carmylie Elusive Dream she produced two champions in her first litter: Champion Rosmoor Honey Do and Champion Rosmoor's Glory Be O'Tuwin, the latter Rosmoor's second Westminster Winners Bitch.

Honey produced three champions in one litter by Champion Romayne's Sportin' Life: Champion Rosmoor's Fancy That (the Tomlins' third Westminster Winners Bitch), Champion Rosmoor Katy-Did, and Champion Rosmoor Hope of Sevenoaks.

Katy won three prestigious Eastern Specialties in a four-month period in 1977-1978: Interstate, Tri-State, and Northern New Jersey. Her two-champion first litter by kennel-mate Champion Rosmoor Robert has been previously mentioned.

Ch. Minstrel Man of Karelane, by Ch. Wandring Minstrel O'Karelane. Owned by Sam and Lois Lippincott, Rustic Kennels.

Rustic

Rustic Kennels are owned by Sam and Lois Lippincott and located at Aliquippa, Pennsylvania.

The foundation bitch here was Champion Apache Sun Dance of Karelane, acquired from Elaine Samuels, Karelane Kennels, in 1966. She produced the Lippincotts' first champion, Rustic's Red Sunset, from a litter of two, sired by Champion Rhoad's Red Domino. "Snoopy," as he was called, retired at four years of age with ten Bests of Breed and three Group placements.

Next the Lippincotts acquired Champion Minstrel Man of Karelane from Elaine Samuels. He finished his title at eighteen months of age, and when he retired he had won Best of Breed twenty times, plus a Group second. He was the sire of Champion Merridon's Chestnut Pebble and the grandsire of Champion Serenade of Rustic, winner of three Bests of Breed and a Group third.

"Sparkle," in turn, produced Champion Karelane's Chances Are, who finished at eighteen months.

Now the Lippincotts are having fun with their newest star, Little Girl Lost, presently being shown and close to the title she will certainly have completed by the time you are reading this.

Rustic is a small kennel, only breeding an occasional litter. The Lippincotts greatly enjoy their dogs and the breed, and pride themselves on *good* temperament.

Above: Ch. Apache Sun Dance of Karelane finishing championship, April 22nd 1968, Hartford County Kennel Club; judge, William L. Kendrick; handler, Elaine Stewart (Karelane Shelties). This Sheltie was the foundation bitch for Rustic Kennels, Sam and Lois Lippincott, Aliquippa, Pennsylvania. **Below:** Ch. Rustic's Red Sunset, by Ch. Rhoad's Red Domino ex Ch. Apache Sun Dance of Karelane, winning Best of Breed at Beaver County Kennel Club, August 7th 1972. Sam and Lois Lippincott, owners, Rustic Shetland Sheepdogs.

197

Sea Isle

One cannot do research for a book about Shetland Sheepdogs and come away without a feeling of tremendous admiration and respect for the Sea Isle Kennels, for the owners Mary Van Wagenen and Evelyn Davis, and for their knowledge of this breed in having perfected so outstandingly balanced, typical, sound moving, and beautiful a strain as that for which Sea Isle has earned fame over numerous generations. Their contribution to Sheltie progress year after year has been awe-inspiring indeed. The tremendous amount of credit due them for the Sheltie they have created, and its impact on former, present, and future generations of the breed, goes far beyond mere words. The two ladies responsible for Sea Isle are talented and knowledgeable and have their values well in place. As breeders they have earned a position at the very top in the annals of American dog show history.

The Sea Isle kennel prefix was registered with the American Kennel Club in 1937. Both owners, however, began their involvement with Shelties considerably earlier than that time. Evelyn Davis had grown up in Swampscott, Massachusetts, a great lover of animals from early childhood and one of the many youngsters whose interest in Collies was fostered by the Albert Payson Terhune stories with the added

Ch. Adoration, Sea Isle Kennels' sable foundation bitch. Adoration, a daughter of Ch. Merrymaker of Pocono, was bred in turn to the three Page's Hill brothers, Ch. Cock O'The North, Ch. Will O'The Mill, and Ch. Kalandar Prince. Her Cock O'The North daughter, Sea Isle Breeze O'The North, was the most important link from then to modern times in the Sea Isle line. Sea Isle Shelties, Evelyn Davis and Mary Van Wagenen, Guilford, Vermont.

impetus of a visit to his kennel, while in her teens. Attending her first dog show, Eastern at Boston in 1927, she saw a breed which evidently intrigued her even more—the Shetland Sheepdog. There she met Catherine Coleman, prominent Sheltie breeder and the first secretary of the American Shetland Sheepdog Association. Miss Coleman also lived in Massachusetts, quite close to the Davis' summer home; thus many a weekend visit was made to Miss Coleman and the Shelties. Then came the occasion when Evelyn Davis visited Anahassitt, seeing the great Wee Laird shortly after his importation. The impression he left on this young fancier was a deep one.

In 1930, Miss Davis, who had been working in Shelburne Falls, Massachusetts, left her job, moving in with her close friend Catherine Coleman. The following year another friend, a lady who was the sister of Laura Delano (a famed breeder of Irish Setters and Long-coated Dachshunds and who was the cousin of Franklin Delano Roosevelt) persuaded the girls to move to a farm which she owned in Newport, New Hampshire, which they did. They remained there nearly eight years until illness forced Miss Coleman's return to Massachusetts and it became necessary for Miss Davis to place a number of their Shelties with other breeders while she herself went to work with other friends, the Tullys, at Alwinton Kennels.

Mary Van Wagenen's mother was a breeder of Newfoundlands, but Mary grew up with a Collie as her companion. In 1932, she attended her first dog show, that of the Westminster Kennel Club, where she saw and, as Evelyn had done, fell in love with that same little dog, Wee Laird. Determined to know more about these "Collies in Miniature" she availed herself of every opportunity, which included reading many articles about Shetland Sheepdogs written by Catherine Coleman. The first Sheltie Specialty Mary Van Wagenen attended was held in conjunction with the 1934 Morris and Essex. Here she became acquainted with Catherine Coleman who told her about Parkswood Little Symphony, the first Sheltie she bought; he went to live with Miss Coleman and Miss Davis as Miss Van Wagenen could not keep a dog with her in New York City.

Little Symphony and Gray Mist of Pocono produced Mary Van Wagenen's first litter. And it was prophetic that even in this first litter she accomplished something exceptional, as one of the puppies became Champion Sea Isle Merle

Legacy who was the first American-bred blue-merle champion.

Mary Van Wagenen selected Sea Isle for a kennel name after having seen that place name listed as a destination on a railroad timetable and liked the sound of it. In 1937, along with registering the kennel name, her acquaintance among Sheltie people started to broaden, bringing lasting friendships which she has treasured through the years. Among these friends were Florence and Nate Levine, professional handlers and Sheltie specialists.

Champion Adoration was purchased by Mary Van Wagenen and Catherine Coleman from Bill Burgess for the pre-inflation price of two hundred dollars. She gained her championship that year. This was at the period when Catherine Coleman became ill, and Evelyn Davis dispersed the kennel. Over the next several years Evelyn, as we have already noted, was working with Shelties at the Tullys. Mary, meanwhile, was thinking longingly of one day living in the country and raising Shelties.

It was in 1942 that these two dedicated Sheltie fanciers formed a partnership, moving to a house which they purchased in Darien, Connecticut. Two years later they left Darien for Vermont—with the postal address of Bernardston, Massachusetts (which has now been changed to Brattleboro, Vermont, although their home is, and right from the first has been, located in Guilford, Vermont). Obviously, this has led to considerable confusion for folks trying to reach them!

We've told you about its background; now let us talk about the Sea Isle breeding ideal as we have found it to be in our historical research. Both Mary Van Wagenen and Evelyn Davis are quoted as saying that a totally balanced dog is their ideal, that the correct Sheltie is like a living work of art, and that placing an overemphasis on any single feature or area is a serious error. They consider balance to be the first consideration, without which all else is lost and which leaves a picture which fails to satisfy. The correctness of this belief has been eloquently substantiated generation after generation through the years as one looks at Sea Isle-bred Shelties!

Quoting an article written awhile back by Charlotte Clem McGowan in which she tells the Sea Isle story, and to which she has kindly permitted us to refer, she states:

> While the Ladies used total balance as
> the goal, a number of considerations

went into the planning of each mating. Evelyn states that they never bred a mediocre dog in hopes of getting something outstanding from it. Each animal selected for breeding had to be of the first rank. They avoided any dog that was coarse, but at the same time also avoided over-refinement. They did not breed from oversize or poor quality. As Mary says, they always demanded balance, quality, soundness and type in any breeding stock.

Whether it was part of the stated plan or not, the dogs used for breeding were also from *producing* lines and individuals. More than one person has seen a Sea Isle pedigree proudly displayed, traced back many generations, with a note of the production of each of the members of the pedigree, especially on the female side. All of the individuals in the pedigree had to have done something production-wise, or been truly outstanding individuals. The breeding plan aimed to build generation by generation. Over a period of nearly four decades, the Ladies bred and showed some of the best dogs in the country. They did this while averaging one or two litters a year and never more than three or four.

Sea Isle Breeze O'The North from the Sea Isle Kennels.

Ch. Sea Isle Summer Breeze, one of the early Sea Isle bitches by Ch. Comet's Gleam O'Wellesley ex Ch. Sea Isle Breeze O'The North. Sea Isle Kennels, owners.

Above: Ch. Sea Isle Sandra and puppy. This daughter of Ch. Golden Note of Nashcrest was the dam of Ch. Sea Isle Serenata. Sea Isle Kennels, Evelyn Davis and Mary Van Wagenen. **Below:** Ch. Sheltieland Kiltie O'Sea Isle, one of the true greats in this breed, at thirteen years of age. This dog had a tremendous influence on Shelties of his own and future generations. Owned by Mary Van Wagenen and Evelyn Davis, Sea Isle Kennels.

We appreciate Charlotte McGowan permitting us to use parts of her article on Sea Isle, and we urge every new breeder to think about and study the Sea Isle philosophy, as it is just about as sure-fire a road to breeding success as can be embarked upon!

A combination of Pocono and Page's Hill Shelties formed the Sea Isle foundation. Champion Adoration, Sea Isle's earliest sable bitch, was a daughter of the wonderful little dog and splendid producer Champion Merrymaker of Pocono, her dam a Tilford-bred bitch. She in turn was bred to each of the Page's Hill brothers: Champion Cock O'The North, Champion Will O'The Mill, and Champion Kalandar Prince. Adoration's Cock O'The North daughter, Sea Isle Breeze O'The North, has had the most important impact on the modern Sheltie from the progeny of these three litters.

Breeze, described as a well-balanced 14½-inch bitch, became the dam of four champions. Bred to Champion Comet's Gleam O'Wellesley, a small sable of Page's Hill lines, she produced the next link to the present in the great Champion Sea Isle Summer Breeze, who in turn was bred to Champion Sheltieland Kiltie O'Sea Isle, thus producing Champion Sea Isle Sandra.

The two most outstanding of the Sea Isle stud dogs were Champion Sheltieland Kiltie O'Sea Isle and Champion Nashcrest Golden Note. Not only was each an outstanding dog, but also they complemented each other in both phenotype and

Ch. Nashcrest Golden Note winning the Working Group at Wilmington Kennel Club, May 1954. Shown by Elizabeth Whelen for Sea Isle Kennels. Photo courtesy of Miss Whelen.

genotype. Charlotte McGowan in her Sea Isle story says,

> Evelyn feels Kiltie had a Mountaineer look. He had a bang-up round muzzle and perfect ears, which were also little ears right on top of his head. Golden Note was a different dog. Like Kiltie, slow to mature. Mary feels his head was similar in many ways to Champion Lingard Sealect Bruce's—longer than Kiltie's, very refined in skull. When in condition he could really move, surely one of the reasons he won eight Working Groups in the days when Shelties rarely placed. His quality was so overwhelming that it was impossible to overlook him.

Kiltie and Note both were combined Page's Hill and Pocono breeding. Note was by Champion Prince George O'Page's Hill, by Kalandar Prince from the Merrymaker daughter, Champion Timberidge Temptress. Kiltie was by a son

of Champion Victory of Pocono from a Mountaineer daughter.

Champion Sea Isle Sandra, continuing the line, was bred to Champion Nashcrest Golden Note. From this came the exquisite Champion Sea Isle Serenata, a bitch who "stands even today as a model for perfection of type." Serenata is described as having been an ideal size, 14½ inches with plenty of substance combined with elegant refinement and the perfect combination of flatness and leanness of skull so essential to the true Sheltie head. Her expression was typically sweet, her body solid and well made. Many tributes have been written to this bitch and her exceptional outstanding qualities. Those who recall her personally say that she held her excellence from the time she was a youngster well into old age. Charlotte McGowan's article describes her as a "national landmark for Sheltie lovers throughout her long life." The only disappointment in connection with this marvelous bitch was that she never produced a daughter to shine in the next generation of great bitches. She did, however, give her owners a son of exceptional merit, who became one of the most outstanding sable sires when bred to daughters of Note, Champion Sea Isle Serenade.

One of three champions from the Note-Serenata combination, Serenade, when seven weeks of age, went to live with a private family who were content to have his breeders take charge of his career when its outstanding potential became obvious. Thus Miss Davis and Miss

Ch. Sea Isle Cadenza, a son of Ch. Nashcrest Golden Note. Owned by Evelyn Davis and Mary Van Wagenen.

Van Wagenen were the guiding spirits behind where he should be shown and to what bitches bred. A limited show career found him a Group winner. And as a sire he produced twenty-nine champions, putting him three ahead of his own sire's twenty-six. Like Note and Kiltie, Serenade not only sired excellent Shelties, but he also sired excellent producers. Sea Isle purchased one of his best sons, Champion Malpsh the Duke of Erle, who in turn sired numerous important winners and producers; included among them was, from a Kiltie daughter, Fair Play of Sea Isle. This dog's show career was a short one, stopped while he was still young as his owners were not quite pleased with the manner in which he moved, which those who knew him personally state improved remarkably as he grew older. Although perhaps not so refined a dog as some others at Sea Isle, he was a sire of outstanding quality. His best-known son was the famed Champion Halstor's Peter Pumpkin, who is the leading sire in the history of this breed (and very likely *all* breeds) with more than 150 champions to his credit, had an impressive show career which included all-breed Best in Show honors and Best of Breed two times at the National, in 1968 and in 1974, and had the admiration of Sheltie lovers everywhere. Peter's dam was the good Serenade daughter Champion Sea Isle Rhapsody of Halstor, who was from a "beautiful, typical Kiltie daughter," Champion Colvidale Soliloquy. Peter, therefore, was really

Above: Fair Play of Sea Isle. Owned by Sea Isle Kennels. **Below:** Ch. Halstor's Peter Pumpkin (left) with his dam, Ch. Sea Isle Rhapsody of Halstor, winning Best Brace in Show at the Eastern Dog Club under Mrs. Augustus Riggs some years ago—what a truly exciting picture!

The famous Ch. Malpsh the Duke of Erle, by Ch. Sea Isle Serenade.

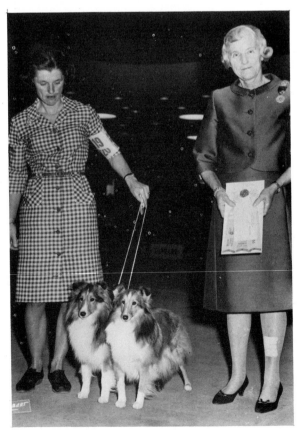

"a fitting culmination of the breeding efforts of Sea Isle as he combined in a most orderly way so many of the best in the line." An interesting sidelight on all this, from Charlotte McGowan's Sea Isle story, is the following:

Peter was officially bred by Edith Overly, but Sea Isle was to get a puppy from the litter and was to select the sire. As it turned out, fate was involved. Rhapsody was to have been bred to Champion Malpsh Great Scot, but he was not willing so Fair Play got the call. When the puppies were quite young, they were brought to Sea Isle but the Ladies decided against taking any of them, or Peter would have become a Sea Isle Sheltie in name as well as heritage.

Ch. Elf Dale Viking taking first in the Working Group at Silver Bay in 1964. Handler, Wayne Baxter; owners, Elf Dale Kennels.

Above: Ch. Sea Isle Rhapsody of Halstor, a Serenade daughter, the dam of Ch. Halstor's Peter Pumpkin. **Below:** Ch. Sea Isle Tay of Eltham, a Serenade son, whelped in 1958 from a three-champion litter of which the dam was the lovely bitch Bagaduce Hannah of Sea Isle.

To review a bit now on the Sea Isle Shelties—Miss Van Wagenen's first, Parkswood Little Symphony, is found in the country's leading blue and tri lines through her daughter, Champion Sea Isle Blue Legacy, who joined Betty Whelen's Poconos. Merle Legacy sired Champion Larkspur of Pocono, top dam in breed history with sixteen champions to her credit. Others produced by Little Symphony include Champion Geronimo Little June, grandam of the famed Best in Show winner Champion Elf Dale Viking, and Sea Isle Dappled Grey, sire of Champion Kingswood Citation who became the sire of ten champions.

Champion Adoration, founder of what is referred to as "the main Sea Isle bitch line," became the dam of Sea Isle Breeze O'The North (by Champion Cock O'The North O'Page's Hill), who produced four Sea Isle champions.

Champion Sea Isle Summer Breeze, the most influential of these, is best remembered as the dam of Champion Sea Isle Sandra, but Summer Breeze was also the dam, in this same litter, of Sea Isle Lady Judith who was bred twice to Champion Nashcrest Golden Note. In the first of these litters came Teaberry Lane Takes a Notion, dam of four Moribrook champions; and in the second was Champion Kildoona Tori of Sea Isle, a group winning bitch who for Timberidge Kennels became a successful winner. She was

Bagaduce Hannah of Sea Isle, the beginning of a second major bitch line at Sea Isle Kennels. A Kiltie daughter from Bagaduce Dinah, she and her descendants produced numerous champions of quality and importance.

the dam of Champion Bilgowan Grenadier and Kiloren Sea Mystery, the latter producing Champion Kiloren Cover Girl of Barwood, dam of Champion Barwood Bold Venture and two other champions. Sea Mystery carries down, as well, through various other Kiloren dogs.

Some of the other Adoration descendants produced winners but do not appear in major pedigrees to any extent. Included among these are Champion Sea Isle Gallant Prince, Sea Isle Gold Prince of Kiloh, Sea Isle Maid O'The Mill, and the latter's son who won the 1950 National Specialty, Champion Sea Isle Peter Pan. Also included are Champion Sea Isle Elizabeth and Champion Sea Isle Rebecca; the latter although a gorgeous bitch was unable to raise puppies due to the aftereffects of a serious bout with distemper.

Bagaduce Hannah of Sea Isle was the foundation of a second major bitch line at Sea Isle. She was a Kiltie daughter from Bagaduce Dinah. Her first litter, by Serenade, produced three dog champions, among them the mahogany sable

Champion Sea Isle Bard of Bagaduce who in turn produced three champions including the noted Champion Meadow Ridge Goodnight Steve (sire of six champions) and the stylish, handsome red bitch Champion Jemima of Bagaduce, grandam of Champion Valdawn's Talk of the Town.

There was a notable bitch in Hannah's Serenade litter, too: Sea Isle Oh Susannah who produced three champions and Sea Isle Do Re Mi who carried the bitch line forward.

Susannah had a son by Champion Notable Lad of Sea Isle. This was Champion Sea Isle Camelot, an elegant and perfectly balanced dog who sired six champions, among them Champion Sea Isle Glengarry, sire of five champions. Then bred to Matchmaker, Susannah produced Champion Sea Isle Sound O'Victory, carrying

Above: Ch. Sea Isle Bard of Bagaduce, a son of Ch. Sea Isle Serenade. **Below:** Ch. Sea Isle Camelot making an important win on June 4th 1961 for Mary Van Wagenen and Evelyn Davis.

Ch. Sea Isle Glengarry taking Best of Winners in December 1963 at Lancaster, California. Sea Isle Kennels, owners.

Ch. Sea Isle Dusky Belle, tri bitch by Ch. Pixie Dell Bright Vision ex Bagaduce Hannah of Sea Isle, an important producer for Malpsh Kennels and Briarwood Kennels as the dam of three champions and two others which produced champions. Bred to Ch. Sea Isle Serenade, she produced Ch. Malpsh the Duke of Erle (sire of nine champions) whose son, Fair Play of Sea Isle, sired Ch. Halstor's Peter Pumpkin. Sea Isle Kennels, Evelyn Davis and Mary Van Wagenen.

along to the Lindhurst dogs. A Sound O'Victory sister, Do Re Mi, was bred to Champion Malpsh the Duke of Erle, producing Champion Sea Isle Westwind and Sea Isle Rosewind, the former of which, along with Champion Sea Isle Sound O'Music (Camelot's sister), went to California breeders, the Robinsons. Rosewind most likely would have finished had it not been that her ears "never seemed to match." Nevertheless she did her breed proud as the dam of three champions and two others who produced champions. Her son by Champion Sea Isle Partner's Choice, Champion Sea Isle March Wind, is the last champion living at Sea Isle. The last of the Sea Isle champion bitches was the beautiful Rosewind daughter by Champion Rorralore Mickey Dazzler, Champion Sea Isle To A Wild Rose. She was winner of the first Colonial Shetland Sheepdog Specialty. A son of hers, Champion Sea Isle Merchant Prince, was sired by Note; and she also was the dam, bred to Dona Hausman's famed Champion Pixie Dell Bright Vision, of the tri bitch, Sea Isle Dusky Belle, who played an important role in Malpsh and Briarwood breeding programs.

Dusky Belle bred to Serenade produced Champion Malpsh the Duke of Erle (sire of nine champions including Champion Gillian Fair of Sea Isle, Champion Beltane Druid April, Champion Mar Jan's Debutante of Waljon, Sea Isle Rosewind, and Fair Play of Sea Isle), Malpsh Her Royal Majesty (five champions), and Pris (five champions).

Ch. Sea Isle To A Wild Rose, by Ch. Rorralore Mickey Dazzler ex a Sea Isle Rosewind daughter, the last Sea Isle bitch champion and winner of the first Colonial Specialty. Evelyn Davis and Mary Van Wagenen, owners, Sea Isle Kennels.

Ch. Gillian Fair of Sea Isle in June 1965. Sea Isle Kennels, Mary Van Wagenen and Evelyn Davis.

Fair Play (Serenade ex Dusky Belle) as we have already mentioned produced Champion Halstor's Peter Pumpkin. Additionally he sired the noted top producer Champion Romayne's Sportin' Life, an especially dominant sire of currently winning Shelties. And Her Royal Majesty is the dam of Champion Malpsh Great Scot, a National Specialty winner, an all-breed Best in Show winner, and an outstanding sire.

Another bitch line which briefly came through at Sea Isle was from E-Danha Manhattan Serenade. She produced Sea Isle Christmas Carol sired by Champion E-Danha Just My Bill, who was then bred to Kiltie and produced Eastertide, the dam of Sea Isle Singing Sands; Singing Sands went to Dorothy Burns' kennel where she became the dam of Timberidge Sandstorm, the dam of Champion Lingard Sealect Bruce; Singing Sands then moved on to establish

Three generations of fabulous Shelties: Ch. Duchess of Clovermead, left, with her sire Ch. Sheltieland Kiltie O'Sea Isle and his dam, right, Ch. Sheltieland Peg o'the Picts—extremely important and influential members of this breed.

Ch. Malpsh Great Scott taking Best of Breed at Trenton Kennel Club, expertly handled by Frank Ashbey. Photo courtesy of John L. Ashbey.

Shetland Sheepdog Association and of the Colonial Shetland Sheepdog Cub. Mary Van Wagenen, the only person in breed history to have four times judged the National Specialty (along with having done most of the other major Specialties in the United States and Canada plus the English Shetland Sheepdog Association Specialty in England) is constantly sought after for judging assignments at prestigious shows; and both ladies are considered to be outstanding sources of information where the breed's history and progress are concerned.

Among those kennels now successfully proceeding along the Sea Isle breeding patterns are such well-known ones as Rorralore (Charlotte McGowan), Beltane (the Currys), Ilemist (Julie Desy Maust), Mistimoor (the Holds), Shu La Le (Sharlene De Fee), Heatherland (Sandra MacIntosh), Romayne (the Danforths), Lobo Dell (Gail Wolfe), Benayr (Susan Bentley), Jade Mist (the Keith Howells), Rockwood (Barbara Kenealy), Barwood (Barbara Thompson), Wit's End (Erica Venier), Chosen (Barbara B. Thompson), Karral (the Ralph Elledges), September (Barbara Linden), Cahaba (Ron Lackey), O'Davak (the Ken Flessas), Wayanet (Betsey Johns), Brandywine (the Boyd Smiths), early Macdega (the Tom Coens), and numerous others.

Sharlene De Fee's Shu La Le Kennel where, bred to Champion Hatfield Sultan of Lorel she produced Champion Shu La Le Sweet Charity and Shu La Le Sultansong of Lorel, both noted producers with multiple champions sired by Champion Halstor's Peter Pumpkin.

Then there was Champion Colvidale Soliloquy, a Kiltie daughter who, bred to Camelot, produced Champion Sea Isle Glengarry, who went to the West with Champion Gillian Fair of Sea Isle where they produced the outstanding bitch Champion Barwood Scotchguard Sonata who, in a litter of five by Serenade, produced Champion Sea Isle Rhapsody of Halstor, the dam of Peter Pumpkin.

Although no longer breeding Shelties, the ladies of Sea Isle retain their active interest in the breed they have loved so long and so dearly. Both are honorary members of the American

Ch. Sea Isle March Wind, the last of the legendary Sea Isle champions still living there. We are told that even as an older dog he is full of the same quality, charm, and grace that brought him early championship honors as a puppy. Mary Van Wagenen and Evelyn Davis, owners, Sea Isle Kennels.

Ch. Macdega Portrait in Black, tri bitch by Ch. Calcurt Luke ex Ch. Lakehill Portrait in Blue, pictured winning at Springfield K.C. in May 1977 under judge Clayre Galye, Gaylord Kennels. Bred by Tom Coen and Steve Barger; owned by Linda Nugent More.

Ch. Severn Spellbinder owned by Linda Nugent More, Pomfret Center, Connecticut.

Severn

Severn Kennels, owned by Linda More at Pomfret, Connecticut, had its start, although unrecognized at the time as such, when Linda's mother sent her, at age eleven, to attend obedience classes with their new Sheltie puppy. Linda's parents had owned Shelties as pets even before Linda's birth, and this daughter of Champion Sheltieland Kiltie O'Sea Isle was the latest in the series. An interest in breed as well as obedience competition developed, and so it was decided to breed this bitch to Champion Nashcrest Golden Note—unwittingly doing what the experienced breeders found to be the highly successful Kiltie-Note cross. The best male puppy was retained and he patiently saw Linda through excursions into breed, obedience, and junior showmanship competition. She comments: "Had I known then what I do now, he would have finished with extreme ease, and quite possibly been a useful sire as well."

However, doggy activities were eclipsed during some years of college, marriage, and babies. When Linda's interest was renewed, she purchased a bitch co-bred by Marlin Roll and Sea Isle: Sea Isle Scalloway Peerie, U.D. Bred to

Ch. Severn Spellbinder, sable dog by Ch. Macdega The Chosen ex Scalloway Kaylie, C.D.X., here at eight and a half months winning over champions under Lynette Saltzman of Catamount Shelties. Spellbinder finished in July 1974 and is the sire of Best in Show winners. Bred and owned by Linda Nugent More.

Severn Smoke On The Water, blue-merle son of Ch. Ridgeside Stormsong ex Severn Petunia Pumpkin. Co-breeders, Madelyn Cirinna and Linda More; owner, Linda More.

Severn Petunia Pumpkin, sable daughter of Ch. Halstor's Peter Pumpkin ex Ch. Macdega Portrait in Black, the dam of Ch. Severn Smoke On The Water. Bred and owned by Linda More; co-owned by Madelyn Tettke Cirinna, Scottfree Shelties.

Champion Malpsh Great Scot, she generously provided Linda with one bitch puppy, Scalloway Kaylie, C.D.X., with eight points toward championship. Kaylie, in turn, was one of the very first bitches bred to the inbred Champion Halstor's Peter Pumpkin son, Champion Macdega The Chosen, and from this litter came Linda's first champion, the beautiful Severn Spellbinder. The latter completed his championship in 1974 and became the sire of two champions, one of them the Best in Show winner, Champion Romayne Special Edition, now in Japan.

At about this time, Linda had decided that since she could keep very few dogs, the best way to have a supply of quality animals to show was to take up handling professionally for others. So it was that her current profession began, and it has meant strictly limiting her own breeding program.

In 1974 a tricolor bitch puppy was purchased by Linda from Tom Coen and Steve Barger, Macdega Portrait in Black, parented by two of her favorite Shelties, Champion Calcurt Luke and the lovely Champion Lakehill Portrait in

Ch. Severn Comedy Tonight, sable bitch by Ch. North-country Westering Son ex Ch. Severn Idle Gossip. Bred by Linda More, Tom Coen and Steve Barger; owned by Joanne Timpany, Sherwood Shelties.

Ch. Severn Idle Gossip, sable bitch by Ch. Calcurt Luke ex Corjo-s Duchess of Severn, finishing at four years of age in July 1979; judge, Richard Greathouse. Owner-handler, Linda More, Severn Kennels.

Blue. This combination yielded a pedigree that was roughly three-quarters Pocono and one-quarter Sea Isle, through Peter Pumpkin. With maturity, Portrait in Black finished easily. Bred back to her grandsire, Peter Pumpkin, she produced Severn Petunia Pumpkin. Very much her father's child, Petunia in turn produced Linda's noted blue, Champion Severn Smoke On The Water, sired by Fred Edlin's excellent Champion Ridgeside Stormsong. Smoke On The Water finished at the American Shetland Sheepdog Association National Specialty in 1981 and a couple of months later was Best of Breed at the Colonial Specialty. He has a number of Best of Breed and Group placements as well. His pedigree contains Peter Pumpkin five times, and he is the sire and grandsire of a number of promising youngsters.

Linda had sold Spellbinder's best sister on a puppy-back basis and requested that she be bred to Champion Calcurt Luke. Her chosen puppy, whelped in December 1974, grew up to become Champion Severn Idle Gossip, winner at eight and a half years of age of two Specialty Best of Opposite Sex awards and several Bests of Breed and Group placements. Idle Gossip has made an art of almost completely avoiding motherhood, but she is the dam of the Working Group-winning bitch Champion Severn Comedy Tonight, owned by Joanne Timpany and sired by Champion Northcountry Westering Son.

At the present time, Linda hopes to carry on her sable line through Comedy Tonight, and the "any other" colors through some youngsters from Portrait in Black and Smoke On The Water.

Ch. Karenwood's Uppercrust, unusually marked blue-merle bitch by Ch. Banchory High Born ex Calcurt Silver Heiress, going Best of Winners at the Colonial Shetland Sheepdog Club Specialty in June 1978; judge, Jo Byrd Parker; handler, Linda More. Bred and owned by Carlene D. Smith, Karenwood Kennels, Braintree, Massachusetts.

Starhaven

It was in 1957 when Carl and Amy Langhorst purchased their first Shetland Sheepdog—an event which led to the foundation of Starhaven Kennels at Goshen, Ohio, and the beginning of a hobby with which they have been continuously involved ever since.

Starhaven's Gay Lady, U.D., this initial purchase, eventually became the grandam of Starhaven's foundation stud dog, Champion Starhaven's Banner, C.D. Lady and her son, Starhaven's Top Kick, C.D.X., were among the best in obedience competition, winning High in Trial on numerous occasions.

The Langhorsts' first show Sheltie was Starhaven's Timberidge Flag, purchased from Timberidge Kennels and carrying the Noralee-Timberidge bloodlines, which became the original foundation for Starhaven. As time passed, other individuals were added from various bloodlines with excellent results. Starhaven has had thirty-eight champions as of August 1983, and a goodly number of them boast obedience titles as well.

Above: Ch. Sooner's Marin o'Waldenwood, by Ch. Kismet's Conquistador ex Ch. Sooner's Jenny Rebecca. Owned by Starhaven Kennels, Carl and Amy Langhorst, Goshen, Ohio. **Below:** Ch. Heatherland's Mr. Kilpatrick, C.D., by Ch. Halstor's Peter Pumpkin, the senior sire at Starhaven Kennels. Carl and Amy Langhorst, owners.

Starhaven's Formal Look, by Ch. Banchory Formal Notice ex Starhaven's Women's Libber, winner of a three-point major from the Puppy Class. Owned by Starhaven Kennels, Carl and Amy Langhorst.

Ch. Starhaven's Georgie Girl, by Ch. Heatherland's Mr. Kilpatrick, C.D., ex Starhaven's Black Beauty, taking Best of Winners and Best of Opposite Sex to finish her championship at the Greater Detroit Shetland Sheepdog Specialty under judge Mrs. Maynard Drury. Owner-handled by Starhaven Kennels, Carl and Amy Langhorst.

Ch. Starhaven's The Main Spark, by Ch. Heatherland's Mr. Kilpatrick ex Starhaven's Spice, the sire of two champions. Owned by Starhaven Kennels, Carl and Amy Langhorst.

Ch. Starhaven's Pieta, by Starhaven's Black Nikki ex Ch. Starhaven's Snow Leopard. Bred and owned by Starhaven Kennels, Carl and Amy Langhorst.

Champion Starhaven's Banner, C.D., was a top producer for the Langhorsts, siring five champions. His grandson, Champion Starhaven's Spook, sired six champions. Currently the top producing senior sire at Starhaven is Champion Heatherland's Mr. Kilpatrick, C.D., a son of Champion Halstor's Peter Pumpkin and himself the sire of five champions. Mr. Kilpatrick's son, Champion Starhaven's The Main Spark, has now sired two champions, a number which will very certainly be added to as time progresses. A daughter of Mr. Kilpatrick's, Champion Starhaven's Georgie Girl, was Best of Winners at a recent Greater Detroit Shetland Sheepdog Club Specialty.

To Mrs. Langhorst's knowledge, Champion Starhaven's Spook is the only sire who has produced three champion tricolor bitches in one litter. They are Champion Starhaven's I'm A Brat Too, Starhaven's Mini Brat, and Starhaven's Black Gold, all of them Specialty winners. As of this writing, Spook is still going strong at the age of eighteen years!

Ch. Starhaven's Tar Baby, by Ch. Starhaven's The Main Spark ex Starhaven's Women's Libber, winning a major under Gerald Schwartz in 1981; shown by Amy Langhorst. Starhaven Kennels, owners, Carl and Amy Langhorst.

Above: Ch. Starhaven's Touch The Sky, multi-breed winner. Bred and owned by Starhaven Kennels, Carl and Amy Langhorst. **Below:** Ch. Ilemist Impromptu, a 1982 champion by Ch. Kensil's Saddle Tramp ex Ch. Ilemist Maybe Someday. Owned by Starhaven Kennels.

Champion Starhaven's Rockin' Robin, C.D., was a High in Trial winner at the Cleveland Shetland Sheepdog Club Specialty and was the sire of two champions. Champion Starhaven's Touch The Sky was the Langhorsts' top breed-winner so far, taking Best of Breed on approximately twenty-three occasions in limited showing over several years' time with placements in the Working Group. The Langhorsts seldom show their dogs in breed, but another breed-winner for them was the tri bitch Champion Starhaven's Black Brat, C.D., a High in Trial winner as well. Brat was a daughter of Banner, and her dam was Champion Sealect Autumn Song. Touch The Sky was sired by the Best in Show dog, Champion Mori-Brook's Icecapade, C.D., and her dam was Champion Starhaven's Miss Behaving, C.D., the dam of four champions.

Currently, Champion Heatherland's Mr. Kilpatrick, C.D., has eighteen Bests of Breed.

Spook's champions were Champion Starhaven's Mini Brat, Champion Starhaven's I'm A Brat Too, Champion Starhaven's Black Gold, Champion Starhaven's Black Talisman, Champion Starhaven Somedays The Blue Spook, and Champion Sealect The Desert Fox.

Banner's champions were Champion Starhaven's Torch, Champion Starhaven's Diamond Lil, C.D., Champion Starhaven's Black Brat, C.D., Champion Starhaven's Black Jack, and Champion Starhaven's Wit of Merrylane.

Ch. Starhaven's Black Brat, C.D., by Ch. Starhaven's Banner, C.D., ex Ch. Sealect Autumn Song, winning Best of Breed from the classes in 1966. The dam of two champions, Brat was Highest in Trial Specialty winner. Owned by Starhaven Kennels, Carl and Amy Langhorst.

Ch. Shawn Dar's Forgot To Tri, by Ch. Cherden Sock It To 'Em ex Shawn Dar's Ebony Elegance. *This is the top producing bi-black dam in breed history.* She is the dam of Ch. SumerSong Hurry Sundown, Ch. Shawn Dar-SumerSong Bi Night, and Ch. Shawn Dar's Bi A Lil' Happiness, all of them multiple Specialty winners. Bred by Andrew and Carolyn Kilham, co-owners with Peggy and Jan Haderlie.

Ch. SumerSong Hurry Sundown, by SumerSong Dance In The Sun ex Ch. Shawn Dar's Forgot To Tri, the foundation sire for SumerSong Shelties and the sire of seven American champions, two Canadian champions, and one Japanese champion. Bred and owned by SumerSong Shelties, Peggy and Jan Haderlie.

SumerSong

SumerSong Shetland Sheepdogs, at Orange, California, are owned by Peggy and Jan Haderlie, whose success as Sheltie breeders has won them admiration from coast to coast.

The Haderlies, from the beginning very much involved with bi-black Shelties, co-own with Shawn Dar Kennels, Andrew and Carolyn Kilham (who bred her), a bitch whom they describe as the "grand matriarch of *both* kennels," Champion Shawn Dar's Forgot To Tri, the top producing black dam in Sheltie history. Among her progeny are Champion SumerSong Hurry Sundown, Champion Shawn Dar-SumerSong Bi Night, and Champion Shawn Dar's Bi A Lil' Happiness, all multiple Specialty winners. Forgot To Tri, "Bye Bye" to her friends, at 12½ years of age is in splendid health and enjoying life. She is a daughter of Champion Cherden Sock It To 'Em from Shawn Dar's Ebony Elegance.

Hurry Sundown, by SumerSong Dance in the Sun (Champion SumerSong Here Comes The Sun ex La Mar's Devil Song O' B-B Jo) from Forgot To Tri, had eight champions to his credit shortly before this book went to press, five of them in the United States, two in Canada, and one in Japan. They are American Champions Sterling Quicksilver (multiple Specialty winner

Ch. Verlyn's You Blew My Mind, by Ch. SumerSong Winter Shadows ex Ch. Verlyn's Character. Breeder-owner, Beverly Malmbory.

Above: Ch. Shawn Dar-SumerSong Bi Night, by Shawn Dar's I've Gotta Be Me ex Ch. Shawn Dar's Forgot To Tri. *This is the first bi-black champion in modern breed history.* He was Reserve Winners Dog at the 1976 National Specialty. Bred by Andrew and Carolyn Kilham; owned by Peggy and Jan Haderlie and Carolyn Kilham. **Below:** Ch. Sumer-Song Winter Shadows, by Ch. Banchory Deep Purple ex SumerSong Kachina. Breeder-owners, SumerSong Shelties, Peggy and Jan Haderlie.

owned by Peggy Stephens), Shawn Dar-Sumer-Song Waltz 'N Bi (multiple Specialty winner co-owned by SumerSong and Shawn Dar), Killybeg Prince of Darkness (Specialty winner owned by Bob and Berkeley Constable), and Rivenwick Rising Silver Sun (finished in sixteen shows and owned by Harriet Smith and Linda Hines); Canadian Champions Tara Hill The Moon Shadow (bred by Bonnie Smith) and Shawn Dar's The Swashbuckler (bred by Carolyn Kilham and owned by Sandy Neil); and Japanese Champion Shawn Dar's Earth Wind and Fire (bred by Carolyn Kilham and owned by Yuji Mihara).

Bi Night, by Shawn Dar's I've Gotta Be Me ex Forgot To Tri, was the first modern bi-black champion in the breed, finishing with an ease and speed which is not always the case with this color. On the way to his title he was Reserve Winners Dog at the American Shetland Sheep-dog National in 1976 under judge Jean Simmonds, and he was Winners Dog the next day at Northern California under Irene Brody. Bred by Shawn Dar and co-owned with SumerSong, this important little dog is now retired and the well-loved family dog of Bob and Barbara Marley.

Bi A Lil' Happiness, another of Forgot To Tri's champions, is a bi-black and quite small,

Ch. Shawn Dar-SumerSong Waltz 'N Bi, by Ch. SumerSong Hurry Sundown ex Shawn Dar's Tri It My Way. Bred by Carolyn Kilham, who co-owns with Peggy and Jan Haderlie, SumerSong Shelties.

measuring 13 5/8 inches. But quality comes through, and the title was easily attained by this one, too. She was bred by Shawn Dar and SumerSong and is now owned by Shawn Dar.

Champion SumerSong Winter Shadows, by Champion Banchory Deep Purple ex the Hurry Sundown daughter SumerSong Kachina, is an outstanding winner and stud dog at SumerSong. This magnificent Sheltie has to his credit at least seven Specialty Show Bests of Breed, twenty-one additional Bests of Breed, and multiple Group placements including two firsts. As a stud dog, he not only is making an important name for himself, but also at least two of his sons, Blue Chip Stock and The Blue Falcon, are doing likewise.

Bi-blues and bi-blacks are the favored colors at SumerSong, and the dogs produced in both of them by this kennel are ones in which to take pride.

The bi-blue bitch SumerSong Silver Pearl, by Ch. Banchory Deep Purple ex Bilori Happy Mother's Day. Bred and owned by Peggy and Jan Haderlie.

SumerSong The Blue Falcon, by Ch. SumerSong Winter Shadows ex SumerSong Bells A Ringing. Bred and owned by SumerSong Shelties, Peggy and Jan Haderlie.

Am. and Can. Ch. Meridian's Miss Behave, Canada's top winning Sheltie in 1968. Owned by Mrs. Ruth E. Lane, Summit Shelties, Centerville, Massachusetts.

Above: Can. Ch. Summit's Gold Dust, C.D., or "Dusty," at twelve years of age winning the Veterans Class at the Canadian Collie and Shetland Sheepdog Specialty Show in Montreal; judge, Mrs. Virginia Hampton; handler, Mrs. Hazel Slaughter. Owned by Mrs. Ruth E. Lane, Summit Shelties. **Below:** Ch. Meridian's Scotch on the Rocks, by Ch. Summit's Golden Rod, C.D., ex Ch. Summit's Forever Amber. Owned at Summit Kennels by Ruth E. Lane.

Summit Lane

Summit Lane Shelties, located at Centerville, Massachusetts, originated in Pointe Claire, Quebec, Canada, in 1959. The owners, Mr. and Mrs. A.C. (Arnold and Ruth) Lane have always loved animals, and prior to the Shelties they had owned several dogs, among them a Collie, a Wire Fox Terrier, and a Cocker Spaniel which Mrs. Lane showed in conformation and obedience. After reading every breed book she could obtain, Mrs. Lane finally decided that she must have a Shetland Sheepdog, and she actually saw her first member of the breed at one of the Montreal Dog Shows in 1950, which made her want one even more. Shortly thereafter a lovely puppy was purchased, a tri bitch, from Mrs. Helen Lovett of Ronas Hill Kennels.

This bitch became Canadian Champion and Canadian Obedience Trial Champion Cinderella Gypsy of Ronas Hill, U.D.T., the first in Canada to gain these combined titles *of any breed;* she was pointed in the United States as well. This bitch was solid Pocono breeding on her sire's side, being by Champion Magic Talisman of Pocono (Champion Tailor Made of Pocono ex Blue Jewel of Pocono) ex Aylmer Chorine (Champion Alford Wee MacGregor ex Bonny Lou), tracing her pedigree back to American and Canadian Champion Lord Lovell O'Page's Hill on her dam's side.

"Cindy" became the dam of five champions, including Canadian Champion Summit's Gold Dust, C.D. The latter handsome dog was the winner of two Groups and many Group placements. An outstanding stud dog, his progeny included Canadian Champion Rosslynn's Ban-Joe of Summit (a Group winner), Summit's Fiesta, C.D., Summit's Forever Amber, Meridian's Gypsy Serenade, Meridian's Gypsy Baron (Specialty Show winner), Bradean's Fancy That, Summit's Golden Promise, U.D.T., Summit's Holiday, and Summit's Night and Day. All of these champions have distinguished accomplishments to their credit.

"Cindy's" champions, in addition to "Dusty," all were winners of the C.D. title as well.

American and Canadian Champion Meridian's Miss Behave is another famous Sheltie from the Lanes' kennel who has prestigious ring accomplishments to her credit. She was Canada's Top Winning Sheltie for 1966. Then there was Champion Summit's Gay Abandon, Top Producing Sheltie Bitch in Canada *of all time,* with thirteen champions to her credit, owned by Mrs. Hazel Slaughter and bred by Ruth E. Lane. Still another important winner was American, Canadian, and Bermudian Champion Cape Winds Breeze, owned by Ruth E. Lane and handled by William Trainor to a splendid career.

The current young star at Summit Shelties as this is written is an exquisite bitch, Winslow Crown Jewels, who won the 1983 Colonial Shetland Sheepdog Futurity, in an entry of ninety, at Danvers, Massachusetts, under judge Mrs. Susan Beacham and handled by Mrs. Rose Chandless. She is among several up-and-coming young bitches which Mrs. Lane will be campaigning in 1984.

Am., Can., and Bda. Ch. Cape Winds Breeze, handled by William Trainor to a fine win under judge Mrs. Nicholas Demidoff. Owned by Ruth E. Lane.

Ch. Stoneridge Copper Melody, by Ch. Fantasy Catcher In The Rye (double grandson of Ch. Halstor's Peter Pumpkin) ex Gia Starlight (Peter Pumpkin granddaughter), the foundation bitch of Evelyn Byer's Velveteen Shelties at El Cajon, California.

Velveteen

Velveteen Shetland Sheepdogs belong to Evelyn Byers of El Cajon, California, and were founded on the bitch Champion Stoneridge Copper Melody, a daughter of Champion Fantasy Catcher In The Rye ex Gia Starlight. This bitch was the pick of her litter and was purchased at a year and a half by Mrs. Byers following her decision to try to establish a line of her own sables.

Prior to the acquisition of "Jenny," as Copper Melody is known, Mrs. Byers had owned and bred two obedience dogs, Dellhree Midnight Lace, C.D.X., and Velveteen Blue Velvet, C.D.X., who had been her first of the breed. Blue Velvet she bred to Champion Esquire's Silver Sovereign, Mrs. Byers keeping the pick bitch, 14½-inch tall Velveteen Forget Me Not. After breeding Forget Me Not three times, trying both line-breeding and outcrossing, she produced several very nice puppies which went oversize at maturity and so could not be shown. Mrs. Byers felt that she would like to try an entirely different line and start out with the sables.

Champion Stoneridge Copper Melody was bred to Champion Esquire's Fringe Benefit, from which Mrs. Byers kept the nicest bitch, Velveteen Gold Dust, who has eleven points. Then she sold "Jenny" on the condition that she get back a litter from her, for which the breeding to Fringe Benefit was repeated. This time she

Above: Dellhree Midnight Lace, C.D.X., and Velveteen Blue Velvet, C.D.X., the first two Shelties owned by Mrs. Evelyn Byers of Velveteen Kennels, who did well for themselves and for their owner in obedience competition. Below: Velveteen Touch of Solid Gold, by Ch. Dorlane's Touch of Class ex Velveteen Tequila Sunrise. One of the lovely Shelties bred and owned by Mrs. Evelyn Byers, Velveteen Kennels.

kept three of the puppies: Velveteen Acapulco Gold, who quickly became a champion; Velveteen Tequila Sunrise, who has nine points including a major as of August 1983; and Champion Velveteen Esquire Aztec Gold, whom she sold at three months of age, not wanting to keep indefinitely two males from the same litter.

Next she bred Velveteen Tequila Sunrise ("Tike") on two occasions to Champion Dorlane's Touch of Class, which produced Velveteen Touch of Copper (five points), Velveteen Touch of Song (five points), and Velveteen Touch of Solid Gold.

Another of the Champion Stoneridge Copper Melody daughters, Velveteen Gold Dust, was bred to Champion Dorlane's Touch of Class twice, producing Velveteen Gold Saddle, Velveteen Gold Fever, Velveteen Gold Dream, and Velveteen Cast in Gold.

As of mid-1983, Evelyn Byers had either owned or bred three champions and four dogs en route to their titles and, of course, the two obedience C.D.X. winners who were her actual introduction to Shelties.

The handsome Ch. Velveteen Acapulco Gold, by Ch. Esquire's Fringe Benefit ex Ch. Stoneridge Copper Melody's second litter. Bred and owned by Evelyn Byers.

Velveteen Tequila Sunrise, with nine points on her championship. Bred and owned by Evelyn Byers.

Velveteen Touch of Song (above) and Velveteen Touch of Copper (below), both with five points toward title, both by Ch. Dorlane's Touch of Class from Velveteen Tequila Sunrise. Homebreds from Evelyn Byers's Velveteen Kennels.

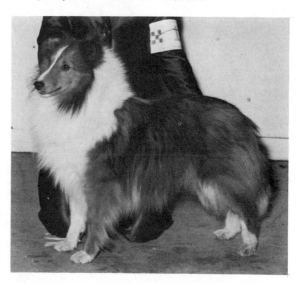

Villager

As has been the case with so many of our fanciers, Lyn B. and Michael J. Reese began their association with Shelties as owners of a pet member of the breed, which they purchased in 1972, a compromise between the Labrador Lyn had wanted and the Collie Mike had envisioned. The decision to purchase a Sheltie was as much the result of fate in the size of their apartment's yard as of anything else. Once hooked as owners of the breed, the next step was involvement with dog shows and the purchase of a show-prospect Peter-Reflection granddaughter in 1976. Probably, however, the true start of Villager Shelties, now located at Visalia, California, was the arrival of "Bobby" in 1979. Purchased as a three-month-old puppy from Kathy Gregor of Grelore Shelties, this handsome dog was sired by Champion Benayr Peter Principle (a Champion September's Rainmaker son) out of Champion

Grelore Ruby Red Dress (a Champion Gerthstone's Jon Christopher daughter). This was a repeat of the breeding that had produced two Sheltie individuals the Reeses tremendously admired, Champion Grelore Helen Hiwater and Champion Grelore Believe It.

Although not particularly fast maturing, Champion Grelore Village Goldsmith, "Robert Redfurred" to his friends, began his show career at the tender age of eleven months, capturing a three-point major at his first show; these points unfortunately were cancelled owing to an incorrect class entry. "Bobby" (or "Bob") would more than make them up later! "Retired" to grow up, he returned to the ring in March of 1980 as a fifteen-month-old, debuting at the Shetland Sheepdog Club of Southern California Specialty, where he was runner-up in the sweepstakes. The next day found him Winners Dog and Best of Opposite Sex over Specials for a four-point major. Four weeks later he won

Am. and Can. Ch. Grelore Village Goldsmith winning the Herding Group at Walla Walla Kennel Club under judge Bob Wilson. Suzi Beacham handling for owners, Lyn and Mike Reese, Visalia, California.

another major, three points this time, before proceeding to lose the last vestige of his puppy coat.

Back in the ring shortly after his second birthday, "Bob" made his first appearance as an adult at the Pacific Northwest Shetland Sheepdog Club Show in January of 1980. There he took a five-point major for Winners Dog and then went on to Best of Winners. The next day he completed his title with the win for another five-point major, going Winners Dog and then Best of Breed over some leading Specials. As if winning his title with four majors were not enough, "Bob" completed his day by taking third in a strong and exciting Working Group.

This first Group placement turned out to have been an omen, for it is now in the Group ring that "Bob" finds the most enjoyment from his dog show career. Although he has always been a non-stop showman (who has kissed more than one judge upon occasion), he seems to especially enjoy the pace and challenge of moving with the larger dogs, not to mention the applause of the crowd. As a two-year-old, he finished Number Nine in the Nation his first year as a Special. In 1982, as a three-year-old, he finished Number Five and is presently Number Three for 1983 under the *Canine Chronicle* System. He is now almost halfway to the Century Club, with his career total standing at forty-eight breed wins, in addition to being a multiple Group-winner and Specialty winner as well, along with being a Canadian champion. His most recent and perhaps most exciting victory to date was the one at Santa Barbara in 1983, where he won the Herding Group.

It is important to realize that "Bob" has never been professionally handled and that all of his successes have been achieved in difficult West Coast competition.

Villager has by choice remained a small kennel, never whelping more than one litter a year or maintaining more than five adult dogs at a time, all of them house dogs. Lyn especially enjoys handling and has finished several Shelties and Collies for others in the past four years.

Currently (mid-1983), there are three adult Shelties living at Villager: "Robert Redfurred" (of course); Villager's Molly Be Good, who needs a major to finish (she is a Champion Gerthstone's Jon daughter out of that first show-prospect); and Villager's Goodtime Girl, a daughter of "Bob" and Molly who already has a Specialty Best in Sweepstakes and seven points to her credit as she nears maturity.

Above: Am. and Can. Ch. Grelore Village Goldsmith winning the Working Group at Kern County on April 4th 1982, judged by Roy Ayres. Susi Gleffe handling for owners Lyn and Mike Reese. **Below:** An exciting occasion! Am. and Can. Ch. Grelore Village Goldsmith is winning the Herding Group at the prestigious Santa Barbara Kennel Club Dog Show, August 1st 1983, under judge Ranier Vuorinen for Lyn and Mike Reese. Bred by Katherine Gregor, "Robert Redfurred," as he is called, is a son of Ch. Benayr Peter Principle ex Ch. Grelore Ruby Red Dress.

Lynnlea's Parade Dress taking Winners Dog at the Des Moines Specialty in September 1982. Owner-handled by Patricia A. Stewart, Chicago, Illinois.

Water's Edge

Water's Edge is one of our newest Shetland Sheepdog Kennels, owner Patricia A. Stewart of Chicago, Illinois, having been showing dogs only since 1982 but already thoroughly "hooked" both on the breed and on the fun offered by participation in the sport. Currently living in a high-rise condominium on Chicago's Lake Shore Drive, it is impossible for her to breed her own dogs in such circumstances. Therefore, her lovely winning dog, Lynnlea's Parade Dress, stands at stud through Barwood Kennels, owned by Barbara Thompson in Mokena, Illinois. As she says, "While it is the best possible arrangement for me at this time, my ultimate goal is to sell the condo and get a house where I can breed Shelties in earnest and start my line on the Sea Isle and Peter Pumpkin lines."

The current dogs at Water's Edge are heavy Sea Isle and Peter on their dam's side and Banchory on their sire's.

Patricia owns Lynnlea's Parade Dress, who currently has thirteen points, three Bests of Breed, one over Specials, and who has been "pulled" (*i.e.*, chosen to remain in the ring, still in competition when the judge settles down to the final six or eight selections from whom the ultimate winners will be chosen) twice in the Working Group. As his owner comments, "I can only imagine what he might have done had he had someone experienced on the end of the lead," for she has handled him herself.

Parade Dress has the distinction of being the only pointed son ever shown of the American Shetland Sheepdog Association National Specialty Best of Breed winner, Champion Lynnlea Forever Amber, C.D., who took the honor in 1983 from the Veterans Class in an entry of about 600 Shelties including seventy-five Specials. She, too, was bred by Ray and Dorothy Christiansen.

Lynnlea's Josh of Water's Edge, by Barwood's Formal Attire ex Ch. Barwood's Ashford Vanity Fair, C.D. Owned by Pat Stewart.

Lynnlea's Parade Dress, by Barwood's Formal Attire ex Ch. Lynnlea Forever Amber, C.D., the only pointed son of Amber, the 1983 National Specialty Best of Breed winner, ever shown. As we write, Parade Dress ("Perry") has thirteen points toward championship, three Bests of Breed (one over Specials from the classes), and was twice pulled in the Working Group. Owner-handled by Patricia A. Stewart.

Rockwood Kintyre Rymin' Simon, by Ch. Rockwood Repeat Performance ex Ch. Our Own Rockwood's Bewitched, taking Winners at Warrenton K.C. in 1983; judge, Bob Wills. Simon has both of his majors. Breeder-owner, Barbara Kenealy.

Above: Ch. Severn Idle Gossip, by Ch. Calcurt Luke ex Corjo's Duchess of Severn, at eight and a half years old taking Best of Opposite Sex from the Veterans Class over an enormous entry at the Colonial Shetland Sheepdog Club Specialty in 1983 under judge George Danforth (Romayne Shelties). Owned by Linda More, she is handled here by Tom Coen as Linda was at her daughter's high school graduation that day. **Below:** Starhaven's FoxBoro Delight, by Ch. Starhaven's Great Xpectation ex Ch. FoxBoro Daydream Believer, taking Winners Bitch for three points at Terre Haute in 1982. Starhaven Kennels, Carl and Amy Langhorst.

Ch. Hoch Haven Maida's Memory, by Ch. Pixie Dell Little Hobo ex Ch. Pixie Dell Charm o'the North, in April 1961. Bred and owned by Mr. and Mrs. Haworth F. Hoch, Sweetbriar Farm.

Ch. Ilakai's Mi Lady Ambassador (left), by Ch. Brigadoon Merri Lou I'm Ready, and Briarwood Jingles Lit'l Tana (right). Both owned by Charlotte Clem McGowan, Rorralore Shelties.

Little Girl Lost, a lovely bitch close to championship as we go to press. Sam and Lois Lippincott, Rustic Kennels.

Winston Crown Jewels, winning the Futurity of the 1983 Colonial Shetland Sheepdog Specialty at Danvers, Massachusetts, handled by Mrs. Rose Chandless; judge, Mrs. Susan Beacham. Owned by Ruth E. Lane and Arnold C. Lane, Summit Shelties.

SWEEPSTAKES OR FUTURITY

TATHAM PHOTO

Rosmoor Star Spangled, a daughter of Ch. Sundowner Mr. Bojangles, with Jennie Tomlin taking Winners Bitch at Agathon Kennel Club in 1982. Owned by Rose and Jennie Tomlin.

Can. and Am. Ch. Lauxly's The Joker Is Wild, blue-merle dog by Sea Isle Nightime o'the Picts ex Meridian's Blues On Parade. A top winner in Canada, Joker won his American title in 1979. Linda More handling for owners Hazel Slaughter of Meridian Shelties in Canada and Ruth Lane of Summit Kennels in the United States.

Ch. Meridian's Hot Shot,
by Am. Ch. Ken-Rob's
Benchmark ex Ch.
Summit's Gay Abandon.
Hazel Slaughter, owner,
Meridian Shelties.

Ch. Sovereign Winning Spirit, sired by Ch. Sovereign Ring's Legacy. Spirit, sire of Am. Ch. Kismet's Saint or Sinner, was sold to Japan after a record winning streak of eighteen straight Bests of Breed in nineteen showings.

Banchory Passport of Pocono. Owned by Elizabeth D. Whelen, Pocono Kennels.

Ch. September Chiffon Ruffles winning one of her five Best Puppy in Breed awards. Owned by Mary MacDonald, Marchwind Kennels.

Ch. Crinan's Star Blazer at fourteen months of age. Homebred owned by Evelyn K. Basnicki, Crinan Shelties.

Am. and Can. Ch. Grelore Village Goldsmith, a 1981 champion by Ch. Benayr Peter Principle ex Ch. Grelore Ruby Red Dress, born December 1978. Bred by Katherine Gregor, this handsome dog is owned by Lyn and Mike Reese.

Above: Two famous Canadian Best in Show winning Shelties. On the left, Ch. Genson's Intrepid Man (Am. and Can. Ch. Gray Dawn Reveille of Sea Isle ex Sheldon Adrienne Faire, C.D.); on the right, Ch. Sheldon Banner Boy (Am. and Can. Ch. Gray Dawn Reveille of Sea Isle ex Sheldon Conversation Piece). Owned by Genson Kennels, Roxanne Ogden and Martha Jolly. **Below:** Can. Ch. Forever Silk Tassel, by Can. Ch. Hi-Hope's Mai'tre De ex Can. Ch. Forever Cafe Royale, C.D. In eight times shown, Tassel has three Bests of Breed (twice from the classes) and four Bests of Opposite Sex. Bred by Leslie B. Rogers and owned by Mrs. Donna Roadhouse.

Ch. Chicwin's Classic Conqueror, by Ch. Sovereign Ring's Legacy ex Ch. Chicwin's Promised Conquest. Breeder-owner, Fred Gordon, Chicwin Shetland Sheepdogs.

Ch. Shadowdale Come Fly With Me pictured at six months of age. Evelyn K. Basnicki.

Ch. Summit's Black as Sin, by Can. and Am. Ch. Banchory Backstop ex Rat's Misty Blue Brat. Owned by Ann Mitchell, Hariann Kennels.

Ch. Chicwin's Chelsea, by Ch. Sovereign Pumpkin of Astolat ex Ch. Chicwin's Promised Victory, exhibiting a gorgeous representation of beautiful head type. This outstanding dog belongs to and was bred by Fred Gordon, Chicwin Shetland Sheepdogs.

CHAPTER FIVE

Shetland Sheepdogs in Canada

Ch. and O.T. Ch. Cinderella Gypsy of Ronas Hill, T.D., Canada's first champion and obedience trial champion and U.D. *in any breed*, she was also pointed in the U.S. This tricolor bitch was the dam of five champions, including Ch. Summit's Gold Dust. All five had obedience titles. Bred by Mrs. G.F. Lovett, Ronas Hill Kennels, Carp, Ontario; owned by Ruth E. Lane, Summit Kennels, Centerville, Massachusetts.

Popularity of Shelties in Canada is very great, the breed enjoying interest there with a keenly enthusiastic following. We are pleased at being able to bring you a comprehensive story of numerous important kennels from there and of some of the dogs who have made Canadian history.

Some Canadian Firsts

Mr. Leslie B. Rogers, from Langley, British Columbia, is a noted historian on Sheltie matters and has very kindly contributed some most interesting information for this chapter. He has written us the following:

The very first Sheltie to win an all-breed Best in Show award in Canada was Champion Tayside Bonnie Prince. He made his historic win at the Alberta Kennel Club on September 6th 1955. At this same show, Bonnie Prince also won Best Brace in Show with his half-sister, and Best Team in Show with three kennel-mates. What a clean sweep! His pedigree was as follows. Sire, International Champion Dempsey's Wee Son of Glen Arden. Dam,

Alford's Miss Tam-O-Shanter. Students of the breed will realize the tremendous impact made by the Alford Kennels who figure in leading kennels of today all across Canada and on both coasts of the U.S.A.

Alford Kennels, no longer in existence, were owned by William Henderson of Toronto.

The first female Best in Show Shetland Sheepdog in Canada was officially known as Champion Hi-Hope's Merry, U.D., American C.D.X., and she was owner-handled by Frances Clark to her Best in Show win. She is the most titled Sheltie to ever achieve such a high award. Her sire and dam were both American-bred Shelties. Sire, American Champion Merrywood Charter Member. Dam, Noralee Naiad, C.D.

Another very famous Sheltie in Canadian History is Champion and Obedience Trial Champion Cinderella Gypsy of Ronas Hill, T.D., born May 14th 1950; bred by Mrs. G.F. Lovett, Ronas Hill Kennels, Ontario; and owned by Ruth E.

A famous Sheltie of the past, the blue-merle female Int. Ch. Pocono Trinket of Windy Oaks, pictured here in May 1948 on the day she finished her U.S.A. championship at Morris and Essex with Best of Winners and Best of Opposite Sex in an entry of fifty-nine. Bred by Elizabeth Whelen, Pocono Shelties; owner, Mrs. G.F. Lovett, Ronas Hill Shelties. Trinket was shown at an American Specialty in the Veterans Class at the incredible age of sixteen and a half years! She was a daughter of Ch. Larkspur of Pocono, top producing female in the breed with sixteen champions.

Lane, Summit Kennels, registered in Canada, now at Centerville, Massachusetts, in the United States.

Gypsy distinguished herself by becoming Canada's first Champion and Obedience Trial Champion and Utility Dog *in any breed,* and she was also pointed in the U.S.A. Additionally she was the dam of five champions, including Champion Summit's Gold Dust, all five also having obedience titles.

Gypsy was by Champion Magic Talisman of Pocono (Champion Tailor Made of Pocono ex Blue Jewel of Pocono) ex Aylmer Chorine (Champion Alford Wee MacGregor ex Bonny Lou). Her conformation successes included a Group first, two Group seconds, four Group thirds, and five Group fourths.

Again a memorable first was scored by American and Canadian Champion Delamantha's Midday Sun, American and Canadian U.D., who became the first Canadian Champion Utility Dog Sheltie to also become a Champion Utility Dog in the United States. Owned and handled by Patricia Houston of Toronto and bred by Carol Watt of the Delamantha Kennels, Midday Sun was born on August 1st, 1975. He gained his

Canadian championship in short order, winning five Bests of Breed , and then started out in obedience, which was a new experience not only for the dog but also for his owner-handler. He was the first dog his owner ever had trained, and he did her proud when he gained his C.D. with qualifying scores of 194 in Novice, 195 in Open, and 195 in Utility. He completed his Canadian U.D. in September 1978.

Coming to the United States, Midday Sun finished his C.D. in only two weekends of competition. Probably the most memorable day in his career was the one on which he gained a four-point major in the United States over sixty-one Shelties, taking Best of Winners; and at the same show he made his first appearance in obedience as an Open contender, coming away highest scoring Sheltie in this class. The following week he won his second major and, again at the same show, completed his American C.D.X., placing third in the class. He finished his American championship in August 1978. Then came Utility Dog competition in the United States, which found Midday Sun with his American U.D. title during the spring of 1979.

Best in Show winner Ch. Sheldon Banner Boy, a son of the litter-sister to Ch. Sheldon This Is The General. He is one of Canada's top Working Group Shelties, with eleven Working Groups to his credit. He is also the sire of eleven champions. Bill and Doreen Randall, owners, Sheldon Shelties.

Best in Show Shelties and Top Sires and Dams

Once again our thanks to Mr. Leslie B. Rogers, owner of the Forever Shelties, this time for the following lists of Canadian Best in Show Shelties of the 1970's and the early 1980's and the leading Canadian Sheltie Sires and Dams (through September 1983, *Dogs in Canada*, the official publication of the Canadian Kennel Club).

Mr. Rogers is a well-known statistician, and we appreciate his sharing with our readers this information, which adds greatly to the interest and value of our Canadian section.

Best in Show Shelties of the 1970's

American and Canadian Champion Terian's Aire Faire (3 Bests in Show)

American and Canadian Champion Gracmar Opin For Victory

American and Canadian Champion Delamantha's Desiderata (3 Bests in Show)

Canadian Champion Elf Dale Royal Ensign

Canadian Champion Cloverleaf's Tri Jet

American and Canadian Champion Timberlawn Blue Haze O'Forelyn

American and Canadian Champion Richmore Roustabout

Canadian Champion Sheldon First Dream, C.D.X.

American and Canadian Champion Reveille's Reflection of Sheldon

American and Canadian Champion Roydon's Indigo of Brookbend

Canadian Champion Meridian's Savoir Faire

Canadian Champion Diamond Lil of Mantoga, C.D.X.

Canadian Champion Jo-Ro's To Sir With Love

Canadian Champion Sheldon Jaunty Justin

American and Canadian Champion Banchory Backstop (3 Bests in Show)

Canadian Champion Alert Highland Lad, C.D.X.

Canadian Champion Sheldon Banner Boy

Canadian Champion Alert Thistle Lass, C.D. 2 Bests in Show)

American and Canadian Champion Iz Charles Rex O'Satelier (2 Bests in Show)

Canadian Champion Sheldon Raspberry Ruffle

Best in Show Shelties of the Early 1980's

Canadian Champion Sheldon Korshelt Classic Look

Canadian Champion Alert Thistle Lass, C.D.

Canadian Champion Sheldon Raspberry Ruffle (2 Bests in Show)

Ch. Meridian's Savoir Faire, by Can. and Am. Ch. Kenrob's Kenny ex Ch. Meridian's Long Shot, winning the Working Dog Specialty in conjunction with Can Save Shows under the late Alva Rosenberg in 1971. This was Canada's Number One Sheltie for 1971. Mrs. Hazel Slaughter, owner.

Canadian Champion Banchory Key Witness (3 Bests in Show)

Canadian Champion Banchory Counterforce

Canadian Champion Satelier's Strike Up the Band

Canadian Champion Banchory Showman of Shaylin

American and Canadian Champion Iz Charles Rex O'Satelier

American and Canadian Champion Sir Joshua of Winslow

Canadian Champion Banchory Eye of the Storm

Canadian Champion Genson's Intrepid Man

Canadian Champion Gallantry Solid Success

Sires of 50 or More Canadian Champions

American and Canadian Champion Reveille's Reflection of Sheldon

Sires of 40 or More Canadian Champions

American Champion Halstor's Peter Pumpkin

Sires of 20 or More Canadian Champions

Canadian Champion Esquire's Casino Royale

Sires of 10 or More Canadian Champions

Canadian Champion Banchory Count Down

American and Canadian Champion Banchory Formal Notice

American and Canadian Champion Banchory High Born

American and Canadian Champion Banchory Backstop

American and Canadian Champion Boydlyn's Andy Devine

Canadian Champion Bronze of Mantoga, U.D.

American Champion Chenterra Thunderation

American and Canadian Champion Cherden Sock It To 'Em

Canadian Champion Delamantha's Daybreak

Canadian Champion Francehill Indigo, U.D.

American and Canadian Champion Graydawn Reveille of Sea Isle

Ch. Gallantry Solid Success taking his first Best of Breed, first time out, from the classes over two Best in Show Specials under judge Lawrence Stanbridge at Evergreen Kennel Club, March 1982. Success, now a Best in Show winner, was just ten months old at this time. Breeder-owner-handler, Mona Stolcz.

Canadian Champion Kel-Lani's Moonshine
American Champion Romayne's Sportin' Life
Canadian Champion Sheldon Presents Michael
Canadian Champion Sheldon Banner Boy
American and Canadian Champion Sheldon This Is The General
Canadian Champion Sovereign Pumpkin of Astolat
Canadian Champion Sovereign Ring's Legacy
Canadian Champion Sunnycrest Black Topper
American and Canadian Champion Terian's Aire Faire
Canadian Champion Timberidge Typesetter, C.D. (17 champions)
Canadian Champion Willow Acres Golden Rocket (16 champions)
Canadian Champion Honeyboy of Callart

Dams of 10 or More Canadian Champions

Canadian Champion Summit's Gay Abandon (13 champions)

Dams of 5 or More Canadian Champions

Canadian Champion Blundell's Peg O' My Heart
Canadian Champion Cloverleaf's Country Charm
Canadian Champion Delamantha's Dove
Canadian Champion Dilhorne Fortune
Canadian Champion Hausenbrook's Mischief Maker (9 champions)

Can. and Am. Ch. Meridian's Miss Behave, by Meridian's Indian Warrior ex Meridian's Indian Legend. Co-owned by Hazel Slaughter and Ruth E. Lane.

Ch. Summit's Gay Abandon, top producing Sheltie bitch in Canada of all time, with thirteen champions to her credit. Bred by Ruth E. Lane in the United States; owned by Mrs. Hazel Slaughter in Canada.

Kel-Lani's Autumn Blaze
Canadian Champion Kel-Lani's Moonglow, C.D.
Canadian Champion Kingsgate Candle in the Rain
Meadow's Orange Marmalade
Satelier's Blessed Event
Canadian Champion Satelier's Rosemary
Canadian Champion Sovereign Song Spinner
American and Canadian Champion Meridian's Miss Behave
Sunnycrest Merry Imp
Canadian Champion Sunnydell Love Story
Canadian Champion Tremur's Autumn Glory
Badgerton's Vain Vanessa (9 champions)
Aylmer Chorine
Canadian Champion Willow Acres Golden Charm, C.D.
Alford Jay Jay's Lassie
Canadian Champion Cinderella Gypsy of Ronas Hill
Doron's Taffy Ann
Canadian Champion Helensdale Wendy
Canadian Champion Minonamee Eugenie

Can. Ch. and O.T.Ch. Grayfield Pepper and Salt, Am. and Bda. C.D., winning first in the Working Group at Sudbury in 1982. Sue Danziger, owner, Cavatina Kennels, Bramalea, Ontario.

Carnwath Cavatina's Rhapsody, by Barwood's Formal Attire ex Ch. Whitegate's On A Clear Day. Owned by Cavatina Shelties, Sue Danziger.

Ch. and O.T.Ch. Grayfield Pepper and Salt, Am. and Bda. C.D., about to make a straight "sit." This is Sue Danziger's beloved "Quincy," at Cavatina Kennels.

Cavatina

Cavatina Shetland Sheepdogs were registered as a kennel in 1980, a new but very conscientious operation owned by Susan Danziger of Bramalea in Ontario.

The kennel started out with Canadian Champion and Obedience Trial Champion Grayfield Pepper and Salt, American and Bermudian U.D. "Quincy," as he is known, was purchased from Audrey Gray of Grayfield Kennels at age seven weeks by Sue Danziger, who from the very beginning had wanted a blue-merle and fell in love with this handsome puppy on sight. He was sired by the Peter Pumpkin son, American Champion Macdega Sergeant Pepper ex Champion Grayfield's Blue Sapphire.

"Quincy" was started in show training and obedience training at an early age. His delight in pleasing his owner made him a happy worker, and he soon sailed through to his C.D. His conformation championship came with ease, too, and he had finished by the time he was just over a year's age. Next came his C.D.X., then his American C.D. with a High in Trial, followed by his Utility Dog degree; then to Bermuda, from where he came home with a C.D. and a High in Trial.

In 1979 "Quincy" made his first appearance in the ring as a Special at a Specialty Show. A

very special moment for a very special dog was when Stanley Saltzman pointed to Susan Danziger with the words "Best of Breed," making "Quincy" the winner. Shown on a limited basis, during 1982 this little dog racked up ten Bests of Breed and four Group placements including a first. He also obtained nine Bermuda points, so is lacking just one point for his title there.

Plans for the future as this book goes to press include more shows, and an American C.D.X. and U.D. tracking degree, competing in open, and who knows what else!

Preceding "Quincy" at Cavatina Kennels was Summit's Stacy, C.D.X., American C.D., bred by Ruth Lane and purchased from Hazel Slaughter.

Breeding at Cavatina was not commenced until 1983 after the acquisition of Carnwath Cavatina's Rhapsody, by Barwood Formal Attire ex Champion Whitegate's On A Clear Day, purchased from Susan Symington of Carnwath Kennels. Now there is a new litter there as we write, by American and Canadian Champion Ridgeside Star Wars ex Rhapsody, with two very promising tri males, Ashly and Michael, looking to the future.

Ch. Chicwin's Promised Jewel, by Ch. Sovereign Ring's Legacy ex Ch. Sovereign Cranberry Red. Bred, owned, and handled by Fred Gordon, Chicwin Shetland Sheepdogs, Sault Ste. Marie, Ontario.

Ch. Sovereign Thornbird, by Ch. Sovereign Ring's Legacy ex Ch. Regency Sweet Brier. Handler, Don Palanio; breeder, Pearl D. Gardeinier; owner, Fred Gordon, Chicwin Shelties.

Chicwin

Chicwin Shetland Sheepdogs are owned by Fred and Sandra Gordon who live at Sault Ste. Marie, Ontario. Chicwin is a bloodline based on many of the top producing dogs of Sovereign Kennels, a kennel that has produced over one hundred Canadian champion Shelties and has existed for more than thirty-four years. Although Chicwin began with one Sheltie in 1974, the Gordons now maintain a breeding force of twenty to twenty-five individuals and has the greatest concentration of Sovereign bloodlines to be found anywhere.

The foundation bitch was Champion Sovereign Cranberry Red. More recently the Gordons have added such fine individuals as Champion Sovereign Pumpkin of Astolat, Champion Sovereign Torch Singer, Champion Sovereign Mystic Charm, Champion Sovereign Ebony Shine, Champion Sovereign Success Story, and Champion Sovereign Thornbird.

Ch. Sovereign Ebony Shine, by Sovereign Curtain Time ex Sovereign Penny Shine. Breeder, Ariel Sleeth; owner, Fred Gordon, Chicwin Kennels.

From the outset of their involvement with Shelties, the Gordons have been serious students of the "Sovereign Predictable Breeding Plan," the genetics breeding program developed and so successfully followed by Mrs. Ariel Sleeth. They credit the use of this plan for the high success which has been theirs within a very short span of time. Not only have the Chicwin dogs been consistent winners, but they also have produced excellent offspring in each generation. Chicwin has produced Specialty winners, Best of Breed winners, Best Puppy in Show winners, and Group winners. To date they have eleven champions carrying the Chicwin prefix, along with many others who are pointed.

Champion Sovereign Chicwin's Panda, Champion Chicwin's Promised Destiny, Champion Chicwin's Promised Jewel, Champion Chicwin's Classic Conqueror, Champion Chicwin's Sweet Honesty, Champion Chicwin's

A lovely head-study of Ch. Chicwin's Promised Destiny, by Ch. Sovereign Ring's Legacy ex Ch. Sovereign Cranberry Red. Breeder-owner, Fred Gordon, Chicwin Shetland Sheepdogs.

Chicwin's Promised Elegance, pointed, by Ch. Sovereign Gonna Fly Now ex Ch. Chicwin's Promised Jewel. Breeder-owner, Fred Gordon, Chicwin Shetland Sheepdogs.

Ch. Chicwin's Sweet Charity, by Sovereign Living Legend ex Ch. Chicwin's Promised Victory. Breeder-owner, Fred Gordon, Chicwin Shetland Sheepdogs.

Ch. Chicwin's Sweet Honesty, by Sovereign Living Legend ex Ch. Chicwin's Promised Victory. Handled by Don Palanio; bred by Fred Gordon; owned by Ariel Sleeth.

Ch. Chicwin's Chelsea, by Ch. Sovereign Pumpkin of Astolat ex Ch. Chicwin's Promised Victory, multiple Best of Breed and Group winner and twice Best Puppy in Show. Don Palanio, handler. Bred and owned by Fred Gordon, Chicwin Shetland Sheepdogs.

Sweet Charity, Champion Chicwin's Diamond Dealer, Champion Chicwin's Promised Victory, Champion Chicwin's Promised Conquest, Champion Chicwin's Country Music, and Champion Chicwin's Chelsea are the Chicwin champions as this is written.

Most notable of them all is Champion Chicwin Chelsea who is a consistent Best of Breed and Group winner. As a puppy she also attained eight Best Puppy in Group wins and twice was Best Puppy in Show. A daughter of Champion Sovereign Pumpkin of Astolat (sire of more than fourteen Canadian champions) ex Champion Chicwin's Promised Victory, she represents the finest of producing bloodlines.

In January 1983, the Gordons purchased from Ariel Sleeth all of the Sovereign bitches, thus assuring themselves of having a broad genetic base enabling assured continuation of line-breeding and producing quality genetically programmed individuals for many generations in the future.

Crinan's Star Blazer, nineteen months old, taking Winners Dog, Best of Winners, then Best of Breed over thirty-six (including eight Specials) at the Dominion Collie and Sheltie booster show, Credit Valley, December 1982; judge, Robert Waters. Owned by Evelyn K. Basnicki, Rexdale, Toronto, Ontario.

Above: Am. and Can. Ch. and O.T.Ch. Delamantha's Midday Sun, Am. and Can. U.D., the sire of Ch. Crinan's Star Blazer. Midday Sun is the first Canadian Sheltie to have won an American championship and U.D. title, and he won both of his majors within a week at the same shows as his obedience successes. Owner-handled in both conformation and obedience by John and Patricia Houston, Toronto, Canada. Photo courtesy of Evelyn Basnicki, owner of his son, Ch. Crinan's Star Blazer. **Below:** Crinan's April Dream, born April 1981, by Am. and Can. Ch. and O.T.Ch. Delamantha's Midday Sun ex Crinan's Keepsake, a full sister to Ch. Crinan's Star Blazer and the dam of Black Velvet at Crinan. Bred by Evelyn K. Basnicki and owned by Pat Blacker Thompson.

Crinan

Crinan Shetland Sheepdogs belong to Evelyn K. Basnicki and are located at Rexdale, Toronto, Ontario. Temperament, type, and structure are the three basic goals here, the owner's belief being that "without these three basics there is no dog."

Top dog in this kennel is the handsome "Echo," Champion Crinan's Star Blazer, 15¼ inches, who was born on April 13th 1981.

A true show dog in temperament as well as quality, "Echo" completed his title with ease, his wins having included Best of Breed at a "booster" show for a five-point major; Best of Winners at Aurora and District under Mrs. P. Stoneham for another five-point win; and at Progressive Kennel Club under Ron Herd, June 1983, Best of Winners for a four-point major.

"Echo" is a son of American and Canadian Champion and Obedience Trial Champion Delamantha's Midday Sun ex Crinan's Keepsake. As we write, he is about to be shown in the United States, in search of his title here, too, which we feel certain he will have earned by the

time you read this book. "Echo's" heritage is a proud one, as his sire, Midday Sun, is the first Canadian Sheltie to have won an American Championship and U.D. title. Owned by John and Patricia Houston of Toronto, this lovely dog, entirely owner-handled in both conformation and obedience, won both his majors within a week and finished his C.D.X. at the same shows as his majors. We wish "Echo" equal success in the United States as enjoyed by his dad.

There are some very exciting puppies at Crinan for whom hopes are high. Among these

This is "Bear" at three months of age. Owned by Evelyn K. Basnicki, Crinan Kennels.

Above: Crinan's Keepsake, by Ch. Shadowdale Come Fly With Me, at ten and a half weeks of age. Evelyn Basnicki, owner. **Below:** Shadowdale's Just A Flying, a 14" bitch by Ch. Crinan's Starblazer ex Shadowdale's Ember Glow, pictured at six months of age. Bred by Mary Curl and owned by Tom Stem.

is "Bear," born February 1983, by Champion Macdega Main Event ex Crinan's Keepsake, who is the dam of Champion Crinan's Star Blazer and was sired by Champion Shadowdale's Come Fly With Me. Still too young to be shown as we write, he is a puppy of unusual potential, a complete "natural," and one whose owner can hardly wait to get him into the ring.

Then there is Star Blazer's daughter, "Sara," a gorgeous tri bitch, 14 inches at nine months. Officially she is Shadowdale's Just A Flying, and she is a daughter of "Echo" from Shadowdale's Ember Glow. On the first day at Aurora in May 1983, she won first in Junior Puppy and Reserve Winners Bitch under judge Eve Whitmore, and on the next day, she was Best Puppy in her breed, under Mrs. P. Stoneham; then in June she won first in Junior Puppy at a big Specialty judged by Ariel Sleeth.

Black Velvet of Crinan, "Sacha," was whelped in May 1982. At six months of age she was shown in the United States, making some good wins in the Puppy Classes. Then at Alberta Kennel Club in Canada, February 11th, 12th, and 13th 1983, she won Junior Puppy and Best Puppy in breed under Captain Bob Wilson of Texas (twenty puppies competing); Winners bitch for five points (twenty-three bitches competing) under Donna Cole; and second out of nine puppies under judge Robert Forsyth.

Since then "Sasha," to her owner's pleasure, has continued to fare well in competition.

251

Forever

The foundation sire for the Forever Kennels, belonging to Leslie B. Rogers, Langley, British Columbia, was the noted American-bred tricolor American Champion Thistlerose Arcwood Aladdin. This dog had a brief, but brilliant, show career in the United States, where his American title was completed with four Bests of Breed, two Working Group firsts, and one second and one fourth in Group. An ear injury necessitated removal of one half an ear, which put an end to what might have been a wonderful Specials career.

Aladdin was the result of a carefully planned breeding of International Champion Blue Quest of Pocono and his daughter, Champion Thistlerose Classic Moderne. Blue Quest was a three-time Best in Show winner in the United States during a period when Shelties were relative strangers to Best in Show awards. Classic

Forever The Skylark at seven months of age. Breeder, Leslie B. Rogers; owner, Karen Zimmerman.

A beautiful painting of a magnificent dog! Ch. Thistlerose Arcwood Aladdin, by Am. and Can. Ch. Blue Quest of Pocono ex Am. Ch. Thistlerose Classic Moderne. This tricolored male was a dominant producer and appears in the pedigree of the top winning male in the history of the breed in the United States, Am. and Can. Ch. Karelane Royal Flush O'Kismet, with thirty-five American Best in Show wins; and the top winning female in the history of the breed in the United States, Am. and Can. Ch. Rosewood Christy The Clown, with seven American Bests in Show. It is an interesting note that both Royal Flush and Christy are blue-merles, and both were breeder-owner-handled to their outstanding records. This painting of Aladdin was done by famed artist and Sheltie breeder Jean Simmonds, Carmylie Kennels. Aladdin was bred by A. and E. Jolly, Thistlerose Shelties, Wisconsin, U.S.A., and was owned by Leslie B. Rogers, Forever Shelties, British Columbia, Canada.

Moderne is one of the leading producing dams in America, having been dam of seven American champions. Aladdin's principal virtues were physical and mental soundness, correct head planes, and excellent movement. A very strong and powerful male, he lived from 1958 to 1972 with never a day of sickness. He was the sire of eleven champions (eight American and three Canadian). His legacy lives on in the Forever Shelties as well as numerous American lines. Mr. Rogers points out that Aladdin appears in the pedigree of the top winning male Shetland Sheepdog and the top winning female Shetland Sheepdog in the history of the breed. Both happen to be blue-merles.

The foundation dam for the Forever Shelties was Lodgewood Ice Blue of Karelane. This 13½-inch blue-merle excelled in head (especially head planes and correct ears) and temperament, and she carried a huge coat of brilliant color. She was a repeat breeding of the American Champion Heir Apparant of Karelane, a noted Working Group and Specialty winner in the eastern United States.

From the two foundation Shelties and their descendants have evolved many champions. One was the famous Champion Forever The Blue Bonnet, a bicolor blue-merle with excellent type and brilliant blue coat, plus wonderful disposition. She produced American Champion Forever Pawthorne Blue Eclipse, another brilliantly colored bicolor who was a Working Group winner from the Puppy Class and in the United States was a Specialty winner. Blue Eclipse pro-

duced American and Canadian Champion Rosewood Christy The Clown, a blue-merle who holds the record as the Top Winning Shetland Sheepdog *female* in the history of the breed, having won, owner-handled, seven American Best in Show awards.

Other Forever champions in bicolor and blue-merle are Champion Forever The Black Bonnet and Champion Blue Flat, C.D.X. (another Working Group winner).

For the sable and white branch of Forever Kennels, the two foundation bitches were a daughter of American and Canadian Champion Pixie Dell Bright Vision, three times Best of Breed at Westminster, and a daughter of one of the leading U.S.A. sable sires, Champion Sea Isle Serenade. From these two females, with judicious blends to Champion Thistlerose Arcwood Aladdin and other family-related males, have resulted many champions, among them Champion Rare Florin O'Forever (sire of champions), Champion Forever Wild Rose (Specialty winner), Champion Forever Autumn Piper, U.D. (a Dual Champion), Champion Forever Autumn Gypsy (Best of Breed winner), Champion Forever Princeling (Best of Breed winner), Champion Forever Jane Eyre (referred to by the fancy as the "$25 champion" as that was the

Two famous Shelties of long ago! This 1960 photo features Day Dream of Ronas Hill, owned by Mrs. G.F. Lovett of Ontario, and Silver Trinket of Ronas Hill (seven points), owned by Leslie B. Rogers of British Columbia. Trinket, born in 1959, had in her pedigree Int. Ch. Blue Quest of Pocono and Int. Ch. Trinket of Windy Oaks. Please note the acceptable blue eyes in Silver Trinket, a color which is permissible only in blue-merle Shelties.

An interesting study of Ch. Forever Autumn Piper, C.D., C.D.X., U.D., and his sister Ch. Forever Autumn Gypsy. Bred by Leslie B. Rogers; owned by Murial Dowling, Canada.

Ch. Forever Cafe Royale, C.D., pictured winning the Blanche Saunders Memorial Challenge Trophy in Obedience. Photo courtesy of Leslie B. Rogers, Forever Shetland Sheepdogs.

Above: Ch. Forever Princeling a 14½″ sable and white son of Am. Ch. Thistlerose Arcwood Aladdin. Breeder-owner-handler, Leslie B. Rogers, Forever Shelties. **Below:** Can. Ch. Forever Rain Whisper, by Am. Ch. September's Rainmaker ex Forever Stylish Miss, a Best Puppy in Show winner under judge Mrs. Doris Wilson. This is a 1982 champion bred by Leslie B. Rogers, Forever Kennels, and owned by Mrs. Donna Roadhouse, Arpeggio Shelties, Aldergrove, British Columbia, Canada.

sum necessary to complete a speedy championship), Champion Loyalty of Forever (multiple Group-winner), Champion Mar-ja's Forever Flame (Group winner from the classes and twice all-breed Best Puppy in Show), Champion Forever Lady Jane, Champion Forever Billy The Kid, Champion Forever Rain Whisper (Best Puppy in Show, all-breeds), and Champion Forever Cafe Royale, C.D. (winner of the Blanche Saunders Memorial Challenge Trophy in Obedience).

Other sable champions were purchased, two of these being Champion Kingsgate The Fire Cat (Working Group winner, twice Best Puppy in Show) and Champion Miskela Destiny O'Forever (Working Group winner from the Puppy Class).

The owner of Forever Shelties, Mr. Rogers, is one of the breed's foremost authorities, highly respected in both the United States and Canada. In his breeding programs, special emphasis always has been placed on correct type along with sound minds in sound bodies. More than forty obedience titles have been earned by Shelties from the Forever bloodlines.

254

Ch. Banchory Birth Right, C.D., by Ch. Banchory The Cornerstone, C.D., ex Banchory Bellisima, winning the Group under W.P. Bowden at Tyee on May 6th 1982. Owner-handled by Mona Stolcz.

Gallantry

Gallantry Shetland Sheepdogs' owner, Mona Stolcz of Victoria, British Columbia, started out, as so many others have done, with no intention of exhibiting in conformation or of breeding. Her first Sheltie, "Val," was an obedience prospect, but she was talked into entering him in a Specialty fun match. The consequences changed her life! "Val" won Best Puppy in Breed. Mona Stolcz was "bitten by the show bug," and, as she says, "my life has literally gone to the dogs."

Unhappily, "Val" never won anything more in conformation, although he earned his C.D. with two High in Trials. So next Mona Stolcz had to buy a show-prospect. Having a background in breeding and exhibiting Siamese cats, she realized the value of purchasing her puppy from a top producing kennel. She wrote to several and spent hours going through the pages of *The Shetland Sheepdog Magazine* and *Sheltie Pacesetter*. Every time a dog caught her eye, it

Ch. Gallantry Solid Success, winner of two Bests of Opposite Sex (including at the 1983 Shetland Sheepdog Club of British Columbia Specialty) and a Best Senior in Sweepstakes at the National Specialty in the United States, at two years of age. Bred and owned by Mona and Lisa Stolcz, Gallantry Kennels.

was of Banchory bloodlines. Thus she decided that Banchory had the outline, look, and prettiness that she wanted.

It took several phone calls before Mona Stolcz was able to convince Donna Harden to sell her an eight-week-old male puppy she had, sired by Champion Banchory The Cornerstone out of a Reflection/Arabesque daughter. To quote Mrs. Stolcz, "Donna was very sweet, finally said yes, and on September 6th 1978, I picked up an incredibly cute ball of fluff from the airport." The ball of fluff grew up to become the widely admired Champion Banchory Birth Right, C.D.!

Excelling in ring presence and attitude, Birth Right finished his championship by taking a Best of Breed from the classes over Specials and went on to a Group second under judge Fred Fraser. Birth Right won a very competitive Working Group his first time out as a Special, under judge Fernandez Cartwright and now has, in limited showing, two Group firsts, one Group second, three Group fourths, twelve Bests of Breed, and two High in Trial awards, the latter with scores of 198 and 198½.

Birth Right has proven a tremendous success as a sire. He is very dominant and his puppies even from outcross bitches of widely dissimilar

Above: Ch. Gallantry Amber Fair winning Best of Breed over two Specials under judge Richard Renihan at Shoreline K.C. in 1983. Amber Fair, a Best Puppy in Show winner, also won two Bests in Puppy Group, one Best of Breed, and eight Bests of Opposite Sex. Bred by Mona and Lisa Stolcz; handled by Sandra Hayward for owner Jean McMillan. **Below:** Ch. Gallantry's Windward Legacy. Bred by Mona Stolcz, Gallantry Shetland Sheepdogs; owned by Jean McMillan.

Ch. Banchory Birth Right, C.D., at four years of age. Owned by Mona Stolcz, Gallantry Shetland Sheepdogs, Victoria, British Columbia.

bloodlines have his look. His siring record to date, in rather limited use, includes: Champion Gallantry Solid Success (a Best in Show winner, Group first winner, multiple Group placer, and seventeen Bests of Breed), Champion Gallantry Amber Fair (Best of Breed winner, Best Puppy in Show and multiple Puppy Group winner), Champion Ronas Hill Eric The Red (Best of Breed winner, Puppy Group winner, and Specialty winner), Champion Gallantry Windward Legacy, Champion Gallantry Spirit of Midnight, Champion Ronas Hill Dixie Melody (Puppy Group winner and Specialty winner), Gallantry Hot Chocolate (ten points), Champion Ronas Hill Serenata (Group placer, Best of Breed and Puppy Group winner), Gallantry Blessington Desiree (five points), Gallantry Highwatch (five points), Cintara Just Imagine (five points), Gallantry Breeze Along (two points), and Gallantry Marquis of Linlithgow (two points).

On October 23rd 1979, Mrs. Stolcz purchased a ten-week-old sable daughter of American and Canadian Champion Wyndcliff The Successor out of an American and Canadian Champion Banchory The Candidate daughter. Destined to become one of Gallantry's top producers, Champion Banchory High Style finished with a Best of Breed over Specials from the classes. She is the dam of the gorgeous young dog, Best in Show winner Champion Gallantry Solid Success

Ch. Banchory High Style, by Am. and Can. Ch. Wyndcliff The Successor ex Banchory Dress Rehearsal, taking Winners Bitch (five points), Best of Winners, and Best of Breed over Specials under judge Joan Morden at Shoreline K.C. in 1981. High Style was pregnant at this time, carrying future Best in Show winner Ch. Gallantry Solid Success and Ch. Gallantry Amber Fair. This win completed her title. Bred by Clare and Donna Harden; handled by Ted Luke for owners Mona and Lisa Stolcz.

Gallantry Hot Chocolate, by Can. Ch. Banchory Birth Right, C.D., ex Banchory Black Magic II, ten points toward title, pictured at eight months of age. Breeder-owners, Mona and Lisa Stolcz, Gallantry Shetland Sheepdogs.

Ch. Gallantry Windward Legacy finishing title under Elmer Grieve at Shoreline K.C. in April 1983. Breeders, Mona and Lisa Stolcz, Gallantry Shelties; handled by Sandra Hayward for owner Jean McMillan.

Champion Harvest Hills Shoeshine Boy out of a daughter of American and Canadian Champion Banchory Formal Notice! The beautiful Banchory Black Magic had some huge wins at the sanctioned matches as a puppy, but, according to Mrs. Stolcz, she "grew herself right out of the show ring." Nevertheless she is another of Gallantry's top producers, being the dam of Champion Gallantry Spirit of Midnight, Gallantry Hot Chocolate (ten points), and Gallantry Nightwatch (five points). Black Magic is expecting her second litter in the fall of 1983, bred again to Birth Right, thus a repeat of the aforementioned.

Having bred their first litter in 1980, Mrs. Stolcz is looking forward with keen anticipation to those which are ahead, some of them being second-generation Gallantry. The kennel is a very small, select one breeding few litters per year. To quote Mrs. Stolcz: "It is with great satisfaction that we watch our puppies taking points and finishing with relative ease. We owe much to Clare and Donna Harden of Banchory Kennels. They gave Gallantry our foundation, and we are forever in their debt."

Ch. Gallantry Spirit of Midnight winning a five-point Best of Winners and Best of Opposite Sex over a Special under judge Gil Sharman at Tyee in 1983. Bred by Mona and Lisa Stolcz; handled by Sandra Hayward for owner Jean McMillan.

and the charismatic Champion Gallantry Amber Fair. The breeding which produced Success and Amber Fair has been repeated; the pick puppy was sold to a fancier in Ontario and at six months of age, from the Junior Puppy Class, started her career with a five-point major by way of Winners bitch, Best of Winners, and Best of Opposite Sex, the latter over a Special—certainly nice going.

Champion Macdega Westerly Breeze was purchased at just over one year of age. She came to Gallantry a finished champion, with two Bests of Breed from the classes and two Puppy Group firsts. Bred to Birth Right, she produced Champion Gallantry Windward Legacy and Gallantry Breeze Along. Currently she is the dam of two champions and three point-winners out of two litters.

While visiting Banchory Kennels in the spring of 1981, a lovely, elegant bi-factored tri puppy caught Mrs. Stolcz's eye. Leaving without her was impossible, especially when Mrs. Stolcz learned she was sired by American and Canadian

Ch. Sheldon Banner Boy, Best in Show dog handled to the top award under judge Howard Tyler by his new owner, Roxanne Ogden. Genson Shelties, Roxanne Ogden and Martha Jolly, Rothesay, New Brunswick, Canada.

Genson

Genson Kennels was established in 1977 by Roxanne Ogden and Martha Jolly of Rothesay, New Brunswick, with the purchase of Sheldon Adrienne Faire, C.D., and the Best in Show dog, Champion Sheldon Banner Boy. This is a relatively new kennel, which is nonetheless making its name and dogs well known among breeders and judges.

The first Sheltie owned by Roxanne Ogden was Sheldon Genson, C.D., the first son of Canadian and Japanese Champion Sheldon This Is The General. The kennel identification, "Genson," was derived from that of this first son of the General.

In their breeding program, Genson is aiming to produce working dogs, physically and mentally able to do a day's work, in keeping with the breed's original purpose. Obviously this is turning out well, judging by the success of Genson homebreds!

From American and Canadian Champion Gray Dawn Reveille of Sea Isle, Roxanne Ogden and Martha Jolly can point with pride to their Best in Show winners Champion Sheldon Banner Boy and Champion Genson Intrepid Man,

who, Roxanne Ogden notes, "give us bone substance, balance and that ever so sweet Sheltie expression." From Champion Sheldon Genson Hat Trick, grandson of American Champion Dorane's Kings Ransom, "we have kept movement and bone, but our head quality has improved, with a beautiful eye and moderate jaw." From Sheldon Adrienne Faire, C.D., "we maintain bone, movement, and natural Sheltie characteristics. Head type is modern with a good back skull." And Champion Hausenbrook Mischief Maker, three-quarters sister to Adrienne, "has a more powerful head, good movement."

Genson Sugar Plum, in mid-1983 with nine points, is nursing a litter by Champion Sheldon Genson Hat Trick. Sugar is a Banner daughter out of a Mischief Maker daughter, and the hope is to produce the balance from Banner and the heads from Hat Trick and Mischief.

In addition to the Best in Show winners Champion Sheldon Banner Boy and Champion Genson Intrepid Man, the Ogden-Jolly duo has a number of other successful winners in both conformation and obedience. These include the

Ch. Genson Intrepid Man, by Am. and Can. Ch. Gray Dawn's Reveille of Sea Isle ex Sheldon Adrienne Faire, C.D., born March 1979. This is a homebred Best in Show winner from Genson Kennels owned by Roxanne Ogden and Martha Jolly.

Can. Ch. Genson's Maggie Muggins, C.D., home-bred by Ch. Sheldon Banner Boy ex Sheldon Adrienne Faire, C.D., Best of Winners all three days on her first weekend out at shows when just six months old, topping which she took Best of Breed over two top-winning Shelties and on to fourth in Working Group on one of these days; Best Puppy in Show one day; and Best Working Puppy twice. Genson Kennels, owners, Roxanne Ogden and Margaret Jolly.

homebreds Champion Genson's Maggie Muggins, C.D. (who had quite a sensational show career as a puppy), Champion Genson's Lady Luck, Champion Genson's Private Treat, Champion Genson's Sweet Selection, and Champion Genson Tri-N-Stop Me, Champion The Sheldon Bright Topaze, C.D., and Champion Genson Hat Trick (the latter two purchased at eight seeks of age)—all having fared well in conformation.

While in obedience, Sheldon Adrienne Faire, C.D., was purchased at three months. Genson's Destiny has gained a C.D.X., Sheldon Genson is a C.D., and Genson's Fair Lady is a C.D. Genson Faire Isle Jubilee is a C.D. winner and has also been High in Trial.

At the present time, Genson is anticipating the show debuts of Sheldon Scottish Sheena's first puppies; they are to come out about the same time as we are writing. She is by American and Canadian Champion Shelando Top Scotch ex Sheldon Adrienne Faire, C.D., thus is to carry on the Adrienne line.

Champion Hausenbrook Mischief Maker, one of Canada's top bitches, purchased when six years of age, is now "retired to the sofa," having done more than her share as an excellent producer.

Ch. Hausenbrooks Mischief Maker and Ch. Genson's Intrepid Man taking Best of Breed and Best Puppy at Ottawa. These are two splendid representatives of the Gensen Shetland Sheepdogs, Roxanne Ogden and Martha Jolly.

Am. and Can. Ch. Bonnicay's Silver Solitaire, by Am. and Can. Ch. Kismet Smash Hit, pictured at his last show in 1975 winning the Working Group over top Best in Show contenders. Lochlana Shetland Sheepdogs, Mr. and Mrs. Gerry Guay, Timmins, Ontario, Canada.

Am. and Can. Ch. Bonnicay's Silver Solitaire pictured winning his first points in the U.S.A., going Best in Show for five points—a very exciting day! Lochlana Shelties, Mr. and Mrs. Gerry Guay.

Lochlana

Lochlana Shetland Sheepdogs are located at Timmins, Ontario, where they are owned by Mr. and Mrs. Gerry Guay, who to date have owned or bred somewhere in the area of close to forty champions, with at least fifteen obedience titleholders also coming from their dogs.

Gerry Guay himself began in dogs when he was just twelve years old, back in 1954. His very first dog was a Collie of excellent bloodlines although not show quality. She was a good producer, though, and lived to seventeen years of age.

Lochlana was registered as the Guays' kennel name on June 4th 1973, and since that time it has become a permanent registration.

As exhibitors, Gerry Guay says that their greatest thrill was showing a dog to second top Sheltie in Canada in 1975. This dog was American and Canadian Champion Bonnicay's Silver Solitaire, half ownership of which the Guays obtained from Bonnie Lafferty of Bonnicay fame. Solitaire became the biggest blue sensation, winning this honor in only seven weekends of showing. As Gerry Guay comments, "Quite a feat for a blue dog with two-tone eyes, plus being only 14½ inches tall, which some breeders felt was too small for a male." As Mr. Guay adds, "Seems strange they would think that, which today seems the preferred

Above: Can. and Am. Ch. Bonnicay's Silver Solitaire at ten months of age. This dog was a Best in Show winner in the United States and was second top Sheltie in Canada for 1975. Lochlana Kennels, owners. **Below:** Can. Ch. Bydard Moor O'Mario, C.D., by Am. and Can. Ch. Philidove Kismet Heir Borne ex Ch. Bydard's Black Mist. This Sheltie figures heavily in the Lochlana pedigrees and breeding program. Photo courtesy of Lochlana Kennels.

Ch. Lochlana Critic's Choice, by Am. and Can. Ch. Banchory Back Stop ex Lochlana Crystal Blue (pointed). Owned by Lochlana Kennels.

size." This obviously points up the changes which can occur in a breed within a few years' time!

Two names appear with great consistency in Lochlana pedigrees. They are those of Champion Banchory High Born and Champion Banchory Heir Borne, the Guays feeling that their best breeding results have come about through concentration on these two dogs plus some of their offspring, including Backstop, among others.

A good representation of Lochlana Shelties is the lovely Champion Lochlana Critic's Choice. This splendid bitch finished her championship undefeated, taking her first five points when only six months old. To date she has produced three champions in one litter.

The Guays have recently purchased one of the last Brig O'Dune dogs from Kathy Spencer. Having a great affection for the late Barbara J. Marr, who owned Brig O'Dune, the Guays were delighted at having the opportunity to purchase this dog when Kathy Spencer decided to offer her for sale. She is Brighton's Brig O'Dune Legacy, and it is hoped that she will produce in the family tradition.

Marchwind

Marchwind Kennels belong to Mary Mac-Donald of Delta, British Columbia, and although a comparatively new kennel, this one has been highly successful within a short period of time. Mrs. MacDonald attributes her success to the fact that she loves reading and finds it quite easy to assimilate information she gains from this source, hers being the type of retentive memory that enables her to literally carry a mental file of pedigrees and other pertinent data regarding her favorite breed. Coupled with this, she has a clear picture of what she likes and does not like in Shelties; thus she has a definite goal for her breeding program. She also gives much credit to Barbara J. Linden, of September Shelties, for her "confidence and kindness" which Mrs. MacDonald has found inestimably helpful. Mrs. Linden's September Kennel was one of the top producers for 1982, and she is breeder-owner of one of the nation's top producing studs.

Mrs. MacDonald's introduction to Shelties came about while she was looking for a family pet. She started out in obedience; then, as so frequently happens, she decided that she wanted a show-quality bitch. This she purchased from a

Ch. Marchwind the Rain Minstrel, Winners Dog and Best Puppy in Specialty at the Shetland Sheepdog Club of B.C. Specialty. Owned and bred by Mary MacDonald, Marchwind Kennels, Delta, British Columbia.

Ch. September Chiffon Ruffles, by Ch. Karral Good Times ex Ch. September Satin Slippers. Bred by Barbara J. and Kenneth A. Linden and owned by Mary MacDonald, Marchwind, Delta, British Columbia, Canada.

September Gypsy Slippers, by Ch. Cahaba's Touch The Wind ex Ch. September's Satin Slippers. Bred by Barbara J. and Kenneth A. Linden and owned by Mary MacDonald, Marchwind Shelties.

local kennel and took to obedience and handling classes. She loved every moment of it! Attending her first Specialty, she saw a gorgeous sable bitch which went on to take Best of Breed that day. Looking in the catalog, she found this bitch to have been sired by Champion September's Rainmaker; at that very moment she decided that she must have a puppy by this dog, as this was definitely "the look" that she wanted to produce in her own kennel.

All of the Marchwind foundation stock is based on that of September Kennels. The bitches presently being bred from there are all "September girls," and Mrs. MacDonald's stud dog is out of a bitch purchased from there and sent back for breeding to Rainmaker. The latter is Marchwind The Rain Minstrel, and hopes are high for his having a bright and exciting future.

Mrs. MacDonald has owned and personally shown Champion September Chiffon Ruffles, Champion Marfray's Wild Blue Yonder, and Champion Hi-Hope MacDee's Marsea, Canadian and American C.D., to their titles. She also is the owner of the Champion September Fresh Face. Her first homebred champion is the lovely Champion Marchwind The Rain Minstrel, by Champion September's Rainmaker ex September Oklahoma Sunrise. Several others, on their way as we write, will probably be champions by the time you are reading this book.

Marchwind is the only Sheltie kennel in Canada based on pure September breeding.

Ch. Marfray's Wild Blue Yonder, by Ch. Harvest Hill's Shoeshine Boy out of Banchory Blueberry Icing. This gorgeous blue dog was purchased after Mrs. MacDonald fell in love with him at a friend's home in Seattle. Although he does not fit into their breeding program at Marchwind, he is a splendid example of correct type and has done extremely well in the show ring. Bred by Mary Frances Hays; owned by Mary MacDonald.

Meridian

Meridian Shetland Sheepdogs are a small hobby kennel operated by Hazel Slaughter of Bois des Filion, Quebec. The breeding here has produced an average of two litters a year for almost three decades, but even with these small numbers, Meridian Shelties have set and broken many records.

With the help and patience of Mrs. Ruth E. Lane of Cape Cod, Massachusetts, two foundation bitches were obtained after seeing Champion Summit's Gold Dust, a very beautiful Sheltie owned by Mrs. Lane (then Mrs. F.H. Mingie) and sired by the legendary American and Canadian Champion Nashcrest Golden Note. Mrs. Slaughter immediately admired Gold Dust's huge, stand-off mahogany coat and decided that was the line on which she wished to base her breeding program. Thus it was that Champion Gypsy Rose of Ronas Hill, American and Canadian C.D. (by Texas Blue of Ronas Hill ex Hieland Melody of Ronas Hill) came to Mrs. Slaughter from Mrs. Helen Lovett's famed Ronas Hill kennels, and Champion Summit's Forever Amber (Champion Summit's Gold Dust, C.D., ex Champion Wee Honey of Ronas Hill) came from Mrs. Lane.

These two bitches immediately produced quality in keeping with their background, and

Can. and Am. Ch. Meridian's Miss Behave, by Meridian's Indian Warrior ex Meridian's Indian Legend, Canada's top Sheltie in 1968 and dam of six champions in all three colors. Co-owned by Mrs. Hazel Slaughter and Mrs. Ruth E. Lane.

Ch. Gypsy Rose of Ronas Hill, Can. and Am. C.D., by Texas Blue of Ronas Hill ex Hieland Melody of Ronas Hill. She was the foundation bitch for Meridian Shelties owned by Mrs. Hazel Slaughter, Bois des Filion, Quebec.

two from Gypsy's first litter sired by Gold Dust were entered in the Dominion Collie and Shetland Sheepdog Association's first Specialty Show in Montreal. The sable male, destined to become Champion Meridian's Gypsy Baron, won the breed over the top winning Specials while his sister, future Champion Meridian's Gypsy Serenade, C.D., went Winners Bitch. Both finished in consecutive shows with Serenade taking a Group fourth and Best Canadian-bred Puppy in Show the day she completed her title. A third Gypsy champion, Meridian's Truly Fair, also had a Best Puppy in Show, in this case in Bermuda.

Amber's first litter by Champion Summit's Golden Rod, C.D., produced Champion Meridian's Gay Tempo, C.D.X., one of the first of several top winning Shelties in Canada for the Meridian Kennels. Shown only ten times, he nonetheless garnered enough points to be Top Sheltie in 1967 with a Best in Show and several Group placements. Tempo was noted for his ground-covering, effortless movement.

Ch. Meridian's Gay Tempo, C.D.X., by Ch. Summit's Golden Rod, C.D., ex Ch. Summit's Forever Amber, a Best in Show dog and Canada's top Sheltie in 1967. Mrs. Hazel Slaughter, owner, Meridian Shetland Sheepdogs, Bois des Filion, P.Q., Canada.

Can. and Bda. Ch. Meridian's Toddy As In Rum (Cape Winds Storm Warning ex Ch. Meridian's Big Shot) winning the first of five Best Puppy in Show awards at the Canadian National Sportsman's Show in 1974 under judge Thelma Brown of California. Mrs. Hazel Slaughter, owner, Meridian Kennels.

The following year an inbred Gypsy granddaughter, the tri Canadian and American Champion Meridian's Miss Behave, topped Shelties in Canada with very limited showing, the latter due to the fact that she took "maternity leave" from the shows to whelp a litter during that year. Miss Behave produced six champions in all three colors. Three of these left their mark in future breedings. Bred back to her grandsire, Gold Dust, Miss Behave produced Champion Summit's Night and Day, a tri who proved an invaluable stud to reduce size; Champion Summit's Gay Abandon, mahogany sable Top Producing Sheltie Bitch of all time in Canada; and Champion Meridian's Blues On Parade, C.D. Additionally, Miss Behave produced Champion Summit's Gay Nineties, owned by Broadley Shelties, Second Top Sheltie in Canada in 1970.

Gay Abandon was sired by American Champion Kenrob's Gay Blade, and her puppies did some remarkable winning. She whelped thirteen champions out of twenty-seven puppies. Three of these were in her first litter of four by Cape Winds Storm Warning (American and Canadian Champion Kenrob's Kenny ex Champion Summit's Holiday). Then she produced an all-champion litter of four when bred again to Kenney, including Champion Meridian's Savoir Faire, Top Winning Sheltie in 1971, winner of a Best in Show and three consecutive Group firsts under Alva Rosenberg (he awarded Savoire Faire Best in the Working Dog Specialty), Winifred Heckman (both a Group and the Best in Show), and Joe Faigel. One littermate, Champion Meridian's Fair Warning owned by Ruth Lane, was a Specialty Show and Best Puppy in Show winner. The other two, Champion Meridian's Vanity Fair (Delting Hill Kennels owners) and Champion Meridian's County Fair (Broadley) were Specialty Show winners on the way to their titles.

Two more champions came from a repeat breeding to Storm Warning, one champion in a litter of one male from a son of Fair Warning and three more from a breeding to American Champion Kenrob's Benchmark. Two of these puppies won Group placements: Champion Meridian's Hot Shot and Champion Meridian's Long Shot. The latter produced Canadian and Bermudian Champion Meridian's Toddy As In Rum who in his puppy year, 1974, five times won Best Puppy in Show plus several Group placements to become the Number Three Top Sheltie in Canada. Long Shot also won the Working Group at eleven years of age at the Ottawa Kennel Club's unofficial all-breed Veterans Show in 1982, which surely speaks well for the lasting powers of this breed—a dog to have been ready for top winning as a puppy still looking his best at eleven years of age.

Miss Behave's last litter was by American Champion Philidove Heir Presumptive, and the

Ch. Meridian's Long Shot, by Am. Ch. Kenrob's Benchmark ex Ch. Summit's Gay Abandon. Owned by Mrs. Hazel Slaughter, Meridian Kennels.

Ch. Summit's Gay Abandon, by Ch. Kenrob's Gay Blade ex Can. and Am. Ch. Meridian's Miss Behave. With thirteen champions, she is Canada's top producing bitch. Mrs. Hazel Slaughter.

Ch. Meridian's Break in the Clouds, by Am. and Can. Ch. Severn Smoke on the Water ex Can. and Bda. Ch. Lauxly's Midnight Madness. This is a new Meridian dog on the show scene. Owned by Mrs. Hazel Slaughter.

resulting two puppies included Meridian's very first ever blue, Champion Meridian's Blues On Parade. "Miss Blue" was bred only twice as she belonged to the Lanes on Cape Cod, both times to the same dog, Champion Sea Isle Night Time o'the Picts, a son of American Champion Wyndcliffe Richmore Striking. She produced four champions, two of which are strongly entrenched behind currently winning Meridian stock. Canadian, American, and Bermudian Champion Lauxly's The Joker Is Wild, C.D., was the Top Winning Sheltie in Canada in 1977 and has produced three champions with some of his grandchildren now making the scene.

With the small numbers kept at Meridian, Canadian and Bermudian Champion Lauxly's Midnight Madness has been the only brood bitch there for the past four years (early 1980's) and was one of the Top Bitches in Canada while being Specialed. Consequently she has had only a few puppies, but three have finished to date, including Champion Meridian's Dark o'the Moon, Champion Meridian's Me and My Shadow, C.D.X., and the newly crowned Champion Meridian's Break In The Clouds, the latter by American and Canadian Champion Severn

Can. and Bda. Ch. Lauxly's Midnight Madness, by Ch. Sea Isle Night Time o'the Picts ex Ch. Meridian's Blues On Parade, Bermuda's only Best in Show Sheltie. Bred and owned by Mrs. Hazel Slaughter, Meridian Kennels.

Smoke on the Water. Midnight Madness, incidentally, is believed to be the only Bermudian Best in Show-winning Sheltie.

Miss Blue's other two champions were not bred but did some enviable winning in show and obedience rings. Champion Meridian's Queen of Spades (Richardson) completed her championship with a Best Puppy in Show on the same day, and Champion Meridian's Song Sung Blue, U.D. (Williams) has had two High in Trials and is one of the most enthusiastic members of Alberta's winning Scent Hurdle Team.

Though these and many other Meridian dogs have set many records in conformation (25% of all puppies bred there have become champions) and in obedience, "the companions that all of our dogs have become has made our years in dog breeding very rewarding," to quote Hazel Slaughter. Meridian is still striving for mentally and physically sound Shelties with "the outline that appears so symmetrical that no part appears out of proportion to the whole," plus that extra-special something that makes a Sheltie stand out above the others.

An extremely capable and popular judge, Hazel Slaughter feels that this occupation for the last few years has only heightened in her mind the necessity of breeding all the true essentials in one package, while having the whole dog balanced. A very knowledgeable "dog lady," Hazel can well take pride in her past accomplishments with Meridian as well as those to which she looks forward in the future.

Sheldon

Sheldon Shetland Sheepdogs, owned by Bill and Doreen Randall at Mount Brydges, Ontario, is a success story which is truly thrilling to read. This couple are a combined effort to develop and maintain the Sheldon line of Shelties in Canada, and their twentieth anniversary as breeders is rapidly approaching as we write these words during mid-1983.

Sheldon Shetland Sheepdogs to date have included no less than six Best in Show winners: American and Canadian Champion Reveille's Reflection of Sheldon (1972 Number One Sheltie in Canada), Champion Sheldon Jaunty Justin (1976 and 1977 Number Two Sheltie in Canada), Champion Sheldon Banner Boy (1977 Number Three Sheltie in Canada), Champion Sheldon First Dream, C.D.X. (1973 Number One Sheltie in Canada), Champion Sheldon Korshelt Classic Look (1980 Number Two Sheltie in Canada), and Champion Sheldon Raspberry Ruffles (1980 Number Three Sheltie in Canada).

The Randalls have bred or owned sixty-eight champions to date (June 1983) in conformation. They have also always had a keen interest in obedience and have bred many High in Trial winners, and their stud dogs have sired numerous obedience champions. A recent statistical record from January 1970 to December 1980 credited Sheldon dogs with twenty-eight C.D. titles, three C.D.X. titles, and one U.D. title. However, as Mrs. Randall notes, a recent update

Best in Show winning Can. and Am. Ch. Reveille's Reflection of Sheldon, the first and to date only Canadian-bred Sheltie to have won Best of Breed at the American Shetland Sheepdog Association National Specialty which he did when only eighteen months of age. He is the sire of more than fifty Canadian champions, including four Best in Show winners, one of them in Japan. Owned by Sheldon Shetland Sheepdogs, Bill and Doreen Randall, Mount Brydges, Ontario.

adds considerably to this list owing to the increasing interest in the obedience field of endeavor.

Among the noteworthy stars at Sheldon we find the Best in Show-winning Canadian and American Champion Reveille's Reflection of Sheldon. As a nine-month-old puppy at his first show he went from the Open Class to Best of Breed, Working Group first, and Best in Show—what a way to start a ring career! At eighteen months of age he won Best of Breed at the American Shetland Sheepdog Association National Specialty, the first and still to date only Canadian-bred Sheltie to gain this honor. Not content with success in the show ring, this superb little dog went on to become Canada's Top Sire in breed history and to date has sired more than fifty champions, including four Best in Show winners and a Best in Show winner in Japan.

Champion Sheldon Crowning Glory, a Specialty Best of Breed winner from the Open Class, is the dam of the aforementioned Japanese Best in Show dog, Canadian, American, and Japanese Grand Champion Sheldon This Is The General. He is also a Specialty Best of Breed winner in Canada and was the first and only import into Japan to win all awards at the Japanese

Am. and Can. Ch. Sheldon This Is The General, a Best of Breed and Specialty winner in Canada and the first and only import into Japan to win all awards at the Japanese Specialty. With thirteen Canadian champions to his credit, he is now proclaimed as Japan's top sire in breed history, so great has been his influence in that country.

Above, left: Sheldon Esmeralda, a daughter of Can., Am., and Jap. Gr. Ch. Sheldon This Is The General, one of the fine producers at Sheldon Kennels, Bill and Doreen Randall. **Above, right:** Ch. Sheldon Korshelt Classic Look, Best in Show winner, Specialty winner, fifty-eight times Best of Breed plus four Working Group firsts and numerous placements. Owned by Sheldon Shelties, Bill and Doreen Randall. **Below:** The Specialty winner, Am. and Can. Ch. Sheldano Top Scotch, purchased by the Randalls when the Sheldano Kennel was dispersed.

Specialty. He also went on to become a sire of note in that country, where he is now proclaimed as Japan's Top Sire in breed history! In Canada he is a leading sire, also, with thirteen champions.

A daughter of The General, Sheldon Esmerelda, was bred back to her grandsire, Champion Reveille's Reflection of Sheldon, from which litter she produced three champion and Best in Show-winning sons, including Champion Sheldon Korshelt Classic Look, a double Specialty winner with fifty-eight Bests of Breed to his credit, four Working Group firsts, and numerous Group placements. This dog is the sire of five champions and quite a number of others who are pointed.

Champion Hausenbrook's Mischief Maker, a Reflection daughter, was bred to Champion Sheldon Korshelt Classic Look, producing the handsome Champion and Japanese Champion Sheldon Royaltye Lookin. This dog completed his Canadian championship in two weekends and his Japanese championship in five weekends and is highly admired by all Japanese breeders and judges. Mischief Maker was purchased by the Randalls as a puppy and played an important role in the Sheldon breeding program, becoming one of Reflection's top producing daughters. Her daughter, Champion Sheldon Raspberry Ruffles, is a triple Best in Show winner and one of Canada's top winning Shelties of all time. Mischief Maker has more pointed offspring on the way to their titles and so has an excellent chance of winding up Canada's top producing bitch.

Sheldon Happy Glow, a daughter of Champion Sheldon Crowning Glory, was bred to

American Champion Shu-La-Le Autumn Son O'Merrimac, a son of American Champion Halstor's Peter Pumpkin, and produced Champion Sheldon Presents Michael. When bred to a General daughter (a sister to Sheldon Esmerelda), he sired the exquisite Specialty winner, Champion Sheldon Michelle MaBelle. Michael also is the sire of Champion Sheldon Raspberry Ruffles and now has a total of sixteen champions to his credit.

The Randalls were pleased about and promptly availed themselves of the opportunity of being able to purchase American and Canadian Champion Shelando Top Scotch when the Shelando Kennel was dispersed. He has proven a tremendous asset to the Sheldon line; and his daughter, Sheldon Gemstone Coronet, a Best of Breed winner her first time out as a puppy, will be playing a serious role in the Sheldon breeding program.

Best in Show Champion Sheldon Banner Boy is from a litter-sister to Champion Sheldon This Is The General. He is one of Canada's top winning Shelties, having won eleven Working Group firsts and having eleven champions already to his credit. Sheldon Fiona Fair is a young daughter of his, presently maturing to play an important role also in the Sheldon line of the future. Her dam is a daughter of Champion Shelando Top Scotch.

The above is a summary of the principal breeding lines at Sheldon Kennels. Occasionally other branches are introduced through these sires and different dams, but the foregoing is the basic program.

Sheldon Gemstone Coronet, Best of Breed-winning daughter of Am. and Can. Ch. Shelando Top Scotch. Coronet will play an important role in the Sheldon breeding program of the future. Bill and Doreen Randall.

O.T. Ch. Carsaig's Bitter Sweet, Am. C.D.X., winning High in Trial in the U.S. at Conewango Valley K.C., June 1980. P. Freeman, breeder; Janet Cameron, owner-handler.

Shiel

Shiel Shetland Sheepdogs had their start in 1975 when Janet A. Cameron of Mississigua, Ontario, acquired the puppy bitch, now Canadian Obedience Trial Champion Carsaig's Bitter Sweet, American C.D.X. She was Ms. Cameron's first Sheltie and her first obedience dog.

In 1979, Bitter Sweet was Canada's Number Two Obedience Dog, all-breeds. She also topped the Working Group in obedience and was entirely owner-trained and owner-handled. This lovely bitch has won numerous High in Trial awards in both Canada and the United States. Currently (summer 1983) Bitter Sweet is in Pennsylvania living temporarily with a friend, Vernon Vogel, who will put on her last leg towards her American Utility title.

"Erin," as Bitter Sweet is known to friends, loves obedience and thoroughly enjoys working in the obedience ring, even at eight years of age displaying a joy for the task not too frequently seen. Her owner says of her, "Erin was truly a thrilling dog to work with and I have been very lucky to have had that experience. She is a once-in-a-lifetime dog."

Adding frosting to the cake is the fact that "Erin's" fantastic temperament has been passed

Ch. Shiel's Sundown, born August 1977. Here judge Libby Babin (Babinett Shelties) is awarding Winners Bitch at Dominion Collie and Shetland Sheepdog Specialty when Sundown was only nine months old. Breeder-owner-handler, Janet Cameron.

on to her offspring. Her grandson, Best in Show winner Champion Shiel's Sunstreak, C.D., brings the same spirit to the conformation ring that Erin brought to the obedience ring.

"Erin" produced two champion daughters, both multi-Best of Breed winners. They are Champion Shiel's Rosie Sunrise, C.D., and Champion Shiel's Sundown, the latter the dam of Best in Show-winning Champion Shiel's Sunstreak, C.D.

Sunstreak has been breeder-owner-handled by Janet Cameron to a very impressive record. In addition to his Best in Show, he has a Group first, a Group third, six Group fourths, thirty-eight Bests of Breed, and one Specialty Best of Opposite Sex—all in Canada. During 1983 or early 1984, Ms. Cameron expects to send him to try his fortunes in the United States, doing so with a handler. Also, he will be more extensively campaigned in Canada during that period.

Only seven months old when he became a champion, Sunstreak is now just reaching his prime. It is interesting that his mother, Champion Shiel's Sundown, also was a puppy champion, completing her title at a Specialty when

Ch. Shiel's Sundown, by Ch. Delamantha's Daybreak ex O.T.Ch. Carsaig's Bitter Sweet, Am. C.D.X., at eleven months of age winning Best Puppy in Working Group under judge Peter Smith. Janet Cameron, breeder-owner-handler.

The Best in Show winner Ch. Shiel's Sunstreak, C.D., by Delamantha's Desideratason ex Ch. Shiel's Sundown, taking a Working Group fourth under judge Dr. C. Lunn, Forest City Kennel Club in 1983. Bred, owned, and handled by Janet A. Cameron.

nine months of age. She has several Bests of Breed to her credit despite limited showing.

Sunstreak is line-bred on the marvelous bitch American and Canadian Champion Delamantha's Desiderata, who won two Canadian Bests in Show and many Specialty Bests of Breed. She is sired by Champion Halstor's Peter Pumpkin.

Shiel has always been a very small kennel, housing no more than three bitches at any one time as all the dogs are house pets. Janet Cameron is striving to breed Shelties that have not only type but also good temperament and good structure, firmly believing that you must have the combination of all three. It is very important to her that she have show dogs who can *move* and who have *style*. As we write this, there are at Shiel several young hopefuls who promise to follow in Sunstreak's footsteps.

Ch. Shiel's Sunstreak, C.D., winner of thirty-eight Bests of Breed. Breeder-owner, Janet Cameron.

Sovereign

The story of Sovereign Shelties began in the late 1940's when Sovereign Collies were being exhibited in the United States. Two Shelties being shown at that time were American Champion Nashcrest Golden Note owned by Mary Van Wagenen and Katie-J's Ronny, then a class dog, owned by Mae Freeman. Ariel Sleeth, owner of Sovereign, so enormously admired those two little Shetland Sheepdogs that she decided to embark on a breeding program of her own Shelties based on the Katie-J and Sea Isle bloodlines. Thus it was, at the close of the 1940's, that American Champion Katie-J's Golden Flame (a sable) and Canadian Champion Dunderraw's Koko (a blue dog by American Champion Sheltieland Little Jack Frost) were purchased by Mrs. Sleeth from the United States. They became the studs for a few selected Katie-J bitches, and Sovereign Shelties were off and running.

The early champions were Champion Sovereign Remember Me (dog,) Champion Sovereign Victorious (bitch), Champion Sovereign Post Script (dog), Champion Sovereign Sure Fire (dog), Champion Sovereign Hootenanny (dog), Champion Sovereign Golden Hour (bitch), Champion Sovereign Fire Chief (dog), Champion Sovereign Flash Fire (dog), Champion

Ch. Sovereign By Jingo (above) and Ch. Sovereign Bonfire (below), littermates by Ch. Sovereign Fire Chief ex Ch. Sovereign Victorious. Both contributed much to the Sovereign winning line. Ariel and Floyd Sleeth, Seeley's Bay, Ontario.

Ch. Sovereign Trailblazer, the sire of many champions. Owned by Jane Farmer, Prince Edward Island.

275

Ch. Sovereign Ring of Fire, sire of five champions. He died at two years of age. Ariel Sleeth, owner, Sovereign Shelties.

Sovereign Golden Conquest (bitch), and Champion Sovereign Melody (bitch).

A bitch named Champion Sovereign Victorious, the dam of six champions, was to greatly influence the next era, which included three champions in one litter (her first) of four puppies. Those produced from Victorious were the dogs Champion Sovereign By Jingo, Champion Sovereign Trailblazer, and Champion Sovereign Folksinger and the bitches Champion Sovereign Bonfire, Champion Sovereign Victory Maid, and Champion Sovereign Gold Tam.

Champion Sovereign Bonfire was the dam of five champions. By Champion Sovereign Fire Chief ex Champion Sovereign Victorious, Bonfire was largely responsible for the direction and success of the next decade. Carrying the type and character so enormously admired by Ariel and Floyd Sleeth, this bitch influenced the line greatly through her top producing daughters, Champion Sovereign Torch Song, Champion Sovereign Flaming Glory, and Champion Sovereign Wee Luv, and through her son Champion Sovereign Ring of Fire who was to die at Cornell at two years of age. These Shelties became the producers to set the type Ariel Sleeth wanted for her Sovereigns.

At this time another purchase brought Canadian Champion Sovereign Pumpkin of Astolat,

by American Champion Halstor's Peter Pumpkin, to Sovereign. His influence was felt for the following ten years when he was sold, still siring, to Chicwin Kennels. The "Sovereign" Peter was litter-brother to American Champion Astolat Galaxy, and he left a rich heritage in his descendants at Sovereign.

Later, another outcross was made in the purchase of Canadian and American Champion Kismet's Royal Sovereign, sired by American Champion Kismet's Conquistador. Royal sired numerous champions in Canada, among them Champion Sovereign Gonna Fly Now who replaced his sire when Royal was sold to the United States.

This era produced: Champion Sovereign Red Blazer (dog), Champion Sovereign Last Word (bitch), Champion Sovereign Ring's Legacy (dog), Champion Sovereign Nitecap of Bonneydoone (dog), Champion Sovereign Burgundy Ale (bitch), Champion Sovereign Song Spinner (bitch), Champion Sovereign Glory B (bitch), Champion Sovereign Cranberry Red (bitch), Champion Sovereign Torch Singer (bitch), Champion Sovereign Brand New Key (dog), Champion Sovereign Winning Spirit (dog), Champion Sovereign So Very Blue (bitch), Champion Sovereign Success Story (bitch), Champion Sovereign Look My Way (bitch), Champion Sovereign Glory Bound (bitch), Champion Sovereign Ring Leader (dog), Champion Sovereign Sundowner (dog), Champion

Sovereign Forget-Me-Not, a five-point Specialty winner who died at one year old. Sovereign Kennels, Ariel and Floyd Sleeth.

Sovereign Close Call, by Sovereign Living Legend ex Sovereign Blue Haven Sprite, with nine points. Ariel Sleeth, breeder; Ariel Sleeth and Fred Gordon, owners.

Ch. Sovereign Dream Maker, by Ch. Sovereign Pumpkin of Astolat ex Sovereign Sandcastle, shown here in 1981 with handler Don Palanio. Dream Maker is the foundation bitch for Lynchill Kennels, Jean Lynch, Fisherville, Ontario.

Ch. Sovereign Bright Idea handled to a Specialty win by daughter Laurie Sleeth. Sovereign Kennels.

Sovereign Ring of Luv, the dam of many champions. Owned by June Trefry. Photo courtesy of Ariel Sleeth.

Ch. Sovereign Ring's Legacy with owner Ariel Sleeth and artist Audrey McNaughton. Shown here is Legacy's portrait being painted during a live television broadcast.

Above: Ch. Sovereign's Thorn Bird, sired by Ch. Sovereign Ring's Legacy, at eleven months of age. Owned by Fred Gordon. **Below:** Ch. Sovereign Gemstone, sired by Ch. Sovereign Ring's Legacy, winner of four Bests of Breed on the way to her title, plus Best Puppy in Show. Ariel and Floyd Sleeth, owners, Sovereign Kennels.

Sovereign Lead My Way (dog), Champion Sovereign Ebony Shine (bitch), Champion Sovereign First Flight (dog), Champion Sovereign Peter Piper (dog), Champion Sovereign Curtain Call (bitch), Champion Sovereign Gonna Fly Now (dog), Champion Sovereign Head Start (bitch), and Champion Sovereign Mystic Charm (bitch).

Whelped after his sire had died, Champion Sovereign Ring's Legacy, by Champion Sovereign Ring of Fire, became the greatest stud dog Sovereign has ever owned. His type, quality, and, above all, his intelligence and worth as a dog have endeared him to all who have known him and most certainly have earned him the respect of the breeders who have used him. The course of dog breeding does not run smoothly, and after losing Legacy's sire at such a young age it was also the Sleeths' misfortune to have Ace stepped on at a dog show while waiting to go in the ring. Broken bones and a slight lameness ended his show career, although as a veteran he did accompany Mrs. Sleeth to the National in San Diego, California, in 1982 to win a fourth in the Veterans Class and a second the following day.

Under the "Sovereign" prefix, Ariel Sleeth has never had a year without homebred champions since beginning with the Shelties in 1949. From then until 1970, there had been more than fifty champions bred, and the total now stands at twice that number. During the late 1960's, Mrs. Sleeth's "predictable breeding program" evolved, and during the 1970's all of the dogs shown were the result of this program. The proof of the program is that from 1970 until the

Above: Ch. Sovereign Glory Bound, by Ch. Sovereign Ring's Legacy, one of the famous winners from Ariel Sleeth's Sovereign Kennels. **Below:** Ch. Sovereign Ebony Shine. Owned by Fred Gordon.

Above: Ch. Sovereign Success Story. Owned by Marlene Lange. **Below:** Sovereign Cappuccino, by Ch. Sovereign Ring's Legacy, at seven months of age. Owned by Dr. Tom Kozina.

end of 1979, fifty-eight champions were bred at Sovereign, despite the fact that the Sleeths had fewer dogs at the latter half of the 1970's than ever before. These figures do not include the large number of dogs finished by others with two Sovereign parents.

Sovereign Kennels are located at Seeley's Bay, Ontario, Canada.

Aust. Ch. Jedemah Sontina Karoly in August 1983. Son of the famous record-breaking Aust. Ch. Jentam Yendys Yelder who has 2,300 C.C. points, fourteen Royal Challenges. "Benji" is, as well, grandson of the renowned Eng. and Aust. Ch. Riverhill Rampion, imported from the United Kingdom, who died at fifteen years of age in 1981, top ranking stud dog for the breed in Australia who has had tremendous influence and been widely used. "Benji" shows promise in following in the pawprints of these famous progenitors. Mrs. Patricia Huggins, owner, The Oaks, New South Wales.

CHAPTER SIX

Shetland Sheepdogs in Australia

Aust. Ch. Pushkin Potomkin, by Can. Ch. Paddy of Chuaig, C.D., ex Aust. Ch. Kanakee Solitude, born October 6th 1975. Bred and owned by B. and D. Flakelar, Pushkin Shetland Sheepdogs, Drummoyne, Sydney, Australia.

Our friends in Australia include many dedicated dog fanciers and excellent breeders, with this country moving ahead each year in the quality of its dogs and thereby of competition at its dog shows. Australian breeders are among the most enthusiastic I have ever known, and it is to their credit that many of them have imported breeding stock from elsewhere to consolidate with their own bloodlines despite the stringent quarantine requirements which make this a long and tedious process.

Now it has reached the point where a number of excellent dogs in various breeds have been exported from Australia to new homes in the United States and elsewhere—usually purchased by fanciers who have visited that country, seen and been impressed by their dogs, and felt that they have quality to contribute to their kennels back home. There is a warm bond and a feeling of mutual respect between Australia and American fanciers, undoubtedly strengthened by the numerous judges from the United States now officiating in Australia and those from Australia in the United States.

Shetland Sheepdogs obviously are sponsored by a strong group of breeders in Australia, with some splendid champions there and good turn-outs in the breed at dog shows. Recently a friend of ours from the United States, Bob Forsyth, has returned from judging the breed (among others) at the Royal Agricultural Society Kennel Control 1983 Spring Show. Seventy-nine Shelties were entered, with many kennels and breeders represented. Best of Breed was the dog Champion Jedemah Sontina Karoly, owned by Mrs. P. Huggins, of The Oaks, New South Wales. He is a son of Australian Champion Jentam Yendys Yeldeh ex Jedemah Tina Maree and was born in May 1979. Reserve Best of Breed was the bitch Champion Bethalice Jasmine, by Lythwood Salvador (an import from the United Kingdom) ex Bethalice Fleurdelys, owned by Doteon Kennels, Queanbeyan, New South Wales.

The largest individual Sheltie entry at this show came from P.J. Mortimer and Mrs. J.I. Mortimer of Badgerys Creek, New South Wales, who had a total of eight on the lists. Included among these were Champion Shelloy Groucho, an Australian-bred bitch by Australian Champion Cardiff Royal Prince ex Areton Summer Joy, born in October 1980; Champion Shelloy Sioux, a daughter of Australian Champion Shelloy Maverick ex Australian Champion Areton Rachel, born in January 1980; two male

Aust. Ch. Pushkin Pravda, by Can. Ch. Paddy of Chuaig ex Aust. Ch. Kanakee Solitude, a widely admired and consistent Australian winner. Bred and owned by Mr. and Mrs. B. Flakelar, Pushkin Shetland Sheepdogs, Sydney.

puppies, by Royal Prince, namely Shelloy Black Boy (from Groucho) and Shelloy Royal Chip (from Shelloy Reign Beau), both born in April 1983; plus three bitches, littermates to Royal Chip, by Royal Prince from Reign Beau.

Mrs. P. Quillan and Miss R. A. Quillan also were well represented at this show. Mrs. Quillan had Arcadia Pardon Me, by Arcadia Look Again ex Australian Champion Arcadia Goodness Me; Arcadia Out 'n About, same breeding as Pardon Me; and a litter-brother to Pardon Me, Arcadia Private Eye. All three were first-prize winners. They represent two different breedings of the same parents. Miss Quillan was showing the Open Bitch, Champion Arcadia Just Looking (Almaroy Black Onyx ex Arcadia Impulse), and Arcadia Look Again, an Impulse son but sired by Almaroy Razzamatazz. The Quillans live at Riverstone in New South Wales.

Several Shelties have completed their championships just as we are writing. They include Champion Belvoir Mighty Moses, who is by Australian Champion Cardiff Royal Prince ex Australian Champion Shelloy Sharese and was born in 1980; Mighty Moses belongs to Mrs. S. U. Ullyott at Dapto, New South Wales.

Australian Champion Toonieglen Trendsetter is the sire of the new Champion Coswick Elsah, owned by H. J. and Mrs. R. H. Standing, Woodberry, New South Wales; Elsah was born in May 1977, from Allenbreck Candy.

Champion Tyrondale Tiffin Time, born in July 1980, has also recently completed championship; Tiffin Time was sired by Australian Champion Tyrondale Tannentella, owned by M. A. and Mrs. C. Colley, Robertson, New South Wales.

Barrie and Denise Flakelar are owners of the Pushkin Shetland Sheepdogs at Sydney in Australia, having come there from Montreal, Canada, where their involvement with Shelties actually began through visiting the Canadian dog shows, those in Bermuda, and such events as Westminster in the United States, plus Crufts in England. When they moved to Australia, early in the 1970's, they took with them a Canadian dog, Canadian Champion Paddy of Chuag, C.D., who was a double grandson of International Champion Honeyboy of Callart, imported into Canada from England. This dog's influence on the breed in Australia has been a beneficial one, as one can see from the photos of the Pushkin Australian-breds included in this book.

It takes one hundred points to make up an Australian champion, twenty-five points being the maximum and six points the minimum a dog can receive at any one show depending on the number of dogs beaten. Champion Pushkin Potamkin retired with well over 1,000 points on his show record; Champion Pushkin Pravda has over 900 points as of December 1983; and Champion Pushkin Posh, a young bitch with much of her career still in the future, is making a fine record, too.

Mrs. Flakelar is herself slowly working on a technical book about Shelties for publication sometime in the future. She comments that in Australia the Sheltie standard is based on England's for the breed. She comments that there is a great deal of controversy, of course, on the subject of size (oversize being a very serious fault and 14 inches for bitches and 14½ for dogs being the desired heights), but breeders are finding that beautiful Shelties of correct, or near-correct, size can be produced with careful breeding.

Shelloy Shetland Sheepdogs, a very select and distinguished kennel in this breed, are owned by Mr. and Mrs. Peter Mortimer at Badgery's Creek, New South Wales.

The Mortimers have, as their foundation dog, the beautiful, dominant, and highly successful import from the United Kingdom, Australian

Champion Cardiff Royal Prince, now twelve years old (in December 1983) but still going strong and still being used at stud. Royal Prince is to be found behind an impressive number of leading Australian champions; obviously, he has placed his stamp upon the breed in that country.

Australian Champion Areton Rachel is the founding bitch at Shelloy. A lovely bitch in her own right, she has won well for her owners, including Best in Show at an important Specialty under United Kingdom breeder and judge Mr. J. Macintosh. Together with Royal Prince she produced two of the current stars on the Australian show scene, Australian Champions Shelloy Maverick and Shelloy Alexandrov, plus she is the grandam of Australian Champion Shelloy Groucho—all much in evidence as one studies show awards!

Australian Champion Shelloy Sioux has lately won the New South Wales Specialty under New Zealand breeder-judge Mr. Sell. Sioux is a Rachel daughter who was sired by Royal Prince ex a Rachel son, Maverick.

Australian Champion Shelloy Groucho, by Royal Prince from Rachel's daughter Areton Summer Joy, was recently awarded Best Bitch in Parade by Mrs. Catherine Jeffries, United Kingdom judge and breeder-owner of Jetsfire Shelties.

Australian Champions Shelloy Maverick, Alexandrov, and Sioux have all won Challenge Certificates at the great and prestigious dog shows at Sidney, these being the Royal Easter event and the Royal Agricultural Society Kennel Control Spring Fair. These are exciting wins, with competition always especially keen.

Shelloy Shetland Sheepdogs are strong in the bloodlines of English and Australian Champion Riverhill Rampion, Champion Blazon of Callart, Champion Lisrouagh Can Can, and Champion Rodanich Rock Mundi. All of these are United Kingdom lines, going back to English Champion Alasdair of Tintobank.

Other Sheltie breeders in New South Wales include Mr. L. C. Whitby of the Amante Kennels at Woonona; Mrs. J. G. Wales of Cherrylea Kennels at Binalong; Mr. D. A. Wheelwright, Fairisle Kennels, Panania; Mrs. D. O. Ashton, Gainess Kennels, Kenthurst; Mrs. C. A. Wylie; Hillswick Kennels, Riverstone; Mrs. J. I. Palinkas, Jupalin Kennels, Nowra; Mr. K. A. Martin, Sandstock Kennels, Wingello; and M. and Mrs. W. Dolbel, Sheildale Kennels, Wottamondara.

Aust. Ch. Pushkin Posh, by Aust. Ch. Shelloy Maverick ex Aust. Ch. Kanakee Solitude, tricolor bitch born September 1980. She is an important winner who has brought many honors to her breeder-owners, Barrie and Denise Flakelar, Pushkin Shetland Sheepdogs, Drummoyne, Sydney.

Ch. SumerSong Winter Shadows, by Ch. Banchory Deep Purple ex SumerSong Kachina, at eleven months of age. This multiple Specialty Show winner is a homebred belonging to Peggy and Jan Haderlie, Orange, California.

CHAPTER SEVEN

Standards
of the Breed

Ch. Wade Gate Honor Bound, who had more than thirty-five Bests of Breed, taking Winners dog, owner-handled by Eugene Cohen, at Westminster in 1976 under judge Mrs. Virginia Hampton.

The standard for a breed of dog is a detailed description of the ideal specimen of that particular breed—a word picture intended to describe in minute detail exactly how this dog should look, act, and gait, as well as what features are the ones important to breed character. This standard describes every feature of the dog, from nose-tip to tail-tip, from topline to paws, placing each in its proper perspective when one surveys the dog as a whole.

The standard of each breed is the product of many years' observation. Our modern standards are based on those which preceded them, the earliest descriptions of the dogs under discussion, usually from the country of their origin. The earliest standards were principally concerned with a dog's working ability as well as his proper conformation to fulfill the tasks for which he had been created. With the passage of time and the increasing appreciation of dogs as companions and as competitors in dog shows, the need came to refine the standards, with the hope of retaining the original desirable traits while at the same time adding modifications and refinements to lead to a more pleasing appearance.

British and Australian Standard

The Australian standard for the Shetland Sheepdog is the same as the British standard.

Characteristics: To enable the Shetland Sheepdog to fulfill its natural bent for sheepdog work, its physical structure should be on the lines of strength and activity, free from cloddiness and without any trace of coarseness. Although the desired type is similar to that of the Rough Collie there are marked differences that must be noted. The expression, being one of the most marked characteristics of the breed, is obtained by the perfect balance and combination of skull and foreface, size, shape, colour and placement of eyes, correct position and carriage of ears, all harmoniously blended to produce that almost indefinable look of sweet, alert, gentle intelligence.

The Shetland Sheepdog should show affection and response to his owner, he may show reserve to strangers but not to the point of nervousness.

General Appearance: The Shetland Sheepdog should instantly appeal as a dog of great beauty, intelligence and alertness. Action lithe

Aust. Ch. Pushkin Potomkin, sable dog by Can. Ch. Paddy of Chuaig, C.D., ex Aust. Ch. Kanakee Solitude. Bred and owned by B. and D. Flakelar, Pushkin Shetland Sheepdogs.

and graceful with speed and jumping power great for its size. The outline should be symmetrical so that no part appears out of proportion to the whole. An abundance of coat, mane and frill, with shapeliness of head and sweetness of expression all combine to present the ideal Shetland Sheepdog that will inspire and secure admiration.

Head and Skull: The head should be refined and its shape when viewed from the top or side is a long blunt wedge tapering from ear to nose. The width of skull necessarily depends upon the combined length of skull and muzzle and the whole must be considered in connection with the size of the dog. The skull should be flat, moderately wide between the ears, showing no prominence of the occipital bone. Cheeks should be flat and merge smoothly into a well rounded muzzle. Skull and muzzle to be of equal length, central point to be the inner corner of the eye. In profile the topline of the skull should be parallel to the topline of the muzzle, but on a higher plane due to a slight but definite stop. The jaws should be clean and strong and with a well developed underjaw. Lips should be tight. Teeth should be sound and level, with an evenly spaced scissor bite.

Eyes: A very important feature giving expression to the dog. They should be of medium size obliquely set and of almond shape. Colour dark brown except in the case of merles, where blue is permissible.

Ears: Should be small and moderately wide at the base, placed fairly close together on the top of the skull. When in repose they should be thrown back, but when on the alert brought forward and carried semi-erect with tips dropping forward.

Neck: The neck should be muscular, well arched and of sufficient length to carry the head proudly.

Body and Quarters: From the withers the shoulder blade should slope at a 45 degree angle, forward and downward to the shoulder joint. At the withers they are separated only by the vertebrae but they must slope outwards to accommodate the desired spring of ribs. The upper arm should join the shoulder blade at as nearly a right angle as possible. The elbow joint to be equi-distant from the ground and the withers. The forelegs should be straight when viewed from the front, muscular and clean, with strong bone. Pasterns strong and flexible. The body is slightly longer from the withers to the root of the tail than the height at the withers, but most of the length is due to the proper angulation of the shoulder and hindquarters. The chest should be deep reaching to the point of the elbow. The ribs well sprung but tapering at their lower half to allow free play of the forelegs and shoulders. The back should be level with a graceful sweep over the loins and the croup should slope gradually to the rear. The thigh should be broad and muscular, the thigh bones to be set into the pelvis at right angles, corresponding to the angle of the shoulder blade. The stifle joint where the femur bone joins the tibia bone must have a distinct angle, hock joint to be clean cut, angular and well let down with strong bone. The hock must be straight when viewed from behind.

Tail: Set on low, tapering bone must reach at least to the hock joint, with abundant hair and slight upward sweep, raised when the dog is moving, but never over the level of the back.

Feet: Oval in shape, soles well padded, toes arched and close together.

Gait: The action of the Shetland Sheepdog should denote speed and smoothness. There should be no pacing, plaiting, rolling or stiff stilted up and down movement.

Coat: Must be double, the outer coat of long hair of harsh texture and straight, the under coat soft (resembling fur) short and close. The mane and frill should be very abundant and forelegs well feathered. Hind legs above the hocks profusely covered with hair, but below the hocks fairly smooth. The mask or face smooth. What are commonly known as smooth coated specimens are barred.

Colour: Tricolours should be an intense black on the body with no signs of ticking, rich tan markings on a tricolour to be preferred. Sables may be clear or shaded, any colour from gold to deep mahogany but in its shade the colour should be rich in tones. Wolf sable and grey colours undesirable. Blue Merles, clear silvery blue is desired, splashed and marbled with black. Rich tan markings to be preferred, but the absence not to be counted as a fault. Heavy black markings, slate coloured or rusty tinge in either top or under coat is highly undesirable. General effect should be blue. White markings may be shown in the blaze, collar, chest frill, legs, stifle and tip of tail. All or some tan markings may be shown on eyebrows, cheeks, legs, stifles and under tail. All or some of the white markings are to be preferred whatever the colour of the dog, but the absence of these markings shall not be considered a fault. Black and White and Black and Tan are also recognised colours. Over markings of patches of white on the body are highly undesirable. The nose black whatever the colour of the dog.

Size: Ideal height measured at the withers 14 inches for bitches, 14½ inches for dogs; anything more than 1 inch above these heights to be considered a serious fault.

Faults: Domed or receding skull; lack of stop; large drooping or pricked ears; over-developed

Aust. Ch. Jedemah Sontina Karoly in October 1983. He won a triple at the three major shows: the Spring Show, the Shetland Sheepdog Specialty, and the Illawarra Collie and Shetland Sheepdog Show; many times won Best Exhibit in Working Dog Group; and recently was runner-up to Best Exhibit in Show, all-breeds. He is the Top Challenge Winning Dog, both 1982 and 1983, Sheltie Club of New South Wales; and he was the club's point-score winner in 1980, 1982, and 1983, and runner-up in 1981. Owned by Mrs. Patricia Huggins, New South Wales.

cheeks; weak jaw; snipy muzzle; not full complement of teeth; crooked forelegs; cow hocks; tail kinked, short, or carried over the back; white coat or white colour predominating. Pink or flesh coloured nose; blue eyes in any other colour than merles. Nervousness. Full or light eye. Undershot or overshot mouth.

Note: Male animals should have two apparently normal testicles fully descended into the scrotum.

Early American Standard

The following is the original standard drawn up in the 1930's by the American Shetland Sheepdog Association.

General Appearance: While the Shetland Sheepdog should resemble an ideal Collie in miniature, it should be borne in mind that this ideal should conform to the Collie type recognized as correct when the Shetland Sheepdog Standard was compiled (about 1915) and the interpretation of this standard is not to follow any subsequent Collie trend that may lead it away from the original intent.

Ch. Rorralore Play Fair, Reserve Dog at the National in 1977. Charlotte Clem McGowan, Rorralore Shelties.

Ch. The Blue Danube, C.D.X., by Ch. Philidove Benevolent Anthony ex Faverdale's Mara Du Printemps, C.D., taking Winners Dog from judge Elizabeth Whelen (of Pocono Shelties) at the American Shetland Sheepdog Association National Specialty in June 1977. "Dan" completed his title later that year. Breeder-owner, Ellen Handel; co-owner Michelle D'Elisiis.

Symmetry: The outline of the Shetland Sheepdog should be so symmetrical that no part appears out of proportion to the whole.

Size: The height of the Shetland Sheepdog should be no less than 12 inches nor more than 15 inches measured at the shoulder. The ideal height being 13½ inches.

Coat: The coat should be double, the outer coat consisting of long, harsh hair, the under coat short, soft and close, like fur. The mane and frill should be abundant, the forelegs well feathered, the hindlegs above the hocks and the brush profusely so. The face and tips of ears should be smooth, the hindlegs below the hocks fairly so. Smooth-coated specimens are barred.

Color: Any color except brindle or solid merle is permissible, the usual colors being sable, black, and blue merle marked with varying amounts of white and tan.

Head: *Skull:* The skull should be flat, moderately wide between the ears, gradually tapering towards the eyes with a slight depression at the stop; the cheeks should not be full or prominent. *Muzzle:* The muzzle should be of fair length tapering to the nose, and must not show

Ch. Macdega Barwood Birthright, American Shetland Sheepdog Association Futurity winner. Courtesy of Thomas W. Coen, Macdega.

weakness or be snipy or lippy. *Jaws* should be clean cut and powerful. *Teeth* should be of good size, sound and level; very slight unevenness is permissible. The nose must be black whatever color the dog may be.

Eyes: Should be of medium size, set somewhat obliquely, of almond shape, and of a brown color except in the case of merles when one or both are frequently blue and white or china. They should be full of intelligence and expression.

Ears: Should be small, moderately wide at the base, placed fairly close together on top of the skull. When in repose they should be folded back into the frill; when on the alert, they should be brought up and carried semi-erect with the tips drooping forward.

Body: *Neck:* The neck should be of fair length, muscular, and somewhat arched. *Forequarters:* The forelegs should be straight and muscular with a fair amount of bone, neither in nor out at the elbows. *Body:* Moderately long with level back and well sprung ribs. *Hindquarters:* The hindquarters should be muscular at the thighs, with loin slightly arched and powerful. *Hindlegs:* Should be clean and sinewy below the hocks with well-bent stifles and hocks well let down.

Feet: The feet should be oval in shape, soles well padded, and the toes arched and close together.

Tail: The tail should be moderately long, carried low when the dog is quiet with a slight up-ward swirl at the end; carried gaily when the dog is excited, but not over the back.

Faults: Domed skull; large, drooping ears; weak jaws; snipy muzzle; full eyes or light eyes except in blue merles; crooked forelegs; cowhocks; tail carried over the back; curly coat; over or undershot mouth.

POINTS

General Appearance

Size	10
Symmetry	10
Coat	10
Total	30

Head

Ears	10
Eyes and expression	10
Skull	5
Muzzle	5
Total	30

Body

Neck	5
Forequarters and forelegs	10
Back	5
Hindquarters and hindlegs	10
Feet	5
Tail	5
Total	40

TOTAL............100

Ch. Jade Mist Twilight Song setting a breed record on the day she finished her championship at nine and a half years of age. Recently a male Sheltie finished, also at nine and a half years of age; he *may* be days older than this one, but she is still the oldest Sheltie *bitch* ever to have finished. Owned by Dr. and Mrs. Keith B. Howell.

Current American Standard

The following is the revision of the original standard and is the one currently in use. It was approved by the American Kennel Club in May 1959.

Preamble: The Shetland Sheepdog, like the Collie, traces to the Border Collie of Scotland, which, transported to the Shetland Islands and crossed with small, intelligent, longhaired breeds, was reduced to miniature proportions. Subsequently crosses were made from time to time with Collies. This breed now bears the same relationship in size and general appearance to the Rough Collie as the Shetland Pony does to some of the larger breeds of horses. Although the resemblance between the Shetland Sheepdog and the Rough Collie is marked, there are differences which may be noted.

General Description: The Shetland Sheepdog is a small, alert, rough-coated, longhaired working dog. He must be sound, agile and sturdy. The outline should be so symmetrical that no part appears out of proportion to the whole. Dogs should appear masculine; bitches, feminine.

Size: The Shetland Sheepdog should stand between 13 and 16 inches at the shoulder. Note: Height is determined by a line perpendicular to the ground from the top of the shoulder blades, the dog standing naturally, with forelegs parallel to line of measurement. *Disqualification:* Heights below or above the desired size range are to be disqualified from the show ring.

Coat: The coat should be double, the outer coat consisting of long, straight, harsh hair; the undercoat short, furry, and so dense as to give the entire coat its "stand-off" quality. The hair on face, tips of ears and feet should be smooth.

Ch. Astolat Stardust, by Ch. Gold Award, winning at the American Shetland Sheepdog Association in June 1966. Mrs. Constance B. Hubbard, owner, Astolat Kennels.

Ch. Chenterra Thunderation, by Chenterra Beauregard ex Chenterra Commotion, one of the top winning Shetland Sheepdogs of all time. This magnificent little dog, shown 228 times, was Best of Breed on 220 occasions, 120 of which were consecutive, and has as well to his credit seventy-eight Working Group firsts, twenty-one all-breed Bests in Show, and twenty-two Specialty Bests in Show. Additionally he has sired twenty champions to date. Handled by Steve Barger; owned by Tetsuo Miyama and Stephen W. Barger.

Mane and frill should be abundant, and particularly impressive in males. The forelegs well feathered, the hind legs heavily so, but smooth below the hock joint. Hair on tail profuse. Note: Excess hair on ears, feet, and on hocks may be trimmed for the show ring. *Faults:* Coat short or flat, in whole or in part; wavy, curly, soft or silky. Lack of undercoat. Smooth-coated specimens.

Color: Black, blue merle, and sable (ranging from golden through mahogany); marked with varying amounts of white and/or tan. *Faults:* Rustiness in a black or a blue coat. Washed out or degenerate colors, such as pale sable and faded blue. Self-color in the case of blue merle, that is, without any merling or mottling and generally appearing as a faded or dilute tri-color. Conspicuous white body spots. Specimens with more than 50 per cent white shall be so severely

penalized as to effectively eliminate them from competition. *Disqualification:* Brindle.

Temperament: The Shetland Sheepdog is intensely loyal, affectionate, and responsive to his owner. However, he may be reserved toward strangers but not to the point of showing fear or cringing in the ring. *Faults:* Shyness, timidity, or nervousness. Stubborness, snappiness, or ill temper.

Head: The head should be refined and its shape, when viewed from top or side, be a long, blunt wedge tapering slightly from ears to nose, which must be black. *Skull and Muzzle:* Top of skull should be flat, showing no prominence of nuchal crest (the top of the occiput). Cheeks should be flat and should merge smoothly into a well-rounded muzzle. Skull and muzzle should be of equal length, balance point being inner corner of eye. In profile the top line of skull should

The great Ch. Halstor's Peter Pumpkin, twice American Shetland Sheepdog Association Best in Show and sire of over 155 American champions. Macdega Kennels, owner, Thomas W. Coen.

parallel the top line of muzzle, but on a higher plane due to the presence of a slight but definite stop. Jaws clean and powerful. The deep, well-developed under-jaw, rounded at chin, should extend to base of nostril. Lips tight. Upper and lower lips must meet and fit smoothly together all the way around. Teeth level and evenly spaced. Scissors bite. *Faults:* Two-angled head. Too prominent stop, or no stop. Overfill below, between, or above eyes. Prominent nuchal crest. Domed skull. Prominent cheekbones. Snipy muzzle. Short, receding, or shallow under-jaw, lacking breadth and depth. Overshot or undershot, missing or crooked teeth. Teeth visible when mouth is closed.

Eyes: Medium size with dark, almond-shaped rims, set somewhat obliquely in skull. Color must be dark, with blue or merle eyes permissible in blue merles only. *Faults:* Light, round, large or too small. Prominent haws.

Ears: Small and flexible, placed high, carried three-fourths erect, with tips breaking forward. When in repose the ears fold lengthwise and are thrown back into the frill. *Faults:* Set too low. Hound, prick, bat, twisted ears. Leather too thick or too thin.

Expression: Contours and chiseling of the head, the shape, set and use of ears, the placement, shape and color of the eyes, combine to

Ch. Macdega Sergeant Pepper, Best in Futurity at the American Shetland Sheepdog Association in 1975. Owned by Macdega, Thomas W. Coen.

Ch. Berridale Alnphyl Brigette, one of the two foundation bitches at Montage Kennels, taking Reserve Winners at the 1978 National; judge, Barbara Curry, Beltane Shelties; handler, Tom Coen. Owner, Christine Machado, Montage Kennels.

produce expression. Normally the expression should be alert, gentle, intelligent and questioning. Toward strangers the eyes should show watchfulness and reserve, but no fear.

Neck: Neck should be muscular, arched, and of sufficient length to carry the head proudly. *Faults:* Too short and thick.

Body: In over-all appearance the body should appear moderately long as measured from shoulder joint to ischium (rearmost extremity of the pelvic bone), but much of this length is actually due to the proper angulation and breadth of the shoulder and hindquarter, as the back itself should be comparatively short. Back should be level and strongly muscled. Chest should be deep, the brisket reaching to point of elbow. The ribs should be well sprung, but flattened at their lower half to allow free play of the foreleg and shoulder. Abdomen moderately tucked up. *Faults:* Back too long, too short, swayed or roached. Barrel ribs. Slab-side. Chest narrow and/or too shallow.

Forequarters: From the withers the shoulder blades should slope at a 45-degree angle forward and downward to the shoulder joints. At the withers they are separated only by the vertebra, but they must slope outward sufficiently to accommodate the desired spring of rib. The upper arm should join the shoulder blade at as nearly

Ch. Rorralore Sportin' Chance, C.D., one of the top Specialty winning Shelties of all time and winner of Best of Breed at Westminster in 1984. Charlotte Clem McGowan, Rorralore Shetland Sheepdogs.

Rockwoods Keepsake, by Ch. Rockwood Repeat Performance ex Ch. Our Own Rockwoods Bewitched, a winner in the 1981 American Shetland Sheepdog Association Futurity. Bred and owned by Barbara M. Kenealy.

as possible a right angle. Elbow joint should be equidistant from the ground or from the withers. Forelegs straight viewed from all angles, muscular and clean, and of strong bone. Pasterns very strong, sinewy and flexible. Dewclaws may be removed. *Faults:* Insufficient angulation between shoulder and upper arm. Upper arm too short. Lack of outward slope of shoulders. Loose shoulders. Turning in or out of elbows. Crooked legs. Light bone.

Feet (front and hind): Feet should be oval and compact with the toes well arched and fitting tightly together. Pads deep and tough, nails hard and strong. *Faults:* Feet turning in or out. Splay-feet. Hare-feet. Cat-feet.

Hindquarters: There should be a slight arch at the loins, and the croup should slope gradually to the rear. The hipbone (pelvis) should be set at a 30-degree angle to the spine. The thigh should be broad and muscular. The thighbone should be set into the pelvis at a right angle corresponding to the angle of the shoulder blade and upper arm. Stifle bones join the thighbone and should be distinctly angled at the stifle joint. The over-all length of the stifle should at least equal the length of the thighbone, and preferably should slightly exceed it. Hock joint should be clean-cut, angular, sinewy, with good bone and strong ligamentation. The hock (metatarsus)

Ch. Rorralore Rejoice, by Ch. Rorralore Sportin' Chance, C.D., ex Rorralore Regret, Winners Bitch at the American Shetland Sheepdog Association National Specialty in 1981. Bred by Charlotte McGowan and Nancy Boomhower; owned by Charlotte Clem McGowan.

Ch. Westwood Tuf Stuff of Coaly, by Ch. Brigadoon Merri Lou I'm Ready, a multiple Best in Show and Specialty winner, pictured here winning the American Shetland Sheepdog Association National Specialty in 1980; judge, Charlotte Clem McGowan; handler, Joe Malloy. Owner, Ruth Lubin.

should be short and straight viewed from all angles. Dewclaws should be removed. Feet (*see* Forequarters).

Tail: The tail should be sufficiently long so that when it is laid along the back edge of the hind legs the last vertebra will reach the hock joint. Carriage of tail at rest is straight down or in a slight upward curve. When the dog is alert, the tail is normally lifted, but it should not be curved forward over the back. *Faults:* Too short. Twisted at end.

Gait: The trotting gait of the Shetland Sheepdog should denote effortless speed and smoothness. There should be no jerkiness, nor stiff, stilted, up-and-down movement. The drive should be from the rear, true and straight, dependent upon correct angulation, musculation, and ligamentation of the entire hindquarter, thus allowing the dog to reach well under his body with his hind foot and propel himself forward. Reach of stride of the foreleg is

dependent upon correct angulation, musculation and ligamentation of the forequarters, together with correct width of chest and construction of rib cage. The foot should be lifted only enough to clear the ground as the leg swings forward. Viewed from the front, both forelegs and hind legs should move forward almost perpendicular to ground at the walk, slanting a little inward at a slow trot, until at a swift trot the feet are brought so far inward toward center line of body that the tracks left show two parallel lines of footprints actually touching a centerline at their inner edges. *There should be no crossing of the feet nor throwing of the weight from side to side. Faults:* Stiff, short steps with a choppy, jerky movement. Mincing steps, with a hopping up and down, or a balancing of weight from side to side (often erroneously admired as a "dancing gait" but permissible in young puppies). Lifting of front feet in hackney-like action, resulting in loss of speed and energy. Pacing gait.

SCALE OF POINTS

General Appearance

Symmetry 10
Temperament 10
Coat 5
Total 25

Head

Skull and stop 5
Muzzle 5
Eyes, ears and expression 10
Total 20

Body

Neck and back 5
Chest, ribs and brisket 10
Loins, croup and tail 5
Total 20

Forequarters

Shoulder 10
Forelegs and feet 5
Total 15

Hindquarters

Hip, thigh and stifle 10
Hocks and feet 5
Total 15

Gait

Gait—smoothness and lack of
waste motion when trotting 5
Total 5

TOTAL 100

DISQUALIFICATIONS

Heights below or above the desired range, i.e. 13-16 inches.
Brindle color.

Ch. Pixie Dell Epicure, born in 1964, a multiple winner of Best in Show, at Specialty Shows, and of the breed at Westminster. He lived to be eighteen years old and was a dog of exceptional excellence. Handled by Mildred B. Nicoll and owned by Mr. and Mrs. A.R. Miller, Scarsdale, New York.

Macdega Marrakech, the bi-black who was Best in Futurity and Best of Winners at the American Shetland Sheepdog Association in 1982. Owned by Macdega Kennels, Thomas W. Coen.

296

Ch. Shadow Hill Blue Dynamic, by Banchory Reflection ex Macdega Under the Rainbow, Best of Winners at the 1980 American Shetland Sheepdog Association Specialty Show. Owned by Debbie Walden; handled by Stephen Barger.

Ch. Karral Good Times at seven months of age winning his class, 6-9 Month Puppy, at the 1980 National Specialty; judge, Charlotte McGowan; handler, Ralph Elledge. Owners, Ralph and Karen Elledge, Karral Shetland Sheepdogs.

Carmylie Cairngold, by Am. and Can. Ch. Carmylie Elusive Dream ex Sable Queen of Carmylie, winning Best Adult at a match show judged by Richard Thomas, Sr., father of Richard Thomas, "John Boy" of *The Waltons*. Cairngold, with five points toward championship, belongs to Jean Simmonds.

Ch. Katie-J's Ronnie, by Am. and Can. Ch. Nashcrest Golden Note ex Katie-J's Colleen, as painted by Jean D. Simmonds. Photo courtesy of Jean D. Simmonds, Carmylie Kennels.

Painting of Ch. Reflections of Sealect by Jean D. Simmonds. Photo courtesy of Jean Simmonds.

Am. and Can. Ch. Banchory High Born, from a painting by Jean D. Simmonds to whom we owe thanks for this photo.

Ch. Kismet's Status Quo, by Ch. Kismet's Conquistador ex Ch. Fiesta's Fazzle Dazzle, Winners Dog at the American Shetland Sheepdog National Specialty in 1976 for five points; judge, Jean Simmonds; handler, Guy Mauldin. Owners, Guy and Thelma Mauldin, Kismet Kennels.

What To Look For in a Sheltie

drawn by

Jean Daniels Simmonds

Being a strong believer in the old Chinese adage regarding the worth of a picture, we did especially want to include some drawings pointing out what to look for in a correct Shetland Sheepdog. Thus my joy was unbounded when Jean Simmonds very graciously granted us permission to use some of the excellent ones from her invaluable book *The Illustrated Shetland Sheepdog Standard*. We feel these to be especially worthy, having been drawn by an obviously talented artist with a thorough knowledge of the Sheltie, and we are proud to present them to our readers. Mrs. Simmonds lives at Chatham, New York, 12037, and her book, revised in 1984, is a valuable addition to any Sheltie fancier's library.

A.K.N.

The body and markings (showing white-factor marking on stifle).

The basic conformation at a glance.

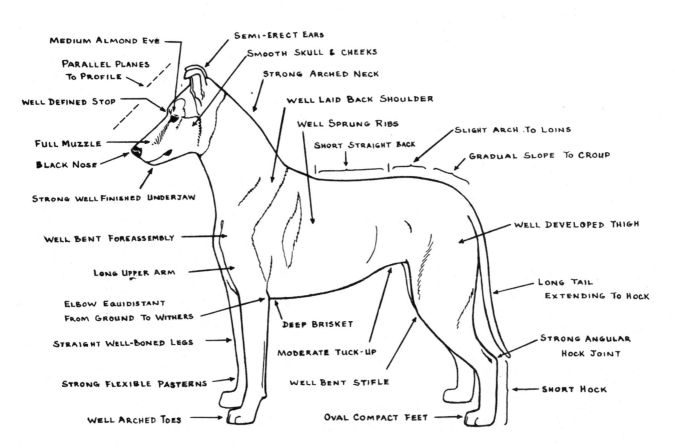

MEDIUM ALMOND EYE
SEMI-ERECT EARS
SMOOTH SKULL & CHEEKS
PARALLEL PLANES TO PROFILE
STRONG ARCHED NECK
WELL DEFINED STOP
WELL LAID BACK SHOULDER
WELL SPRUNG RIBS
SLIGHT ARCH TO LOINS
FULL MUZZLE
SHORT STRAIGHT BACK
GRADUAL SLOPE TO CROUP
BLACK NOSE
STRONG WELL FINISHED UNDERJAW
WELL DEVELOPED THIGH
WELL BENT FOREASSEMBLY
LONG UPPER ARM
LONG TAIL EXTENDING TO HOCK
ELBOW EQUIDISTANT FROM GROUND TO WITHERS
DEEP BRISKET
STRAIGHT WELL-BONED LEGS
STRONG ANGULAR HOCK JOINT
MODERATE TUCK-UP
STRONG FLEXIBLE PASTERNS
WELL BENT STIFLE
SHORT HOCK
WELL ARCHED TOES
OVAL COMPACT FEET

Black and White

Sable

Blue-merle

Tricolor

Correct general appearance—male.

Correct general appearance—female.

The correct head—profile.

Correct head—top view.

Correct head—front view.

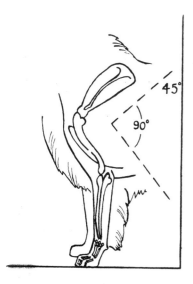
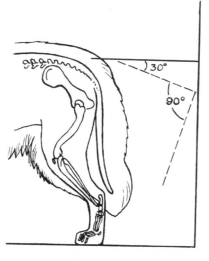
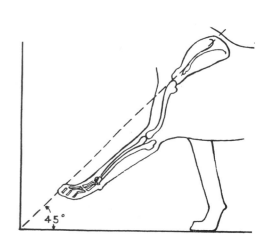

Diagram of proper shoulder angulation.

Diagram of proper rear angulation.

Diagram showing how extension of shoulder placement determines forward reach of front leg.

Correct position of single-tracking, showing where proper break occurs. Legs are straight from breaking point to ground and are moving in direct line of travel.

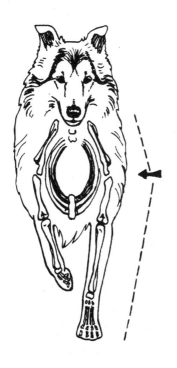
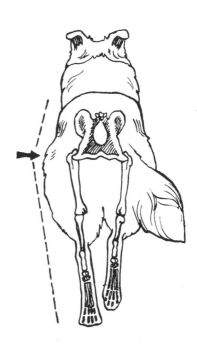

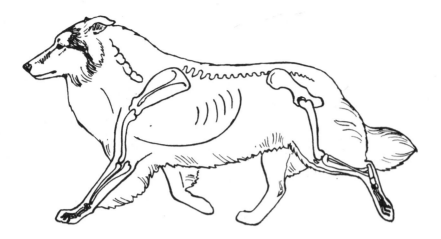

Position I

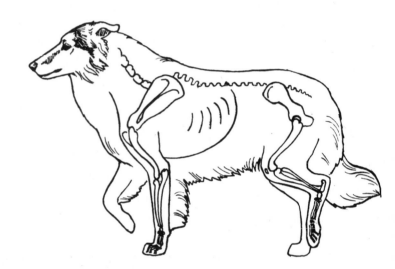

Position II

The correct trot—side view. Feet lifted just enough to clear the ground. Free flowing movement, with no apparent effort. Full reach of front, strong drive to rear.

Correct rear movement during slow trot (left) and fast trot (right).

Correct front (left) and correct rear (right).

Am. and Can. Ch. Rosewood Christy The Clown, top winning bitch in Shetland Sheepdog history, taking her fifth Best in Show at Olympic Kennel Club. Owned by Rosemary Petter, Rosewood Shelties.

Ch. Lakehill Portrait In Blue, by Ch. Kiloren Night Apache ex Kiloren Moonbeam, twice Best of Opposite Sex at the National Specialty, once when ten years of age. Blue was the dam of three champions, one of which was Best of Winners at the National. Owner, Stephen W. Barger.

Above: Ch. Mainstay Rumor Has It, by Ch. Macdega Mainstay ex Montage Pardon My Past, finished in six shows with all Specialty wins! Co-owned by Jo Ann McNeal and Stephen W. Barger. **Below:** Can. and Jap. Ch. Sheldon Royaltye Lookin completed his title in Canada in two weekends and his Japanese championship in five weekends. Bred by Sheldon Kennels, Bill and Doreen Randall.

Ch. Legacy Steela Breeze, born in 1980, taking Best of Opposite Sex at the American Shetland Sheepdog Association National Specialty in 1983. A grandson of Ch. Banchory Deep Purple, this dog has made a prestigious record for breeder-owner Nancy Howard. Handled by Lloyd H. Graser, Jr.

Belle Mount Wee Duke of Orange and Ch. Belle Mount Wee Tobias, the sensational Sheltie brace which is frequently winning Best Working Brace and Best Brace in Show as this book is written. Owned and handled by Alice A. Burhans, Belle Mount Shelties.

Am., Can., and Bda. Ch. Astolat Jupiter, C.D., by Ch. Astolat Galaxy, C.D. (by Peter Pumpkin) ex Park Crest Cinnamon Twist (Peter granddaughter). Jupiter is a fifth generation descendant of Ch. Frigate and became a champion in 1979. Constance B. Hubbard, owner, Astolat Kennels.

Ch. Rorralore Play Fair, by Ch. Fair Play of Sea Isle ex Rorralore Mary Rose, Reserve Winners at the American Shetland Sheep-dog Association Specialty in 1977. Charlotte McGowan, owner, Rorralore Shelties.

Ch. Shamont Ruby Slippers, multiple all-breed and Specialty Best in Show winner. Owned by Macdega Kennels, Thomas W. Coen.

Am., Can., and Bda. Ch. Lauxly's The Joker Is Wild, by Can. Ch. Sea Isle Night Time o'the Picts ex Ch. Meridian's Blues on Parade, C.D. This is one of the outstanding Shelties belonging to Mrs. Hazel Slaughter, Meridian Kennels.

Ch. Severn Smoke On The Water, at three years of age, winning the Colonial Shetland Sheepdog Club Specialty in June 1981; judge, Miss Olwyn Gwynne-Jones from England. Handled at this show by Martha Bjorkman; bred by Linda More and Madelyn Cirinna; owned by Linda More, Severn Kennels.

Above: Ch. Birch Hollow Once Upon A Time pictured winning under Ernest Loeb. This multiple Group and Specialty Show winner was Best of Breed at Westminster in 1983. Owned by Mildred B. Nicoll, Birch Hollow.
Below: Ch. Kismet's Status Quo taking Best of Breed at the American Shetland Sheepdog Association National Specialty in 1981. Owner-handled by Guy Mauldin for himself and Thelma Mauldin, Kismet Shelties.

Gene Cohen winning Best of Breed with his gorgeous and consistent Ch. Wade Gate Honor Bound, known to friends as "Bounty."

316

Ch. Rorralore Sportin' Chance, C.D., taking Best of Breed in 389 entries at the Colonial Shetland Sheepdog Specialty, National week, 1983. Owner-handled by Charlotte Clem McGowan.

Ch. Rickgarbob Dianamation, by Ch. Chenterra Thunderation ex Rickgarbob Katie. Dianamation finished in three months during 1979 and was top winning Sheltie bitch in the United States in 1979. Bred and owned by Rickgarbob Shelties, Bob Carlough and Mrs. Marie Carlough.

Ch. Chenterra Thunderation winning one of his numerous Bests in Show with his handler Steve Barger.

Ch. Benayr Chimera Colloquy taking Best of Breed at San Gabriel Valley Kennel Club, April 1978. This lovely bitch, owned by Susan Bentley, was also Best of Breed at the American Shetland Sheepdog Association National in 1976.

Ch. Lynnlea Forever Amber, C.D., pictured at eight years of age when she had just completed her championship two weeks before the 1983 National Specialty, where she won Best of Breed over seventy-five Specials and close to six hundred Shelties from the Veterans Class! Owned by Ray and Dorothy Christiansen, Lynnlea Kennels.

CHAPTER EIGHT

Some Comments on Sheltie Type

by Leslie B. Rogers

Am. Ch. Forever Pawthorne Blue Eclipse, a bi-blue female who was a Working Group winner from the Puppy Class. She was the dam of Am. and Can. Ch. Rosewood Christy The Clown. Bred by Leslie B. Rogers and owned by Linda Crutcher. Photo courtesy of Mr. Rogers.

When one speaks of "type" in referring to a purebred dog, one has in mind the combination of features upon which the standard of that breed places particular emphasis, the characteristics which combine to make that breed and its members unique to the point that they are instantly recognizable as such. A good type dog is one which adheres closely to the dog described in the standard; one lacking type, or poor in type, is a dog which does not meet the standard's requirement.

In judging Shetland Sheepdogs, or in selecting them for the foundation of a breeding program, type should always be foremost in one's mind. A dog lacking correct type can never be outstanding and can never accumulate the wins or produce future generations which will do so.

Mr. Leslie Rogers is a Sheltie breeder of note and a popular judge. We feel that his following comments, which are revised and updated from articles he wrote many years ago for a magazine, *Shetland Sheepdog*, which is no longer in publication, deserve to be included here for their value and interest to our readers, and we are delighted at having his permission for us to use them.

A.K.N.

Some breeders consistently produce winning stock year after year. Their winning strain pro-

duces results for others who show their stock, winning with these dogs at shows which may be located far across the country in distant areas from the home kennel. Such a breeder can bask in the satisfaction of having produced a winning type.

A winning breeder has thorough knowledge of the breed standard and knows to a hair precisely the virtues and faults of his dogs and their immediate ancestors. The progeny from each breeding is carefully studied and evaluated. A follow-up examination is made of the litter of each of its members upon maturity. Strong and weak points at that time are evaluated, and tendencies to produce certain virtues and/or faults are carefully noted for the future.

Dogs of winning type usually possess most of the following virtues:

Balance: This is the key point. The profile outline must be pleasing, with nicely arched neck and correctly proportioned back length blending into smooth rear quarters. Correct size and specific breed characteristics are taken into consideration in order to show the pleasing overall appearance.

Movement: This should be smooth rather than jerky or prancing. True movement both coming and going is extremely important.

Showmanship: This is a definite must. A good specimen who is not inclined to show, who stands there bored, ears flattened, is definitely at a disadvantage. Shelties of a winning type show happily and naturally. They do not possess timid natures. A confident, self-assured showman who responds well to both the lead and the liver stands out in any group.

Head and Expression: A pleasing head and expression add greatly to the overall appearance. Correct expression is best seen in Shelties of good temperament. Timid, shy and nervous Shelties cannot show correct expression. Natural ears, not those exhibiting obvious work, correctly set and well carried are extremely important and generally enhance the overall picture of balance and good type.

Breeders with a winning type know exactly when to show their dogs to best advantage. They do not show good dogs when they are out of coat or condition. Sending your out-of-coat Sheltie into the ring is like sending a soldier to battle without his armour. A well-groomed Sheltie has a definite advantage over one whose grooming is inadequate and who therefore fails to present a pleasing picture.

Breeders who continue to show and win do not develop fads on specific points. They do not sacrifice good overall type and balance in order to overcome one weakness. For example, a wise breeder realizes that the development of his winning strain has taken a great deal of time, thought and study. Any minor improvement will only become possible after a long time and very careful selection and breeding.

Shelties of winning type are *easily* recognizable. Their pleasing overall balance and happy nature appeals on sight to everyone. It is not necessary to study them in detail before reaching the conclusion that these are *typical* specimens. Their obvious virtues stand out clearly, proclaiming the fact that they are *truly* winning type.

Since Shelties are a "coat breed," *i.e.*, their coats are among their most beautiful and characteristic assets, understanding of a *correct* coat is of importance in the overall consideration of type. For a number of years I have offered a trophy for the best coated Sheltie at our annual Specialty [Author's note: This is a Canadian Specialty; trophies of this type are not listed at A.K.C. point shows], for which the premium list states: "Trophy to be awarded to the Best Coated Shetland Sheepdog on the basis of quality, quantity, condition, texture, etc." Each year we acquire the services of a qualified specialist judge to evaluate our regular conformation classes as well as the special classes. Some years the award for the Best Coated Sheltie has been given to an excessively coated Sheltie who had *quantity* of coat *only*, which sometimes seems to be confused with quality.

Can. Ch. Forever Silk Tassel "in action," moving out as a Sheltie should. This lovely young winner was bred by Leslie B. Rogers and is owned by Donna Roadhouse, Arpeggio Shelties, Aldengrove, British Columbia, Canada.

Ch. Miskela Destiny O'Forever winning a Working Group at only eight months of age. Destiny finished with three Best of Breed wins over Specials under judges from three different countries—America, Canada, and Australia—truly a representative opinion! Breeder, Leslie B. Rogers; owner, Lois Greenlay. Photo courtesy of Mr. Rogers.

My interpretation of correct coat in a Shetland Sheepdog involves the following:

Coat Type: The coat must be *double*, consisting of both an under and an outer coat. The short, thick undercoat is necessary to achieve the "stand off" quality—often not seen *correctly*. The outer coat must be long, straight and *harsh*. Both undercoat and outer coat must be evident.

Coat Pattern: The correct coat forms a distinct pattern blending smoothly together to form a beautiful overall picture. The hair on the face, ear-tips and feet should be smooth. Mane and frill should be abundant, especially in males. Well-feathered forelegs, smooth hocks, and profuse hair on tail form the overall pattern. Excessive coat, such as leg feathering dragging on the floor, bushiness on the head or an overcoated, ragmop appearance, is faulty. The correct pattern is lost and the general appearance is out of balance.

Coat Texture: The outer coat should be long, straight and *harsh*. The undercoat short, furry and *dense*.

Coat Condition: A healthy coat, glossy and shimmering under lights, reflects the condition of its owner. A soft, heavy coat, artificially made

Best in Show winner Ch. Gallantry Solid Success pictured winning his tenth Best of Breed, over three Specials, at just two years of age; judge, Leslie Rogers. Breeder- owner- handler, Mona Stolcz, Gallantry Shetland Sheepdogs.

BEST OF BREED
NANAIMO
KENNEL CLUB
SPRING 1983

Forever The Blackberry Belle, by Banchory Adonis o'Forever ex Ch. Forever The Blue Bonnet, being selected for an important award by the famous J. Nate Levine, a leading American professional handler and Sheltie breeder who contributed inestimably to the breed with his Page's Hill dogs. Leslie B. Rogers, owner-handler, Forever Shelties, Langley, British Columbia.

Ch. Mar-ja's Forever Flame, a Working Group winner from the classes and two times Best Puppy in Show, all-breeds. Along with a kennelmate, Forever Jenne, Flame was stolen and despite extensive investigation, no trace of either dog was ever found—truly a heartbreaker! Bred by Leslie B. Rogers; owned by Marjorie Jarocki.

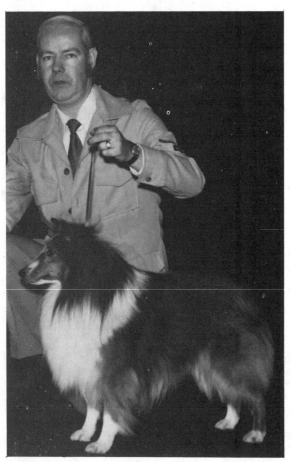

harsh by stale beer or chemical preparations, cannot reflect a healthy gloss. It will also feel incorrect to the knowledgeable hand. A healthy coat is usually the result of good feeding, outdoor exercise, and a dog being a good "doer."

Coat Colour: Some may question the importance of putting colour down as a component of correct coat. I feel that it is very important. A *good* sable colour (*gold* through *mahogany*), *deep* black *with* rich tan markings in a tri-colour; and a *definite* blue colour with *distinct* merling add greatly to the qualities of the Sheltie coat. Pale sables, rusty tri-colours, and faded blue merles are definite coat faults and should be penalized accordingly.

Some of the coat faults that I have noticed in Shelties over the past years are as follows:

Coat Texture: A) *Undercoat and Outer Coat* —Many lack correct undercoat, resulting in lack of the "stand off" quality. Once having seen a truly correct "stand off" coat, its beauty will not soon be forgotten. At one time an eleven-year-old Champion Sheltie stayed at my place for a week. He arrived looking perfectly groomed. His living quarters consisted of a large, grassy paddock with a dog house in it. During his entire stay he lived outdoors, weathering several rainstorms. When he went home, his coat still looked perfectly groomed and in ideal condition. The coat's correct texture maintained this appearance. The long, straight, harsh outer coat shed the rain; the short, thick, furry undercoat

Leslie B. Rogers, owner of Forever Shelties, judging the dog he refers to as "top tri-colour Sheltie of all time" with twenty-six Bests in Show: Ch. Chenterra Thunderation. Owned at that period by Stephen Barger and Thomas Coen who is handling.

prevented the penetration of the water. His correct coat would enable him to carry out his functions as a sheep dog who must brave all weather, all conditions to fulfill his purpose. B) *Soft coat*—Have you ever seen what a heavy rain can do to a soft, silky coat? In just minutes the dog is sodden and bedraggled. The water can be squeezed from this type of coat, for it has acted as an absorbent sponge. Such a coat would severely hinder a Sheltie called upon to fulfill his purpose in life, acting as a herding dog. Therefore it is atypical. Wavy, curly coats are also faulty. Unfortunately, spray starches and similar preparations may remove all visual traces from sight. However, the texture is wrong, and this is very obvious to the fingers of a knowledgeable judge.

Shelties with smooth, flat coats considered to be smooth coated are not often seen, but they are around. Such Shelties generally only have a slight trace of feathering or frill, accompanied by a short, smooth body coat. These dogs lack proper undercoat and development of the outer coat.

Pattern or Fit of the Coat: I have seen Sheltie males with a truly abundant mane and frill but lacking hair on the rear quarters. Such Shelties appear heavy in front and over balanced. The coat has an incorrect pattern if this is a permanent condition.

A Sheltie with a correctly textured coat, with the proper pattern and the right quantity, can be said to have a well-fitted coat. Everything is in balance and the eye is not drawn just to one particular area.

Colour Faults: A) *Sables*—Paleness of colour rather than gold through mahogany. These dogs appear almost straw colour, making it sometimes difficult to trace even the white markings. B) *Tri-colours*—Rusty blacks, or pale tan markings. C) *Blue-merles.* Faded blue. Lack of merling or mottling. A mouse-like colour (dilute tri-colour) with white markings is very undesirable in any breeding program. D) *Bi-black.* Rustiness in the black body coat. A harsh coat on a bi-black is difficult to find. E) *Bi-blue.* Rustiness in the blue or black colour; lack of merling; too little blue colour, causing a faded appearance. F) *White markings.* Conspicuous white body spots. A coat with more than 50% white is so severely penalized as to practically eliminate the dog from competition. Some Shelties have some rather unfortunate facial markings which may detract from the expression. G) *Brindle.* This colour is a disqualification, and I have never seen one. H) *Tan markings.* Generally speaking, the richer the tan the better, since this enhances the overall appearance and expression of both blue merles and tri-colours. Faded, yellow-tan markings are unattractive and undesirable.

It should be noted that tan markings are *optional, not* an absolute requirement as some breeders seem to believe. Blue merles without tan are what we refer to as Bi-blues. A Bi-black is a black and white Sheltie with no tan markings whatsoever. The Sheltie standard states *nothing* about colour preferences. All colours are equally desirable with the exception of the one disqualification—brindle!

325

Dona Hausman, well-known breeder, exhibitor, and judge, in an informal moment with her handsome Ch. Meadow Ridge Hello Bunny in 1975.

CHAPTER NINE

Random Thoughts on Judging Shelties

by Dona Hausman

Ch. Carmylie If Bi Chance, by Philidove Neva Can Say Goodby ex Carmylie Black Lace, the first bi-black champion bitch in breed history in the United States. Jean D. Simmonds, owner, Carmylie Shelties.

In planning for this book, one of our first thoughts was "who would be a good person to write about judging the breed?" And of course the name we came up with was that of Dona Hausman. She is a widely respected judge of numerous breeds, but at the same time she is considered by Sheltie breeders to be a specialist, owing to her long association with the breed as a breeder, owner, exhibitor, as well as a judge. We are honored that she accepted our invitation to participate in *The Book of the Shetland Sheepdog* and take tremendous pride in presenting her remarks.

A.K.N.

In my opinion, breed type is the foremost consideration when judging Shelties. Of course a dog with a disqualification, or one with a disfiguring fault, cannot be considered winning quality even if it possesses those requisites of correct type: a beautiful head and expression along with the overall balance of the whole dog which makes him unique and a true Sheltie. As in many breeds, showmanship and a very long and full coat help to create a lovely picture. But getting down to basics, it is still the head which says "this dog is a Shetland Sheepdog."

Careful, and knowledgeable, examination of the head is of great importance. Do feel the top half of the ears for any weighting, and also ascertain that there is no horizontal line across the ear near the halfway mark, or about where it creases, for such a line is telling you that the ear has certainly been altered as a muscle runs perpendicular and therefore this cannot be a normal crease. Then pay attention to where the stop is placed, as it should be right between the eyes. Also look for depth of muzzle. You want to see a strong muzzle, but in proportion, and never so wide as to make the head look chunky. Remember, too, that while blue eyes, or one brown eye and one blue eye, are acceptable in a blue dog they are a very serious fault in the tris or sables. Should the eyes look wet, or be tearing, take a long look at the pupils, for if they are enlarged, then atropine could have been used (this treatment makes the eyes appear darker and also smaller).

A good coat can hide many faults, so feel right through it for conformation of the shoulders, making sure that they are correctly sloping rather than straight. Then be sure that correct spring of rib exists by this same method. Remember the importance of coat texture, feeling carefully for that. If the coat feels like a bris-

Ch. Sutter's Golden Masquerade, a gorgeous winning Sheltie. Owned by Dona Hausman, Meadow Ridge Kennels.

tle brush, it has probably been sprayed with starch.

Should the dog possess a beautiful red-sable face but coat on the neck and legs of a far lighter sable, you can suspect that color has been added to the face. Check the front legs carefully for correct bone and desired width of chest. Sometimes, when doing this, one finds the front legs practically coming "out of the same hole" so to speak.

If you have a blue with a lot of sable running through the body coat, this indicates poor color breeding, especially if the hair roots are blue and the ends sable. Exhibitors will tell you this is

Caper Hills I Have Dreamed, by Am. and Can. Ch. Severn Smoke On The Water ex Caper Hills Could It Be Magic, C.D., at seven months of age taking Best of Winners under Mrs. Dona Hausman at Mobile Kennel Club in 1981. Lynette Smith and Bitsy Adkins, breeder-owners.

Int. Ch. Astolat Gold Award, Int. C.D., by Ch. Astolat Golden Symbol ex Scotswold Gretta, winning at Penn Treaty in 1965 under judge Mrs. Dona Hausman. Owner-handled by Mrs. Constance B. Hubbard, Astolat Kennels.

caused by the water. But if the white on the dog is white, why should not the blue be blue?

When the Sheltie is on the ground, do not "pussy-foot" up to him, but walk up in a normal manner, say "Hi," and look at whatever you want to examine. Also do not squat alongside the dog, as this may never before have been done to him.

Condition in a Herding breed is of tremendous importance, as a really fat, soft dog could never work all day, and neither could a thin, frail dog. Also, a very fat dog is ruined in outline, movement, and general appearance.

When a dog is being gaited I like to see it move right along, and I hate to see one hanging back and not keeping abreast of the handler.

There is no size difference between dogs and bitches, but the bitches have a bit more refinement in head than do the dogs.

Should you feel the necessity of measuring, be sure that the wicket is correctly adjusted and lies, as it should, across the shoulders (withers) and not the neck. The top of the shoulders is quite far back on a dog with a nice long neck and is the spot where the wicket should measure. Also make certain that the dog is set up (the handler must do this to the judge's satisfaction) with the legs really under the dog in a parallel line, because if the legs are placed with the feet at all forward, this will make the dog measure less than the actual height if placed normally. The A.K.C. ruling states that it is the handler who must set up the dog; the judge may not participate in doing so, but the judge must give directions and ascertain that the dog is set up in proper position—all very important things to be remembered as you judge this breed!

"Getting the feel of it." This darling baby, by Ch. Chenterra Thunderation ex Ch. Marwal Bluesette, is sitting proudly in one of Dad's Best in Show trophies in 1978. Who knows what the future may bring for this promising youngster?

CHAPTER TEN

Selection of a Shetland Sheepdog

Jade Mist puppy at seven weeks of age. Owned by Dr. and Mrs. Keith B. Howell. Photo by Virginia Kay.

Once you have made the decision that the Shetland Sheepdog is the breed of dog you wish to own, the next important step for you is to determine the right Sheltie to best satisfy your needs. Do you prefer to start out with a puppy, with an adult dog, or with one partially mature? Do you prefer a male or a female? What type of dog do you wish—one for show or for competition in obedience? Are you looking for a Sheltie for breeding, possibly as the foundation for a kennel? Do you simply want one for companionship, to be a family pet?

A decision should be reached about these matters prior to your contacting breeders; then you can accurately describe your requirements and the breeder can offer you the most suitable dog for your purposes. Remember that with any breed of dog, as with any other major purchase, the more care and forethought you invest when planning, the greater the pleasure and satisfaction likely to result.

Referring to a dog as a "major investment" may possibly seem strange to you; however, it is an accurate description. Generally speaking, a sizable sum of money is involved, and you are assuming responsibility for a living creature, taking on all the moral obligations this involves. Assuming that everything goes well, your Sheltie will be a member of your family for a

dozen or more years, sharing your home, your daily routine, and your interests. The happiness and success of these years depend largely on the knowledge and intelligence with which you start the relationship.

Certain ground rules apply to the purchase of a dog, regardless of your intentions for its future. Foremost among these is the fact that no matter what you will be doing with the dog, the best and most acceptable place at which to purchase a Shetland Sheepdog is a kennel specializing in that breed. Even though pet shops occasionally have Shetland Sheepdog puppies for sale, they are primarily concerned with *pet* stock, puppies with meaningless pedigrees. When you buy from a breeder you are getting a dog that has been the result of parents very carefully selected as individuals and as to pedigree and ancestry. For such a breeding, a dog and a bitch are chosen from whom the breeder hopes to achieve show type dogs that upgrade both his own kennel's quality and that of the breed generally. Much thought has been given to the conformation and temperament likely to result from the combination of parents and bloodlines involved, for the breeder wants to produce sound, outstanding dogs that will further the respect with which he is regarded in the Shetland Sheepdog world. A specialist of this sort is interested in

331

raising *better* dogs. Since it is seldom possible to keep all the puppies from every litter, fine young stock becomes available for sale. These puppies have flaws so slight in appearance as to be unrecognizable as such by other than the trained eye of a judge or a specialist on Shelties. These flaws in no way affect the strength or future good health of these Shelties; they simply preclude success in the show ring. The conscientious breeder will point them out to you when explaining why the puppy is being offered for sale at "pet price." When you buy a Sheltie like this, from a knowledgeable, reliable breeder, you get all the advantages of good bloodlines with proper temperament, careful rearing, and the happy, well-adjusted environment needed by puppies who are to become satisfactory, enjoyable adults. Although you are not buying a show dog or show prospect, puppies raised in the same manner have all the odds in their favor to become dogs of excellence in the home where they will bring great pleasure.

If you are looking for a show dog, obviously everything I have said about buying only from a specialized Sheltie breeder applies with even

Kathy Hubbard with a litter of puppies sired by Ch. Frigate's Emblem of Astolat. Two of them became champions: Ch. Astolat Good Luck on the left and Champion Astolat Future Emblem in the center. Mrs. Constance B. Hubbard, owner, Astolat Kennels.

A Carmylie puppy owned by Jean D. Simmonds.

greater emphasis. Show-type dogs are bred from show-type dogs of proven producing lines and are the result of serious study, thought, and planning. They do *not* just happen.

Throughout the pages of this book are the names and locations of dozens of reliable Sheltie breeders. Should it so happen that no one has puppies or young stock available to go at the moment you inquire, it would be far wiser to place your name on the waiting list and see what happens when the next litter is born than to rush off and buy a puppy from some less desirable source. After all, you do not want to repent at leisure.

Another source of information regarding recognized Sheltie breeders is the American Kennel Club, 51 Madison Avenue, New York, NY 10010. A note or phone call will bring you a list of breeders in your area.

Still another source of information is a professional handler. They have many contacts and might be able to put you in touch with a breeder and/or help you choose a dog.

The moment you even start to think about purchasing a Sheltie, it makes sense to look at, observe, and study as many members of the breed as possible prior to taking the step. Acquaint yourself with correct type, soundness and beauty before making any commitments. Since

Blue-merle Sheltie pup owned by Macdega Kennels, Thomas W. Coen.

you are reading this book, you have already started on that route. Now add to your learning by visiting some dog shows if you can. Even if you are not looking for a show dog, it never hurts to become aware of how such a dog appears and behaves. Perhaps at the shows you will meet some breeders from your area with whom you can discuss the breed and who you can visit.

If you wish your Sheltie to be a family dog, the most satisfactory choice often is a female. Females make gentle, delightful companions and usually are quieter and more inclined not to roam than males. Often, too, they make neater house dogs, being easier to train. And they are of at least equal intelligence to the males. In the eyes of many pet owners, the principal objection to having a bitch is the periodic "coming in season." Sprays and chlorophyll tablets that can help to cut down on the nuisance of visiting canine swains stampeding your front door are available; and, of course, I advocate spaying bitches who will not be used for show or breeding, with even the bitches who are shown or bred

Merry Christmas, as expressed by these handsome Marchwind puppies. These are five of the seven puppies from the Ch. September's Rainmaker litter which produced Ch. Marchwind The Rain Minstrel, pictured at extreme right. Mary MacDonald, owner, Marchwind Kennels.

Three-month-old litter by Barwood's Formal Attire ex Harvest Hills Holly of Pocono. Elizabeth D. Whelen, Pocono Kennels.

Above: A handsome homebred son of Ch. Candega Main Event ex Crinan's Keepsake, at three months of age in May 1983. Owner-breeder, Evelyn K. Basnicki, Crinan Shelties. **Below:** Jade Mist Sunbrite Cedar at nine and a half weeks of age. Owned by Dr. and Mrs. Keith B. Howell.

being spayed when their careers in competition or in the whelping box have come to a close. Bitches who have been spayed, preferably before four years old, remain in better health later on in life, because spaying almost entirely eliminates the dangers of breast cancer. Spaying also eliminates the messiness of spotting on rugs and furniture, which is annoying in a household companion.

To many, however, a dog (male) is preferable. The males do seem to be more strongly endowed with true breed character. But do consider the advantages and disadvantages of both males and females prior to deciding which to purchase.

If you are buying your Sheltie as a pet, a puppy is usually preferable, as you can teach it right from the beginning the ways of your household and your own schedule. Two months is an ideal age at which to introduce the puppy into your home. Older puppies may already have established habits of which you will not approve and which you may find difficult to change. Besides, puppies are such fun that it is great to share and enjoy every possible moment of their process of growing up.

When you are ready to buy, make appointments with as many Sheltie breeders as you have been able to locate in your area for the purpose of seeing what they have available and discussing the breed with them. This is a marvelous learning experience, and you will find the majority of breeders are willing and happy to spend time

"Christmas Angels!" These two darling baby Shelties are owned by Starhaven Kennels, Carl and Amy Langhorst.

334

Meridian puppies, including Ch. Meridian High Noon. Owned by Mrs. Hazel Slaughter.

with you, provided that you have arranged the visit in advance. Kennel owners are busy folks with full schedules, so do be considerate about this courtesy and call on the telephone before you appear.

If you have a choice of more than one kennel where you can go to see the dogs, take advantage of that opportunity instead of just settling for and buying the first puppy you see. You may return to your first choice in the long run, but you will do so with greater satisfaction and authority if you have seen the others before making the selection. When you look at puppies, be aware that the one you buy should look sturdy, bright-eyed, and alert, with an inquisitive, friendly attitude. The puppy's coat should look clean and glossy. Do not buy a puppy that seems listless or dull, is strangely hyperactive, or looks half sick. The condition of the premises where the puppies are raised is also important as you want your puppy to be free of parasites; don't buy a puppy whose surroundings are dirty and ill kept.

One of the advantages of buying at a kennel you can visit is that you are thereby afforded the opportunity of seeing the dam of the puppies and possibly also the sire, if he, too, belongs to the breeder. Sometimes you can even see one or more of the grandparents. Be sure to note the

Lochanora Southern Accent, by Ch. Madselin's Grand Slam ex Banchory Badgerton Babe, at eight weeks of age. Breeders, Cathy and Gerry Grafstrom; owners, George and Melanie Williams, Lakeland, Florida.

temperament of these Shelties as well as their conformation.

If there are no Sheltie breeders within your travelling range, or if you have not liked what you have seen at those you've visited, do not hesitate to contact other breeders who are recommended to you even if their kennels are at a distance and to purchase from one of them if you are favorably impressed with what is offered. Shipping dogs is done with regularity nowadays and is reasonably safe, so this should not present a problem. If you are contacting a well-known, recognized breeder, the puppy should be fairly described and represented to you. Breeders of this caliber want you to be satisfied, both for the puppy's sake and for yours. They take pride in their kennel's reputation, and they make every effort to see that their customers are pleased. In this way you are deprived of the opportunity of seeing your dog's parents, but even so you can buy with confidence when dealing with a specialized breeder.

Every word about careful selection of your pet puppy and where it should be purchased applies twofold when you set out to select a show dog or the foundation stock for a breeding kennel of

SumerSong puppies, by Ch. SumerSong Winter Shadows ex SumerSong Easter Robin, at nine weeks of age. Bred and owned by Peggy and Jan Haderlie.

A grandson of Ch. Galaxy and Ch. Headliner showing all the charm of Astolat Sheltie puppies. Mrs. Constance B. Hubbard, owner, Astolat Kennels.

are dogs that perhaps may never finish their championships but which should do a bit of winning for you in the classes: a blue ribbon here and there, perhaps Winners or Reserve occasionally, but probably nothing truly spectacular. Obviously the hardest to obtain, and the most expensive, are dogs in the first category, the truly top grade dogs. These are never plentiful as they are what most breeders are working to produce for their own kennels and personal enjoyment and with which they are loathe to part.

A dog of championship quality is easier to find and less expensive, although it still will bring a good price. The least difficult to obtain is a fair show dog that may pick up some points here and there but will mostly remain in class placements. Incidentally, one of the reasons that breeders are sometimes reluctant to part with a truly excellent show prospect is that in the past people have bought this type of dog with the promise it will be shown, but then the buyer has changed his mind after owning the dog awhile, and thus the dog becomes lost to the breed. It is really not fair to a breeder to buy a dog with the understanding that it will be shown and then renege on the agreement. Please, if you select a dog that is available only to a show home, think it over carefully prior to making a decision; then buy

your own. You look for all the things already mentioned but on a far more sophisticated level, with many more factors to be taken into consideration. The standard of the Shetland Sheepdog must now become your guide, and it is essential that you know and understand not only the words of this standard but also their application to actual dogs before you are in a position to make a wise selection. Even then, if this is your first venture with a show-type Sheltie, listen well and heed the advice of the breeder. If you have clearly and honestly stated your ambitions and plans for the dog, you will find that the breeders will cooperate by offering you something with which you will be successful.

There are several different degrees of show dog quality. There are dogs that should become top flight winners which can be campaigned for Specials (Best of Breed competition) and with which you can hope to attain Herding Group placements and possibly even hit the heights with a Best in Show win. There are dogs of championship quality which should gain their titles for you but are lacking in that "extra something" to make them potential Specials. There

Happy Glen's Red Baron at ten weeks of age when he weighed seven pounds and measured 9 7/8". Hopes are high for a good show career as this son of Happy Glen's Royal Dream from Banchory Bit O'Stone looks most promising. Happy Glen Kennels, breeder-owners, Barbara and Marvin Ross.

Sterling's Enchanted Spirit at seven weeks of age—a future show dog! Debra Elkin, owner, Enchanted Shelties.

to "make haste slowly;" mistakes can be expensive, and the more you have studied the breed, the better equipped you will be to avoid them.

As you make inquiries among various breeders regarding the purchase of a show dog or a show prospect, keep these things in mind. Show-prospect puppies are less expensive than fully mature show dogs. The reason for this is that with a puppy there is the element of chance, for one never can be absolutely certain exactly how the puppy will develop, while the mature dog stands before you as the finished product— "what you see is what you get"—all set to step out and win.

There is always the risk factor involved with the purchase of a show-type puppy. Sometimes all goes well and that is great. But many a swan has turned into an ugly duckling as time passes, and it is far less likely that the opposite will occur. So weigh this well and balance all the odds before you decide whether a puppy or a mature dog would be your better buy. There are times, of course, when one actually has no choice in the matter; no mature show dogs may be available for sale. Then one must either wait awhile or gamble on a puppy, but please *be aware that gambling is what you are doing.*

Banchory A Blue Nun, by Ch. Banchory Deep Purple ex Banchory Night Glow, at four months of age. Owned by Jerry and Chris Machado, Montage Kennels.

the dog only if you will be willing to give it the opportunity to prove itself in the show ring as the breeder expects.

If you want a show dog, obviously you are a person in the habit of attending dog shows. Now this becomes a form of schooling rather than just a pleasant pastime. Much can be learned at the Sheltie ringside if one truly concentrates on what one sees. Become acquainted with the various winning exhibitors. Thoughtfully watch the judging. Try to understand what it is that causes some dogs to win and others to lose. Note well the attributes of the dogs, deciding for yourself which ones you like, giving full attention to attitude and temperament as well as conformation. Close your ears to the ringside "know-it-alls" who have only derogatory remarks to make about each animal in the ring and all that takes place there. You need to develop independent thinking at this stage and should not be influenced by the often entirely uneducated comment of the ringside spoilsports. Especially make careful note of which exhibitors are campaigning winning homebreds—not just an occasional "star" but a series of consistent quality dogs. All this takes time and patience. This is the period

Puppies at Legacy Kennels.
Owned by Nancy Howard.

If you do take a show-prospect puppy, be guided by the breeder's advice when choosing from among what is offered. The person used to working with a bloodline has the best chance of predicting how the puppies will develop. Do not trust your own guess on this; rely on the experience of the breeder. For your own protection, it is best to buy puppies whose parents' eyes have been certified clear.

Although initially more expensive, a grown show dog in the long run often proves to be the far better bargain. His appearance is unlikely to change beyond weight and condition, which depend on the care you give him. Also to your advantage, if you are a novice about to become an exhibitor, is that a grown dog of show quality almost certainly will have been trained for the ring; thus, an inexperienced handler will find such a dog easier to present properly and in winning form in the ring.

If you plan to have your dog campaigned by a professional handler, have the handler help you locate and select a future winner. Through their numerous clients, handlers usually have access to a variety of interesting show dogs; and the usual arrangement is that the handler buys the dog, resells it to you for the price he paid, and at the same time makes a contract with you that the dog shall be campaigned by this handler throughout the dog's career.

Rosmoor Once Again, by Ch. Macdega Proof Positive ex Ch. Rosmoor Night Sprite. Bred and owned by Rose and Jennie Tomlin.

Lynnlea's Parade Dress at eight months of age. Owned by Patricia A. Stewart.

If the foundation of a future kennel is what you have in mind as you contemplate the purchase of a Sheltie, concentrate on one or two really excellent bitches, not necessarily top show bitches but those representing the finest producing Shetland Sheepdog lines. A proven matron who has already produced show type puppies is, of course, the ideal answer here, but, as with a mature show dog, a proven matron is more difficult to obtain and more expensive since no one really wants to part with so valuable an asset. You just might strike it lucky, though, in which case you will be off to a flying start. If you do not find such a matron available, do the next best thing and select a young bitch of outstanding background representing a noted producing strain, one that is herself of excellent type and free of glaring faults.

Great attention should be paid to the background of the bitch from whom you intend to breed. If the information is not already known to you, find out all you can about the temperament, character, and conformation of the sire and dam, plus eye rating. A person just starting in dogs is wise to concentrate on a fine collection of bitches

Two promising young hopefuls at Marwal Kennels, Margaret and Walt Huening.

Macdega Blue Note, by Ch. Chenterra Thunderation ex Banchory Blue Petal, at five months of age. Owned by Rickgarbob Shelties, Bob Carlough and Mrs. Marie Carlough.

Starhaven's Ice Castles, by Ch. Chenterra Thunderation ex Ch. Starhaven's Singing the Blues, four months of age when this photo was taken, now en route to championship having four points including a major. Starhaven Kennels, Carl and Amy Langhorst.

A promising Meridian puppy, a daughter of Am. and Can. Ch. Severn Smoke on the Water ex Ch. Grayfield Black Velvet, sold to Harry Mitchell (Hariann Kennels). This pup grew up to become Ch. Meridian's Velvet Feelin' and produced a champion in her first litter.

and to raise a few litters sired by leading *producing* studs. The practice of buying a stud dog and then breeding everything you have to that dog does not always work out. It is better to take advantage of the availability of splendid stud dogs for your first few litters.

In summation, if you want a family dog, buy it young and raise it to the habits of your household. If you are buying a show dog, the more mature it is the more certain you can be of the future. If you are buying foundation stock for a breeding program, bitches are better than dogs,

Mountaincrest's Sparkler, still a puppy here but already a winner. Owned by Mountaincrest Shetland Sheepdogs, Mrs. Frances Ruth Williams.

Happy Glen's Centerfold, by Happy Glen's Royal Dream ex Banchory Bit O'Stone, at eleven months of age. Bred and owned by Happy Glen Kennels, Marvin and Barbara Ross.

Gallantry Hot Chocolate at four months of age, Bred and owned by Mona and Lisa Stolcz.

Caper Hill's Hello Again, by Ch. Banchory Deep Purple ex Can. Ch. Banchory Picture Perfect, at ten weeks of age. Bred and owned by Lynette Smith.

but they must be from the finest *producing* bloodlines.

Regarding price, you should expect to pay up to a few hundred dollars for a healthy pet Sheltie puppy and more than that for a show-type puppy with the price rising accordingly as the dog gets older. A grown show dog can run well into four figures if of finest quality, and a proven brood matron will be priced according to the owner's valuation and can also run into four figures.

When you buy a purebred Shetland Sheepdog dog or puppy that you are told is eligible for registration with the American Kennel Club, you are entitled to receive, from the seller, an application form that will enable you to register your dog. If the seller cannot give you the application, you should demand and receive an identification of your dog consisting of the breed, the registered names and numbers of the sire and dam, the name of the breeder, and the dog's date of birth. If the litter of which your Sheltie is part has been recorded with the American Kennel Club, then the litter number is sufficient identification.

Do not accept a verbal promise that registration papers will be mailed to you. Demand a registration application form or proper identification. If neither is supplied, do not buy the dog. These words are to be especially heeded if you are buying show dogs or breeding stock.

A tricolor puppy and a blue-merle puppy. Courtesy of Macdega, Thomas W. Coen.

CHAPTER ELEVEN

Caring for a Sheltie Puppy

Whispering secrets! These puppies are Pineknoll's Golden Tiger (left) and DuryVoe Now and Then (right). Courtesy of Jean D. Simmonds, Carmylie.

Ownership of a dog entails a great deal of responsibility. You must be willing and prepared to provide your pet with shelter, food, training, and affection. With proper attention and care, your pet will become a loving member of the family and a sociable companion to be enjoyed for many years to come.

Advance Preparation

The moment you decide to become the owner of a Shetland Sheepdog puppy is not one second too soon to start planning for the new family member in order to make the transition period more pleasant for yourself, your household, and the puppy.

The first step in preparation is a bed for that puppy and a place where you can pen him up for rest periods. I am a firm believer that every dog should have a crate of its own right from the very beginning. This will fill both of the previously mentioned requirements, and the puppy will come to know and love this crate as his special haven. Crates are ideal, for when you want the puppy to be free, the crate door stays open. At other times, you securely latch it and know that the puppy is safe from harm, comfortable, and out of mischief. If you plan to travel with your dog, his crate comes along in the car; and, of course, to travel by plane, the dog must be put in a crate. If you show your dog, or take him to obedience, what better place to keep him when you are not working with him than in his crate? No matter how you look at it, a crate is a very sensible, sound investment in your puppy's comfort, well-being, and safety— not to mention your own peace of mind.

The crates we prefer are the sturdy wooden ones with removable side panels. These wooden crates are excellent for cold weather, with the panels in place, and they work equally well for hot weather when the solid panels are removed, leaving just the wire sides for better ventilation. Crates made entirely of wire are all right in the summer, but they provide no protection from drafts or winter chills. I intensely dislike solid aluminum crates due to the manner in which aluminum reflects surrounding temperatures. If it is cold, so is the metal of the crate. If it is hot, that too is reflected, sometimes to the point that one's fingers can be burnt when handling it. For this reason I consider them unsuitable.

When you choose the puppy's crate, be certain that it is roomy enough not to be outgrown as your Sheltie matures. He should have sufficient height in which to stand up comfortably and sufficient area to stretch out full length when relaxed. When the puppy is young, give him shredded newspapers as his first bed. In time, the news-

Ch. Starhaven's Tar Baby with her rabbit friend "Glorious." Owned by Starhaven Kennels, Carl and Amy Langhorst.

papers can be replaced with a mat or turkish towels. Carpet remnants are great for the bottom of the crate as they are inexpensive and in case of accidents can be easily replaced. Once the dog has matured past the chewing stage, a pillow or a blanket for something soft and comfortable is an appreciated luxury in the crate.

Sharing importance with the crate is a safe area where the puppy can exercise and play. If you have a yard of your own, then the fenced area in which he can stay outdoors safely should be ready and waiting upon his arrival. It does not need to be a vast area, but it should have shade and be secure. Do have the fenced area planned and installed *before* bringing the puppy home if

Belle Mount puppies in the summer play yard. Alice A. Burhans.

you possibly can do so; this is far more sensible than putting it off until a tragedy occurs. As an absolute guarantee that a dog cannot dig his way out under the fence, an edging of cinder blocks tight against the inside bottom of it is very practical protection. If there is an outside gate, a key and padlock are a *must* and should be *used at all times*. You do not want to have the puppy or dog set free in your absence either purposely or through carelessness. I have seen people go through a fence and then just leave the gate ajar. So for safety's sake, keep the gate locked so that only someone responsible has access to its opening.

The ultimate convenience, of course, is if there is a door in your house situated so that the fence can be installed around it, thereby doing away with the necessity for an outside gate. This arrangement is ideal, because then you need never be worried about the gate being left unlatched. This arrangement will be particularly appreciated during bad weather when, instead of escorting the dog to wherever his fenced yard is, you simply open the house door and he exits directly into his safe yard. In planning the fenced area, do give serious thought to the use of stockade fencing for it, as it really does work out well.

When you go to pick up your Sheltie, you should take a collar and lead with you. Both of these should be appropriate for the breed and age of the dog, and the collar should be one that fits him now, not one he has to grow into. Your

Ch. Jade Mist Woodwind Chimes at nine and a half weeks of age. Owned by Dr. and Mrs. Keith B. Howell.

new Sheltie also needs a water dish (or two, one for the house and one for outside) and a food dish. These should preferably be made from an unbreakable material. You will have fun shopping at your local pet shop for these things, and I am sure you will be tempted to add some luxury items of which you will find a fascinating array. For chew things, either Nylabone or real beef bones (leg or knuckle cut to an appropriate size, the latter found as soup bones at most butcher shops or supermarkets) are safe and provide many hours of happy entertainment, at the same time being great exercise during the teething period. Rawhide chews can be safe, too, if made under the proper conditions. There was a problem, however, several years back owing to the chemicals with which some of the rawhide chew products had been treated, so in order to take no chances, avoid them. Also avoid plastic and rubber toys, *particularly* toys with squeakers. If you want to play ball with your Sheltie, select a ball that has been made of very tough construction; Shelties have strong jaws. Even then do not leave the ball with the puppy alone; take it with you when you finish the game. There are also some nice "tug of war" toys which are fun when you play with the dog. But again, do not go off and leave them to be chewed in privacy.

Too many changes all at once can be difficult for a puppy. Therefore, no matter how you eventually wind up doing it, for the first few days keep him as nearly as you can on the

Belle Mount yearlings. Alice A. Burhans.

routine to which he is accustomed. Find out what brand of food the breeder used, how frequently and when the puppies were fed, and start out by doing it that way yourself, gradually over a period of a week or two making whatever changes suit you better.

Of utmost precedence in planning for your puppy is the selection of a good veterinarian whom you feel you can trust. Make an appointment to bring the puppy in to be checked over on your way home from the breeder's. Be sure to obtain the puppy's health certificate from the breeder, along with information regarding worming, shots, and so on.

With all of these things in order, you should be nicely prepared for a smooth, happy start when your puppy actually joins the family.

Above: Ch. Banchory High Style, by Am. and Can. Ch. Windcliff The Successor ex Banchory Dress Rehearsal, pictured at ten weeks of age. Bred by Clare and Donna Harden; owned by Mona and Lisa Stolcz. **Below:** Starhaven's Double Take, a Specialty class winner, pictured at two months of age. Starhaven Kennels, Carl and Amy Langhorst.

Above: Jade Mist Sheltie puppies at seven weeks of age. Dr. and Mrs. Keith B. Howell, owners. **Below:** Christmas 1971 at Carmylie. Jean D. Simmonds.

Four-week-old puppies, by Ch. Candega Main Event. Evelyn K. Basnicki, Crinan Kennels, breeder-owner-photographer.

Joining the Family

Remember that as exciting and happy as the occasion may be for you, the puppy's move from his place of birth to your home can be a traumatic experience for him. His mother and littermates will be missed. He will perhaps be slightly frightened or awed by the change of surroundings. The person he trusted and depended on will be gone. Everything, thus, should be planned to make the move easy for him, to give him confidence, to make him realize that yours is a pretty nice place to be after all.

Never bring a puppy home on a holiday. There just is too much going on, with people and gifts and excitement. If he is honoring "an occasion" (a birthday, for example), work it out so that his arrival will be a few days before or, better still, a few days after the big occasion. Then he will be greeted by a normal routine and will have your undivided attention. Try not to bring the puppy home during the evening. Early morning is the ideal time, as then he has the opportunity of getting acquainted, and the first strangeness wears off before bedtime. You will find it a more peaceful night that way, I am sure. Allow the puppy to investigate his surroundings under your watchful eye. If you already have a pet in the household, carefully watch that things are going smoothly between them, so that the relationship gets off to a friendly start; otherwise, you may quickly have a lasting problem. Be careful not to let your older pet become jealous by paying more attention to the newcomer than to him. You want a friendly start. Much of the future attitude of each toward

Above: "Do I have to sit with her?" Sesame and daughter Princess are owned by Belle Mount Shelties, Alice A. Burhans. **Below:** Marwal puppies in 1977. Margaret and Walt Huening, owners.

Jade Mist puppies meet the telephone. Dr. and Mrs. Keith B. Howell.

the other depends on what takes place that first day.

If you have children, again, it is important that the relationship start out well. Should the puppy be their first pet, it is assumed that you have prepared them for it with a firm explanation that puppies are living creatures to be treated with gentle consideration, not playthings to be abused and hurt. One of my friends raised her children with the household rule that should a dog or puppy belonging to one of the children bite one of the children, the child would be punished, not the dog, as Mother would know that the child had in some way hurt the dog. I must say that this strategy worked out very well, as no child was ever bitten in that household and both daughters grew up to remain great animal lovers. Anyway, on whatever terms you do it, please bring your children up not only to *love* but also to *respect* their pet, with the realization

The bi-blue puppy Caper Hills Song Without End, by Am. and Can. Ch. Banchory Deep Purple ex Can. Ch. Banchory Picture Perfect. Bred by Lynette Smith; owned by SumerSong Shelties.

"Take time to smell the flowers" would seem to be what seven-week-old Sterling's Enchanted Spirit is saying. Owned by Debra Elkin.

Above: Starhaven's Summer Symphony and her "deer" friend Rachel. Summer is grown up now and well on the way toward her title. Carl and Amy Langhorst, owners, Starhaven Kennels. **Below, left:** September Champagne, by Ch. September's Rainmaker ex September Winter Wildflower, as a young puppy, with his owner's son Sean (on the left) and Sean's friend Jordy. **Right:** September Champagne with Mark MacDonald. Bred by Barbara J. and Kenneth A. Linden; owned by Mary MacDonald and Barbara Linden.

Above: Jason Haderlie with a SumerSong puppy.
Below: SumerSong Blue Chip Stock, by Ch. Sumer-Song Winter Shadows ex SumerSong Amazing Grace, at twelve weeks of age. Breeders, Peggy and Jan Haderlie; owner, E.L. Robinson.

that dogs have rights, too. These same ground rules should also apply to visiting children. I have seen youngsters who are fine with their own pets unmercifully tease and harass pets belonging to other people. Children do not always realize how rough is too rough, and without intending to, they may inflict considerable pain or injury if permitted to ride herd on a puppy.

If you start out by spoiling your new puppy, your puppy will expect and even demand that you continue to spoil it in the future. So think it out carefully before you invite the puppy to come spend its first night at your home in bed with you, unless you wish to continue the practice. What you had considered to be a one-night stand may be accepted as just great and expected for the future. It is better not to start what you may consider to be bad habits which you may find difficult to overcome later. Of course, a lovely Shetland Sheepdog is not all that bad on the bed, particularly on a chilly night, but be sure you will like it that way before you introduce the puppy to the idea!

Severn Save The Last Dance, blue-merle puppy bitch by Ch. Banchory Deep Purple, the top-producing blue sire in the breed, ex Ch. Macdega Portrait in Black. This litter of one is pictured at the adorable age of seven weeks. Bred and owned by Linda More.

Socialization and Training

Socialization and training of your new baby Sheltie actually starts the second you walk in the door with him, for every move you make should be geared toward teaching the puppy what is expected of him and, at the same time, building up his confidence and feeling of being at home.

The first step is to teach the puppy his name and to come when called by it. No matter how flowery or long or impressive the actual registered name may be, the puppy should also have a short, easily understood "call name" which can be learned quickly and to which he will respond. Start using this call name immediately, and use it in exactly the same way each time that you address the puppy, refraining from the temptation to alternate various forms of endearment, pet names, or substitutes which will only be confusing to him.

Using his name clearly, call the puppy over to you when you see him awake and looking about for something to do. Just a few times of this, with a lot of praise over what a "good dog" he is when he responds, and you will have taught him to come to you when he hears his name; he knows that he will be warmly greeted, petted, and possibly even be given a small snack.

As soon as the puppy has spent a few hours getting acquainted with his new surroundings, you can put a light collar on the puppy's neck, so that he will become accustomed to having it on.

Ch. Marwal Struttin' the Blues, by Am. and Can. Ch. Macdega Mainstay ex Ch. Marwal Bluesette, at four months of age—what a lovely puppy head-study! This is one of the excellent homebreds from Marwal Kennels, Margaret and Walt Huening.

Carmylie Bi Inkling as a baby. Jean D. Simmonds, Carmylie Shelties.

He may hardly notice it, or he may make a great fuss at first, rolling over, struggling, and trying to rub it off. Have a tasty tidbit or two on hand with which to divert his attention at this period, or try to divert his attention by playing with him. Soon he no longer will be concerned about that strange new thing around his neck.

The next step in training is to have the puppy become accustomed to the lead. Use a lightweight lead, attached to the collar. Carry him outdoors where there will be things of interest to investigate; then set him down and see what happens. Again, he may appear hardly to notice the lead dangling behind him, or he may make a fuss about it. If the latter occurs, repeat the diversion attempts with food or a toy. As soon as the puppy has accepted the presence of the lead, pick up the end of it and follow after him. He may react by trying to free himself, struggling to slip his head through the collar, or trying to bite at the lead. Coax him, if you can, with kind words and petting. In a few moments, curiosity regarding his surroundings and an interesting smell or two should start diverting him. When this takes place, do not try at first to pull on him or guide his direction. Just be glad that he is walking with the lead on and let him decide where to go. When he no longer seems to resent the lead, try gently to direct him with short little tugs in the direction you would like him to travel. Never jerk him roughly, as then he will become frightened and fight harder; and never pull steadily or attempt to drag him, as this immediately triggers a battle of wills with each of you pulling in an opposite direction. The best method is a short, quick, gentle jerk, which, repeated a few times, should get him started off with you. Of course, continue to talk encouragingly to him and offer him "goodies" until he gets started. Repetition of the command "Come" should accompany all of this.

Once this step has been mastered and walks are taken on the lead pleasantly and companionably, the next step is to teach him to remain on your left-hand side. Use the same process as you used to teach him to respond correctly while on the lead, this time repeating the word "Heel." Of course, all of this is not accomplished in one day; it should be done gradually, with short work periods each time, letting the puppy know when he pleases you. The exact length of time required for each puppy varies and depends on the aptitude of each individual puppy.

Housebreaking a puppy is more easily accomplished by the prevention method than by the cure. Try to avoid "accidents" whenever you can rather than punishing the puppy once they have occurred. Common sense helps a great deal. A puppy will need to be taken out at regularly spaced intervals: first thing in the morning directly from his bed, immediately after meals, after he has napped, or whenever you notice that he is "looking for a spot." Choose roughly the same place outdoors each time that you take the puppy out for this purpose, so that a pattern will be established. If he does not go immediately, do not just return him to the house as chances are that he will go the moment he is back inside. Try to be patient and remain out with him until you get results; then praise him enthusiastically and both of you can return indoors. If you catch the puppy having an "accident," pick him up firmly, sharply say, "No!" and rush him outside. If you do not see the accident occur, there is little point of doing anything beyond cleaning it up, as once it has happened and been forgotten, the puppy will likely not even realize why you are angry with him.

Your Sheltie puppy should form the habit of spending a certain amount of time each day in his crate, even when you are home. Sometimes the puppy will do this voluntarily, but if not, he should be taught to do so. Lead the puppy by the collar over to the crate, and then gently push him inside firmly saying "Down" or "Stay" as you fasten the door. Whatever command you

Jade Mist Sunbrite Cedar at nine and a half weeks of age. Owned by Dr. and Mrs. Keith B. Howell.

Two adorable Sheltie babies, by Ch. Cherden's Sock It To Em ex Velveteen Forget Me Not, with their Halloween pumpkin. Owned by Evelyn Byers.

use, always make it the same word for each act every time. Repetition is the big thing in training, and the dog must learn to associate a specific word or phrase with each different thing he is expected to do. When you mean "Sit," always say exactly that. "Stay" should mean that the dog should remain where he was when you gave the command. "Down" means something else again. Do not confuse the dog by shuffling the commands, as you will create confusion for him and a problem for yourself by having done so.

As soon as he has received his immunization shots, take your Sheltie puppy with you wherever and whenever possible. Nothing else can equal this close association for building up self-confidence and stability in a young dog. It is extremely important that you spend the time necessary for socialization, particularly if you are planning on the puppy becoming a show dog.

Take your Sheltie in the car, so that he will learn to enjoy riding without becoming carsick, as can happen to a dog unused to the car's motion. Take him everywhere you go, provided you are certain he will not be unwelcome or create any difficulties by his presence: visiting friends and relatives (if they like dogs and do not have house pets of their own who will consider your puppy an intruder), to busy shopping centers (always keeping him on his lead), or just walking around the streets of your town. If someone admires him, as always seems to happen under these circumstances, encourage that person to

Ch. Jade Mist Windspell at three and a half months of age. Dr. and Mrs. Keith B. Howell, **Jade Mist Shelties.**

Ch. SumerSong Winter Shadows, by Ch. Banchory Deep Purple ex SumerSong Kachina, at eight months of age. Bred and owned by Peggy and Jan Haderlie, SumerSong Shetland Sheepdogs.

pet or talk with him; becoming accustomed to people in this manner always seems especially beneficial in instilling self-confidence. You want your puppy to develop a relaxed, happy canine personality and like the world and its inhabitants. The most debilitating thing for a puppy's self-confidence is excessive sheltering and pampering. Keeping a growing puppy always away from strange people and strange dogs may well turn him into a nervous, neurotic dog— surely the last thing anyone can enjoy as a pet.

Make obedience training a game with your puppy while he is extremely young. Try to teach him the meaning of and expected responses to the basic terms such as "Come," "Stay," "Sit," "Down," and "Heel," along with the meaning of "No" even while he is still too young for formal training, and you will be pleased and proud of the good manners that he will exhibit.

Nylabone® is the perfect chewing pacifier for young dogs in their teething stage and even for older dogs to help satisfy that occasional urge to chew. Unlike many other dog bones on the market today, Nylabone® does not splinter or fall apart; it will last indefinitely and as it is used it frills, becoming a doggie toothbrush that cleans teeth and massages gums.

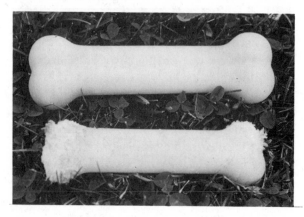

Ch. Marchwind The Rain Minstrel, by Ch. September's Rainmaker ex September Oklahoma Sunrise (a Ch. September The Provider daughter). This young dog has several Best Puppy in Breed awards and a five-point Specialty Winners Dog, as well as Best Puppy at Specialty, and is widely admired for his excellent expression. Soon to be seriously campaigned, he has been held back to await full coat and maturity. Owned and bred by Mary MacDonald, Delta, British Columbia.

Feeding

There was a time when providing good, nourishing food for our dogs involved a far more complicated routine and time-consuming process than people now feel is necessary. The old belief was that the daily rations should consist of fresh beef, vegetables, cereal, egg yolks, and cottage cheese as basics, with such additions as brewer's yeast and other vitamin supplements.

During recent years, however, many attitudes have been changed regarding the necessity, or even the desirability, of this procedure. We still give eggs, cottage cheese, and supplements to the diet, but the basic methods of feeding dogs have changed; and the changes are definitely for the better in the opinion of many an authority. The school of thought now is that you are doing your dogs a definite service when you feed them some of the fine commercially prepared dog foods in preference to your own home-cooked concoctions.

The reasoning behind this new outlook is easy to understand. The production of dog food has grown to be a major industry, participated in by some of the best known, most highly respected names in the dog fancy. These trusted firms do turn out excellent products. People are feeding their dogs these preparations with confidence, and the dogs are thriving, prospering, and keeping in top condition. What more could we want or ask?

There are at least a half dozen absolutely splendid dry foods which can be mixed with water or broth and served to your dog, either "as is" or with the addition of fresh or canned meat. There is a variety of canned meat preparations for your dog, either 100% meat to be mixed with kibble or complete prepared dinners, a combination of both meat and cereal. There are several kinds of "convenience foods," these in packets which you open and dump out into the dog's dish. It is just that simple. The "convenience foods" are neat and easy for you when travelling, but generally speaking we prefer to feed a dry food mixed with hot water, to which we usually add canned meat (although leftover meat scraps or ground beef are sometimes added instead of the canned meat). Actually we feel that the canned meat, with its added fortifiers, is more beneficial to the dogs than the fresh meat. However, the two can be used alternately or, if you prefer and your dogs do well on it, by all means use ground beef.

Dogs enjoy variety in the meat part of their diet, which is easy to provide with the canned meat. The canned meats available include all sorts of beef (chunk, ground, stewed, and so on), lamb, chicken, liver, and numerous concoctions of several of these blended together.

There also is prepared food geared to every age bracket of your dog's life, from puppyhood

SumerSong Winter Dream, by Ch. SumerSong Winter Shadows ex SumerSong Amazing Grace, at twelve weeks of age. Bred and owned by Sumer-Song Shetland Sheepdogs, Peggy and Jan Haderlie.

Ch. Severn Idle Gossip at three months of age. Linda More, owner, Severn Kennels.

Ch. Jade Mist Suntide at three and a half months of age showing us a marvelous head. Jade Mist Kennels, Dr. and Mrs. Keith B. Howell.

A beautiful head-study of Ch. Jade Mist Suntide at a mature age. Owned by Dr. and Mrs. Keith B. Howell.

on through old age, with special additions or modifications to make it especially nourishing and beneficial. The dogs of yesteryear never had it so good during the canine dinner hour because these foods are tasty and geared to meet the dog's gastronomical approval.

Additionally, contents and nutritional values are clearly listed on the labels, and careful instructions for feeding exactly the right amount for the size and weight of each dog are also given.

With the great choice of dog foods available today, we do not feel that the addition of vitamins is necessary; but if you do, there are several highly satisfactory vitamin products available at pet shops. These products serve as tasty treats along with being beneficial.

Of course there is no reason not to cook up something for your Sheltie's dinner if you would feel happier doing so, but it seems to us superfluous when such truly satisfying rations are available at so much less expense and trouble.

How often you feed is a matter of how a schedule works out best for you and for your dog or dogs. Many owners prefer to feed their dogs once a day. Others feel that twice daily is better for the digestion and more satisfying to the dog, particularly if he is a family member who stands around and watches the preparation of family meals. The important thing is that you *do not*

Banchory A Blue Nun with her brother Ch., Banchory Color My World. Photo courtesy of the Machados, Montage Kennels.

Marwal puppies in 1981. Margaret and Walt Huening, owners.

overfeed, as overfeeding can bring on many canine problems.

Until they are about twelve weeks old, fully weaned puppies should be fed four times daily. Each morning and evening, a Sheltie pup needs a meal of kibble soaked in hot water, broth, or soup to which either canned or fresh raw beef has been added. At noontime and bedtime, condensed milk mixed with an equal amount of water to which a bit of dry kibble has been added can be given. The amounts should be adjusted to the individual puppy's weight and appetite.

As the pup grows older, from three to six months of age, cut back to three meals, increasing the size of each. At six months of age, the pup should be fed twice daily, and at twelve months, if you wish, you may cut back to one daily feeding with a biscuit or two morning and evening. If you do feed just once daily, it should be given by early afternoon.

Remember that fresh, cool water should always be available to your dog. This is of utmost importance to his good health throughout his lifetime.

Krook

Ch. Macdega Portrait in Black, a lovely head-study showing excellent expression in a tricolor. Linda Nugent More, owner, Severn Kennels.

CHAPTER TWELVE

Grooming the Shetland Sheepdog

by Linda More

Ch. Severn Comedy Tonight, finished in 1980. Shown that summer seven times as a Special, she won seven consecutive Bests of Breed and five Group placements including this first during August under Tom Stevenson. Comedy Tonight was Number Two Sheltie for 1980, despite this very limited showing. Bred by Linda More, Tom Coen, and Steve Barger; handled by Linda More; owned by Joanne Timpany. Sherwood Shelties, Auburn, Maine.

Very special pride is taken in presenting Sheltie breeder and professional handler Linda More's thoughts and suggestions on correct grooming of a Sheltie. She is a thoroughly knowledgeable and experienced "Sheltie person" whose dogs always look impeccable. We feel that her words will be tremendously helpful to our readers, and we thank Linda for the time and thought she put into doing this chapter for us.

A.K.N.

Your basic healthy Sheltie is as much a "wash and wear" dog as any long-coated breed can be. The correct coat texture sheds dirt and moisture and does not mat easily. For the average pet Sheltie, a good brushing once a week or so will keep him tidy and neat most of the year.

Good grooming of your Sheltie starts with good health. Freedom from parasites such as worms, fleas and ticks, and good nutrition are all essential. Shelties are generally easy to care for, a result perhaps of their original island heritage, needing as a rule no special supplements to a good balanced diet. Your veterinarian's good advice and your attention to basic sanitation will help to keep parasites under control. And you can easily provide the most important "supplement" to your Sheltie's happiness and consequent well-being: attention and approval from his chosen people.

General Good Care

General good care of the external dog is relatively simple. Equip yourself with a few basic tools: a good quality pin brush with medium length pins set firmly in the base, a steel comb, a slicker brush, straight barber shears (I prefer the 7½-inch size), nail clippers, and styptic powder. Other items you may wish to have, depending on what you wish to do with your dog, will be mentioned as we go through the grooming procedure.

Shelties are not as a rule bathed frequently. If you wish to give your dog a bath, say perhaps after a romp in the swamp or a roll in some aromatic dead thing in the woods, or if the dog is simply very dirty or, as is sometimes the case, the coat is a rather oily one, use a good quality shampoo, made for dogs, and lukewarm water. Perhaps the most important step is to be sure to thoroughly rinse *all* the suds out of the coat, as soap not removed can irritate. After rinsing,

Ch. Stonewall Michelangelo, blue-merle son of Ch. Banchory Thunder Blue ex Banchory Gypsy Queen, a Specialty winner who finished his championship in 1977. Bred and owned by Edward Sanchez, Stonewall Shelties, Texas. Photo courtesy of Linda More.

There is a "right way" to brush your dog for best effect. Sometimes called "linebrushing," the technique is to start at the head of the dog, more or less part the coat backwards in small sections as you go along, and brush the coat forward *from the base* of the hairs to the tips. Getting right down to the skin is most important for both health and appearance. If the coat is dry, you may wish (and if you are grooming for show you *will* wish) to mist the hair with a spray of water from a spray bottle as you work along. This will not only add to the apparent fullness of the coat but also is good for the hair, preventing breakage as you brush and cleaning the hair as well. It is more helpful to train your Sheltie to lie quietly on his side while you brush, and in fact most dogs enjoy this relaxed position once they are accustomed to it. If you are planning to show your dog, and perhaps even if you are not, you will want to acquire or make a grooming table of a convenient height for you, with a non-slip surface. There are a couple of sizes available commercially. Personally I prefer the larger size so that I can spread all my "stuff" around and still have room for the dog, but the smaller size may

squeeze as much water out of the coat as possible, and then towel dry the dog. In warm weather, or if you have a nice toasty spot to put the dog, you can simply let him dry naturally. If you do this, you will need to brush through the coat when it is still just damp to properly separate the hair and lay it in the direction you wish it to dry. If you plan to use a dryer, you can put the dog in an open crate and set the dryer to blow on him for a while; then brush while the coat is still a bit damp. Or, if you wish to blow-dry the dog while brushing, section by section, this will result in a lovely appearing coat, especially if it is on the short or soft side. Remember, however, that done too often, bathing can dry out the hair and damage it.

Being a double-coated breed, Shelties do, indeed, shed heavily at times. No amount of prayers and stratagems will prevent the dead coat from falling out when its time has come, and it is best to hasten it along and get the process over with. A fairly warm bath will help to loosen the dead coat, and when the dog is dry, a hearty brushing will be necessary. You may want to resort to using a large comb to assist in removing the dead hair.

Ch. Severn Idle Gossip exhibiting lovely head and expression. Idle Gossip has won multiple Group placements, plus two Bests of Opposite Sex at Specialty shows when eight and a half years old. Linda More, owner, Severn Kennels.

Severn Gathering Moonbeams, C.D., blue-merle daughter of Ch. Ridgeside Stormsong ex Ch. Macdega Portrait in Black. Bred by Linda More who co-owns her with Madelyn Cirinna.

be enough for neater people! It is certainly more convenient to lug around and to store.

All Shelties should have their toenails cut regularly, including the dewclaws, if these were not removed shortly after birth. In white nails it is easy to see where the blood vessel inside the nail ends, and in general you will want to cut the nail straight across as close to the tip of the blood vessel as you can come. If the nails are done frequently, they can be kept comfortably short without having to cut the blood vessel; but if they are neglected, the vein will grow right along with the nail and cutting the nails back to a respectable length will cause some bleeding. In addition, very often the toenails are black and you may inadvertently cut the vein from time to time. Keep some styptic powder on hand, and if bleeding does occur, press some powder against the end of the nail. If the bleeding is fairly heavy, a piece of cotton dipped in styptic and then pressed to the nail will help greatly.

The Sheltie's teeth should also be cleaned regularly to remove the accumulated tartar that causes gum problems and doggy breath. This is easy to do with a dental scaler, but rather than go into detail here I would suggest you ask your vet for instructions, or go to an experienced breeder who can show you the correct technique. It is

Ch. Romayne's Summer Seascape, sable bitch by Ch. September's Rainmaker ex Ch. Romayne's Sportin' Chance, finished in January 1981. Seascape, a breed-winner with Group placements, is pictured at Lehigh Valley in 1980, winning under judge Miss Elaine Samuels, Karelane Kennels. Handler, Linda More; breeders, G. and T. Danforth.

important to avoid lacerating or bruising the gums while scraping the teeth.

Trimming the Sheltie

Before discussing trimming the Sheltie for show, let us cover something that is fundamental to a healthy pet as well as show dog: *feet*! Many Shelties grow a lot of extra hair on their feet, and pet owners as well as show exhibitors should keep the feet neatly trimmed for the dog's health. First, with a very fine comb (a flea comb will do nicely), comb out any tangles in the hair between the toes. You may be surprised to see how much hair is actually jammed into this space! Now turn the foot over, and with the straight shears trim out the hair between the pads, and trim around the outside edges of the pad. Comb down the hair on the top of the foot, and with the dog standing naturally, again trim around the bottom edges of the pads. If there are tufts sticking out anywhere, my own preference

here is to use thinning or tapering shears (my favorites are forty-six-tooth single-edged tapering shears), holding them perpendicular to the table, points down, and snipping off the stray bits of hair to achieve a neat but compact look. If you are trimming for show, remember that the Sheltie foot is correctly an *oval* foot, not a round one. Judicious trimming can help to correct the appearance of a less than perfect foot.

Perhaps the first rule of trimming should be to bear in mind that you can't put the hair back after you have cut it off! You must have a picture in mind of the look you are trying to achieve and proceed slowly. An artistically trimmed Sheltie should look neatened but natural, not barbered; your goal is to enhance the dog's virtues and to avoid calling attention to his less wonderful features.

Heads and ears must be considered together, as together they so much contribute to—or detract from—the essential "Sheltie look." My

Ch. Severn Spellbinder, who became a champion in 1974, pictured at Mid-Arizona Shetland Sheepdog Club Specialty in March 1978; judge, Marlin Roll, Mar-Jan Kennels; handled by Nioma Stoner (now Nioma S. Coen). Bred and owned by Linda More.

Ch. Rorralore Sportin' Chance, C.D., Best in Show and multiple Specialty winner and winner of Best of Breed at Westminster in 1984. Owned by Mrs. Charlotte Clem McGowan.

own method is to start on the ears, though there are as many ways to trim as there are trimmers. First, comb the hair on the back of the ear to the outside. Looking at the ear from the front, trim down the outside edge with the fine, tapering shears. How far down you trim will depend on your preference and on what looks best for the dog; if the ear is well set and pretty, I like to go just as far as the point where the longer frill starts. Trim around the tip of the ear, and partway down the inside edge, as appropriate. If the dog has a sizeable "weed patch" growing on the lower inside edge, you may thin there. If the hair on the backs of the ears is very long, I shorten it a bit with the tapering shears, but taking off too much hair gives an ugly, scalped appearance. I like to blend the ears with the longer fluff at the base by hand pulling as much of the fluff as needed (it pulls very easily) rather than doing a lot of cutting. If the ears break a bit too low, trim

most of the hair from the inside of the ear flaps; if they break too high, trim only enough to neaten. If you trim too heavily on the back, inside, or in front of the ears, you will find that you will have the unfortunate distinction of creating the "startled rabbit" look which does not fit in the sweet, typical Sheltie appearance!

From the ears, I move to the skull, starting with the sides. Many Shelties grow hair quite thickly on their heads and can give the impression of being far heavier in head than they are. First, comb through the hair on the entire skull with the fine comb; this will remove any loose undercoat. You can use the tapering shears on the sides of the skull behind the eyes, laying the shears flat against the dog's head and thinning the hairs right at the base, in horizontal lines. Take only one snip with the thinning shears on each line as you may make holes or marks. Comb the hair flat with the fine comb and study the

Ch. Severn Smoke On The Water, blue-merle son of Ch. Ridgeside Stormsong ex Severn Petunia Pumpkin, at two and a half years of age. Smoke finished taking Best of Winners at the American Shetland Sheepdog Association Specialty, March 1981, under judge Jean D. Simmonds, Carmylie Kennels; he also has numerous Group placements. Bred by Linda More and Madelyn Cirinna; owned by Linda More, Severn Kennels.

results before going on. If there is more to come, you might make a few vertical cuts, again only one snip per line, and then comb again. If at any point you are not sure whether to cut more, wait a day or so and then decide after you see how the trim job fits your dog.

Next, consider the fringe of hair growing in front of the ears. If the ears break low, you may wish to thin or shorten this hair to "open the ear up" and make it appear less low. If the hair is too plentiful and bushy, trimming can lighten the appearance of the head.

The Sheltie's topskull should be flat. If your dog's skull is not flat, or if there is a bush of hair causing it to appear high or bumpy, you may again use the thinning shears to trim the hair in the area above the eyes. Be very careful not to thin too far forward into the eyebrows; these help to create the stop as seen in profile and also affect the appearance of the eyeset. Again, trim the hair by thinning at the base and make only one cut per line, the lines being along the length of the head, *not* across it.

Do notice that, in all the trimming on the head, too heavy trimming will cause changes in the color of the hair, particularly on sables. This is because the brown hairs have bands of different shades, darker at the tips and lighter nearer the skin. Consequently, trimming by cut-

ting the ends off the hairs instead of thinning will create choppy-looking lighter patches that lend a contrived rather than a natural look.

Remove the facial whiskers by snipping them off at the base. Do not use your good barber shears for this as it will quickly dull them; instead you might use an older pair, or a small pair of scissors perhaps with blunt ends. After doing the whiskers, look at your Sheltie's lip-line. An attractive, straight lip-line adds greatly to the profile, and an unattractive one may be improved somewhat by trimming appropriately. With the barber shears, very carefully trim the longer hairs from the edges of the lips, being watchful that you do not cut so much that the corners of the mouth appear to turn down in a sulky-looking way.

The preceding basic head and ear trimming will take you into the ring with a dog that will look most presentable if you have done a careful, adequate job. Naturally, there are many more "tricks" and techniques that can be applied. If possible, learn even the basic trimming by watching someone whose dogs always look pleasing and well groomed, and always strive for a natural, soft look.

Show exhibitors and pet owners, too, may wish to do some trimming on their Shelties' lower legs. The amount of trimming done does vary with geography, and you might want to see how the dogs in your area are done prior to starting your own. On the front legs, I prefer to simply taper the hair from the heel of the foot to the fuller feathering on the legs. On the rear legs, below the hock, many dogs grow quite a lot of fuzzy, irregular hair which can be considerably neatened. Brush this through with the slicker; then comb it straight out. Trim it to an even length with the thinning shears, avoiding the "scalped" look but remembering, too, that **Shelties are not supposed to be bulky dogs with massive legs.**

Trimming of the body coat to any extent is not an approved procedure for Shelties, although there has been a marked increase in the use of it in recent years. Scissored coats are easy to identify as the cut hair has a frizzy, hacked-off look, and there may be color changes as well as texture changes. The area most frequently under attack is the "rump lump" or bushy pile of hair many Shelties grow over their hips. This hair can distort the outline and apparent balance of the dog, but there are ways of taming it without barbering. First, brush through the area thoroughly and then follow this with a good combing, doing small strips at a time so as not to

cause the dog discomfort. This may remove some extra undercoat, which is the purpose, and it will help to flatten the hair. You may next "comb" as before but this time with a stripping knife (I use the kinds appropriate to doing Setters and Spaniels, and are fairly dull) which will pull out more undercoat. Thinning the hair with thinning shears is a last resort only, because of the long-term effect; as the thinned hairs grow back they will be short and unmanageable. This in turn leads to more thinning, and when the dog sheds there will be gaping holes filled with bristly bits of hair.

Grooming at the Show

You will want to go through your show grooming routine at home before your first show to see just how long it will take. If you groom your dog too long before his appearance in the ring, some of the fresh effect will be lost; you also do not want to exhaust and bore your dog by keeping him on the table for too long a time.

Whether or not you have washed your dog's legs at home, using a powdered chalk substance will give them a fresh and fluffy look. If they are clean, you can spray them lightly with water and towel in, or you may use one of the so-called

Ch. Checkerchance John Harvard, a sable male by Ch. Romayne Sportin' Life ex Aylmere Annastasia, finishing under judge Joe Gregory, handled by Linda More, at Danville Kennel Club in 1982. Bred and owned by Rose Backus and Patricia Wright.

Ch. Aylmere Brookview Gold Bond, sable male by Ch. Romayne Sportin' Life ex Aylmere Annastasia, finished in January 1983. Gold Bond is pictured here winning under judge Chester Collier, handled by Linda More. Bred and owned by Rose Backus and Patricia Wright.

"waterless" shampoos to clean the legs. Towel them until they are only damp. With a bristle brush, brush the chalk or cornstarch into the hair, against the grain, up to the elbows of the front legs and up to the hock on the rear legs. You may do this even in brown areas as you are going to brush out most of this substance, using the slicker brush. If the legs are still rather damp, you may need to wait until they are dry.

Next, you will brush your dog, and this is probably the single most important step in having your dog look his best. No amount of artful trimming and chalking will make up for lack of a well-brushed and well-fitted, fresh-looking coat. Spray the coat with water and massage it in with your hands, right down to the skin. Proceed to brush through your dog as you have done at home, from the skin out, misting with additional water as needed. Pay special attention to sides and back of the neck. If the fluffy hair behind the ears tends to clump, you can shake a little baby

powder in and brush it through with the slicker to help separate it. After doing the belly and both sides, stand your dog up and do his back, finishing by brushing the hair down to give a level topline. If the "rump lump" is still a bit out of control, lay a towel over it and leave it while doing the ruff and chest. You will want to spend more extra time brushing the mane and ruff to make the hair stand out and frame your dog's face. Put the collar or leash on the dog before you finish and work it in to the hair so that it will not disturb the lines of the coat. Using a block of soft, white chalk, whiten your dog's blaze or snippet, if he has one, and his chin. Fluff the legs once more, being sure that there is no excess chalk left that will fly out in the ring and get your dog excused from competition. Put the dog on the floor, let him shake, and then re-arrange the coat as necessary with the brush. Good luck!

The exquisite bitch Ch. Sea Isle Serenata, by Ch. Nashcrest Golden Note ex Ch. Sea Isle Sandra, considered by many today still to be a model of classic type for her breed. Bred back to her sire, Serenata produced a litter of three champion sons which included one of the breed's greatest sable sires, Ch. Sea Isle Serenade. Sea Isle Kennels, Mary Van Wagenen and Evelyn Davis, owners.

Sweet Harmony of Edlen as a puppy. Edlen Shelties, owned by Edmund and Helen Scherer.

Ch. Bran Gay Cricket, nine years old, by Ch. Cherdon Light My Fire ex Esthof Misty Morn, the latter the first Sheltie owned by Gayle Eads and the one who started Bran Gay Kennels. Cricket is the first champion from the first Bran Gay litter, and she finished July 25th 1975.

Sweet Harmony of Edlen taking a four-point major as she goes Winners bitch, Best of Winners, and Best of Opposite Sex (over a Special) at Western Pennsylvania K.C. in 1983. Edmund and Helen Scherer, owners, Edlen Kennels.

Belle Mount puppy all set to jet to his new home. Alice A. Burhans.

Ch. Chosen Jubilation, C.D., taking Winners Dog under judge John Honig at Concho K.C., at eight months of age. Handled by Barbara B. Thompson.

BEST
OF OPP. SEX

RAMAPO
KENNEL CLUB INC.

KLEIN   OCT 15, 1978

SumerSong Silver Patterns at nine weeks of age. Bred by Peggy and Jan Haderlie, SumerSong Shetland Sheepdogs.

Facing page: Ch. Catamount Caress going Winners Bitch and Best of Opposite Sex as a puppy at Ramapo in 1978. Owner-handled by Lynette Saltzman.

Ch. Markris Red Baron of Edlen, a son of Ch. Kerrylance Bossman, C.D.X., the beginning of Edlen Shetland Sheepdogs owned by Edmund and Helen Scherer.

Ch. Gallantry Solid Success, a future Best in Show Dog, at three months of age. Mona Stolcz, Gallantry Shetland Sheepdogs.

Above: Future champion SumerSong Winter Shadows, a very handsome puppy by Ch. Banchory Deep Purple ex SumerSong Kashina, at eight weeks of age. Bred and owned by Peggy and Jan Haderlie, SumerSong Shelties. **Below:** Ch. SumerSong Winter Shadows at three years of age.

MONA

The Best in Show winner, Ch. Gallantry Solid Success, at twenty-two months of age. Owned by Mona Stolcz, Gallantry Shetland Sheepdogs.

Above: Ch. Jade Mist Down Memory Lane at three months of age. Owned by William and Suzanne McCullough. **Below:** Gallantry Amber Fair at three months of age. Breeders, Mona Stolcz and Lisa Stolcz; owner, Jean McMillan.

Ch. Fran-Dor's Kelty, an exciting young Sheltie from Fran-Dor Kennels, Doris A. Homsher.

Ch. Benayr Lil Tartan O'Conendale at his first dog show. Eddie Abramowitz handled him to Best Puppy (pictured) at the Chicagoland Specialty for owner Eugene Cohen, Conendale Shelties.

Happy Glen's Grand Stand, by Ch. Banchory Stand Back, C.D., ex Shannansy Flicker O'Flame, taking Best Puppy in Show at the Shetland Sheepdog Club of Greater Denver. Owned by Barbara and Marvin Ross.

Arista Malashel's May Flower at ten weeks of age. Owned by Elaine Wishnow.

Sheltie pups from Belle Mount Kennels, Alice A. Burhans.

Above: Starhaven's Collector's Item, winner of a four-point major under Lee Reasin and a Specialty Best in Sweepstakes winner, pictured as a two-month-old puppy. Starhaven Kennels, owners, Carl and Amy Langhorst. **Below:** A lovely three-month-old son of Ch. Candega Main Event. Note the beautiful *untouched* ears. Owned by breeder, Evelyn M. Basnicki.

Shelties and kids go great together! And with ducklings, too! Snapped at Carmylie, thanks to Jean D. Simmonds.

Below, left: Designed Bi Pocono, by Ch. Karelane Royal Flush O'Kismet ex Ch. Harvest Hills Ribbons 'n' Lace with Betty Whelen, Pocono Kennels. **Below, right:** Thornedge Kensington Spice, sable, and Kensington Benchmark, tricolor, with Rhea Butler in 1982. Photo by Four Winds.

Bran Gay Unchained Melody, by Bran Gay Golden Quest ex Lady Sandstorm, at her very first show, 6-9 Class, where she was Best in Sweepstakes and Reserve Winners Bitch in an entry of ninety-eight in the regular classes. Sweepstakes judge, Mrs. Jack Fowler; Specialty judge, Sandi MacIntosh. Brandol and Gayle Eads, owners, Bran Gay Shelties.

CHAPTER THIRTEEN

Showing Your Shetland Sheepdog

Mr. and Mrs. A.R. Miller's renowned winner Ch. Pixie Dell Epicure, at Newtown Kennel Club in 1965.

The groundwork for showing your Sheltie has been accomplished with your careful selection and purchase of your future show prospect. If it is a puppy, we assume that you have gone through all the proper preliminaries of good care, which actually should be the same whether the puppy is a pet or a future show dog, with a few extra precautions in the case of the latter.

General Considerations

Remember that a winning dog must be kept in trim, top condition. You want him neither too fat nor too thin, so do not spoil his figure and his appearance, or his appetite for proper nourishing food, by allowing family members or guests to be constantly feeding him "goodies." The best "treat" of all is a small wad of ground raw beef or one of the packaged dog "goodies." To be avoided are ice cream, potato chips, cookies, cake, candy, and other fattening items which will cause the dog to gain weight. A dog in show condition must never be fat, nor must he be painfully thin to the point of his ribs fairly sticking through the skin.

The importance of temperament and showmanship cannot possibly be overemphasized. These two qualities have put many a mediocre dog across, while lack of them can ruin the career of an otherwise outstanding specimen. So, from the day your dog or puppy arrives home, socialize him. Keep him accustomed to being with people and to being handled by people. Encourage your friends and relatives to "go over" him as the judges will in the ring, so that at the shows this will not be a strange, upsetting experience. Practice showing his "bite" (the manner in which his teeth meet) deftly and quickly. It is quite simple to spread the lips apart with your fingers, and the puppy should be accustomed and willing to accept this from you or from the judge, without struggle. Some judges ask the exhibitors to handle the mouths, showing them bite, rather than doing it themselves. These are the considerate judges who prefer not to risk spreading any possible virus infections by taking their hands from one dog's mouth to another's; but the old-fashioned judges still persist in doing the latter, so the dog should be prepared for either.

Take your future show dog with you in the car, so that he will love riding and not become carsick when he travels. He should associate going in the car with pleasure and attention. Take him where it is crowded: downtown, shopping malls, or, in fact, anywhere you go where dogs are permitted. Make the expeditions fun for him by frequent petting and words of praise; do not

385

Little bit of Luck of Edlen illustrating what can happen to a coat when playing with kennelmates—to be strictly avoided if planning soon to show your Sheltie! Owned by Edmund and Helen Scherer.

just ignore him as you go about your errands or other business.

Do not overly shelter your future show dog. Instinctively you may want to keep him at home, especially while a young puppy, where he is safe from germs or danger; but this can be foolish on two counts. To begin with, a dog kept away from other dogs or other environments builds up no natural immunity against all the things with which he will come in contact at the dog shows. Actually it is wiser to keep him well up-to-date on all protective "shots" and then allow him to become accustomed to being among other dogs and dog owners. Also, a dog who never goes among people, to strange places, or among strange dogs, may grow up with a timidity of spirit that will cause you deep problems when his show career gets under way.

Assuming that you will be handling the dog personally, or even if he will be professionally handled, it is important that a few moments of each day be spent practicing dog show routine. Practice "stacking," or "setting him up," as you have seen the exhibitors do at the shows you've attended, and teach him to hold this position once you have him stacked to your satisfaction. Make the learning pleasant by being firm but lavish in your praise when he behaves correctly. Work in front of a mirror for setting up practice; this enables you to see the dog as the judge does

Ch. September Chiffon Ruffles showing off a pretty profile. Owned by Mary MacDonald, Marchwind Shetland Sheepdogs.

The double merle nine-week-old puppy Sumer-Song In White Satin (above), by Ch. SumerSong Winter Shadows ex SumerSong Silver Pearl, and ten-week-old SumerSong Wild Violets (below), by Ch. SumerSong Winter Shadows ex SumerSong Reminiscence, a blue-merle to trifactored sable breeding. SumerSong Shelties, breeder-owners, Peggy and Jan Haderlie.

and to learn what corrections need to be made by looking at the dog from that angle.

Teach your Sheltie to gait at your side, at a moderate rate of speed on a loose lead. When you have mastered the basic essentials at home, then look for and join a training class for future work and polishing up your technique. Training classes are sponsored by show-giving clubs in many areas, and their popularity is steadily increasing. If you have no other way of locating

one, perhaps your veterinarian may know of one through some of his clients; but if you are sufficiently aware of the dog show world to want a show dog, you will probably be personally acquainted with other fanciers who will share information of this sort with you.

Accustom your show dog to being in a crate (which you should be doing, even if the dog is to be only a pet). He should be kept in the crate "between times" for his own well-being and safety.

A show dog's teeth must be kept clean and free of tartar. Hard dog biscuits can help toward this. If tartar does accumulate, see that it is removed promptly by your veterinarian. Bones are not suitable for show dogs once they have their second teeth as they tend to damage and wear down the tooth enamel (bones are all right for puppies, as they help with the teething process).

Above: Black Velvet at Crinan, by Ch. Candega City Lights ex Crinan's April Dream, at nine weeks of age. Evelyn K. Basnicki, owner. **Below:** Ch. Jade Mist Suntide, at nine months of age, winning his first points from the Bred-by-Exhibitor Class. Dr. and Mrs. Keith B. Howell, owners.

Debra Elkin with Valdawn's Sterling Nugget, by Ch. Shylove's Tobias The Spirited ex Hiland Chatterbox of Deesown, at twelve weeks old making match show debut. Note how well trained in show procedure this very young puppy already is!

Match Shows

Your Shetland Sheepdog's first experience in show ring procedure should be at match show competition. There are several reasons for this. First of all, this type of event is intended as a learning experience for both the puppies and for the exhibitors; thus you will feel no embarrassment if your puppy misbehaves or if your own handling technique is obviously inept. There will be many others in that same position. So take the puppy and go, and the two of you can learn together what it is like actually to compete against other dogs for the approval of the judge.

Another reason for beginning a show career at match shows is the matter of cost. Entries at the point shows nowadays cost over ten dollars. True, there are many clubs who reduce this fee by a few dollars for the Puppy Classes (but by no means do all of them), but even so it is silly to throw this amount away when you know full well your puppy will not yet have the ring presence to hold his own. For the match shows, on the other hand, the entry fee is usually less than five dollars, so using those shows as a learning ground for you and your puppy certainly makes better sense. Another advantage of match shows is that advance entries for them are seldom necessary, and even those clubs having them usually will accept additional entries the morning of the show. If you wake up feeling like taking the puppy for an outing, you can go right ahead. The entries at point shows, however, close about two and a half weeks in advance.

You will find the judges more willing to discuss your puppy with you at a match show than during the day of a full and hectic point show; one of their functions, when officiating at a match, is to help new exhibitors with comments and suggestions. We might wish that we could do so at the point shows; but, generally speaking, our schedules do not permit this time to be taken. Unless you stay until the judge's working day is ended, it is often difficult to get even a few words with him. The informality of match shows makes it far easier to get a judge's verbal opinion there; and since judges at these events are usually professional handlers or

Ch. Bran Gay Melody Maker at four and a half months of age at her first puppy match where she won first prize. Brandol and Gayle Eads, owners, Bran Gay Shelties.

A playpen full of baby Shelties awaiting their turn in the match show ring. Edlen Kennels, Edmund and Helen Scherer.

already licensed judges who are working toward applying for additional breeds, the opinions should be knowledgeable and helpful.

As with training classes, information regarding match shows can be obtained from breeders in your area, your local kennel club if there is one, your veterinarian, or, of course, the person in charge of your training class, if you belong to one. The A.K.C. can also furnish this information; and if your local newspaper carries a pet column, announcements of such coming events will almost certainly appear there.

Ch. Meridian's Toddy As In Rum, by Cape Winds Storm Warning ex Ch. Meridian's Long Shot, pictured completing his puppy show career with his fifth Best Puppy in Show award, this one under Collie and Shetland Sheepdog specialist Virginia Hampton, at the Working Dog Specialty. His four other Best Puppy in Show wins were under Mrs. Thelma Brown, Vincent Perry, Heywood Hartley, and Mrs. Ramona Van Court. He was bred, owned, and is handled here by Mrs. Hazel Slaughter, Meridian Kennels.

Point Shows

Entries for American Kennel Club licensed or member point shows must be made in advance. This must be done on an official entry blank of the show-giving club and then filed either in person or by mail with the show superintendent (or show secretary) in time to reach the latter's office prior to the published closing date and hour or the filling of the advertised quota. These entries should be written out clearly and carefully, signed by the owner of the dog or his agent (your professional handler), and must be accompanied by the entry fee; otherwise they will not be accepted. Remember, it is not when the entry blank leaves your hands or is postmarked that counts but the time that the entry arrives at its destination. If you are relying on the postal system, bear in mind that it is not always reliable, and waiting until the last moment may cause your entry to arrive too late for acceptance. Leave yourself a bit of leeway by mailing *early*.

A dog must be entered at a dog show in the name of the actual owner at the time of entry closing date for that specific show. If a registered dog has been acquired by a new owner, the dog must be entered in the name of that new owner at any show for which entries close following the date of purchase, regardless of whether or not

Ch. Chicwin's Chelsea as a puppy at Barrie in 1982. Don Palanio, handler; Fred Gordon, breeder-owner.

The very handsome Ch. Marwal Steppin' Out in 1983 at about ten months of age. This excellent young dog completed his title at eleven months of age from the Puppy Classes. Breeders, Margaret and Walt Huening; owner, Diane Bostwick.

the new owner has actually received the registration certificate indicating that the dog is registered in the new owner's name. State on the entry form whether or not the transfer application has been mailed to the American Kennel Club, and it goes without saying that the latter should be promptly attended to when you purchase a registered dog.

When you fill out your entry blank, be sure to type, print, or write legibly, paying particular attention to the spelling of names, correct registration numbers, and so on. Sign your name as owner *exactly*—not one time as Jane Doe, another as Jane C. Doe, and another as Mrs. John Doe.

Puppy Classes are for dogs or bitches that are six months of age and under twelve months, were whelped in the United States, and are not champions. The age of a puppy is calculated up to and inclusive of the first day of a show you are entering. For example, the first day a dog whelped on January 1st is eligible to compete in a Puppy Class at a show is July 1st of the same year; and he may continue competing in Puppy Classes up to and including a show on December 31st of the same year, but he is *not* eligible to

Ch. Montage Alnphyl Trinket, by Ch. Banchory The Candidate ex Carmylie Candle Dancer, shown finishing. Handled by Joe Malloy for owners Jerry and Chris Machado, Montage Kennels.

Ch. Carmylie Carioca of Kaher, by Ch. Halstor's Peter Pumpkin ex Carmylie Scottish Charm, finishing title at Wampanoag Kennel Club in 1981. Owner-handler, Jean D. Simmonds.

compete in a Puppy Class at a show held on or after January 1st of the following year.

The Puppy Class is the first one in which you should enter your puppy, for several reasons. To begin with, a certain allowance for behavior is made in recognition of the fact that they *are* puppies and lack show experience; a puppy who is immature or displays less than perfect ring manners will not be penalized so heavily as would be the case in an adult class such as Open. It is also quite likely that others in the Puppy Class will be suffering from the same puppy problems as your own; all of the puppies will be pretty much on equal footing where age and ring assurance are concerned. A puppy shown in the same class with fully matured Shelties who are experienced in the show ring looks all the more young and inexperienced and thus is far less likely to gain the judge's admiration than in a class where the puppy does not seem out of place. There are many good judges who will take a smashing good puppy right from the Puppy Class on through to Winners, but more often than not, this puppy

Ch. Chicwin's Chelsea, by Ch. Sovereign Pumpkin of Astolat ex Ch. Chicwin's Promised Victory, a multiple Best of Breed and Group winner and twice Best Puppy in Show. Bred and owned by Fred Gordon, Chicwin Kennels.

on an unlimited number of occasions but also in Bred-by-Exhibitor, American-bred, or Open and still remain eligible for Novice. But he may no longer be shown in Novice when he has won three blue ribbons in that class, when he has won even one blue ribbon in either Bred-by-Exhibitor, American-bred, or Open, or even a single championship point.

In determining whether or not a dog is eligible for the Novice Class, keep in mind the fact that previous wins are calculated according to the official published date for closing of entries, not by the date on which you may actually have made the entry. So if, in the interim, between the time you made the entry and the official closing date, your dog makes a win causing it to become ineligible for Novice, change your class *immediately* to another for which your Sheltie will be eligible. The Novice Class always seems to have the fewest entries of any class, and therefore it is a splendid "practice ground" for you and your young Sheltie while you both are getting the "feel" of being in the ring.

Bred-by-Exhibitor Class is for dogs whelped in the United States or, if individually registered in

started the day and was "discovered" by the judge right where it belonged, in the Puppy Class. Another bonus of using Puppy Class is the fact that numerous clubs offer a reduced entry fee to those competing in it; this certainly is beneficial because showing dogs is becoming increasingly expensive.

One word of caution on entering the Puppy Class: carefully check the classification, as in some cases it is divided into a 6-9 months old section and a 9-12 months old section; if this is the case you will have to ascertain that your puppy is entered in the correct section for the age he will be on the day of the show.

The Novice Class is for dogs six months of age and over, whelped in the United States or in Canada, who *prior to* the official closing date for entries have *not* won three first prizes in the Novice Class, any first prize at all in the Bred-by-Exhibitor, American-bred, or Open Classes, or one or more points toward championship. The provisions for this class are confusing to many people, which is probably the reason it is so infrequently used. A dog may win any number of first prizes in the Puppy Class and still retain his eligibility for Novice. He may place second, third, or fourth not only in Novice

Ch. Macdega Proof Positive at ten months of age winning Best of Breed en route to third in the Group, handled by Jane Hammett. Breeders, Chris Machado and Tom Coen; owners, Jerry and Chris Machado, Montage Kennels.

Can. Ch. Millbrook Macalester Lad, by Ch. Rockwoods Nite Enchantment, C.D., ex Romayne's Millbrook Gold Gem, Am. and Can. C.D., with fourteen points including both majors in the U.S. Handled by Barbara M. Kenealy; bred and owned by Barbara and Lowell Olson, M.D.

the American Kennel Club Stud Book, for dogs whelped in Canada that are six months of age and over, are not champions, and are owned wholly or in part by the person or the spouse of the person who was the breeder or one of the breeders of record. Dogs entered in this class must be handled *in this class* by an owner or by a member of the immediate family of the owner. Members of an immediate family for this purpose are husband, wife, father, mother, son, daughter, brother, or sister. This is the class which is really the "breeder's showcase," the one which breeders should enter with special pride, to show off their achievements. It is *not necessary* for the winner of Bred-by-Exhibitor to be handled by an owner or a member of the owner's family in the Winners Class, where the dog or bitch *may be handled by whomsoever the exhibitor may choose*, including a professional handler.

The American-bred Class is for all dogs excepting champions, six months of age or older,

who were whelped in the United States by reason of a mating which took place in the United States.

The Open Class is for any dog six months of age or older (this is the only restriction for this class). Dogs with championship points compete in it; dogs who are already champions can do so; dogs who are imported can be entered; and, of course, American-bred dogs compete in it. This class is, for some strange reason, the favorite of exhibitors who are "out to win." They rush to enter their pointed dogs in it, under the false impression that by so doing they assure themselves of greater attention from the judges. This really is not so; and it is my feeling that to enter in one of the less competitive classes, with a better chance of winning it and then getting a second crack at gaining the judge's approval by return-

Am. and Mex. Ch. Dan-Dee's Samantha, by Ch. Windemere's Bold Venture ex Ch. Dan Dee's Portrait in Gold, in 1966. Samantha, owned by Marjorie Sutter who is handling, was at that time dam of Ch. Sutter's Golden Masquerade and Sutter's Golden Temptation. She completed both her American and Mexican titles in 1967. Photo courtesy of Lee Reasin.

ing to the ring in the Winners Class, can often be a more effective strategy.

One does not enter for the Winners Class. One earns the right to compete in it by winning first prize in Puppy, Novice, Bred-by-Exhibitor, American-bred, or Open. No dog who has been defeated on the same day in one of these classes is eligible to compete in Winners, and every dog who has been a blue-ribbon winner in one of them and not defeated in any of the others *must* do so. Following the selection of the Winners Dog or the Winners Bitch, the dog or bitch receiving that award leaves the ring. Then the dog or bitch who placed second in the class,

Above: Ch. Jade Mist Woodwind Chimes taking Reserve Winners Bitch at the Interstate Shetland Sheepdog Club Specialty at Wilmington, Delaware, April 1978, one week before finishing. Dr. and Mrs. Keith B. Howell, owners, Jade Mist Shelties. **Below:** Ch. Valdawn's Double Talk, by Ch. Valdawn's Krackerjack ex O'Canonach Jubilee Misty, taking Reserve Winners. Bred by Kay Searle who is co-owner with Sharon Kenealy.

Above: Ch. Serenade of Rustic, by Ch. Wandring Minstrel Man O'Karelane ex Sweet Melody of Rustic, taking Best of Winners. Sam and Lois Lippincott, owners. **Below:** Ch. Starhaven's Great Xpectation, by Ch. Starhaven's The Main Spark ex Ch. Starhaven's Singing The Blues, Reserve Winners Dog at the SCIOTO Shetland Sheepdog Club Specialty in 1982. Owned by Starhaven Kennels, Carl and Amy Langhorst.

unless previously defeated by another dog or bitch at the same show, re-enters the ring to compete against the remaining first-prize winners for Reserve. The latter award means that the dog or bitch receiving it is standing by "in reserve" should the one that received Winners be disallowed through any technicality when the awards are checked at the American Kennel Club. In that case, the one that placed Reserve is moved up to Winners, at the same time receiving the appropriate championship points.

Winners Dog and Winners Bitch are the awards which carry points toward championship with them. The points are based on the number of dogs or bitches actually in competition; and the points are scaled one through five, the latter being the greatest number available to any dog or bitch at any one show. Three-, four-, or five-point wins are considered majors. In order to become a champion, a dog or bitch must win two majors under two different judges, plus at least one point from a third judge, and the additional points necessary to bring the total to fifteen. When your dog has gained fifteen points as described above, a certificate of championship will be issued to you, and your Sheltie's name will be published in the list of new champions which appears monthly in *Pure-Bred Dogs/ American Kennel Gazette*, the official publication of the American Kennel Club.

The scale of championship points for each breed is worked out by the American Kennel Club and reviewed annually, at which time the number required in competition may be either changed (raised or lowered) or remain the same. The scale of points for all breeds is published annually in the May issue of the *Gazette*, and the current ratings for each breed within that area are published in every dog show catalog.

Carmylie Taplrac Nellie Bi, bi-blue female by Taplrac Sound of Silence ex Ch. Carmylie Polly Paintbrush, with eight points including a major, here taking Winners Bitch at Onondaga Kennel Club, November 1981. Owned and shown here by Jean Simmonds, Carmylie Kennels.

Ch. Calico Lace of Pocono winning Best of Opposite Sex at Colorado Specialties in 1983. Elizabeth D. Whelen, owner-handler, Pocono Kennels.

When a dog or a bitch is adjudged Best of Winners, its championship points are, for that show, compiled on the basis of which sex had the greater number of points. If there are two points in dogs and four in bitches and the dog goes Best of Winners, then *both* the dog and the bitch are awarded an equal number of points, in this case four. Should the Winners Dog or the Winners Bitch go on to win Best of Breed, additional points are accorded for the additional Shelties defeated by so doing, provided, of course, that there were entries specifically for Best of Breed competition, or Specials, as these specific entries are generally called. If your dog or bitch takes Best of Opposite Sex after going Winners, points are credited according to the number of the same sex defeated in both the regular classes and Specials competition. Many a one- or two-point class win has grown into a major in this manner.

Moving further along, should your Sheltie win the Herding Group from the classes (in other words, if it has taken either Winners Dog or Winners Bitch, Best of Winners, and Best of Breed), you then receive points based on the greatest number of points awarded to any breed included within that Group during that show's competition. Should the dog's winning streak also include Best in Show, the same rule of thumb

On the left, Am. and Can. Ch. Offshore Fromaneer, by Am. and Can. Ch. Browne Acres Brigadier ex Ch. Tinker Vegas Night Life, born in 1964. Bred and owned by Dr. Diane M. Leschner. On the right, Am. and Can. Ch. Browne Acres Brigadier. Photo from Lee Reasin's collection.

Ch. Rockwoods The Hustler, by Ch. Shylove Tobias The Spirited ex Ch. Valdawn Chit Chat of Rockwood, Best of Breed at Mispillion Kennel Club in 1979. Bred by Barbara Kenealy; co-owned by Barbara Kenealy and Shirley Bond.

applies, and your Sheltie receives points equal to the highest number of points awarded to any other dog of any breed at that event.

Best of Breed competition consists of the Winners Dog and the Winners Bitch, who automatically compete on the strength of those awards, in addition to whatever dogs and bitches have been entered specifically for this class for which champions of record are eligible. Shelties who, according to their owner's records, have completed the required number of points for a championship after closing of entries for the show but whose championships are unconfirmed, may be transferred from one of the regular classes to the Best of Breed competition, provided this transfer is made by the show superintendent or show secretary *prior to the start of judging at the show.*

This has proven an extremely popular new rule, as under it a dog can finish on Saturday and then be transferred and compete as a Special on Sunday. It must be emphasized that the change *must* be made a half hour *prior* to the start of the day's judging, which means to the start of *any* judging at the show, not your individual breed.

In the United States, Best of Breed winners are entitled to compete in the Variety Group which includes them. This competition is not mandatory; it is a privilege which Sheltie exhibitors should value. The dogs winning *first* in each Variety Group *must* compete for Best in Show.

Non-regular classes are sometimes included at the all-breed shows, and they are almost invariably included at Specialty shows. These include Stud Dog Class and Brood Bitch Class, which are judged on the quality of the offspring (usually two) accompanying the sire or dam. The quality of the latter two is beside the point; it is the youngsters that count, and the qualities of *both* are averaged to decide which sire or dam is the best and most consistent producer. Then there is the Brace Class (which, at all-breed shows, moves along to Best Brace in each Variety Group and then Best Brace in Show), which is judged on the similarity and evenness of appearance of the two members of the brace. In other words, the Shelties should look like identical twins in size, color, and conformation and should move together almost as a single dog, one person handling with precision and ease. The same applies to the Team competition except that four dogs are involved and, if necessary, two handlers.

The Veterans Class is for the older dog, the minimum age of whom is usually seven years. This class is judged on the quality of the dogs, as

Above: Ch. Karalane Royal Flush O'Kismet, by Ch. Banchory High Born ex Ch. Kismet's Cee Dee Pollyanna, taking Best in Show at Fort Worth Kennel Club in 1980 for Guy and Thelma Mauldin, Kismet Kennels. **Below:** The most famous team of dogs in all show history: Timberidge Truth of Pocono, C.D.; Ch. Sea Isle Merle Legacy, C.D.; Ch. Bil-Bo-Dot Blue Flag of Pocono; and Ch. Penstemon of Beech Tree, C.D. These Shelties won Best Team in Show no less than four times at Westminster *successively,* in 1940, 1941, 1942, and 1943, and also won at various other events, including Specialties of the American Shetland Sheepdog Association, always beautifully handled by their owner Elizabeth D. Whelen. Miss Whelen won Best Team in Show with four of her Shelties at Westminster again in 1953, which must give her the record for this accomplishment by one exhibitor in Westminster competition.

Ch. Rockwood Repeat Performance, by Ch. Rockwoods Bac Talk ex Shylove Rockwood Show Off, C.D., Best of Breed at the Tri State Shetland Sheepdog Specialty. Bred, owned, and handled by Barbara M. Kenealy.

Ch. Pixie Dell Epigram, famous Group winner born in 1965. Owned by Mr. and Mrs. A.R. Miller.

the winner competes for Best of Breed, and, on a number of occasions, has been known to win it. So the point is *not* to pick the oldest looking dog, as some seem to think, but the best specimen of the breed, exactly as throughout the regular classes.

Then there are Sweepstakes and Futurity Stakes, sponsored by many Specialty clubs, sometimes as part of their shows and sometimes as separate events. The difference between the two is that Sweepstakes entries usually include dogs and bitches from six to eighteen months of age, and entries are made at the usual time as others for the show, while for a Futurity the entries are bitches nominated when bred and the individual puppies entered at or shortly following their birth.

Ch. Montage Seasconset Sophia, by Ch. Northcountry Westering Son ex Ch. Berridale Alnphyl Brigette, winning at the Southern California Specialty, handled by Jerry Machado. Bred and owned by Jerry and Chris Machado.

Am. and Can. Ch. Markris Red Baron of Edlen winning Best of Breed in 1973, at four years of age. Owned by Edmund and Helen Scherer.

Junior Showmanship

If there is a youngster in your family between the ages of ten and seventeen, I can suggest no better or more rewarding a hobby than having a Sheltie to show in Junior Showmanship competition. This is a marvelous activity for young people. It teaches responsibility, good sportsmanship, the fun of competition where one's own skills are the deciding factor of success, proper care of a pet, and how to socialize with other young folks. Any youngster may experience the thrill of emerging from the ring a winner and the satisfaction of a good job done well.

Your Sheltie is an outstandingly satisfactory breed of dog for Junior Showmanship competition. His amiability and desire to please make him cooperative, and his comparatively simple show preparation make him an easy dog for a youngster to keep looking well to take into the ring.

Shelties and juniors work well together, thus are often to be seen in the winners circle.

Entry in Junior Showmanship is open to any boy or girl who is at least ten years old and under seventeen years old on the day of the show. The Novice Junior Showmanship Class is open to youngsters who have not already won, at the time the entries close, three firsts in this class. Youngsters who have won three firsts in Novice may compete in the Open Junior Showmanship Class. Any junior handler who wins his third first-place award in Novice may participate in the Open Class at the same show, provided that the Open Class has at least one other junior handler entered in it. The Novice and Open Classes may be divided into Junior and Senior Classes. Youngsters between the ages of ten and twelve, inclusively, are eligible for the Junior division; and youngsters between thirteen and seventeen, inclusively, are eligible for the Senior division. Any of the foregoing classes may be separated into individual classes for boys and for girls. If such a division is made, it must be indicated on the premium list. The premium list also indicates the prize for Best Junior Handler, if such a prize is being offered at the show. Any youngster who wins a first in any of the regular classes may enter the competition for this prize, provided the youngster has been undefeated in any class at that show.

Junior Showmanship Classes, unlike regular conformation classes in which the dog's quality is judged, are judged entirely on the skill and ability of the junior handling the dog. Which dog is best is not the point—it is which youngster does the best job with the dog that is under consideration. Eligibility requirements for the dog being shown and other detailed information can be found in *Regulations for Junior Showmanship*, issued by the American Kennel Club.

A junior who has a dog that he or she can enter in both Junior Showmanship and conformation classes has twice the opportunity for success and twice the opportunity to get into the ring and work with the dog. Shelties and juniors work well together, and this combination has often wound up in the winner's circle.

Pre-Show Preparation

Preparation of the things you will need as a Sheltie exhibitor should not be left until the last moment. They should be planned and arranged for at least several days before the show in order for you to relax and be calm as the countdown starts.

The importance of the crate has already been discussed, and we assume it is already in use. Of equal importance is the grooming table, which we are sure you have already acquired for use at home. You should take it along with you, as your dog will need final touches before entering the ring. If you do not have one yet, a folding table with a rubber top is made specifically for this purpose and can be purchased from the concession booths found at most dog shows. Then you will need a sturdy tack box (also available at the show's concessions) in which to carry your brush, comb, scissors, nail clippers, whatever you use for last minute clean-up jobs, cotton swabs, first-aid equipment, and anything else you are in the habit of using on the dog, such as a leash or two of the type you prefer, some well-cooked and dried-out liver or any of the small packaged "dog treats" your dog likes for use as "bait" in the ring, and a turkish towel.

Take a large thermos or cooler of ice, the biggest one you can accommodate in your vehicle, for use by "man and beast." Take a jug of water (there are lightweight, inexpensive ones available at all sporting goods shops) and a water

Happy Glen's Royal Dream, by Ch. Windhover Sweet Music Man ex Happy Glen's Flaming Fantasy, one of the excellent Shelties owned by Happy Glen Kennels, Barbara Ross and Marvin G. Ross.

dish. If you plan to feed the dog at the show, or if you and the dog will be away from home more than one day, bring food from home so that he will have the type to which he is accustomed.

You may or may not have an exercise pen. Personally, I think that one is a *must*, even if you have only one dog. While the shows do provide areas for exercise of the dogs, these are among the best places to come into contact with any illnesses that may be going around, and I feel that having a pen of your own for your dog's use is excellent protection. Such a pen can be used in other ways, too, such as a place other than the crate in which to put the dog to relax and a place in which the dog can exercise at rest areas or motels during your travels. A word of caution: never tie a dog to an exercise pen or leave him unattended in it while you wander off, as the pens are not sufficiently secure to keep the dog there should he decide to leave, at least not in most cases. Exercise pens are also available at the dog show concession booths should you not already have yours when you reach the dog's first show. They come in a variety of heights and sizes.

Bring along folding chairs for the members of your party, unless all of you are fond of standing, as these are almost never provided by the show-giving clubs. Have your name stamped on the chairs so there will be no doubt as to whom the chairs belong. Bring whatever you and your family enjoy for drinks or snacks in a picnic

SumerSong Bi Power, one of the many noted Shelties at SumerSong Kennels, Peggy and Jan Haderlie.

Lynnlea's Josh of Water's Edge, by Barwood's Formal Attire ex Ch. Barwood's Ashford Vanity Fair, C.D. Pat Stewart of Chicago, Illinois, owns this handsome dog.

basket or cooler, as show food, in general, is expensive and usually not great. You should always have a pair of boots, a raincoat, and a rain hat with you (they should remain permanently in your vehicle if you plan to attend shows regularly), as well as a sweater, a warm coat, and a change of shoes. A smock or big cover-up apron will assure that you remain tidy as you prepare the dog for the ring. Your overnight case should include a small sewing kit for emergency repairs, headache and indigestion remedies, and any personal products or medications you normally use.

In your car you should always carry maps of the area where you are headed and an assortment of motel directories. Generally speaking, we have found that Holiday Inns are the friendliest about taking dogs. Some Ramadas and some Howard Johnsons do so cheerfully (the Ramadas indicate on each listing in their directory whether or not pets are welcome). Best Western usually frowns on pets (not all of them but enough to make it necessary to find out which do). Some of the smaller chains welcome pets. The majority of privately owned motels do not.

Have everything prepared the night before the show to expedite your departure. Be sure that the dog's identification and your judging program and other show information are in your purse or briefcase. If you are taking sandwiches, have them ready. Anything that goes into the car the night before will be one thing less to be concerned with in the morning. Decide upon what you will wear and have it out and ready. If there is any question in your mind about what to wear, try on the possibilities before the day of the show; don't risk feeling you may want to change when you see yourself dressed a few moments prior to departure time! In planning your outfit, wear something simple that will make an attractive background for your Sheltie, providing contrast to his color, calling attention to the *dog* rather than to yourself. Sports clothes always seem to look best at a dog show. What you wear on your feet is important, as many types of flooring are slippery, and wet grass, too, can present a hazard as you move the dog. Make it a rule to wear rubber soles and low or flat heels in the ring, so that you can move along smartly.

Your final step in pre-show preparation is to leave yourself plenty of time to reach the show that morning. Traffic can get extremely heavy as one nears the immediate vicinity of the show, finding a parking place can be difficult, and other delays may occur. You'll be in better humor if you can take it all in your stride without the pressure of watching every second because you figured the time too closely.

Gay Acres Glory of Mainstay, sable bitch by Ch. Sunnybrook's Heritage Spirit ex Mainstay This Moment In Time. Glory has points from the Puppy Class. Bred by Stephen Barger and Joan and Terry Pavey; owned by Mrs. Florence W. Roberts and Stephen W. Barger.

Harbot Lite Cajun Queen, one of the Ardencaple Shelties belonging to Mr. and Mrs. Willard K. Denton.

Day of the Show

From the moment of your arrival at the dog show until after your Sheltie has been judged, keep foremost in your mind the fact that he is your purpose for being there. You will need to arrive in advance of the judging in order to give him a chance to exercise after the trip to the show and take care of personal matters. A dog arriving in the ring and immediately using it for an exercise pen hardly makes a favorable impression on the judge. You will also need time to put the final touches on your dog, making certain that he goes into the ring looking his very best.

When you reach ringside, ask the steward for your arm-card with your Sheltie's entry number on it and anchor it firmly into place on your arm with the elastic provided. Make sure that you are where you should be when your class is called. The fact that you have picked up your arm-card does not guarantee, as some seem to think, that the judge will wait for you more than a minute or two. Judges are expected to keep on schedule, which precludes delaying for the arrival of exhibitors who are tardy.

Even though you may be nervous, assume an air of cool, collected calm. Remember that this is a hobby to be enjoyed, so approach it in that state of mind. The dog will do better, too, as he will be quick to reflect your attitude.

If you make a mistake while presenting the dog, don't worry about it—next time you'll do better. Do not be intimidated by the more expert or experienced exhibitors. After all, they, too, were once newcomers.

Always show your Sheltie with an air of pride. An apologetic attitude on the part of the exhibitor does little to help the dog win, so try to appear self-confident as you gait and set up the dog.

The judging routine usually starts when the judge asks that the dogs be gaited in a circle around the ring. During this period the judge is watching each dog as it moves along, noting style, topline, reach and drive, head and tail carriage, and general balance. This is the time to keep your mind and your eye on your dog, moving him at his most becoming gait and keeping your place in line without coming too close to the dog ahead of you. Always keep your dog on the inside of the circle, between yourself and the judge, so that the judge's view of the dog is unobstructed.

Calmly pose the dog when requested to set up for examination. If you are at the head of the line and many dogs are in the class, do not stop half-

Ch. Chenterra Thunderation with his handler, Steve Barger, as he relaxes in the ring while awaiting his turn.

way down the end of the ring and begin stacking the dog. Go forward enough so that sufficient space is left for the other dogs. Simple courtesy demands that we be considerate and give others a chance to follow the judge's instructions, too.

Space your Sheltie so that on all sides of the dog the judge will have room in which to make his examination; this means that there must be sufficient room between each of the dogs for the judge to move around. Time is important when you are setting up your Sheltie, so practice in front of a full-length mirror at home, trying to accustom yourself to "getting it all together" correctly in the shortest possible time. When you set up your Sheltie, you want his forelegs well under the dog, feet directly below the elbows, toes pointing straight ahead, and hindquarters extended *correctly*. not overdone (stretched too far behind) or with the hind feet further forward than they should be. You want the dog to look "all of a piece," head carried proudly on a strong neck, correct topline, hindquarters nicely angulated, the front straight and true, and the dog standing firmly on his feet.

Listen carefully as the judge instructs the manner in which the dog is to be gaited, whether it is straight down and straight back; down the ring,

across, and back; or in a triangle. The latter has become the most popular pattern with the majority of judges. "In a triangle" means down the outer side of the ring to the first corner, across that end of the ring to the second corner, and then back to the judge from the second corner, using the center of the ring in a diagonal line. Please learn to do this pattern without breaking at each corner to twirl the dog around you, a senseless maneuver we sometimes have noted. Judges like to see the dog move in an *uninterrupted* triangle, as they get a better idea of the dog's gait.

It is impossible to overemphasize that the gait at which you move your Sheltie is tremendously important, and considerable thought and study should be given to the matter. At home, have someone move the dog for you at different speeds so that you can tell which shows him off to best advantage. Your Sheltie should travel with powerful reach and drive, head up, and tail an extension of the firm, unbroken topline. Galloping or racing around the ring is out of character for a Sheltie and unbecoming to almost any dog.

Do not allow your Sheltie to sidetrack, flop, or weave as you gait him, and do not let him pull so

A candid photo, taken by a spectator at ringside, of the Best in Show winner Ch. Shiel's Sunstreak, C.D. Bred and owned by Janet A. Cameron.

Ch. Merri-Lon Count On Me of Edlen. Owned by Edlen Kennels, Edmund and Helen Scherer.

Ch. Calico Lace of Pocono, by Ch. Karelane Royal Flush O'Kismet ex Ch. Harvest Hills Ribbons 'n Lace, in 1982. Elizabeth D. Whelen, Pocono Kennels.

that he appears to lean on the lead as you are gaiting him. He should move in a straight line, displaying strength and power. That is your goal as you work with him on a lead in preparation for his show career.

Baiting your dog should be done in a manner which does not upset the other Shelties in the ring or cause problems for their handlers. A tasty morsel of well-cooked and dried-out liver is fine for keeping your own dog interested, but discarded on the ground or floor, it can throw off the behavior of someone else's dog who may attempt to get it. So please, if you drop liver on the ground, pick it up and take it with you when you have finished.

When the awards have been made, accept yours courteously, no matter how you may actually feel about it. To argue with a judge is unthinkable, and it will certainly not change the decision. Be gracious, congratulate the winners if your dog has been defeated, and try not to show your disappointment. By the same token, please be a gracious winner; this, surprisingly, sometimes seems to be even more difficult.

If you already show your Sheltie, if you plan on being an exhibitor in the future, or if you simply enjoy attending dog shows, there is a book, written by me, which you will find to be an invaluable source of detailed information about all aspects of show dog competition. This book is *Successful Dog Show Exhibiting* (T.F.H. Publications, Inc.) and is available wherever the one you are now reading was purchased.

Ch. Jezebel the Golden Gem, by Forecaster Scarlet Duke ex Oaklawn's Golden Nymph, whelped in September 1962. Breeder, Dorothy I. Swena; owner, Timothy L. Nagao. Photo from Lee Reasin's collection.

Ch. Nashcrest Golden Note, Best of Breed, and Ch. Va-Gore's Bright Promise, Best of Opposite Sex, at the Interstate Shetland Sheepdog Association Specialty in May 1954. Golden Note handled for Sea Isle Kennels by Betty Whelen, Bright Promise for Mr. and Mrs. George Howard by J. Nate Levine. Photo courtesy of Miss Whelen.

Ch. Neilly O'Havic, sable bitch by Ch. Malpsh Great Scott ex Moll Flanders O'Havic, finished in 1975, pictured at Holyoke that February under judge Ernest Loeb. It is believed that she was the last of her famous producing sire's get to finish. Owned by Richard and Nancy Hildreth, Cindahope Kennels, Ashland, Massachusetts.

A most gorgeous Sheltie—Ch. Sea Isle Serenade, the Group-winning Golden Note son who sired twenty-nine American champions. Sea Isle Kennels, Mary Van Wagenen and Evelyn Davis.

The very famous Ch. Banchory High Born, a tricolor by Ch. Philidove Heir Presumptive ex Tiree Hall Solo's High-Lite, born in February 1968. High Born, the second top producing Sheltie of all time with seventy-four champions, is shown here winning Best of Breed. Bred by Rosemary Shrauger; owned by Kismet Kennels, Guy and Thelma Mauldin.

Ch. Tiger Adonis, from Ch. Forecaster Golden Dawn, with his sire Ch. Elf Dale Viking (left). Viking, a Sheltie great during the 1960's, was a Best in Show and Working Group winner who also gained 170 Bests of Breed, among other honors. In 1963, the year this photo is dated, Viking was Number Five all-breeds. Courtesy of Lee A. Reasin.

Ch. Astolat Enchantor with handler Frank Ashbey winning at Hunterdon Hills Kennel Club in 1969 under judge Arnold Wolf. Photo courtesy of John L. Ashbey.

Ch. Nashcrest Golden Note taking Best of Breed at the Cleveland Specialty in 1954 for Sea Isle Kennels. The judge is Mrs. Nichols, owner of the famous Walnut Hall Shetland Sheepdogs. Photo courtesy of Betty Whelen.

Ch. Wade Gate Honor Bound, owner-handled by Eugene Cohen, taking Winners Dog at the Shetland Sheepdog Club of Greater Detroit Specialty in 1977 under judge Charlotte Clem McGowan.

Ch. Heatherland's Mr. Kilpatrick, C.D., pictured winning his third major, under specialist judge Lynn Anderson. A son of Ch. Halstor's Peter Pumpkin, Mr. Kilpatrick is the sire of five champions. Starhaven Kennels, owners, Carl and Amy Langhorst.

"Lordy," Ch. Conendale Lord of Astolat, winning under the late Alva Rosenberg. Handled by his owner Gene Cohen.

Lynnlea's Parade Dress going Best of Breed in Specials and pulled in the Working Group at Northeastern Indiana Kennel Club; judge, Mrs. Robert Thomas. Breeders, Ray and Dorothy Christiansen; handler-owner, Pat Stewart.

Above: Ch. Rosmoor Katy-Did, by Ch. Romayne Sportin' Life ex Ch. Rosmoor Honey-Do, one of three champions in one litter and herself the dam of two champions. Katy-Did was the winner of the Interstate Specialty in 1977, the Tri State Specialty in 1978, and the New Jersey Specialty in 1978. Bred by Rose and Don Tomlin and owned by Rose and Jennie Tomlin, Rosmoor Kennels. **Below:** Montage Moment By Moment, by Ch. Macdega Proof Positive ex Banchory I'll Stand By, taking Winners Bitch at the Harrisburg Specialty judged by Connie Hubbard; Tom Coen handling. Bred and owned by Jerry and Chris Machado.

Above: Ch. Ridgeside Stormsong, blue-merle son of Ch. Chenterra Thunderation ex Pixie Dell Indigo Melody, bred and owned by Dr. Alfred Edlin, Ridgeside Kennels in New Jersey, who is also a noted Borzoi breeder-owner-exhibitor. Stormsong finished in April 1978, when this photo was taken, with two Specialty majors along the way. Younger half-brothers to Stormsong are Am. Ch. Ridgeside Star Wars, sire and grandsire of winners, and Ch. Ridgeside Starship. **Below:** Ch. Macdega The Piano Man, a well-known sire, winning Best in Show. Owned by Thomas W. Coen, Macdega Shelties.

Above: Head-study of a fully mature Ch. Marwal Struttin' the Blues in 1983, the year he finished. Margaret and Walt Huening. **Below:** Ch. Rorralore Star Echo, by Ch. Brigadoon Merri Lou I'm Ready ex Ch. Rorralore Anne Boleyn, dam of Ch. Rorralore Star Envoy. Echo is shown here handled by Cheryl Willacker to a Herding Group first under judge Henry Stoecker at Licking River in 1983. Bred and owned by Charlotte Clem McGowan.

Ch. Sovereign Success Story, by Can. and Am. Ch. Kismet's Smash Hit ex Sovereign Irish Coffee, winning Best of Breed. Success Story is the dam of champions. Bred by Ariel Sleeth; owned by Fred Gordon, Chicwin Kennels.

Ch. Marwal Bluesette, a lovely bitch born in 1976 and finished in 1983. Bluesette is the dam of Ch. Marwal Struttin' the Blues. Marwal Kennels, owners, Margaret and Walt Huening.

Ch. Exeter Hills Suzy's Imprint, by Ch. Kings Bridge Sweet William ex Ch. Exeter Hills Oh Suzanna, finished with three majors won under Specials judges in 1982. Here Imprint is winning under Mrs. Dorothy Welsh, handled by co-owner Carl Langhorst. Starhaven Kennels, Carl and Amy Langhorst.

Banchory By Invitation Only taking Winners Dog at the Pacific Northwest Specialty in 1983 under judge Jo Byrd Parker; handler, Chris Machado. Owners, Jerry and Chris Machado.

Banchory A Blue Nun at the Pacific Northwest Specialty in 1981 taking five points under judge Virginia Lynn; handled by Clare Harden for Jerry and Chris Machado, Montage Kennels.

Multiple Best in Show winner, Ch. Banchory Rebel Blue taking the final points for title at Santa Cruz Kennel Club in 1980 under judge Lou Harris; handler, Chris Machado. At the time Rebel Blue was owned by the Machados but was later sold and now belongs to Dr. Richard McConnell.

Ch. Harvest Hills Ribbon 'n Lace, by Ch. Banchory Deep Purple ex Harvest Hills Twilight Tear, taking Winners Bitch at the Greater Milwaukee Shetland Sheepdog Club Specialty under judge Jo Parker. Elizabeth D. (Betty) Whelen is the owner-handler of this top producer and premier brood bitch for Pocono.

Ch. Rorralore Sportin' Chance, C.D. (left) winning the Stud Dog Class with his kids Ch. Rockwood's Gold Strike, Ch. Beltane All That Jazz, and Beltane Second Edition at the Colonial Shetland Sheepdog Specialty in 1983. Owner-handled by Charlotte McGowan.

Belle Mount Wee Silver Shore, Am. and Can. C.D., born July 13th 1981, finished his American C.D. with a High in Trial (score 199) at Holyoke in November 1982, Novice A., judged by Edwin Keppler. His American and Canadian titles were obtained in three straight shows. "Shortie" qualified for the Dog Obedience Trial Championship sponsored by Gaines and attended the Gaines Eastern Regional Competition in September 1983. He is the first Belle Mount-bred Sheltie to participate in the Gaines events. He was rated Number Thirty-two in the nation's top forty obedience Shelties in 1982. "Shortie" scored his High in Trial award at the second largest obedience trial in the East (and ninth largest in the country), in an actual entry of 254 dogs. Bred by Alice A. Burhans; exclusively trained and handled by Linda McAuley.

CHAPTER FOURTEEN

Obedience and Shetland Sheepdogs

Ch. and O.T.Ch. Grayfield Pepper and Salt, Am. and Bda. C.D., by Am. Ch. Macdega Sergeant Pepper ex Ch. Grayfield's Blue Sapphire. Owned by Sue Danziger, Cavatina Kennels.

Both beauty and brains are combined in a Shetland Sheepdog, and the result is a multitalented, versatile dog. Aside from possessing championship qualities, proven in the show ring, Shelties also exhibit intelligence, stamina, and a fine temperament—qualities which make this breed excel in obedience and several specialized fields of work.

Obedience

For its own protection and safety, every dog should be taught, at the very least, to recognize and respond promptly to the commands "Come," "No," "Down," "Sit," and "Stay." Doing so might at sometime save the dog's life and, in less extreme circumstances, will certainly make him a better-behaved, more pleasant member of society. If you are patient and enjoy working with your dog, study some of the good books available on the subject of obedience and then teach your Sheltie these basic manners. If you need the stimulus of working with a group, find out where obedience training classes are held (your dog's veterinarian, your dog's breeder, or a dog-owning friend can tell you) and you and your Sheltie can join up. Alternatively, you could let someone else do the training by sending the dog to class, but this is not very rewarding, because you lose the opportunity of working with your dog and developing a rapport between the two of you.

If you are going to do it yourself, there are some basic rules which you should follow. You must remain calm and confident in attitude. Never lose your patience or temper and frighten or punish your dog unjustly. Never resort to cruelty. Be quick and lavish with praise each time a command is correctly followed. Make it fun for your dog, and he will be eager to please you by responding correctly. Repetition is the keynote, but it should not be continued without recess to the point of tedium. Limit the training sessions to ten- or fifteen-minute periods at a time.

Formal obedience training can be followed, and very frequently is, by entering the dog in obedience competition to work toward an obedience degree, or several of them, depending on the dog's aptitude and your own enjoyment. Obedience trials are held in conjunction with the majority of conformation dog shows, as Specialty events, and in conjunction with Sheltie Specialties. If you are working alone with your dog, a list of trial dates might be obtained from your dog's veterinarian, your dog's breeder, or a dog-owning friend; or write to the American Kennel Club. The A.K.C. *Gazette* carries a monthly listing of all members or licensed dog shows and obedience trials to be held during the coming months in the United States. If you have been working with a training class, you will find information readily available regarding dates and locations of trials.

The basic goals for which one works in the formal American Kennel Club obedience trials are the following titles: Companion Dog (C.D.), Companion Dog Excellent (C.D.X.), and Utility Dog (U.D.). These degrees are earned by gaining three "legs," or qualifying scores, at each level of competition. The degrees must be earned in order, with one completed prior to starting work on the next. For example, a dog must have attained C.D. before starting work on C.D.X.; then C.D.X. must be completed before work on

Ch. Vanity Fair of Carmylie, C.D., by Ch. Sea Isle Serenade ex Ch. Kawartha's Fair Game. Jean D. Simmonds, owner.

Jennie Tomlin, twelve years old, performing off-lead heeling in 1978 with Rosmoor Winter Wind O'Tuwin, C.D., by Ch. Waldenwood Bonny's Blue Clyde ex Rosmoor Night Lark. Breeders, Rose Tomlin and Tony Tumlin; owner, Mimi Denton.

U.D. is started. The ultimate title attainable in obedience is Obedience Trial Champion (O.T.Ch.).

When you see the letters "C.D." following a dog's name, you will know that the dog has satisfactorily completed the following exercises: heel on leash, stand for examination, heel free, recall, long sit, and long stay. "C.D.X." indicates tests have been passed in all of the above plus heel free, drop on recall, retrieve over high jump, broad jump, long sit, and long stay. "U.D." indicates that the dog has additionally passed tests in scent discrimination (leather article), scent discrimination (metal article), signal exercises, directed retrieve, directed jumping, and group stand for examination.

The letters "O.T.Ch." are the abbreviation for the only obedience title which precedes rather than follows a dog's name. To gain an obedience trial championship, a dog who already holds a Utility Dog degree must win a total of one hundred points and must win three firsts, under three different judges, in Utility and Open B Class. Fulfilling these requirements is certainly no small achievement but rather one in which to take tremendous pride.

There is also a Tracking Dog title (T.D.) which can be earned at tracking trials, and a dog who has this title can then take a Tracking Dog

Badgerton Red Riot o'Carmylie, C.D.X., with his son. Red Riot has eight points including both majors. Carmylie Shelties owned by Jean D. Simmonds.

Excellent test which, if passed successfully, permits the dog to be known as a Tracking Dog Excellent (T.D.X.) In order to pass the Tracking Dog tests, the dog must follow the trail of a stranger along a path on which the trail was laid between thirty minutes and two hours previously. Along this trail there must be more than two right-angle turns, at least two of which are well out in the open where no fences or other boundaries exist for the guidance of the dog or the handler. The dog wears a harness and is connected to the handler by a lead twenty to forty feet in length. Inconspicuously dropped at the end of a track is an article to be retrieved, usually a glove or a wallet, which the dog is expected to locate and the handler to pick up. "T.D.X." is gained through completion of a more difficult version of the Tracking Dog test, with longer tracks being used and more turns through which the dog must work satisfactorily.

The owner of a dog holding the U.D. title and the T.D. title may then use the letters "U.D.T." following the dog's name. If the dog has gained his U.D. title and his T.D.X. title, then the letters "U.D.T.X." may follow his name, indicating that he is a Utility Dog and Tracker Excellent.

Am. and Can. Ch. Carmylie Shine On High, Am. and Can. C.D., by Banchory Heatherland On High ex Katie-J's Early Bird, headed for the water. Jean Simmonds, owner, Carmylie Kennels.

Above: Miss Polly Porter of Bagaduce Shelties and Mrs. W. Taylor Day, both very active early obedience exhibitors, with two champion daughters of Ch. Merrymaker of Pocono. Photo courtesy of Betty Whelen. **Below:** Sarn-Dee's Pride O'Mar-Bil-Hal, C.D., by Dawn's Blue Jester O'Mar-Bil-Hal ex Bonnie Carol O'Argyle's Pride, born October 6th 1964 and known as "Magic." Breeder, Bill Greenhalgh; owner, Mrs. Claude Roberts. Photo courtesy of Lee Reasin.

Some Outstanding Obedience Shelties

Throughout the pages of this book, in word and picture, you will note references to the good work done by Shelties in obedience competition. The quick intelligence of this breed, plus their desire to please, makes them especially trainable and fun to work with—a fact which has obviously been appreciated by owners in both the United States and Canada. It is especially nice noting the number of conformation champions which also possess obedience titles. Truly, in this breed "brains and beauty" definitely are compatible!

In a recent issue of *Pure-Bred Dogs/American Kennel Gazette*, there was a listing of the Top Twenty-five Obedience Dogs through 1982, figured on their lifetime records. Three Shetland Sheepdogs appear on this list. We find, in seventh place, Obedience Trial Champion Amstad Regimental Piper, owned by M.S. Stokely, Jr., and Helen M. Stokely. In eleventh place we find Obedience Trial Champion Car-A-Lam's Easy Rider, owned by Anna M. Arranda. And in seventeenth place, Obedience Trial Champion Seago's Tiny Tip, owned by Mrs. Carol D. Seago.

The leading Sheltie in obedience competition for 1982 was Obedience Trial Champion Andronama's Velvet Mariposa, owned by B.E. McCaleb. This Sheltie had eight High in Trial awards and many other exciting wins during the year.

Ch. Victory of Pocono, C.D.X., by Ch. Merrymaker of Pocono ex Sunny Girl of Anahassitt, dam of four champions and one of the breed's early greats. Elizabeth D. Whelen, owner, Pocono Kennels.

Am., Can., Mex. Ch. and O.T.Ch. Merriley's Steely Dan, Am., Can., and Mex. U.D., on his way to a Group first at Cabrillo Kennel Club, May 17th 1980, judged by Fred Young. This famous dog was nine years old when this photo was taken. Owned by Gene and Karen Dickinson and Maryann A. Morley, Woodland Hills, California.

Ch. Alandie Blue Lily, C.D.X., Best of Breed at the Shetland Sheepdog Club of Southern California Specialty Show in 1952. Photo courtesy of Lee Reasin.

Malashel's Autumn Amberglo, U.D., Can. C.D.X. "Alice" is taking one of the jumps at the Shetland Sheepdog Club of Northern New Jersey in April 1979. Owned by Elaine Wishnow.

"Taking the jumps." Ch. Merry Meddler of Pocono, C.D.X., 14½", by Ch. Merrymaker of Pocono, C.D., ex Ch. Merry Memory of Pocono. Bred and owned by Elizabeth D. Whelen, Pocono Kennels.

Badgerton Red Riot of Carmylie, C.D.X., at work. Jean D. Simmonds, owner, Carmylie Kennels.

Starhaven's Mel-O-D Miss, C.D., with her owner Laura McCoy, after winning Highest in Trial at their first show. Bred by Starhaven Kennels.

Ch. Starhaven's Rockin' Robin, C.D., sire of two champions, shown winning High in Trial at Cleveland Shetland Sheepdog Specialty with Amy Langhorst. Starhaven Kennels, owners, Carl and Amy Langhorst.

Ch. Forever Blue Flag, Int. C.D., an owner-handled Working Group winner. Bred by Leslie B. Rogers and owned by Karen Parker.

Ch. Conendale Challenger O'Akirene, finished with three majors, two Bests of Breed from the classes, and a third in Working Group. He also won first place at the graduation of his sub-novice class in obedience. This is one of the Shelties owned by Gene Cohen at the time of his sudden death of a heart attack. Challenger, who had eight points at the time, was left to Gene's good friend Constance Hubbard of Astolat Shelties, and finished in four shows.

Ch. Victory of Pocono, C.D.X., and Ch. Larkspur of Pocono on T.V. in Philadelphia. Betty Whelen, owner.

Ch. Hi-Hope MacDee's Marsea, Can. and Am. C.D., by Ch. Hi-Hope's Mai Tre De ex Hi-Hope Princess Laurel. A Canadian champion, Marsea is also a talented obedience dog, having a *Dog World* Award in her C.D. titles and also a High in Trial on one of her American legs. She was high in class for all of her Canadian and U.S. legs for C.D., and she is now working toward C.D.X. and Utility degrees. Bred by E.H. and Frances Clark; owned by Mary MacDonald.

Ch. Rorralore Zodiac, C.D.X., by Ch. Katie-J's Ronnie ex Ch. Hatfield's Stardust, sire of five champions. Charlotte McGowan, owner, Rorralore Kennels.

Shylove Rockwood Show Off, C.D., by Ch. Whipporwil Grand Master ex Shyloves Tinker Bell, dam of five champions as of February 1983. Owned by Barbara M. Kenealy.

Ch. Banchory Stand Back, C.D., winning the Stud Dog Class with Happy Glen's Autumn Amber and Happy Glen's Bit O'An O'Tolin, his pups from Banchory Bit O'Stone. Owned by Happy Glen Shelties.

Left to right: Ch., Rockwoods Sweet Charity, Ch. Our Own Rockwoods Bewitched, and Ch. Rockwoods Nite Enchantment, C.D.—three of the many outstanding Shelties belonging to Barbara M. Kenealy, Rockwood Kennels.

A group of 4-H girls showing Shelties and Labrador Retrievers, owned by Arnold C. Lane and Ruth E. Lane, at a 4-H obedience class during the Barnstable County Fair.

Am. and Can. Ch. Carmylie Shine On High, Am. and Can. C.D., and Dury Vee Summerwind playing "Labrador Retrievers" in tandem. Owned by Judy Brown. Photo courtesy of Jean D. Simmonds.

Malashel's Fortune Cookie, U.D., Can. C.D. Owned by Elaine Wishnow.

The first Sheltie top Dog Team (above) and Relay Team (below), at Orange Empire Dog Club, October 1967. Photos courtesy of Lee Reasin.

Limestone City Kennel Club, Novice B Obedience Class. First is Malashel's Autumn Amberglo, U.D., Can. C.D.X., by Ch. Valdawn's Krackerjack ex Trumark's Little Miss Tammy, U.D., Can. C.D.X. Amberglo is a *Dog World* award winner and a pointed Obedience Trial champion and has many High in Trials and High Scoring Sheltie. Second is Trumark's Little Miss Tammy, U.D., Can. C.D.X., by Am. and Can. Ch. Mor Jan's Destiny Maker. Little Miss Tammy gained her Canadian C.D.X. at eleven years of age with three first placements. Third is Lingard My Precious Peach, C.D.X., Can. C.D., by Ch. Lingard Sealect Bruce ex Lingard Dark Mist. Elaine Wishnow, owner.

Am., Can., and Mex. Ch. and O.T.Ch. Merriley's Steely Dan, Am., Can., and Mex. U.D., by Ch. Sundowner Mr. Bojangles, C.D. (by Ch. Tentagle David Copperfield ex Ch. Tentagel The Genie) ex Brig O'Dunes Blueberry Bunny (by Ch. Brig O'Dunes Partial Eclipse ex Ch. Brig O'Dunes Amoret) one of the breed's true greats. Bred by Cathleen D. Loesch; owned by the Dickinsons and Maryann Morley.

A Very Special Sheltie
Am., Can., and Mex. Ch. and O.T.Ch. Merriley's Steely Dan, Am., Can., and Mex. U.D.

American, Canadian, Mexican Champion and Obedience Trial Champion Merriley's Steely Dan, American, Canadian, and Mexican U.D., was born on November 8th 1974, at the Harvest Hill Kennels of Cathy Loesch. He was sired by the noted tricolor Champion Sundowner Mr. Bojangles, C.D., ex the lovely bi-blue Brig O'Dunes Blueberry Bunny. Danny was a "stud fee puppy" slated to go to Maryann Morley when he was twelve weeks old.

As scheduled, Danny was sent to California at the proper time, where he matured into a most handsome young dog and was entered to begin his show career at the Ventura County Kennel Club in July 1975. As fate would have it, Karen Dickinson was sitting at ringside that day, and she and Danny met when the little dog climbed into her lap by way of greeting.

So deep an impression had Danny made upon Karen Dickinson, of Woodland Hills, California, that she found her thoughts returning frequently to him, and she wondered if it might prove possible for her to purchase him. Maryann Morley did not want to entirely relin-

quish Danny's ownership, but an arrangement was finally worked out by which her name would remain as co-owner on the registration papers, but that for all intents and purposes Danny would belong to the Dickinsons and remain with Karen as her own dog.

Danny started out in conformation competition under his new ownership in 1976, not too auspiciously, as quite plainly he was not happy at being there. Karen Dickinson had on two previous occasions, once with a Collie and once with another Sheltie, proceeded with obedience training prior to the show ring, and so she decided to try this method with Danny since it had been successful with both the Collie and with the Sheltie, American, Canadian, and Mexican Champion Lobo Dell's Charm Bracelet, American, Canadian, and Mexican U.D.

Karen and Danny started novice training in May 1976. To quote Danny's owner, "I feel knowing one's dog to be the key to all obedience training. Most important is a good heeling dog. The dog should heel happily and smoothly and in an accurate heel position. He should sit quietly and straight on each halt. By July we were scoring 199's in matches."

Danny became a Canadian C.D. that summer with all first place scores and the bonus of a *Dog World* Award, plus nine points toward his Canadian championship. Then he went on to the Oregon Circuit where Danny quickly gained his American championship.

Still, despite having gained considerable self-confidence from these experiences, Danny obviously lacked the true love of being a show dog. For further socialization, Karen Dickinson took him with her to school, permitting him to run with her students during gym class, making it a game he enjoyed. Exuberance and sparkle began to shine as Danny enjoyed being the center of so much attention, which carried over now when he found himself in a dog show ring.

In 1977, Danny obtained his Mexican C.D. with another *Dog World* Award. He also won his first Mexican Best in Show and High in Trial, *both on the same day*. Then he came back home to the United States, where he attained his American C.D. with a third *Dog World* Award and three first-place scores of 198, 199, and 198. Additionally, Danny placed second in Novice in

the 1977 Gaines U.S. Western Regional Competition, with an average score of 198.7 and went on in December to place second in Novice in the 1978 Gaines U.S. Dog Obedience Classic with an average of 198.8.

The official beginning of "Steely Dan, Super Showman" took place in 1978 when Danny teamed up with handler Pam Stage. With Pam and her husband, Leroy, Danny travelled in style, sharing their motorhome as an honored guest and special friend. By now he was a sparkling show dog, "giving" every moment in the ring. By the end of 1978, he had accumulated twenty-eight Best of Breed wins. He completed his American C.D.X. with still a fourth *Dog World* Award, and all first place scores of 198½, 198½, and 199. He rounded out the year with ten High in Trial awards. Also, during 1978, he received another Mexican Best in Show, his Canadian championship, his Canadian C.D.X. with a fifth *Dog World* Award, a first place in

Am., Can., and Mex. Ch. and O.T.Ch. Merriley's Steely Dan, Am., Can., and Mex. U.D., in an obedience picture, at eight years of age. Gene and Karen Dickinson and Maryann Morley, owners, Woodland Hills, California.

Am., Can., and Mex. Ch. and O.T.Ch. Merriley's Steely Dan, Am., Can., and Mex. U.D., winning his one hundredth Best of Breed award! Cathleen D. Loesch, breeder, and the Dickinsons and Maryann Morley, owners, of this beautiful and talented dog.

Open in the 1978 Gaines U.S. Western Regional Competition, and an award of "Best in the West" by the *Collie-Sheltie Review.*

During 1979, Danny and Pam won three all-breed Bests in Show, nineteen Group placements, and thirty-six Best of Breed awards bringing their Best of Breed total to sixty-four. Danny also gained two additional Mexican Bests in Show, one of which included a High In Trial and the completion of his Mexican C.D.X. And again he was selected "Best in the West" by the *Collie-Sheltie Review.*

In the autumn of 1979, Danny developed serious bladder problems which necessitated scraping of the bladder wall in an effort to correct the condition and avoid formation of bladder stones. Danny made a good recovery, and all was considered to be well when in 1980 emergency surgery was needed for a bladder stone which was as large as a golf ball. Again he made a quick recovery and returned to the conformation ring, where he added an additional twenty-five Best of Breed awards including twelve Group placements and bringing his total of Bests of Breed to eighty-nine.

In 1981, Danny started out to try for his U.D. His first score was 195½ for the first leg to that title. Then things took a turn for the worse, his scores fell back, and he was obviously working

with difficulty. Two days after that he was in the hospital for emergency surgery for bladder stones and a blocked urethra. This time his recovery was a slow one, and great concern was felt by his owners.

Some two months later Danny did re-enter competition to complete his U.D., with a third straight leg of 194. During that summer he also finished his Canadian U.D. and his Mexican U.D., rounding out all the goals which had been set for him, while also obtaining another Best in Show and another High in Trial in Mexico on the same day. He then travelled with his handler to gain eleven more Best of Breed awards, enabling him to join the Century Club of U.S. winners who have gained Best of Breed 100 times. In the beginning of 1982, he gained his Obedience Trial championship for his greatest triumph of all, that of becoming America's first multiple Best in Show dog *of any breed* to also gain the honor of an Obedience Trial championship!

Danny is retired and enjoying fine health as we write this during September 1983. His well-wishers throughout the Sheltie world join forces in admiration for his accomplishments and hope that he will set still another Sheltie record—one for longevity and happiness over many years to come.

Ch. and O.T.Ch. Merriley's Steely Dan taking High in Trial with a score of 199½ at the National Specialty, February 24, 1982.

An informal pose of Mary Mac-
Donald's Can. Ch. Hi-Hope
MacDee's Marsea, Can. and Am.
C.D.

Can. Ch. and O.T.Ch. Grayfield Pep
per and Salt, Am. and Bda. C.D., a
Peter Pumpkin grandson being by
Am. Ch. Macdega Sergeant Pepper
ex Ch. Grayfriar's Blue Sapphire.
Owned by Susan Danziger, Cavatina
Kennels.

Above, left: Badgerton Red Riot o'Carmylie, C.D.X., and son. Jean D. Simmonds, owner, Carmylie Kennels. **Above, right:** Ch. Halstor's Peter Pumpkin (left), top sire in the breed, with his dam, Ch. Sea Isle Rhapsody of Halstor. Peter Pumpkin was bred by Edith Overly and owned by Tom Coen, Rhapsody was bred by Sea Isle Kennels and owned by Edith Overly and Charlotte McGowan. **Below:** Ch. Banchory Birth Right, C.D., Number Twelve Sheltie in Canada in 1982 and sire of six champions including a Best in Show winner and seven point winners. Bred by Clare and Donna Harden; owned by Mona and Lisa Stolcz.

Above: Ch. Shiel's Sunstreak, C.D., winning Best in Show at Ontario County Kennel Club in 1983; judge, Peter Smith. Breeder-owner-handler, Janet A. Cameron. **Below:** O.T. Ch. Carsaig's Bitter Sweet, Am. C.D.X., by Cannobie Black as Coal ex Sunnydell Small Talk, born in June 1975, winning High in Trial (score 198) owner-handled under judge Howard Ward at Grey Bruce in 1982. Breeder P. Freeman; owner, Janet A. Cameron.

Caper Hills Could It Be Magic, C.D., by Am. and Can. Ch. Banchory Deep Purple ex Can. Ch. Banchory Picture Perfect, shown winning second place for her third straight leg with owner Jane De Voe and a score of 195½ on the last run-off for first. She is the dam of two current winners, Caper Hills I Mean To Shine and Caper Hills I Have Dreamed. Bred by Lynette Smith, Caper Hill Shelties.

437

Ch. Sherwyn's Chasing The Blues, by Ch. Rockwoods Nite Enchantment, C.D., ex Ch. Pecheis Gwendolyn Blue, sire of six champions at the time of this writing. Barbara M. Kenealy handling for breeder-owners Fredna and Rhonda Picherd.

Ch. Marwal Steppin' Out, by Am. and Can. Ch. Sir Joshua of Winslow ex Marwal Bobbin' Along, finished in 1983 at eleven months of age with all his wins from the Puppy Class. Bred by Margaret and Walt Huening; owned by Diane Bostwick.

Below, left: Bran Gay Memory Maker, the dam of three champions. Owned by Brandol and Gayle Eads, Bran Gay Shelties. **Below, right:** Marwal Bobbin' Along, a daughter of Ch. Macdega Barwood Birthright ex Ch. Barwoods Symphony, the dam of Ch. Marwal Steppin' Out. She was acquired for Marwal Kennels in 1980 by Margaret and Walt Huening.

Brood Bitch Class, 1980 American Shetland Sheepdog Association Specialty, San Antonio, Texas: dam, Am. and Can. Ch. Caper Hills Song Sung Blue; first daughter, Caper Hills Shandoah Windsong; second daughter, Am. and Can. Ch. Macdega Gift of Song—both daughters sired by Banchory Reflection. Lynette Smith, breeder-owner. An interesting

note is that the brother of these two progeny bitches was sold to Japan after a broken leg ruined his show career. His first year at stud found him with, from only two offspring, one champion, the Best Specials Bitch and Reserve Winners Bitch at the Japanese National the following year. He is Caper Hill's I Write The Songs.

Above: Three puppies from a litter sired by Ch. September's Rainmaker pictured taking first, second, and third in a large Puppy Class at a match show: from left to right, Marchwind Moondancer, Ch. Marchwind The Rain Minstrel, and Marchwind Majestic Prince. Bred by Mary MacDonald, Marchwind Kennels. **Below:** Puppies sired by Ch. Sovereign Ring's Legacy. These handsome youngsters owned by Donna Biggs.

Kismet Classic of Pocono, by Ch. Karelane Royal Flush O'Kismet ex Valmora's Black Witch, top Pocono stud dog as of 1981. Elizabeth D. Whelen, owner.

Ch. Calcurt Luke, sire of twenty-one champions. Owned by Thomas W. Coen, Macdega.

Caper Hills I Like Dreamin', eight months old, by Caper Hills I Mean To Shine ex Caper Hills Song Without End, pictured at her first match. Bred and owned by Lynette Smith.

Above, left: Ch. Carmylie Jillian Lauradon, right, with her two pups, Ryan and Raini. Jean D. Simmonds, owner. **Above, right:** Sovereign Living Legend, by Ch. Sovereign Ring's Legacy ex Ch. Sovereign Mystic Charm, the sire of four champions and many more point winners. Sovereign Kennels, Ariel and Floyd Sleeth. **Below:** Ch. Philidove Kismet Heir Borne; sire of ten champions. Owned by Guy Mauldin and Irene Brody.

Rockwell

Above, left: Darling puppies whose dam is Velveteen Gold Dust. Mrs. Evelyn Byers, owner. **Above, right:** Caper Hills Song Without End, bi-blue puppy by Am. and Can. Ch. Banchory Deep Purple ex Can. Ch. Banchory Picture Perfect, at two and a half months of age. Bred by Lynette Smith; owned by SumerSong Shelties. **Below:** Ch. Starhaven's IBN Blue, by Best in Show winning Ch. Mori-Brook's Icecapade, C.D., ex Ch. Starhaven's Black Brat, C.D. (Highest in Trial winner), the sire of three champions. Starhaven Kennels, owners, Carl and Amy Langhorst.

Velveteen Gold Dust, the "pick" from Evelyn Byers's first litter by Ch. Esquire's Fringe Benefit ex Champion Stoneridge Copper Melody, with eleven points.

Am. and Can. Ch. Banchory Deep Purple, who has become the top producing blue-merle sire in Sheltie history with eighteen champions just prior to our going to press. Dr. and Mrs. Dale Gouger, owners, Cedarhope Kennels.

CHAPTER FIFTEEN

Breeding Shetland Sheepdogs

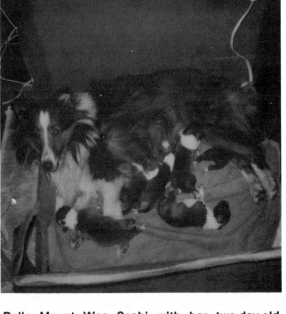

Belle Mount Wee Sophi with her two-day-old puppies. Alice A. Burhans, owner, Belle Mount Kennels.

Breeding good dogs requires a lot of hard work. It is not easy to produce dogs who conform as closely as possible to the standard, and it takes years to develop a strain of good and successful dogs. A lot of time and effort must go into choosing the stud dog and brood bitch, and then more time must be spent with the litter once it arrives.

The Stud Dog

Choosing the best stud dog to complement your bitch is not an easy task. The principal factors to be considered are the stud's quality and conformation and his pedigree. The pedigree lists the various bloodlines involved with the ancestry of the dog. If you are a novice in the breed, I would suggest that you seek advice from some of the more experienced breeders who are old-timers in the fancy and thus would be able to discuss with you some of the various dogs behind the one to which you are planning to breed your bitch. Many times such people accurately recall in minute detail the dogs you need to know about, perhaps even having access to photos of them. And do be sure to carefully study the photos in this book, as they show representatives of important Sheltie bloodlines.

It is extremely important that the stud's pedigree be harmonious with that of your bitch.

Do not just rush out and breed to a current winner, with no regard for whether or not he can reproduce his quality. Take time to check out the progeny being sired by the dog, or dogs, under your consideration. A dog that has sired nothing of quality for others probably will do no better for you, unless, of course, it is a young stud just starting out; such a stud may not have had the opportunity to produce much of anything, good or bad, thus far. Do you want to waste your bitch's time on an unknown quantity? Wouldn't you prefer to use a dog with a good producing record? You may get a little-known or unproven dog for a less expensive stud fee, but is that really sensible?

Breeding dogs is not a moneymaking proposition. By the time you pay a stud fee, take care of the bitch during gestation, whelp the litter, and raise and care for the puppies (including shots, and food, among other things) until they reach selling age, you will be fortunate if you break even on the cost of the litter. Therefore, it is foolish to skimp on the stud fee. Let nothing influence your selection except that the dog be best suited to your bitch in background and conformation, with the best producing record, regardless of the cost. It is just as expensive to raise mediocre puppies as good ones, and you will certainly fare better financially if you have show-prospect puppies to sell than if you come up with nothing but pets, which you will probably wind up selling for far less than you had intended or you'll end up giving away to get them good homes. Remember, the only excuse for breeding and bringing puppies into the world is an honest effort to improve the breed. So in choosing the stud you use, remember that the best, most suitable one you can find with an impressive producing record will almost certainly be by far the greatest bargain in the long run.

You will have to decide on one of three courses to follow in planning the breeding of your bitch: inbreeding, line-breeding, or outcrossing. Inbreeding is normally considered to be father to daughter, mother to son, or sister to brother. Line-breeding is combining two dogs belonging originally to the same strain or family of Shelties, descended from the same ancestors, such as half-brother to half-sister, niece to uncle, granddaughter to grandsire, and so on. Outcross breeding is using a dog and a bitch of completely different bloodlines with no mutual ancestors, or only a few, and these far back, if at all.

Each of these methods has advantages and disadvantages; each has supporters and detractors. I would say that line-breeding is probably the safest, the most generally approved, and the most frequently used with the desired results. Thus, I would say, it is perfect for the novice breeder because it is the easiest to figure out, especially until one has acquired considerable experience with the breed and the various bloodlines of which it consists.

Ch. Rockwoods Nite Enchantment, C.D., four times Peter breeding, by Ch. Rockwoods Bac Talk (sire of six champions) ex Shylove's Rockwood Show Off, C.D. (dam of five champions). Bred and owned by Barbara M. Kenealy, Our Own Rockwood Kennels.

Twelve-year-old Banchory Bi Jingo of Carmylie, by Ch. Thistlerose Arcwood Aladdin ex Lodgewood Queen of Banchory, the foundation of the Carmylie bi-color strain. Jean D. Simmonds, owner, Carmylie Shelties.

Inbreeding should be left for the experienced, very sophisticated breeder who knows the line extremely well and thus is in a position to evaluate the probable results. Outcrossing is normally done when you are trying to bring in a specific feature or trait, such as better movement, better head type, superior bone or substance, or better personality or temperament.

Everyone sincerely interested in breeding dogs wants to develop a line of their own, but this is not accomplished overnight. It takes at least several generations before you can claim to have done so, and during this time the close study of bloodlines and the observation of individual dogs are essential. Getting to know and truthfully evaluate the dogs with which you are working will go a long way in helping you preserve the best in what you have while at the same time remove weaknesses.

As a novice breeder, your wisest bet is to start by acquiring one or two bitches of the finest quality and background you can buy. In the beginning, it is really foolish to own your own stud dog; you will make out better and have a wider range of dogs with which to work if you pay a stud fee to one of the outstanding producing Shelties available to service your bitch. In order to be attractive to breeders a stud dog must be well known, must have sired at least one champion (and usually one that has attracted considerable attention in Specials competition), and must have winning progeny in the ring; this

Four generations of Shelties at Belle Mount: Lena, Sesame, Buccalena, and Princess. Alice A. Burhans, owner.

Above: Ch. Banchory Blue Mist of Pocono, by Ch. Sundowner Mr. Bo Jangles ex Horizon White Ice, litter-sister to Ch. Banchory Deep Purple. This was Betty Whelen's first champion in her first search for dogs carrying her original Pocono lines when she decided to return to breeding in the 1970's. **Below:** The marvelous Ch. Sea Isle Serenade, the sire of twenty-nine American champions, as an older dog.

represents a large expenditure of time and money before the dog begins to bring in returns on your investment. So start out by paying a stud fee a few times to use such a dog, or dogs, retaining the best bitch out of each of your first few litters and breeding those once or twice before you seriously think of owning your own stud dog. By that time, you will have gained the experience to recognize exactly what sort of dog you need for this purpose.

A future stud dog should be selected with the utmost care and consideration. He must be of very high standard as he may be responsible for siring many puppies each year, and he should not be used unless he clearly has something to contribute to the breed and carries no hereditary disease. Ideally, he should come from a line of excellent Shelties on both sides of his pedigree, the latter containing not only *good* dogs but also ones which are *proven successful producers of quality.* The dog himself should be of sufficient quality to hold his own in competition in his breed. He should be robust and virile, a keen stud dog who has proved that he is able to transmit his best qualities to his progeny. Do not use an unsound dog or a dog with a major or outstanding fault. Not all champions seem able to pass along their individual splendid quality and, by the same token, occasionally one finds a dog who never finished but who does sire puppies better than himself *provided that his pedigree is star-studded with top producing dogs and bitches.* Remember, too, that the stud dog cannot do it alone; the bitch must have what it takes too, although I must admit that some stud dogs, the truly dominant ones, can consistently produce

Five generations of Sea Isle champions: left to right, Ch. Sea Isle Summer Breeze; her daughter, Ch. Sea Isle Sandra; her daughter, Ch. Sea Isle Serenata; her granddaughter, Ch. Sea Isle Memorytime; and her sire, Champion Sea Isle Cadenza, Serenade's litter-brother. Photo courtesy of Charlotte MacGowan.

Ch. Chisterling Smoke Screen, by Ch. Chisterling Smoke Signal ex Ch. Sherrilion Lark O'Wadegate, the sire of four champions. Bred and owned by Don K. Combee, Chisterling Shelties.

type and quality regardless of the bitch or her background. Great studs like this, however, are few and far between.

If you are the proud owner of a promising young stud dog, one that you have either bred from one of your own bitches or that you have purchased after much serious thought and deliberation, do not permit him to be used for the first time until he is about a year old. The initial breeding should be to a proven matron, experienced in what is expected of her and thus not likely to give the stud a bad time. His first encounter should be pleasant and easy, as he could be put off breeding forever by a maiden bitch who fights and resents his advances. His first breeding should help him develop confidence and assurance. It should be done in quiet surroundings, with only you and one other person (to hold the bitch) present. Do not make a circus of it, as the first time will determine your stud's attitude and feeling about future breeding.

Your young stud dog must allow you to help with the breeding, as later there will be bitches who will not be cooperative and he will need to develop the habit of accepting assistance. If,

Ch. Severn Spellbinder, by Ch. Macdega The Chosen ex Scalloway Kaylie, C.D.X., at nine months of age in June 1974. Spellbinder is the sire of Best in Show winners. Owned by Linda Nugent More, Severn Kennels.

right from the beginning, you are there helping and praising him, he will expect and accept this as a matter of course whenever it may be necessary.

Before you introduce the dogs, be sure to have some K-Y Jelly at hand (this is the only lubricant that should be used) and either a stocking or a length of gauze with which to muzzle the bitch should it seem necessary, as you do not want either yourself or your stud dog bitten. Once they are "tied," you will be able to remove the muzzle, but, for the preliminaries, it is best to play it safe by muzzling her.

The stud fee is paid at the time of the breeding. Normally a return service is offered should the bitch fail to produce. Usually one live puppy is considered to be a litter. In order to avoid any misunderstanding regarding the terms of the breeding, it is wise to have a breeding certificate which both the owner of the stud and the owner of the bitch should sign. This should spell out quite specifically all the conditions of the breeding, along with listing the dates of the matings (usually the bitch is bred twice with one day in between, especially if she is a maiden bitch). The owner of the stud should also at this time provide the owner of the bitch with a copy of the stud dog's pedigree, if this has not previously been done.

Sometimes a pick-of-the-litter puppy is taken instead of a stud fee, and this should be noted on the breeding certificate along with such terms as at what age the owner of the stud dog is to select the puppy and whether it is to be a dog puppy, a bitch puppy, or just the "pick" puppy. All of

this should be clearly stated to avoid any misunderstandings later on.

In almost every case, the bitch must come to the stud dog for breeding. Once the owner of the bitch decides to what stud dog she will preferably be bred, it is important that the owner of the stud be contacted immediately to discuss the stud fee, terms, approximate time the bitch is due in season, and whether she will be shipped in or brought to the stud owner. Then, as soon as the bitch shows signs of coming into season, another phone call to the stud owner must follow to finalize the arrangements. I have experienced times when the bitch's owner has waited until a day or two before the bitch should be bred to contact me, only to meet with disappointment owing to the dog's absence from home.

Above: Ch. Carmylie Rosmoor Silvertip, a champion producer by Ch. Nathan Hale of Carmylie ex Rosmoor Winter Wind of Tuwin, C.D. Owned by Jean D. Simmonds. Below: Ch. Rockwoods Bac Talk, sire of six champions. Owned and shown by Barbara M. Kenealy, Rockwood Kennels.

Ch. Sovereign Pumpkin of Astolat, by Am. Ch. Halstor's Peter Pumpkin ex Am. Ch. Astolat Stardust, sire of fourteen Canadian champions plus numerous pointed offspring. Bred by Constance B. Hubbard; owned by Fred Gordon, Chicwin Kennels.

It is essential that the stud owner have proper facilities for housing the bitch while she is there. Nothing can be more disheartening than to have a bitch misbred or, still worse, to have her get away and become lost. Unless you can provide safe and proper care for visiting bitches, do not offer your dog at public stud.

Owning a stud dog is no easy road to riches, as some who have not experienced it seem to think; making the dog sufficiently well known is expensive and time-consuming. Be selective in the bitches you permit this dog to service. It takes two to make the puppies; and while some stud dogs do seem almost to achieve miracles, it is a general rule that an inferior bitch from a mediocre background will probably never produce well no matter how dominant and splendid may be the stud to whom she is bred. Remember that these puppies will be advertised and perhaps shown as sired by your dog. You do not want them to be an embarrassment to yourself or to him, so do not accept just any bitch who comes along in order to get the stud fee. It may prove far too expensive in the long run.

A stud fee is generally based on the going price of one show-type puppy and on the sire's record as a producer of winners. Obviously, a stud throwing champions in every litter is worth a greater price than a dog that sires mediocre pup-

One of the most influential sires in American Sheltie history, Ch. Sheltieland Kiltie O'Sea Isle, by Bogota Blaze ex Ch. Sheltieland Peg o'the Picts. Sea Isle Kennels, owners.

pies. Thus a young stud, just starting his career as a sire, is less expensive before proven than a dog with, say, forty or fifty champions already on the record. And a dog that has been used more than a few times but has no winning progeny should, it goes without saying, be avoided no matter how small the fee; he will almost certainly be a waste of your bitch's time.

I do not feel that we need to go into the actual breeding procedure here, as the experienced fancier already knows how it should be handled and the novice should not attempt it for the first time by reading instructions in a book. Plan to have a breeder or handler friend help you until you have become accustomed to handling such matters or, if this is not practical for you, it is very likely your veterinarian can arrange to do it for you or get someone from his staff to preside.

Ch. Sovereign Ring's Legacy, by Ch. Sovereign Ring of Fire, the greatest stud dog ever owned by Sovereign Kennels, famous producers of more than one hundred Sheltie champions. Ariel and Floyd Sleeth, owners.

Back row, left to right: Ch. Rockwoods Nite Enchantment, C.D., Ch. Rockwood Repeat Performance, and Rockwood Sensitive Prince (nine points); middle row, left to right: Ch. Rockwood Sylvan Seafaran Man and Ch. Alician Rockwood Talk Bac; front row, mom and pa: Shylove Rockwood Show Off, C.D., and Ch. Rockwoods Bac Talk. This handsome group owned by Barbara M. Kenealy, Our Own Rockwood.

If a complete "tie" is made, that breeding should be all that is actually necessary. However, with a maiden bitch, a bitch who has "missed" (failed to conceive) in the past, or one who has come a long distance, most people like to give a second breeding, allowing one day to elapse in between the two. This second service gives additional insurance that a litter will result; and if the bitch is one with a past record for misses, sometimes even a third mating takes place in an effort to take every precaution.

Once the "tie" has been completed, be sure that the penis goes back completely into its sheath. The dog should be offered a drink of water and a short walk, and then he should be put in his crate or kennel somewhere alone to settle down. Do not permit him to mingle with the other males for a while, as he will carry the odor of the bitch about him and this could result in a fight.

The bitch should not be allowed to urinate for at least an hour. In fact, many people feel that she should be "upended" (held with her rear end above her front) for several minutes following the "tie" in order to permit the sperm to travel deeper. She should then be offered water, crated, and kept quiet.

There are no set rules governing the conditions of a stud service. They are whatever the owner of the stud dog chooses to make them. The stud fee is paid for the act, not for the litter;

Ch. Philidove Heir Presumptive and his then three-month-old daughter Ch. Philidove Carmylie In A Mist. Photo courtesy of Jean D. Simmonds, Carmylie.

Ch. Barwood's Bonanza o'Merri Lon, by Ch. Sea Isle's Serenade ex Ch. Kiloren Cover Girl of Barwood, C.D., the sire of three champions. Bred by Barbara Thompson; owned by Karen and Ralph Elledge.

and if a bitch fails to conceive, this does not automatically call for a return service unless the owner of the stud sees it that way. A return service is a courtesy, not something that can be regarded as a right, particularly as in many cases the failure has been on the part of the bitch, not the stud dog. Owners of a stud in whom they take pride and whom they are anxious to have make records as the sire of numerous champions, however, are usually most generous in this respect; and I do not know of any instances where this courtesy has been refused when no puppies resulted from the breeding. Some stud owners insist on the return service being given to the same bitch only, while others will accept a different bitch in her place if the owner wishes, particularly if the original one has a previous record for missing.

When a bitch has been given one return breeding and misses again, the stud owner's responsibility has ended. If the stud dog is one who consistently sires puppies, then obviously the bitch is at fault; and she will quite likely never conceive, no matter how often or to how many different studs she is bred. It is unreasonable for the owner of a bitch to expect a stud's owner to give more than one return service.

Four of the magnificent Shelties at Rorralore Kennels in 1967: left to right, Ch. Rorralore Zodiac (dog), Ch. Rorralore Faerie Queen (bitch), Rorralore Mistris Myne (bitch), and the dam of all three, Ch. Hatfield's Stardust. Photo courtesy of Lee Reasin.

Above: Belle Mount Wee Sesame and his daughter Belle Mount Wee Princess. Alice A. Burhans, owner, Belle Mount Kennels. **Below:** Ch. Carmylie Jillian Lauradon (left) with daughter, Wildaire Raini. Owned by Jean D. Simmonds.

The Brood Bitch

One of the most important purchases you will make in dogs is the selection of your foundation brood bitch, or bitches, on whom you plan to base your breeding program. You want marvelous bloodlines representing top producing strains; you want sound bitches of basic quality, free of any hereditary problems.

Your Sheltie bitch should not be bred until her second period in season; but if she starts her season at an extra early age, say, barely over six months of age and then for the second time just past one year of age you would be wise to wait until her third heat. The waiting period can be profitably spent carefully watching for the ideal stud to complement her own qualities and be compatible with her background. Keeping this in mind, attend dog shows and watch the males who are winning and, even more important, siring the winners. Subscribe to any dog magazines which include Shelties and study the pictures and stories accompanying them to familiarize yourself with dogs in other areas of which you may have not been aware. Be sure to keep in mind that the stud should be strong in the bitch's weak points; carefully note his progeny to see if he passes along the features you want and admire. Make special note of any offspring from bitches with backgrounds similar to your bitch's; then you can get an idea of how well the background fits with his. When you see a stud dog that interests you, discuss your bitch with the owner and request a copy of his dog's pedigree for your study and perusal.

When you have made a tentative choice, contact the stud's owner to make the preliminary arrangements regarding the stud fee (whether it will be in cash or a puppy), approximate time the

Three of the bitches at Montage Kennels: left to right, Ch. Berridale Alnphyl Brigette, Ch. Berridale A Touch of Class, and Ch. Macdega Cotton Blossom. Owned by the Machados.

bitch should be ready, and so on. Find out, too, the requirements (such as health certificates, and tests) the stud owner has regarding bitches accepted for breeding. If you will be shipping the bitch, find out which airport and airline should be used.

The airlines will probably have special requirements, too, regarding conditions under which they will or will not take dogs. These requirements, which change from time to time, include such things as crate size and type they will accept. Most airlines have their own crates available for sale which may be purchased at a nominal cost, if you do not already have one that they consider suitable. These are made of fiberglass and are the safest type in which to ship a dog. Most airlines also require that the dog be at the airport two hours before the flight is scheduled to depart and that the dog is accompanied by a health certificate from your veterinarian, including information about rabies inoculation. If the airline does not wish to accept the bitch because of extreme temperature changes in the weather but will do so if you sign a waiver stating that she is accustomed to them and should have no problem, think it over carefully before doing so, as you are thus relieving them of any responsibility should the bitch not reach her destination alive or in good condition. And always insure the bitch when you can.

Normally the airline must be notified several days in advance for the bitch's reservation, as only a limited number of dogs can be accommodated on each flight. Plan on shipping the bitch on her eighth or ninth day, but if at all possible arrange it so that she avoids travelling on the

Above: Ch. Kawartha's Fair Game, by Champion Sheltieland Kiltie o'Sea Isle ex Kawartha's Sabrina Fair, the dam of five champions. Owned by Jean D. Simmonds. **Below:** Ch. Pixie Dell Blue Thistle, dam of Ch. Pixie Dell Thistledown, Ch. Pixie Dell Bairn of Cluaron, Ch. Pixie Dell Lavender Blue, and Ch. Catamount Magic Dragon. Owned by Mr. and Mrs. A.R. Miller.

Ch. Sea Isle Serenata, famous daughter of Ch. Nashcrest Golden Note ex Ch. Sea Isle Sandra, one of the key bitches in the Sea Isle line. Bred back to her sire Golden Note, she produced the famous dog Ch. Sea Isle Serenade, sire of twenty-nine American champions. Sea Isle Kennels, Evelyn Davis and Mary Van Wagenen.

weekend when schedules are not always the same and freight offices are likely to be closed.

It is important that whenever possible you ship your bitch on a flight that goes directly to the airport which is her destination. It is not at all unusual, when stopovers are made along the way, for a dog to be removed from the plane with other cargo and either incorrectly loaded for the next leg of the flight or left behind. Take every precaution that you can against human error!

It is simpler if you can plan to bring the bitch to the stud dog. Some people feel that the trauma of the plane trip may cause the bitch not to conceive; others just plain prefer not sending them that way. If you have a choice, you might do better to take the bitch in your own car where she will feel more relaxed and at ease. If you are doing it this way, be sure to allow sufficient time for the drive to get her to her destination at the correct time for the breeding. This usually is any time from the eighth to the fourteenth day, depending on the individual bitch and her cycle. Remember that if you want the bitch bred twice, you must allow a day in between the two services. Do not expect the stud's owner to put you up during your stay. Find a good, nearby motel that accepts dogs, and make a reservation for yourself there.

Just prior to your bitch's season, you should make a visit to your veterinarian with her. Have her checked for worms, make sure that she is up-to-date on all her shots, and attend to any other

tests the stud owner may have requested. The bitch may act and be perfectly normal up until her third or fourth week of pregnancy, but it is better for her to have a clean bill of health before the breeding than to bother her after it. If she is overweight, right now is when you should start getting the fat off her; she should be in good hard condition, neither fat nor thin, when bred.

The day you've been waiting for finally arrives, and you notice the swelling of her vulva, followed within a day or two by the appearance of a colored discharge. Immediately call the stud's owner to finalize arrangements, advising whether you will ship her or bring her, the exact day she will arrive, and so on. Then, if she is going by plane, as soon as you know the details, advise the stud owner of the flight number, the time of arrival, and any other pertinent information. If you are shipping the bitch, the check for the stud fee should be mailed now. If the owner of the stud dog charges for his trips to the airport, for picking the bitch up and then returning her, reimbursement for this should either be included with the stud fee or sent as soon as you know the amount of the charge.

Ch. Chicwin's Promised Victory, by Ch. Sovereign Gonna Fly Now ex Ch. Chicwin's Promised Jewel, dam of several Canadian champions, including Ch. Chicwin's Chelsea. Bred and owned by Fred Gordon, Chicwin Shetland Sheepdogs.

Kismet's Rubaiyyat, by Ch. Ken-Robs Bobbie ex Ch. Kismet's Coquette, the dam of thirteen champions. Bred by Guy A. and Thelma J. Mauldin; owned by Burt B. Pardue and Guy A. Mauldin.

If you are going to ship your bitch, do not feed her on the day of the flight; the stud's owner will do so when she arrives. Be sure that she has had access to a drink of water just before you leave her and that she has been exercised prior to being put in her crate. Place several layers of newspapers, topped with some shredded papers, on the bottom of the crate for a good bed. The papers can be discarded and replaced when she reaches her destination prior to the trip home. Rugs and towels are not suitable for bedding material as they may become soiled, necessitating laundering when she reaches her destination. A small towel may be included to make her feel more at home if you wish. Remember to have her at the airport two hours ahead of flight time.

If you are driving, be sure to arrive at a reasonable time of day. If you are coming from a distance and get in late, have a good night's sleep before contacting the stud's owner first thing in the morning. If possible, leave the children and relatives at home; they will not only be in the way, but also most stud owners definitely object to too many people around during the actual breeding.

Once the breeding has been completed, if you wish to sit and visit for a while, that is fine; but do not leave the bitch at loose ends. Take her to

Ch. Starhaven's Singing The Blues, by Ch. Starhaven's IBN Blue ex Starhaven's Bit of A Brat, dam of Ch. Starhaven's Great Xpectations. Owned by Starhaven Kennels, Carl and Amy Langhorst.

her crate in the car where she can be quiet (you should first, of course, ascertain that the temperature is comfortable for her there and that she has proper ventilation). Remember that she should not urinate for at least an hour following the breeding.

If you have not already done so, pay the stud fee now, and be sure that you receive your breeding certificate and a copy of the dog's pedigree if you do not have one.

Now you are all set to await, with happy anticipation, the arrival of the puppies.

Above: Marwal Bobbin' Along in 1982. "Robin" is a daughter of Ch. Macdega Barwood Birthright (Am. and Can. Ch. Macdega Mainstay ex Ch. Barwood's Treasure) from Ch. Barwoods Symphony (Ch. Chenterra Thunderation ex Ch. Barwoods Rhapsody). She is the dam of Ch. Marwal Steppin' Out. Bred by Margaret Huening; owned by Diane Bostwick. **Below:** Ch. Chisterling Extra Special with her daughter, Chisterling Special Dream. Breeder-owner, Don K. Combee.

Above: A lovely Sheltie head-study of Ch. Jade Mist Woodwind Chimes, dam of four champions. Owned by Dr. and Mrs. Keith B. Howell. **Below:** Ch. Carmylie Polly Paintbrush (center) and her two pointed daughters, Carmylie Taplrac Nelli Bi (left) and Taplrac Carmylie Blueprint (right). Carmylie Shelties, Jean Simmonds.

Pedigrees

To anyone interested in the breeding of dogs, pedigrees are the basic component with which this is best accomplished. It is not sufficient to just breed two nice-looking dogs to one another and then sit back and await outstanding results. Chances are they will be disappointing, as there is no equal to a scientific approach to the breeding of dogs if quality results are the ultimate goal.

We have selected for you pedigrees of Shetland Sheepdog dogs and bitches who either are great producers or have come from consistently outstanding producing lines. Some of these dogs are so dominant that they have seem-

ed to "click" with almost every strain or bloodline. Others, for best results, need to be carefully line-bred. The study of pedigrees and breeding is both a challenge and an exciting occupation.

Even if you have no plans to involve yourself in breeding and just anticipate owning and loving a dog or two, it is fun to trace back the pedigree of your dog, or dogs, to earlier generations and thus learn the sort of ancestors behind your own. Throughout this book you will find a great many pictures of dogs and bitches whose names appear in these pedigrees, enabling you not only to trace the names in the background of your Shetland Sheepdog but also to see what the forebears look like.

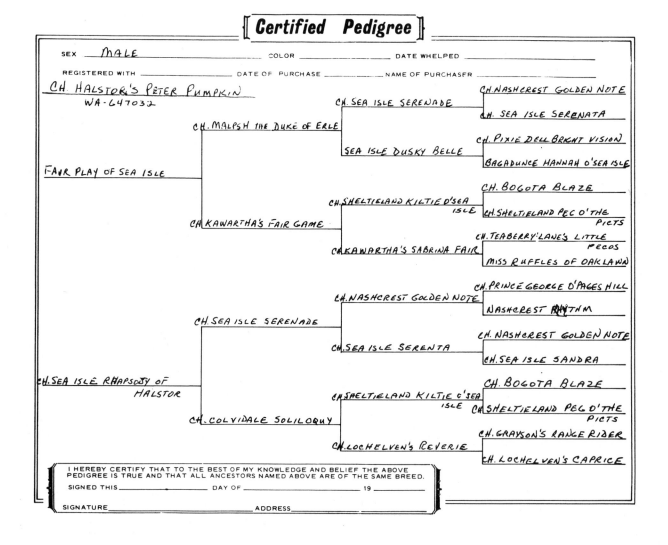

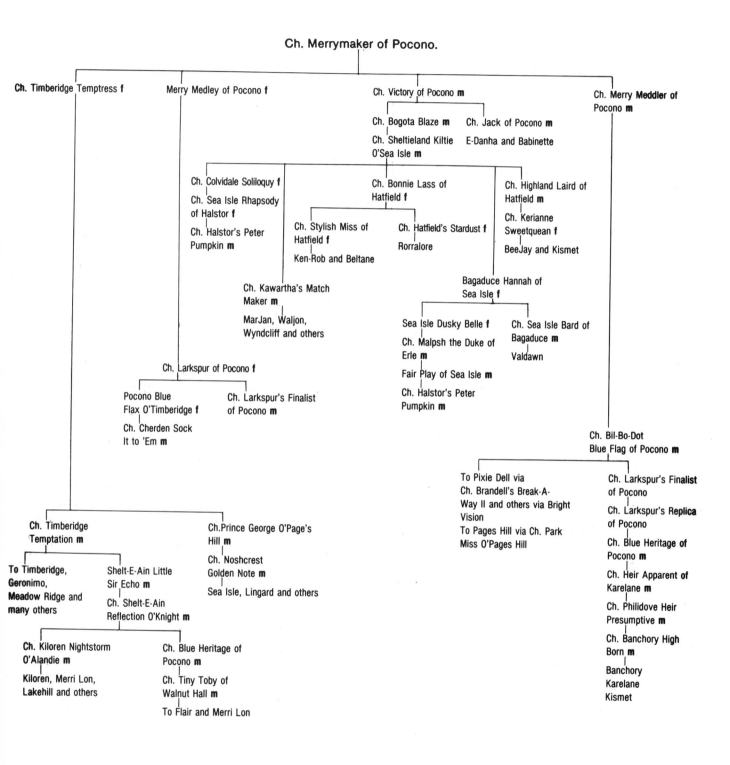

Ch. Merrymaker of Pocono.

Ch. Timberidge Temptress **f**

Merry Medley of Pocono **f**

Ch. Victory of Pocono **m**

Ch. Merry Meddler of Pocono **m**

Ch. Bogota Blaze **m**   Ch. Jack of Pocono **m**

Ch. Sheltieland Kiltie   E-Danha and Babinette
O'Sea Isle **m**

Ch. Colvidale Soliloquy **f**

Ch. Bonnie Lass of
Hatfield **f**

Ch. Highland Laird of
Hatfield **m**

Ch. Sea Isle Rhapsody
of Halstor **f**

Ch. Kerianne
Sweetquean **f**

Ch. Halstor's Peter
Pumpkin **m**

Ch. Stylish Miss of
Hatfield **f**

Ch. Hatfield's Stardust **f**

BeeJay and Kismet

Ken-Rob and Beltane

Rorralore

Ch. Kawartha's Match
Maker **m**

Bagaduce Hannah of
Sea Isle **f**

MarJan, Waljon,
Wyndcliff and others

Sea Isle Dusky Belle **f**

Ch. Sea Isle Bard of
Bagaduce **m**

Ch. Malpsh the Duke of
Erle **m**

Valdawn

Ch. Larkspur of Pocono **f**

Fair Play of Sea Isle **m**

Pocono Blue
Flax O'Timberidge **f**

Ch. Larkspur's Finalist
of Pocono **m**

Ch. Halstor's Peter
Pumpkin **m**

Ch. Cherden Sock
It to 'Em **m**

Ch. Bil-Bo-Dot
Blue Flag of Pocono **m**

To Pixie Dell via
Ch. Brandell's Break-A-
Way II and others via Bright
Vision
To Pages Hill via Ch. Park
Miss O'Pages Hill

Ch. Larkspur's Finalist
of Pocono

Ch. Larkspur's Replica
of Pocono

Ch. Timberidge
Temptation **m**

Ch. Prince George O'Page's
Hill **m**

Ch. Blue Heritage of
Pocono **m**

Ch. Noshcrest
Golden Note **m**

Ch. Heir Apparent of
Karelane **m**

To Timberidge,
Geronimo,
Meadow Ridge and
many others

Shelt-E-Ain Little
Sir Echo **m**

Sea Isle, Lingard and others

Ch. Philidove Heir
Presumptive **m**

Ch. Shelt-E-Ain
Reflection O'Knight **m**

Ch. Banchory High
Born **m**

Ch. Kiloren Nightstorm
O'Alandie **m**

Ch. Blue Heritage of
Pocono **m**

Banchory
Karelane
Kismet

Kiloren, Merri Lon,
Lakehill and others

Ch. Tiny Toby of
Walnut Hall **m**

To Flair and Merri Lon

f = female

m = male

The family tree of Elizabeth D. Whelen's great Ch. Merrymaker of Pocono.

WD006114
INDIVIDUAL REG. NO.

Certificate of Pedigree

Danny
CALL NAME

CH. & OTCH. Merriley's Steely Dan
REGISTERED NAME OF DOG

BREED Shetland Sheepdog   DATE WHELPED November 8, 1974   SEX Male

BREEDER Cathleen D. Loesch   ADDRESS 5625 64th Street, Snohomish, WA

OWNER Karen Dickinson (co-owned by   ADDRESS 5715 Oakdale Ave, Woodland Hills,

GENERAL DESCRIPTION Blue Merle   Maryann Morley)   CA, 91367

SIRE

CH. Tentagle David Copperfield
- CH. Diamond's Robert Bruce
  - CH. Lingard Sealect Bruce
    - CH. Nashcrest Golden Note
    - Timberidge Sandstorm
  - CH. Diamond's Black Velvet
    - CH. Tess's Trump Card of Wadmalaw
    - CH. Diamond's Lady Gold-ment
- Tentagel Mrs. Robinson
  - CH. Diamond's Robert Bruce
    - CH. Lingard Sealect Bruce
    - CH. Diamond's Black Velvet
  - CH. Sharlin's Penny Brite
    - CH. Pixie Dell Bright Vision
    - CH. Sharlins Tempting Teressa

CH. Sundowner Mr. Bojangles C.D.

REG. NO. ....

CH. Tentagel The Genie
- CH. Vikingsholm Vilhelm
  - CH. E-Danha Just My Bill
    - CH. E-Danha Overture
    - CH. E-Danha Fanciful Wish
  - CH. Gigi of Holly Hill
    - CH. Kawartha's Match Maker
    - Sheltie Glen Wee Topaz
- CH. Sharlin's Oh-Suzanna
  - CH. Pixie Dell Bright Vision
    - CH. Brandell's Break-A-Way II
    - CH. Va-Gore's Bright Promise
  - CH. Forecaster Francesca
    - CH. Forecaster Son of Heidi
    - Geronimo Golden Gossimer

DAM

CH. Brig O'Dune's Partial Eclipse
- CH. Cherden Sock It To 'Em
  - CH. Diamond's Robert Bruce
    - CH. Lingard Sealect Bruce
    - CH. Diamond's Black Velvet
  - Julaine's Wood Mist O'Cherden
    - Banchory Phantom O'Four Winds
    - Banchory Golden Glow
- CH. Banchory Mist O'Brigadoon C.D.
  - CH. Hallmark the Black Watch
    - CH. Tiny Toby of Walnut Hall
    - Hallmark's Heirloom of Pocono
  - CH. Lodgewood Tempo Primo
    - Kiloren Footprints
    - Lodgewood Sonata

Brig O'Dunes Blueberry Bunny

REG. NO. ....

CH. Brig O'Dunes Amoret Bi-Azure
- CH. Cherden Sock It To 'Em
  - CH. Diamond's Robert Bruce
    - CH. Lingard Sealect Bruce
    - CH. Diamond's Black Velvet
  - Julaine's Wood Mist O'Cherden
    - Banchory Phantom O'Four Winds
    - Banchory Golden Glow
- CH. Banchory Mist O'Brigadoon C.D.
  - CH. Hallmark the Black Watch
    - CH. Tiny Toby of Walnut Hall
    - Hallmark's Heirloom of Pocono
  - CH. Lodgewood Tempo Primo
    - Kiloren Footprints
    - Lodgewood Sonata

I HEREBY CERTIFY THAT THIS PEDIGREE IS TRUE AND CORRECT
TO THE BEST OF MY KNOWLEDGE AND BELIEF

SIGNED _____

DATE July 1 , 19 82

464

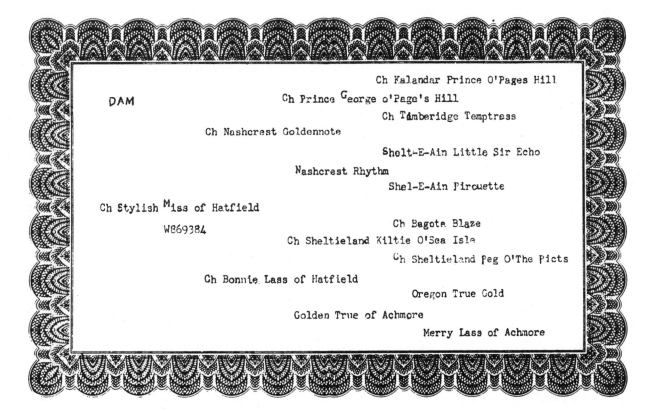

```
                                              Ch Merrymaker of Pocono C.D.
SIRE                       Ch Victory of Pocono
                                              Sunny Girl of Anahassitt
            Ch Bagota Blaze
                                           Ch Rockwood Laddie
                        Bravo of Tavistock
                                           Black Thimble of Tavistock
Ch Sheltieland Kiltie O'Sea Isle
       W 91729                             Ch Kim O'Page's Hill
                        Ch Mountaineer O'Pages Hill
                                           Coquette O'Page's Hill
            Ch Sheltieland Peg O'The Picts
                                           Melchoir of Anahasitt
                        Ch Pinafore O'The Picts
                                           Ch Petticoat O'The Picts
```

```
                                              Ch Kalandar Prince O'Pages Hill
DAM                       Ch Prince George o'Page's Hill
                                              Ch Timberidge Temptress
            Ch Nashcrest Goldennote
                                           Shelt-E-Ain Little Sir Echo
                        Nashcrest Rhythm
                                           Shel-E-Ain Pirouette
Ch Stylish Miss of Hatfield
       W869384                             Ch Bagota Blaze
                        Ch Sheltieland Kiltie O'Sea Isle
                                           Ch Sheltieland Peg O'The Picts
            Ch Bonnie Lass of Hatfield
                                           Oregon True Gold
                        Golden True of Achmore
                                           Merry Lass of Achmore
```

Pedigree—SHETLAND SHEEPDOG—Ch. Frigate's Emblem of Astolat, A.K.C. W-55,439

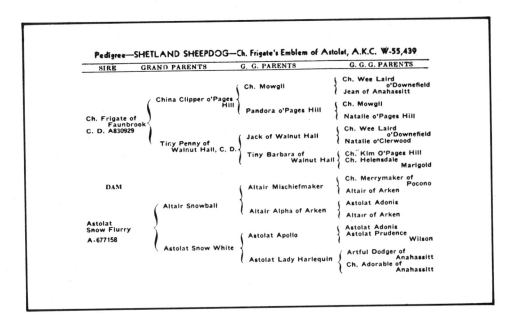

SIRE	GRAND PARENTS	G. G. PARENTS	G. G. G. PARENTS
Ch. Frigate of Faunbrook C. D. A830929	China Clipper o'Pages Hill	Ch. Mowgli	Ch. Wee Laird o'Downefield
			Jean of Anahassitt
		Pandora o'Pages Hill	Ch. Mowgli
			Natalie o'Pages Hill
	Tiny Penny of Walnut Hall, C. D.	Jack of Walnut Hall	Ch. Wee Laird o'Downefield
			Natalie o'Clerwood
		Tiny Barbara of Walnut Hall	Ch. Kim O'Pages Hill
			Ch. Helensdale Marigold
DAM	Altair Snowball	Altair Mischiefmaker	Ch. Merrymaker of Pocono
			Altair of Arken
Astolat Snow Flurry A-677158		Altair Alpha of Arken	Astolat Adonis
			Altair of Arken
	Astolat Snow White	Astolat Apollo	Astolat Adonis
			Astolat Prudence Wilson
		Astolat Lady Harlequin	Artful Dodger of Anahassitt
			Ch. Adorable of Anahassitt

This is the pedigree of the Sheltie Can. & Amer. CH. ASTOLAT GOLD AWARD, WA-378,416

	GRAND PARENTS	GREAT-GRANDPARENTS	GREAT-GREAT-GRAND PARENTS
SIRE — CH. Astolat Golden Symbol	CH. Frigate's Emblem of Astolat	CH. Frigate of Faunbrook, C. D.	China Clipper o'Page's Hill
			Tiny Penny of Walnut Hall
		Astolat Snow Flurry	Altair Snowball
			Astolat Snow White
	Astolat Marigold	CH. Wayfarer of Pocono	CH. Timberidge Temptation
			Sunny Girl of Anahassitt
		Astolat Emblem of Hope	CH. Frigate's Emblem of Astolat
			Gay Princess Taffeta
DAM — Scotswold Gretta	CH. Bykenhall St. Andrew	CH. Astolat Future Emblem	CH. Frigate's Emblem of Astolat
			Astolat Emblem of Hope
		Falkirk's Wee Merrie Sprite	CH. Pixie Doll Firebrand
			CH. Timberidge Penelope
	CH. Timberidge Scarlet Phantasy	CH. Noralee Forecaster	CH. Noralee Bronze Nugget
			Noralee Indian Summer
		CH. Timberidge Black Eyed Susan	CH. Timberidge Temptation
			Timberidge Topsy

CERTIFIED PEDIGREE OF CH. ASTOLAT GALAXY—WB-759,849

	Grand Parents	Great-Grand Parents	Great-Great-Grand Parents
SIRE — CH. Halstor's Peter Pumpkin	Fair Play of Sea Isle	CH. Malpsh The Duke of Erle	CH. Sea Isle Serenade
			Sea Isle Dusky Belle
		CH. Kawartha's Fair Game	CH. Sheltieland Kiltie o' Sea Isle
			CH. Kawartha's Sabrina Fair
	CH. Sea Isle Rhapsody of Halstor	CH. Sea Isle Serenade	CH. Nashcrest Golden Note
			CH. Sea Isle Serenata
		CH. Colvidale Soliloquy	CH. Sheltieland Kiltie o' Sea Isle
			CH. Lochlevin's Reverie
DAM — CH. Astolat Stardust	CH. Astolat Gold Award, Int. CD.	CH. Astolat Golden Symbol	CH. Frigate's Emblem of Astolat
			Astolat Marigold
		Scotswold Gretta	CH. Bykenhall St. Andrew
			CH. Timberidge Scarlet Phantasy
	CH. Piper's Pride of Astolat	CH. Gay Piper o'Pages Hill	CH. Magnet o'Pages Hill
			Dark Blossom o'Pages Hill
		Astolat Symbol's Primrose	CH. Astolat Golden Symbol
			Astolat Emblem of Hope

466

Certified Pedigree of CAN. & AMER. CH. ASTOLAT ENCHANTOR WA-829,139

	GRAND PARENTS	GREAT-GRANDPARENTS	GREAT-GREAT-GRAND PARENTS
SIRE CHAMPION LINGARD SEALECT BRUCE	CHAMPION Int. Nashcrest Golden Note	CHAMPION Prince George o' Pages Hill	CH. Kalendar Prince o' Pages Hill / CH. Timberidge Temptress
		Nashcrest Rhythm	CH. Shelt-E-Ain Little Sir Echo / Shelt-E-Ain Pirouette
	Timberidge Sandstorm	Geronimo Prince Royal	Geronimo Prince Charming / Silversheen Miss Priss
		Sea Isle Singing Sands	CH. Sea Isle Cadenza / Sea Isle Eastertide
DAM CHAMPION ASTOLAT PEGGY of FAUNBROOK, C.D.	CHAMPION Browne Acres Statesman	CHAMPION Geronimo Little Hi-Lite	CH. Geronimo Crown Prince / Timberidge Black Aster
		Browne Acres Ballad	CH. Nashcrest Golden Note / CH. Browne Acres Blossom
	Faunbrook Nonnie	Nashcrest Golden Note	CH. Prince George o' Pages Hill / Nashcrest Rhythm
		CHAMPION Gay Adventure of Karelane	CH. Frigate of Faunbrook, CD. / CH. Wayfarer's Girl of Pocono

CERTIFIED PEDIGREE OF CH. ASTOLAT HEADLINER, C.D.—WB-692,443

	Grand Parents	Great-Grand Parents	Great-Great-Grand Parents
SIRE Amer. Ber. Can. Mex. & Col. Champion Astolat Gold Award, Int. CD. WA-378,416	CH. Astolat Golden Symbol	CH. Frigate's Emblem of Astolat	CH. Frigate of Faunbrook, CD. / Astolat Snow Flurry
		Astolat Marigold	CH. Wayfarer of Pocono / Astolat Emblem of Hope
	Scotswold Gretta	CH. Bykenhall St. Andrew	CH. Astolat Future Emblem / Falkirk's Wee Merrie Sprite
		CH. Timberidge Scarlet Phantasy	CH. Noralee Forecaster / CH. Timberidge Black-Eyed Susan
DAM Atolat Maytime	CH. Astolat Enchantor WB-246,024	CH. Lingard Sealect Bruce	CH. Nashcrest Golden Note / Timberidge Sandstorm
		CH. Astolat Peggy of Faunbrook, CD.	CH. Browne Acres Statesman / Faunbrook Nonnie
	Astolat Springtime	Astolat Bronze Mark	Astolat Zorro / Astolat Magic Moment
		Bright Flash o' Page's Hill	Legacy o'Pages Hill / Alicia o'Pages Hill

This is the pedigree of the Sheltie Can. & Amer. CH. ASTOLAT GOLDEN TOUCH, WA-735,449

	GRAND PARENTS	GREAT-GRANDPARENTS	GREAT-GREAT-GRAND PARENTS
SIRE CAN. Amer. & Bermuda CH. Astolat Gold Award	CH. Astolat Golden Symbol	CH. Frigate's Emblem of Astolat	CH. Frigate of Faunbrook, CD. / Astolat Snow Flurry
		Astolat Marigold	CH. Wayfarer of Pocono / Astolat Emblem of Hope
	Scotswold Gretta	CH. Bykenhall St. Andrew	CH. Astolat Future Emblem / Falkirk's Wee Merrie Sprite
		CH. Timberidge Scarlet Phantasy	CH. Noralee Forecaster / CH. Timberidge Black Eyed Susan
DAM Astolat Symbol's Radience	CH. Astolat Golden Symbol	CH. Frigate's Emblem of Astolat	CH. Frigate of Faunbrook, CD. / Astolat Snow Flurry
		Astolat Marigold	CH. Wayfarer of Pocono / Astolat Emblem of Hope
	Lorrie of Astolat	Magnet's Charmer of Astolat	CH. Magnet o'Pages Hill / CH. Astolat Emblem's Onyx
		Astolat Emblem's Radience	CH. Frigate's Emblem of Astolat / Falkirk's Radience

Sire

Am/Can.CH.Banchory Deep Purple
WD 381631
REG. NO. ....

- CH.Sundowner Mr.Bojangles,CD.
  - CH.Tentagel David Copperfield
    - CH.Diamond'sRobert Bruce
      - CH.Lindgard Sealect Bruce
      - CH.Diamond'sBlack Velvet
    - Tentagel Mrs.Robinson
      - CH.Diamond's Robert Bruce
      - CH.Sharlin's Penny Brite
  - CH.Tentagel the Genie
    - CH.Vikingsholm Vilhelm
      - CH.E-Danna Just My Bill
      - Gigi of Holly Hill
    - CH.Sharlin'sOhSuzanna
      - CH.Pixie Dell Bright Vision
      - CH.Forecaster Francesa
- Horizon White Ice
  - CH.Banchory Thunder Blue
    - CH.Cherden Sock It TO'Em
      - CH.Diamond's Robert Bruce
      - Juliane's Woodmist O'Cherden
    - Clan Duncan Banchory Blustle
      - CH.Cherden Sock It To'Em
      - Banchory Half Moon
  - Banchory Flash of Blue
    - CH.Banchory High Born
      - CH.Philidove Heir Presumptive
      - Tiree Hall Solo's High Lite
    - Banchory Pamper of Maywood
      - CH.Philidove Heir Presumptive
      - CH.Banchory Blueberry Muffin

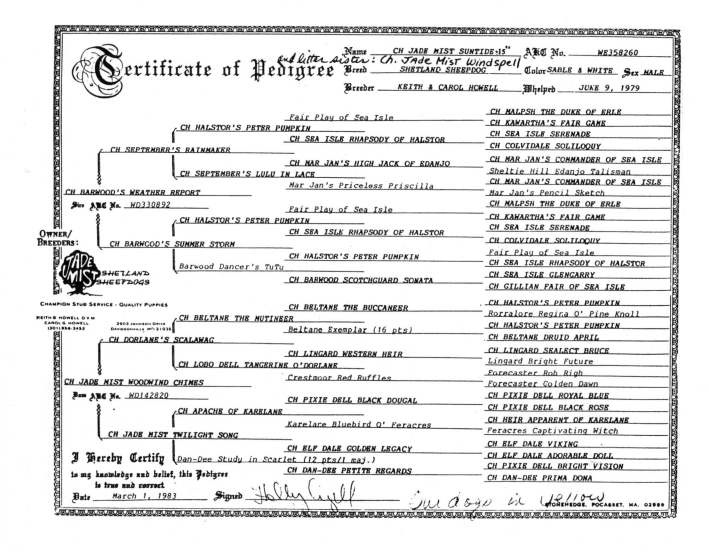

Certificate of Pedigree

Name: CH JADE MIST SUNTIDE 15" *and litter sister: Ch. Jade Mist Windspell* AKC No. WE358260

Breed SHETLAND SHEEPDOG   Color SABLE & WHITE   Sex MALE

Breeder KEITH & CAROL HOWELL   Whelped JUNE 9, 1979

Owner/Breeders:

JADE MIST SHETLAND SHEEPDOGS

CHAMPION STUD SERVICE · QUALITY PUPPIES

KEITH B HOWELL DVM
CAROL G HOWELL
(301) 956-3452
2903 JOHNSON DRIVE
DAVIDSONVILLE MD 21035

- CH BARWOOD'S WEATHER REPORT (Sire AKC No. WD330892)
  - CH SEPTEMBER'S RAINMAKER
    - CH HALSTOR'S PETER PUMPKIN
      - Fair Play of Sea Isle
        - CH MALPSH THE DUKE OF ERLE
        - CH KAWARTHA'S FAIR GAME
      - CH SEA ISLE RHAPSODY OF HALSTOR
        - CH SEA ISLE SERENADE
        - CH COLVIDALE SOLILOQUY
    - CH SEPTEMBER'S LULU IN LACE
      - CH MAR JAN'S HIGH JACK OF EDANJO
        - CH MAR JAN'S COMMANDER OF SEA ISLE
        - Sheltie Hill Edanjo Talisman
      - Mar Jan's Priceless Priscilla
        - CH MAR JAN'S COMMANDER OF SEA ISLE
        - Mar Jan's Pencil Sketch
  - CH BARWOOD'S SUMMER STORM
    - CH HALSTOR'S PETER PUMPKIN
      - Fair Play of Sea Isle
        - CH MALPSH THE DUKE OF ERLE
        - CH KAWARTHA'S FAIR GAME
      - CH SEA ISLE RHAPSODY OF HALSTOR
        - CH SEA ISLE SERENADE
        - CH COLVIDALE SOLILOQUY
    - Barwood Dancer's TuTu
      - CH HALSTOR'S PETER PUMPKIN
        - Fair Play of Sea Isle
        - CH SEA ISLE RHAPSODY OF HALSTOR
      - CH BARWOOD SCOTCHGUARD SONATA
        - CH SEA ISLE GLENGARRY
        - CH GILLIAN FAIR OF SEA ISLE
- CH JADE MIST WOODWIND CHIMES (Dam AKC No. WD142820)
  - CH DORLANE'S SCALAWAG
    - CH BELTANE THE MUTINEER
      - CH BELTANE THE BUCCANEER
        - CH HALSTOR'S PETER PUMPKIN
        - Rorralore Regina O' Pine Knoll
      - Beltane Exemplar (16 pts)
        - CH HALSTOR'S PETER PUMPKIN
        - CH BELTANE DRUID APRIL
    - CH LOBO DELL TANGERINE O'DORLANE
      - CH LINGARD WESTERN HEIR
        - CH LINGARD SEALECT BRUCE
        - Lingard Bright Future
      - Crestmoor Red Ruffles
        - Forecaster Rob Righ
        - Forecaster Colden Dawn
  - CH JADE MIST TWILIGHT SONG
    - CH APACHE OF KARELANE
      - CH PIXIE DELL BLACK DOUGAL
        - CH PIXIE DELL ROYAL BLUE
        - CH PIXIE DELL BLACK ROSE
      - Karelane Bluebird O' Feracres
        - CH HEIR APPARENT OF KARELANE
        - Feracres Captivating Witch
    - Dan-Dee Study in Scarlet (12 pts/1 maj.)
      - CH ELF DALE GOLDEN LEGACY
        - CH ELF DALE VIKING
        - CH ELF DALE ADORABLE DOLL
      - CH DAN-DEE PETITE REGARDS
        - CH PIXIE DELL BRIGHT VISION
        - CH DAN-DEE PRIMA DONA

I Hereby Certify to my knowledge and belief, this Pedigree is true and correct.

Date March 1, 1983   Signed _____

STONEHEDGE, POCASSET, MA. 02559

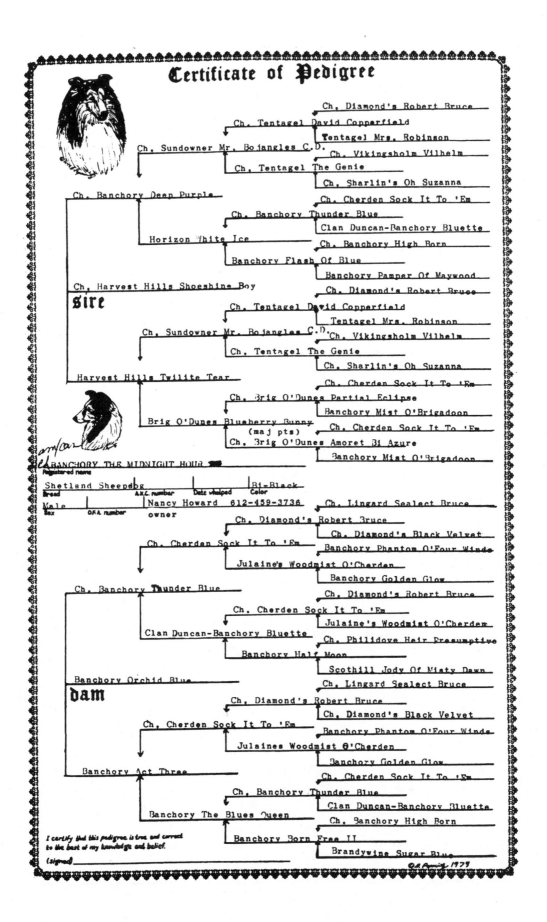

Certificate of Pedigree

Ch. Diamond's Robert Bruce

Ch. Tentagel David Copperfield

Tentagel Mrs. Robinson

Ch. Sundowner Mr. Bojangles C.D.

Ch. Vikingsholm Vilhelm

Ch. Tentagel The Genie

Ch. Sharlin's Oh Suzanna

Ch. Banchory Deep Purple

Ch. Cherden Sock It To 'Em

Ch. Banchory Thunder Blue

Clan Duncan-Banchory Bluette

Horizon White Ice

Ch. Banchory High Born

Banchory Flash Of Blue

Banchory Pamper Of Maywood

Ch. Harvest Hills Shoeshine Boy

Ch. Diamond's Robert Bruce

sire

Ch. Tentagel David Copperfield

Tentagel Mrs. Robinson

Ch. Sundowner Mr. Bojangles C.D.

Ch. Vikingsholm Vilhelm

Ch. Tentagel The Genie

Ch. Sharlin's Oh Suzanna

Harvest Hills Twilite Tear

Ch. Cherden Sock It To 'Em

Ch. Brig O'Dunes Partial Eclipse

Banchory Mist O'Brigadoon

Brig O'Dunes Blueberry Bunny

(maj pts)

Ch. Cherden Sock It To 'Em

Ch. Brig O'Dunes Amoret Bi Azure

Banchory Mist O'Brigadoon

Registered name CH. BANCHORY THE MIDNIGHT HOUR

Breed Shetland Sheepdog | **Color** Bi-Black

Sex Male | **A.K.C. number** | **Date whelped** | **O.F.A. number**

owner Nancy Howard 612-459-3736

Ch. Lingard Sealect Bruce

Ch. Diamond's Robert Bruce

Ch. Diamond's Black Velvet

Ch. Cherden Sock It To 'Em

Banchory Phantom O'Four Winds

Julaine's Woodmist O'Cherden

Banchory Golden Glow

Ch. Banchory Thunder Blue

Ch. Diamond's Robert Bruce

Ch. Cherden Sock It To 'Em

Julaine's Woodmist O'Cherden

Clan Duncan-Banchory Bluette

Ch. Philidove Heir Presumptive

Banchory Half Moon

Scothill Jody Of Misty Dawn

Banchory Orchid Blue

Ch. Lingard Sealect Bruce

dam

Ch. Diamond's Robert Bruce

Ch. Diamond's Black Velvet

Ch. Cherden Sock It To 'Em

Banchory Phantom O'Four Winds

Julaines Woodmist O'Cherden

Banchory Golden Glow

Banchory Act Three

Ch. Cherden Sock It To 'Em

Ch. Banchory Thunder Blue

Clan Duncan-Banchory Bluette

Banchory The Blues Queen

Ch. Banchory High Born

Banchory Born Free II

Brandywine Sugar Blue

I certify that this pedigree is true and correct
to the best of my knowledge and belief.

(signed) _____

O.A. Armig 1979

INDIVIDUAL REG. NO.

Tobyy

CALL NAME

Certified Pedigree

LITTER REG. NO.

A.K.C.

REGISTERED WITH

CH. BELLE MOUNT WEE TOBIAS

REGISTERED NAME OF DOG

BREED SHETLAND SHEEPDOG **DATE WHELPED** FEBRUARY 8, 1976 **SEX** MALE

BREEDER ALICE A. BURHANS **ADDRESS** R.D. 3, Box 104-B, TROY, NEW YORK 12180 Tel. 518-279-3831

OWNER **ADDRESS**

GENERAL DESCRIPTION SABLE AND WHITE

SIRE

AM/CAN. CH. ASTOLAT GALAXY, C.D.

REG. NO. WB-759849

- Ch. Halstor's Peter Pumpkin
  - Fair Play of Sea Isle
    - Ch. Malpsh The Duke of Erle
      - Ch. Sea Isle Serenade
      - Sea Isle Dusky Belle
    - Ch. Kawartha's Fair Game
      - Ch. Sheltieland Kiltie O'Sea Isle
      - Ch. Kawartha's Sabrina Fair
  - Ch. Sea Isle Rhapsody of Halstor
    - Ch. Sea Isle Serenade
      - Am/CanCh. Nashcrest Golden Note
      - Ch. Sea Isle Serenata
    - Ch. Colvidale Soliloquy
      - Ch. Sheltiland Kiltie O'Sea Isle
      - Ch. Lochlevin's Reverie

- Ch. Astolat Stardust
  - Int. Ch. Astolat Gold Award, Int. C.D.
    - Ch. Astolat Golden Symbol
      - Ch. Frigate's Emblem of Astolat
      - Astolat Marigold
    - Scotswold Gretta
      - Ch. Bykenhall St. Andrew
      - Ch. Timberidge Scarlet Phantasy
  - Ch. Piper's Pride of Astolat
    - Ch. Gay Piper O'Pages Hill
      - Ch. Magnet O'Pages Hill
      - Dark Blossom O'Pages Hill
    - Astolat Symbol's Primrose
      - Ch. Astolat Golden Symbol
      - Astolat Emblem of Hope

DAM

BELLE MOUNT WEE LENA, C.D.

REG. NO. WR249929

- Fair Play of Sea Isle
  - Ch. Malpsh The Duke of Erle
    - Ch. Sea Isle Serenade
      - Am/Can. Ch. Nashcrest Golden Note
      - Ch. Sea Isle Serenata
    - Sea Isle Dusky Belle
      - Ch. Pixie Dell Bright Vision
      - Bagaduce Hannah of Sea Isle
  - Ch. Kawartha's Fair Game
    - Ch. Sheltieland Kiltie O'Sea Isle
      - Ch. Bogota Blaze
      - Ch. Sheltieland Peg O'The Pict
    - Ch. Kawartha's Sabrina Fair
      - Ch. Sheltieland Kiltie O'Sea Isle
      - Miss Ruffles of Oak-Lawn

- Belle Mount Wee Gypsy, C.D.
  - Kylo Clowning Wee Macgregor
    - Ch. Sea Isle Cadenza
      - Am/Can. Ch. Nashcrest Golden Note
      - Ch. Sea Isle Serenata
    - Geronimo Diamond Lass of Kylo
      - Ch. Geronimo Son Key
      - Ch. Geronimo Diamond Lil
  - Dunderraw's Zulu Queen
    - Ch. Sheltieland Little Jack Frost
      - Feracres Blueberry Pie
      - Sheltieland Abalone O'Sea Isle
    - Fraser's Pocketsize
      - Runlee Post Patrol
      - Runlee Pinther

I HEREBY CERTIFY THAT THIS PEDIGREE IS TRUE AND CORRECT
TO THE BEST OF MY KNOWLEDGE AND BELIEF

SIGNED _____

DATE _____, 19_____

470

INDIVIDUAL REG. NO.
Cookie-bush
CALL NAME

Certified Pedigree

WM608033
LITTER REG. NO.
A.K.C.
REGISTERED WITH

BELLE MOUNT WEE DUKE OF ORANGE
REGISTERED NAME OF DOG

BREED SHETLAND SHEEPDOG   DATE WHELPED MAY 20, 1979   SEX **male**

BREEDER Alice A. Burhans   ADDRESS RD 3, Box 104-B, Troy, New York 12180
   518-279-3831
OWNER   "   "   "   ADDRESS

GENERAL DESCRIPTION   sable and white

SIRE

BELLE MOUNT WEE SESAME
(5 pts.)
REG. NO. WD171149

- Belle Mount Wee Gourmet (ptd)
  - CH. HALSTOR'S PETER PUMPKIN
    - Fair Play of Sea Isle
      - CH. MALPSH THE DUKE OF ERLE
      - CH. KAWARTHA'S FAIR GAME
    - CH. SEA ISLE RHAPSODY OF HALSTOR
      - CH. SEA ISLE SERENADE
      - CH. COLVIDALE SOLILOQUY
  - Belle Mount Wee Jessie
    - CH. BELTANE THE BUCCANEER
      - CH. HALSTOR'S PETER PUMPKIN
      - Rorralore Regina O'Pine Knoll
    - BELLE MOUNT WEE LENA, C.D. (5 pts.)
      - Fair Play of Sea Isle
      - BELLE MOUNT WEE GYPSY, CD
- Belle Mount Wee Buccalena (pts.)
  - CH. BELTANE THE BUCCANEER
    - CH. HALSTOR'S PETER PUMPKIN
      - Fair Play of Sea Isle
      - CH. SEA ISLE RHAPSODY OF HALSTOR
    - Rorralore Regina O'Pine Knoll
      - CH. MALPSH GREAT SCOTT
      - CH. RORRALORE CURSE KATE
  - BELLE MOUNT WEE LENA, C.D. (5 pts.)
    - Fair Play of Sea Isle
      - CH. MALPSH THE DUKE OF ERLE
      - CH. KAWARTHA'S FAIR GAME
    - BELLE MOUNT WEE GYPSY, CD
      - Kylo Clowning Wee Macgregor
      - Dunderraw's Zulu Queen

DAM

LAKEHILL WEE RACHEL, C.D. (5 pts)
REG. NO. WG496084

- CH. CALCURT LUKE
  - CH. HALSTOR'S PETER PUMPKIN
    - Fair Play of Sea Isle
      - CH. MALPSH THE DUKE OF ERLE
      - CH. KAWARTHA'S FAIR GAME
    - CH. SEA ISLE RHAPSODY OF HALSTOR
      - CH. SEA ISLE SERENADE
      - CH. COLVIDALE SOLILOQUY
  - Calcurt Black Angie
    - Black Laird of Calcurt
      - Silver Talisman of Pocono
      - CH. LINGARD BLUE HEATHER
    - Calcurt Molly Fitchett
      - AM/CAN. CH. TOPO GIGIO
      - Jomar's Happy Miss Tam
- Lakehill Special Request
  - CH. BLUE QUEST OF POCONO
    - CH. LARKSPUR'S FINALIST OF POCONO
      - CH. BILBODOT BLUE FLAG OF POCONO
      - CH. LARKSPUR OF POCONO
    - Blue Silhouette of Pocono
      - CH. DEMPSAY'S BLUE BILL
      - CH. BLUE TREASURE OF POCONO
  - Kiloren Moonbeam
    - CH. KILOREN NIGHTSTORM O'ALANDIE
      - CH. SHELT-E-AIN REFLECTION O' Knight
      - Crazy Quilt of Pocono
    - Kiloren Larkspur's Memory
      - CH. KILOREN NIGHT APACHE
      - Crazy Quilt of Pocono

I HEREBY CERTIFY THAT THIS PEDIGREE IS TRUE AND CORRECT
TO THE BEST OF MY KNOWLEDGE AND BELIEF

SIGNED *Alice A. Burhans*
DATE _____, 19___

471

Certified Pedigree

INDIVIDUAL REG. NO.	REGISTERED NAME OF DOG	LITTER REG. NO.
Hyacinth	BELLE MOUNT WEE HYACINTH	**AKC**
CALL NAME		REGISTERED WITH

BREED **SHETLAND SHEEPDOG** DATE WHELPED **MARCH 28, 1980** SEX **female**

BREEDER **Alice A. Burhans** ADDRESS **RD 3, Box 104-B, Troy, N.Y. 12180**

OWNER **Breeder** ADDRESS **(518)279-3831**

GENERAL DESCRIPTION **BLUE MERLE, WHITE AND TAN**

SIRE

CH. CHENTERRA THUNDERATION
REG. NO. WC-647,582

Chenterra Beauregard C.D.

- CH. TENTAGEL MR. PRESIDENT C.D.X.
  - CH. DIAMOND'S REDBUD
    - CH. SEA ISLE SERENADE
    - CH. DIAMOND'S BLACK VELVET
  - CH. SHARLINS PENNY BRITE
    - CH. PIXIE DELL BRIGHT VISION
    - CH. SHARLINS TEMPTING TERESSA
- Tentagel The Cheer Leader
  - CH. HALSTOR'S PETER PUMPKIN
    - Fair Play of Sea Isle
    - CH. SEA ISLE RHAPSODY OF HALSTOR
  - Tambrae Cinnamon Toast
    - CH. BROWNE ACRES PRINCE CONSORT
    - Browne Acres Back Talk

Chenterra Commotion

- Lanlee's Chenterra Citation
  - CH. HALSTOR'S PETER PUMPKIN
    - Fair Play of Sea Isle
    - CH. SEA ISLE RHAPSODY OF HALSTOR
  - Aron-Kae Song of Spring
    - CH. MAR JAN'S MUSIC MAKER O' WALJON
    - CH. SPARKLING SHERRY OF ARON KAE
- Tentagel The Cheer Leader
  - CH. HALSTOR'S PETER PUMPKIN
    - Fair Play of Sea Isle
    - CH. SEA ISLE RHAPSODY OF HALSTOR
  - Tambrae Cinnamon Toast
    - CH. BROWNE ACRES PRINCE CONSORT
    - Browne Acres Back Talk

BELLE MOUNT SHELTIES

Shetland Sheepdogs - Bred to the Standard

DAM

BELLE MOUNT WEE ELISABETH (6 pts)
REG. NO. WD103113

CH. PHILIDOVE BENEVOLENT ANTHONY

- AM/CAN.CH. BANCHORY HIGH BORN
  - CH. PHILIDOVE HEIR PRESUMPTIVE
    - CH. HEIR APPARENT OF KARELANE
    - Wansor's Flashy Flame
  - Tiree Hall Solo's High Lite
    - CH. BADGERTON WIT O'MEADOW RIDGE
    - CH. LOCHINDAL SOLO OF TIREE HALL
- CH. PHILIDOVE CARMYLIE IN A MIST
  - CH. PHILIDOVE HEIR PRESUMPTIVE
    - CH. HEIR APPARENT OF KARELANE
    - Wansor's Flashy Flame
  - Banchory Bi Jingo of Carmylie
    - CH. THISTLEROSE ARCWOOD ALADDIN
    - Lodgewood Queen of Banchory

LAKEHILL WEE RACHEL, C.D. (5 pts)

- CH. CALCURT LUKE
  - CH. HALSTOR'S PETER PUMPKIN
    - Fair Play of Sea Isle
    - CH. SEA ISLE RHAPSODY OF HALSTOR
  - Calcurt Black Angie
    - Black Laird of Calcurt
    - Calcurt Molly Fitchett
- Lakehill Special Request
  - CH. BLUE QUEST OF POCONO
    - CH. LARKSPUR'S FINALIST OF POCONO
    - Blue Silhouette of Pocono
  - Kiloren Moonbeam
    - CH. KILOREN NIGHTSTORM O'ALANDIE
    - Kiloren Larkspur's Memory

I HEREBY CERTIFY THAT THIS PEDIGREE IS TRUE AND CORRECT TO THE BEST OF MY KNOWLEDGE AND BELIEF

SIGNED _Alice A. Burhans_

DATE _____ , 19_____

Certified Pedigree

WF078133
INDIVIDUAL REG. NO.
Eloise
CALL NAME

WM796553
LITTER REG. NO.
AKC
REGISTERED WITH

REGISTERED NAME OF DOG
BELLE MOUNT WEE ELOISE

BREED **SHETLAND SHEEPDOG**　　DATE WHELPED **Julyy 25 1981**　　SEX **female**

BREEDER **ALICE A. BURHANS**　　ADDRESS **R.D. 3, BOX 104-B, TROY, N.Y. 12180**

OWNER **breeder**　　ADDRESS

GENERAL DESCRIPTION **Blue merle, white and tan**

SIRE

CH. PIXIE DELL BAIRN OF CLUARON
REG. NO. **WC127140**

- Dawn's Kwik Silver O'Marble Hall
  - CH.KILOREN'S NIGHTSTORM O'ALANDIE
  - Gilshaw Dawn Adventure
- O'Melren Blue Sabre
  - CH.THE LONE RANGER OF POCONO
  - Silver Gift of Pocono
- Hallmark's Black Legacy
- Black Sabre of Pocono
  - Moribrook's Voyager
    - CH.MORIBROOK'S GOLDEN NOTION
    - CH.MORIBROOKE'S CUTE COOKIE
  - Blue Creek's Michelle of Pocono
    - Alfran's Sandman Replica
    - Ken Sta Cherry Girl
  - Glynell's Jacque Kay

- CH.PIXIE DELL ROYAL BLUE
  - CH.DARK STREAM O'PAGES HILL
  - CH.KATIE-J'S BLUE DAWN OF POCONO
- CH.PIXIE DELL BLACK DOUGAL
  - CH.PIXIE DELL MR. MACDUFF
  - Pixie Dell Firebird
- CH.PIXIE DELL BLACK ROSE
- CH. PIXIE DELL BLUE THISTLE
  - CH. PIXIE DELL ROYAL BLUE
    - CH. DARK STREAM O'PAGES HILL
    - CH.KATIE-J'S BLUE DAWN OF POCONO
  - Pixie Dell Blue Heather
    - CH.PIXIE DELL MR. MACDUFF
    - CH. PIXIE DELL BLACK TULIP
  - Pixie Dell Black Orchid

BELLE MOUNT SHELTIES
Shetland Sheepdogs - Bred to the Standard

DAM

BELLE MOUNT WEE HYACINTH
REG. NO. **WE895491**

- CH.CHENTERRA THUNDERATION
  - Chenterra Beauregard C.D.
    - CH.TENTAGEL MR. PRESIDENT C.D.X.
      - CH. DIAMOND'S REDBUD
      - CH.DIAMOND'S BLACK VELVET
    - Tentagel The Cheer Leader
      - CH.HALSTOR'S PETER PUMPKIN
      - Tambrae Cinnamon Toast
  - Lanlee's Chenterra Citation
    - CH.HALSTOR'S PETER PUMPKIN
    - Aron-Kae Song of Spring
  - Chenterra Commotion
    - Tentagel The Cheer Leader
      - CH.HALSTOR'S PETER PUMPKIN
      - Tambrae Cinnamon Toast

- AM/CAN.CH. BANCHORY HIGH BORN
  - CH.PHILIDOVE HEIR PRESUMPTIVE
  - Tiree Hall Solo's High Lite
- CH.PHILIDOVE BENEVOLENT ANTHONY
  - CH.PHILIDOVE CARMYLIE IN A MIST
    - CH.PHILIDOVE BENEVOLENT ANTHONY
    - Banchory Bi Jingo of Carmylie
- BELLE MOUNT WEE ELISABETH (6 pts.)
  - CH. CALCURT LUKE
    - CH. HALSTOR'S PETER PUMPKIN
    - Calcurt Black Angie
  - LAKEHILL WEE RACHEL, C.D. (5 pts.)
    - Int.CH.BLUE QUEST OF POCONO
    - Kiloren Moonbeam
  - Lakehill Special Request

I HEREBY CERTIFY THAT THIS PEDIGREE IS TRUE AND CORRECT
TO THE BEST OF MY KNOWLEDGE AND BELIEF

SIGNED _Alice A. Burhans_

DATE _____, 19____

88K—Rev. 6-1-77

473

Certified Pedigree

WD-033560
INDIVIDUAL REG. NO.

Memory
CALL NAME

BranGay Memory Maker
REGISTERED NAME OF DOG

DATE WHELPED Sept. 5, 1974

SEX Female

LITTER REG. NO.

AKC
REGISTERED WITH

BREED _____ ADDRESS _____

BREEDER _____ ADDRESS _____

OWNER _____ ADDRESS _____

GENERAL DESCRIPTION _____

SIRE

CH. Lingard Sealect Bruce

INT/ CH. Nashcrest Golden Note
— CH. Prince George O'Page's Hill
— — CH. Kalandar Prince O'Page's Hill
— — CH. Timberidge Temptress
— Nashcrest Rhythm
— — Shelt-E-Ain Little Sir Eco
— — Shelt-E-Ain Pirouette

Timberidge Sandstorm
— Geronimo Prince Royal
— — Geronimo Prince Charming
— — Silversheen Miss Priss
— Sea Isle Singing Sands
— — CH. Sea Isle Cadenza
— — Sea Isle Eastertide

Lingard Golden Idol (pt.)

REG. NO. ....

CH. Lingard Sealect Bruce
INT/ CH. Nashcrest Golden Note
— — CH. Prince George O'Page's Hill
— — Nashcrest Rhythm
— Timberidge Sandstorm
— — Geronimo Prince Royal
— — Sea Isle Singing Sands

Lingard Gold Dust
— CH. Sea Isle Serenade
— — INT/ CH. Nashcrest Golden Note
— — CH. Sea Isle Serenata
— Burnbrae Gold Echo O'Timewol
— Badgerton Whiz O'Meadow Ridge
— — CH. Katie-J's Ronny
— — CH. Badgerton Pantomine Patsy

WAYNE THE ALL-PRO LINE

DAM

CH. Cherden Light My Fire

CH. Diamond's Robert Bruce
— CH. Lingard Sealect Bruce
— — INT/ CH. Nashcrest Golden Note
— — Timberidge Sandstorm
— CH. Diamond's Black Velvet
— — CH. Tess's Trump Card of Wadmalaw
— — CH. Diamond's Lady Goldmont

Julaines Woodmist O'Cherden
— Banchory Phantom O'Four Winds
— — Catamount Excalibur
— — Banchory Midnight Mist
— Banchory Golden Glow
— — CH. Banchory Royal Heritage, C.D
— — CH. Banchory Mae West

BranGay Georgie Girl
REG. NO WC-32 9256
Died at 2 hours.
SISTER of CH. BranGay ticket

Esthof Copper Merchant C.D.
— CH. Elf Dale Mr. Wonderful
— — CH. Elf Dale Viking
— — Merry Dale
— Faharaby Dark Donna
— — CH. Faharaby Replica of Don Juan
— — Lingard Bluebell

Esthof Misty Morn (pts.)
— Sand Bag
— — Elf Dale Mity Mite
— — Elf Dale Dinah Mite
REPEAT of Mr. Wonderful
— Miss Vickey Lynn
— Tijuana Lola
— — CH. Robrovin The Ginger Bread Boy
SISTER of (CH. Elf Dale Good Lookin')
— — Sheladah's Velvet Dream
SIRE: CH. Thistlrose Hrewood Aladdin

I HEREBY CERTIFY THAT THIS PEDIGREE IS TRUE AND CORRECT
TO THE BEST OF MY KNOWLEDGE AND BELIEF

SIGNED Gayle Pado

DATE _____ , 19 ___

86K—Rev. 6-1-77

Certified Pedigree

INDIVIDUAL REG. NO. _Jessica + Sugar_

LITTER REG. NO.

CALL NAME _Jessica + Sugar_

REGISTERED NAME OF DOG _CH. BranBay Jessica + CH. BranGay Sweet Vision_

REGISTERED WITH

BREED _Shetland Sheepdog_ DATE WHELPED SEX _Female_

BREEDER _Brandol + Gayle Eads_ ADDRESS _1105 W. Grove St. Rialto, Calif. 92376_

(7N) 820-1419

OWNER ADDRESS

GENERAL DESCRIPTION

SIRE

CH. Halstor's Peter Pumpkin

CH. Scotspride Legionaire

REG. NO. ....

- Fair Play of Sea Isle
  - CH. Malosh The Duke of Erle
    - CH. Sea Isle Serenade
    - Sea Isle Dusky Bell
  - CH. Kawartha's Fair Game
    - CH. Sheltieland Kiltie O'Sea Isle
    - CH. Kawarth's Sabrina Fair
- CH. Sea Isle Rhapsody of Halstor
  - CH. Sea Isle Serenade
    - CH. Nashcrest Golden Note
    - CH. Sea Isl Serenata
  - CH. Colvidale Soliloquy
    - CH. Sheltieland Kiltie O'Sea Isle
    - CH. Lochelven's Reverie
- Deb's Little Jo O'Rosamba
  - CH. Hallydell Maestro Shelby, C.D.X.
    - CH. Lindhurst Shenandoah
      - CH. Sea Isle Sound O'Victory
      - Glenelm Sparkle
    - Lincrest Holiday Sonata, C.D.
      - CH. Pixie Dell Bright Vision
      - Len Dee Miss Sassy
  - Metco's Cheerleader
    - Aron Kae Band Leader
      - CH. Mar Jan Music Maker
      - CH. Mar Jan Rorralor Riddle
    - Pats Echo Victoria
      - CH. Scotchguard Sea Chantey
      - Pat Golden Shelli

WAYNE THE ALL-PRO LINE

DAM

CH. Cheenden Light My Fire

CH. BranGay Cricket

REG. NO. ....

- CH. Diamond's Robert Bruce
  - CH. Lingard Senlect Bruce
    - INT'L CH. Nachcrest Golden Note
    - Timberidge Sandstorm
  - CH. Diamond's Black Velvet
    - CH. Tess's Trump Card of Wadmalaw
    - CH. Diamond's Lady Goldmont
- Julaines Woodmist D'Cheenden
  - Banchory Phantom D'Four Winds
    - Catamount Excalibur
    - Banchory Midnight Mist
  - Banchory Golden Glow
    - CH. Banchory Royal Heritage, C.D.
    - CH. Banchory Mae West
- Esthef Copper Merchant, C.D.
  - CH. Elf Dale Mr. Wonderful
    - CH. Elf Dale Viking
    - Merry Dale
  - Faharaby Dark Donna
    - CH. Faharaby Replica of Don Juan
    - Lingard Bluebell
- Esthef Misty Morn pts.
  - Sand Bag
    - Elf Dale Mity Mite
    - Elf Dale Dinah
  - Miss Vickey Lynn
    - Tijuana Lola
      - CH. Robrovin The Ginger Bread Boy
      - Sheladah's Velvet Dream

I HEREBY CERTIFY THAT THIS PEDIGREE IS TRUE AND CORRECT TO THE BEST OF MY KNOWLEDGE AND BELIEF

SIGNED _Gayle Eads_

DATE _June 14_ , 19 _85_

88K-Rev. 6-81

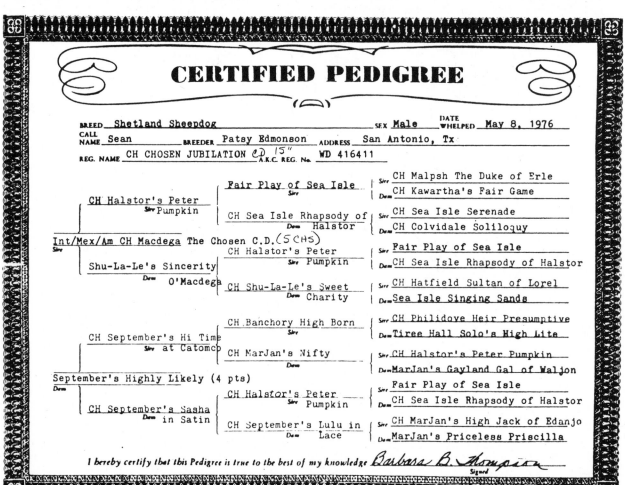

Certificate of Pedigree

Registered Name: Krock On Wood of Edlen
Kennel Name: Buddy
Sex: Male
Breed: Sheltie

A.K.C.R.R. No.
A.K.C. Litter No.
R.K.C.R.R. No.
C.K.C.R.R. No.
P.B.R.R. No.
Date of Birth:
Birthplace:
Breeder: Helen Scherer
Address: 7245 Sandy Lk Rd
City: Ravenna, OH 44266

GENERAL DESCRIPTION
Color and Marking: Sable & white
Weight:
Height at Shoulder: about 15½"
Temperament: Excellent
House-broken:

Grand Parents:

Sire: (1) Am.Can. Ch. Markris Red Baron of Edlen

Ch. Kerrylance Bossman CDX *Sire (3)*
Kerrylance Witacism *Dam (4)*

Dam: (2) Tiny Dian of Walnut Hall

Ch. Tiny Tuck of Walnut Hall *Sire (5)*
Tiny Amanda of Walnut Hall *Dam (6)*

Great Grand Parents:

Ch. Beach Cliff's Roc-Sycamore *Sire(7)*
Badgerton Your Ladyship *Dam (8)*
Badgerton Zem Zem CD *Sire (9)*
Ch. Starhaven's Wit of Kerrylance *Dam (10)*
Ch. Lingard Sealect Brucs *Sire (11)*
Elizabeth of Pocono (tri) *Dam (12)*
Ch. Tiny Toby of Walnut Hall *Sire (13)*
Tiny Judith of Walnut Hall *Dam (14)*

Great Great Grand Parents:

Ch. Roc-Sycamore Minute Man *Sire (15)*
Roc-Sycamore Bronze Gypsy *Dam (16)*
Ch. Badgerton Proud Prince *Sire (17)*
Katie-J's Princess Patti *Dam (18)*
Ch. Badgerton Proud Prince CD *Sire (19)*
Badgerton Sassy Sally *Dam (20)*
Ch. Starhaven's Banner CD *Sire (21)*
Starhaven's Proud Promise *Dam (22)*
Ch. Nashcrest Golden Note *Sire (23)*
Timberidge Sandstorm *Dam (24)*
Ch. Tiny Toby of Walnut Hall *Sire (25)*
Rojay's Starfire *Dam (26)*
Ch. Blue Heritage of Pocono *Sire (27)*
Tiny Leatha of Walnut Hall *Dam (28)*
Ch. Brown Acres Statesman *Sire (29)*
Tiny Leatha of Walnut Hall *Dam (30)* tri

I Hereby Certify that to the best of my knowledge and belief the above Pedigree is true and that all persons named above are of the same breed.

Signed this _____ day of _____, 19___
Address _____

CERTIFIED PEDIGREE

BREED: Shetland Sheepdog
SEX: Male
DATE WHELPED: May 8, 1976
CALL NAME: Sean
BREEDER: Patsy Edmonson
ADDRESS: San Antonio, Tx
REG. NAME: CH CHOSEN JUBILATION CD 15"
A.K.C. REG. No.: WD 416411

Int/Mex/Am CH Macdega The Chosen C.D. (5 CHS) *Sire*

- CH Halstor's Peter Pumpkin *Sire*
  - Fair Play of Sea Isle *Sire*
    - CH Malpsh The Duke of Erle *Sire*
    - CH Kawartha's Fair Game *Dam*
  - CH Sea Isle Rhapsody of Halstor *Dam*
    - CH Sea Isle Serenade *Sire*
    - CH Colvidale Soliloquy *Dam*
- Shu-La-Le's Sincerity O'Macdega *Dam*
  - CH Halstor's Peter Pumpkin *Sire*
    - Fair Play of Sea Isle *Sire*
    - CH Sea Isle Rhapsody of Halstor *Dam*
  - CH Shu-La-Le's Sweet Charity *Dam*
    - CH Hatfield Sultan of Lorel *Sire*
    - Sea Isle Singing Sands *Dam*

September's Highly Likely (4 pts) *Dam*

- CH September's Hi Time at Catomco *Sire*
  - CH Banchory High Born *Sire*
    - CH Philidove Heir Presumptive *Sire*
    - Tiree Hall Solo's High Lite *Dam*
  - CH MarJan's Nifty *Dam*
    - CH Halstor's Peter Pumpkin *Sire*
    - MarJan's Gayland Gal of Waljon *Dam*
- CH September's Sasha in Satin *Dam*
  - CH Halstor's Peter Pumpkin *Sire*
    - Fair Play of Sea Isle *Sire*
    - CH Sea Isle Rhapsody of Halstor *Dam*
  - CH September's Lulu in Lace *Dam*
    - CH MarJan's High Jack of Edanjo *Sire*
    - MarJan's Priceless Priscilla *Dam*

I hereby certify that this Pedigree is true to the best of my knowledge
Signed: Barbara B. Thompson

BARB & MARV ROSS
S-706 EVANSVL BOXE
EVANSVILLE, WYO.
88686

INDIVIDUAL REG. NO.

CALL NAME

Certified Pedigree

Sir Toby Happy Man
REGISTERED NAME OF DOG

WL 937586
LITTER REG. NO.

A. K. C.
REGISTERED WITH

BREED Shetland Sheepdog   DATE WHELPED April 10, 1972   SEX Male

BREEDER Marvin O. & Barbara L. Ross   ADDRESS Box 360, Evansville, Wyo. 82636

OWNER   ADDRESS

GENERAL DESCRIPTION Brown & White (Sable)

SIRE

Sir Sabestian's Little Toby C.D.
REG. NO. WB 416394

Sir Sabestian of Milord

- Ch.Thistlerose Milord
  - INT. Ch.Nashcrest Golden Note
    - Ch.Prince George O'Pag's Hill
    - Nashcrest Rhythm
  - Ch.Thistlerose Temple Belle
    - Ch.Geronimo Guardsman O'Norake
    - Honoretta of Lynwood
- Honey Maid of Silver Swan
  - Ch.Ronas Hill Eric The Red
    - Can.Ch.Ronas Hill Frolic
    - Can.Ch.Jewel of Ronas Hill
  - High Jinx Frolicking Night
    - High Jinx of Windy Knoll C.D.
    - Victoria's Bonnie Mactavish

Bevs Little Heidie

- High Jinx of Windy Knoll C.D.
  - CH.Thistlerose Dark Vindicator
    - Ch.The Lone Ranger of Pocono
    - Thistlerose Blue Belle
  - Cindi Lynn Snowpuff
    - Ch.Badgerton Alert Alec
    - Charvel's Golden Taffy
- Golden Contessa
  - Highland's Golden Rebel
    - Brown Acres Beauregard
    - Brown Acres Golden Girl
  - Richter's Ginger Flower
    - Tamoshanter Sabre Jet
    - Tamoshanter Dina

DAM

Ross's Happy Girl
REG. NO. WB 646515

Gra-John's Whiz Kid

- Ch.Gra-John's Country Gentleman
  - Ch.Gra-John's Little-G-Man
    - Ch.Gra-John's Little Sir Echo
    - Ch.Gra-John's Diamond Lill
  - Gra-John's Dark Angel
    - Darlington's Chuckles
    - Dixie Rose of Ronas Hill
- Ch.Gra-John's Diamond Lill
  - Ch.Gilmanor Three Cheers
    - Ch.Gilmanor Sugar Daddy
    - Astolat Liberty Belle
  - Ch.Gra-John's Little Tim Tam
    - Ch.Gilmanor Sugar Daddy
    - Tiny Herdsman's Lady Cricket 5Pts

Gra-John's Red Angel

- Ch.Gra-John's Little-G-Man
  - Ch.Gra-John's Little Sir Echo
    - Ch.Gilmanor Sugar Daddy
    - Tiny Herdsman's Lady Cricket
  - Ch.Gra-John's Diamond Lill
    - Ch.Gilmanor Three Cheers
    - Ch.Gra-John's Little Tim Tam
- Gra-John's Dark Angel
  - Darlington's Chuckles
    - Int.Ch. Blue Quest of Pocono
    - Int.Ch.Dixie Charmer of Ronas Hill
  - Dixie Rose of Ronas Hill
    - Peter of Ronas Hill
    - Larkspur of Ronas Hill

I HEREBY CERTIFY THAT THIS PEDIGREE IS TRUE AND CORRECT
TO THE BEST OF MY KNOWLEDGE AND BELIEF

SIGNED _____

DATE _____ 19____

477

Certified Pedigree of

HAPPY GLEN'S STARTING STONE
REGISTERED NAME & NO.

BREED __SHETLAND SHEEPDOG__   DATE WHELPED __FEB. 17, 1978__   SEX __MALE__

BREEDER __BARBARA & MARVIN ROSS__ ADDRESS __Box 13-1A EVANSVILLE, WY   82636__

OWNER __Susan Ashridge & Marvin Ross__ ADDRESS __Box 8005" Shirley Basin WY 82615__   CALL NAME __"STREAK"__

GENERAL DESCRIPTION __Mahoganey Sable & White (Tri-Factore)__

SIRE AM/CAN BER

- CH HALSTOR'S PETER PUMPKIN
  - FAIR PLAY OF SEA ISLE
    - CH MALPSH THE DUKE OF EARL
      - CH SEA ISLE SERENADE
      - SEA ISLE DUSKY BELLE
    - CH KAWARTHA'S FAIR GAME
      - CH SHELTIELAND KILTIE O'SEA ISLE
      - CH KAWARTHA'S SABRINA FAIR
  - CH. SEA ISLE RHAPSODY OF HALSTOR AM/CAN BER
    - CH SEA ISLE SERENADE
      - INT. CH NASHCREST BOLDEN NOTE
      - CH SEA ISLE SERENATA
    - CH. COLVIDALE SOLILOQUY
      - CH SHELTIELAND KILTIE O'SEA ISLE
      - CH LOCHLEVEN'S REVERIE

- CH BANCHORY THE CORNERSTONE C.D.
  - REG. NO................
  - CH BANCHORY HIGH BORN
    - CH PHILIDOVE HEIR PRESUMPTIVE
      - CH HEIR APPARENT OF KARE LANE
      - WANSOR'S FLASHY FLAME
    - TIREE HALL'S SOLO HIGH LITE
      - CH BADGERTON WIT O'MEADOW RIDGE
      - CH LOCHINDAAL SOLO OF TIREE HALL
  - BANCHORY HIGH GLOW
    - CH BANCHORY ROYAL HERITAGE
      - CH THISTLROSE ARLWOOD ALADIN
      - BANCHORY BIT OF GOLD
    - BANCHORY ALL-A-GLOW
      - BRIAR WOOD'S BELL'S-A-RINGING
        - AM/CAN. CH MALPSH GREAT SCOTT
        - SEA ISLE DUSKY BELLE

DAM

- AM/CAN CH ILEMIST IMPOSSIBLE DREAM C.D.X.
  - CH. HALSTOR'S PETER PUMPKIN AM/CAN BER
    - FAIR PLAY OF SEA ISLE
      - CH. MALPSH DUKE OF ERLE
      - CH KAWARTHA'S FAIR GAME
    - CH SEA ISLE RHAPSODY OF HALSTOR
      - CH SEA ISLE SERENADE
      - CH COLVIDALE SOLILOQUY
  - AM/CAN CH. LINDHURST CHRISTMAS CAROL
    - CH LINDHURST TRADEMARK
      - CH NORALEE HARVESTOR OF WALTON
      - CH LINDHURST SARABANDE
    - CH LINDHURST LOVELY LULLABY
      - CH HARLINE'S GOLDEN BOY
      - LOCHELVEN'S SOLILOQUY

- SHANNASY FLICKER OF FLAME C.D. (8 PT.)
  - REG. NO.............
  - CH KEN-ROB'S PARTNERS
    - CH SEA ISLE SERENADE
      - INT. CH NASHCREST GOLDEN NOTE
      - CH SEA ISLE SERENATA
    - CH STYLISH MISS OF HATFIELD
      - INT. CH NASHCREST GOLDEN NOTE
      - CH BONNIE LASS OF HATFIELD
  - SHANNASY I'M SOMEBODY
    - CH SEA ISLE SERENADE
      - INT. CH. NASHCREST GOLDEN NOTE
      - CH SEA ISLE SERENATA
    - DIAMOND'S GOLDEN DAWN
      - CH DIAMOND'S BLACK VELVET
        - CH. TESS'S TRUMP CARD OF WADMALAW
        - CH DIAMOND'S LADY GOLDMONT

I HEREBY CERTIFY THAT THIS PEDIGREE IS TRUE AND CORRECT
TO THE BEST OF MY KNOWLEDGE AND BELIEF.

SIGNED __Barbara Ross__

DATE __Feb 17__ 19 __78__

Certified Pedigree

HAPPY GLEN PRESENTS

WE889505

INDIVIDUAL REG. NO.

CALL NAME **BOY**

REGISTERED NAME OF DOG **HAPPY GLEN'S ROYAL DREAM**

BREED **SHETLAND SHEEPDOGS** DATE WHELPED **FEB 19 1981**

OWNER **BARBARA ROSS & MARVIN O ROSS**

ADDRESS **S-702 EV. RT. BOX 2, EVANSVILLE, WYO. 82636 (307) 237-7017**

GENERAL DESCRIPTION **SABLE & WHITE**   SEX **MALE**

SIRE
CH WINDHOVER SWEET MUSIC MAN
REG. NO. ....

- BANCHORY REFLECTION
  - CH BANCHORY HIGH BORN
    - CH PHILADOVE HEIR PRESUMPTIVE
      - CH HEIR APPARENT OF KARELANE
      - WANSOR'S FLASY FLAME
    - TIREE HALL SOLO'S HIGH LITE
      - CH BADGERTON WIT'O MEADOW RIDGE
      - CH LOCHINDAEL SOLO OF TIREE HALL
  - BANCHORY HIGH GLOW
    - CH BANCHORY HIGH BORN
      - CH PHILADOVE HEIR PRESUMPTIVE
      - TIREE HALL SOLO'S HIGHT-LITE
    - BANCHORY ALL-A-GLOW
      - CH BANCHORY ROYAL HERITAGE C.D
      - BRIAWOOD BELLS-A-RINGING
- WINDHOVER AFTERNOON DELIGHT 14 pt.
  - CH HALSTOR'S PETER PUMKIN
    - FAIR PLAY OF SEA ISLE
      - CH MALPSH THE DUKE OF ERLE
      - CH KAWARTHA'S FAIR GAME
    - CH SEA ISLE RHAPSODY OF HALSTOR
      - CH SEA ISLE SERENADE
      - CH COLVIDALE SOLILOQUY
  - CRYSTLBROOK WINDHOVER ZELDA
    - CH HALSTOR'S PETER PUMPKIN
      - FAIR PLAY OF SEA ISLE
      - CH SEA ISLE RHAPSODY OF HALSTOR
    - TOMAR CARMYLIE LOVES MUSIC

MARVIN & BARBARA ROSS
S-702 Evansville Rt., Box 2
Evansville, WY 82636
(307) 237-7017

SHELTIES

DAM
HAPPY GLEN'S FLAMING FANTASY
REG. NO. ....

- CH BANCHORY STAND BACK C.D.
  - AM/CAN CH BANCHORY BACK STOP
    - BANCHORY REFLECTION (4pt.)
      - AM/CAN CH BANCHORY HIGH BORN
      - BANCHORY HIGH GLOW
    - BANCHORY FOXY LADY
      - BANCHORY BLACK GOLD
      - BANCHORY WHIPPED CREAM
  - BANCHORY ANGELIQUE
    - CH HALSTOR'S PETER PUMKIN
      - FAIR PLAY OF SEA ISLE
      - CH SEA ISLE RHAPSODY OF HALSTOR
    - BANCHORY HIGH GLOW
      - AM/CAN CH BANCHORY HIGH BORN
      - BANCHORY ALL-A-GLOA
- SHANNASY FLICKER OF FLAME C.D. (8pt.)
  - AM/CAN CH ILEMIST IMPOSSIBLE DREAM C.D.
    - CH HALSTOR S PETER PUMKIN
      - FAIR PLAY OF SEA ISLE
      - CH SEA ISLE RHAPSODY OF HALSTOR
    - AM/CAN CH LINDHURST CHRISTMAS CAROL
      - CH LINDHURST TRADEMARK
      - CH LINDHURST LOVELY LULLABY
  - SHANNASY I'M SOMEBODY
    - CH KEN-ROBS PARTNERS CHOICE
      - CH SEA ISLE SERENADE
      - CH STYLISH MISS OF HATFIELD
    - DIAMOND'S GOLDEN DAWN
      - CH SEA ISLE SERENADE
      - CH DIAMOND'S BLACK VELVET

I HEREBY CERTIFY THAT THIS PEDIGREE IS TRUE AND CORRECT
TO THE BEST OF MY KNOWLEDGE AND BELIEF

SIGNED *Barbara Ross*

DATE _____ Jan 1 _____ , 19 82

479

```
                                            Ch Kalandar Prince O'Pages Hill
                        Ch Prince George O'Pages Hill
                                            Ch Timberidge Temptess
        Int Ch   Nashcrest Golden Note
                                                Shel-E-Ain Sir Echo
                        Nashcrest Rythym
                                                Shel-E-Ain Pirouette
Ch Stylish Miss of Hatfield
    W-869384                                Ch  Bagota Blaze
                        Ch Sheltieland Kiltie O'Sea Isle
                                            Ch Sheltieland Peg O'The Picts
        Ch Bonnie Lass of Hatfield
                                                Oregon True Gold
                        Golden True of Achmore
                                                Merry Lass of Achmore
```



```
                                                    Ch. Hatfield Sultan of Lorel
    CH. KEN-ROBS PARTNERS CHOICE        Sept 17, 1965    Ken-Robs LI'L Miss Stylish


                                            Ch Kalanda Prince O'Pages Hill
                        Ch Prince George O'Pages Hill
                                            Ch Timberidge Temptess
        Int Ch Nashcrest Golden Note
                                                Shel-E-Ain Little Sir Echo
                        Nashcrest Rythym
                                                Shel-E-Ain Pirouette
    Ch Sea Isle Serenade
        W-807488                              Ch Prince George O'Fages Hill
                        Int Ch Nashcrest Golden Note
                                            Nashcrest Rythym
                Ch Sea Isle Serenta
                                            Ch Sheltieland Kiltie O'Sea Isle
                        Ch Sea Isle Sandra
                                            Ch Sea Isle Summer Breeze
```

SIRE

Ch Kalanda Prince O' Pages Hill

CH Prince George O'Pages Hill

CH Timberidge Temptess

Int CH Nashcrest Golden Note

Shelt-E- Ain Little Sir Echo

Nashcrest Rythym

Shelt E-Ain Pirouette

Ch Sea Isle Serenade

Ch Prince George O'Pages Hill

IntCh Nashcrest Golden Note

Nashcrest Rythym

Ch Sea Isle Serenta

Ch Shetieland Kiltie O'Sea Isle

Ch Sea Isle Sandra

Ch Sea Isle Summer Breeze

DAM

Ch Victory of Pocono

Ch Bagota Blaze

Bravo of Taristock

Ch Sheltieland Kiltie O'Sea Isle

Ch Mountaineer O'Pages Hill

Ch Sheltieland Peg O' The Picts

Ch Pinafore O'The Picts

Ch Bonnie Lass Of Hatfield

Ch The Cheif Geronimo

Oregon True Gold

Gadabouts Strawberry Blonde

Golden True of Achmore

Ch Massapoag Topper

Merry Lass Of Achmore

Massapoag Folly of Faunbrock

481

KISMET KENNELS

GUY AND THELMA MAULDIN
RT 2 BOX 83 T   RICHMOND TEXAS 77469

Ch. Banchory High Born WB-165909
REGISTERED NAME & NO.

BREED __Shetland Sheepdog__ DATE WHELPED __February 27, 1968__ SEX __M__

BREEDER __Rosemary Shrauger__ ADDRESS _____

OWNER __Guy A. & Thelma Mauldin__ ADDRESS __Rt. 2, Box 83 T, Richmond TX 77469__

GENERAL DESCRIPTION __Tri-color__

SIRE

REG. NO. ....

- Ch. Heir Apparent of Karelane
  - Ch. Blue Heritage of Pocono
    - Ch. Shelt-E-Ain Reflection
      - Ch. Shelt-E-Ain Black Knight O'Knight
      - Shelt-E-Ain Lucky Penny
    - Ch. Larkspur's Replica of Pocono
      - Ch. Larkspur's Finalist of Pocono
      - Abendruhe Carolynann's Pixie
  - Karelane Fair Lady of Pocono
    - Shelcort Knight in Armour
      - Ch. Shelcort Saltine Warrior
      - Ch. Formal Note of Shelcort
    - Robinette of Pocono
      - Katie-I's Rob Robin
      - Shelcort Life of the Party

- Ch. Philidove Heir Presumptive
  - Ch. Magnet's Royalty of Astolat
    - Ch. Magnet O'Page's Hill
      - Ch. Musket O'Pages Hill
      - Alicia O'Page's Hill
    - Ch. Astolat Emblem's Onyx
      - Ch. Frigates Emblem of Astolat
      - Ch. Lady Libby
  - Wansor's Flashy Flame
    - Astolat Emblem's Radience
      - Ch. Frigate's Emblem of Astolat
        - Ch. Frigate of Faunbrook CD
        - Astolat Snow Flurry
      - Falkirk's Radience
        - Ch. Pixie Dell Firebrand
        - Ch. Falkirk's Whimsical Susie

DAM

REG. NO. ....

- Ch. Badgerton Wit O'Meadow Ridge
  - Ch. Katie-J's Ronny
    - Ch. Nashcrest Golden Note
      - Ch. Prince George O'Page's Hill
      - Nashcrest Rhythm
    - Katie'J's Colleen
      - Katie'I's Golden Nugget
      - Ch. Badgerton Lassie
  - Ch. Badgerton Pantomime Patsy
    - Ch. Sea Isle Serenade
      - Ch. Nashcrest Golden Note
      - Ch. Sea Isle Sandra
    - Ch. Badgerton Impersonator
      - Ch. Geronimo Crown Prince
      - Am.Can.Ch. Badgerton Flirt UD

- Tiree Hall Solo's High-Lite
  - Flying Kilt O'Lochindaal
    - Ch. Thistlerose V.I.P.
      - Ch. Thistlerose Sir Reginald
      - Ch. Thistlerose Classic Moderne
    - Thistlerose Modern Miniature
      - Ch. Thistlerose Showmaster
      - Thistlerose Heatherbell
  - Ch. Lochindaal Solo of Tiree Hall
    - Ch. Sheltilore Diablo
      - Robin Hood of Kenloch
      - Sheltilore After Dark
    - Alnphyll Ginger Gumdrop
      - Chari of Al-N-Phyll
        - Ch. Timberidge Target
        - Timberidge Letitia

I HEREBY CERTIFY THAT THIS PEDIGREE IS TRUE AND CORRECT
TO THE BEST OF MY KNOWLEDGE AND BELIEF.

SIGNED _____

DATE _____ 19___

KISMET KENNELS

GUY AND THELMA MAULDIN
RT 2 BOX 83 T   RICHMOND TEXAS 77469

CH.KISMET'S CONQUISTADOR WC810358

REGISTERED NAME & NO.

BREED __Shetland Sheepdog__ DATE WHELPED __December 15, 1973__ SEX __Male__

BREEDER __Guy A. & Thelma J. Mauldin__ ADDRESS __Rt. 4, Box 83 T, Richmond, TX 77469__

OWNER __Same__ ADDRESS _____

GENERAL DESCRIPTION __14-1/2" Mahogany Sable__

SIRE
Ch.Banchory High Born
REG. NO. WB165909

- Ch.Philidove Heir Presumptive
  - Ch.Heir Apparent of Karelane
    - Ch.Blue Heritage of Pocono
      - Ch.Shelt-E-Ain Reflection
      - Ch.Larkspur's Replica of Pocono
    - Karelane Fair Lady of Pocono
      - Shelcort Knight in Armour
      - Robinette of Pocono
  - Wansor's Flashy Flame
    - Ch.Magnet's Royalty of Astolat,CDX
      - Ch.Magnet O'Page's Hill
      - Ch.Astolat Emblem's Onyx
    - Astolat Emblem's Radiance
      - Ch.Frigate's Emblem of Astolat
      - Falkirk's Radiance
- Tiree Hall Solo's High-Lite
  - Ch.Badgerton Wit O'Meadow Ridge
    - Ch.Katie J's Ronny
      - Ch.Nashcrest Golden Note
      - Katie I's Colleen
    - Ch.Badgerton Pantomime Patsy
      - Ch.Sea Isle Serenade
      - Ch.Badgerton Impersonator
  - Ch.Lochindaal Solo of Tiree Hall
    - Flying Kilt O'Lochindaal
      - Ch.Thistlerose V.I.P.
      - Thistlerose Modern Minature
    - Al-N-Phyll Ginger Gumdrop
      - Ch.Sheltilore Diablo
      - Chari of Al-N-Phyll

DAM
Cee Dee's Annandale
REG. NO. WB869849

- Ch.Diamond's Robert Bruce
  - Ch.Lingard Sealect Bruce
    - Ch.Nashcrest Golden Note
      - Ch.Prince George O'Page's Hill
      - Nashcrest Rhythm
    - Timberidge Sandstorm
      - Geronimo Prince Royal
      - Sea Isle Singing Sands
  - Ch.Diamond's Black Velvet
    - Ch.Tess's Trump Card of Wadmalaw
      - Ch.Timberidge Target
      - Titian Tess of Wadmalaw
    - Ch.Diamond's Lady Goldmont
      - Ch.Geronimo Son Rey
      - Ch.Geronimo Diamond Lil
- Cee Dee's Sandwick,CD
  - Ch.Cee Dee's Squire
    - Glenelm's Comanche Brave
      - Ch.Lindhurst Comanchero
      - Glenelm's Honey Chile
    - Glenelm's Wistful Dottie
      - Ch.Lindhurst Trademark
      - Melodylane Sprite of Eltham
  - Wynfield's Best Try
    - Ch.Twin Willow's Bright Future
      - Ch.Malpsh the Duke of Erle
      - Hieland Molly Stark
    - Wynfield's Best Bet
      - Piper Glen's Ebony Prince
      - Sunnycrest Golden Lassie

I HEREBY CERTIFY THAT THIS PEDIGREE IS TRUE AND CORRECT
TO THE BEST OF MY KNOWLEDGE AND BELIEF.

SIGNED _Thelma J. Mauldin_

DATE __March 26,__ 19 __80__

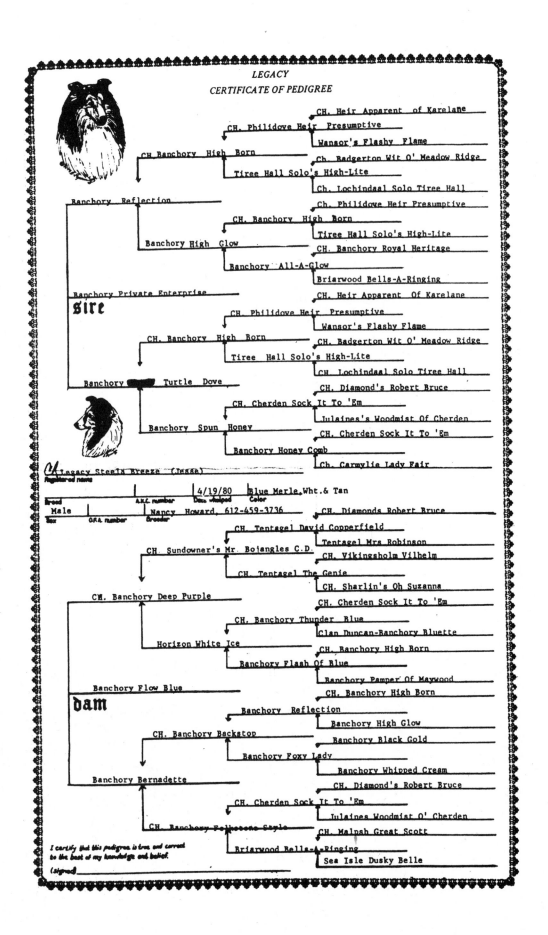

LEGACY
CERTIFICATE OF PEDIGREE

CH. Heir Apparent of Karelane
CH. Philidove Heir Presumptive
Wansor's Flashy Flame
CH Banchory High Born
Ch. Badgerton Wit O' Meadow Ridge
Tiree Hall Solo's High-Lite
Ch. Lochindaal Solo Tiree Hall
Banchory Reflection
Ch. Philidove Heir Presumptive
CH. Banchory High Born
Tiree Hall Solo's High-Lite
Banchory High Glow
CH. Banchory Royal Heritage
Banchory All-A-Glow
Briarwood Bells-A-Ringing
Banchory Private Enterprise
CH. Heir Apparent Of Karelane

sire

CH. Philidove Heir Presumptive
Wansor's Flashy Flame
CH. Banchory High Born
CH. Badgerton Wit O' Meadow Ridge
Tiree Hall Solo's High-Lite
CH Lochindaal Solo Tiree Hall
Banchory Turtle Dove
CH. Diamond's Robert Bruce
CH. Cherden Sock It To 'Em
Julaines's Woodmist Of Cherden
Banchory Spun Honey
CH. Cherden Sock It To 'Em
Banchory Honey Comb
Ch. Carmylie Lady Fair

CH Legacy Steals Breeze (Jesse)
Registered name

	4/19/80	Blue Merle,Wht.& Tan
Breed	A.K.C. number	Date whelped / Color
Male		CH. Diamonds Robert Bruce
Sex / O.F.A. number	Nancy Howard, 612-459-3736 / Breeder	

CH. Tentagel David Copperfield
Tentagel Mrs Robinson
CH. Sundowner's Mr. Bojangles C.D.
CH. Vikingsholm Vilhelm
CH. Tentagel The Genie
CH. Sharlin's Oh Suzanna
CH. Banchory Deep Purple
CH. Cherden Sock It To 'Em
CH. Banchory Thunder Blue
Clan Duncan-Banchory Bluette
Horizon White Ice
CH. Banchory High Born
Banchory Flash Of Blue
Banchory Pamper Of Maywood
Banchory Flow Blue
CH. Banchory High Born

dam

Banchory Reflection
CH. Banchory Backstop
Banchory High Glow
Banchory Black Gold
Banchory Foxy Lady
Banchory Whipped Cream
Banchory Bernadette
CH. Diamond's Robert Bruce
CH. Cherden Sock It To 'Em
Julaines Woodmist O' Cherden
CH. Banchory Folkstone Style
CH. Malpsh Great Scott
Briarwood Bells-A-Ringing
Sea Isle Dusky Belle

I certify that this pedigree is true and correct
to the best of my knowledge and belief.

(signed)

484

Pedigree

CH. MADSELIN'S GRAND SLAM	MALE	March 20, 1978
REGISTERED NAME	SEX	WHELPED

SHETLAND SHEEPDOG	WE 609351	" MATT "
BREED	A. K. C. No.	CALL NAME

Susan ~~Johnson~~ Jensen		Blue Merle & White
BREEDER		COLOR

Parents	Grand Parents	Great Grand Parents	Great Gr. Grand Parents

CH. PHILADOVE HEIR PRESUMPTIVE

CH. BANCHORY HIGH BORN

Tired Hall Solo's High Lite

Banchory Reflection
Grand Sire

CH. BANCHORY HIGH BORN

Banchory High Glow

Banchory All-A-Glow

CH. BANCHORY BACKSTOP
SIRE
Reg. No. _____

CH. BANCHORY HIGH BORN

Banchory Black Gold

Banchory Silver Fanfare

Banchory Foxy Lady
Grand Dam

CH. CHERDEN SOCK IT TO'EM CD

Banchory Whipped Cream

Julaine Oceon Blue

CH. DIAMOND'S ROBERT BRUCE

CH. CHERDEN SOCK IT TO'EM CD

Julaine's Woodmist O'Cherden

CH. BANCHORY THUNDER BLUE
Grand Sire

CH. CHERDEN SOCK IT TO'EM CD

Clan-Duncan Banchory Bluette

Banchory Half Moon

Can.Ch. Banchory Misty Blue
DAM
Reg. No. _____

CH. DIAMOND'S ROBERT BRUCE

CH. CHERDEN SOCK IT TO'EM CD

Julaine's Woodmist O'Cherden

Banchory Blue Torch
Grand Dam

CH. BANCHORY HIGH BORN

Banchory Flash of Blue

Banchory Pamper of Maywood

⌘ This Certifies That, the above Pedigree is true and correct to the best of my knowledge and belief.

Date of Purchase _____

Signed _____

Name of Purchaser _____

485

Certified Pedigree

CALL NAME JOSH

REGISTERED WITH A K C

CH MARWAL JOSHUA OF JERICHO
REGISTERED NAME OF DOG

BREED Shetland Sheepdog   **DATE WHELPED** November 10, 1975   **SEX** Male

BREEDER Margaret L. Huening   **ADDRESS** RD#2 Charlton Road, Ballston Spa, New York 12020

OWNER Margaret L. Huening   **ADDRESS** RD#2 Charlton Road, Ballston Spa, New York 12020

GENERAL DESCRIPTION Sable

SIRE

CH Calcurt Luke
REG. NO. WC106684

- CH Halstor's Peter Pumpkin
  - Fair Play Of Sea Isle
    - CH Malpsh The Duke Of Erle
      - CH Sea Isle Serenade
      - Sea Isle Dusky Belle
    - CH Kawartha's Fair Game
      - CH Sheltieland Kiltie O' Sea Isle
      - CH Kawartha's Sabrina Fair
  - CH Sea Isle Rhapsody Of Halstor
    - CH Sea Isle Serenade
      - CH Nashcrest Golden Note
      - CH Sea Isle Serenata
    - CH Colvidale Soliloquy
      - CH Sheltieland Kiltie O' Sea Isle
      - CH Lochelven's Reverie
- Calcurt Black Angie
  - Black Laird Of Calcurt
    - Silver Talisman Of Pocono
      - CH Tiny Toby Of Walnut Hall
      - Calico Maid Of Pocono
    - CH Lingard Blue Heather
      - CH Lingard Blue Boy
      - George's Creek Sally Lou
  - Calcurt Molly Fitchett
    - CH Topo Gigio
      - Badgerton Red Riot O' Carmylie
      - Carmylie Honey Bear
    - Jomar's Happy Miss Tam
      - Carmylie El Toro Of Tyria
      - Tyria Red Riot

DAM

Marwal's Pennies From Heaven
REG. NO. WC422123

- CH Carmylie Elusive Dream
  - CH Halstor's Peter Pumpkin
    - Fair Play Of Sea Isle
      - CH Malpsh The Duke Of Erle
      - CH Kawartha's Fair Game
    - CH Sea Isle Rhapsody Of Halstor
      - CH Sea Isle Serenade
      - CH Colvidale Soliloquy
  - Jomar Carmylie Love's Magic
    - CH Katie J's The Gay Prince
      - CH Katie J's Ronny
      - Katie J's Sweet Sue
    - CH Jomar Carmylie Bundle Of Love
      - Carmylie Comanche
      - Jomar's Heather Dee
- Princess Lana Of Marwal
  - Kiloren Friendly Persuasion II
    - CH Ken-Rob's Kenny
      - CH Malpsh Great Scott
      - CH Stylish Miss Of Hatfield
    - Kiloren Kirstie
      - CH Sea Isle Serenade
      - Kiloren Sea Mystery
  - Shel-T-Lane Cutey
    - CH T. Torbit Of The Rim Rocks
      - CH Ebb Tide Of Tobruk
      - Glengyle's Tid Bit O' Clar Mar
    - Sondra Lane's Tinker Toy
      - Dorisu's Ebony Challenge
      - Lillegard Facination

Certified Pedigree

WD575788
INDIVIDUAL REG. NO.

WM329420
LITTER REG NO

BECKY
CALL NAME

AKC
REGISTERED WITH

CH MARWAL BLUESETTE
REGISTERED NAME OF DOG

BREED Shetland Sheepdog	DATE WHELPED July 11, 1976 SEX Female
BREEDER Margaret L. Huening	ADDRESS RD#2 Charlton Road, Ballston Spa, New York 12020
OWNER Margaret L. Huening	ADDRESS RD#2 Charlton Road, Ballston Spa, New York 12020

GENERAL DESCRIPTION   Blue Merle

SIRE

CH Chenterra Thunderation
REG. NO. WC647582

- Chenterra Beauregard CD
  - CH Tentagel Mr. President CD
    - CH Diamond's Redbud
      - CH Sea Isle Serenade
      - CH Diamond's Black Velvet
    - CH Sharlin's Penny Brite
      - CH Pixie Dell Bright Vision
      - CH Sharlin's Tempting Teressa
  - Tentagel The Cheerleader
    - CH Halstor's Peter Pumpkin
      - Fair Play Of Sea Isle
      - CH Sea Isle Rhapsody Of Halstor
    - Tambrae Cinnamon Toast
      - CH Browne Acres Prince Consort
      - Browne Acres Back Talk
- Chenterra Commotion
  - Lanlee's Chenterra Citation
    - CH Halstor's Peter Pumpkin
      - Fair Play Of Sea Isle
      - CH Sea Isle Rhapsody Of Halstor
    - Aron-Kae Song Of Spring
      - CH Marjan's Music Maker O' Waljon
      - CH Sparkling Sherry Of Aron-Kae
  - Tentagel The Cheerleader
    - CH Halstor's Peter Pumpkin
      - Fair Play Of Sea Isle
      - CH Sea Isle Rhapsody Of Halstor
    - Tambrae Cinnamon Toast
      - CH Browne Acres Prince Consort
      - Browne Acres Back Talk

DAM

Rallyround Lady Ice
REG. NO. WC546950

- Banchory High Power
  - Am/Can CH Banchory High Born
    - CH Philidove Heir Presumptive
      - CH Heir Apparent Of Karelane
      - Wansor's Flashy Flame
    - Tiree Hall Solo's High-Lite
      - CH Badgerton Wit O' Meadow Ridge
      - CH Lochindaal Solo Of Tiree Hall
  - Banchory A Taste Of Honey
    - Am/Can CH Cherden Sock It To 'Em
      - CH Diamond's Robert Bruce
      - Julaine's Woodmist O' Cherden
    - Banchory Bright Lights CDX
      - CH Banchory Royal Heritage
      - CH Carmylie Lady Fair
- Banchory A-Blue-Delight
  - Am/Can CH Cherden Sock It To 'Em
    - CH Diamond's Robert Bruce
      - CH Lingard Sealect Bruce
      - CH Diamond's Black Velvet
    - Julaine's Woodmist O'Cherden
      - Banchory Phantom O' Four Winds
      - Banchory Golden Glow
  - Banchory Pamper Of Maywood
    - CH Philidove Heir Presumptive
      - CH Heir Apparent Of Karelane
      - Wansor's Flashy Flame
    - CH Banchory Blueberry Muffin
      - CH Thistlerose Arcwood Aladdin
      - Lodgewood Sonata

487

Certified Pedigree

INDIVIDUAL REG NO WF281025

CALL NAME ANDY

LITTER REG NO WM886443

REGISTERED WITH A K C

REGISTERED NAME OF DOG CH Marwal Steppin' Out

BREED Shetland Sheepdog **DATE WHELPED** July 12, 1982 **SEX** Male

BREEDER Margaret L. Huening **ADDRESS** RD#2 Charlton Road, Ballston Spa, New York 12020

OWNER Diane Bostwick **ADDRESS** 231 N. Elmira St., Sayre, PA 18840

GENERAL DESCRIPTION Sable

SIRE

Am/Can CH Sir Joshua Of Winslow
REG. NO. WE103117

- CH Romayne Sportin' Life
  - Fair Play Of Sea Isle
    - Am/Can CH Malpsh The Duke Of Erle
      - CH Sea Isle Serenade
      - Sea Isle Dusky Belle
    - CH Kawartha's Fair Game
      - CH Sheltieland Kiltie O'Sea Isle
      - CH Kawartha's Sabrina Fair
  - CH Beltane Romayne
    - CH Halstor's Peter Pumpkin
      - Fair Play Of Sea Isle
      - CH Sea Isle Rhapsody of Halstor
    - Beltane High Barbaree
      - CH Halstor's Peter Pumpkin
      - CH Beltane Holly Golightly
- Trefoil Dazzling Rose
  - CH Rorralore Mickey Dazzler
    - Can CH Willow-Acres Golden Encore
      - Willow-Acres Golden Note
      - Willow-Acres Golden Coin
    - CH Rorralore Curst Kate
      - CH Rorralore Robert The Bruce
      - CH Hatfield's Stardust
  - Trefoil Aim For Love
    - CH Lingard Sealect Bruce
      - Am/Can CH Nashcrest Golden Note
      - Timberidge Sandstorm
    - Ken-Rob's Call Me Candee
      - CH Ken-Rob's Kenny
      - Ken-Rob's Call Girl

DAM

Marwal Bobbin' Along
REG. NO. WE580597

- CH Macdega Barwood Birthright
  - Am/Can CH Macdega Mainstay
    - CH Chenterra Thunderation
      - Chenterra Beauregard CD
      - Chenterra Commotion
    - Macdega Leave It To Beaver
      - CH Calcurt Luke
      - CH Kenset Rare Vintage
  - CH Barwoods Treasure
    - CH Halstor's Peter Pumpkin
      - Fair Play Of Sea Isle
      - CH Sea Isle Rhapsody Of Halstor
    - CH Barwood Scotchguard Sonata
      - CH Sea Isle Glengarry
      - CH Gillian Fair Of Sea Isle
- CH Barwoods Symphony
  - CH Chenterra Thunderation
    - Chenterra Beauregard CD
      - CH Tentagel Mr. President CDX
      - Tentagel The Cheerleader
    - Chenterra Commotion
      - Lanlee's Chenterra Citation
      - Tentagel The Cheerleader
  - CH Barwoods Rhapsody
    - CH Halstor's Peter Pumpkin
      - Fair Play Of Sea Isle
      - CH Sea Isle Rhapsody Of Halstor
    - CH Barwood Scotchguard Sonata
      - CH Sea Isle Glengarry
      - CH Gillian Fair Of Sea Isle

Breeder Dona Hausman
Owner Barbara M. Kenealy

Certificate of Pedigree of

Meadow Ridge Rockwood It's Me
Dam 3 CHs

			Ch. Brandell's Bric A Brac
		Ch. Brandells Break-A-Way	
			Brandell's Bettina of Tobruc
	Ch. Pixie Dell Bright Vision		
			Ch. Musket O'Page's Hill
		Ch. Va-Gore's Bright Promise	
			Ch. Creole Babe O'Page's Hil
Ch. Sutter's Golden Masquerade			
Sire			Ch. JimJonArd Geronimo
		Ch. Wendemere's Bold Venture	
			Brown Acres Bouffant
	Ch. Dan-Dee's Samantha		
			Ch. Elf Dale Golden Legacy
		Ch. Dan-Dee's Portrait In Gold	
			DanD's Merry Maggie

			Ch. Brandell's Bric A Brac
		Ch. Brandell's Break A Way	
			Brandell's Bettina of Tobruc
	Ch. Pixie Dell Bright Vision		
			Ch. Musket O'Page's Hill
		Ch. Va-Gor's Bright Promise	
			Ch. Creole Babe O'Pages Hill
Meadow Ridge Star Light			
Dam			Ch. Elf Dale Viking
		Ch. Elf Dale Golden Legacy	
			Ch. Elf Dale Adorable Doll
	Meadow Ridge Venus		
			Ch. Pixie Dell Bright Vision
		Ch. Meadow Ridge Bright Holiday	
			Birch Hollow Destiny

Philidove Reg.

286 CANAL ROAD · PORT JEFFERSON STATION, N. Y. 11776

Pedigree Certificate

Name __CH.PHILIDOVE KISMET HEIR BORNE__   A.K.C. # _____   Sex: __M.__   Breeder: __IRENE BRODY__

Breed __SHETLAND SHEEPDOG__   Color: __BLUE MERLE, TAN & WHITE__   Whelped: __7/26/72__

SIRE	SIRE	SIRE	SIRE
AM. & CAN. CH. BANCHORY HIGH BORN	CH.PHILIDOVE HEIR PRESUMPTIVE	CH.HEIR APPARENT OF KARELANE	SIRE CH.BLUE HERITAGE OF POCONO
			DAM KARELANE FAIR LADY OF POCONO
		DAM WANSOR'S FLASHY FLAME	SIRE CH.MAGNET'S ROYALTY OF ASTOLAT
			DAM ASTOLAT EMBLEM'S RADIENCE
	DAM TIREE HALL SOLO'S HIGH LITE	SIRE CH.BADGERTON WIT O' MEADOW RIDGE	SIRE CH.KATIE J'S ROMY
			DAM CH.BADGERTON PANTOMINE PATSY
		DAM CH.LOCHINDAAL SOLO OF TIREE HALL	SIRE FLYING KILT O' LOCHINDAAL
			DAM AL- N- PHYLL GINGER GUMDROP
DAM CH. PHILIDOVE CARMYLIE IN A MIST	SIRE CH. PHILIDOVE HEIR PRESUMPTIVE	SIRE CH. HEIR APPARENT OF KARELANE	SIRE CH.BLUE HERITAGE OF POCONO
			DAM KARELANE FAIR LADY OF POCONO
		DAM WANSOR'S FLASHY FLAME	SIRE CH.MAGNET'S ROYALTY OF ASTOLAT
			DAM ASTOLAT EMBLEM'S RADIENCE
	DAM BANCHORY BI JINGO OF CARMYLIE	SIRE CH. THISTLEROSE ARROWOOD ALLADIN	SIRE CH.BLUE QUEST OF POCONO
			DAM CH.THISTLEROSE CLASSIC MODERNE
		DAM LODGEWOOD QUEEN OF BANCHORY	SIRE CH.TINY TOBY OF WALNUT HALL
			DAM LODGEWOOD CHIP OF CLOUDMERE

THIS PEDIGREE IS CERTIFIED TO BE CORRECT TO THE BEST OF MY KNOWLEDGE AND BELIEF.

Signed_____   Date_____

OUR OWN ROCKWOOD
SHETLAND SHEEPDOGS

MRS. BARBARA M. KENEALY
77 Grand View Drive Ridgefield, CT 06877
Telephone: (203) 438-6189

| BREED | SHETLAND SHEEPDOG | COLOR AND/OR MARKINGS | SABLE & WHITE | SEX | MALE | DATE WHELPED | MAY 24, 1973 |

CALL NAME: RASCAL BREEDER: BARBARA KENEALY ADDRESS:

REG. NAME: CH. ROCKWOOD'S BAC TALK A.K.C. REG. No. WC-577387 SELLER:

Sire 6 CH

CH. ROCKWOOD'S BAC TALK
├─ CH. HALSTOR'S PETER PUMPKIN (Sire)
│   ├─ FAIR PLAY OF SEA ISLE (Grand Sire)
│   │   ├─ CH. MALPSH THE DUKE OF ERLE
│   │   │   ├─ CH. SEA ISLE SERENADE
│   │   │   │   ├─ CH. NASHCREST GOLDEN NOTE
│   │   │   │   └─ CH. SEA ISLE SERENATA
│   │   │   └─ SEA ISLE DUSKY BELLE
│   │   │   ├─ CH. PIXIE DELL BRIGHT VISION
│   │   │   └─ BAGADUCE HANNAH OF SEA ISLE
│   │   └─ CH. KAWARTHA'S FAIR GAME
│   │   ├─ CH. SHELTIELAND KILTIE O'SEA ISLE
│   │   │   ├─ CH. BOGOTA BLAZE
│   │   │   └─ CH. SHELTIELAND PEG O'THE PICTS
│   │   └─ CH. KAWARTHA'S SABRINA FAIR
│   │   ├─ CH. TEABERRY LANE'S LITTLE PECOS
│   │   └─ MISS RUFFLES OF OAK-LAWN
│   └─ CH. SEA ISLE RHAPSODY OF HALSTOR (Grand Dam)
│   ├─ CH. SEA ISLE SERENADE
│   │   ├─ CH. NASHCREST GOLDEN NOTE
│   │   │   ├─ CH. PRINCE GEORGE O'PAGE'S HILL
│   │   │   └─ NASHCREST RHYTHM
│   │   └─ CH. SEA ISLE SERENATA
│   │   ├─ CH. NASHCREST GOLDEN NOTE
│   │   └─ CH. SEA ISLE SANDRA
│   └─ CH. SHELTIELAND KILTIE O'SEA ISLE
│   ├─ CH. BOGOTA BLAZE
│   └─ CH. SHELTIELAND PEG O'THE PICTS

Certificate of Pedigree

CH. ROCKWOODS TALK TO ME (Dam)
├─ CH. VALDAWN'S TALK OF THE TOWNE (Grand Sire)
│   ├─ CH. VALDAWN'S KRACKERJACK
│   │   ├─ CH. COLVIDALE SOLILOQUY
│   │   │   ├─ CH. LOCHELVEN'S REVERIE
│   │   │   │   ├─ CH. GRAYSON'S RANGE RIDER
│   │   │   │   └─ CH. LOCHELVEN'S CAPRICE
│   │   │   └─ CH. PIXIE DELL EPICURE
│   │   │   ├─ CH. PIXIE DELL PENROD
│   │   │   └─ PIXIE DELL EPIC, C.D.
│   │   └─ CH. JEMIMA OF BAGADUCE
│   │   ├─ CH. SEA ISLE BARD OF BAGADUCE
│   │   └─ STARLITE'S VIKING MIST
│   └─ O'CANONACH JUBILEE MISTY
│   ├─ CH. MALPSH TEXAS LONER
│   │   ├─ CH. KAWARTHA'S MATCH MAKER
│   │   └─ CH. MALPSH AUTUMN GOLD
│   └─ LINGARD LAURIE O'JUBILEE
│   ├─ CH. LINGARD SEALECT BRUCE
│   └─ CH. BROWNE ACRES BUTTERSCOTCH
└─ MEADOW RIDGE ROCKWOOD IT'S ME (Grand Dam)
    ├─ CH. SUTTER'S GOLDEN MASQUERADE
    │   ├─ CH. PIXIE DELL BRIGHT VISION
    │   │   ├─ CH. BRANDELL'S BREAK-A-WAY II
    │   │   └─ CH. VA-GORE'S BRIGHT PROMISE
    │   └─ CH. DAN-DEE'S SAMANTHA
    │   ├─ CH. WENDEMER'S BOLD VENTURE
    │   └─ CH. DAN-DEE'S PORTRAIT IN GOLD
    └─ MEADOW RIDGE STAR LIGHT
        ├─ CH. PIXIE DELL BRIGHT VISION
        │   ├─ CH. BRANDELL'S BREAK-A-WAY II
        │   └─ CH. VA-GORE'S BRIGHT PROMISE
        └─ MEADOW RIDGE VENUS
            ├─ CH. ELF DALE GOLDEN LEGACY
            └─ CH. MEADOW RIDGE BRIGHT HOLIDAY

I hereby certify that this Pedigree is true to the best of my knowledge _____ Signed

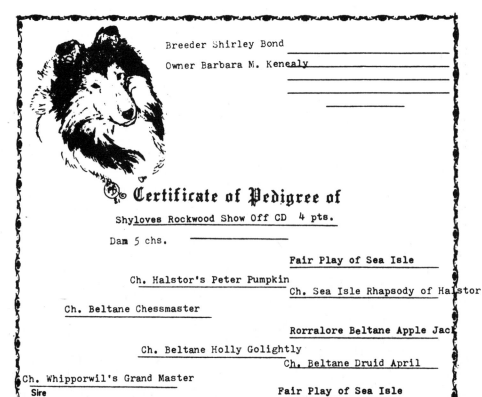

Breeder Shirley Bond

Owner Barbara M. Kenealy

Certificate of Pedigree of

Shyloves Rockwood Show Off CD 4 pts.

Dam 5 chs.

```
                                                    Fair Play of Sea Isle
                         Ch. Halstor's Peter Pumpkin
                                                    Ch. Sea Isle Rhapsody of Halstor
        Ch. Beltane Chessmaster
                                                    Rorralore Beltane Apple Jack
                         Ch. Beltane Holly Golightly
                                                    Ch. Beltane Druid April
Ch. Whipporwil's Grand Master
    Sire                                            Fair Play of Sea Isle
                         Ch. Halstors Peter Pumpkin
                                                    Ch. Sea Isle Rhapsody of Halstor
        Whipporwil's Pumpkin Seed
                                                    Ch. Lingard Select Bruce
                         Malpsh Wee Lass of Whipporwil
                                                    Malpsh Priss


                                                    Ch. Malpsh The Duke of Erle
                         Fair Play of Sea Isle
                                                    Ch. Kawartha's Fair Game
        Ch. Halstors Peter Pumpkin
                                                    Ch. Sea Isle Serenade
                         Ch. Sea Isle Rhapsody of Halstor
                                                    Ch. Colvidale Soliloquy
Shyloves Tinker Bell
    Dam                                             Ch. Pixie Dell Epicure
                         Ch. Valdawn's Krackerjack
                                                    Ch.Jemina of Bagaduce
        Valdawn's Frisky Fawn
                                                    Ch. Mapsh Texas Loner
                         O'Canonach Jubilee Misty
                                                    Lingard Laurie O'Jubilee
```

492

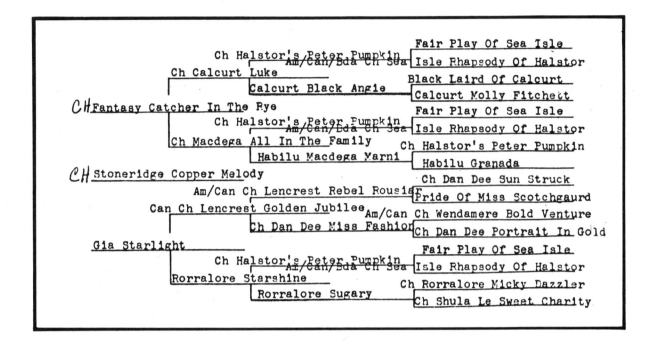

```
                    Ch Halstor's Peter Pumpkin        Fair Play Of Sea Isle
       Ch Calcurt Luke     Am/Can/Bda Ch Sea   Isle Rhapsody Of Halstor
                                               Black Laird Of Calcurt
               Calcurt Black Angie             Calcurt Molly Fitchett
CH Fantasy Catcher In The Rye                  Fair Play Of Sea Isle
                    Ch Halstor's Peter Pumpkin        Isle Rhapsody Of Halstor
       Ch Macdega All In The Family   Am/Can/Bda Ch Sea
                                      Ch Halstor's Peter Pumpkin
               Habilu Macdega Yarni            Habilu Granada
CH Stoneridge Copper Melody                    Ch Dan Dee Sun Struck
               Am/Can Ch Lencrest Rebel Rousier Pride Of Miss Scotchgaurd
       Can Ch Lencrest Golden Jubilee   Am/Can Ch Wendamere Bold Venture
               Ch Dan Dee Miss Fashion  Ch Dan Dee Portrait In Gold
       Gia Starlight                           Fair Play Of Sea Isle
                    Ch Halstor's Peter Pumpkin        Isle Rhapsody Of Halstor
               Rorralore Starshine  Am/Can/Bda Ch Sea
                                      Ch Rorralore Micky Dazzler
               Rorralore Sugary              Ch Shula Le Sweet Charity
```

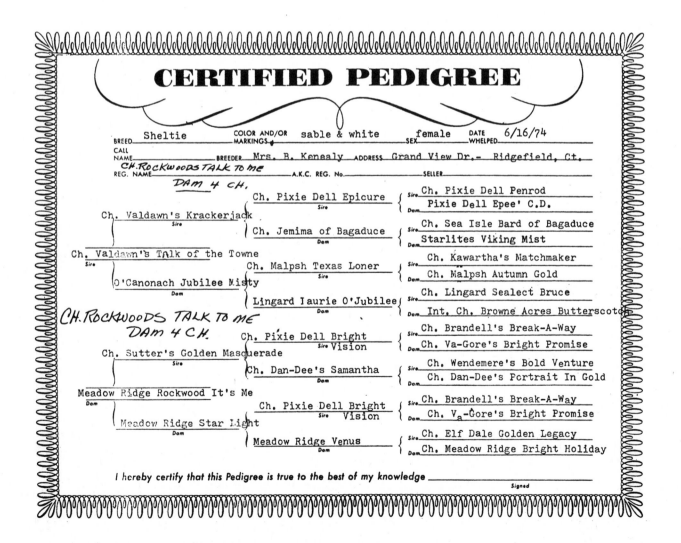

CERTIFIED PEDIGREE

| BREED | Sheltie | COLOR AND/OR MARKINGS | sable & white | SEX | female | DATE WHELPED | 6/16/74 |

CALL NAME _____ BREEDER Mrs. B. Kenealy ADDRESS Grand View Dr. - Ridgefield, Ct.

REG. NAME *CH. ROCKWOODS TALK TO ME* _____ A.K.C. REG. No. _____ SELLER _____

DAM 4 CH.

```
                                              Sire Ch. Pixie Dell Penrod
                       Ch. Pixie Dell Epicure
                            Sire                Dam  Pixie Dell Epee' C.D.
       Ch. Valdawn's Krackerjack
            Sire                              Sire Ch. Sea Isle Bard of Bagaduce
                       Ch. Jemima of Bagaduce
                            Dam                 Dam  Starlites Viking Mist
Ch. Valdawn's Talk of the Towne
    Sire                                      Sire Ch. Kawartha's Matchmaker
                       Ch. Malpsh Texas Loner
                            Sire                Dam  Ch. Malpsh Autumn Gold
       O'Canonach Jubilee Misty
            Dam                               Sire Ch. Lingard Sealect Bruce
                       Lingard Laurie O'Jubilee
                            Dam                 Dam  Int. Ch. Browne Acres Butterscotch
```

CH. ROCKWOODS TALK TO ME
   DAM 4 CH.

```
                                              Sire Ch. Brandell's Break-A-Way
                       Ch. Pixie Dell Bright
                            Sire   Vision       Dam  Ch. Va-Gore's Bright Promise
       Ch. Sutter's Golden Masquerade
            Sire                              Sire Ch. Wendemere's Bold Venture
                       Ch. Dan-Dee's Samantha
                            Dam                 Dam  Ch. Dan-Dee's Portrait In Gold
Meadow Ridge Rockwood It's Me
    Dam                                       Sire Ch. Brandell's Break-A-Way
                       Ch. Pixie Dell Bright
                            Sire   Vision       Dam  Ch. Va-Gore's Bright Promise
       Meadow Ridge Star Light
            Dam                               Sire Ch. Elf Dale Golden Legacy
                       Meadow Ridge Venus
                            Dam                 Dam  Ch. Meadow Ridge Bright Holiday
```

I hereby certify that this Pedigree is true to the best of my knowledge _____

Signed

493

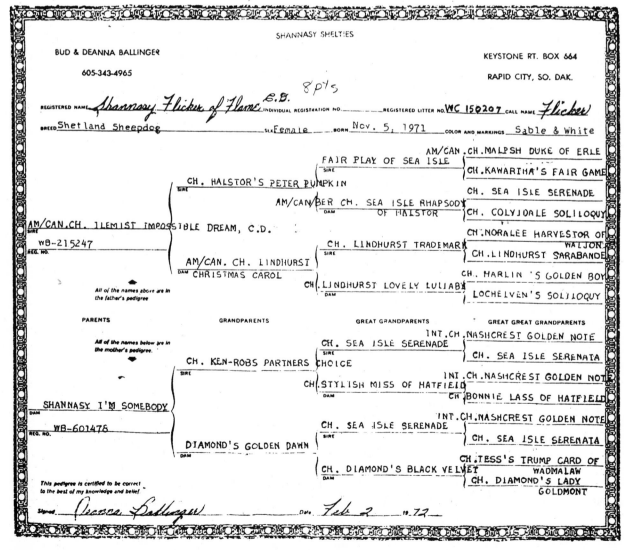

CH. RORRALORE SPORTIN' CHANCE C.D.

Ch. Romayne's Sportin' Life
- Fair Play of Sea Isle
  - Ch. Malpsh The Duke of Erle
    - Ch. Sea Isle Serenade
    - Sea Isle Dusky Belle
  - Ch. Kawartha's Fair Game
    - Ch. Sheltieland Kiltie O' Sea Isle
    - Ch. Kawartha's Sabrina Fair
- Ch. Beltane Romayne
  - Ch. Halstor's Peter Pumpkin
    - Fair Play of Sea Isle
    - Ch. Sea Isle Rhapsody of Halstor
  - Beltane High Barbaree
    - Ch. Halstor's Peter Pumpkin
    - Ch. Beltane Holly Golightly

Jeanie of Mary Dell (4 Chs.)
- Ch. Rorralore Mickey Dazzler
  - Can. Ch. Willow Acres Golden Encore
    - Willow Acres Golden Note
    - Willow Acres Golden Coin
  - Ch. Rorralore Curl Kate
    - Ch. Rorralore Robert The Bruce
    - Ch. Hatfield's Stardust
- Beech Tree Cindy of Mary Dell (2 Chs.)
  - Ch. Brevstar's Rocket of Helreg
    - Ch. Willow Acres Curtain Call
    - Helreg's Starlette
  - Beech Tree Do It Yourself
    - Ch. Hallmark's The Black Watch
    - Altimar Morning Star

RORRALORE

Charlotte Clem McGowan
(617) 969-5756

78 Clements Road
Newton, MA 02158

Shipping: Boston, Logan International

SHANNASY SHELTIES

BUD & DEANNA BALLINGER

605-343-4965

KEYSTONE RT. BOX 664

RAPID CITY, SO. DAK.

REGISTERED NAME *Shannasy Flicker of Flame* C.D. 8 pts INDIVIDUAL REGISTRATION NO. _____ REGISTERED LITTER NO. WC 150207 CALL NAME *Flicker*

BREED Shetland Sheepdog   SEX Female   BORN Nov. 5, 1971   COLOR AND MARKINGS Sable & White

AM/CAN.CH. ILEMIST IMPOSSIBLE DREAM, C.D.
REG. NO. WB-215247

- All of the names above are in the father's pedigree
- CH. HALSTOR'S PETER PUMPKIN
  - FAIR PLAY OF SEA ISLE (SIRE)
    - AM/CAN.CH.MALPSH DUKE OF ERLE
    - CH.KAWARTHA'S FAIR GAME
  - AM/CAN/BER CH. SEA ISLE RHAPSODY OF HALSTOR (DAM)
    - CH. SEA ISLE SERENADE
    - CH. COLYJDALE SOLILOQUY
- AM/CAN. CH. LINDHURST CHRISTMAS CAROL (DAM)
  - CH. LINDHURST TRADEMARK (SIRE)
    - CH.NORALEE HARVESTOR OF WALJON
    - CH.LINDHURST SARABANDE
  - CH. LINDHURST LOVELY LULLABY (DAM)
    - CH. HARLIN'S GOLDEN BOY
    - LOCHELVEN'S SOLILOQUY

PARENTS	GRANDPARENTS	GREAT GRANDPARENTS	GREAT GREAT GRANDPARENTS

All of the names below are in the mother's pedigree.

SHANNASY I'M SOMEBODY
REG. NO. WB-601478

- CH. KEN-ROBS PARTNERS CHOICE (SIRE)
  - CH. SEA ISLE SERENADE (SIRE)
    - INT.CH.NASHCREST GOLDEN NOTE
    - CH. SEA ISLE SERENATA
  - CH.STYLISH MISS OF HATFIELD (DAM)
    - INT.CH.NASHCREST GOLDEN NOTE
    - CH BONNIE LASS OF HATFIELD
- DIAMOND'S GOLDEN DAWN (DAM)
  - CH. SEA ISLE SERENADE (SIRE)
    - INT.CH.NASHCREST GOLDEN NOTE
    - CH. SEA ISLE SERENATA
  - CH. DIAMOND'S BLACK VELVET (DAM)
    - CH.TESS'S TRUMP CARD OF WADMALAW
    - CH. DIAMOND'S LADY GOLDMONT

This pedigree is certified to be correct to the best of my knowledge and belief.

Signed *Deanna Ballinger*   Date Feb 2 19 72

494

Starhaven

SHETLAND SHEEPDOGS · ARABIAN HORSES
2229 Goshen Pike - Goshen, Ohio 45122
PHONE: 513-625-7844

BREED Shetland Sheepdog COLOR AND/OR MARKINGS Tricolor SEX Male BORN 10-10-62

CALL NAME Banner BREEDER Carl A. and Amy Langhorst, Starhaven Kennels

REG. NAME Ch. Starhaven's Banner, C.D. REG. No. VA329945 OWNER Breeder

	Ch. Noralee Leader O'Roc-Sycamore	Ch. Noralee Bronze Nugget
		Ch. Noralee Autumn Shadow
Roc-Sycamore Brass Tacks (SIRE)	Tri-Acre's Emblemet	Ch. Frigate's Emblem of Astolat
		Ch. Harline's Babsie
Ch. Alfran's Amber Talisman (SIRE)		
	Ch. Noralee Leader O'Roc-Sycamore	Ch. Noralee Bronze Nugget
		Ch. Noralee Autumn Shadow
Ch. Alfran Wee Amber Midge (DAM)	Green Acre Golden Sunrise	Ch. Roc-Sycamore Minute Man
		Green Acre Bronze Belle
	Ch. Noralee Leader O' Roc-Sycamore	Ch. Noralee Bronze Nugget
		Ch. Noralee Autumn Shadow
Starhaven's Top Kick, C.D.X. (SIRE)	Gay Lady V, U.D.	Blithewood Robin
		Lena's Princess Peggy
Starhaven's Feathers (DAM)		
	Timberidge Trader of Kiloren	Ch. Kinswood Citation
		Timberidge Letitia
Timberidge Starhaven's Flag (DAM)	Timberidge Twostep	Ch. Nashcrest Golden Note
		Ch. Timberidge Black Velvet

I hereby certify that this Pedigree is true to the best of my knowledge **Amy Langhorst**

Starhaven

SHETLAND SHEEPDOGS · ARABIAN HORSES
2229 Goshen Pike - Goshen, Ohio 45122
PHONE: 513-625-7844

BREED Shetland Sheepdog COLOR AND/OR MARKINGS Sable & White SEX Male BORN 1-27-76

CALL NAME "George" BREEDER Sandra MacIntosh

CHANGED REG. NAME Heatherland's Mr. Kilpatrick, C.D. REG. No. WD435852 OWNER Carl A. & Amy Langhorst

	Ch. Malpsh the Duke of Erle	Ch. Sea Isle Serenade
		Sea Isle Dusky Belle
Fair Play of Sea Isle (SIRE)	Ch. Kawartha's Fair Game	Ch. SheltieLand Kiltie O'Sea Isle
		Ch. Kawartha's Sabrina Fair
Ch. Halstor's Peter Pumpkin (SIRE)		
	Ch. Sea Isle Serenade	Ch. Nashcrest Golden Note
		Ch. Sea Isle Serenata
Ch. Sea Isle Rhapsody of Halstor (DAM)	Ch. Colvidale Soliloquy	Ch. Sheltieland Kiltie O'Sea Isle
		Ch. Lochelven's Reverie
	Ch. Carmylie Elusive Dream	Ch. Halstor's Peter Pumpkin
		Jomar Carmylie Loves Magic
Ch. Heatherland's Simon Says (SIRE)	Katie J's Early Bird	Ch. Katie J's The Gay Prince
		Ch. Katie J's Sally Jean
Heatherland's Angel Face (DAM)		
	Ch. Heatherland's Simon Says	Ch. Carmylie Elusive Dream
		Katie J's Early Bird
Heatherland's Buffy St. Marie (DAM)	Macdega Pen & Ink	Ch. Philidove Heir Presumptive
		Ch. Lakehill Portrait in Blue

I hereby certify that this Pedigree is true to the best of my knowledge **Amy Langhorst**

495

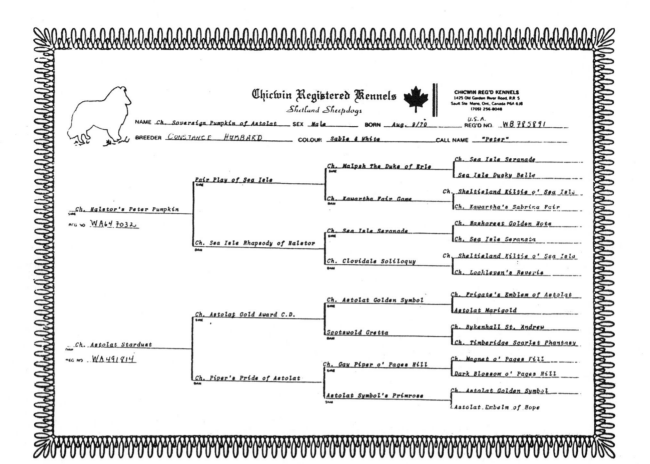

Chicwin Registered Kennels
Shetland Sheepdogs

NAME *Ch. Sovereign Pumpkin of Astolat* SEX *Male* BORN *Aug. 9/70* U.S.A. REG'D NO. *WB 785891*
BREEDER *CONSTANCE HUBBARD* COLOUR *Sable & White* CALL NAME *"Peter"*

CHICWIN REG'D KENNELS
1425 Old Garden River Road, R.R. 5
Sault Ste. Marie, Ont., Canada P6A 6J8
(705) 256-8048

			Ch. Sea Isle Serenade
		Ch. Nalpsh The Duke of Erle	
	Fair Play of Sea Isle		Sea Isle Dusky Belle
			Ch. Sheltieland Kiltie o' Sea Isle
		Ch. Kawartha Fair Game	
Ch. Halstor's Peter Pumpkin			Ch. Kawartha's Sabrina Fair
REG NO WA64 7032			Ch. Nashcrest Golden Note
		Ch. Sea Isle Serenade	
	Ch. Sea Isle Rhapsody of Halstor		Ch. Sea Isle Serenata
			Ch. Sheltieland Kiltie o' Sea Isle
		Ch. Clovidale Soliloquy	
			Ch. Lochleven's Reverie
			Ch. Frigate's Emblem of Astolat
		Ch. Astolat Golden Symbol	
	Ch. Astolat Gold Award C.D.		Astolat Marigold
			Ch. Bykenhall St. Andrew
		Scotswold Gretta	
Ch. Astolat Stardust			Ch. Timberidge Scarlet Phantasy
REG NO WA 491814			Ch. Magnet o' Pages Hill
		Ch. Gay Piper o' Pages Hill	
	Ch. Piper's Pride of Astolat		Dark Blossom o' Pages Hill
			Ch. Astolat Golden Symbol
		Astolat Symbol's Primrose	
			Astolat Emblem of Hope

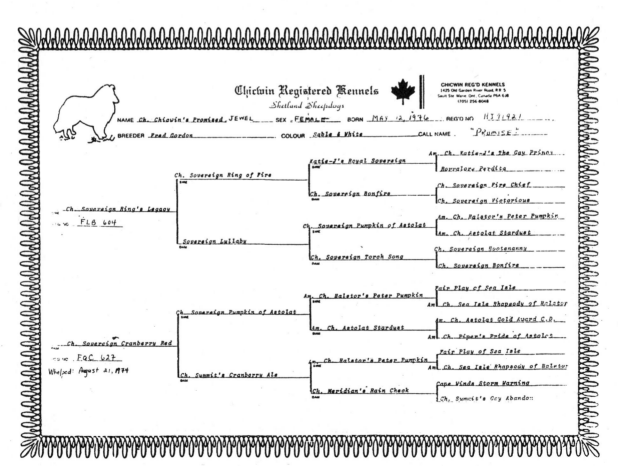

Chicwin Registered Kennels
Shetland Sheepdogs

NAME *Ch. Chicwin's Promised Jewel* SEX *FEMALE* BORN *MAY 12, 1976* REG'D NO. *HJ 91921*
BREEDER *Fred Gordon* COLOUR *Sable & White* CALL NAME *"Promise"*

CHICWIN REG'D KENNELS
1425 Old Garden River Road, R.R. 5
Sault Ste. Marie, Ont., Canada P6A 6J8
(705) 256-8048

			Am. Ch. Katie-J's the Gay Prince
		Katie-J's Royal Sovereign	
	Ch. Sovereign Ring of Fire		Rorralore Perdita
			Ch. Sovereign Fire Chief
		Ch. Sovereign Bonfire	
Ch. Sovereign Ring's Legacy			Ch. Sovereign Victorious
REG NO FLB 604			Am. Ch. Halstor's Peter Pumpkin
		Ch. Sovereign Pumpkin of Astolat	
	Sovereign Lullaby		Am. Ch. Astolat Stardust
			Ch. Sovereign Hootenanny
		Ch. Sovereign Torch Song	
			Ch. Sovereign Bonfire
			Fair Play of Sea Isle
		Am. Ch. Halstor's Peter Pumpkin	
	Ch. Sovereign Pumpkin of Astolat		Am. Ch. Sea Isle Rhapsody of Halstor
			Am. Ch. Astolat Gold Award C.D.
		Am. Ch. Astolat Stardust	
Ch. Sovereign Cranberry Red			Am. Ch. Piper's Pride of Astolat
REG NO FQC 627			Fair Play of Sea Isle
Whelped: August 21, 1974		Am. Ch. Halstor's Peter Pumpkin	
	Ch. Summit's Cranberry Ale		Am. Ch. Sea Isle Rhapsody of Halstor
			Cape Winds Storm Warning
		Ch. Meridian's Rain Check	
			Ch. Summit's Coy Abandon

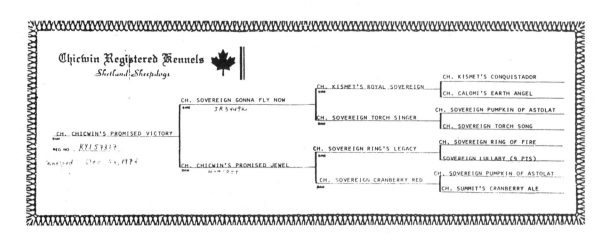

Chicwin Registered Kennels
Shetland Sheepdogs

CH. CHICWIN'S PROMISED VICTORY
REG. NO. KX157317
Whelped Dec 29, 1978

- CH. SOVEREIGN GONNA FLY NOW — JR34492
  - CH. KISMET'S ROYAL SOVEREIGN
    - CH. KISMET'S CONQUISTADOR
    - CH. CALOMI'S EARTH ANGEL
  - CH. SOVEREIGN TORCH SINGER
    - CH. SOVEREIGN PUMPKIN OF ASTOLAT
    - CH. SOVEREIGN TORCH SONG
- CH. CHICWIN'S PROMISED JEWEL
  - CH. SOVEREIGN RING'S LEGACY
    - CH. SOVEREIGN RING OF FIRE
    - SOVEREIGN LULLABY (9 PTS)
  - CH. SOVEREIGN CRANBERRY RED
    - CH. SOVEREIGN PUMPKIN OF ASTOLAT
    - CH. SUMMIT'S CRANBERRY ALE

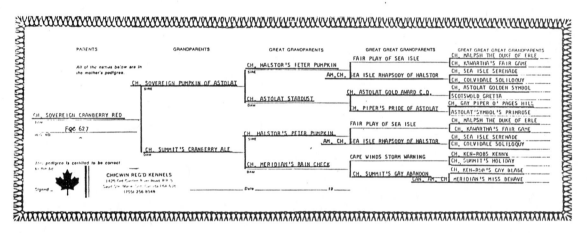

PARENTS	GRANDPARENTS	GREAT GRANDPARENTS	GREAT GREAT GRANDPARENTS	GREAT GREAT GREAT GRANDPARENTS

All of the names below are in the mother's pedigree.

CH. SOVEREIGN CRANBERRY RED — Fge 627

- CH. SOVEREIGN PUMPKIN OF ASTOLAT
  - CH. HALSTOR'S PETER PUMPKIN
    - FAIR PLAY OF SEA ISLE
      - CH. MALPSH THE DUKE OF ERLE
      - CH. KAWARTHA'S FAIR GAME
    - AM. CH. SEA ISLE RHAPSODY OF HALSTOR
      - CH. SEA ISLE SERENADE
      - CH. COLVIDALE SOLILOQUY
  - CH. ASTOLAT STARDUST
    - CH. ASTOLAT GOLD AWARD C.D.
      - CH. ASTOLAT GOLDEN SYMBOL
      - SCOTSWOLD GRETTA
    - CH. PIPER'S PRIDE OF ASTOLAT
      - CH. GAY PIPER O' PAGES HILL
      - ASTOLAT SYMBOL'S PRIMROSE
- CH. SUMMIT'S CRANBERRY ALE
  - CH. HALSTOR'S PETER PUMPKIN
    - FAIR PLAY OF SEA ISLE
      - CH. MALPSH THE DUKE OF ERLE
      - CH. KAWARTHA'S FAIR GAME
    - AM. CH. SEA ISLE RHAPSODY OF HALSTOR
      - CH. SEA ISLE SERENADE
      - CH. COLVIDALE SOLILOQUY
  - CH. MERIDIAN'S RAIN CHECK
    - CAPE WINDS STORM WARNING
      - CH. KEN-ROBS KENNY
      - CH. SUMMIT'S HOLIDAY
    - CH. SUMMIT'S GAY ABANDON
      - CH. KEN-ROB'S GAY BLADE
      - CAN. AM. CH. MERIDIAN'S MISS BEHAVE

This pedigree is certified to be correct by me to

CHICWIN REG'D KENNELS
1425 Fort Frances N Sault Ste. Marie, R.R. 5
Sault Ste. Marie, Ont. Canada P6A 6J8
(705) 256-8048

Signed _____ Date _____ 19___

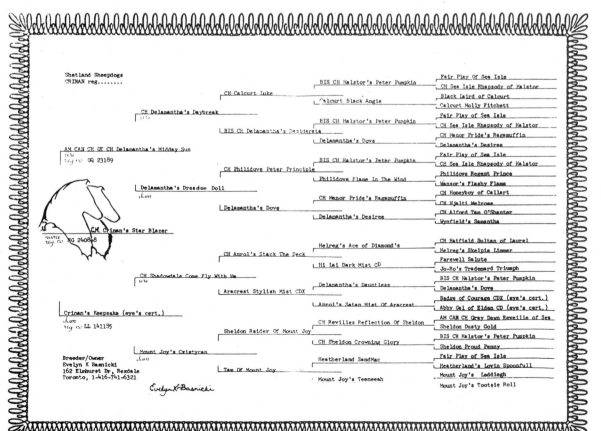

Shetland Sheepdogs
CRINAN reg........

CH Crinan's Star Blazer
reg. no. HG 240848

- AM CAN CH OT CH Delamantha's Midday Sun
  reg. no. OB 23189
  - CH Delamantha's Daybreak
    - CH Calcurt Luke
      - BIS CH Halstor's Peter Pumpkin
        - Fair Play Of Sea Isle
        - CH Sea Isle Rhapsody of Halstor
      - Calcurt Black Angie
        - Black Laird of Calcurt
        - Calcurt Molly Fitchett
    - BIS CH Delamantha's Desiderata
      - BIS CH Halstor's Peter Pumpkin
        - Fair Play Of Sea Isle
        - CH Sea Isle Rhapsody of Halstor
      - Delamantha's Dove
        - CH Manor Pride's Ragamuffin
        - Delamantha's Desiree
  - Delamantha's Dresden Doll
    - CH Philidove Peter Principle
      - BIS CH Halstor's Peter Pumpkin
        - Fair Play Of Sea Isle
        - CH Sea Isle Rhapsody of Halstor
      - Philidove Flame In The Wind
        - Philidove Regent Prince
        - Wansor's Flashy Flame
    - Delamantha's Dove
      - CH Manor Pride's Ragamuffin
        - CH Honeyboy of Callart
        - CH Hjalti Melrose
      - Delamantha's Desiree
        - CH Alford Tam O'Shanter
        - Wynfield's Samantha
- Crinan's Keepsake (eye's cert.)
  reg. no. LL 141195
  - CH Shadowdale Come Fly With Me
    - CH Anrol's Stack The Deck
      - Helreg's Ace of Diamond's
        - CH Hatfield Sultan of Laurel
        - Helreg's Skelpie Limmer
      - Hi Lai Dark Mist CD
        - Farewell Salute
        - Jo-Ro's Tredemard Triumph
    - Aracrest Stylish Mist CDX
      - Delamantha's Dauntless
        - BIS CH Halstor's Peter Pumpkin
        - Delamantha's Dove
      - Anrol's Satan Mist Of Aracrest
        - Badge of Courage CDX (eye's cert.)
        - Abby Gel of Elden CD (eye's cert.)
  - Mount Joy's Cristycan
    - Sheldon Raider Of Mount Joy
      - CH Revilles Reflection Of Sheldon
        - AM CAN CH Gray Dawn Reveille of Sea
        - Sheldon Dusty Gold
      - CH Sheldon Crowning Glory
        - BIS CH Halstor's Peter Pumpkin
        - Sheldon Proud Penny
    - Tam Of Mount Joy
      - Heatherland SandMac
        - Fair Play of Sea Isle
        - Heatherland's Lovin Spoonfull
      - Mount Joy's Teeneeah
        - Mount Joy's Laddiegh
        - Mount Joy's Tootsie Roll

Breeder/Owner
Evelyn K Basnicki
162 Elmhurst Dr, Rexdale
Toronto, 1-416-741-6321

Evelyn K Basnicki

497

Breed: SHETLAND SHEEPDOG

Ch. Name: SOVEREIGN RING'S LEGACY
CERF #SS-532/79-59

CKC Reg No.: FLB604

Born: 16 JUN 74

Colour: SABLE & WHITE

Sex: MALE

Breeder: MRS. ARIEL J. SLEETH, KINGSTON, ONTARIO.

Owner: MRS. ARIEL J. SLEETH, KINGSTON, ONTARIO.

1 Sire: CH. SOVEREIGN RING OF FIRE
CNS778

   3 KATIE-J'S ROYAL SOVEREIGN
874839 (USA: WB513468)

      7 AM. CH. KATIE-J'S THE GAY PRINCE
(USA: WA303697)

      8 RORRALORE PERDITA
(USA: WB157677)

   4 CH. SOVEREIGN BONFIRE
565607

      9 CH. SOVEREIGN FIRE CHIEF
495256

      10 CH. SOVEREIGN VICTORIOUS
459329

2 Dam: SOVEREIGN LULLABY
DSC290

   5 CH. SOVEREIGN PUMPKIN OF ASTOLAT
874836 (USA: WB785891)

      11 AM. CH. HALSTOR'S PETER PUMPKIN
(USA: WA647032)

      12 AM. CH. ASTOLAT STARDUST
(USA: WA491814)

   6 CH. SOVEREIGN TORCH SONG
737892

      13 CH. SOVEREIGN HOOTENANNY
606056

      14 CH. SOVEREIGN BONFIRE
565607

The Seal of The Canadian Kennel Club affixed hereto certifies that this Pedigree was officially compiled from Canadian Kennel Club records.

18 APR 75   AD

Shadowdale's Just A' Flying
nume reg no

WHELPED SEPT. 27 1982

CKC CRINAN"S STAR BLAZER
sire reg no NG240848
OWNER CRINAN SHELTIES R.
EVELYN K. BASNICKI 741-6321

AMCAN CH OT CH DELAMANTHA"S MIDDAY SUN
sire

  CH DELAMANTHA"S DAYBREAK

    CH CALCURT LUKE
      BIS CH HALSTOR"S PETER PUMPKIN
      CALCURT BLACK ANGIE
    BIS CH DELAMANTHA"S DESIDERATA
      BIS CH HALSTOR"S PETER PUMPKIN
      DELAMANTHA"S DOVE

  DELAMANTHA"S DRESIDEN DOLL
    CH PHILIDOVE PETER PRINCIPLE
      BIS CH HALSTOR"S PETER PUMPKIN
      PHILIDOVE FLAME IN THE WIND
    DELAMANTHA"S DOVE
      CH MANOR PRIDE"S RAGAMUFFIN
      DELAMANTHA"S DESIREE

CRINAN"S KEEPSAKE EYE"S CERT.
dam

  CH SHADOWDALE COME FLY WITH ME
    CH ANROL"S STACK THE DECK
      HELREG"S ACE OF DIAMOND"S
      HI LAI DARK MIST CD
    ARACREST STYLISH MIST CDX
      DELAMANTHA"S DAUNTLESS
      ANROL"S SATAN MIST OF ARACREST

  MOUNT JOY"S CRISTYCAN
    SHELDON RAIDER OF MOUNT JOY
      CH REVILLES REFLECTION OF SHELDON
      CH SHELDON CROWNING GLORY BIS
    TAM OF MOUNT JOY
      HEATHERLAND SANDMAC
      MOUNT JOY"S TEENEEAH

SHADOWDALE"S EMBER GLOW
dam reg. no. KL111930 MARY CURL
SHADOWDALE R. 426-4792

CH SHADOWDALE COME FLY WITH ME
sire

  CH ANROL"S STACK THE DECK
    HELREG"S ACE OF DIAMOND"S
      CH HATFIELD SULTAN OF LAUREL
      HELREG"S SKELPIE LIMMER
    HI LAI DARK MIST CD
      FAREWELL SALUTE
      JO-RO"S TRADEMARK"S TRIUMPH

  ARACREST STYLISH MIST CDX
    DELAMANTHA"S DAUNTLESS
      BIS CH HALSTOR"S PETER PUMPKIN
      DELAMANTHA"S DOVE
    ANROL"S SATAN MIST OF ARACREST EYE &HIP CERT.
      BADGE OF COURAGE CDX EYE & HIP CERT
      ABBY GAL OF EDLEN CD EYE & HIP CERT

DELAMANTHA"S DRESIDEN DOLL
dam

  CH PHILIDOVE PETER PRINCIPLE
    BIS CH HALSTOR"S PETER PUMPKIN
      FAIR PLAY OF SEA ISLE
      CH SEA ISLE RHAPSODY OF HALSTOR
    PHILIDOVE FLAME IN THE WIND
      PHILIDOVE REGENT PRINCE
      WANSOR"S FLASHY FLAME

  DELAMANTHA"S DOVE
    CH MANOR PRIDE"S RAGAMUFFIN
      CH HONEYBOY OF CALLART
      CH HJALTI MELROSE
    DELAMANTHA"S DESIREE
      CH ALFORD TAM O"SHANTER
      WYNFIELD"S SAMANTHA

CERTIFIED PEDIGREE

Name of Dog	CH MACDEGA PROOF POSITIVE	Sex MALE Reg. No. WE082263
Breed	SHETLAND SHEEPDOG	Color BLUE MERLE WHITE AND TAN
Date Whelped	JUNE 8 1978	Breeder CHRISTINE E POWER AND THOMAS W COEN

```
                                                                    7  CHENTERRA BEAUREGARD CD
                                                                        WC105207  4-73
                                  3   CH CHENTERRA THUNDERATION
                                      WC647582  2-75                    CHENTERRA COMMOTION
                                                                    8   WC304541  12-73
         RIDGESIDE STAR WARS                                        9  MAC ARDSLEIGH ENSIGN
  Sire-1  WD861666  12-78                                               WA589161  11-68

                                                                       PIXIE DELL INDIGO MELODY
                                                                       WB926701  9-74
                                  4                                 10     PIXIE DELL BLUE HEATHER
                                                                        WA303809  3-65

                                                                    11  CH SUNDOWNER MR BOJANGLES CD
                                  5   CH BANCHORY DEEP PURPLE            WB964301  2-73
                                      WD381631  6-77
                                                                       HORIZON WHITE ICE
         BANCHORY A BLUE NUN                                        12   WC923392  8-76
  Dam-2  WD647351  12-78                                            13  CH CHERDEN SOCK IT TO 'EM CD
                                                                        WB236839  2-70
                                  6   BANCHORY NIGHT GLOW
                                      WC820321  7-77                    BANCHORY HIGH GLOW
                                                                    14  WC017403  2-73
```

The Seal of The American Kennel Club affixed hereto certifies that
this pedigree has been compiled from official Stud Book records.

Date Issued   9-3-80 MS

Ch. Macdega Proof
Positive at two years of
age. This stunning
grandson of Ch.
Chenterra Thunderation
and Ch. Banchory Deep
Purple is owned by Jerry
and Chris Machado,
Montage Kennels.

499

Gestation, Whelping, and the Litter

When your bitch has been bred and is back at home, remain ever watchful that no other male gets to her until at least the twenty-second day of her season has passed. Prior to that time, it will still be possible for an undesired breeding to take place, which, at this point, would be catastrophic. Remember, she actually can have two separate litters by two different dogs, so *be alert and take care.*

In all other ways, the bitch should be treated quite normally. It is not necessary for her to have any additives to her diet until she is at least four to five weeks pregnant. It is also unnecessary for her to have additional food. It is better to underfeed the bitch this early in her pregnancy than to overfeed her. A fat bitch is not an easy whelper, so by "feeding her up" during the first few weeks, you may be creating problems for her.

Controlled exercise is good, and necessary, for your pregnant bitch. She should not be permitted to just lie around. At about seven weeks, the exercise should be slowed down to several sedate walks daily, not too long and preferably on the leash.

In the fourth or fifth week of pregnancy, calcium may be added to the diet; and at seven weeks, the one meal a day may be increased to two meals with some nutritional additives in each. Canned milk may be added to her meals at this time.

A week before she is due to whelp, your Sheltie bitch should be introduced to her whelping box, so that she will have accustomed herself to it and feel at home there by the time the puppies arrive. She should be encouraged to sleep there and be permitted to come and go as she pleases. The box should be roomy enough for her to lie down and stretch out in it; but it should not be too large or the pups will have too much room in which to roam, and they may get chilled if they move too far away from the warmth of their mother. Be sure that there is a "pig rail" for the box, which will prevent the puppies from being crushed against the side of the box. The box should be lined with newspapers, which can easily be changed as they become soiled.

The room where the whelping box is placed, either in the home or in the kennel, should be free from drafts and should be kept at about

Banchory A Blue Nun in whelp with her litter by Ch. Macdega Proof Positive, a son back to mother breeding. Owned by Jerry and Chris Machado, Montage Shelties.

Alice with her newborn puppy. Miss Elaine Wishnow, owner.

eighty degrees Fahrenheit. It may be necessary during the cold months to install an infrared lamp in order to maintain sufficient warmth, in which case guard against the lamp being placed too low or too close to the puppies.

Keep a big pile of newspapers near the box. You'll find that you never have enough of these when there is a litter, so start accumulating them ahead of time. A pile of clean towels, a pair of scissors, and a bottle of alcohol should also be close at hand. Have all of these things ready at least a week before the bitch is due to whelp, as you never know exactly when she may start.

The day or night before she is due, the bitch will become restless; she'll be in and out of her box and in and out of the door. She may refuse food, and at this point her temperature will start to drop. She will start to dig and tear up the newspapers in her box, shiver, and generally look uncomfortable. You alone should be with her at this time (or one other person who is an experienced breeder, to give you confidence if this is one of your first litters). The bitch does not need an audience or any extra people around. This is not a sideshow, and several people hovering over the bitch may upset her to the point where she may hurt the puppies. Stay nearby, but do not fuss too much over her. Keep a calm attitude; this will give her confidence. Eventually she will settle down in her box and begin to pant; shortly thereafter she will start to have contractions and soon a puppy will begin to emerge, sliding out with one of the contractions.

The mother immediately should open the sac and bite the cord and clean up the puppy. She will also eat the placenta, which you should permit. Once the puppy is cleaned, it should be placed next to the bitch, unless she is showing signs of having another one immediately. The puppy should start looking for a nipple on which to nurse, and you should make certain that it is able to latch on and start doing so at once.

If a puppy is a breech birth (*i.e.*, born feet first), then you must watch carefully that it is delivered as quickly as possible and the sac removed very quickly, so that the puppy does not drown. Sometimes even a normally positioned birth will seem extremely slow in coming. Should either of these events occur, you might take a clean towel and, as the bitch contracts, pull the puppy out, doing so gently and with utmost care. If the bitch does not open the sac and cut the cord, you will have to do so. If the puppy shows little sign of life, make sure the mouth is free of liquid and then, using a Turkish towel or terry cloth, massage the puppy's chest, rubbing back and forth quite briskly. Continue this for about fifteen minutes. It may be necessary to try mouth-to-mouth breathing. Open the puppy's jaws and, using a finger, depress the tongue which may be stuck to the roof of the puppy's mouth. Then blow hard down the puppy's throat. Bubbles may pop out of its nose, but keep on blowing. Rub with the towel again across the chest, and try artificial respiration, pressing the sides of the chest together, slowly and rhythmically, in and out, in and out. Keep trying one method or the other for at least fifteen minutes (actual time—not how long it seems to you) before giving up. You may be rewarded with a live puppy who otherwise would not have made it.

If you are able to revive the puppy, it should not be put with the mother immediately, as it should be kept extra warm for a while. Put it in a cardboard box near a stove, on an electric heating pad, or, if it is the time of year when your heat is running, near a radiator until the rest of the litter has been born. Then it can be put in with the others.

The bitch may go for an hour or more between puppies, which is fine as long as she seems comfortable and is not straining or contracting. She should not be allowed to remain unassisted for more than an hour if she does continue to contract. This is when you should call your veterinarian, whom you should have alerted ahead of time of the possibility so that he will be somewhere within easy reach. He may want the bitch brought in so that he can examine her and perhaps give her a shot of Pituitrin. In some cases, the veterinarian may find that a Caesarean operation is necessary, because a puppy may be lodged in some manner that makes normal delivery impossible. This can occur due to the size of a puppy or may be due to the fact that the puppy is turned wrong. If any of the foregoing occurs, the puppies already born must be kept warm in their cardboard box, which should have been lined with shredded newspapers in advance and which should have a heating pad beneath it.

Ch. Jade Mist Woodwind Chimes with her litter of six males and one female sired by Ch. Barwood's Weather Report. Dr. and Mrs. Keith B. Howell, owners.

Assuming that there have been no problems, and the bitch has whelped normally, you should insist that she go outside to exercise, staying just long enough to make herself comfortable. She can be offered a bowl of milk and a biscuit, but then she should settle down with her family. Be sure to clean out the whelping box and change the newspapers so that she will have a fresh bed.

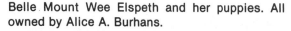

Belle Mount Wee Elspeth and her puppies. All owned by Alice A. Burhans.

Belle Mount Wee Betsey with her puppies. Alice A. Burhans, Belle Mount Kennels.

Valdawn's Heather of Rockwood, who has one leg toward her C.D., with her babies. Owned by Debra Elkin, Enchanted Shetland Sheepdogs.

If the mother lacks milk at this point, the puppies will need to be fed by hand, kept very warm, and held against the mother's teats several times a day in order to stimulate and encourage the secretion of her milk, which will probably start shortly.

Unless some problem arises, there is little you need do about the puppies until they become three to four weeks old. Keep the box clean with fresh papers. When the puppies are a couple of days old, the papers should be removed and

Turkish towels should be tacked down to the bottom of the box so that the puppies will have traction when they move. This is important.

If the bitch has difficulties with her milk supply, or if you should be so unfortunate as to lose the bitch, then you must be prepared to either hand-feed or tube-feed the puppies if they are to survive. We prefer the tube method as it is so much faster and easier. If the bitch is available, it is better that she continue to clean and care for the puppies in the normal manner, except for

Ten-day-old Shetland Sheepdog puppies. Owned by Miss Elaine Wishnow.

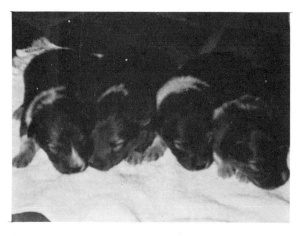

Two-week-old Enchanted Sheltie puppies. Owned by Debra Elkin.

the food supplements you will provide. If she is unable to do this, then after every feeding, you must gently rub each puppy's abdomen with wet cotton to induce urination, and the rectum should be gently rubbed to open the bowels.

Newborn puppies must be fed every three or four hours around the clock. The puppies must be kept warm during that time. Have your veterinarian show you how to tube-feed. Once learned it is really quite simple, fast, and efficient.

After a normal whelping, the bitch will require additional food to enable her to produce sufficient milk. She should be fed twice daily now, and some canned milk should be available to her several times during the day.

Sixteen-day-old Sheltie puppies. Elaine Wishnow, owner.

Annie at nineteen days of age. Miss Elaine Wishnow, owner, Malashel Shelties.

When the puppies are two weeks old, you should clip their nails, as they are needle-sharp at this point and can hurt or damage the mother's teats and stomach as the pups hold on to nurse.

Between three and four weeks of age, the puppies should begin to be weaned. Scraped beef (prepared by scraping it off slices of raw beef with a spoon, so that none of the muscle or gristle is included) may be offered in very small quantities a couple of times daily for the first few days. If the puppy is reluctant to try it, put a little on your finger and rub it on the puppy's lips; this should get things going. By the third day, you can mix in ground puppy chow with warm water as directed on the package, offering it four times daily. By now the mother should be kept out of the box and away from the puppies for several hours at a time. After the puppies reach five weeks of age, she should be left in with them only overnight. By the time they are six weeks old, the puppies should be entirely weaned and the mother should only check on them with occasional visits.

Most veterinarians recommend a temporary DHL (distemper, hepatitis, leptospirosis) shot when the puppies are six weeks old. This remains effective for about two weeks. Then, at eight weeks, the series of permanent shots begins for the DHL protection. It is a good idea to discuss with your vet the advisability of having

Seven-week-old puppies enjoying their playpen. Note the merry expressions of these babies by Ch. Rockwoods The Hustler ex Valdawn's Heather of Rockwood. Bred by Debra Elkin.

your puppies inoculated against the dreaded parvovirus at the same time. Each time the pups go to the vet for shots, you should bring stool samples so that they can be examined for worms. Worms go through various stages of development and may be present in a stool sample even though the sample does not test positive. So do not neglect to keep careful watch on this.

The puppies should be fed four times daily until they are three months old. Then you can cut back to three feedings daily. By the time the puppies are six months old, two meals daily are sufficient. Some people feed their dogs twice daily throughout their lifetime, while others cut back to one meal daily when the puppy reaches one year of age.

The ideal time for Sheltie puppies to go to their new homes is when they are between eight and twelve weeks old, although some puppies successfully adjust to a new home when they are six weeks of age. Be certain that they go to their future owners accompanied by a description of the diet you've been feeding them and a schedule of the shots they have received and those they still need. These should be included with a registration application and a copy of the pedigree.

Sterling's Enchanted Spirit, by Ch. Rockwoods The Hustler ex Valdawn's Heather of Rockwood, at three weeks of age. This promising baby belongs to Debra Elkin.

Ch. Philidove Benevolent Anthony, by Ch. Banchory High Born ex Ch. Philidove Carmylie In A Mist. Handled by Steve Barger; owned by Irene Brody.

CHAPTER SIXTEEN

You and Your Sheltie

A truly beautiful pen and ink sketch of Am. and Can. Ch. Caper Hills Song Sung Blue done by Marna Obermiller of California. Lynette Smith, breeder-owner, Caper Hill Shelties.

Shetland Sheepdogs have enjoyed a steady rise in popularity since they first appeared in the world of purebred dogs, and today they rank in the top ten most popular dog breeds. There is good reason for this popularity, for Shelties are versatile dogs and excel as house pets and as dog show and obedience competitors. Though owning a Sheltie does entail certain responsibilities, these responsibilities are a pleasure to fulfill for such a personable breed of dog.

The Shetland Sheepdog Personality

If you have never owned a Sheltie and are considering doing so, I am sure that you will be well pleased if you select this as your future breed. Shelties are most intelligent, sweet, loving little dogs; loyal and devoted; and a joy to own.

The breed is of a convenient size, no matter where you live—not too large to manage happily in a city apartment and not too small to enjoy the outdoor life of a country dog. They are sturdy, long-lived dogs, very important when one considers how quickly the lifetime of a beloved pet seems to pass. You will note mention in many places of members of this breed still "going strong" in their upper teens!

The Sheltie is one of the easiest "coated" breeds to keep groomed. As Linda More says,

their coats, though luxuriant and beautiful to the eye, are very much of the "wash and wear" variety, requiring little more for a pet than a weekly brushing. Attention to the feet, and an occasional bath, and you are "in business" with a glamorous looking little dog of great beauty.

The Sheltie is gentle and quiet around the house. His alertness, however, makes him very much an "on-the-spot" watch dog, quick to give the alarm should he hear an intruder or sense danger to his family.

There are countless obedience stars in the Sheltie world, for due to his quick intelligence and desire to please, the Sheltie has been outstandingly successful in this area. If you wish to have just a well-trained pet, he will quickly learn what is expected. And if you hanker for the thrill of competition, he will almost surely "do you proud" in obedience classes once trained for this purpose.

Their natural sweetness of disposition and devotion to family make Shelties a perfect pet for children. Their patience seems almost endless with youngsters, whom they obviously adore. They also become deeply devoted to the adult family members and are quite happy so long as they are at your side.

The Sheltie is not a breed disposed to roam. While for his own safety, no dog should ever be turned loose unrestricted, you will not find the Sheltie constantly trying to escape you and slip away, winding up lost.

One of the breeds known as "good doers," Shelties have easy-to-please appetites and seem to thrive nicely so long as they receive a balanced diet.

They are sturdy enough to enjoy outdoor exercise while at the same time are equally happy snoozing at your feet or by the fire. From every point of view they are an ideal breed to own: one of the most beautiful, intelligent, faithful, and hardy members of our canine world.

Belle Mount Wee Renee in her favorite pose. Alice Burhans, Belle Mount Kennels.

Jason Haderlie with Ch. SumerSong Winter Shadows, both three years old. Peggy and Jan Haderlie.

Ch. Severn Idle Gossip enjoying a romp at Severn Kennels. Owned by Linda More.

"Playing ball." Two of the Carmylie Shelties enjoying a game. Jean D. Simmonds, owner.

Valdawn's Sterling Nugget, who seems to have just opened a gift package. Owned by Kathleen Searle and David Nytray.

From Lee Reasin's collection comes this fantastic Christmas card from Merrywood Kennels which he kindly is sharing with our readers.

An informal snapshot showing the beautiful quality and type of Ch. Ken-Rob's Gay Blade. Owned by Ken-Rob Shelties, Kenneth E. Poole and Robert W. White.

Responsibilities of Shetland Sheepdog Owners

Whether you are a one-dog owner, the owner of a show kennel, one involved in obedience, or a breeder, there are definite responsibilities—to your dog or dogs, to your breed, and to the general public—involved which should never be overlooked or taken lightly.

It is inexcusable for anyone to breed dogs promiscuously, producing unneeded litters. The only time a responsible breeder plans a litter is when it is *needed* to carry on a bloodline or to provide dogs for which this breeder has very definite plans, including orders for at least half the number of puppies which will probably be born. Every healthy puppy deserves a good and loving home, assuring its future well-being. No puppy should be born to an uncertain future on someone's assumption that there will be no problem selling or otherwise finding a home for it, as very definitely this is not always easy. Overpopulation is the dog world's most heartbreaking tragedy. Those of us who love dogs should not add to it by carelessly producing more. If you have any reason to feel that the puppies may not be assured of homes, don't breed the bitch; wait for a more propitious time. Certainly no Sheltie breeder likes the thought of

running around frantically trying to find someone who will take puppies off his hands, even if they must be given away. The latter usually is not a good idea anyway, as many people cannot resist saying "yes" to something which costs nothing, regardless of whether or not they really want it. As the Sheltie grows larger and demands more care, their enthusiasm wanes to the point that the dog soon is left to roam the streets where he is subject to all sorts of dangers, and the owner simply could not care less. If one pays for something, one seems to respect it more.

One litter at a time is all that any breeder should produce, making sure that all those puppies are well provided for prior to breeding for another litter. Breeders should do all in their power to ascertain that the home to which each of his puppies goes is a *good* home, one that offers proper care, a fenced in area, and a really enthusiastic owner. I have tremendous respect for those breeders who make it a point to check carefully the credentials of prospective purchasers, and I firmly believe that all breeders should do likewise on this important point. I am certain that no breeder wants any Sheltie puppy to wind up in an animal shelter, in an experimental laboratory, or as a victim of a speeding car. While complete control of such situations may not be possible, it is at least our responsibility to make every effort to turn our puppies over to people who have the same outlook as our own where love of dogs and responsibility toward them are concerned and who realize that

Ch. Carmylie Polly Paintbrush, by Ch. Banchory Deep Purple ex Ch. Carmylie As If Bi Chance, just relaxing. Owned by Jean D. Simmonds, Carmylie Shelties.

Two Shelties, Forever Gypsy and Forever Sabrina, pictured on the Aleutian Islands in April 1972. Owner, Leslie B. Rogers, Forever Kennels.

Another marvelous Merrywood Christmas greeting. Shared with us by Lee Reasin.

the ownership of a dog involves care, not neglect.

It is the breeder's responsibility to sell every puppy with the understanding that should the new owner find it necessary to place the dog elsewhere, you, the breeder, must be contacted immediately and given the opportunity to take back the dog or to help in finding it a new home. Many a dog starting out in what has seemed a good home has, under unforeseen circumstances, been passed along to others, only to wind up in exactly the sort of situation we most want to avoid. Keep in touch with what is happening to your dogs after they are sold.

The final obligation every dog owner shares, be there just one dog or many, is that of leaving detailed and up-to-date instructions in our wills about what is to become of our animals in the event of our death. Far too many of us are apt to procrastinate and leave this matter unattended to, feeling that everything will work out all right or that "someone will see to them." The latter is not too likely to happen, at least not to the benefit of the dogs, unless the owner makes absolutely certain that all will be well for them in the future.

If you have not already done so, please get together with your lawyer and set up a clause in your will specifying what is to be done with each and every dog you own and to whom each will be entrusted (after first ascertaining that this person is willing and able to assume the responsibility); also include details about the location of all registration papers, pedigrees, and kennel records, along with ways of identifying each dog. Just think of the possibilities of what might happen otherwise!

It is not wise to count on family members, unless they share your involvement with the dogs. In many cases our relatives are not the least bit "dog-oriented," perhaps they think we're a trifle crazy for being such enthusiasts, and they might absolutely panic at the thought of suddenly having even *one* dog thrust upon them. They might mean well, and they might try; but it is unfair to them and to the dogs to leave the one stuck with the other!

If you travel a great deal with your dogs, another wise idea is to post prominently in your vehicle and carry in your wallet the name, address, and telephone number of someone to be called to take charge of them in case of an accident. Of course, this should be done by prearrangement with the person named. We have such a friend, and she has a signed check of ours to be used in case of an emergency or accident when we are travelling with our dogs; this check

Two stunning Shelties! Ch. Carrico's Port of Entry, a tricolor, and Ch. Hallinwood Robin of Marl, a sable, appeared in this Davidow advertisement for *Vogue* magazine. Owned by the Ardencaple Kennels, Mr. and Mrs. Willard K. Denton.

Ch. Ardencaple's Cute Trick from a 1953 painting by Jeanne Mellin. Mr. and Mrs. Willard K. Denton, owners, Ardencaple Kennels.

will be used to cover her expenses to come and take over the care of our dogs should anything happen to make it impossible for us to do so.

The registration certificates of all our dogs are enclosed in an envelope with our wills, and the person who will be in charge knows each of them, and one from the other, so there will be no identification problem. These are all points to be considered, for which provision should be made.

We also owe an obligation to our older dogs who too often are disregarded. It disgusts me that so many supposedly great dog lovers think nothing of getting an older dog, even though well, happy, and enjoying life, out of the way to make room for younger show prospects or additional puppies. The people I consider to be genuine dog lovers are the ones who permit their dogs to live out their lives in comfort as loved, respected members of the household or kennel. How quickly some of us seem to forget the pleasures these dogs have brought us with exciting wins and the devotion they have shown to us and our families!

So much for our responsibility to our dogs, but we also owe a responsibility to our breed: to keep up its quality and to protect its image. Every Shetland Sheepdog breeder should breed only from and for high-grade stock and should guard against the market being flooded with excess puppies. We should display good sportsmanship and concern for the dogs at all times, and we should involve ourselves whenever possible in activities beneficial to the breed.

To the general public we owe the consideration of good dog ownership. Our dogs should not be permitted to run at large and annoy others. Dogs should not be left barking endlessly, tied outside or closed in the house. We should pick up after our dogs, as required in most cities, when we exercise them where people must walk. We should, in other words, enjoy our dogs without allowing them to infringe on those who may be less enthusiastic.

Kerrylance Gypsy Mol of Edlen gives us a big smile. One of the Edlen Shelties.

Ch. Hallinwood Robin Hood of Marl and Hallinwood Token with some of the Ardencaple puppies. All owned by Mr. and Mrs. Willard K. Denton.

Travelling With Your Shetland Sheepdog

When you travel with a dog, you must always remember that everyone does not necessarily share your love of dogs and that those who do not, strange creatures though they may seem, have their rights too. These rights, on which we should not encroach, include not being disturbed, annoyed, or made uncomfortable by the presence and behavior of other people's pets. Sheltie owners, since theirs is an intelligent and easily trained breed, should have the dog well schooled in proper canine behavior by the time maturity is reached. Your dog should not jump enthusiastically on strangers, no matter how playful or friendly the dog's intentions. We may love having them do this to us, but it is unlikely that someone else will share our enthusiasm, especially in the case of muddy paws on delicate or light-colored clothes which may be soiled or damaged. A sharp "Down" from you should be promptly obeyed, as should be "Sit," "Stay," and "Come."

If you expect to take your Sheltie on many trips, he should have, for your sake and for his, a crate of appropriate size for him to relax in comfortably. In cases of emergency or accident, a crated dog is far more likely to escape injury. Left in a parked car, a crated dog should have the car windows fully open in hot weather, thus being assured sufficient ventilation. For your own comfort, a dog in a crate does not hang from the car window, climb over you and your passengers, and shed hair on the upholstery. Dogs quickly become accustomed to their crates, especially when started with one, as they should be, from puppyhood. Both you and the dog will have a more enjoyable trip when you provide him with this safeguard.

If you do permit your dog to ride loose in the car, see to it that he does not hang from the windows. He could become overly excited by something he sees and jump out; he could lose his balance and fall out should you stop short or swerve unexpectedly; he could suffer an eye injury induced by the strong wind generated by the moving car. All of these unnecessary risks can so easily be avoided by crating!

Never, ever, under any circumstances, should a dog be permitted to ride uncrated in the back end of an open pick-up truck. I have noted, with disgust and horror, that some people do transport their dogs in this manner, and I think it cruel and shocking. How easily such a dog can be thrown out of the car by sudden jolts or an impact! And I am sure that many dogs have jumped out at the sight of something exciting along the way, quite possibly into the path of an oncoming car. Some unthinking individuals tie the dog, probably not realizing that if he were to

Can. Ch. Ridgeside Star Wars, by Ch. Chenterra Thunderation ex Pixie Dell Indigo Melody. Handled by Steve Barger; owned by Gulie Krook.

Rebecca Burhans, then eight years old, sheltered by her Shelties at the 1972 Hartford benched dog show. Belle Mount Kennels.

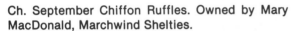

Ch. September Chiffon Ruffles. Owned by Mary MacDonald, Marchwind Shelties.

jump under those circumstances, his neck could be broken, he could be dragged alongside the vehicle or get under its wheels, or he could be hit by another vehicle. If you are for any reason taking your dog *anywhere* in an open back truck, *please* have sufficient regard for that dog to provide a crate to protect him. Also please remember that with or without a crate, a dog riding exposed to the sun in hot weather can really suffer and have his life endangered by the heat.

If you are staying in a hotel or motel with your dog, please exercise him somewhere other than in the parking lot, along the walkways, or in the flower beds of the property. People walking to and from their rooms or cars really are not thrilled at "stepping in something" left by your dog and should not be subjected to the annoyance. Should an accident occur, pick it up with tissues or a paper towel and deposit it in a proper receptacle; don't just let it remain there. Usually there are grassy areas on the sides or behind motels where dogs can be exercised with no bother to anyone. Use those places rather than the busy, more conspicuous, carefully tended areas. If you are becoming a dog show enthusiast, you will eventually need an exercise pen to take with you to the show. They are ideal to use when staying

Two handsome Shelties adorning a post card, so old that it had been mailed with a 1 ¢ postage stamp. From A.K.N.'s collection.

at motels, too, as they permit you to limit the dog's roaming space and to pick up after him easily. Should you have two or more dogs, such a convenience is truly a "must!"

Never leave your dog unattended in a room at a motel unless you are absolutely, positively, sure that he will stay quiet and not destroy anything. You do not want a long list of complaints from irate fellow-guests, caused by the annoying barking or whining of a lonesome dog in strange surroundings or an overzealous watch dog barking furiously each time a footstep passes the door. And you certainly do not want to return to

torn curtains or bedspreads, soiled rugs, or other embarrassing (and sometimes expensive) evidence of the fact that your dog is not really house-reliable.

If yours is a dog accustomed to travelling with you and you are positive that his behavior will be acceptable when left alone, that is fine. But if the slightest uncertainty exists, the wise course is to leave him in the car while you go to dinner or elsewhere and then bring him into the room when you are ready to retire for the night.

When you travel with a dog, it is sometimes simpler to take along his food and water from

These three exquisite Shelties are, left to right, Ch. Rorralore Anne Boleyn, Ch. Rorralore Mickey Dazzler, and Rorralore Queen Anne's Lace. All bred and owned by Charlotte Clem McGowan, Rorralore Kennels.

home rather than to buy food and to look for water while you travel. In this way he will have the rations to which he is accustomed and which you know agree with him, and there will be no problems due to different drinking water. Feeding on the road is quite easy now, at least for short trips, with all the splendid dry prepared foods and high quality canned meats available, not to mention the "just remove it from the packet" convenience foods. And many types of lightweight, refillable water containers can be bought at many types of stores.

If you are going to another country, you will need a health certificate from your veterinarian for each dog you are taking with you, certifying that each has had rabies shots within the required length of time preceding your visit.

Remember that during the summer, the sun's rays can make an inferno of a closed-up car in a matter of minutes, so always leave windows open enough that there is sufficient ventilation for the dog. Again, if your dog is in a crate, this can be done easily and with safety. Remember, too, that leaving the car in a shady spot does not mean that it will remain shaded. The position of the sun changes quickly, and the car you left nicely shaded half an hour earlier may be in the full glare of the sun upon your return. Be alert and be cautious.

When you travel with your dog, be sure to take a lead and use it, unless he is completely and thoroughly obedience trained. Even if the dog is trained, however, using a lead is a wise precaution against his getting lost in strange territory. I am sure that all of us have seen in the "Lost and Found" columns the sad little messages about dogs who have gotten away or been lost during a trip, so why take chances?

"A Gift of Love." This is the title Betty Whelen has given this beautiful photograph, taken by Rhea Butler, of Betty with the adorable puppy Designed Bi Pocono. Elizabeth D. Whelen, Pocono Shetland Sheepdogs.

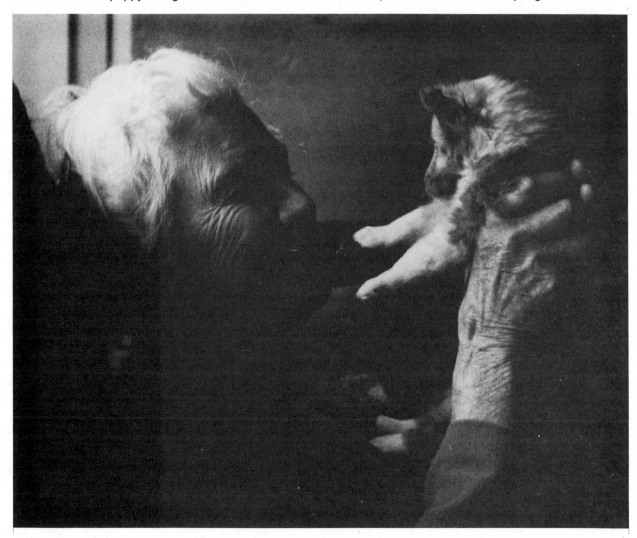

517

A lovely head-study of Ch. Rickgarbob Jonathan, by Ch. Gerthstone's Jon Christopher ex Rickgarbob Lotsa Luck. Jonathan finished at sixteen months of age from the Bred-by-Exhibitor Class. Bred and owned by Rickgarbob Shelties, Mrs. Marie Carlough and Bob Carlough.

CHAPTER SEVENTEEN

Veterinarian's Corner

by Joseph P. Sayres, D.V.M.

Ch. Macdega Chasing Rainbows, by Ch. Chenterra Thunderation ex Macdega Blue Portrait. Handled by Steve W. Barger and owned by Tetsuo Miyama.

Until recent years, there has been a lot of misunderstanding and even animosity between veterinarians and breeders. Some distrust arose on the breeder's part because most veterinarians were not familiar with, or even interested in learning about, purebred dogs. Some of the problems encountered were peculiar to certain breeds and some would crop up at inconvenient times. Veterinarians were then beset by breeders who thought that they knew more about the medical problems of their dogs than the vets did. The veterinarians very often were called only for emergencies or when it was too late to save a sick dog that had been treated too long by people in the kennel. Another problem was that many breeders had never included veterinary fees in their budgets and were slow to pay their bills, if indeed they paid them at all.

Fortunately, these problems, to a large extent, have been solved. Education and better communication between breeders and veterinarians have eliminated most areas of friction.

Today, veterinary education and training have advanced to a point paralleling that of human standards. This resulted from advances in the field of Veterinary Science in the last two decades. Sophisticated diagnostic procedures, new and advanced surgical techniques, and modern well-equipped hospitals all make for improved medical care for our dogs.

Educated breeders now realize that, while they may know more about the general husbandry of their dogs and the unique traits of the Shetland Sheepdog, they should not attempt to diagnose and treat their ailments.

In choosing your veterinarian, be selective. He or she should be friendly, should be interested in your dogs, and, in the case of breeders, should be interested in your breeding programs. Veterinarians should be willing to talk freely with you. Such things as fees, availability for emergencies, and what services are and are not available should be discussed and understood before a lasting relationship with your veterinarian can be established.

You can expect your veterinarian's office, clinic, or hospital to be clean, free of undesirable odors, well equipped, and staffed by sincere, friendly personnel who willingly serve you at all times. All employees should be clean, neat in appearance, and conversant with whatever services you require. You may also expect your dog to be treated carefully and kindly at all times by the doctor and his staff.

Your veterinarian should participate in continuing education programs in order to keep up with changes and improvements in his field. He should also be aware of his limitations. If he doesn't feel confident in doing certain procedures, he should say so and refer you to qualified individuals to take care of the problem. Seeking second opinions and consultation with specialists on difficult cases is more the rule than the exception nowadays. That is as it should be.

You will know that if your veterinarian is a member of the American Animal Hospital Association, he and his facility have had to measure up to high standards of quality and are subjected to inspections every two years.

Many excellent veterinarians and veterinary hospitals by choice do not belong to the American Animal Hospital Association. You can satisfy your curiosity about these places by taking guided tours of the facilities and learning by word of mouth about the quality of medicine practiced at these hospitals.

So far, we have discussed only what you should expect from your veterinarian. Now, let's discuss what the veterinarian expects from his clients.

Most of all, he expects his clients to be open and frank in their relations with him. He doesn't like to be double-checked and second-guessed behind his back. He also wants you to handle your pet so that he, in turn, can examine him. He also expects you to leash your dog, to control him, and to keep him from bothering other pets in the room. He expects to be paid a fair fee and to be paid promptly for services rendered. Fees in a given area tend to be consistent, and variations are due only to complications or unforeseen problems. Medicine is not an exact science; therefore, things unpredictable can happen.

If you are dissatisfied with the services or fees, then ask to discuss these things in a friendly manner with the doctor. If his explanations are not satisfactory or he refuses to talk to you about the problem, then you are justified in seeking another doctor.

The veterinarian expects to provide his services for your animals during regular hours whenever possible. But he also realizes that in a kennel or breeding operation, emergencies can occur at any time, and his services will be needed at off hours. You should find out how these emergencies will be handled and be satisfied with the procedures.

No veterinarian can be on duty twenty-four hours of every day. Today, cooperative veterinarians group together to take turns covering each other's emergency calls. Some cities have emergency clinics that operate solely to take care of those catastrophes that seem usually to happen in the middle of the night or on weekends.

Ch. Nathan Hale of Carmylie, by Deltam's In Sunshine Or Shadow ex Carmylie Gentian Bluefringe, one of the many fine Shelties owned by Jean D. Simmonds.

My conclusion, after thirty years of practice, is that most disagreements and hard feelings between clients and veterinarians are a result of a breakdown in communication. Find a veterinarian that you can talk to and can be comfortable with, and you'll make a valuable friend.

In using veterinary services to their best advantage, I believe that you will find that prevention of diseases and problems is more important than trying to cure these things after they occur. In other words, an ounce of prevention is worth a pound of cure.

Congenital Defects

Shetland Sheepdogs have their share of congenital defects. From the publication *Congenital Defects in Dogs* published by Ralston Purina Company, as well as other reliable sources, the following conditions are listed as congenital defects in Shetland Sheepdogs:

a. Cataracts, Bilateral—Opacity of the lenses of the eyes.

b. Central Progressive Retinal Atrophy—Causes loss of central vision at three to five years of age. Difficulty in seeing stationary objects. Vision better in dim light.

c. Choroidal Hypoplasia—Underdevelopment of a vascular coat of the eye.

d. Coloboma—Defect in ocular tissues.

e. Cryptorchidism—Non-descent of testicles.

f. Dwarfism—Achondroplasia.

g. Ectasia Syndrome—Defective retinal development.

h. Epidermolysis Bullosa—Onset at two to four months old. Signs: baldness, redness of the skin, and a blistering reaction of the skin to trauma. Cause unknown.

i. Hemophilia A — Factor VIII Deficiency—Prolonged bleeding episodes.

j. Hip Dysplasia—Deformed hip joints. See section on this subject near end of chapter.

k. Nasal Solar Dermatitis—Lack of skin pigment on nose predisposes to the disease.

l. Patent Ductus Arteriosus—Non-closure of vessels between aorta and pulmonary artery.

m. "Walleye"—Blue and white iris.

Vaccines

By proper and vigilant vaccination programs, the following contagious diseases can be eliminated: distemper, hepatitis, parainfluenza, leptospirosis, rabies, and parvovirus enteritis.

The vaccination schedule described below should be set up and strictly followed to prevent infectious diseases.

Distemper: Vaccinate when six to eight weeks old, with the second inoculation to be given at twelve to sixteen weeks of age. Revaccinate annually.

Hepatitis (Adenovirus): Follow the same schedule as for distemper.

Parainfluenza (Kennel cough): Follow the same schedule as for distemper.

Leptospirosis: Give first vaccine at nine weeks of age. Revaccinate with second DHLP (distemper, hepatitis, leptospirosis, parainfluenza) at twelve to sixteen weeks of age. Revaccinate annually.

Rabies: Give first inoculation at three to four months of age; then revaccinate when one year old, and at least every three years thereafter. If dog is over four months old at the time of the first vaccination, then revaccinate in one year and then once every three years thereafter.

Parvovirus: Give first vaccine at seven to eight weeks of age, second vaccine four weeks later, and third vaccine four weeks later. Duration of immunity from three injections established at one year at the time of this writing. See explanation below. Revaccinate annually.

Vaccines used are all modified live virus vaccines except for leptospirosis, which is a killed bacterium. New and improved vaccines to immunize against parvovirus have appeared recently. The long-awaited modified live virus vaccine of canine origin was made available recently. It is safe and will produce immunity lasting one year.

Other communicable diseases for which no vaccine has been perfected as yet are: canine coronavirus, canine rotavirus, and canine brucellosis.

Infectious and Contagious Diseases
Distemper

Distemper is caused by a highly contagious, airborne virus. The symptoms are varied and

Ch. Valdawn Chit Chat of Rockwood, by Ch. Valdawn's Krackerjack ex O'Canonach Jubilee Misty. Photo courtesy of Barbara M. Kenealy.

Ch. Astolat Emblem's Rhoda. Bred by Constance Hubbard; owned by Mr. and Mrs. Willard K. Denton.

may involve all of the dog's systems. A pneumonic form is common, with heavy eye and nose discharges, coughing, and lung congestion. The digestive system may be involved as evidenced by vomiting, diarrhea, and weight loss. The skin may show a pustular type rash on the abdomen. Nervous system involvement is common, with convulsions, chorea, and paralysis as persistent symptoms. This virus may have an affinity for nerve tissue and cause encephalitis and degeneration of the spinal cord. These changes, for the most part, are irreversible and death or severe crippling ensues.

We have no specific remedy or cure for distemper; and recoveries, when they occur, can only be attributed to the natural resistance of the patient, good nursing care, and control of secondary infections with antibiotics.

That's the bad news about distemper. The good news is that we rarely see a case of distemper in most areas today because of the efficiency of the vaccination program. This is proof that prevention by vaccination has been effective in almost eradicating this dreaded disease.

Hepatitis

Hepatitis is another contagious viral disease affecting the liver. This is not an airborne virus and can only be spread by contact. Although rarely seen today because of good prevention by vaccination programs, this virus is capable of producing a very acute, fulminating, severe infection and can cause death in a very short time. Symptoms of high temperature, lethargy, anorexia, and vomiting are the same as for other diseases. Careful evaluation by a veterinarian is necessary to confirm the diagnosis of this disease.

The old canine infectious hepatitis vaccine has been replaced by a canine adenovirus type 2 strain vaccine which is safer and superior. The new vaccine seems to be free of post-vaccination complications such as blue eyes, shedding of the virus in the urine, and some kidney problems.

Parainfluenza

This is commonly called kennel cough. It is caused by a throat-inhabiting virus that causes an inflammation of the trachea (windpipe) and larynx (voice box). Coughing is the main symptom and fortunately it rarely causes any other systemic problems. The virus is airborne and highly contagious, and it is the scourge of boarding kennels. A vaccine is available that will protect against this contagious respiratory disease and should be given as part of your vaccination program, along with the distemper, hepatitis, leptospirosis, and parvovirus shots. Pregnant bitches should not be vaccinated against parainfluenza because of the possibility of infecting the unborn puppies. As there may be more than one infectious agent involved in contagious upper respiratory diseases of dogs, vaccination against parainfluenza is not a complete guarantee to protect against all of them.

Leptospirosis

This is a disease that seriously affects the kidneys of dogs, most domestic animals, and man. For this reason, it can become a public health hazard. In urban and slum areas, the disease is carried by rats and mice in their urine. It is caused by a spirochete organism which is very resistant to treatment. Symptoms include fever, depression, dehydration, excess thirst, persistent vomiting, occasional diarrhea, and jaundice in the latter stages. Again, it is not always easy to diagnose so your veterinarian will have to do some laboratory work to confirm it.

We see very few cases of leptospirosis in dogs and then only in the unvaccinated ones. The vaccine is generally given concurrently with the distemper and hepatitis vaccinations. Preventive inoculations have resulted in the almost complete eradication of this dreaded disease.

Rabies

This is a well-known virus-caused disease that is almost always fatal and is transmissible to man and other warm-blooded animals. The virus causes very severe brain damage. Sources of the infection include foxes, skunks, and raccoons, as well as domesticated dogs and cats. Transmission is by introduction of the virus by saliva into bite wounds. Incubation in certain animals may be from three to eight weeks. In a dog, clinical signs will appear within five days. Symptoms fall into two categories, depending on what stage the disease is in when seen. We have the dumb form and the furious form. There is a change of personality in the furious form; individuals become hypersensitive and overreact to noise and stimuli. They will bite any object that moves. In dumb rabies, the typical picture of the loosely hanging jaw and tongue presents itself. Diagnosis is confirmed only by a laboratory finding the virus and characteristic lesions in the brain. All tissues and fluids from rabid animals should be considered infectious and you should be careful not to come in contact with them. Prevention by vaccination is a must because there is no treatment for rabid dogs.

Canine Parvovirus (CPV)

This is the newest and most highly publicized member of the intestinal virus family. Cat distemper virus is a member of the same family but differs from canine parvovirus biologically, and it has been impossible to produce this disease in dogs using cat virus as the inducing agent; and conversely canine parvovirus will not produce the disease in a cat. However, vaccines for both species will produce immunity in the dog. The origin of CPV is still unknown.

Canine parvovirus is very contagious and acts rapidly. The main source of infection is contaminated bowel movements. Direct contact between dogs is not necessary, and carriers such as people, fleas, and medical instruments may carry and transmit the virus.

The incubation period is five to fourteen days. The symptoms are fever, severe vomiting and diarrhea, often with blood, depression, and dehydration. Feces may appear yellowish gray streaked with blood. Young animals are more severely affected, and a shock-like death may occur in two days. In animals less than six weeks old, the virus will cause an inflammation of the heart muscle, causing heart failure and death. These pups may not have diarrhea. A reduction in the number of white blood cells is a common finding early in the disease.

The virus is passed in the feces for one to two weeks and may possibly be shed in the saliva and urine also. This virus has also been found in the coats of dogs. The mortality rate is unknown.

Ch. Carmylie Jillian Lauradon, by Ch. Heatherland's Simon Says ex Carmylie Cinnamon Flare. Jean D. Simmonds, Carmylie Shelties.

Dogs that recover from the disease develop an immunity to it. Again, the duration of this immunity is unknown.

Control measures include disinfection of the kennels, animals, and equipment with a 1 to 30 dilution of Clorox and isolation of sick individuals.

Treatment is very similar to that for coronavirus, namely: intravenous fluid therapy, administration of broad spectrum antibiotics, intestinal protectants, and good nursing care.

Transmission to humans has not been proven.

Clinical studies have proven that vaccination with three injections of the new modified live virus vaccine of canine origin, with four weeks between injections, will be over ninety percent effective. Recent work at the James A. Baker Institute for Animal Health at Cornell University has shown that maternally derived antibodies can interfere with the immunizing properties of our vaccines for as long as fifteen to sixteen weeks. This means that some of our puppies, especially those from dams with good immunity, will not become susceptible to successful vaccination until they are sixteen weeks old. It is also known that the maternal protection afforded

Banchory By Invitation Only, blue-merle and white dog by Banchory The Midnight Hour II (Ch. Harvest Hill's Shoeshine Boy ex Banchory Orchid Blue) ex Banchory Montage Mona Lisa (Ch. Banchory Formal Notice ex Banchory A Blue Nun), at one and a half years of age. Bred by Clare and Donna Harden; owned by Jerry and Chris Machado, Montage Kennels.

these puppies, while enough to prevent successful vaccination, may not be enough to protect them from an exposure to the virus. The best advice is to give our puppies three inoculations of a canine origin modified live virus vaccine four weeks apart, starting when they are eight weeks old. Then, hope for the best and revaccinate annually.

Canine Coronavirus (CCV)

This is a highly contagious virus that spreads rapidly to susceptible dogs. The source of infection is through infectious bowel movements. The incubation period is one to four days, and the virus will be found in feces for as long as two weeks. It is hard to tell the difference sometimes between cases of diarrhea caused by coronavirus and parvovirus. Coronavirus generally is less severe or causes a more chronic or sporadic type of diarrhea. The fecal material may be orange in color and have a very bad odor; occasionally, it will also contain blood. Vomiting sometimes precedes the diarrhea, but loss of appetite and listlessness are consistent signs of the disease. Fever may or may not be present. Recovery is the rule after eight to ten days, but treatment with fluids, antibiotics, intestinal protectants, and good nursing care are necessary in the more severe watery diarrhea cases. Dogs that survive these infections become immune but for an unknown length of time.

To control an outbreak of this virus in a kennel, very stringent hygienic measures must be taken. Proper and quick disposal of feces, isolation of affected animals, and disinfection with a 1 to 30 dilution of Clorox are all effective means of controlling an outbreak in the kennel.

There is no vaccine yet available for prevention of canine coronavirus. Human infections by this virus have not been reported.

Canine Rotavirus (CRV)

This virus has been demonstrated in dogs with a mild diarrhea but again with more severe cases in very young puppies. Very little is known about this virus.

A milder type of diarrhea is present for eight to ten days. The puppies do not run a temperature and continue to eat. Dogs usually recover naturally from this infection. There is no vaccine available for this virus.

Canine Brucellosis

This is a disease of dogs that causes both abortions and sterility. It is caused by a small bacterium closely related to the agent that causes

Ch. Velveteen Esquire Aztec Gold, a son of Ch. Esquire's Fringe Benefit ex Ch. Stoneridge Copper Melody. Bred by Evelyn Byers.

undulant fever in man and abortion in cows. It occurs worldwide.

Symptoms of brucellosis sometimes are difficult to determine, and some individuals with the disease may appear healthy. Vague symptoms such as lethargy, swollen glands, poor hair coat, and stiffness in the back legs may be present. This organism does not cause death and may stay in the dog's system for months and even years. The latter animals, of course, have breeding problems and infect other dogs.

Poor results in your breeding program may be the only indication that brucellosis is in your kennel. Apparently normal bitches abort without warning. This usually occurs forty-five to fifty-five days after mating. Successive litters will also be aborted. In males, signs of the disease are inflammation of the skin of the scrotum, shrunken testicles, and swollen tender testicles. Fertility declines and chronically infected males become sterile.

The disease is transmitted to both sexes at the time of mating.

Other sources of infection are aborted puppies and birth membrane and discharge from the womb at the time of abortions.

Humans can be infected, but such infections are rare and mild. Unlike in the dog, the disease in humans responds readily to antibiotics.

Diagnosis is done by blood testing, which should be done carefully. None of the present tests are infallible and false positives may occur.

The only certain way that canine brucellosis can be diagnosed is by isolating the *B. canis* organism from blood or aborted material and for this, special techniques are required.

Treatment of infected individuals has proven ineffective in most cases. Sterility in males is permanent. Spaying or castrating infected pets should be considered as this will halt the spread of the disease and is an alternative to euthanasia.

At present, there is no vaccine against this important disease.

Our best hope in dealing with canine brucellosis is prevention. The following suggestions are made in order to prevent the occurrence of this malady in your dogs.

a. Test breeding stock annually and by all means breed only uninfected animals.

b. Test bitches several weeks before their heat periods.

c. Do not bring any new dogs into your kennel unless they have had two negative tests taken a month apart.

d. If a bitch aborts, isolate her, wear gloves when handling soiled bedding, and disinfect the premises with Roccal.

e. If a male loses interest in breeding or fails to produce after several matings, have him checked.

f. Consult your veterinarian for further information about this disease; alert other breeders and support the research that is going on at the James A. Baker Institute for Animal Health at Cornell University.

Head-study of Ch. Philidove Heir Presumptive. Handled by Steve Barger; owned by Irene Brody.

External Parasites

The control and eradication of external parasites depends on the repeated use of good quality insecticide sprays or powders during the warm months. Make a routine practice of using these products at seven-day intervals throughout the season. It is also imperative that sleeping quarters and wherever the animal habitates be treated also.

Fleas

These are brown, wingless insects with laterally compressed bodies and strong legs, and they are bloodsuckers. Their life cycle comprises eighteen to twenty-one days from egg to adult flea. They can live without food for one year in high humidity but die in a few days in low humidity. They multiply rapidly and are more prevalent in the warm months. They can cause a severe skin inflammation in those individuals that are allergic or sensitive to the flea bite or saliva of the flea. They can act as a vector for many diseases and do carry tapeworms. Control measures must include persistent, continual use of flea collars or flea medallions, or sprays or powders. The dog's bedding and premises must also be treated because the eggs are there. Foggers, vacuuming, or professional exterminators may have to be used. All dogs and cats in the same household must be treated at the same time.

Ticks

There are hard and soft species of ticks. Both species are bloodsuckers and at times cause severe skin inflammations on their host. They act as a vector for Rocky Mountain Spotted Fever, as well as other diseases. Hibernation through an entire winter is not uncommon. The female tick lays as many as one thousand to five thousand eggs in crevices and cracks in walls. These eggs will hatch in about three weeks and then a month later become adult ticks. Ticks generally locate around the host's neck and ears and between the toes. They can cause anemia and serious blood loss if allowed to grow and multiply. It is not a good idea to pick ticks off the dogs because of the danger of a reaction in the skin. Just apply the tick spray directly on the ticks which then die and fall off eventually. Heavily affected dogs should be dipped every two weeks in an anti-parasitic bath. The premises, kennels, and yards should be treated every two weeks during the summer months, being sure to apply the insecticide to walls and in all cracks and crevices. Frequent or daily grooming is effective in finding and removing ticks.

Lice

There are two kinds of lice, namely the sucking louse and the biting louse. They spend their entire life on their host but can be spread by direct contact or through contaminated combs and brushes. Their life cycle is twenty-one days, and their eggs, known as nits, attach to the hairs of the dog. The neck and shoulder region, as well as the ear flaps, are the most common areas to be inhabited by these pesky parasites. They cause itchiness, some blood loss, and inflammation of the skin. Eradication will result from dipping or dusting with methyl carbonate or Thuron once a week for three to four weeks. It is a good idea to fine-comb the dogs after each dip to remove the dead lice and nits. Ask your veterinarian to provide the insecticides and advice or control measures for all of these external parasites.

Mites

Less commonly occurring parasitic diseases such as demodectic and sarcoptic mange, caused by mites, should be diagnosed and treated only by your veterinarian. You are wise to consult your doctor whenever any unusual condition occurs and persists in your dog's coat and skin. These conditions are difficult to diagnose and treat at best, so that the earlier a diagnosis is obtained, the better the chances are for successful treatment. Other skin conditions such as ringworm, flea bite allergy, bacterial infections, eczemas, and hormonal problems, among others, all have to be considered.

Internal Parasites

The eradication and control of internal parasites in dogs will occupy a good deal of your time and energy.

Ch. Banchory Strike Me Silver, by Ch. Banchory Formal Notice ex Banchory Ice Follies. Owned by Tetsuo Miyama and Stephen Barger.

Puppies should be tested for worms at four weeks of age and then six weeks later. It is also wise to test them again six weeks following their last worm treatment to be sure the treatments have been successful. Annual fecal tests are advisable throughout your dog's life. All worming procedures should be done carefully and only with the advice and supervision of your veterinarian. The medicants used to kill the parasites are, to a certain extent, toxic, so they should be used with care.

Ascarids

These include roundworms, puppy worms, stomach worms, and milk worms. Puppies become infested shortly after birth and occasionally even before birth. Ascarids can be difficult to eradicate. When passed in the stool or thrown up, they look somewhat like cooked spaghetti when fresh or like rubber bands when they are dried up. Two treatments at least two weeks apart will eliminate ascarids from most puppies. An occasional individual may need more wormings according to the status in its system of the life cycle of the worm at the time of worming. Good sanitary conditions must prevail and immediate disposal of feces is necessary to keep down the worm population.

Hookworms

Hookworms are bloodsuckers and also cause bleeding from the site of their attachment to the lining of the intestine when they move from one site to another. They can cause a blood-loss type of anemia and serious consequences, particularly in young puppies. Their life cycle is direct and their eggs may be ingested or pass through the skin of its host. Treatment of yards and runs where the dogs defecate with 5% sodium borate solution is said to kill the eggs in the soil. Two or three worm treatments three to four weeks apart may be necessary to get rid of hookworms. New injectable products administered by your veterinarian have proven more effective than remedies used in the past. Repeated fecal examinations may be necessary to detect the eggs in the feces. These eggs pass out of the body only sporadically or in showers, so that it is easy to miss finding them unless repeated stool testing is done. As is true with any parasite, good sanitary conditions in the kennel and outside runs will help eradicate this worm.

Whipworms

These are a prevalent parasite in some kennels and in some individual dogs. They cause an intermittent mucousy type diarrhea. As they live only in the dog's appendix, it is extremely difficult to reach them with any worm medicine given by mouth. Injections seem to be the most effective treatment, and these have to be repeated several times over a long period of time to be effective. Here again, repeated fresh stool samples must be examined by your veterinarian to be sure that this pest has been eradicated. Appendectomies are indicated in only the most severe chronic cases. The fact that cleanliness is next to godliness cannot be emphasized too often; it is most important in getting rid of this parasite.

Tapeworms

They are another common internal parasite of dogs. They differ in the mode of their transmission as they have an indirect life cycle. This means that part of their cycle must be spent in an intermediate host. Fleas, fish, rabbits, and field mice all may act as an intermediate host for the tapeworm. Fleas are the most common source of tapeworms in dogs, although dogs that live near water and may eat raw fish and hunting dogs that eat the entrails of rabbits may get them from those sources. Another distinguishing feature of the tapeworm is the suction apparatus which is the part of the head which enables the tapeworm to attach itself to the lining of the intestine. If, after worming, just the head remains, it has the capability of regenerating into another worm. This is one reason why tapeworms are so difficult to get rid of. It will require several treatments to get the entire parasite out of a dog's system. These worms are easily recognized by the appearance of their segments which break off and appear on top of a dog's feces or stuck to the hair around the rectal area. These segments may appear alive and mobile at times, but most often they are dead and dried up when found. They look like flat pieces of rice and may be white or brown when detected. Elimination of the intermediate host is an integral part of any plan to rid our dogs of this worm. Repeated wormings may be necessary to kill all the adult tapeworms in the intestine.

Heartworms

Heartworm disease is caused by an actual worm that goes through its life cycle in the blood stream of its victims. It ultimately makes its home in the right chambers of the heart and in the large vessels that transport the blood to the lungs. They vary in size from 2.3 inches to 16

inches. Adult worms can survive up to five years in the heart.

By its nature, this is a very serious disease and can cause irreversible damage to the lungs and heart of its host. Heart defect and lung pathology soon result in serious problems for the dog.

The disease is transmitted and carried by female mosquitoes that have infected themselves after biting an infected dog; they then pass it on to the next dog with which they come in contact.

The disease has been reported wherever mosquitoes are found, and cases have been reported in most of the United States. Rare cases have been reported in man and cats. It is most prevalent in warmer climates where the mosquito population is the greatest, but hotbeds of infection exist in the more temperate parts of the United States and Canada also.

Concerted effort and vigorous measures must be taken to control and prevent this serious threat to our dog population. The most effective means of eradication I believe will come through annual blood testing for early detection, by the use of preventive medicine during mosquito exposure times, and also by ridding our dogs' environment of mosquitoes.

Annual blood testing is necessary to detect cases that haven't started to show symptoms yet and thus can be treated effectively. It also enables your veterinarian to prescribe safely the preventive medicine to those individuals that test negative. There is a ten to fifteen percent margin of error in the test, which may lead to

Ch. Hallinwood Robin Hood of Marl from a 1954 painting by Jeanne Mellin. Mr. and Mrs. Willard K. Denton, owners, Ardencaple Kennels.

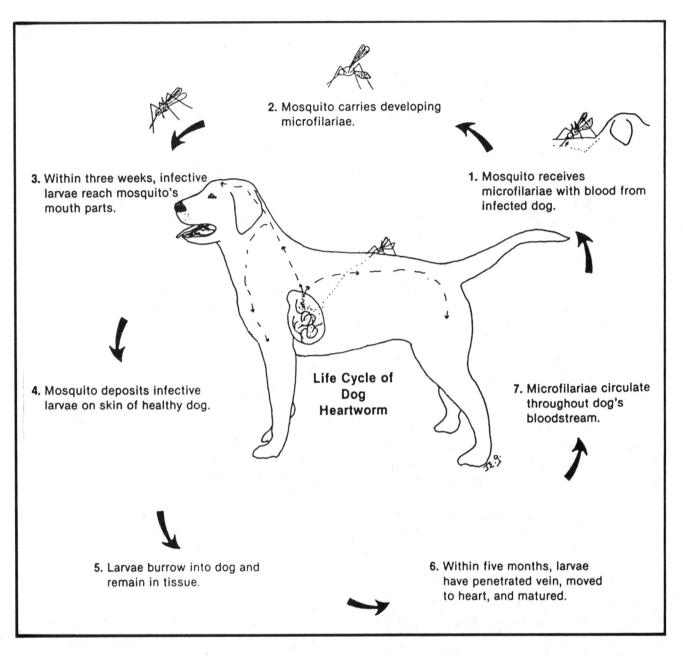

Life Cycle of Dog Heartworm

1. Mosquito receives microfilariae with blood from infected dog.

2. Mosquito carries developing microfilariae.

3. Within three weeks, infective larvae reach mosquito's mouth parts.

4. Mosquito deposits infective larvae on skin of healthy dog.

5. Larvae burrow into dog and remain in tissue.

6. Within five months, larvae have penetrated vein, moved to heart, and matured.

7. Microfilariae circulate throughout dog's bloodstream.

some false negative tests. Individuals that test negative but are showing classical symptoms of the disease such as loss of stamina, coughing, loss of weight, and heart disease should be further evaluated with chest X-rays, blood tests, and electrocardiograms.

Serious consequences may result when the preventive medication is given to a dog that already has heartworm in his system. That is why it is so important to have your dog tested annually before starting the preventive medicine.

In order to be most effective, the preventive drug diethylcarbamazine should be given in daily doses of 2.5 mg. to 3 mg. per pound of body weight or 5 mg. per kilogram of body weight of your dog. This routine should be started fifteen days prior to exposure to mosquitoes and be continued until sixty days after exposure. Common and trade names for this drug are Caricide, Styrid-Caricide, and D.E.C. It comes in liquid and tablet forms.

This drug has come under criticism by some breeders and individuals who claim that it affects fertility and causes some serious reactions. Controlled studies have shown no evidence that the drug produces sterility or abnormal sperm count or quality. Long-term studies on reproduction, when the drug was given at the rate of 4.9 mg. per pound of body weight (two times the preventive dose level) for two years, showed no signs of toxic effects on body weight maintenance, growth rate of pups, feed consumption, conception rate, numbers of healthy pups whelped, ratio of male to female pups, blood counts, and liver function tests. It is reported to be a well-tolerated medication, and many thousands of dogs have benefitted from its use. From personal experience, I find only an occasional dog who will vomit the medicine or get an upset stomach from it. The new enteric coated pills have eliminated this small problem.

However, if you still don't want to give the preventive, especially to your breeding stock, an alternative procedure would be to test your dogs every six months for early detection of the disease, so that it can be treated as soon as possible.

Heartworm infestation can be treated successfully. There is a one to five percent mortality rate from the treatment. It can be expected that treatment may be completed without side effects if the disease hasn't already caused irreversible problems in the heart, lungs, liver, kidneys, or other organs. Careful testing, monitoring, and supervision is essential to success in treatment. Treatment is far from hopeless these days and if the disease is detected early enough, a successful outcome is more the rule than the exception.

In conclusion, remember that one case of heartworm disease in your area is one too many, especially if that one case is your dog. By following the steps mentioned here, we can go a long way in ridding ourselves of this serious threat to our dogs.

Home Remedies and First Aid

You have repeatedly read here of my instructions to call your veterinarian when your animals are sick. This is the best advice I can give you. There are a few home remedies, however, that may get you over some rough spots while trying to get professional help.

I think it is a good idea to keep on hand some medical supplies in a first aid kit. The kit should contain the following items: a roll of cotton, gauze bandages, hydrogen peroxide, tincture of metaphen, cotton applicator swabs, BFI powder, rectal thermometer, adhesive tape, boric acid ointment and crystals, tweezers, and a jar of petroleum jelly.

A word here on how to take a dog's temperature may be in order. Always lubricate the thermometer with petroleum jelly and carefully insert it well into the rectum. Hold it in place for two to three minutes and then read it. The thermometer should be held firmly so that it doesn't get sucked up into the rectum.

To administer liquid medicines to dogs, simply pull the lips away from the side of the mouth, making a pocket for depositing the liquid. Slightly tilt the dog's head upward and he will be able to swallow the liquid properly. Giving liquids by opening the mouth and pouring them directly on the tongue is an invitation to disaster because inhalation pneumonia can result. Putting it in the side of the mouth gives the dog time to hold it in his mouth and then swallow it properly.

Tablets are best administered by forcing the dog's mouth open, and pushing the pill down over the middle of the tongue into the back of his mouth. If put in the right place, a reflex tongue reaction will force the pill down the throat and thus be swallowed. There is no objection to giving the pills in favorite foods as long as you carefully determine that the medicine is surely swallowed with the food.

Vomiting

To stop vomiting, mix one tablespoon of table salt to one pint of water and dissolve the salt thoroughly; then give one tablespoonful of the mixture to the patient. After waiting one hour, repeat the procedure and skip the next meal. The dog may vomit a little after the first dose, but the second dose works to settle the stomach. This mixture not only provides chlorides but also acts as a mild astringent and many times in mild digestive upsets will work to stop the vomiting.

Diarrhea

In the case of adult Shelties, give one or two tablespoons of Kaopectate or Milk of Bismuth every four hours. Use one-third of this dosage for puppies. Skip the next meal, and if diarrhea persists, then start a bland diet of boiled ground lean beef and boiled rice in the proportions of half and half. Three or four doses of this medicine should suffice. If the diarrhea persists and, particularly, if accompanied by depression, lethargy, and loss of appetite, your veterinarian should be consulted immediately. With all these new viral-caused diarrheas floating around, time is of the essence in securing treatment.

Mild Stimulant

Dilute brandy half and half with water, add a little sugar, and give a tablespoonful of the mixture every four to five hours. For puppies over three months old, reduce the dosage to a teaspoonful of the mixture every four to five hours.

Mild Sedative

Dilute brandy half and half with water, add a little sugar, and give a tablespoon of the mixture every twenty to thirty minutes until the desired effect is attained. For puppies over three months old, reduce the dosage to a teaspoonful of the mixture every twenty to thirty minutes.

Using brandy for both sedation and stimulation is possible by varying the time interval between doses. Given every four to five hours, it's a stimulant; but given every twenty to thirty minutes it acts as a sedative.

Minor Cuts and Wounds

Cleanse them first with soap and water, preferably Tincture of Green Soap. Apply a mild antiseptic such as Bactine or Tincture of Metaphen two or three times daily until healed. If the cut is deep, and fairly long and bleeding, then a bandage should be applied until professional help can be obtained.

Whenever attempting to bandage wounds, first apply a layer or two of gauze over the cleaned and treated wound. Then apply a layer of cotton and then another layer or two of gauze. The bandage must be snug enough to stay on but not so tight as to impair the circulation to the body part. Adhesive tape should be applied over the second layer of gauze to keep the bandage as clean and dry as possible until you can get your dog to the doctor.

Tourniquets should be applied only in cases of profusely bleeding wounds. They are applied tightly between the wound and the heart, in addition to the pressure bandage that should be applied directly to the wound. The tourniquet must be released and reapplied at fifteen-minute intervals.

Burns

Application of ice or very cold water and compresses is the way to treat a skin burn. Apply cold packs as soon as possible and take the dog immediately to your vet.

Frostbite

Frostbite is a rarely occurring problem. The secret in treating this condition is to restore normal body temperature gradually to the affected parts. In other words, use cold water, then tepid water, to thaw out the area slowly and restore circulation. In cases of severe freezing or shock due to bitter cold temperature, take the animal to the veterinarian as soon as possible.

Abscesses and Infected Cysts

Obvious abscesses and infected cysts that occur between the toes may be encouraged to drain by using hot boric acid packs and saturated

Ch. Jade Mist Windspell, gorgeous example of the Jade Mist Shelties, Dr. and Mrs. Keith B. Howell.

dressings every few hours until professional aid can be secured. The boric acid solution is made by dissolving one tablespoon of crystals to one pint of hot water. Apply frequently to the swollen area. Further treatment by a veterinarian may involve lancing and thoroughly draining and cleaning out the abscess cavity. As most abscesses are badly infected, systemic antibiotics are generally indicated.

Heatstroke or Heat Exhaustion

A word about the serious effects of heat on a dog is timely. It never ceases to amaze me how many people at dog shows have to be warned and advised not to leave their dogs in cars or vans on a warm day.

A dog's heat-regulating mechanism is not nearly as efficient as ours. Consequently, dogs feel the heat more than we do. Keep them as cool and as well ventilated as possible in hot weather. Another inducement for shock is taking your dog out of a cool air-conditioned vehicle and exposing him immediately to the hot outdoors. Make that change as gradual as you can because a rapid change can cause a shock-like reaction.

In cases of suspected heatstroke, which manifests itself with very high body temperatures (as high as 106° to 108°F. sometimes), severe panting, weakness, shaking, and collapse, act quickly to get him into a cold bath or shower or put ice-cold compresses on his head. Then, again without delay, rush him to the nearest veterinarian for further treatment. Prevention is the key here and with a little common sense, heatstroke and exhaustion can be avoided.

Poisons

Many dogs are poisoned annually by unscrupulous people who hate dogs. Many others are victims of poisoning due simply to the careless use of rat and ant poisons, insecticides, herbicides, anti-freeze solutions, drugs, and so forth. Dogs also frequently eat poisonous plants, either in the house or outdoors, which can lead to serious consequences. Common sources of these toxic products are named below.

Plants that can be a source of poison for dogs include the following (this list contains only the most common ones): daffodils, oleanders, poinsettias, mistletoe, philodendron, delphiniums, monkshood, foxglove, iris, lilies of the valley, rhubarb, spinach, tomato vines, sunburned potatoes, rhododendron, cherry, peach, oak, elderberry, black locust, jack-in-the-pulpit, Dutchman's-breeches, water hemlock, mush-

Am. and Can. Ch. Bonnicay's Silver Solitaire, a noted Best in Show dog, at eight and a half years of age. Owned by Lochlana Shelties.

rooms, buttercups, poison hemlock, nightshade, jimson weed, marijuana, locoweed, and lupine. Also, grain contaminants can exist in dog food. The most common ones are ergot, corn cockle, and grotolaria.

Poisonous animals include such snakes as vipers, rattlesnakes, copperheads, water moccasins, and the coral snake. Lizards like the Gila monster and Mexican beaded lizard are bad. Some toads, spiders, insects, and fish also are potential sources of trouble.

Chemicals comprise perhaps the largest and most common source of poisoning in our environment. These are hazards that our dogs may be exposed to every day. Careful handling and awareness of these products are essential.

Toxic materials are found in arts and crafts supplies, photographic supplies, and automotive and machinery products and include such things as antifreeze and de-icers, rust inhibitors, brake fluids, engine and carburetor cleaners, lubricants, gasoline, kerosene, radiator cleaners, and windshield washers. Cleaners, bleaches and polishes, disinfectants, and sanitizers all contain products that potentially are dangerous.

Even health and beauty aids may contain toxic materials if ingested in large enough quantities: some bath oils, perfumes, corn removers, deodorants, anti-perspirants, athlete's foot remedies, eye makeup, hair dyes and preparations, diet pills, headache remedies, laxatives, liniments, fingernail polish removers, sleeping pills, suntan lotions, amphetamines, shaving lotions, colognes, shampoos, and certain ointments.

Paints and related products also can be dangerous. Caulking compounds, driers, thinners, paints, paint brush cleaners, paint and varnish removers, preservatives, and floor and wood cleaners all fit into the category.

Pest poisons for the control of birds, fungi, rats, mice, ants, and snails all can be toxic and sometimes fatal to dogs.

Miscellaneous items like fire extinguishers and non-skid products for slippery floors can be unsafe. Almost all solvents like carbon tetrachloride, benzene, toluene, acetone, mineral spirits, kerosene, and turpentine are bad.

The previous paragraphs serve only to illustrate how many products in our everyday environment exist which can be hazardous or fatal to our dogs.

In cases of suspected poisoning, be aware of what to do until professional help can be obtained:

a. Keep the animal protected, quiet, and warm.

b. If a contact is on the skin, eye, or body surface, cleanse and flush the area with copious amounts of water. Do this also if the dog gets something in his eye. Protect him from further exposure.

c. Inducing vomiting may be dangerous and should be done only on the advice of a veterinarian. Giving peroxide may induce vomiting in some cases. It is better to allow the animal to drink as much water as he wants. This will dilute the poison. Giving milk or raw egg whites is helpful many times to delay absorption of the toxic products.

Do not attempt to give anything by mouth if the patient is convulsing, depressed, or unconscious.

Do not waste time getting veterinary service. Take any vomited material and suspected causative agents, and their containers with you to the vet. When the suspected product is known, valuable time can be saved in administering specific treatment.

A word to the wise should be sufficient. Keep away from your dog all products that can harm him in any way.

Whelping

We cannot leave the subject of emergencies without considering the subject of whelping. Most bitches whelp without any problems. It is wise, however, to watch them closely during this time. I feel that no bitch should go more than two hours in actual labor without producing a puppy. This includes the time before the first one as well as between puppies. If more than two hours elapse, then the dam should be examined by a veterinarian. It will then be determined if she is indeed in trouble or is just a slow whelper. This rule of thumb gives us time to find out if there is a problem, what it may be, and have time to save both dam and puppies in most cases.

It is good practice to have your bitches examined for pregnancy three and a half to four weeks after mating, as well as at term around the fifty-eighth to fifty-ninth day. These procedures will enable the veterinarian to discover any troubles that may occur during pregnancy, as well as alert him as to when the whelping is going to take place. Knowing this, he can plan to provide service, if needed during off hours.

Bitches that are difficult to breed, miss pregnancies, or have irregular reproductive cycles should have physical exams including laboratory tests to determine the cause of the trouble. These tests may be expensive, but a lot of breeding and sterility problems due to sub-par physical condition, hormonal imbalances, or hypo-thyroidism can be corrected. If a valuable bitch is restored to her normal reproductive capacity, the reward more than offsets the medical costs.

Another important thing to remember about whelping and raising puppies is to keep them warm enough. This means a room temperature

Sheltie pups in bi-black, blue-merle, and tricolor by Ch. SumerSong Winter Shadows ex Carmylie Kaher Bi-Now. Owned by Jean D. Simmonds, Carmylie.

Austr. Ch. Jedemah Sontina Karoly in October 1983. Best of Breed at the Royal Canbera Show, this lovely dog won his first C.C. at eight months of age and gained his title in March 1982. Throughout 1983 he has taken the C.C. on the majority of his ring appearances and had a total of 747 challenge points at the close of 1983. Owned by Mrs. Patricia Huggins, New South Wales.

of 80° to 85°F. for the first ten days to two weeks until the puppies are able to generate their own body heat. Be sure the dam keeps them close; leave a light burning at night for the first week so she won't lose track of any of them or accidentally lie on one of them. Chilling remains the biggest cause of death of newborn puppies. Other causes are malnutrition, toxic milk, hemorrhage, and viral and bacterial infections. Blood type incompatibilities have been understood lately as causes of trouble.

Consultation with your veterinarian concerning these and any other breeding problems you've had in the past may result in the solution of these problems. This may result in larger litters with a higher survival rate.

Care of the Older Dog

Providing medical services from cradle to grave is the slogan of many veterinarians, and rightly so. The average life expectancy for our dogs these days is about thirteen years. Sad to say, this is a short time compared to our life span. Larger breeds historically do not live as long as the medium-sized or smaller breeds. However, I think that with proper care your Sheltie should be expected to reach this expectancy.

Probably the most common ailments in older dogs are arthritis, kidney disease, heart problems, and cataracts; hip dysplasia may also become evident as the dog ages.

Arthritis

When your pet has trouble getting up in the morning, jumping up, or going upstairs, you can bet that some form of a joint problem is starting. Giving one enteric coated aspirin tablet three times a day for five days very often will help these individuals. This dosage is for adult dogs. It is relatively free of side effects and as long as nothing else is wrong, your dog will get a bit of relief.

Kidney Disease

Signs of kidney weakness are excessive drinking, inability to hold urine through the night, loss of weight, lack of appetite, and more than occasional bouts of vomiting and diarrhea. If any of these signs present themselves, it would be worthwhile to have a checkup. Very often corrective measures in diet and administering some medicine will prolong your dog's life.

Heart Problems

Some form and degree of heart problems exist in a lot of older animals. Symptoms of chronic congestive heart failure consist of a chronic cough, especially after exercise, lack of stamina, lethargy, abdominal enlargement, and labored breathing at times. If diagnosed and treated early in the disease, many heart patients live to a ripe old age.

Cataracts

Cataracts form in the lenses of most, if not all, old dogs. They are a part of the normal aging process. Total blindness from cataracts generally does not result for a long time. Distant and peripheral vision remain satisfactory for the expected life span of the dog. Rarely is total blindness produced by these aging cataracts before the dog's life expectancy is reached. There is no effective treatment for cataracts other than their surgical removal which is not recommended in the older patient that has any vision at all left.

Hip Dysplasia

Even though hip dysplasia rarely occurs in Shetland Sheepdogs, all dog owners should be aware of the condition and its symptoms.

It is becoming more evident that most of the arthritis in older dogs in large breeds is the result of problems in bone growth and development when the individual was very young. Problems such as panosteitis, hip dysplasia, elbow dysplasia, and osteochondrosis dessicans all are often precursors of arthritis.

At any rate, hip dysplasia seems to be a developmental condition and not a congenital anomaly. It is thought to be an inherited defect, with many genes being responsible for its development. Environmental factors also enter into the severity of the pathology in the hip joints. Nutrition during the growth period has been an important factor. Overfeeding and over-supplementation of diets have caused an abnormal growth rate with overweight puppies. These individuals, if they were susceptible to hip dysplasia in the first place, show more severe lesions of hip dysplasia. Restricted feeding of growing dogs is necessary for normal bone growth and development.

Signs of hip dysplasia vary from one dog to another, but some of the more common ones are difficulty in getting up after lying for awhile, rabbit-like gait with both rear legs moving forward at the same time when running, lethargy, and walking with a swaying gait in the rear legs. In many cases, a period of pain and discomfort at nine months to one year of age will resolve itself; and even though the dysplasia is still there, most of the symptoms may disappear.

It is recommended that dysplastic individuals not be bred, that they not be allowed to become overweight, and that they have moderate exercise.

The selection of dysplastic-free individuals for breeding stock eventually will result in the production of sounder hip joints in affected breeds. This factor, of course, is only one consideration in the breeding and production of an overall better Shetland Sheepdog.

Canine Nutrition

After mentioning the problem of overfeeding and oversupplementation of puppies' diets with vitamins and minerals in the discussion of hip dysplasia, a few words about canine nutrition are in order.

It is generally agreed that great strides have been made in canine nutrition in the past few years and that most of our well-known commercial dog foods provide all the essential ingredients of a well-balanced diet for our dogs. Probably the greatest problem is providing good quality protein in proper proportions. It behooves us to read dog food labels and to know

what we are feeding and how much is necessary to provide the requirements for a lean healthy individual. The tendencies in our society today are to overfeed and under exercise both our dogs and ourselves.

We must know the energy content or caloric value of the foods we are feeding. Then we must determine the energy requirements of our dogs. These will vary with time and circumstances. Your adult Shetland Sheepdog requires about twenty-five to thirty calories per pound of body weight daily for maintenance.

Generally speaking for the average adult Shetland Sheepdog house dog, a diet consisting of 16% high quality protein, 10% fat, and 44% carbohydrates is a good mix. For the working dogs, dogs being shown, or pregnant bitches, increase the protein and fat percentages by about 25% and decrease the carbohydrate proportion by 25%. To meet the needs of the increased stress of growth in young puppies and nursing bitches, the protein and fat components should be increased yet another 10 to 15% and the percentage of carbohydrates should be decreased by the same amount. Any stress situation means a rise in caloric requirement. For example, in the case of pregnancy, it is advisable to increase the amount of food intake by 20% after four weeks of gestation and by 75% after six weeks of gestation, and so forth.

We are assuming that the vitamins and minerals in the foods used are complete and balanced.

You may have to combine, mix, and juggle various types and brands of food to attain the desired diet, but don't despair; it can be done. Prescription and special diet foods are available through your veterinarian. These probably cost more initially but may pay off in the long run.

As to exactly how much to feed each individual dog, no one can give you a magic formula that works in all cases. My best advice is to use common sense and a scale. The guidelines on dog food containers have a tendency to be over-inflated. It is better to err on the low side than to overfeed. Remember, keep your dog slim and fit with a proper diet and plenty of exercise. That's not a bad idea for your own well-being also.

Ch. Carmylie Polly Paintbrush, by Ch. Banchory Deep Purple ex Ch. Carmylie As If Bi Chance. Jean D. Simmonds, owner.

Index

This index is composed of three separate parts: an index of names of people, an index of kennels, and a general index.

Names

A

Abramowicz, Eddie, 103, 105, 379
Adamson, Peggy, 184
Adkins, Bitsy, 328
Ain, Toby, 173
Alexander, Art (Mr. and Mrs.), 173
Allen, J.A. (Mrs.), 16
Allen, Mr. and Miss, 16
Alters, Sandra, 136
Anderson, Cheryl, 95
Anderson, Lynn, 409
Arranda, Anna M., 420
Ashbey, Frank, 36, 37, 41, 43, 73, 102, 207, 408
Ashbey, John, 36, 43
Ashton, D.O. (Mrs.), 283
Atkins, Dorothy, 49, 68
Ayres, Roy, 223

B

Babin, Elizabeth (Libby), 103, 273
Backus, Rose, 367, 368
Bailey, Lee (Mr. and Mrs.), 128-29
Bailey, Rhea Jane, *See* Butler, Rhea
Barger, Stephen (Steve) W., 53, 64, 69, 114, 144-47, 153, 208, 209, 210, 291, 297, 306, 307, 318, 325, 361, 401, 402, 506, 514, 519, 526, 527
Basnicki, Evelyn K., 236, 238, 250-51, 334, 349, 382, 387
Baxter, Wayne, 34, 35, 203
Beacham, Susan (Suzi), 219, 222, 230
Beadley, Cindy, 85
Beckwith, Mrs., 167
Bentley, Susan, 207, 319
Biggs, Donna, 442
Billings, Michele, 135
Bjorkman, Martha, 314
Bond, Shirley, 111, 183, 396
Bonney, Leonard W. (Mrs.), 186
Boomhower, Nancy, 189, 294
Bostwick, Diane, 153, 390, 439, 461
Bowden, W.P., 255
Bowie, Dr., 11-12
Brackett, Lloyd, 67
Brainard, Constance, 40
Brody, Irene, 131, 140, 141, 216, 445, 506, 526
Brooks, Teresa M., 45
Brown, J.W., 45
Brown, Judith C., 88, 89, 427

Brown, Thelma, 266, 389
Burgess, Bill, 199
Burhans, Alice A., 74-77, 309, 346, 347, 349, 371, 381, 416, 449, 451, 457, 502, 508
Burhans, Rebecca, 74, 76-7, 515
Burns, Dorothy, 206
Butler, Bob, 128, 179
Butler, Rhea, 128-30, 179, 383
Butterfield, Nancy, 195
Byers, Evelyn, 220-21, 355, 446, 447, 525
Byrd, Barbara, 137

C

Cameron, Janet, 272-74, 403, 436
Campbell, Shawn, 79
Carey, Gerald J., 35
Carlough, Bob, 180-82, 318, 341, 518
Carlough, Marie, 180-82, 318, 341, 518
Carr, George W., 39
Carrico, Louis, 172
Carroll, Glennis and Buddy, 63
Carroll, Jesse R. and Glennis, 68, 69
Carter, Jean, 40
Cartright, Fernandez, 117, 256
Cathcart, Elizabeth, 193, 195
Cavallaro, Ginny, 147
Chandless, Rose, 219, 230
Chappell, Frank (Mr. and Mrs.), 175, 193
Character, Buddy (Mr. and Mrs.), 68
Charlton, Mrs., 20
Chenoweth, Jody, 146-47
Christiansen, Ray and Dorothy, 139, 224, 320, 410
Cirinna, Madelyn, 209, 314, 363, 366
Clark, Anne Rogers, 145
Clark, Mr., 15
Clark, E.H. and Frances, 424
Clark, Frances, 241
Cleveland, Brian, 135
Cleveland, Florence B., 32, 34, 35
Coen, Nioma S., 364
Coen, Thomas W., 49, 53, 140-43, 145, 147, 207, 208, 209, 210, 227, 289, 292, 293, 296, 311, 325, 333, 344, 361, 392, 411, 435, 443

Cohen, Eugene (Gene), 73, 102-105, 182, 285, 316, 379, 409, 410, 424
Cole, Donna, 251
Coleman, Catherine, 27, 28, 31, 32, 39, 164, 198
Colley, M.A. and Mrs. C., 282
Collier, Chester, 368
Combee, Don K., 60, 61, 96-9, 452, 461
Combs, Arthur, 170
Combs, Arthur (Dr. and Mrs.), 128
Constable, Bob and Berkeley, 216
Cooley, Mrs., 34
Copland, A. (Mrs.), 17
Cornell, Betty M., 69
Cox, A.R., 16
Cronin, Carol, 178
Cross, C. Ashton (Mrs.), 15
Crutcher, Linda, 321
Curl, Mary, 251
Curry, Barbara, 189, 293
Currys, the, 187, 207

D

Danforth, G. and T., 51, 207, 363
Danforth, George, 227
Daniels, Valerie, 121, 155
Danziger, Susan, 246-47, 417, 434
Davis, Evelyn, 198-207, 368, 406, 459
Davis, Linda and Charles, 122
Davis, Mary, 189
Dawson, E. (Miss), 15
Day, Oscar, 40
Day, W. Taylor (Mrs.), 420
De Fee, Sharlene, 207
De Voe, Jane, 437
De Witt, Anne, 83
del Guercio, Mrs., *See* Fry, Fredericka
D'Elisiis, Michelle, 288
Demidoff, Nicholas (Mrs.), 219
Denton, Mimi, 172, 418
Denton, Willard K. and Mimi, 18, 37, 42, 49, 64, 65-9, 173, 194, 402, 512, 513, 522, 528
Devaney, Peter, 190
Dickenson, K., 95
Dickinson, Gene and Karen, 421, 430-32
Dolbel, M. and W., 283

Dowling, Murial, 253
Downey, Larry, 177
Dreer, William F. (Mrs.), 17, 27, 28-30, 39, 40, 162, 163-64
Drury, Maynard (Mrs.), 213

E
Eads, Brandol and Gayle, 50, 384, 388, 439
Eads, Cindy, 82
Eads, Cosette, 83
Eads, Gayle, 369
Eads, Wendy, 82
Eaves, Margaret D., 19-22
Edlin, Alfred (Fred), 211, 411
Edmiston, E.C. (Mrs.), 46
Edmonson, Patsy, 100
Edwards, Harkness, 28
Elkin, Debra, 59, 111-12, 338, 350, 388, 503, 504, 505
Elledge, Karen and Ralph, 124-25, 207, 297, 456
Elledge, Ralph, 297
Elliott, Becky, 193

F
Faigel, Joe, 267
Farmer, Jane, 275
Fennel, Caryl, 52, 100, 101
Ferry, Peg, 171
Fisher, Helen Miller, 138
Flakelar, Barrie and Denise, 281, 282, 283, 286
Flessas, Ken and Ann, 188
Forsyth, Jane Kamp, 145
Forsyth, Robert (Bob), 251, 281
Foster, Dorothy (Dot) Allen, 30, 31, 165, 170, 171
Foster, Rex B., 34
Fowler, Jack (Mrs.), 384
Fraser, Fred, 256
Freeman, Mae, 87, 173, 275
Freeman, P., 272, 436
Freeman, Ralph and Mae, 88
Frothingham, Robert (Mr. and Mrs.), 162, 179
Fry, Fredericka, 16, 27, 39, 40
Funke, Gladys A., 40

G
Gallagher, William W., 18, 29, 30-31, 32, 33, 162-63
Galye, Clayre, 208
Gardeinier, Pearl D., 247
Garvin, Florence, Mabel, and Anthony, 40
Gleffe, Susi, 223
Gollow, Marybeth, 177

Gordon, Fred, 238, 240, 247-49, 277, 278, 279, 390, 392, 412, 454, 459
Gordon, Fred and Sandra, 247
Gouger, Dale (Dr. and Mrs.), 95, 448
Grafstrom, Cathy and Gerry, 335
Graham, Esther, 172
Graham, P., 95
Graham, Walter J., 40
Graser, Jr., Lloyd H., 308
Graser, Lloyd, H., 132
Gray, Audrey, 246
Gray, Mrs., 39
Greathouse, Richard, 210
Greenhaigh, Bill, 420
Greenlay, Lois, 323
Gregor, Katherine (Kathy), 222, 223, 236
Gregory, Joe, 50, 367
Grey, M. (Miss), 15
Guay, Gerry (Mr. and Mrs.), 261-62
Gunzel, Lynn, 185
Gwynne-Jones, Olwyn, 314

H
Haderlie, Jason, 352, 508
Haderlie, Peggy and Jan, 215-17, 284, 336, 352, 356, 357, 373, 375, 387, 400, 508
Haegele, Barbara, 46
Haegele, Richard, 46
Hall, Betty, 114
Hall, Elizabeth, 188
Hall, Jack P. and Flora C., 47
Hammett, Jane, 147, 392
Hampton, Virginia, 218, 285, 389
Handel, Ellen, 288
Hansch, Earle E. (Dr. and Mrs.), 35
Hansch, Sallie, 44, 46
Harden, Clare, 414
Harden, Clare and Donna, 257, 258, 348, 435, 524
Harden, Donna Tidswell, 95, 116, 158, 256
Harris, Lou, 414
Harrison, T. (Mrs.), 15
Hartley, Heywood, 389
Hastings, Bob, 48
Hausman, Dona (Mrs. James E.), 54, 154-56, 183, 205, 326, 327, 328, 329
Hausman, James, 154
Hays, Mary Frances, 264
Hayward, Sandra, 256, 258
Heckman, Winifred, 266
Heinen, Harry, 171
Henderson, William, 241

Herd, Ron, 250
Hildreth, Richard and Nancy, 405
Hillman, Lois, 158
Hines, Linda, 216
Hoch, Haworth F. (Mr. and Mrs.), 118-20, 171, 228
Hoggan, Mr., 15
Holbrook, Bill, 45
Holds, the, 207
Holt, Jill and Tap, 188
Homsher, Doris A., 113, 379
Honig, John, 371
Hough, Florence L., 40
Houston, John and Patricia, 250, 251
Houston, Patricia, 242
Howard, George (Mr. and Mrs.), 154, 405
Howard, Nancy, 135-36, 308, 339
Howell, Keith B. and Carol, 58, 121-23, 207, 289, 331, 334, 347, 348, 350, 354, 355, 358, 387, 394, 461, 502, 531
Huband, B. (Mrs.), 15
Hubbard, Constance (Connie), 29, 70-73, 96, 102, 103, 105, 164, 169, 290, 310, 329, 332, 337, 411, 424, 454, 522
Hubbard, Kathy, 332
Huening, Margaret, 461
Huening, Margaret and Walt, 63, 150-53, 341, 349, 353, 359, 390, 412, 439
Huggins, Patricia, 280, 281, 287, 534
Huhn, Mrs., 164
Humphries, E.P. (Miss), 12
Hunloke, Mrs., 15
Hurlburt, Helen A., 135
Hydon, Elsie, 65

I
Illg, M., 95
Inguaggiato, Pat, 52

J
Jackson, Carl and Barbara, 46
Jarocki, Marjorie, 324
Jeffries, Catherine, 283
Jensen, Susan, 50, 137
Jewett, Marcella, 138
Jitosho, Yasko, 85
Johns, Betsy, 207
Johnson, Jan, 100
Johnson, Virgil, 35
Jolly, A. and E., 252
Jolly, Martha, 237, 259-60
Jones, J.D., 94

K

Kay, Jane, 83
Kazar, Patty, 176
Keith, Mr., 15
Kenealey, Barbara, 111, 112, 183-85, 207, 226, 294, 393, 396, 397, 425, 426, 438, 450, 453, 455
Kenealy, Barbara and Robert, 184
Kenealy, Sharon, 394
Kennedy, Stephanie, 175
Keppler, Edwin, 416
Kettles, Jr., Richard C., 166
Keyburn, Claire Barnet, 171
Kilham, Andrew and Carolyn, 215, 216
Kilham, Carolyn, 216, 217
Knoop, A. Peter, 103
Kodner, Denise, 51
Koranko, June, 178
Kozina, Tom, 279
Krook, Gulie, 147, 514
Kuhn, Charles A. (Mr. and Mrs.), 6
Kulneski, Shirley, *See* Bond, Shirley
Kurlburg, Alice, 185

L

Lackey, Ron, 207
Lafferty, Bonnie, 261
Lafore, John, 174
Lane, Arnold C. and Ruth, 218-19, 230, 231, 268, 426
Lane, Ruth E., 241-42, 245, 247, 265, 267
Lange, Marlene, 279
Langhorst, Carl and Amy, 212-14, 227, 334, 341, 346, 348, 351, 382, 394, 409, 413, 423, 446, 460
Leach, Carol, 177, 178
Leckington, Susan and Harlan, 185
Leeds, Mr., 162
Leschner, Diane M., 396
Levine, Florence, 36
Levine, Florence and Nate, 199
Levine, J. Nate, 28, 31, 40, 92, 159, 162, 163, 167, 175, 324, 405
Linden, Barbara, 207
Linden, Barbara J. and Kenneth A., 263, 264, 351
Lippincott, Sam and Lois, 197, 229, 394
Loeb, Ernest, 125, 315, 405
Loesch, Cathleen (Cathy) D., 95, 430, 432
Loggie, Mr., 15, 27
Lopina, Louise, 48
Lovett, Helen (Mrs. G.F.), 11, 218, 241, 242, 253
Lubin, Ruth, 295

Luke, Ted, 257
Lunn, C., 274
Lynch, Jean, 277
Lynn, Virginia, 414

M

McAuley, Linda, 416
McCaleb, B.E., 420
McChesney, E.H., 27
McConnell, Betty, 37
McConnell, Richard, 414
McCoy, Laura, 423
McCoy, Virginia, 129
McCullough, William and Suzanne, 122, 123, 378
MacDonald, Mark, 351
MacDonald, Mary, 235, 263-64, 333, 351, 357, 386, 424, 434, 442, 515
MacDonald, Sean, 351
McGee, Ron, 52
McGowan, Charlotte Clem, 186-90, 199-200, 201, 203, 207, 228, 288, 293, 294, 295, 297, 310, 317, 365, 409, 412, 415, 425, 435, 516
MacGregor, Mr., 16
McGuire, Lila, 175
Machado, Chris, 293
Machado, Chris and Jerry, 62, 63, 157-58, 338, 359, 391, 392, 398, 411, 413, 414, 458, 499, 500, 524
Macintosh, J. (Mr.), 283
MacIntosh, Sandra (Sandi), 207, 384
McLaughlin, Allan B., 29
McMillan, Jean, 256, 258, 378
McMurrich, K.D. (Mrs.), 27
McNaughton, Audrey, 278
McNeal, JoAnn, 147, 307
Malloy, Joe, 103, 105, 295, 391
Malmbory, Beverly, 216
Mann, Eleanor, 164
Marks, Joseph, 195
Marley, Bob and Barbara, 216
Marr, Barbara J., 262
Martin, Hayden, 82
Martin, K.A. (Mr.), 283
Mauldin, Guy, 130, 132, 134, 299, 315, 445, 460
Mauldin, Guy and Thelma, 8, 56, 131-34, 299, 315, 397, 406, 460
Maust, Julie, 189, 207
Mellin, Jeanne, 68, 69, 512, 528
Merrill, Harry O. (Mr. and Mrs.), 48
Mihara, Yuji, 216
Milbank, Samuel, 171
Miller, A. Raymond and Marie, 154, 159-61, 173, 175, 296, 385, 398, 458

Miller, Marie K., 79
Mills, Agnes, 40
Mingie, F.H. (Mrs.), *See* Lane, Ruth E.
Mitchell, Ann, 239
Mitchell, Harry, 342
Miyama, Tetsuo, 53, 144, 145, 146, 153, 291, 519, 527
Montgomery, Miss, 16, 29, 164, 165
Morden, Joan, 257
More, Linda Nugent, 51, 53, 85, 105, 208-11, 227, 231, 314, 352, 358, 360, 361, 362, 363, 364, 366, 367, 368, 453, 507, 508
Morey, Mary Jane, 129
Morgan, Gerry A. (Mrs.), 40
Morley, Joan, 44
Morley, Maryann, 421, 430-32
Mortimer, Peter J. and J.I., 281, 282-83
Murr, Louis, 39

N

Neil, Sandy, 216
Nicholas, Anna K., 159
Nichols, Jr., H.W. (Mr. and Mrs.), 39, 42
Nichols, Jr., Katherine (Mrs. H.W.), 28
Nichols, Mrs., 33, 176, 408
Nichols, Willis H. (Mr. and Mrs.), 17, 31, 171, 174, 175
Nicoll, Mildred B., 77, 78-79, 159, 160, 296, 315
Nicoll, Pamela (Pam) J., 78, 79
Noe, James, 101
Nytray, David, 509

O

Obermiller, Marna, 507
O'Bryan, Vance Callan (Mrs.), 32-34
O'Connell, Karol A., 36
Ogden, Roxanne, 237, 259-60
Oishi, Irene, 137
Okayama, Guy, 83
Okayama, Guy and Judy, 81
Olson, Barbara and Lowell, 393
Olson, Donna, 84
Overly, Edith, 189, 435

P

Paine, Bob and Nancy, 189
Palanio, Don, 247, 249, 277, 390
Palinkas, J.I. (Mrs.), 283
Pardue, Burt B., 460
Parker, A.A., 39
Parker Jo Byrd, 211, 413, 415

Parker, Karen, 423
Parkhurst, Don and Margaret, 45
Parkhurst, T.D., 45
Patterson, R.L., 33
Pavey, Joan and Terry, 114, 146, 401
Perry, Vincent, 92, 389
Petersen, Mrs., 174
Petter, Brenda, 192
Petter, Linda, 191
Petter, Rosemary, 191-92, 305
Phillips (May), Fran, 174
Picherd, Fredna and Rhonda, 438
Pickhardt, Ed, 36
Pierce, E.C. (Mr.), 12, 15, 16
Pilzer, Jo Anne, 183, 185
Poole, Blanche, 186, 187
Poole, Blanche and Kenneth, 186
Poole, Kenneth E., 126-27, 510
Porter, Polly, 420

Q

Quillan, P. (Mrs.), 282
Quillan, R.A. (Miss), 282

R

Ramsay, J.C. (Mrs.), 17
Ramsey, Mr., 15
Randall, Bill and Doreen, 243, 269-72, 307
Randolph, Kathy, 138
Reasin, Lee, 35, 382
Reed, Mr. and Mrs., 173, 174
Reese, Lyn B. and Michael J., 222-23, 236
Reeves, Natalie, 172
Reinertsen, Helen, 44
Rejholic, Joan J., 26
Renihan, Richard, 256
Richardson, Benjamin, 40
Riddle, Maxwell, 132
Riepe, Barbara, 46
Riggs, Augustus (Mrs.), 202
Roadhouse, Donna, 237, 254, 322
Roberts, Claude (Mrs.), 420
Roberts, Florence W., 401
Roberts, Melvin and Florence, 114
Roberts, Percy, 68
Robinson, E.L., 352
Robinsons, the, 205
Robson, Alan (Mrs.), 129, 171, 173, 174
Rogers, Byron (Mrs.), 27
Rogers, Felicity and Patience, 19
Rogers, Leslie B., 237, 241, 243, 252-54, 321, 322, 323, 324, 325, 423, 511
Roland, Jeanne, 176

Roll, Marlin, 208, 364
Rosenberg, Alva, 33, 243, 266, 410
Ross, Barbara and Marvin, 55, 115-17, 337, 342, 380, 400
Ross, Betty W., 45
Ross, Rita, 116
Rowlands, Irene C., 45

S

Sagebeer, Josephine, 42
Saltzman, Lynette, 209, 372
Saltzman, Stanley, 103, 247
Saltzman, Stanley and Lynette, 92-4
Samuels, Elaine, 169, 174, 197, 363
Sanchez, Edward, 362
Sanders, Frank and Velma, 34
Saunders, James, 31
Saunders, Mr., 16
Savitch, Betty, 193
Scherer, Edmund and Helen, 106-10, 369, 370, 374, 386, 389, 399, 404
Schultz, Marilyn, 189
Schwartz, Gerald, 214
Seago, Carol D., 420
Searle, Kathleen (Kay), 394, 509
Searle, Kathleen and Herbert, 111
Sell, Mr., 283
Shanaberger, J. Edward (Mrs.), 40
Sharman, Gil, 258
Shaw, R. Stephen, 155
Sherman, J.G. (Mr.), 27
Shrauger, Rosemary, 406
Simmonds, Jean Daniels, 59, 86-91, 196, 216, 252, 298, 299, 300, 327, 332, 345, 348, 353, 366, 383, 391, 395, 418, 419, 422, 435, 445, 450, 453, 457, 458, 461, 509, 510, 520, 523, 533, 536
Skarda, Langdon, 48, 145
Slaughter, Hazel, 218, 219, 231, 232, 243, 245, 247, 265-69, 312, 335, 389
Sleeth, Ariel, 248, 249, 251, 275-79, 412
Sleeth, Ariel and Floyd, 275, 276, 278, 279, 445, 455
Sleeth, Laurie, 277
Smith, Bonnie, 216
Smith, Boyd (Mr. and Mrs.), 207
Smith, Carlene D., 211
Smith, H., 95
Smith, Harriet, 216
Smith, James L. and Lynette, 84-85
Smith, Lynette, 328, 343, 350, 356, 437, 440, 444, 446, 507
Smith, Peter, 273, 436
Smith, Seaver, 74

Sparrow, E.E. (Mrs.), 13
Spencer, Kathy, 262
Spill, C.J. (Mr. and Mrs.), 40
Stage, Leroy, 431
Stage, Pam, 431-32
Stanbridge, Lawrence, 244
Standing, H.J. and R.H., 282
Stanek, John, 80
Staples, Mr. and Mrs., 174
Stem, Tom, 251
Stephens, Peggy, 216
Stettinius, E.R. (Mr.), 27
Stevenson, Tom, 361
Stewart, Elaine, 197
Stewart, Patricia A., 139, 224, 225, 340, 401, 410
Stoecker, Henry, 412
Stokely, Helen M., 420
Stokely, Jr., M.S., 420
Stolcz, Mona, 244, 255-58, 323, 374, 376
Stolcz, Mona and Lisa, 255, 256, 257, 258, 343, 348, 378, 435
Stoneham, P. (Mrs.), 250, 251
Stoner, Nioma, See Coen, Nioma S.
Stonington, Natalie, 40
Sutter, Marjorie, 393
Symington, Susan, 247

T

Taynton, Ruth, 168
Terhune, Albert Payson, 144, 162, 198
Thatcher, Mrs., 20
Thomas, Robert (Mrs.), 410
Thomas, Sr., Richard, 298
Thompson, Barbara, 207, 224, 456
Thompson, Barbara B., 100-101, 207, 371
Thompson, Mr., 15
Thompson, Pat Blacker, 250
Thynne, B. (Miss), 13, 15, 16, 17
Timpany, Joanne, 53, 210, 211, 361
Tod, M.C. (Mrs.), 16
Tomlin, Jennie, 231, 418
Tomlin, Rose, 418
Tomlin, Rose and Don, 193, 196, 411
Tomlin, Rose and Jennie, 193-96, 231, 340, 411
Trainor, William, 219
Travis, Frances L., 48
Travis, Richard D., 48
Trefry, June, 277
Troups, the, 152
Trullinger, James Walker, 72, 156
Tuff, Marjorie, 183
Tullys, the, 198, 199

Tumlin, Tony, 193, 418
Tyler, Howard, 47, 104, 259

U
Ullyott, S.U. (Mrs.), 282

V
Van Court, Ramona, 389
Van Wagenen, Mary, 39, 165, 166, 189, 190, 198-207, 275, 368, 406, 459
Venier, Erica, 207
Vogel, Vernon, 272
Von Thaden, Thelma, 62
Vuorinen, Ranier, 223

W
Wadsworth, Bill and Helen, 189
Walden, Debbie, 297
Wales, J.G. (Mrs.), 283
Wallace, Mary, 129
Wallace, Mary Ellen and Bill, 128
Walter, Carole and Gordon, 130
Wander, Mrs., 29

Ward, Howard, 436
Warhurst, Bill, 183
Warren, I. (Mrs.), 16
Waters, Robert, 250
Watt, Carol, 242
Welsh, Dorothy, 130, 413
Wernsman, Lil and Charles, 171
Wheelwright, D.A. (Mr.), 283
Whelen, Elizabeth (Betty) D., 10, 16, 29, 30, 38, 39, 41, 42, 66, 67, 68, 71, 98, 107, 129, 130, 154, 162-79, 201, 203, 234, 242, 288, 334, 383, 395, 397, 404, 405, 415, 420, 422, 424, 451, 463, 517
Whitby, L.C. (Mr.), 283
White, Robert W., 53, 126-27, 510
Whitmore, Eve, 251
Wilbraham, Mrs., 21
Wilcox, Janet, 191
Wilk, Joan, 88
Wilkinson, J. (Miss), 15
Willacker, Cheryl, 412
Williams, Frances Ruth, 14, 19, 23-25, 49, 342

Williams, George and Melanie, 50, 137-38, 335
Wills, Laura, 130
Wills, Robert (Bob), 43, 128, 226
Wilson, Bob, 222
Wilson, Capt. Bob, 251
Wilson, Doris, 254
Wirkus, Howard G. and Rosalie, 184
Wishnow, Elaine, 148-49, 381, 422, 427, 501, 503, 504
Wolcott, Dianne, 145
Wolf, Arnold, 408
Wolfe, Gail, 207
Woodring, Jon, 125
Wray, Neva, 163
Wright, Patricia, 367, 368
Wright, S.W., 40
Wylie, C.A. (Mrs.), 283

Y
Young, Fred, 421

Z
Zane, Arthur, K., 132

Kennels

(Page references in **bold** face indicate location of kennel story.)

A
Add-A-Bit, 166
Akirene, 137
Alandie, 44
Albelarm, 171
Alderbourne (Pekingese), 15
Alford, 241
Alwinton, 198
Amante, 283
Anahassitt, 27, 28-30, 162, 163-64, 198
Ardencaple, 18, **65-69**, 173, 194, 402, 512, 513, 528
Arken (Afghan Hounds), 171
Arpeggio, 254, 322
Arthea, 128
Astolat, **70-73**, 96, 102, 105, 164, 290, 310, 329, 332, 337, 424

B
Babinett, 273
Bagaduce, 29, 78, 420
Banchory, 84, 115, 158, 179, 258
Barwood, 207, 224
Beach Cliff, 29, 30, 31
Belle Mount, **74-77**, 309, 346, 347, 349, 371, 381, 449, 451, 457, 502, 508, 515

Beltane, 186, 187, 207, 293
Benayr, 207
Bil-Bo-Dot, 168
Birch Hollow, **78-79**, 315
Bonnicay, 261
Bran Gay, 50, **80-83**, 369, 384, 388, 439
Brandywine, 207
Briarwood, 205
Brig O'Dune, 262
Broadley, 266, 267
Browne Acres, 175

C
Cahaba, 207
Caper Hill, **84-85**, 437, 507
Captivator, 29
Carmylie, 59, **86-91**, 252, 298, 327, 332, 345, 348, 353, 366, 383, 395, 419, 422, 435, 450, 461, 509, 510, 523, 533
Carnwath, 247
Catamount, **92-4**, 209
Cavatina, **246-47**, 417, 434
Cedarhope, **95**, 448
Checkerchance, 188
Cherrylea, 283
Chicwin, 238, 240, **247-49**, 276, 392, 412, 454, 459

Chisterling, **96-9**, 452
Chosen, **100-101**, 207
Cindahope, 405
Clerwood, 16
Cleveland and Callan, 32
Conendale, **102-105**, 379
Crinan, 236, **250-51**, 334, 349

D
Dan-Dee, 121
Delamantha, 242
Delting Hill, 267
Diamond, 137
Doteon, 281
Dury Voe, 88

E
E-Danha, 150
Edlen, **106-10**, 369, 370, 374, 389, 404, 513
Elf Dale, 34
Eltham Park, 12, 16, 28
Enchanted, 59, **111-12**, 338, 503

F
Faharaby, 193
Fairisle, 283
Far Sea, 27

Feracres, 171
Forecaster, 35
Forever, 243, **252-54**, 324, 325, 511
Fran-Dor, **113**, 379

G
Gainess, 283
Gallantry, **255-58**, 323, 374, 376
Gay Acres, **114**
Gaylord, 208
Genson, 237, **259-60**
Geronimo, 32, 34, 35
Glenara (Collies and Scottish Terriers), 162
Grayfield, 246
Grelore, 222

H
Happy Glen, **115-17**, 337, 342, 400, 425
Hariann, 239, 342
Harvest Hill, 95, 430
Hatfield, 186
Heatherland, 88, 207
Hillswick, 283
Hoch Haven, 19, **118-20**, 228

I
Ilemist, 187, 189, 207

J
Jade Mist, 58, **121-23**, 207, 331, 348, 350, 355, 358, 394, 531
Jetsfire, 283
Jupalin, 283

K
Kambrae, 47
Karelane, 169, 197, 363
Karenwood, 211
Karral, **124-25**, 207, 297
Katie-J, 87, 88, 275
Ken-Rob, **126-27**, 510
Kensington, **128-30**
Kiloh, 163
Kiloren, 150, 173, 204
Kismet, 8, 56, **131-34**, 299, 315, 397, 406
Kyleburn, **19-22**

L
Legacy, **135-36**, 339
Lindhurst, 205
Lobo Dell, 189, 207
Lochanora, **137-38**
Lochlana, **261-62**, 532
Longleigh, 29
Longworth, 129

Lynchill, 277
Lynnlea, **139**, 320

M
Macdega, 49, **140-43**, 207, 289, 292, 296, 311, 333, 344, 411, 443
Mainstay, 87, **144-47**
Malashel, **148-49**, 504
Malpsh, 205
Marchwind, 235, **263-64**, 333, 386, 442, 515
Mar-Jan, 364
Marwal, 63, **150-53**, 341, 349, 353, 359, 412, 439
Meadow Ridge, 78, **154-56**, 161, 183, 328
Melwaig, 20
Meridian, 231, 232, **265-69**, 312, 335, 342, 389
Merri-Lon, 124
Merrywood, 509, 511
Midnitesun, 21
Mistimoor, 207
Montage, 62, **157-58**, 293, 338, 359, 391, 392, 414, 458, 499, 500, 524
Moribrook, 129, 203
Mountaincrest, 19, 23, **24-25**, 49, 342

N
Noralee, 30, 32, 35, 164

O
O' the Picts, 32-34
Our Own Rockwood, *See* Rockwood

P
Page's Hill, 29, 30-31, 33, 163, 324
Peabody, 16
Pixie Dell, 30, 32, 78, 79, **159-61**, 173, 175
Pocono, 10, 16, 29, 30, 38, 41, 71, 130, **162-79**, 203, 234, 242, 288, 334, 383, 395, 404, 415, 420, 422, 451, 517
Pushkin, 281, 282, 283, 286

R
Rickgarbob, **180-82**, 318, 341, 518
Ridgeside, 411
Riverhill, 19
Rockwood, **183-85**, 207, 426, 450, 453, 455
Romayne, 207, 227
Ronas Hill, 218, 241, 242, 265
Rorralore, **186-90**, 207, 228, 288, 293, 310, 425, 457, 516

Rosewood, **191-92**, 305
Rosmoor, **193-96**, 411
Rustic, **197**, 229

S
Sandstock, 283
Scottfree, 209
Sea Isle, 141, 165, 167, **198-207**, 208, 275, 368, 405, 406, 408, 435, 452, 454, 459
September, 207, 263, 264
Severn, **208-11**, 314, 358, 360, 362, 366, 453, 508
Shawn Dar, 215, 216, 217
Sheildale, 283
Shelando, 271, 272
Sheldon, 243, **269-72**, 307
Shelert, 19
Shelloy, 282-83
Shelmar, 169, 171
Sheltieland, 27
Sherwood, 210, 361
Shiel, **272-74**
Shu La Le, 207
Shylove, 183
Someday, 187
Sovereign, 247, 248, 249, **275-79**, 445, 455
Starhaven, **212-14**, 227, 334, 341, 346, 348, 351, 382, 394, 409, 413, 423, 446, 460
Stonewall, 362
SumerSong, **215-17**, 336, 350, 352, 356, 357, 373, 375, 387, 400, 446
Summit Lane, **218-19**, 230, 231, 241-42
Sunnybank Farm (Collies), 162
Sunset, 32
Sweetbriar Farm, *See* Hoch Haven

T
Tambrae, 35
Terian, 88
Thistlerose, 252
Tilford, 16
Timberidge, 30, 35, 165, 203, 212

V
Velveteen, **220-21**
Villager, **222-23**

W
Waldenwood, 152
Walnut Hall, 17, 28, 31, 42, 171, 176, 408
Water's Edge, **224**
Wayanet, 207
Wit's End, 207

General

A

Abscesses, 531-32

Adenovirus, *See* Hepatitis

American Kennel Club, 27, 332, 343, 389, 391, 395, 399, 417

American Shetland Sheepdog Association, 39-40

American-bred Class, 393

Arthritis, 534

Artificial respiration, 501-502

Ascarids, 527

Australia, Shelties in, 280-83

B

Bait, 404

Baths, 361-62

Beds, *See* Crates

Best in Show Shelties, Canadian, 243-44

Best of Breed competition, 395-97

Brace Class, 397

Bred-by-Exhibitor Class, 392-93

Breech birth, 501

Breeding, 20-22, 77, 141, 190, 199, 248, 259, 269, 274, 278-79, 449-505, 510-11

Breeding problems, 501-502, 533-34

British Shetland Sheepdog Breeders Association, 13

Brood bitch, 457-61

Brood bitch, care of, 500-504, 533

Brood Bitch Class, 397

Brood bitch, purchase of a, 341, 450, 457

Brucellosis, canine, 524-25

Burns, 531

C

Caesarean section, 502

Canadian firsts, 241-42

Cataracts, 534

Century Club, 35-36

Chew things, 347

Children, Shelties and, 350, 352

Clifford Pat, 15

Collar, 346, 353

Collie, 11-13

Collie Club of Great Britain, 13

Collie-Sheltie Review, 432

Colonial Shetland Sheepdog Club, 190, 207

Congenital defects, 520-21

Congenital Defects in Dogs, 520

Contagious diseases, infectious and, 521-25

Coronavirus, canine, 524

Cost, 331, 338, 343

Crates, 345-46, 354, 387, 514

Cuts, 531

Cysts, infected, 531-32

D

Dams, top Canadian, 245

Diarrhea, 530

Dishes, food and water, 347

Distemper, 521-22

Dog Team, top Sheltie, 428

Dog World, 37, 144

Dogs in Canada, 243

E

English Shetland Sheepdog Club, 13, 18

Exercise areas, 346

Exercise pens, 400

F

Feeding, 347-48, 357-59, 385, 535

Feet, care of, 364

Female or male, 333-34

First aid kit, 530

Fleas, 526

Frostbite, 531

Futurity Stakes, 398

G

Gait, 387, 402-404

Gestation, 500-501

Grooming, 361-68

H

Hand-feeding, 503-504

Heart problems, 534

Heartworms, 528-30

Heat exhaustion, 532

Heatstroke, 532

Helensdale Laddie, 31

Hepatitis, 522

Herding Group competition, 395-97

Hip dysplasia, 534-35

History in Australia, 281-83

History in Canada, 241-79

History in England, 15-25

History in the United States, 27-40

History on Shetland Islands, 11-13

Hookworms, 527

Housebreaking, 354

I

Illustrated Shetland Sheepdog Standard, 91, 300-304

Inbreeding, 450

Infectious and contagious diseases, 521-25

Interstate Shetland Sheepdog Club, 105

J

James A. Baker Institute for Animal Health, 525

Judging, 167, 172

Judging routine, 402

Judging Shelties, 327-29

Junior Showmanship, 399

K

Kennel Club (British), 13, 15

Kennel cough, *See* Parainfluenza

Kennels, American, 65-224

Kennels, Australian, 281-83

Kennels, British, 19-25

Kennels, Canadian, 246-79

Kidney disease, 534

L

Lead, 346, 353

Leptospirosis, 523

Lerwick Rex, 27

Lice, 526-27

Life expectancy, 534

Line-breeding, 450

Litter, care of, 503-505, 533-34

Love Is A Many Splendored Thing, 78, 79

M

Male or female, 333-34

Mange, 527

Match shows, 388-89

Medicine, administering, 530

Merriley's Steely Dan, 430-32

Mites, 527

Mohawk Shetland Sheepdog Club, 127

Movement, *See* Gait

Mowgli, 30-31, 163

N

Nails, care of, 363, 505

Name, breed, 12-13

Novice Class, 392

Nutrition, *See* Feeding

543

O

Obedience degrees, 418-19
Obedience Shelties, top, 420
Obedience trials, 417-18
Off To The Shows, 162
Older dogs, care of, 512-13, 534-35
Open Class, 393-94
Origin, 11
Other pets, Shelties and, 349-50
Outcrossing, 450

P

Pacific Northwest Shetland
    Sheepdog Club, 34
Parainfluenza, 522-23
Parasites, external, 526-27
Parasites, internal, 527-30
Parvovirus, canine, 523-24
Pedigrees, 462-99
Personality, 507-508
Pet-quality puppies, 332, 334
Petroon Dog Training Club, 75
Point Shows, 390-98
Poisons, 532-33
Puppies, care of, 345-59, 503-505,
    527
Puppies, pet-quality, 332, 334
Puppies, purchasing, 334-40, 343
Puppies, show-quality, 338, 340
Puppy Class, 391-92
Purchase of a dog, 331-43
*Pure-Bred Dogs/American Kennel
    Gazette,* 395, 417-18, 420

R

Rabies, 523
Registration, 343
Regulations for Junior Showmanship,
    399
Relay Team, top Sheltie, 428

Remedies, home, 530-34
Responsibilities of owners, 510-13
Rotavirus, canine, 524

S

Santiago Shetland Sheepdog Club
    of Southern California, 80
Scottish Shetland Sheepdog Club,
    13, 18
Sedative, mild, 531
Shedding, 362
Sheltie Pacesetter, 138, 255
Sheltieland Thistle, 31
Shetland Sheepdog, 321
Shetland Sheepdog Magazine, 255
Shipping dogs, 336, 458-59, 460
Show dog, purchase of a, 332, 336-40
Showing, 385-404
Showing, grooming for, 367-68
Showing, preparations for, 400-401
Show-prospect puppies, 338, 340
Sires, top Canadian, 244-45
Socialization, 353-56, 385-86
Spaying, 333-34
Stacking, 386, 402-403
Standard, American (current), 290-96
Standard, American (early), 288-89
Standard, Australian, 285-88
Standard, British (current), 285-88
Standard, British (early), 17-18
Standard, comments on American,
    178-79; *See also* Type, Sheltie
Standard, comments on Australian,
    282
Standard, illustrations of American,
    300-304
Standards, Sheltie, 285-96
Stimulant, mild, 530
Stud dog, 449-56
Stud Dog Class, 397

Stud dog, purchase of a, 342, 450-52
Successful Dog Show Exhibiting, 404
Sweepstakes, 398

T

Tapeworms, 528
Teeth, care of, 363-64, 387
Temperament, 85, 97, 190, 274, 385
Temperature, taking, 530
Ticks, 526
Tourniquets, 531
Training, 353-56, 417
Training, obedience, 417
Training, show, 385-87, 403
Travelling, 355, 512, 514-17
Toy Collie, 12
Toys, 347
Tracking Trials, 418-19
Tube-feeding, 503-504
Type, Sheltie, 321-25

V

Vaccinations, 505, 521
Vaccines, 521
Veterans Class, 397-98
Veterinarian, choosing a, 348, 519-20
Vitamins, 358, 535
Vomiting, 530

W

Weaning, 505
Whelping, 501-502, 533-34
Whelping box, 500-501
Whipworms, 527-28
Wills, 511-12
Winners Class, 394-95
Worms, tests for, 527
Wounds, 531